Signals and Communication Technology

This series is devoted to fundamentals and applications of modern methods of signal processing and cutting-edge communication technologies. The main topics are information and signal theory, acoustical signal processing, image processing and multimedia systems, mobile and wireless communications, and computer and communication networks. Volumes in the series address researchers in academia and industrial R&D departments. The series is application-oriented. The level of presentation of each individual volume, however, depends on the subject and can range from practical to scientific.

Indexing: All books in "Signals and Communication Technology" are indexed by Scopus and zbMATH

For general information about this book series, comments or suggestions, please contact Mary James at mary.james@springer.com or Ramesh Nath Premnath at ramesh.premnath@springer.com.

Werner Henkel

Channel Coding

Springer

Werner Henkel
Constructor University
Bremen, Germany

ISSN 1860-4862 ISSN 1860-4870 (electronic)
Signals and Communication Technology
ISBN 978-3-032-08235-0 ISBN 978-3-032-08236-7 (eBook)
https://doi.org/10.1007/978-3-032-08236-7

This Springer imprint is published by the registered company Springer Nature Switzerland AG
The registered company address is: Gewerbestrasse 11, 6330 Cham, Switzerland

To
Ulrike,
Ake and Erik,
Antonia and Claudius

Preface

This book has evolved from my coding lecture taught at different universities, namely University of Kaiserslautern, Vienna University of Technology (TU Wien), City University Bremen (Hochschule Bremen), and finally, Constructor University, formerly known as IUB or Jacobs University Bremen, step-wise extending and updating the corresponding lecture notes. One can certainly observe manifold influences or contributions from my own Ph.D. advisor, Bernhard Dorsch, and from colleagues like Robert Calderbank or Jack Wolf to name two prominent ones. However, I will not be able to name all dear colleagues and friends that I have had the pleasure to be in touch with and learn from. Among them are great contributors to our field, many of which have become friends over the years, just as Jim Massey, Dan Costello, Shu Lin, Rolf Johannesson, David Declercq, Claude Berrou, Rüdiger Urbanke, Li Ping, Francis Lau, Hans-Andrea Loeliger, Gerhard Kramer, Martin Bossert, Han Vinck, Johannes Huber, Joachim Hagenauer, Volker Kühn, to just mention some in a more or less random order.

I should acknowledge the many contributions of my Ph.D. students and also undergraduate and graduate students in my lecture, pointing me to typos and other issues. I had the luck to have extremely talented students around and working with them was a real pleasure.

The book is tailored to an advanced course, typically in a graduate program, where at my current university, we were also able to offer it in the last year of undergraduate studies. We are covering almost all essential aspects of classical and modern coding theory. Given the constraints of one or even two semesters, some details had to be limited or omitted, but the text provides the basis for further studies. We hope to also offer some intuitive understanding here and there.

Chapters 1 and 2 provide introductory material talking about channels and metrics as well as the essential information theoretic background, respectively. It can, of course, not be a complete information theory treatment. Hereto, we recommend a separate course based on typical IT books, just as the ones by Cover and Thomas or Csiszár and Körner.

Thereafter, the book first follows the traditional block and convolutional code separation to finally dissolve the strict separation. We start with simple block codes and essential definitions in Chap. 3, immediately moving over to Convolutional Codes in three Chapters, deferring the required mathematics for algebraic block codes to a later chapter.

Chapter 4 introduces Convolution Codes and their formal and graphical representation, Chap. 5 adds the decoding algorithms, such as Viterbi, SOVA, and BCJR. Puncturing and Pruning complete the chapter. In Chap. 6, we give an overview over sequential, tree-based decoding.

Trellis-Coded Modulation and Trellis Shaping follow in Chaps. 7 and 8, respectively. This finalizes the convolutional-coding-based part. Later, the block-coding-related part will also be terminated with coded modulation and shaping.

Chapter 9 provides the mathematical foundation for algebraic block codes which are finite fields, so-called Galois fields. They are not only the basis for block codes, but also for Cryptology and random number generation.

Reed-Solomon (RS) codes, as found in manifold applications directly (one may just think of the error correction for a CD or DVD) or as outer codes in a concatenation, are described in Chap. 10, introducing them as polynomial interpolation.

The treatment of RS decoding likewise begins with interpolation, this time an exponential one, to thereafter introduce the Berlekamp-Massey and Euclidean algorithms. Chapter 10 is concluded discussing error values. Bose-Chaudhuri-Hocqhenghem (BCH) codes follow as subfield subcodes of RS codes in Chap. 11.

"Modern" coding schemes are treated in Chap. 12, extending the codeword length as required from Information Theory to approach Capacity. Among the discussed modern coding schemes are Turbo, LDPC, and Polar codes.

Chapter 13 offers a short excursion to network-related coding. Error probabilities and coding bounds are then discussed in Chaps. 14 and 15, respectively.

As one of the links between block and convolutional codes, Chap. 16 offers construction possibilities for trellises of block codes, thereby allowing to use trellis-based maximum-likelihood (or MAP) decoders for block codes.

Multilevel Coded Modulation and Shaping by Shell Mapping are finalizing the treatment of this share in Chaps. 17 and 19, respectively, with an intermediate introduction of Lattices in Chap. 18 making use of multilevel code designs.

The book concludes with a collection of exercises and corresponding solutions.

Opening quotes for chapters and sections shall not be interpreted as following any political orientation, religion, belief, or opinion. They were found to fit and highlight contents, although however, they were originally phrased in a totally different context.

Bremen, Germany Werner Henkel
June 2025

Competing Interests The author has no competing interests to declare that are relevant to the content of this manuscript.

Contents

About the Author

Werner Henkel received his Diploma and Dr.-Ing. (Ph.D.) degree from Darmstadt University of Technology (TUD) in May 1984 and June 1989, respectively. After that, he worked at Deutsche Telekom's R&D Labs in Darmstadt. During this time, he spent a sabbatical at AT&T Bell Laboratories (later Lucent). In turn, he continued his career at the Telecommunications Research Center Vienna and achieved a professorship at the City University Bremen. He taught Coding Theory at this University, and at the universities of Kaiserslautern and Vienna, alike. Since September 2003 he has been a professor for electrical engineering at Constructor University, formerly Jacobs University and International University of Bremen chairing the ECE program from its existence until 2022. He was elected Dean from April 2012 to June 2014. He had visiting positions at Old Dominion University (ODU), in Norfolk, Virginia and at the Technical University of Denmark (DTU), Copenhagen, Denmark, in Spring 2015 and Fall 2025, respectively. Dr. Henkel was involved in organizing or serving on the technical program committees of: ISIT 1997, IEEE J-SAC, June 2002, International Zurich Seminar 2004, EUSIPCO 2004 and 2007, ICC 2006, 2017–2026, CNS 2025, Turbo Symposia (ISTC) 2008, 2010, 2014, 2016, 2018, 2020/21, 2023, IWCMC 2022 Sec. Symp., GC 2022 WS '5GBeyond', INFOCOM Wireless-Sec 2023, Globecom 2024 IEEE NExtG Wisec, and SampTA 2013. During his career, he has published on the following topics: coding, iterative decoding, unequal error protection, coded modulation, joint source-channel coding, network coding, frame synchronization, channel modeling, impulse noise, DSL, power-line communication, single- and multicarrier transmission, multi-user communication, MIMO, DNA analysis, physical-layer security, and TEMPEST. Moreover, he has been teaching the following courses: Coding Theory; Information Theory; Data Compression, Compressive Sensing, and Modern Coding; Digital Signal Processing; Signals and Systems; Digital Communication, Wireline Communication (DSL). Other courses include Measurement Automation; Circuits; and Statistical Analysis and Simulation.

Chapter 1
Channels, Channel Models, and Metrics

Das Pferd frisst keinen Gurkensalat
Probing the first telephone channel with a nonsense phrase:
The horse does not eat cucumber salad.

Philipp Reis, 1861

This first chapter provides an introduction into the topic, starting from a distinction from neighboring fields. Some typical channels will be described, metrics will be defined as distance measures, and based on simple linear block codes, the basic block-coding definitions will be compiled. Following this chapter, however, block codes will first be put aside and convolutional codes will be treated, instead. A comprehensive treatment will then follow after an introduction into the necessary algebraic framework in Chap. 9. Convolutional codes can be explained without the tools of discrete algebra and thus, only for didactic reasons, these codes are treated first.

1.1 Distinction Between Channel Coding and Related Topics

Very often, the term ‘coding’ is used with a different meaning. A clear definition and distinction to other topics is therefore put at the beginning of this channel coding text. We distinguish the following four areas that have either similar names or some other relation:

1. Line coding
2. Source coding
3. Channel coding
4. Cryptology.

W. Henkel, *Channel Coding*, Signals and Communication Technology,
https://doi.org/10.1007/978-3-032-08236-7_1

Line coding has been in practical use for a very long time, almost from the beginning of digital communications over AC-coupled copper pairs. Line coding provides the required spectral shaping, especially in the form of a spectral null at DC. A manifold of block- and sequence-oriented procedures have been developed. This will not be the focus of this work. Nevertheless, the corresponding metric will be defined in Sect. 1.4, and in Sect. 8.3, line coding will serve as a possible application of Trellis-Shaping. A comprehensive treatment of line codes can, e.g., be found in [1].

Source coding is a means of reduction of redundancy or irrelevance in a signal or in data. On one hand, such measures comprise methods that do not modify the contained information, such as the well-known Huffman algorithm [2] and the variants of the Lempel-Ziv-Algorithms [3–5], which are widely used under names like 'compress', 'zip', or 'gzip' and are part of almost every computer software installation.[1] On the other hand, there are procedures that take the subjective properties of the recipient into account. Irrelevant signal components are eliminated, which is not regarded as disturbance or at least is considered to be tolerable. Audio (speech, music) and video coding algorithms are widely used in modern transmission systems. [7] provides a collection of audio and video-coding algorithms. More recent books are [8–10] for audio and [11, 12] for video coding.
For a information-theoretic treatment of source coding, the reader is referred to [13].

Channel coding provides error protection by means of a suitable addition of redundancy to the signal or data. At first sight, this is counterproductive to Source Coding. Source coding eliminates less structured redundancy, whereas channel coding adds redundancy in such a structured way that it allows for error detection and correction. The different algorithms for channel coding will be treated in this book. We divide into block- and sequence-based methods, i.e., block and convolutional codes.

All different kinds of coding need not be seen as separate and independent. Actually, there are tight relations between them. Often, it proves to be more efficient, to combine source and channel coding or to provide spectral shaping, i.e., line coding, by means of special channel coding.

Cryptology appears to be somewhat aside from signal and data transmission. Nevertheless, there exist strong links between cryptology and channel coding. Both disciplines make use of the same mathematical bases, the discrete algebra, and, they even use the same algorithms. However, the aim of cryptology is not related to the reduction or introduction of redundancy. Cryptology is devoted to the secure transmission of information, avoiding unauthorized access of third parties, and the authentication. With crypto algorithms in place, there exist additional requirements for source and channel coding to ensure that signal redundancy does not allow for easier decryption. An introduction is given by [14–16].

In this book, cryptographic methods will not be treated and will be considered as part of the source and destination.

---

[1] As more recent work, a paper by Willems et al. [6] may be mentioned.

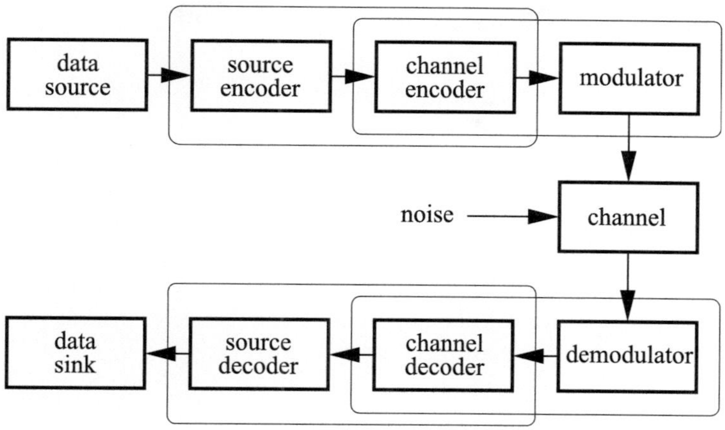

Fig. 1.1 The transmission path

1.2 Components of a Transmission System

Figure 1.1 shows the succession of source coding, channel coding, and modulation in a transmit path. This should not lead to the impression of separate and independent components. A common design of source and channel coding and of channel coding and modulation (coded modulation) is indeed usually the better approach. These aspects will also be discussed in this book. Especially, the chapters on convolutional codes and the chapters on block codes will be concluded with the corresponding coded modulation schemes.

1.3 Channels and Their Modeling

Before we proceed to channel coding itself, this section provides some basic knowledge of typical exemplary channels.

1.3.1 Additive White Gaussian Noise (AWGN)

This is the most commonly used channel idealization. It is assumed that additive noise samples are the output of a random process that has a Gaussian density and whose samples are statistically independent.

The Gaussian density is known to be

$$p(r|v) = \frac{1}{\sqrt{2\pi\sigma_n^2}} e^{-\frac{(r-v)^2}{2\sigma_n^2}}. \tag{1.1}$$

σ_n can be written as $\sigma_n = 1/\sqrt{2E_s/N_0}$ when normalizing the signal energy. For 2-PSK, this would mean ± 1 instead of $\pm\sqrt{E_s}$. N_0 denotes the one-sided power spectral density. The derivation of this density and the corresponding standard deviation at the output of a 'matched' filter can be found in almost every standard book on transmission systems and will therefore not be handled here. Instead we refer to, e.g., Gitlin et al. [17], Blahut [18], and Barry et al. [19].

1.3.2 Binary Erasure Channel (BEC)

The binary erasure channel models errors at known positions. It is suitable, e.g., to describe packet loss in data networks. It is also used a lot in proofs for LDPC codes, since they become more tractable and often, results appear transferable to other channels. Figure 1.2 shows the BEC, where Δ denotes the erasure.

1.3.3 Binary Symmetric Channel (BSC)

The binary symmetric channel as given in Fig. 1.3 is the typical channel model of binary transmission without any analog information, i.e., at the output of a binary quantizer.

In the case of an underlying Gaussian channel (AWGN), a source with a binary signal alphabet $\{+\sqrt{E_s}, -\sqrt{E_s}\}$ (normalized $\{+1, -1\}$), and a hard quantization with a threshold in the middle, we obtain using the densities

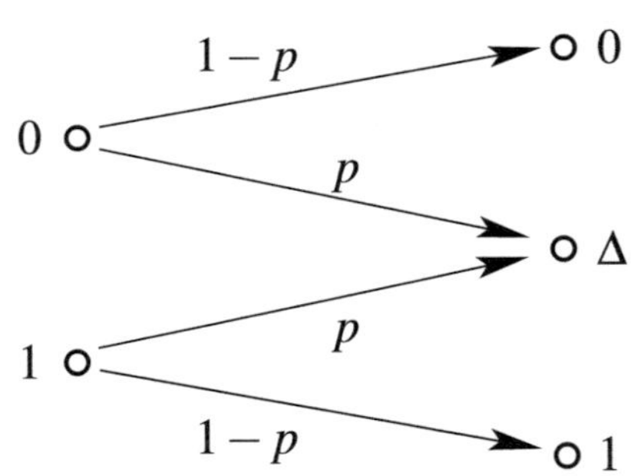

Fig. 1.2 Binary erasure channel

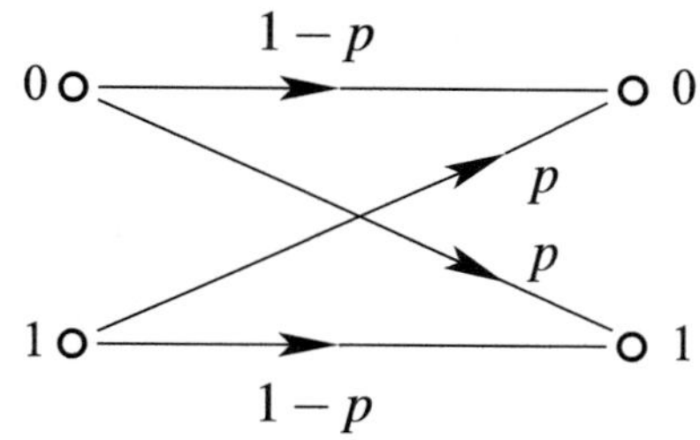

Fig. 1.3 Binary symmetric channel

$$P(r| \pm 1) = \frac{1}{\sqrt{2\pi\sigma_n^2}} e^{-\frac{(r\mp 1)^2}{2\sigma_n^2}}$$

the error probability p of the corresponding binary symmetric channel as

$$\begin{aligned} p &= \int_0^\infty p(y| - 1)dy = \int_0^\infty \frac{1}{\sqrt{2\pi\sigma_n^2}} e^{-\frac{(y+1)^2}{2\sigma_n^2}} dy = \frac{1}{\sqrt{\pi}} \int_{\frac{1}{\sqrt{2\sigma_n^2}}}^\infty e^{-t^2} dt \\ &= \frac{1}{2}\text{erfc}\left(\frac{1}{\sqrt{2}\sigma_n}\right) = Q\left(\frac{1}{\sigma_n}\right) \\ &= \frac{1}{2}\text{erfc}\left(\sqrt{\frac{E_s}{N_0}}\right) = Q\left(\sqrt{\frac{2E_s}{N_0}}\right) \end{aligned} \tag{1.2}$$

with

$$\text{erf}(x) = \frac{2}{\sqrt{\pi}} \int_0^x e^{-t^2} dt, \tag{1.3}$$

$$\text{erfc}(x) = 1 - \text{erf}(x) = \frac{2}{\sqrt{\pi}} \int_x^\infty e^{-t^2} dt, \tag{1.4}$$

$$Q(x) = \frac{1}{\sqrt{2\pi}} \int_x^\infty e^{-t^2/2} dt = \frac{1}{2} \cdot \text{erfc}(x/\sqrt{2}). \tag{1.5}$$

When transmitting a word of length N over the binary symmetric channel, the probability of e erroneous bits at arbitrary positions is

$$p(e) = \binom{N}{e} p^e (1-p)^{N-e}. \tag{1.6}$$

In case a code would be able to correct t errors, the probability of error-free correction would be

$$p_{corr} = \sum_{e \le t} \binom{N}{e} p^e (1-p)^{N-e}. \tag{1.7}$$

Correspondingly,

$$p_{nocorr} = 1 - p_{corr} = \sum_{e>t} \binom{N}{e} p^e (1-p)^{N-e}. \tag{1.8}$$

is the probability of not being able to correct, i.e., the block-error probability .

1.3.4 Gilbert-Elliott Model of a Channel with Memory

The Gilbert-Elliott model shown in Fig. 1.4 is a Markov model of first order and is specified by transition probabilities between two states that are usually denoted as 'good' or 'bad'. It is a suitable simplifying model for a mobile communications channel with shadowing and extreme changes between very good channel conditions with a low bit error probability p_{bG} and a very bad channel state with a bit error probability of p_{bB} near 0.5. The states thus represent different bit error probabilities.

Markov models are described by means of their transition matrix:

$$\begin{pmatrix} p_G(t_0+T) \\ p_B(t_0+T) \end{pmatrix} = \begin{pmatrix} 1-q_1 & q_2 \\ q_1 & 1-q_2 \end{pmatrix} \begin{pmatrix} p_G(t_0) \\ p_B(t_0) \end{pmatrix}, \tag{1.9}$$

with the probabilities $p_G(t)$ and $p_B(t)$ that the channel is in state G and B, respectively, at time t.

Such $n \times n$-transition matrices fulfill $\sum_{i=1}^{n} q_{ij} = 1$, where q_{ij} are the transition probabilities.

The average burst length, i.e., the average time to remain in state B is

$$\sum_{i=0}^{\infty} 1 \cdot (1-q_2)^i = \frac{1}{1-(1-q_2)} = 1/q_2. \tag{1.10}$$

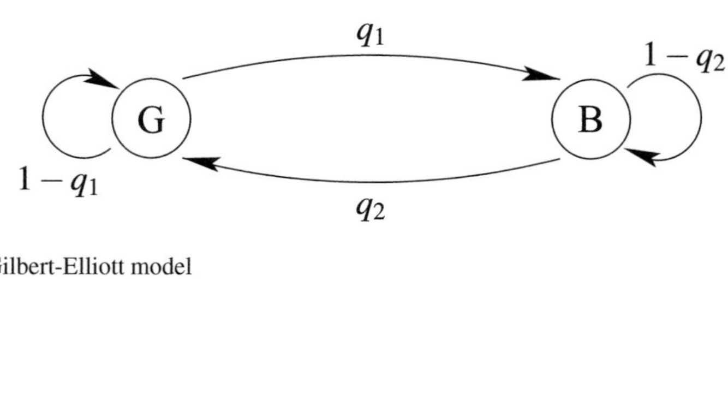

Fig. 1.4 Gilbert-Elliott model

The following averaging provides an alternative derivation.

$$\sum_{i=0}^{\infty}(i+1)\cdot q_2\cdot(1-q_2)^i = 1/q_2 \tag{1.11}$$

Correspondingly, the average gap length, i.e., the average burst separation is $1/q_1$. The average bit error probability is given by

$$p = \frac{\frac{1}{q_2}p_{bB} + \frac{1}{q_1}p_{bG}}{\frac{1}{q_2} + \frac{1}{q_1}} = \frac{q_1 p_{bB} + q_2 p_{bG}}{q_1 + q_2} \tag{1.12}$$

1.3.5 Fading Channels

After having described a simplifying model of a channel with memory that may be suited as a simple model of a fading channel, we will now shortly derive the distribution of so-called small-scale fading. These are the statistics that result from a manifold of scattered components and leads to faster variations. Shadowing and changes that depend on larger objects or the landscape are denoted as large-scale fading. It follows a log-normal density and will not be described in here. A more detailed treatment of the mobile channel can be found in [20, 21].

In case of many scatter paths that are combined at the receiver, we obtain the received signal

$$\begin{aligned} r(t) &= \sum_i \alpha_i(t)\cos(\omega_c t - \theta_i(t)) \\ &= a_I(t)\cos(\omega_c t) + a_Q(t)\sin(\omega_c t). \end{aligned} \tag{1.13}$$

with

$$a_I(t) = \sum_i \alpha_i(t)\cos(\theta_i(t))$$

$$a_Q(t) = \sum_i \alpha_i(t)\sin(\theta_i(t)) \qquad \theta_i(t) = \omega_c \cdot \tau_i(t)$$

Assuming $\alpha_i(t)$ to be i.i.d. (independent and identically distributed) and $\theta_i(t)$ to be equally distributed within the interval $[0, 2\pi]$, it follows from the central limit theorem that $a_I(t)$ and $a_Q(t)$ will be statistically independent zero mean Gaussian random variables with variance σ_a^2.

The probability density of the fading amplitude (envelope)

$$a = \sqrt{a_I^2 + a_Q^2} \tag{1.14}$$

results in

$$p_F(a) = \frac{a}{\sigma_a^2} e^{-\frac{a^2}{2\sigma_a^2}}. \tag{1.15}$$

In the following, a short proof is provided.

Proof The proof is based on the transformation rule

$$p(y = f(x)) = \sum_{x:x=f^{-1}(y)} p(x) \Big/ \left| \frac{df(x)}{dx} \right| \tag{1.16}$$

and the fact that the sum of two random variables is described by the convolution of their densities.

Squaring of the I and Q components $y = f(x) = x^2 \longrightarrow df/dx = 2x = 2\sqrt{y}$ yields

$$\frac{1}{\sqrt{2\pi\sigma_a^2}} \cdot 2 \cdot \frac{1}{2\sqrt{y}} \cdot e^{-\frac{y}{2\sigma_a^2}}, \quad y \geq 0 \tag{1.17}$$

The convolution of the densities results in

$$\int_0^y \frac{1}{2\pi\sigma_a^2} \frac{1}{\sqrt{t}} e^{-\frac{t}{2\sigma_a^2}} \cdot \frac{1}{\sqrt{y-t}} e^{-\frac{y-t}{2\sigma_a^2}} dt = \frac{1}{2\pi\sigma_a^2} e^{-\frac{y}{2\sigma_a^2}} \int_0^y \frac{1}{\sqrt{t(y-t)}} dt =$$

$$= \frac{1}{2\pi\sigma_a^2} e^{-\frac{y}{2\sigma_a^2}} \underbrace{[-\arcsin(1-2t/y)]_{t=0}^{t=y}}_{=\pi} =$$

$$= \frac{1}{2\sigma_a} e^{-\frac{y}{2\sigma_a^2}}, \quad y \geq 0. \tag{1.18}$$

A further application of the transformation rule with $a = f(y) = \sqrt{y} \longrightarrow df/dy = 1/(2a)$ yields the **Rayleigh** density.

$$p_F(a) = \frac{a}{\sigma_a^2} e^{-\frac{a^2}{2\sigma_a^2}}. \tag{1.19}$$

The phase of the fading $\Phi = \arctan \frac{a_Q}{a_I}$ is equally distributed within the interval $[0, 2\pi]$. □

If there should be a strong direct path (line of sight, typical for maritime mobile communication), the so-called **Rice Fading** is obtained. The fading amplitude follows to be

$$a = \sqrt{(A + a_I)^2 + a_Q^2}. \tag{1.20}$$

It can be shown that

$$p_F(a) = 2a(1+K)e^{(K+a^2(1+K))} I_0(2a\sqrt{K(K+1)}) \quad \text{with} \quad I_0(x) = \sum_{k=0}^{\infty} \left(\frac{x^k}{2^k k!} \right)^2 . \tag{1.21}$$

I_0 is the modified Bessel function of first kind and order zero and the Rice factor $K = \frac{A}{2\sigma_a^2}$ describes the share of the direct path. The phase will not be equally distributed any more.

1.3.6 Some Other Channels

To mention just a few other channel conditions, there are many non-white noise environments like the one due to NEXT and FEXT (Near-End Crosstalk and Far-End Crosstalk) between wire pairs in twisted-pair cables. Due to common clocks, such disturbances may even have cyclostationary properties.

Impulse noise caused by relays, electrical engines, lightning, etc., are a counterpart to Fading. In Fading the signal amplitude suddenly drops, whereas with impulse noise, the noise amplitude suddenly becomes very high. Both disturbances may lead to error bursts.

Jamming denotes an intentional impairment in different flavors, e.g., impulsive, narrow-band, or even as repeat-back jamming, where spreading sequences are determined to also use them for jamming.

Furthermore, there are disturbances due to quantization and nonlinearities.

1.4 Metrics

Wer misst, misst Mist.

Who measures, measures crap.

In order to take different channel properties into account, corresponding distance measures have been defined that are called *metrics*, which is not meant in a mathematical strict sense. Later, we will discuss the choice of a suitable metric for special applications. In this section, we will just present the most important ones and intuitively, their possible application should become evident.

The mathematical metric definition would be

Definition 1.1 Elements $x, y, z, \ldots$ from a set M, denoted as a metric space, a non-negative number $D[x, y]$ is associated with that must have the following properties

1. $D[x, x] = 0$,
2. $D[x, y] = D[y, x] \neq 0$, if $x \neq y$ (commutativity),
3. $D[x, z] \leq D[x, y] + D[y, z]$ (triangular inequality).

$D[x, y]$ is denoted as *distance*.

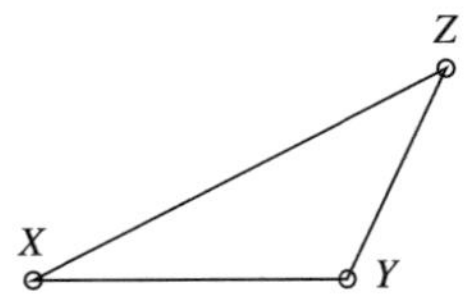

For our purposes, the fulfillment of the triangular inequality is usually not important. We thus still call a distance measure a metric, even if the triangular inequality is not fulfilled.

1.4.1 Euclidean Distance

The Euclidean distance fulfills all the axioms of a metric and is thus a real metric in strict mathematical sense. The squared Euclidean distance is contained in the Gaussian density. The probability of a certain received value is then dependent on the (squared) Euclidean distance from the transmitted symbol.

Definition 1.2 The **Euclidean distance** d_E between two vectors **a** and **b** of length n with components $a_i, b_i \in \mathbb{R}$ is given by

$$d_E^2 = \sum_{i=0}^{i=n} (a_i - b_i)^2 \tag{1.22}$$

Complex components a_i and b_i can be regarded as twice as long vectors with real components.

1.4.2 Hamming Distance

In case of bursty noise, where only the number of disturbed symbols is of interest, or if a (binary) hard quantization is carried out at the receiver, the Hamming distance will be the suitable distance measure.

Definition 1.3 The **Hamming distance** d_H between two vectors **a** and **b** of length n with components a_i and b_i that may be elements of an arbitrary number field, are given as the number of different components.

(A somewhat more formal description would be the cardinality $d_H = |M|$ of the set $M = \{j|a_j \neq b_j\}$.)

Definition 1.4 The **Hamming weight** w_H of a vector is the number of components different from zero.

(More formal: $w_H = |M|$, with $M = \{j|a_j \neq 0\}$)

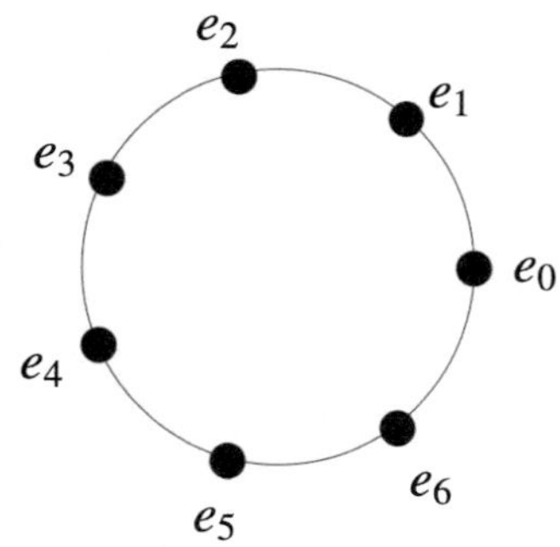

Fig. 1.5 Illustration of the Lee distance

1.4.3 Lee Distance

To understand the meaning of the Lee distance, one should think of signal points equally spaced on the unit circle, similar to a PSK. For this signal set, it can be useful to have a measure for the shortest distance between two points given in segments of the circle.

Definition 1.5 Let a set M with cardinality $|M| = q$ be completely ordered with elements $a_0 < a_1 < a_2 < ... < a_{q-1}$. The Lee distance is then given as

$$d_L^1(a_i, a_j) = \min\{|j - i|, |q + i - j|, |q + j - i|\}, \quad a_i, a_j \in M. \tag{1.23}$$

For vectors $\mathbf{w}$ and $\mathbf{v}$ of length n with components $w_k, v_k \in M$, the Lee metric is then given by

$$d_L^n(\mathbf{w}, \mathbf{v}) = \sum_{k=1}^{n} d_L^1(w_k, v_k). \tag{1.24}$$

For illustration, one may determine the Lee distance of two points in Fig. 1.5.

1.4.4 Product Distance

The so-called product distance shows up in the computation of the pairwise error probability between two valid code sequences (for Fading channels).

Definition 1.6 Let L be the length of an error event (burst) and let $\boldsymbol{a}$, b be two valid code sequences. The **product distance** is then defined as

$$d_\Pi^2 = \prod_{\substack{k=1 \\ d_k \neq 0}}^{L} d_k^2(a_k, b_k). \tag{1.25}$$

The product distance thus is the Lth power of the geometric mean of the quadratic Euclidean distances of L different sequence components.

1.4.5 Running Digital Sum (RDS)

This metric is applied in line coding and is thus a little aside from the other metrics listed before. Since line coding will be handled together with channel coding, it will nevertheless be mentioned here.

The discrete Fourier transform (DFT) is given by

$$F_k = \sum_{i=0}^{n-1} f_i e^{-j\frac{2\pi}{n}ik}. \tag{1.26}$$

The power at DC, i.e., at $f = 0$ is then given by

$$P(0) = \frac{1}{n^2} F_0^2 = \frac{1}{n^2} \left[\sum_{i=0}^{n-1} f_i \right]^2. \tag{1.27}$$

Definition 1.7 The **Running Digital Sum** $\mathrm{RDS}(n)$ after n symbols is defined to be

$$\mathrm{RDS}(n) = \sum_{i=0}^{n-1} f_i. \tag{1.28}$$

Theorem 1.1 *A spectral null at DC ($f = 0$) is obtained if the Running Digital Sum does not grow without limits.*

This follows directly from (1.27) and taking the limit $n \to \infty$: if $\mathrm{RDS} \le S$

$$\lim_{n\to\infty} \frac{1}{n^2} \left[\sum_{i=0}^{n-1} f_i \right]^2 \le \lim_{n\to\infty} \frac{1}{n^2} S^2 = 0. \tag{1.29}$$

The RDS, however, does not have an important property of a metric. It has a sign, i.e., it is not non-negative. Therefore, the variance of the RDS may be used as a metric, instead. This will then be minimized.

Zeros at other positions of the power density spectrum can easily be obtained by applying the shift properties of the Fourier transform to the metric specification.

References

1. A. Bluschke, *Digitale Leitungs- und Aufzeichnungscodes (in German)*. Berlin, Offenbach: VDE-Verlag, 1992.
2. D. A. Huffman, "A method for the construction of minimum-redundancy codes," *Proceedings of the Institute of Radio Engineers*, vol. 40, no. 9, pp. 1098–1101, September 1952.
3. J. Ziv and A. Lempel, "A universal algorithm for sequential data compression," *IEEE Transactions on Information Theory*, vol. 23, no. 3, pp. 337–343, May 1977.
4. J. Ziv and A. Lempel, "Compression of individual sequences via variable-rate coding," *IEEE Transactions on Information Theory*, vol. 24, no. 5, pp. 530–536, Sep. 1978.
5. T. Welch, "A technique for high-performance data compression," *Computer*, vol. 17, no. 6, pp. 8–19, June 1984.
6. F. M. J. Willems, Y. M. Shtarkov, and T. J. Tjalkens, "The context-tree weighting method: basic properties," *IEEE Transactions on Information Theory*, vol. 41, no. 3, pp. 653–664, May 1995.
7. N. S. Jayant and P. Noll, *Digital Coding of Waveforms – Principles and Applications to Speech and Video*. Englewood Cliffs (NJ): Prentice Hall, 1984.
8. W. B. Kleijn and K. K. Paliwal, *Speech Coding and Synthesis*. Amsterdam: Elsevier, 1995.
9. A. Gersho and R. M. Gray, *Vector Quantization and Signal Compression*. Boston, Dordrecht, London: Kluwer, 1992.
10. N. Jayant, J. Johnston, and R. Safranek, "Signal compression based on models of human perception," *Proceedings of the IEEE*, vol. 81, no. 10, pp. 1385–1422, Oct 1993.
11. R. J. Clarke, *Transform Coding of Images*. Academic Press, 1985.
12. J.-R. Ohm, *Digitale Bildcodierung, Repräsentation, Kompression und Übertragung von Bildsignalen (in German)*. Berlin: Springer, 1995.
13. R. M. Gray, *Source Coding Theory*. Boston: Kluwer, 1990.
14. A. Beutelspacher, *Kryptologie (in German)*. Braunschweig: Vieweg, 1996.
15. A. Beutelspacher, J. Schwenk, and K. Wolfenstetter, *Moderne Verfahren der Krypotgraphie - von RSA zu Zero-Knowledge (6.Aufl., in German)*. Vieweg, 2006.
16. A. J. Menezes, S. A. Vanstone, and P. C. V. Oorschot, *Handbook of Applied Cryptography*, 1st ed. Boca Raton, FL, USA: CRC Press, Inc., 1996.
17. R. D. Gitlin, J. F. Hayes, and S. B. Weinstein, *Data Communications Principles*. New York, NY, USA: Plenum Press, 1993.
18. R. E. Blahut, *Digital Transmission of Information*. Owego, NY: Addison Wesley, 1990.
19. J. R. Barry, D. G. Messerschmitt, and E. A. Lee, *Digital Communication: Third Edition*. Norwell, MA, USA: Kluwer Academic Publishers, 2003.
20. J. R. Barry, D. G. Messerschmitt, and E. A. Lee, "Rayleigh fading channels in mobile digital communication systems Part I: Characterization," *IEEE Communications Magazine*, vol. 35, no. 7, pp. 90–100/136–146, July/Sept 1997.
21. B. Sklar and F. J. Harris, *Digital Communications: Fundamentals and Applications*, 3rd ed. Upper Saddle River, NJ, USA: Prentice Hall, 2020.

Chapter 2
Introduction to Information Theory

> Frequently the messages have meaning; that is they refer to or are correlated according to some system with certain physical or conceptual entities. These semantic aspects of communication are irrelevant to the engineering problem.
>
> Claude E. Shannon, 1948

Information Theory has its major foundation in the mentioned paper by Shannon [1]. In here, we provide the basics that will be needed in later chapters. For a more concise coverage, the reader is referred to standard IT texts, e.g., the ones by Cover and Thomas [2] or Csiszár and Körner [3].

2.1 Information, Entropy, Joint and Conditional Entropies

Shannon's [1] (Hartley's [4]) **Information** measure in 'bit' is defined as

$$I(x_i) = \log_2 (1/P(x_i)) = -\log_2 P(x_i). \tag{2.1}$$

The **Entropy** $H(X)$ is defined as the average information

$$H(X) = \sum_{x_i \in X} P(x_i) \cdot I(x_i) = \sum_{x_i \in X} P(x_i) \cdot \log (1/P(x_i)). \tag{2.2}$$

It describes the number of binary messages necessary to describe the outcome of a statistical experiment. It expresses the average uncertainty.

W. Henkel, *Channel Coding*, Signals and Communication Technology,
https://doi.org/10.1007/978-3-032-08236-7_2

Fig. 2.1 Binary entropy function

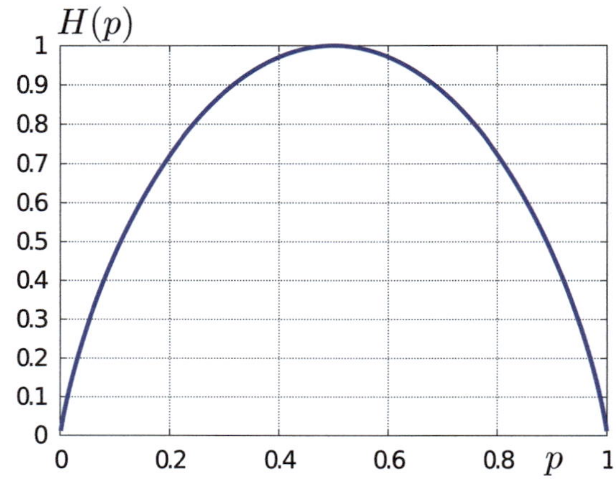

The binary entropy function for a Bernoulli(p) source with probabilities p and $1 - p$ is then

$$H(p) = p \cdot \log \frac{1}{p} + (1-p) \log \frac{1}{1-p} \quad =: h(p), \tag{2.3}$$

which is shown in Fig. 2.1. As indicated, we write the binary entropy function as lower-case $h(p)$.

Note the symmetry. The biggest uncertainty is reached at $p = 0.5$.

The Joint Entropy for two random variables, e.g., channel input and output is then

$$H(X, Y) = -\sum_{x \in \mathcal{X}} \sum_{y \in \mathcal{Y}} P(x, y) \log P(x, y) = -E\{\log P(X, Y)\}. \tag{2.4}$$

The **conditional entropy** is defined as

$$\begin{aligned} H(Y|X) &= \sum_{x \in \mathcal{X}} P(x) \cdot H(Y|X = x) \\ &= -\sum_{x \in \mathcal{X}} P(x) \sum_{y \in \mathcal{Y}} P(y|x) \log P(y|x) \\ &= -\sum_{x \in \mathcal{X}} \sum_{y \in \mathcal{Y}} P(x, y) \log P(y|x) \\ &= -E_{P(x,y)} \{\log P(Y|X)\}. \end{aligned} \tag{2.5}$$

The relation between the individual, joint, and conditional entropies are given by the so-called **Chain Rule**,

$$H(X, Y) = H(X) + H(Y|X). \tag{2.6}$$

Since the entropy is a logarithmic quantity, this follows directly from Bayes' rule ,

$$P(X, Y) = P(X) \cdot P(Y|X) = P(Y) \cdot P(X|Y). \tag{2.7}$$

For a set of random variables, we obtain the following theorem.

Theorem 2.1 Chain Rule *for a collection of random variables*

$$H(X_1, X_2, \ldots, X_n) = \sum_{i=1}^{n} H(X_i|X_{i-1}, \ldots, X_1) \tag{2.8}$$

Proof

$$\begin{aligned}
H(X_1, X_2) &= H(X_1) + H(X_2|X_1) \\
H(X_1, X_2, X_3) &= H(X_1) + H(X_2, X_3|X_1) \\
&= H(X_1) + H(X_2|X_1) + H(X_3|X_2, X_1) \\
&\vdots \\
H(X_1, X_2, \ldots, X_n) &= H(X_1) + H(X_2|X_1) + \cdots + H(X_n|X_{n-1}, \ldots, X_2, X_1) \\
&= \sum_{i=1}^{n} H(X_i|X_{i-1}, \ldots, X_1)
\end{aligned}$$

□

From this, we also obtain the **Independence Bound**.

Theorem 2.2 *Let X_i, $i = 1, \ldots, n$ be n random variables. As an upper bound for the joint entropy, we obtain the entropy for independent random variables*

$$H(X_1, X_2, \ldots, X_n) \leq \sum_{i=1}^{n} H(X_i), \tag{2.9}$$

Proof By the chain rule for entropies,

$$H(X_1, X_2, \ldots, X_n) = \sum_{i=1}^{n} H(X_i|X_{i-1}, \ldots, X_1) \leq \sum_{i=1}^{n} H(X_i).$$

The theorem follows from $H(X) \geq H(X|Y)$. □

2.2 Typical Sequences and the Asymptotic Equipartition Property (AEP)

We look into the binary coin-flipping situation first with p, the probability for head and $q = 1 - p$, the probability for tail. Let us consider approximating the actual mean by the estimate $r_n = \frac{\sharp heads}{\sharp flips} = \frac{k}{n}$.

Theorem 2.3 *Chebyshev's inequality*

$$P\left(|r_n - \mu_r| > \epsilon\right) = P\left(|r_n - p| > \epsilon\right) \leq \frac{\sigma^2}{\epsilon^2} = \frac{pq}{n\epsilon^2}, \tag{2.10}$$

σ^2 and $\mu_r = p$ being the variance and mean of r_n, respectively, and $\epsilon > 0$. This tells us that the probability of the deviation of the estimate from the actual mean decreases with n. This is called the **Asymptotic Equipartition Property (AEP)** and is valid for long sequences of random variables. We will study only the case of i.i.d. random variables, although AEP is also valid for other classes of sequences, especially ergodic sequences.

AEP splits the set of sequences in typical and untypical ones. Although the typical ones will be much less than the whole set, its probability will sum up to almost one. This effect will be more pronounced with increasing sequence length.

Thus, reducing ϵ and increasing n would make the probability diminish that an untypical sequence would be used. Hence, only typical sequences would need to be encoded. The set will be much smaller and also the corresponding code sequence can be much shorter.

Proof of Chebyshev's inequality

$$\begin{array}{ll}
\text{Discrete case} & \text{Continuous case} \\
\sigma^2 = \sum\limits_{-\infty}^{\infty}(x-\mu)^2 P_X(x) & \sigma^2 = \int_{-\infty}^{\infty}(x-\mu)^2 f_X(x)dx \\
\quad > \sum\limits_{|x-\mu|\geq\epsilon}(x-\mu)^2 P_X(x) & \quad > \int_{|x-\mu|\geq\epsilon}(x-\mu)^2 f_X(x)dx \\
\quad > \sum\limits_{|x-\mu|\geq\epsilon}\epsilon^2 P_X(x) & \quad > \int_{|x-\mu|\geq\epsilon}\epsilon^2 f_X(x)dx \\
\quad = \epsilon^2 \cdot \sum\limits_{|x-\mu|\geq\epsilon} P_X(x) & \quad = \epsilon^2 \cdot \int_{|x-\mu|\geq\epsilon} f_X(x)dx \\
\quad = \epsilon^2 \cdot P\left(|x-\mu| \geq \epsilon\right) & \quad = \epsilon^2 \cdot P\left(|x-\mu| \geq \epsilon\right)
\end{array} \tag{2.11}$$

$$\Longrightarrow P\left(|x-\mu| \geq \epsilon\right) < \sigma^2/\epsilon^2 \tag{2.12}$$

We still need to show that $\sigma^2 = \frac{pq}{n}$.
Let $p_n(k)$ be the probability of obtaining k heads amongst n trials,

$$p_n(k) = \binom{n}{k} p^k q^{n-k} = \frac{n!}{(n-k)!k!} p^k q^{n-k}. \tag{2.13}$$

We note that

$$\sigma^2 = E\left\{\left(\frac{k}{n} - p\right)^2\right\} = \frac{1}{n^2} \cdot E\left\{(k - np)^2\right\} = \frac{1}{n^2}\sum_{k=0}^{n}(k - np)^2 p_n(k) \tag{2.14}$$

$$\begin{aligned}
n^2\sigma^2 &= \sum_{k=0}^{n} k^2 p_n(k) - 2np\sum_{k=0}^{n} kp_n(k) + n^2p^2 \\
&= \sum_{k=0}^{n} k^2 p_n(k) - 2n^2p^2 + n^2p^2 \\
&= \sum_{k=0}^{n} k^2 p_n(k) - n^2p^2
\end{aligned}$$

$$\begin{aligned}
\sum_{k=0}^{n} k^2 p_n(k) &= \sum_{k=1}^{n} k\frac{n!}{(n-k)!(k-1)!}p^k q^{n-k} \\
&= \sum_{k=1}^{n}(k-1)\cdot\frac{n!}{(n-k)!(k-1)!}p^k q^{n-k} + \sum_{k=1}^{n}(1)\cdot\frac{n!}{(n-k)!(k-1)!}p^k q^{n-k} \\
&= \sum_{k=2}^{n}\frac{n!}{(n-k)!(k-2)!}p^k q^{n-k} + \sum_{k=1}^{n}\frac{n!}{(n-k)!(k-1)!}p^k q^{n-k}
\end{aligned}$$

substituting $k' = k - 2$ in the first term, leads to

$$\begin{aligned}
&= \sum_{k'=0}^{n-2}\cdot\frac{n!}{(n-k'+2)!k!}p^{k'+2}q^{n-k'-2} + \sum_{k=1}^{n}\frac{n!}{(n-k)!(k-1)!}p^k q^{n-k} \\
&= n(n-1)p^2(p+q)^{n-2} + \sum_{k=1}^{n}\frac{n!}{(n-k)!(k-1)!}p^k q^{n-k} \\
&= n(n-1)p^2 + \sum_{k=1}^{n} k\cdot\frac{n!}{(n-k)!(k)!}p^k q^{n-k} \\
&= n(n-1)p^2 + np = n^2p^2 - np^2 + np \\
&= n^2p^2 + np(1-p) = n^2p^2 + npq
\end{aligned} \tag{2.15}$$

leads to

$$n^2\sigma^2 = n^2p^2 + npq - n^2p^2 = npq \Longrightarrow \sigma^2 = \frac{pq}{n}. \tag{2.16}$$

Note: The typical sequence set has in total the highest probability. Its element sequences need not necessarily have higher probability than sequences in the non-typical set. For example, obtaining np head outputs from the coin experiment would be typical, but the probability of having n times a heads output would actually be bigger for an unfair coin with $p > 1/2$!

Let $X_1, X_2, \ldots, X_n$ be a sequence of i.i.d. random variables, e.g., n coin flipping experiments. The probability of a certain sequence will be

$$P_{\mathbf{X}}(\mathbf{x}) = \prod_{i=1}^{n} P_X(x_i). \tag{2.17}$$

We say that the event $\mathbf{x} = x_1, x_2, \ldots, x_n$ is an ϵ-typical sequence, if the arithmetic mean of its information values

$$-\frac{1}{n}\log P_{\mathbf{X}}(\mathbf{x}) = -\frac{1}{n}\sum_{i=1}^{n}\log P_X(x_i) = -\frac{1}{n}\sum_{i=1}^{n} I_X(x_i) \tag{2.18}$$

differs from the stochastic average of $I_X(x)$, the entropy, only by ϵ. □

Definition 2.1 The set $\mathcal{A}_\epsilon$ of ϵ-typical sequences $\mathbf{x} = x_1, x_2, \ldots, x_n$ is defined as

$$\mathcal{A}_\epsilon(X) := \left\{\mathbf{x} : \left|-\frac{1}{n}\log P_{\mathbf{X}}(\mathbf{x}) - H(X)\right| \leq \epsilon\right\} \tag{2.19}$$

The equipartition property will be formulated as follows:

Theorem 2.4 *For each $\epsilon > 0$ exists an $n \in \mathbb{N}$, such that $\mathcal{A}_\epsilon(X)$ has the following properties:*

1. $P(\mathcal{A}_\epsilon(X)) \geq 1 - \epsilon$,
2. $\mathbf{x} \in \mathcal{A}_\epsilon(X) \Rightarrow \left|-\frac{1}{n}\log P_{\mathbf{X}}(\mathbf{x}) - H(X)\right| \leq \epsilon$,
3. $(1-\epsilon)2^{n(H(X)-\epsilon)} \leq |\mathcal{A}_\epsilon(X)| \leq 2^{n(H(X)+\epsilon)}$.

Proof 1. Follows from the convergence of $-\frac{1}{n}\log P_{\mathbf{X}}(\mathbf{x})$ in the definition of $\mathcal{A}_\epsilon(X)$.
2. Follows from the definition of $\mathcal{A}_\epsilon(X)$.
3. Follows from

$$1 \geq \sum_{\mathcal{A}_\epsilon(X)} P_{\mathbf{X}}(\mathbf{x}) \geq \sum_{\mathcal{A}_\epsilon(X)} 2^{-n(H(X)+\epsilon)} = |\mathcal{A}_\epsilon(X)| \cdot 2^{-n(H(X)+\epsilon)} \tag{2.20}$$

and

$$1-\epsilon \leq \sum_{\mathcal{A}_\epsilon(X)} P_{\mathbf{X}}(\mathbf{x}) \leq \sum_{\mathcal{A}_\epsilon(X)} 2^{-n(H(X)-\epsilon)} = |\mathcal{A}_\epsilon(X)| \cdot 2^{-n(H(X)-\epsilon)}. \tag{2.21}$$

We made use of the second property, obtaining

$$2^{-n(H(X)+\epsilon)} \leq P_{\mathbf{X}}(\mathbf{x}) \leq 2^{-n(H(X)-\epsilon)}. \tag{2.22}$$

□

Shannon's source coding theorem [1] follows from the third property in Theorem 2.4, since the cardinality of the typical sequences and with it the corresponding minimum number of representing bits $\log_2(|\mathcal{A}_\epsilon(X)|)$ is given by the entropy. In here, we do not discuss source coding much, but the AEP property will be addressed again.

2.3 Mutual Information and Channel Capacity

Links between information quantities and error probabilities between a transmitted value X and received one Y is provided by Fano's lemma.

Lemma 2.1 Fano's lemma *Let X and Y be random variables with values from the set $\mathcal{X} = \{x_1, x_2, \ldots, x_\nu\}$, with $\nu = |\mathcal{X}|$. Furthermore, let $P_e = P(X \neq Y)$.*
We then obtain

$$H(X|Y) \leq h(P_e) + P_e \log_2(\nu - 1). \tag{2.23}$$

Proof We make use of an error indicator

$$Z = \begin{cases} 0, \text{ if } X = Y \\ 1, \text{ if } X \neq Y. \end{cases}$$

From the chain rule, we know

$$H(XZ|Y) = H(X|Y) + H(Z|XY) = H(X|Y),$$

where the final equality is due to the fact that X and Y uniquely determine Z. Furthermore,

$$\begin{aligned} H(X|Y) &= H(XZ|Y) \\ &= H(Z|Y) + H(X|YZ) \quad \text{(chain rule)} \\ &\leq H(Z) + H(X|YZ). \end{aligned}$$

First, we note that $H(X|Y, Z = 0) = 0$, since X is uniquely defined. There are $\nu - 1$ cases with $Z = 1$, leading to

$$H(X|Y, Z = 1) \leq \log_2(\nu - 1).$$

Thus,

$$H(X|YZ) \leq P(Z = 1) \log_2(\nu - 1) = P_e \log_2(\nu - 1).$$

Finally, we insert $H(Z) = h(P_e) = -P_e \log_2 P_e - (1 - P_e) \log_2(1 - P_e)$. □

We may give some intuition behind Fano's lemma

$$H(X|Y) \leq h(P_e) + P_e \log_2(\nu - 1).$$

Let $H(X|Y)$ be the information that is needed to determine X when Y is known. One way to do this, is to check if $X = Y$. If this is the case, we are done. If, however, $X \neq Y$, $\nu - 1$ possibilities are left for X. The first step, i.e., determining if $X = Y$, requires $h(P_e)$ bit. If $X \neq Y$, which occurs with the probability P_e, at most $\log_2(\nu - 1)$ further bits will be needed.

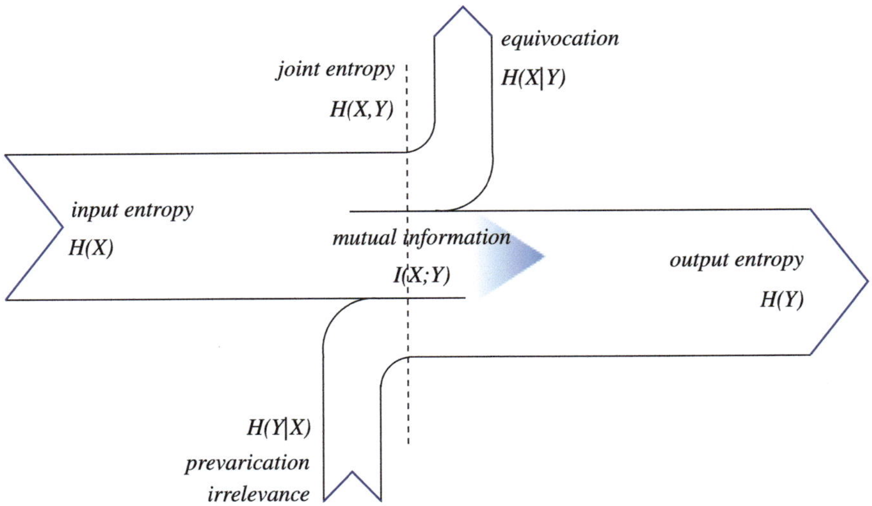

Fig. 2.2 Mutual information, irrelevance, and equivocation

After having discussed the link between error probability and the lost information named Equivocation, we are deriving the information that is left to link source and channel, the **Mutual Information** $I(X, Y)$ as illustrated in Fig. 2.2. Following this figure, we find

$$I(X;Y) := H(X) - H(X|Y) \tag{2.24}$$

$$= \sum_{x \in \mathcal{X}} P(x) \cdot \log \frac{1}{P(x)} - \sum_{x \in \mathcal{X}} \sum_{y \in \mathbb{Y}} P(x,y) \cdot \log \frac{1}{P(x|y)} \tag{2.25}$$

$$= \underbrace{\sum_{x \in \mathcal{X}} \sum_{y \in \mathbb{Y}} P(x,y)}_{P(x)} \cdot \log \frac{1}{P(x)} - \sum_{x \in \mathcal{X}} \sum_{y \in \mathbb{Y}} P(x,y) \cdot \log \frac{1}{P(x|y)} \tag{2.26}$$

$$= \sum_{x \in \mathcal{X}} \sum_{y \in \mathbb{Y}} P(x,y) \cdot \underbrace{\log \frac{P(x|y)}{P(x)}}_{=:I(x;y)} \tag{2.27}$$

$$= \sum_{x \in \mathcal{X}} \sum_{y \in \mathbb{Y}} P(x,y) \cdot \log \frac{P(x,y)}{P(x) \cdot P(y)} = \ldots \tag{2.28}$$

$$= H(Y) - H(Y|X) = I(Y;X). \tag{2.29}$$

$I(X;Y)$ depends on the probability distribution of the source and the channel matrix. Here, we assumed the Discrete Memoryless Channel (DMC), which will later be generalized for continuous alphabets at the received and/or the transmitter, then moving to probability density functions. In Information Theory, a reformulation with Kullback-Leibler divergence is introduced, which we will not require in here.

With this, we define the

Definition 2.2 Channel Capacity

$$C = \sup_{P(x)} I(X; Y) \tag{2.30}$$

This means the Channel Capacity is the supremum of the mutual information over all possible probability distributions of the input alphabet.

In line with the Chain Rule for entropies, we also have the **Chain Rule for the Mutual Information**

Theorem 2.5

$$I(X_1, X_2, \ldots, X_n; Y) = \sum_{i=1}^{n} I(X_i; Y|X_{i-1}, X_{i-2}, \ldots, X_1) \tag{2.31}$$

Proof

$$\begin{aligned} I(X_1, X_2, \ldots, X_n; Y) &= H(X_1, X_2, \ldots, X_n) - H(X_1, X_2, \ldots, X_n|Y) \\ &= \sum_{i=1}^{n} H(X_i|X_{i-1}, X_{i-2}, \ldots, X_1) \\ &\quad - \sum_{i=1}^{n} H(X_i|X_{i-1}, X_{i-2}, \ldots, X_1, Y) \\ &= \sum_{i=1}^{n} I(X_i; Y|X_{i-1}, X_{i-2}, \ldots, X_1) \end{aligned}$$

□

As examples, we determine the Capacities for the BSC and BEC that we had introduced in the previous chapter. The BSC is again depicted in Fig. 2.3, now in two equivalent forms. Here. the "+" stands for a modulo-2 sum, i.e., XOR.

$$\begin{aligned} I(X; Y) &= H(Y) - H(Y|X) && (2.32) \\ &= H(Y) - \sum_{x} P(x) \cdot H(Y|X = x) && (2.33) \\ &= H(Y) - \sum_{x} P(x) \cdot h(p) && (2.34) \\ &= H(Y) - h(p) && (2.35) \\ &\leq 1 - h(p) && (2.36) \end{aligned}$$

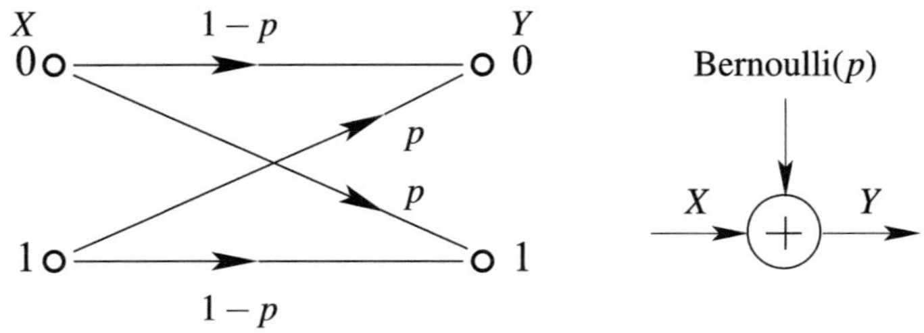

Fig. 2.3 Binary symmetric channel (BSC)

Fig. 2.4 Capacity of the BSC

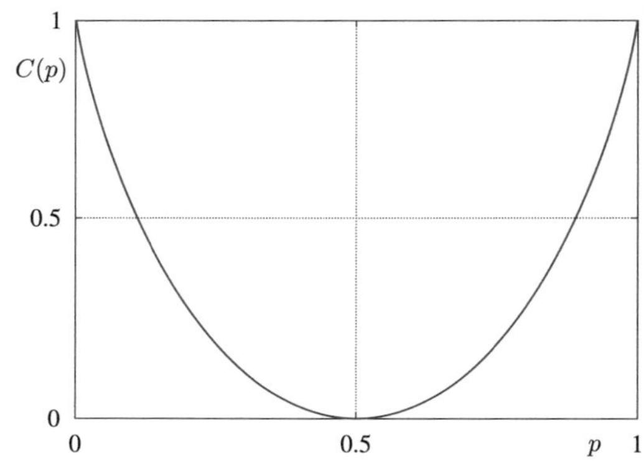

Fig. 2.5 The binary erasure channel (BEC)

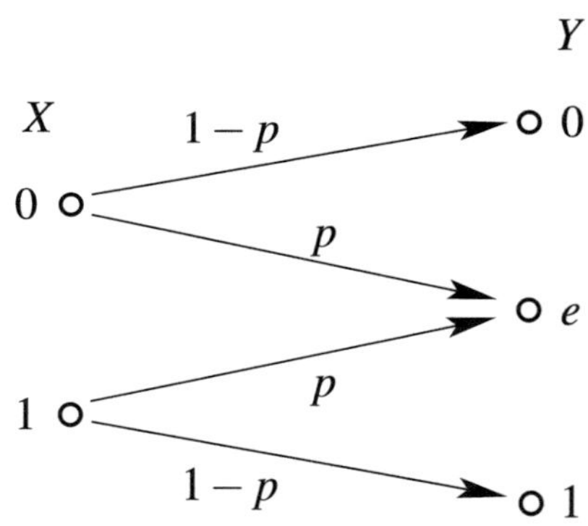

Hence, the Capacity is given by

$$C_{BSC} = 1 - h(p), \tag{2.37}$$

drawn in Fig. 2.4.

Now to the erasure channel, again depicted in Fig. 2.5.

We can subdivide this channel into two direct paths (ideal channel) with a probability $(1 - p)$ and a completely disturbed one with probability p.

$$C_{BEC} = (1 - p) \cdot 1 + p \cdot 0 = 1 - p \tag{2.38}$$

For the proof of the channel coding theorem and the converse to the coding theorem, we refer to standard IT references. The proof of the channel coding theorem is either based on jointly typical sequences or Gallager's error exponent. The converse to the coding theorem uses Fano's lemma. The first shows that the error probability can be made small for large ($N \to \infty$) block lengths. The latter shows that the error probability cannot be made arbitrarily small if the rate exceeds the Capacity.

2.4 Channel Capacities of Common Modulation Formats Under Additive White Gaussian Noise (AWGN)

Using modulation methods just as PAM, ASK, PSK, or QAM means a discrete input and a continuous output. For the Capacity derivations, we follow [5]. We already know that for a DMC, i.e., discrete input x_i and a discrete output y_j, the mutual information is given by

$$I(X;Y) = \sum_{i=1}^{M_x}\sum_{j=1}^{M_y} P(x_i, y_j)\log_2\left(\frac{P(x_i, y_j)}{P(x_i)\cdot P(y_j)}\right), \tag{2.39}$$

where M_x and M_y denote the numbers of transmit and receive values. Using Bayes' theorem, we obtain

$$I(X;Y) = \sum_{i=1}^{M_x} P(x_i)\sum_{j=1}^{M_y} P(y_j|x_i)\log_2\left(\frac{P(x_i)\cdot P(y_j|x_i)}{P(x_i)\cdot P(y_j)}\right) \tag{2.40}$$

and finally with the total probability theorem,

$$I(X;Y) = \sum_{i=1}^{M_x} P(x_i)\sum_{j=1}^{M_y} P(y_j|x_i)\log_2\left(\frac{P(y_j|x_i)}{\sum\limits_{i'=1}^{M_x} P(x_{i'})P(y_j|x_{i'})}\right). \tag{2.41}$$

For a continuous output, we replace the summation by an integration to obtain

$$C = \max_{P(x_i)} I(X;Y) = \max_{P(x_i)} \sum_{i=1}^{M_x} P(x_i)\int_{-\infty}^{+\infty} p(y|x_i)\log_2\frac{p(y|x_i)}{\sum\limits_{i'=1}^{M_x} P(x_{i'})p(y|x_{i'})}dy. \tag{2.42}$$

Note that upper-case and lower-case, P and p, stand for probability-mass function and probability density function, respectively. We consider the case of an AWGN channel with a density

$$p(y|x_i) = e^{-\frac{|y-x_i|^2}{2\sigma_n^2}} \cdot \begin{cases} \frac{1}{\sqrt{2\pi\sigma_n^2}} & \text{one-dimensional (PAM)} \\ \frac{1}{2\pi\sigma_n^2} & \text{two-dimensional (PSK, QAM)} \end{cases} . \tag{2.43}$$

Assuming equiprobable input signals, i.e., $P(x_i) = 1/M_x$, we obtain

$$C = 1/M_x \cdot \sum_{i=1}^{M_x} \int_{-\infty}^{+\infty} p(y|x_i) \left[\log_2 \left(\frac{p(y|x_i)}{\sum_{i'=1}^{M_x} p(y|x_{i'})} \right) + \log_2(M_x) \right] dy \tag{2.44}$$

$$= \log_2(M_x) - 1/M_x \cdot \sum_{i=1}^{M_x} \int_{-\infty}^{+\infty} \left\{ \begin{matrix} \frac{1}{\sqrt{2\pi\sigma_n^2}} \\ \frac{1}{2\pi\sigma_n^2} \end{matrix} \right\} \cdot e^{-\frac{|y-x_i|^2}{2\sigma_n^2}} \log_2 \left[\frac{\sum_{i'=1}^{M_x} e^{-\frac{|y-x_{i'}|^2}{2\sigma_n^2}}}{e^{-\frac{|y-x_i|^2}{2\sigma_n^2}}} \right] dy.$$

Substituting $w = y - x_i$ yields

$$C = \log_2(M_x) - 1/M_x \cdot \sum_{i=1}^{M_x} \int_{-\infty}^{+\infty} \left\{ \begin{matrix} \frac{1}{\sqrt{2\pi\sigma_n^2}} \\ \frac{1}{2\pi\sigma_n^2} \end{matrix} \right\} \cdot e^{-\frac{|w|^2}{2\sigma_n^2}} \cdot \log_2 \left[\frac{\sum_{i'=1}^{M_x} e^{-\frac{|w+x_i-x_{i'}|^2}{2\sigma_n^2}}}{e^{-\frac{|w|^2}{2\sigma_n^2}}} \right] dw. \tag{2.45}$$

Before suitable math packages became available, such integrals were solved by writing $\int \ldots \exp[-\frac{|w|^2}{2\sigma_n^2}]dw$ as an expectation $E\{\ldots\}$ for Monte-Carlo integration. We are still showing this, since also modern math routines may have some numerical issues. The curves shown later, however, were computed using Mupad.

$$C = \log_2(M_x) - 1/M_x \cdot \sum_{i=1}^{M_x} E \left\{ \log_2 \left[\sum_{i'=1}^{M_x} e^{-\frac{|w+x_i-x_{i'}|^2 - |w|^2}{2\sigma_n^2}} \right] \right\} \tag{2.46}$$

We show Capacity results for M-PAM, M-PSK, and M-QAM in Figs. 2.6, 2.7, and 2.8, respectively. In there, note

$$\text{SNR} = E_s/N_0 = E(|s_i|^2)/E(|w|^2) = \begin{cases} E(|s_i|^2)/\sigma_n^2 & \text{one-dimensional (PAM),} \\ E(|s_i|^2)/2\sigma_n^2 & \text{two-dimensional (PSK, QAM).} \end{cases} \tag{2.47}$$

When discussing the mutual information for continuous output, instead of a probability mass functions, we went for probability densities that come with a unit. However, since the same unit appears in numerator and denominator in Eq. (2.42), they cancel out. For the entropies alone, one defines the so-called differential entropy,

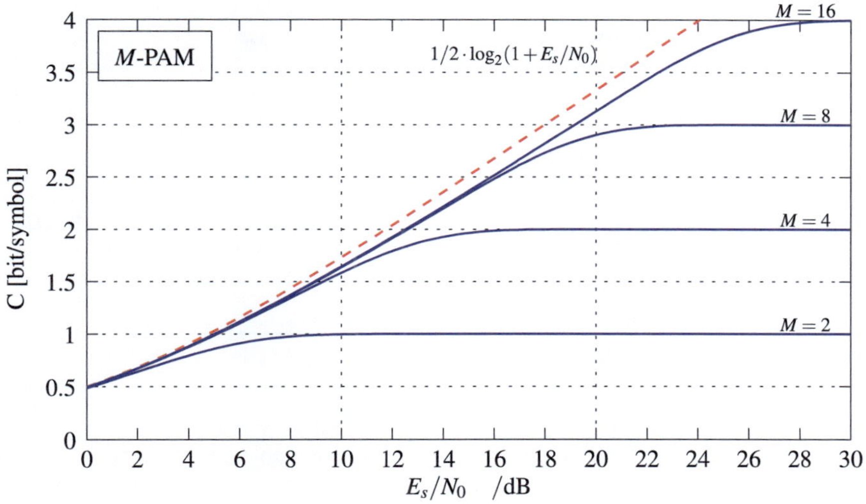

Fig. 2.6 Channel capacities for one-dimensional M-PAM dependent on the SNR=E_s/N_0

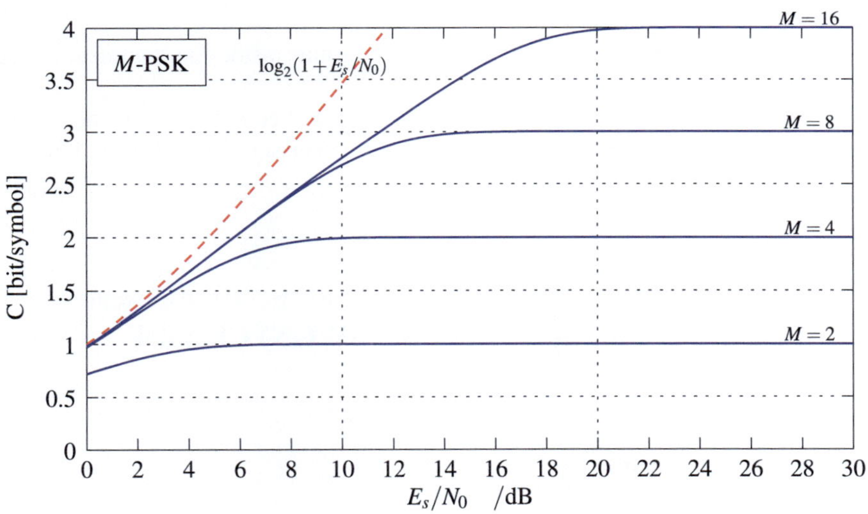

Fig. 2.7 Channel capacities for two-dimensional M-PSK dependent on the SNR=E_s/N_0

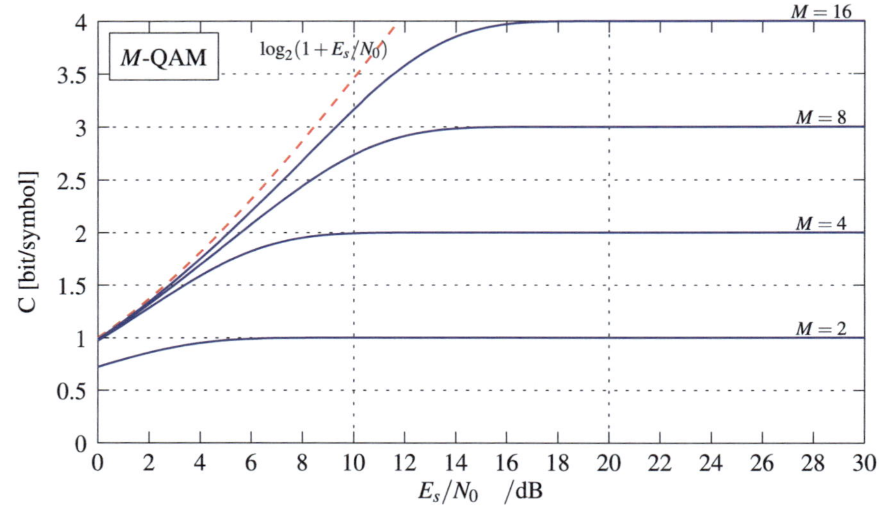

Fig. 2.8 Channel capacities for two-dimensional M-QAM dependent on the SNR=E_s/N_0

as described in the following section, despite the unit inside the argument of the logarithm.

In the following section, we will also derive the dashed red upper bounds in the Capacity figures, representing the Capacities for a Gaussian input distribution, i.e., not discrete.

2.5 Differential Entropy and Capacity of the Time-Discrete Additive White Gaussian Noise (AWGN) Channel

In the following, we use lower-case $f(x)$, $g(x)$, and $h(x)$ to denote densities.

Definition 2.3 We define

$$H(X) := -\int_{-\infty}^{\infty} f_X(x) \log f_X(x) dx \tag{2.48}$$

as the **differential entropy** as of a continuous random variable X with a density $f_X(x)$.

Note the problem regarding the physical interpretation, since $f(x)$ has a unit in the argument of the logarithm. One may, of course, introduce some normalization.

As we already did in the previous section, we can still define the **Mutual Information** without unit problems, since they are canceling out.

Definition 2.4 The Mutual Information for continuous input and output is defined as

$$I(X;Y) := \int_{-\infty}^{\infty}\int_{-\infty}^{\infty} f_{X,Y}(x,y)\log\frac{f_{X|Y}(x|y)}{f_X(x)}dxdy \tag{2.49}$$

with

$$H(X|Y) := -\int_{-\infty}^{\infty}\int_{-\infty}^{\infty} f_{X,Y}(x,y)\log f_{X|Y}(x|y)dxdy. \tag{2.50}$$

We still have the relation

$$I(X;Y) = H(X) - H(X|Y) \geq 0. \tag{2.51}$$

However, we cannot say anything about signs of the individual differential entropies.

Let us now discuss the Differential Entropy in the Gaussian case with

$$f_X(x) = \frac{1}{\sqrt{2\pi\sigma^2}}e^{-\frac{(x-\mu)^2}{2\sigma^2}}. \tag{2.52}$$

The Differential Entropy follows to be

$$\begin{aligned} H(X) &= -\int_{-\infty}^{\infty}\frac{1}{\sqrt{2\pi\sigma^2}}e^{-\frac{(x-\mu)^2}{2\sigma^2}}\log\left[\frac{1}{\sqrt{2\pi\sigma^2}}e^{-\frac{(x-\mu)^2}{2\sigma^2}}\right]dx \\ &= \log\sqrt{2\pi\sigma^2}\int_{-\infty}^{\infty}\frac{1}{\sqrt{2\pi\sigma^2}}e^{-\frac{(x-\mu)^2}{2\sigma^2}}dx + \\ &\quad +\frac{\log e}{2\sigma^2}\int_{-\infty}^{\infty}(x-\mu)^2\frac{1}{\sqrt{2\pi\sigma^2}}e^{-\frac{(x-\mu)^2}{2\sigma^2}}dx \\ &= \frac{1}{2}\log(2\pi\sigma^2) + \frac{\log e}{2\sigma^2}\sigma^2 = \frac{1}{2}\log(2\pi e\sigma^2). \end{aligned} \tag{2.53}$$

We will now show that the Gaussian distribution is the one with the highest differential entropy. We first need the following

Lemma 2.2 *Let $f_X(x)$ and $g_X(x)$ be two densities with the same mean and standard deviation (variance) and let*

$$h_X(x) = \frac{1}{\sqrt{2\pi\sigma^2}}e^{-\frac{(x-\mu)^2}{2\sigma^2}}. \tag{2.54}$$

When the integrals exist, we obtain

$$-\int_{-\infty}^{\infty} f_X(x)\cdot\log h_X(x)dx = -\int_{-\infty}^{\infty} g_X(x)\cdot\log h_X(x)dx. \tag{2.55}$$

Proof For convenience, we replace log by ln which are just related by a factor.

$$
\begin{aligned}
-\int_{-\infty}^{\infty} f_X(x)\cdot \ln h_X(x)dx &= \int_{-\infty}^{\infty} f_X(x)\cdot \left[\ln\sqrt{2\pi\sigma^2}+\frac{(x-\mu)^2}{2\sigma^2}\right]dx\\
&= \ln\sqrt{2\pi\sigma^2}+\frac{1}{2\sigma^2}\int_{-\infty}^{\infty}(x-\mu_f)^2 f_X(x)dx+\\
&+\frac{\mu_f-\mu}{\sigma^2}\int_{-\infty}^{\infty}(x-\mu_f)f_X(x)dx\\
&+\frac{(\mu_f-\mu)^2}{2\sigma^2}\int_{-\infty}^{\infty} f_X(x)dx\\
&= \ln\sqrt{2\pi\sigma^2}+\frac{\sigma_f^2+(\mu_f-\mu)^2}{2\sigma^2} \qquad (2.56)
\end{aligned}
$$

μ_f and σ_f are the mean and variance, respectively, for $f_X(x)$. Since they were said to be equal to μ_g and σ_g, respectively, we have already proven the lemma. □

We are now prepared for the following

Theorem 2.6 *The Gaussian distribution maximizes the differential entropy amongst all distributions with a given mean μ and variance σ^2.*

Proof

$$
\begin{aligned}
H(X)-\frac{1}{2}\log(2\pi e\sigma^2) &=\\
&= -\int_{-\infty}^{\infty} f_X(x)\log f_X(x)dx+\int_{-\infty}^{\infty} h_X(x)\log h_X(x)dx \qquad (2.57)\\
&= -\int_{-\infty}^{\infty} f_X(x)\log f_X(x)dx+\int_{-\infty}^{\infty} f_X(x)\log h_X(x)dx\\
&= \int_{-\infty}^{\infty} f_X(x)\log\frac{h_X(x)}{f_X(x)}dx\\
&\le \int_{-\infty}^{\infty} f_X(x)\left[\frac{h_X(x)}{f_X(x)}-1\right]\log(e)\,dx\\
&= \left(\int_{-\infty}^{\infty} h_X(x)dx-\int_{-\infty}^{\infty} f_X(x)dx\right)\cdot\log e=0 \qquad (2.58)
\end{aligned}
$$

□

The next step towards the Capacity of the Additive White Gaussian Noise channel is to express the Mutual Information for the Gaussian source and channel. Let $Y = X + Z$.

$$I(X;Y) = H(Y) - H(Y|X) \tag{2.59}$$

$$\begin{aligned} H(Y|X) &= -\int_{-\infty}^{\infty}\int_{-\infty}^{\infty} f_{X,Y}(x,y)\log f_{Y|X}(y|x)dxdy \\ &= -\int_{-\infty}^{\infty}\int_{-\infty}^{\infty} f_X(x)f_{Y|X}(y|x)\log f_{Y|X}(y|x)dxdy \\ &= -\int_{-\infty}^{\infty}\int_{-\infty}^{\infty} f_X(x)f_Z(y-x)\log f_Z(y-x)dxdy \\ &= \int_{-\infty}^{\infty} f_X(x)H(Z)dx = H(Z) \end{aligned} \tag{2.60}$$

Theorem 2.7 *For $Y = X + Z$ and normal variates X and Z with variances S and N, respectively, we obtain*

$$I(X;Y) = \frac{1}{2}\log\left(1 + S/N\right). \tag{2.61}$$

Proof Y has a variance of $S + N$. We thus obtain

$$I(X;Y) = H(Y) - H(Z) = \frac{1}{2}\log\left[2\pi e(S+N)\right] - \frac{1}{2}\log\left[2\pi eN\right] = \frac{1}{2}\log\left(1 + S/N\right). \tag{2.62}$$

□

The **Channel Capacity time-discrete AWGN**[1] **channel** results from maximizing the Mutual Information

$$C = \sup_{f_X(x)} I(X;Y). \tag{2.63}$$

Usually, the average power is limited (one may additionally have to obey PSD or peak-power constraints)

$$E\{X^2\} = \int_{-\infty}^{\infty} x^2 f_X(x)dx \leq E. \tag{2.64}$$

Theorem 2.8 *The Channel Capacity of a time-discrete, memoryless channel with additive Gaussian noise with a variance of N and average power limit E of the input signal is*

$$C = \frac{1}{2}\log\left(1 + E/N\right). \tag{2.65}$$

Proof Since $I(X;Y) = H(Y) - H(Z)$, we just have to maximize $H(Y)$, which we know should be Gaussian with variance $E + N$. If the sum of two random variables is Gaussian, each single one will also be Gaussian [6]. We thus know that the input distribution should also be Gaussian with variance E. □

---

[1] The AWGN (Additive White Gaussian Noise) channel is the worst "disturbing" in the sense that it is the most "uncertain", since $H(Z)$ is maximum for a given variance.

2.6 Capacity of the Band-Limited Additive Gaussian Noise Channel

For the band-limited case, we use the sampling theorem to be able to directly make use of the results of the previous section. Let us assume a sampling frequency ω_0 and a strictly band-limited signal with $F(j\omega) = 0$ for $|\omega| \geq \omega_0/2$. Sampling, regarded as the multiplication with the Dirac sequence $x_\delta(t)$, means a convolution in frequency domain, thereby periodically repeating $F(j\omega)$.

$$f(t) \cdot \frac{2\pi}{\omega_0} \sum_{k=-\infty}^{+\infty} \delta(t - kT) \circ\!\!-\!\!\bullet\ 2\pi \cdot \sum_{k=-\infty}^{+\infty} F(j\omega - k\omega_0) \tag{2.66}$$

One ideally recovers the original signal using a rectangular brick-wall filter

$$r(t) = \frac{\omega_0}{2\pi} \frac{\sin(\omega_0/2 \cdot t)}{\omega_0/2 \cdot t} \circ\!\!-\!\!\bullet\ R(f) = \begin{cases} 1 \text{ for } |\omega| < \omega_0/2 \\ 0 \text{ for } |\omega| \geq \omega_0/2. \end{cases} \tag{2.67}$$

This sinc impulse response has equidistant zeros at multiples of $T = \frac{2\pi}{\omega_0}$, except for $t = 0$.

Feeding this filter with the sequence of samples, from the convolution in time domain, we obtain

$$f(t) = [x_\delta(t) \cdot f(t)] * r(t) = \sum_{k=-\infty}^{\infty} f(kT) \cdot \frac{\sin(\omega_0/2 \cdot (t - kT))}{\omega_0/2 \cdot (t - kT)}. \tag{2.68}$$

This is the well-known interpolation formula, recovering the time-continuous function from its samples.

Writing $\omega_0 = 2\pi \cdot 2 \cdot W$ with the edge frequency W,

$$f(t) = \sum_{k=-\infty}^{\infty} f(kT) \cdot \frac{\sin(\pi \cdot (2Wt - k))}{\pi \cdot (2Wt - k)}. \tag{2.69}$$

Let $Z(t)$ be a Gaussian process with a rectangular two-sided power-density spectrum

$$N(f) = \begin{cases} N_0/2, & |f| < W \\ 0, & |f| \geq W. \end{cases} \tag{2.70}$$

Since $R_Z(\tau) \circ\!\!-\!\!\bullet\ N(f)$,

$$R_Z(\tau) = E\{Z(t + \tau)Z(t)\} = \sigma_Z^2 \frac{\sin(2\pi W\tau)}{2\pi W\tau}, \tag{2.71}$$

where $\sigma_Z^2 = N_0 W$.

This means that the autocorrelation between two successive Nyquist samples is zero. The Nyquist samples of a Gaussian process with a brick-wall spectrum are independent Gaussian distributed random variables.

Let us consider a time interval τ and n being the number of samples within this interval ($n = 2W\tau$). This means n parallel time-discrete independent Gaussian channels, each with a Channel Capacity of

$$C_k = \frac{1}{2} \log\left(1 + \frac{S}{N_0 \cdot W}\right), \tag{2.72}$$

with the average power

$$S = \frac{1}{n} \sum_{k=0}^{n-1} E\{X_k^2\} \tag{2.73}$$

and the noise power $N_0 \cdot W$, N_0 being the power spectral density and W the bandwidth. We observe that

$$S/W = 2 \cdot S \cdot \tau/n = 2 \cdot E_s. \tag{2.74}$$

E_s is the energy per symbol (sample). With this, we finally obtain

$$C_k = \frac{1}{2} \log\left(1 + \frac{E_s}{N_0/2}\right). \tag{2.75}$$

The total Capacity of all n channels follows to be

$$\sum_{k=1}^{n} C_k = W\tau \log\left(1 + \frac{S}{N_0 W}\right). \tag{2.76}$$

The Capacity per time unit in bit/s is finally given by

$$C_t = \lim_{\tau\to\infty} C/\tau = W \log\left(1 + \frac{S}{N_0 W}\right). \tag{2.77}$$

In our derivation, we had used a one-sided noise PSD N_0, which would be corresponding 2-sided one with $N_0/2$ as given in Eq. (2.70). If defining the 2-sided noise PSD as N_0, then Eq. (2.75) would read

$$C = \frac{1}{2} \log_2\left[1 + \frac{S}{N}\right] = \frac{1}{2} \log_2\left[1 + \frac{2E_s W}{N_0 2W}\right] = \frac{1}{2} \log_2\left[1 + \frac{E_s}{N_0}\right]. \tag{2.78}$$

Note also that for a 2-dimensional case (I/Q), one would have to apply a factor of 2, leading to

$$C = \log_2 \left[1 + \frac{S}{N} \right] = \log_2 \left[1 + \frac{2E_s W}{N_0 2W} \right] = \log_2 \left[1 + \frac{E_s}{N_0} \right]. \quad (2.79)$$

2.7 Bhattacharyya's Bound for Maximum-Likelihood Decoding

As discussed more in the later Sect. 5.2.4, Maximum-Likelihood detection or decoding stands for maximizing the probability $P(Y|X)$, i.e., the output of a channel given the input, which is aligned with the channel description.

Let the number of possible messages w_i be M, i.e., we may think of the messages $w_i \in \{1, 2, \dots M\}$[2]. At the receiver, we estimate (decide for) the transmitted symbol $\hat{w}$ from some received $\mathbf{y}$. We define a region that leads to the same decision as

$$\mathcal{D}_i := \{\mathbf{y} : g(\mathbf{y}) = w_i\}. \quad (2.80)$$

The block-error probability P_B can be written as

$$P_B = \sum_{i=1}^{M} P_B(W = w_i) \cdot P_W(w_i), \quad (2.81)$$

with $P_B(W = w_i) = P(\hat{W} \neq W)|W = w_i)$

$$P_B(W = w_i) = \sum_{\mathbf{y} \notin \mathcal{D}_i} P_{\mathbf{Y}|\mathbf{X}}(\mathbf{y}|\mathbf{x}_i), \quad \text{with } \mathbf{x}_i = \mathbf{x}(w_i). \quad (2.82)$$

Let us study the binary case with two messages, $M = 2$, i.e.,

$$P_B(W = 1) = \sum_{\mathbf{y} \in \mathcal{D}_2} P_{\mathbf{Y}|\mathbf{X}}(\mathbf{y}|\mathbf{x}_1). \quad (2.83)$$

We multiply this by $\sqrt{P_{\mathbf{Y}|\mathbf{X}}(\mathbf{y}|\mathbf{x}_2)/P_{\mathbf{Y}|\mathbf{X}}(\mathbf{y}|\mathbf{x}_1)}$, which is greater or equal to one, if $\mathbf{y} \in \mathcal{D}_2$. We obtain

$$\begin{aligned} P_B(W = 1) &\leq \sum_{\mathbf{y} \in \mathcal{D}_2} P_{\mathbf{Y}|\mathbf{X}}(\mathbf{y}|\mathbf{x}_1) \cdot \sqrt{P_{\mathbf{Y}|\mathbf{X}}(\mathbf{y}|\mathbf{x}_2)/P_{\mathbf{Y}|\mathbf{X}}(\mathbf{y}|\mathbf{x}_1)} \\ &= \sum_{\mathbf{y} \in \mathcal{D}_2} \sqrt{P_{\mathbf{Y}|\mathbf{X}}(\mathbf{y}|\mathbf{x}_2) \cdot P_{\mathbf{Y}|\mathbf{X}}(\mathbf{y}|\mathbf{x}_1)} \\ &\leq \sum_{\mathbf{y}} \sqrt{P_{\mathbf{Y}|\mathbf{X}}(\mathbf{y}|\mathbf{x}_2) \cdot P_{\mathbf{Y}|\mathbf{X}}(\mathbf{y}|\mathbf{x}_1)}. \end{aligned} \quad (2.84)$$

[2] Note that from the following chapter onward, M will be used in a differing meaning, namely the number of parity symbols.

We can now simply sum over all $\mathbf{y}$.

In case of the discrete memoryless channel (DMC), we can write

$$\begin{aligned}
P_B(W = w_i) &\leq \sum_{y_1} \cdots \sum_{y_n} \sqrt{\prod_{l=1}^{n} P_{Y|X}(y_l|x_{1l}) \cdot P_{Y|X}(y_l|x_{2l})} \\
&= \sum_{y_1} \cdots \sum_{y_n} \prod_{l=1}^{n} P_{Y|X}^{1/2}(y_l|x_{1l}) \cdot P_{Y|X}^{1/2}(y_l|x_{2l}) \\
&= \sum_{y_1} P_{Y|X}^{1/2}(y_1|x_{11}) P_{Y|X}^{1/2}(y_1|x_{21}) \cdot \sum_{y_2} P_{Y|X}^{1/2}(y_2|x_{12}) P_{Y|X}^{1/2}(y_2|x_{22}) \cdots \\
&\quad \cdots \sum_{y_n} P_{Y|X}^{1/2}(y_n|x_{1n}) P_{Y|X}^{1/2}(y_n|x_{2n}) \\
&= \prod_{l=1}^{n} \sum_{y_l} \sqrt{P_{Y|X}(y_l|x_{1l}) \cdot P_{Y|X}(y_l|x_{2l})}. \qquad (2.85)
\end{aligned}$$

If we use this to describe P_B regardless of the input distribution, this is the **Bhattacharyya Bound** for Maximum-Likelihood decoding.

Example 2.1 The repetition code over the BSC

A repetition code has the two codewords $\mathbf{x}_1 = (0, 0, \ldots, 0)$ and $\mathbf{x}_2 = (1, 1, \ldots, 1)$. Let the length be n. We assume a binary symmetric channel (BSC) with an error probability of p. We get

$$\sqrt{P_{Y|X}(0|0) P_{Y|X}(0|1)} + \sqrt{P_{Y|X}(1|0) P_{Y|X}(1|1)} = 2\sqrt{p(1-p)}. \qquad (2.86)$$

Bhattacharyya's bound will be

$$P_B \leq \left(2\sqrt{p(1-p)}\right)^n \approx 2^n p^{n/2}. \qquad (2.87)$$

Exact for even n:

$P_B = \sum_{i=n/2+1}^{n} \binom{n}{i} p^i (1-p)^{n-i} + \frac{1}{2}\binom{n}{n/2} p^{n/2}(1-p)^{n/2} \approx \frac{1}{2}\binom{n}{n/2} p^{n/2}(1-p)^{n/2}$ $\approx \frac{1}{2}\binom{n}{n/2} p^{n/2}$.

Example 2.2 The repetition code over the erasure channel with erasure probability δ

$$\begin{aligned}
&\sqrt{P_{Y|X}(0|0) P_{Y|X}(0|1)} + \sqrt{P_{Y|X}(\Delta|0) P_{Y|X}(\Delta|1)} + \sqrt{P_{Y|X}(1|0) P_{Y|X}(1|1)} \\
&\qquad = \sqrt{(1-\delta) \cdot 0} + \sqrt{\delta \cdot \delta} + \sqrt{0 \cdot (1-\delta)} = \delta \qquad (2.88)
\end{aligned}$$

Bhattacharyya's bound:

$$P_B \leq \delta^n \qquad (2.89)$$

The actual probability will, however, be $P_B = 1/2 \cdot \delta^n$.

We now generalize to more than two codewords with

$$P_B(W = w_i) \leq \sum_{j=1, j \neq i}^{M} P(\mathbf{Y} \in \mathcal{D}_j | W = w_i). \tag{2.90}$$

We thus obtain **Bhattacharyya's bound** for the general case using the previous one as an upper bound for each of the sum terms.

$$P_B(W = w_i) \leq \sum_{j=1, j \neq i}^{M} \prod_{l=1}^{n} \sum_{y_l} \sqrt{P_{Y|X}(y_l|x_{il}) \cdot P_{Y|X}(y_l|x_{jl})}, \quad \text{for } i = 1, 2, \ldots, M \tag{2.91}$$

The bound for P_B is dependent on i and thus we also have a dependency on the source statistics. However, we can always use

$$P_B \leq \max_{1 \leq i \leq M} P_B(W = w_i) \tag{2.92}$$

as an upper bound, which may be loose when the number of codewords is big.

2.8 Rate-Distortion Theory

This section will provide an introduction to rate-distortion theory that will later provide us with the means to determine the shape of the so-called Shannon limit over the SNR.

Let us represent a subset of values x by some $\hat{x}$. For illustration in the Euclidean space, one may think of a vector quantizer (Lloyd-Max quantizer, k-means alg., Linde-Buzo-Gray alg.), where the codebook entry representative would be the conditional mean of a Voronoi region, denoting the quantizer region assigned to the same $\hat{x}$.

Definition 2.5 Let us first define a distortion as a mapping

$$d{:}\mathcal{H} \times \hat{\mathcal{H}} \longrightarrow \mathbb{R}^+ \tag{2.93}$$

from the set of source alphabet-reproduction alphabet pairs into the set of non-negative real numbers. The distortion $d(x, \hat{x})$ is a measure of the cost of representing the symbol x by the symbol $\hat{x}$.

Especially, using the Hamming distance,

$$d(x, \hat{x}) = \begin{cases} 0 \text{ if } x = \hat{x} \\ 1 \text{ if } x \neq \hat{x}, \end{cases} \tag{2.94}$$

the **Hamming distortion** is defined as a probability of error distortion, since

$$E\{d(X, \hat{X})\} = P(X \neq \hat{X}). \tag{2.95}$$

For the continuous case, one often uses the **Squared error distortion**

$$d(x, \hat{x}) = (x - \hat{x})^2. \tag{2.96}$$

The distortion between vectors $\mathbf{x}$ and $\hat{\mathbf{x}}$ of length N is defined by

$$d(\mathbf{x}, \hat{\mathbf{x}}) = \frac{1}{N} \sum_{i=1}^{N} d(x_i, \hat{x}_i). \tag{2.97}$$

For the encoding and decoding sequence, we formulate as follows.

Definition 2.6 A $(2^{NR}, N)$ rate-distortion code of length N and rate $R = K/N$ consists of an encoding function

$$f_N : \mathcal{H}^N \longrightarrow \{1, 2, \ldots, 2^{NR}\}, \tag{2.98}$$

and a decoding (reproduction) function

$$g_N : \{1, 2, \ldots, 2^{NR}\} \longrightarrow \hat{\mathcal{H}}^N. \tag{2.99}$$

The distortion associated with the $(2^{NR}, N)$ code is defined as

$$D = E\{d(\mathbf{X}, g_N(f_N(\mathbf{X})))\}, \tag{2.100}$$

where the expectation is with respect to the probability distribution on X, i.e.,

$$D = \sum_{\mathbf{x}} p(\mathbf{x}) d(\mathbf{x}, g_N(f_N(\mathbf{x})). \tag{2.101}$$

We require some more definitions.

Definition 2.7 The set of N-tuples $g_N(1), g_N(2), \ldots, g_N(2^{NR})$, denoted by $\hat{\mathbf{x}}(1), \hat{\mathbf{x}}(2), \ldots, \hat{\mathbf{x}}(2^{NR})$, constitutes the codebook, and $f_N^{-1}(1), \ldots, f_N^{-1}(2^{NR})$ are the associated assignment (Voronoi) regions.

A rate-distortion pair (R, D) is said to be achievable, if there exists a sequence of $(2^{NR}, N)$ rate-distortion codes (f_N, g_N) with $\lim_{N \to \infty} E\{d(\mathbf{X}, g_N(f_N(\mathbf{X}))) \leq D$

The rate-distortion region for a source is the closure of the set of achievable rate-distortion pairs (R, D).

The rate-distortion function $R(D)$ is the infimum of rates R such that (R, D) is in the rate-distortion region of the source for a given distortion D.

The distortion-rate function $D(R)$ is the infimum of all distortions D such the (R, D) is in the rate-distortion region of the source for a given rate R.

Definition 2.8 The *information rate-distortion function* $R^{(I)}(D)$ for a source X with distortion measure $d(x,\hat{x})$ is defined as

$$R^{(I)}(D) = \min_{p(\hat{x}|x):\sum_{x,\hat{x}} p(x)\cdot p(\hat{x}|x)\cdot d(x,\hat{x})\le D} I(X;\hat{X}),$$

where the minimization is over all conditional distributions $p(\hat{x}|x)$ for which the joint distribution $p(x,\hat{x}) = p(x)\cdot p(\hat{x}|x)$ satisfies the expected distortion constraint.

Theorem 2.9 *The rate-distortion function for an i.i.d. source X with distribution $p(x)$ and bounded distortion function $d(x,\hat{x})$ is equal to the associated information rate-distortion function. Thus,*

$$R(D) = R^{(I)}(D) = \min_{p(\hat{x}|x):\sum_{x,\hat{x}} p(x)\cdot p(\hat{x}|x)\cdot d(x,\hat{x})\le D} I(X;\hat{X})$$

is the minimum achievable rate at distortion D.

Calculation of the rate-distortion function — the binary case

Theorem 2.10 *The rate-distortion function for a Bernoulli(p) source with Hamming distortion is given by*

$$R(D) = \begin{cases} h(p) - h(D), & 0 \le D \le \min(p, 1-p) \\ 0, & D > \min(p, 1-p). \end{cases} \tag{2.102}$$

Proof First lower-bound $I(X;\hat{X})$

$$\begin{aligned} I(X;\hat{X}) &= H(X) - H(X|\hat{X}) \\ &= h(p) - H(X \oplus \hat{X}|\hat{X}) \\ &\ge h(p) - H(X \oplus \hat{X}) = h(p) - h(D), \end{aligned} \tag{2.103}$$

since $P(X \ne \hat{X}) \le D$ and $h(D)$ increases with D for $D \le 1/2$.

We now construct probabilities for $\hat{X}$ such that equality is achieved. Let $r = P(\hat{X}=1)$ and $1-r = P(\hat{X}=0)$ and note that $p = P(X=1)$ and $(1-p) = P(X=0)$ (Fig. 2.9).

$$r(1-D) + (1-r)D = p \implies r = \frac{p-D}{1-2D}$$

If $D \le p \le 1/2$, then $P(\hat{X}=1) \ge 0$ and $P(\hat{X}=0) \ge 0$. We then have

$$\begin{aligned} I(X;\hat{X}) &= H(X) - H(X|\hat{X}) \\ &= h(p) - h(D), \end{aligned} \tag{2.104}$$

and the expected distortion is $P(X \ne \hat{X}) = D$.

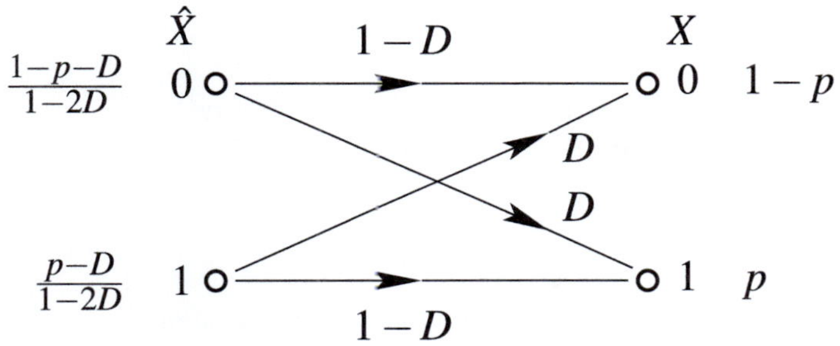

Fig. 2.9 Hamming distortion

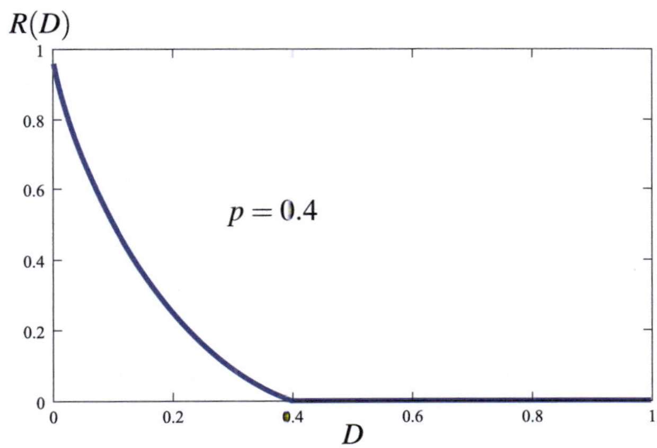

Fig. 2.10 Rate-distortion function for the Hamming distortion and Bernoulli(p) source

If $D \geq p$, then we can achieve $R(D) = 0$ by letting $\hat{X} = 0$ with probability 1. In this case, $I(X; \hat{X}) = 0$ and $D = p$. Similarly, if $D \geq 1 - p$, we can achieve $R(D) = 0$ by setting $\hat{X} = 1$ with probability 1.

Hence, the rate-distortion function for a binary source is

$$R(D) = \begin{cases} h(p) - h(D), & 0 \leq D \leq \min(p, 1-p) \\ 0, & D > \min(p, 1-p). \end{cases}$$

□

Figure 2.10 shows the rate-distortion function.

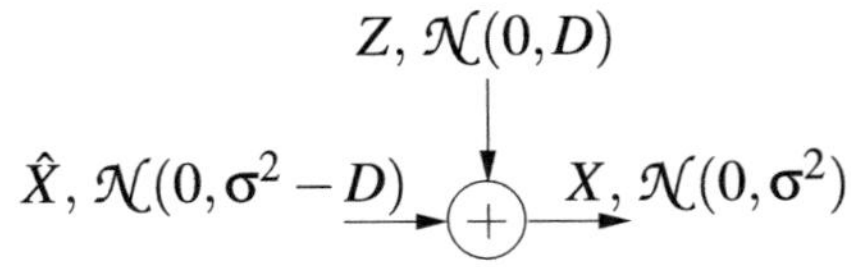

Fig. 2.11 Squared-error distortion

Calculation of the rate-distortion function — the Gaussian case

Theorem 2.11 *The rate-distortion function for a $\mathcal{N}(0, \sigma^2)$ source with squared-error distortion D is*

$$R(D) = \begin{cases} \frac{1}{2}\log\frac{\sigma^2}{D}, & 0 \le D \le \sigma^2 \\ 0, & D > \sigma^2 \end{cases} \tag{2.105}$$

Proof

$$\begin{aligned} I(X;\hat{X}) &= H(X) - H(X|\hat{X}) \\ &= \frac{1}{2}\log(2\pi e\sigma^2) - H(X-\hat{X}|\hat{X}) \\ &\ge \frac{1}{2}\log(2\pi e\sigma^2) - H(X-\hat{X}) \\ &\ge \frac{1}{2}\log(2\pi e\sigma^2) - H(\mathcal{N}(0, E\{(X-\hat{X})^2\})) \\ &= \frac{1}{2}\log(2\pi e\sigma^2) - \frac{1}{2}\log\left(2\pi e E\{(X-\hat{X})^2\}\right) \\ &= \frac{1}{2}\log(2\pi e\sigma^2) - \frac{1}{2}\log\left(2\pi e D\}\right) = \frac{1}{2}\log(\sigma^2/D) \end{aligned} \tag{2.106}$$

Let us consider the following *test channel* (note the duality between Channel Capacity and rate distortion!), where $\hat{X}$ and Z are independent. We obtain (Fig. 2.11)

$$I(X;\hat{X}) = \frac{1}{2}\log(\sigma^2/D).$$

If $D > \sigma^2$, we choose $\hat{X} = 0$ with probability 1, achieving $R(D) = 0$. □

Figure 2.12 shows the rate-distortion function.

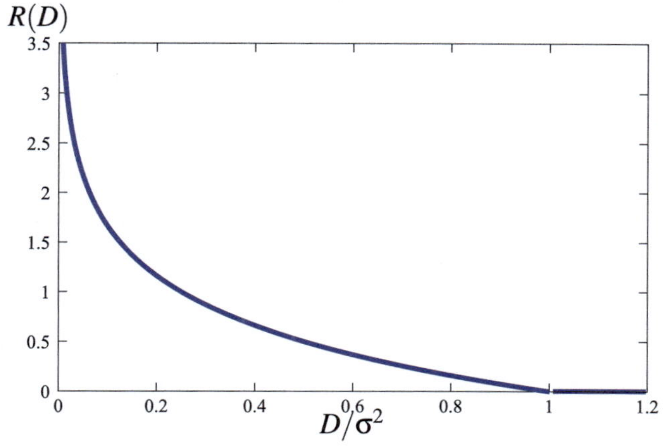

Fig. 2.12 Rate-distortion function for the squared-error distortion and a Gaussian $\mathcal{N}(0, \sigma^2)$ source

References

1. C. E. Shannon, "A mathematical theory of communication," *Bell System Technical Journal*, vol. 27, no. 3, pp. 379–423, 1948. [Online]. Available: https://onlinelibrary.wiley.com/doi/abs/10.1002/j.1538-7305.1948.tb01338.x
2. T. M. Cover and J. A. Thomas, *Elements of Information Theory (Wiley Series in Telecommunications and Signal Processing)*. New York, NY, USA: Wiley-Interscience, 2006.
3. I. Csiszár and J. Körner, *Information Theory: Coding Theorems for Discrete Memoryless Systems*, 2nd ed. Cambridge University Press, 2011.
4. R. V. L. Hartley, "Transmission of information," *Bell System Technical Journal*, vol. 7, pp. 535–563, 1928. [Online]. Available: https://api.semanticscholar.org/CorpusID:109872947
5. G. Ungerboeck, "Channel coding with multilevel/phase signals," *IEEE Transactions on Information Theory*, vol. 28, no. 1, pp. 55–67, 1982.
6. H. Cramer, *Random Variables and Probability Distributions*. Cambridge, England: Cambridge University Press, 1970, vol. Cambridge Tracts in Mathematics No. 36.

Chapter 3
Basic Coding Definitions and Some Block Codes

Selten habt ihr mich verstanden,
Selten auch verstand ich euch,
Nur wenn wir im "**Code**" (Kot) uns fanden,
So verstanden wir uns gleich.

Heinrich Heine

Ye could not understand mine ire,
Nor I the tales that ye did tell,
*But when we met within the "**Code**" (mire),*
We knew each other very well.

3.1 First Basic Coding Facts

Definition 3.1 A codeword of a block code with length N consists of K information symbols $I_j \in \mathbb{F}$ and M parity symbols $P_j \in \mathbb{F}$, where $\mathbb{F}$ is an arbitrary number field. The ratio $R = K/N$ is the **code rate**. More generally, it can be defined as $R = \log_2 |C|/N$, where $|C|$ denotes the cardinality of the code C, i.e., the number of codewords in the set C.

(Remark: Codes over groups or rings will not been described.)

$$\underbrace{\boxed{I_0 \,|\, I_1 \,|\, I_2 \,|\, \cdots \,|\, I_{K-1} \,\|\, P_0 \,|\, P_1 \,|\, \cdots \,|\, P_{M-1}}}_{N}$$

An information block will thus be extended by a redundant part by applying a linear or even nonlinear operation. This should allow the correction (or just detection)

W. Henkel, *Channel Coding*, Signals and Communication Technology,
https://doi.org/10.1007/978-3-032-08236-7_3

of errors that may have occurred during transmission. We speak of a **systematic code** if the information is directly part of the codeword, without any modification.

The most important code parameter is its minimum Hamming distance.

Definition 3.2 The **minimum Hamming distance** of a code C is given by

$$d_{Hm} = \min_{\substack{\boldsymbol{c}_i, \boldsymbol{c}_j \in C \\ i \neq j}} d_H(\boldsymbol{c}_i, \boldsymbol{c}_j). \tag{3.1}$$

Practically, especially such codes are applied that have a linear relation between information and redundancy.

Definition 3.3 A **linear code** C with codewords $\boldsymbol{c}_i \in C$, whose components are elements of the field $\mathbb{F}$ have the property

$$a \cdot \boldsymbol{c}_i + b \cdot \boldsymbol{c}_j \in C, \quad a, b \in \mathbb{F} \tag{3.2}$$

The distance properties, i.e., the distances to other codewords are thus independent from the actual reference codeword. This leads to an important property of linear codes:

Theorem 3.1 *The minimum Hamming distance d_{Hm} between the codewords of a linear Code C is equal to its* **minimum Hamming weight** w_{Hm}.

$$d_{Hm} = \min_{\mathbf{c} \neq 0} w_H(\mathbf{c}) = w_{Hm} \tag{3.3}$$

Proof

$$d_{Hm} = \min_{\substack{\mathbf{c}_i, \mathbf{c}_j \in C \\ i \neq j}} d_H(\mathbf{c}_i, \mathbf{c}_j) = \min_{\substack{\mathbf{c}_i, \mathbf{c}_j \in C \\ i \neq j}} d_H(\mathbf{c}_i - \mathbf{c}_j, 0) = \min_{\substack{\mathbf{c} \in C \\ \mathbf{c} \neq 0}} w_H(\mathbf{c}) \tag{3.4}$$

□

Theorem 3.2 *A code with the minimum distance d_{Hm} allows for the correction of $\lfloor (d_{Hm} - 1)/2 \rfloor$ errors. For even d_{Hm}, $(d_{Hm} - 2)/2$ errors can be corrected. Additionally, $d_{Hm}/2$ errors can be detected.*

For illustration, see Fig. 3.1.

Theorem 3.3 (Singleton bound [1]) *The minimum distance and the minimum weight of a linear (N, K) code is limited by*

$$d_{Hm} = w_{Hm} \leq 1 + N - K = 1 + M. \tag{3.5}$$

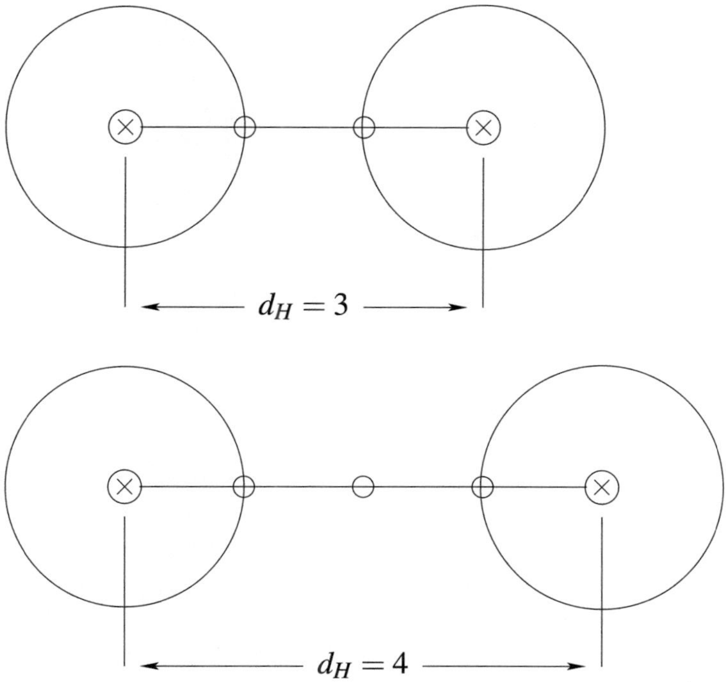

Fig. 3.1 Illustration of the correction capabilities dependent on the minimum distances

Fig. 3.2 Illustration of the Singleton bound

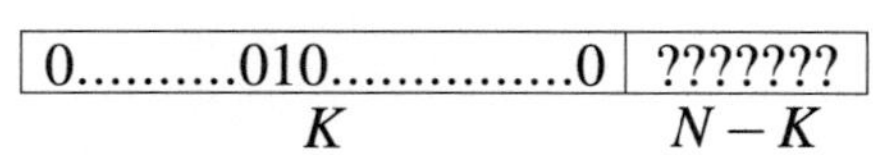

Note: Codes are usually specified by the three parameters (N, K, d_{Hm}).

Proof Let the minimum weight of a codeword be d_{Hm}.
We now consider a systematic codeword with just one information symbol different from zero and $N - K$ parity symbols (see Fig. 3.2). We obtain the maximum weight to be $1 + N - K$. (qed.) □

The binary parity-check code is a simple example, where a mod-2 sum of all information bits is attached as an even parity bit. At the receiver, a single error (or an odd number of errors) can easily been detected by just adding up all received bits modulo 2.

3.2 Matrix Description of the Coding and the Decoding of Linear Block Codes

Since the relation between parity and information part of a codeword should be linear, it should be possible to check if a word belongs to the code by just applying M equations. To this end, a **parity-check matrix H** is defined.

Definition 3.4 The parity-check matrix $\mathbf{H}$ is an $(N-K)\times N$ matrix that fulfills the following equation for all codewords $\mathbf{c}$ from a code C.

$$\mathbf{H}\begin{pmatrix} c_0 \\ c_1 \\ c_2 \\ \vdots \\ c_{N-1} \end{pmatrix} = \mathbf{H}\mathbf{c}^T = \mathbf{0}. \tag{3.6}$$

The parity-check matrix of the parity code would be $\mathbf{H} = (1, 1, 1, \ldots, 1)$.

Let us now consider a code that cannot just be used to detect an error, but also is able to correct a single error — the **Hamming code**. We are only discussing the Hamming code of length $N = 7$. A possible parity-check matrix would be

$$\mathbf{H} = \begin{pmatrix} 0001111 \\ 0110011 \\ 1010101 \end{pmatrix}. \tag{3.7}$$

In this formulation, the result of the parity-check equations, denoted as **syndrome**, has the nice property that the error position of a single error is obtained in binary notation.

Let, e.g., $\mathbf{r} = (1, 0, 0, 1, 0, 0, 0)$ be a received word. We then obtain

$$\mathbf{s}^T = \mathbf{H}\mathbf{r}^T = \begin{pmatrix} 0\,0\,0\,1\,1\,1\,1 \\ 0\,1\,1\,0\,0\,1\,1 \\ 1\,0\,1\,0\,1\,0\,1 \end{pmatrix}\begin{pmatrix} 1 \\ 0 \\ 0 \\ 1 \\ 0 \\ 0 \\ 0 \end{pmatrix} = \begin{pmatrix} 1 \\ 0 \\ 1 \end{pmatrix} \quad \text{mod } 2. \tag{3.8}$$

Note that inverting bit $5 = 101_2$ leads to a zero syndrome. If there is just one error, then the location is directly specified by the syndrome.

The parity-check equations can also be graphically illustrated, as shown in Fig. 3.3.

Each circle stands for a parity-check equation. The error location can be seen from the overlap of non-zero parity-check equations.

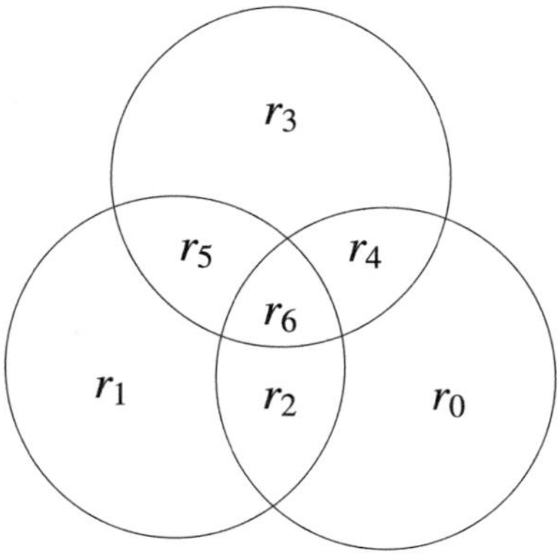

Fig. 3.3 A graphical illustration of the parity-check equations of the Hamming code of length $N = 7$

We have seen that the syndrome follows from a linear combination of the columns of **H**. The columns will be selected by the error locations. Superimposed valid codewords will be eliminated by the parity-check matrix. To be able to correct t errors, i.e., to ensure a minimum Hamming distance of $d_{Hm} = 2t + 1$, a number of $d_{Hm} - 1 = 2t$ columns of the **H** matrix have to be linearly independent. With less linearly independent columns, it would be possible to move from one valid codeword to another with a smaller number of errors. This means, in other words, that a valid codeword with the minimum weight d_{Hm} leads to a linear combination of d_{Hm} columns of the parity-check matrix. This linear combination should result in the zero vector. This should, however, not be the case with a lower weight. Otherwise, this would also be a valid codeword and would mean that the code would have a lower minimum distance = minimum weight.

3.3 Equivalent Representations of the Parity-Check Matrix

It is important to note that the parity-check matrix can appear in a manifold of equivalent representations. Since valid codewords always lead to a zero syndrome in (3.6), an equivalent representation can be obtained by linearly combining the rows of the parity-check matrix. The **H** matrix of the Hamming code in (3.7) may, e.g., be modified by the following linear combinations:

$$\begin{aligned} I + II &\longrightarrow I \\ I + III &\longrightarrow II \\ I + II + III &\longrightarrow III \end{aligned}$$

leading to the **systematic form**

$$\begin{array}{cccc|ccc} 0 & 1 & 1 & 1 & 1 & 0 & 0 \\ 1 & 0 & 1 & 1 & 0 & 1 & 0 \\ 1 & 1 & 0 & 1 & 0 & 0 & 1 \end{array} = (\boldsymbol{A} \mid \boldsymbol{I}) \tag{3.9}$$

A identity matrix $\boldsymbol{I}$ appears on the right-hand side. We obtain a coding rule that allows to derive the parity positions 4–6 from the information positions 0–3.

Furthermore, the columns of the **H** matrix may be exchanged. However, this comes with a permutation of the codeword positions. A **cyclic representation** can be obtained as follows:

$$\begin{array}{ccccccc} 1 & 1 & 1 & 0 & 1 & 0 & 0 \\ 0 & 1 & 1 & 1 & 0 & 1 & 0 \\ 0 & 0 & 1 & 1 & 1 & 0 & 1 \end{array} \tag{3.10}$$

Definition 3.5 A code C is called **cyclic**, if for $(c_0, c_1, \ldots, c_{N-1}) \in C$ also follows $(c_1, c_2, \ldots, c_{N-1}, c_0) \in C$.

Up to now, we only discussed the Hamming code with parameters ($N = 7$, $K = 4$, $d_H = 3$). The properties of binary Hamming codes of other lengths are gathered in the following table.

Properties of Hamming codes	
Length:	$N = 2^M - 1$
Number of parity positions:	M
Number of information pos. (dimension):	$K = 2^M - 1 - M$
Minimum Hamming distance:	$d_{Hm} = 3$

The parity-check equations relate parity-check and information symbols (bits). e.g., we obtain from the parity-check equations with the **H**-Matrix from (3.9)

$$\begin{aligned} c_4 &= c_1 + c_2 + c_3 \\ c_5 &= c_0 + c_2 + c_3 \\ c_6 &= c_0 + c_1 + c_3 \end{aligned} \tag{3.11}$$

Let $c_i, i = 0..3$ be the information positions taken to be the unit vectors. We then obtain the four codewords

$$\begin{array}{cccc|ccc} c_0 & c_1 & c_2 & c_3 & c_4 & c_5 & c_6 \\ \hline 1 & 0 & 0 & 0 & 0 & 1 & 1 \\ 0 & 1 & 0 & 0 & 1 & 0 & 1 \\ 0 & 0 & 1 & 0 & 1 & 1 & 0 \\ 0 & 0 & 0 & 1 & 1 & 1 & 1 \end{array} \tag{3.12}$$

These are also the four linearly independent code vectors that span the vector subspace of the code.

Theorem 3.4 *The code C of length N and dimension K results from a linear combination of K linearly independent codewords. These linearly independent codewords constitute the so-called* **generator matrix**

Hence, codewords are obtained by the product

$$\mathbf{c} = \mathbf{iG} \tag{3.13}$$

In systematic representation, one can easily derive the corresponding **G**-Matrix for a given **H**-Matrix:

Theorem 3.5 *Let a parity-check matrix* $\mathbf{H}$ *be given in the form* $\mathbf{H} = [\boldsymbol{A}|\boldsymbol{I}_{\mathbf{N-K}}]$. *Then the corresponding generator matrix* $\mathbf{G}$ *follows to be* $\mathbf{G} = [\boldsymbol{I}_{\mathbf{K}}| - \mathbf{A}^{\mathbf{T}}]$.

Proof From $\mathbf{Hc}^{\mathrm{T}} = \mathbf{0} \Longrightarrow$

$$[\boldsymbol{A}|\boldsymbol{I}_{N-K}]\begin{pmatrix} c_0 \\ \vdots \\ c_{N-1} \end{pmatrix} = 0$$

$$\begin{pmatrix} c_K \\ \vdots \\ c_{N-1} \end{pmatrix} = -\boldsymbol{A}\begin{pmatrix} c_0 \\ \vdots \\ c_{K-1} \end{pmatrix} = -\boldsymbol{A}\begin{pmatrix} i_0 \\ \vdots \\ i_{K-1} \end{pmatrix}$$

With

$$\begin{pmatrix} c_0 \\ \vdots \\ c_{K-1} \end{pmatrix} = \boldsymbol{I}_K\begin{pmatrix} i_0 \\ \vdots \\ i_{K-1} \end{pmatrix},$$

we obtain

$$\begin{pmatrix} c_0 \\ \vdots \\ c_{N-1} \end{pmatrix} = \left[\frac{\boldsymbol{I}_K}{-\boldsymbol{A}}\right]\begin{pmatrix} i_0 \\ \vdots \\ i_{K-1} \end{pmatrix}.$$

Taking the transposes, we finally obtain

$$\mathbf{c} = \mathbf{iG} \quad \text{with} \quad \mathbf{G} = [\boldsymbol{I}_{\mathbf{K}}| - \boldsymbol{A}^{\mathbf{T}}]\,.$$

□

3.4 Equivalent Representations of the Generator Matrix

Similar to the modifications of the parity-check matrix in Sect. 3.3, we observe: linear combinations of codewords are still valid codewords. This means that linear combinations of the rows of the generator matrix do not change the code. Permutations of the columns, however, do also mean a corresponding permutation of the bit positions in the codeword. This has to be taken into consideration for the parity-check matrix, as well.

3.5 Extending Codewords

One often used extension is the attachment of an additional parity position, thereby increasing the codeword length by one. If the original code had an odd minimum Hamming distance (weight), the minimum distance (weight) will be increase by one, as well.

For the parity equations one additional parity sum is required. The new parity-check matrix $\mathbf{H}$ will be

$$\mathbf{H_e} = \begin{pmatrix} 1 \ 1 \ 1 \ldots & 1 \\ & 0 \\ & 0 \\ \mathbf{H} & \vdots \\ & 0 \end{pmatrix} \tag{3.14}$$

The extended Hamming code with the parameters (8,4,4) has an $\mathbf{H}$ matrix

$$\begin{array}{cccc|cccc|c} 1&1&1&1&1&1&1&1&1 \\ \hline 0&1&1&1&1&0&0&0&0 \\ 1&0&1&1&0&1&0&0&0 \\ 1&1&0&1&0&0&1&0&0 \end{array} \tag{3.15}$$

As far as the generator matrix $\mathbf{G}$ is concerned, this just means the extension by one parity position, which results from the modulo-2 sum of all other positions.

$$\begin{array}{cccc|ccc|c} 1&0&0&0&0&1&1&1 \\ 0&1&0&0&1&0&1&1 \\ 0&0&1&0&1&1&0&1 \\ 0&0&0&1&1&1&1&0 \end{array} \tag{3.16}$$

This extended Hamming code is also the first-order Reed-Muller code of length 2^3.

3.6 Reed-Muller Codes

An early description of the repetition code?

But let your speech be, Yea, yea; Nay, nay:
and whatsoever is more than these is of the evil one

Matthew 5:37

An 'r-th order' Reed-Muller code RM(r, m) of length 2^m can be defined by a blocked generator matrix as follows

$$\mathbf{G} = \begin{pmatrix} \mathbf{G_0} \\ \mathbf{G_1} \\ \vdots \\ \mathbf{G_r} \end{pmatrix}, \tag{3.17}$$

where $\mathbf{G_0}$ is the all-ones vector of length 2^m (repetition code!). $\mathbf{G_1}$ is an $m \times 2^m$ matrix consisting of all binary m-tuples appearing only once. $\mathbf{G_l}$ $(2 \leq l \leq r)$ results from all different products of l rows of $\mathbf{G_1}$.

The number of information bits is thus

$$K = 1 + \binom{m}{1} + \cdots + \binom{m}{r}. \tag{3.18}$$

The minimum Hamming distance d_{Hm} is $d_{Hm} = 2^{m-r}$ (without proof).

As an example, we show the generator matrix of the 3rd order RM code of length $2^4 = 16$:

$$\mathbf{G} \begin{cases} \mathbf{G}_0 = \begin{bmatrix} 1111111111111111 \end{bmatrix} = [\mathbf{c}_0] \\ \mathbf{G}_1 = \begin{bmatrix} 0000000011111111 \\ 0000111100001111 \\ 0011001100110011 \\ 0101010101010101 \end{bmatrix} = \begin{bmatrix} \mathbf{c}_1 \\ \mathbf{c}_2 \\ \mathbf{c}_3 \\ \mathbf{c}_4 \end{bmatrix} \\ \mathbf{G}_2 = \begin{bmatrix} 0000000000001111 \\ 0000000000110011 \\ 0000000001010101 \\ 0000001100000011 \\ 0000010100000101 \\ 0001000100010001 \end{bmatrix} = \begin{bmatrix} \mathbf{c}_1\mathbf{c}_2 \\ \mathbf{c}_1\mathbf{c}_3 \\ \mathbf{c}_1\mathbf{c}_4 \\ \mathbf{c}_2\mathbf{c}_3 \\ \mathbf{c}_2\mathbf{c}_4 \\ \mathbf{c}_3\mathbf{c}_4 \end{bmatrix} \\ \mathbf{G}_3 = \begin{bmatrix} 0000000000000011 \\ 0000000000000101 \\ 0000000000010001 \\ 0000000100000001 \end{bmatrix} = \begin{bmatrix} \mathbf{c}_1\mathbf{c}_2\mathbf{c}_3 \\ \mathbf{c}_1\mathbf{c}_2\mathbf{c}_4 \\ \mathbf{c}_1\mathbf{c}_3\mathbf{c}_4 \\ \mathbf{c}_2\mathbf{c}_3\mathbf{c}_4 \end{bmatrix}. \end{cases} \tag{3.19}$$

Obviously,

$$\text{RM}(0, m) \subset \text{RM}(1, m) \subset \text{RM}(2, m) \subset \text{RM}(3, m). \tag{3.20}$$

Search for the generator matrix of the extended Hamming code (16, 11, 4) inside the Reed-Muller RM(3, 4) generator matrix!

3.7 Perfect Codes

Theorem 3.6 Sphere-packing or Hamming bound:
Let a code with parameters (N, K) have a correcting capability of t.
Binary case:

$$2^K \left(1 + \binom{N}{1} + \binom{N}{2} + \cdots + \binom{N}{t}\right) \leq 2^N \tag{3.21}$$

Non-binary case over a field with q elements.

$$q^K \left(1 + \binom{N}{1}(q-1) + \binom{N}{2}(q-1)^2 + \cdots + \binom{N}{t}(q-1)^t\right) \leq q^N \tag{3.22}$$

This theorem [2] follows from simple counting of all possible vectors within an n-dimensional 'sphere' of 'radius' t according to Fig. 3.4. These are all possible vectors of weight less or equal to t. All vectors inside of all correction spheres follow from a multiplication with 2^K, the number of codewords. This number, of course, has always to be smaller than the number of all possible vectors of length n. The non-binary case is an obvious extension, since there are $q-1$ possible error values.

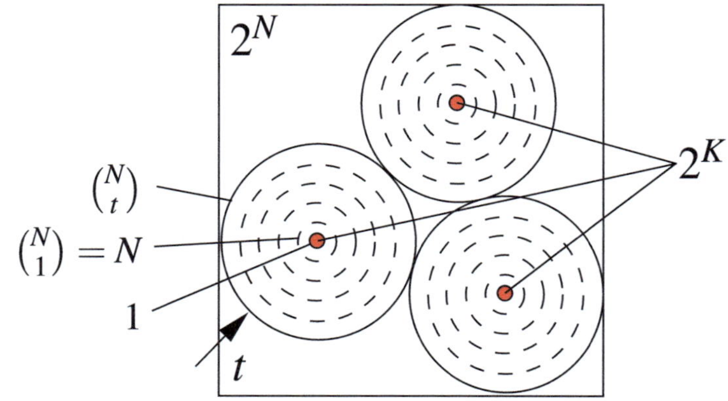

Fig. 3.4 Illustration of the sphere-packing bound

Definition 3.6 A **perfect code** fulfills the Hamming bound with equality, i.e., no words are left outside of the decoding spheres.

Only three different code classes do exist that are perfect:

1. binary repetition code with odd length N
2. Hamming codes
3. binary and ternary Golay code.

The **repetition code**, as the name implies, has a generator matrix

$$\mathbf{G} = \underbrace{(1, 1, 1, \ldots, 1)}_{N} \tag{3.23}$$

and the parity-check matrix

$$\mathbf{H} = \begin{pmatrix} 1\,1 & 0 & 0 \cdots 0 \\ 1\,0 & 1 & 0 \quad\; 0 \\ 1\,0 & 0 & 1 \quad\; 0 \\ \vdots & & \ddots \\ 1\,0 \cdots & 0 & 0 \;\; 1 \end{pmatrix} \tag{3.24}$$

The repetition code is **dual** to the parity-check code, hence, the above G and H matrices of the repetition code are the same as the H and G matrices of the parity-check code, respectively.

Definition 3.7 Let the generator and parity-check matrices of a code C be $\mathbf{G}$ and $\mathbf{H}$, respectively. Its dual code $C^{\perp}$ has a generator matrix $\mathbf{G}^{\perp} = \mathbf{H}$ and a parity-check matrix $\mathbf{H}^{\perp} = \mathbf{G}$.

We have

$$\begin{aligned} \mathbf{H}\,\mathbf{G}^T &= 0 \\ \mathbf{G}\,\mathbf{H}^T &= 0 \end{aligned} \tag{3.25}$$

Golay codes

The binary Golay code has the parameters (23, 12, 7), extended (24, 12, 8), and the ternary one has the parameters (11, 6, 5).

Theorem 3.7 *The extended binary Golay code is* **self-dual**, *i.e.,* $\mathbf{G}_{24}^{\perp} = \mathbf{G}_{24}$.

Note that duality is not the same as orthogonality. There is no orthogonality in finite fields. In [3], Massey defines so-called linear codes with complementary duals to model orthogonality to some extent. To make the difference clear, consider the scalar product of two vectors $\mathbf{a}$ and $\mathbf{b}$. If $\mathbf{a} \cdot \mathbf{b}^H = 0$, one would conclude the two vectors to be orthogonal when the components are real or complex. Now consider multiplying tow exemplary vectors

$$\begin{bmatrix} 0\,1\,1\,0\,1\,0\,1 \end{bmatrix} \begin{bmatrix} 0 \\ 1 \\ 1 \\ 0 \\ 1 \\ 0 \\ 1 \end{bmatrix} = 0 \quad \text{modulo } 2$$

The vectors are the same and hence not orthogonal. We obtain a zero result for all vectors of even weight. We clearly see that the notion of orthogonality is not suitable for finite fields, e.g., for the binary number field. This also means that projection to find a least-squares optimum over the reals or complex numbers does not have a counterpart over finite fields.

The self-dual generator matrix of the binary extended Golay code is shown in (3.26).

$$\mathbf{G_{24}} = \left(\begin{array}{c|cccccccccccc|ccccccccccc}
1 & 1 & & & & & & & & & & & & 1 & 1 & & 1 & 1 & 1 & & & & 1 & \\
1 & & 1 & & & & & & & & & & & & 1 & 1 & & 1 & 1 & 1 & & & & 1 \\
1 & & & 1 & & & & & & & & & & 1 & & 1 & 1 & & 1 & 1 & 1 & & & \\
1 & & & & 1 & & & & & & & & & & 1 & & 1 & 1 & & 1 & 1 & 1 & & \\
1 & & & & & 1 & & & & & & & & & & 1 & & 1 & 1 & & 1 & 1 & 1 & \\
1 & & & & & & 1 & & & & & & & & & & 1 & & 1 & 1 & & 1 & 1 & 1 \\
1 & & & & & & & 1 & & & & & & 1 & & & & 1 & & 1 & 1 & & 1 & 1 \\
1 & & & & & & & & 1 & & & & & 1 & 1 & & & & 1 & & 1 & 1 & & 1 \\
1 & & & & & & & & & 1 & & & & 1 & 1 & 1 & & & & 1 & & 1 & 1 & \\
1 & & & & & & & & & & 1 & & & & 1 & 1 & 1 & & & & 1 & & 1 & 1 \\
1 & & & & & & & & & & & 1 & & 1 & & 1 & 1 & 1 & & & & 1 & & 1 \\
 & & & & & & & & & & & & 1 & 1 & 1 & 1 & 1 & 1 & 1 & 1 & 1 & 1 & 1 & 1
\end{array}\right) \tag{3.26}$$

3.8 Decoding with the Standard Array

The standard array is a table of all q^N words with components from a field with q elements. The first row consists of the codewords, starting from the all-zero word. Along the columns, error vectors will be added to the codewords, until all possible q^N vectors are tabulated. If one would stop at the error-correcting capability t (given the **designed distance**) as the maximum weight of error vectors, a non-complete error correction will be represented by the table. Non-tabulated words would not be assigned to codeword and would thus stay uncorrected. The error vectors that are added to the zero codeword are called **coset leaders**, the corresponding row is the **coset**. Cosets have the same distance properties as the original code, but they are nonlinear (no zero codeword). The columns down to the error pattern with weight t are denoted as **decoding spheres**. Limiting the decoding to such spheres is called bounded minimum distance (BMD) decoding. The standard array outlines two decoding options, namely pointing upward to the codeword or to the left, to the coset leader, i.e., the error pattern.

Standard array:

			decoding sphere	
	$\mathbf{0}$	$\mathbf{c}_2$	$\mathbf{c}_3$	$\cdots\ \mathbf{c}_{q^k}$
	$\mathbf{0}+\mathbf{e}_1$	$\mathbf{c}_2+\mathbf{e}_1$	$\mathbf{c}_3+\mathbf{e}_1$	$\cdots\ \mathbf{c}_{q^k}+\mathbf{e}_1$
coset	$\mathbf{0}+\mathbf{e}_2$	$\mathbf{c}_2+\mathbf{e}_2$	$\mathbf{c}_3+\mathbf{e}_2$	$\cdots\ \mathbf{c}_{q^k}+\mathbf{e}_2$
	$\vdots$			$\vdots$
	$\mathbf{0}+\mathbf{e}_j$	$\mathbf{c}_2+\mathbf{e}_j$	$\mathbf{c}_3+\mathbf{e}_j$	$\cdots\ \mathbf{c}_{q^k}+\mathbf{e}_j$
	$\mathbf{0}+\mathbf{e}_{j+1}$	$\mathbf{c}_2+\mathbf{e}_{j+1}$	$\mathbf{c}_3+e_{j+1}$	$\cdots\ \mathbf{c}_{q^k}+\mathbf{e}_{j+1}$
	$\vdots$		$\vdots$	
	$\mathbf{0}+\mathbf{e}_l$	$\mathbf{c}_2+\mathbf{e}_l$	$\mathbf{c}_3+\mathbf{e}_l$	$\cdots\ \mathbf{c}_{q^k}+\mathbf{e}_l$
	coset leader			

$$j = \sum_{i=1}^{t} \binom{N}{i} (q-1)^i$$

References

1. R. Singleton, "Maximum distance q-nary codes," *IEEE Transactions on Information Theory*, vol. 10, no. 2, pp. 116–118, 1964.
2. R. W. Hamming, "Error detecting and error correcting codes," *The Bell System Technical Journal*, vol. 29, no. 2, pp. 147–160, 1950.
3. J. Massey, "Linear codes with complementary duals," *Discrete mathematics*, vol. 106/107, pp. 337–342, 1992.

Chapter 4
Convolutional Codes I—Representation and Formal Description

... more efficient algorithms have been found for using channel measurement information (i.e., soft decisions) in the decoding of convolutional codes than in the decoding of block codes.

Jack Wolf, 1978

4.1 Formal Description of Convolutional Codes

4.1.1 Basic Definitions and Infinite Generator and Parity-Check Matrices

The name 'convolutional codes' is due to the fact that the input-output relation is a convolution. The encoder structures are similar to digital filters. However, the additions will not be over the real or complex numbers, but over a discrete finite alphabet. In the binary case addition is modulo 2.

In contrast to block codes, convolutional codes operate on and output infinitely long sequences that are, of course, blocked in practice. The means of blocking are 'truncation', 'termination', or 'tail biting' which will be treated in Sect. 5.2.5. However, convolutional codes consist of a framing structure that results from the generation of n output symbols from k input symbols.

In Fig. 4.1, we show an example for the case $k = 1$ and $n = 2$, i.e., a code of rate $R = 1/2$.

This convolutional code has constraint length of four and a memory of three.

W. Henkel, *Channel Coding*, Signals and Communication Technology,
https://doi.org/10.1007/978-3-032-08236-7_4

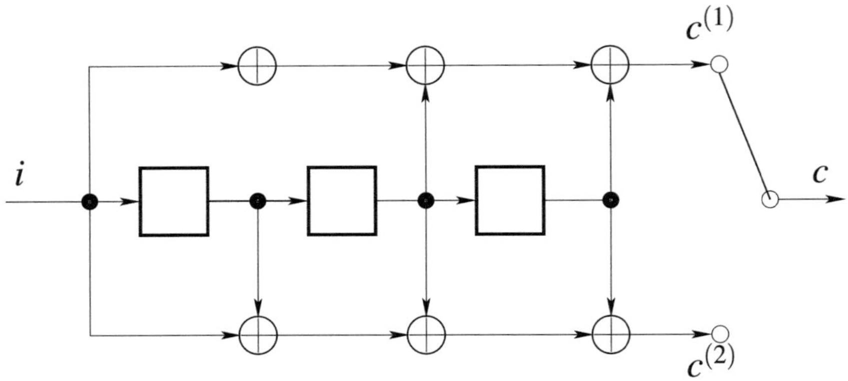

Fig. 4.1 Convolutional code of rate 1/2

Definition 4.1 The **constraint length** L specifies the maximum time interval out of the input sequence that influences an output sample. The **memory** m is the number of memory cells for each input sequence and is thus $m = L - 1$.

In case of a binary convolutional code, the maximum number of required memory cells equals $m \cdot k$. Some authors include the multiplication by k in their numbers for the constraint length and the memory.

The taps of the shift register of the example in Fig. 4.1 can be described with the generators

$$\begin{aligned} g^{(1)} &= (1\,0\,1\,1) = (g_0^{(1)}\; g_1^{(1)}\; g_2^{(1)}\; g_3^{(1)}) \\ g^{(2)} &= (1\,1\,1\,1) = (g_0^{(2)}\; g_1^{(2)}\; g_2^{(2)}\; g_3^{(2)})\,. \end{aligned} \tag{4.1}$$

If we would use the usual matrix representation of block codes, we would obtain a banded, infinitely long generator matrix.

$$(c_0^{(1)}\, c_0^{(2)}\, c_1^{(1)}\, c_1^{(2)}\, c_2^{(1)}\, c_2^{(2)}\, \ldots) = \tag{4.2}$$

$$= (i_0\, i_1\, i_2\, \ldots) \cdot \begin{pmatrix} g_0^{(1)} g_0^{(2)} & g_1^{(1)} g_1^{(2)} & g_2^{(1)} g_2^{(2)} & & \cdots & g_m^{(1)} g_m^{(2)} & & \\ & g_0^{(1)} g_0^{(2)} & g_1^{(1)} g_1^{(2)} & g_2^{(1)} g_2^{(2)} & & \cdots & g_m^{(1)} g_m^{(2)} & \\ & & g_0^{(1)} g_0^{(2)} & g_1^{(1)} g_1^{(2)} & g_2^{(1)} g_2^{(2)} & & \cdots & g_m^{(1)} g_m^{(2)} \\ & & \ddots & & & & \ddots & \\ & & & & \ddots & & & \ddots \end{pmatrix}$$

This matrix equation corresponds to the two convolutions

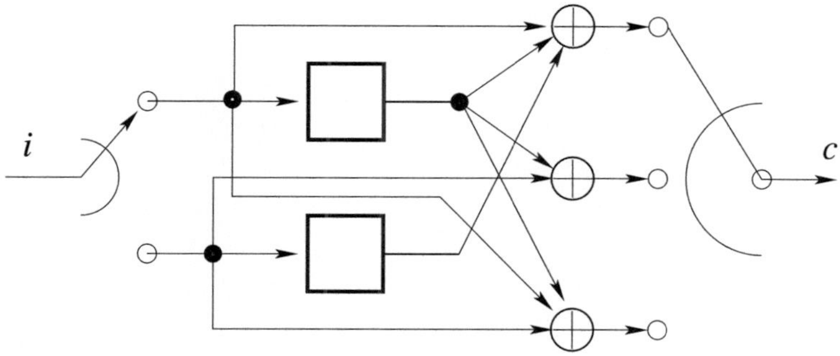

Fig. 4.2 Convolutional encoder of rate 2/3

$$\mathbf{c}^{(1)} = \mathbf{i} \star \mathbf{g}^{(1)} \Longleftrightarrow c_l^1 = \sum_{j=0}^{m} i_{l-j} g_j^{(1)} ,$$

$$\mathbf{c}^{(2)} = \mathbf{i} \star \mathbf{g}^{(2)} \Longleftrightarrow c_l^2 = \sum_{j=0}^{m} i_{l-j} g_j^{(2)} . \tag{4.3}$$

Compute the output sequence for $\mathbf{i} = (1\,1\,0\,0\,1\,0\,0\,0\,\ldots)$!
We now study an example with $k = 2$ given in Fig. 4.2.
Here, the generators are

$$\begin{array}{lll} \mathbf{g}_1^{(1)} = (1\,1) & \mathbf{g}_1^{(2)} = (0\,1) & \mathbf{g}_1^{(3)} = (1\,1) \\ \mathbf{g}_2^{(1)} = (0\,1) & \mathbf{g}_2^{(2)} = (1\,0) & \mathbf{g}_2^{(3)} = (1\,0) . \end{array} \tag{4.4}$$

This would lead to a generator set of equations

$$(c_0^{(1)}, c_0^{(2)}, c_0^{(3)}, c_1^{(1)} c_1^{(2)} c_1^{(3)} \ldots) =$$

$$= (i_{1,0}\, i_{2,0}\, i_{1,1}\, i_{2,1}\, i_{1,2}\, i_{2,2} \ldots) \begin{pmatrix} 101\;111 & & \\ 011\;100 & & \\ & 101\;111 & \\ & 011\;100 & \\ & & 101\;111 \\ & & 011\;100 \\ & & & \ddots \end{pmatrix} . \tag{4.5}$$

For arbitrary k, n, and m, we obtain a banded, infinite generator matrix with rectangular sub-matrices of the form

$$\mathbf{G} = \begin{pmatrix} g_{1,0}^{(1)}g_{1,0}^{(2)}\cdots g_{1,0}^{(n)} & g_{1,1}^{(1)}g_{1,1}^{(2)}\cdots g_{1,1}^{(n)} & \cdots & g_{1,m}^{(1)}g_{1,m}^{(2)}\cdots g_{1,m}^{(n)} & & \\ g_{2,0}^{(1)}g_{2,0}^{(2)}\cdots g_{2,0}^{(n)} & g_{2,1}^{(1)}g_{2,1}^{(2)}\cdots g_{2,1}^{(n)} & \cdots & g_{2,m}^{(1)}g_{2,m}^{(2)}\cdots g_{2,m}^{(n)} & & \\ \vdots & \vdots & \cdots & \vdots & & \\ g_{k,0}^{(1)}g_{k,0}^{(2)}\cdots g_{k,0}^{(n)} & g_{k,1}^{(1)}g_{k,1}^{(2)}\cdots g_{k,1}^{(n)} & \cdots & g_{k,m}^{(1)}g_{k,m}^{(2)}\cdots g_{k,m}^{(n)} & & \\ & g_{1,0}^{(1)}g_{1,0}^{(2)}\cdots g_{1,0}^{(n)} & g_{1,1}^{(1)}g_{1,1}^{(2)}\cdots g_{1,1}^{(n)} & \cdots & g_{1,m}^{(1)}g_{1,m}^{(2)}\cdots g_{1,m}^{(n)} & \\ & g_{2,0}^{(1)}g_{2,0}^{(2)}\cdots g_{2,0}^{(n)} & g_{2,1}^{(1)}g_{2,1}^{(2)}\cdots g_{2,1}^{(n)} & \cdots & g_{2,m}^{(1)}g_{2,m}^{(2)}\cdots g_{2,m}^{(n)} & \\ & \vdots & \vdots & \cdots & \vdots & \\ & g_{k,0}^{(1)}g_{k,0}^{(2)}\cdots g_{k,0}^{(n)} & g_{k,1}^{(1)}g_{k,1}^{(2)}\cdots g_{k,1}^{(n)} & \cdots & g_{k,m}^{(1)}g_{k,m}^{(2)}\cdots g_{k,m}^{(n)} & \\ & & \ddots & & & \ddots \end{pmatrix}. \tag{4.6}$$

Systematic convolutional encoding, i.e., a convolutional encoding where the information symbols are directly part of the output sequence, would have a generator matrix with the following structure [1]:

$$\mathbf{G} = \begin{pmatrix} \mathbf{I}\ \mathbf{P}_0\ \mathbf{0}\ \mathbf{P}_1\ \mathbf{0}\ \mathbf{P}_2 \cdots\cdots \mathbf{0}\ \mathbf{P}_m & & \\ \quad \mathbf{I}\ \mathbf{P}_0\ \mathbf{0}\ \mathbf{P}_1\ \ \mathbf{0}\ \ \mathbf{P}_2 \cdots\cdots \mathbf{0}\ \mathbf{P}_m & & \\ \qquad \mathbf{I}\ \mathbf{P}_0\ \ \mathbf{0}\ \ \mathbf{P}_1\ \ \mathbf{0}\ \ \mathbf{P}_2 \cdots\cdots \mathbf{0}\ \mathbf{P}_m & & \\ \qquad\qquad \ddots & & \ddots \end{pmatrix}. \tag{4.7}$$

The corresponding parity-check matrix would be

$$\mathbf{H} = \begin{pmatrix} \mathbf{P_0^T} & -\mathbf{I} & & & & & & & & \\ \mathbf{P_1^T} & \mathbf{0} & \mathbf{P_0^T} & -\mathbf{I} & & & & & & \\ \mathbf{P_2^T} & \mathbf{0} & \mathbf{P_1^T} & \mathbf{0} & \mathbf{P_0^T} & -\mathbf{I} & & & & \\ \vdots & & & & & & & & & \\ \mathbf{P_m^T} & \mathbf{0} & \mathbf{P_{m-1}^T} & \mathbf{0} & \cdots & \cdots & \mathbf{P_0^T} & -\mathbf{I} \cdots & & \\ & & \mathbf{P_m^T} & \mathbf{0} & \mathbf{P_{m-1}^T} & \mathbf{0} & \cdots & \cdots \mathbf{P_0^T} & -\mathbf{I} \cdots & \\ & & & & \mathbf{P_m^T} & \mathbf{0} & \mathbf{P_{m-1}^T} & \mathbf{0} & \cdots\cdots \mathbf{P_0^T} & -\mathbf{I} \cdots \\ & & & & & & \ddots & & & \end{pmatrix}. \tag{4.8}$$

Check that $\mathbf{GH}^T = \mathbf{0}$!
The principle structure of systematic encoding is shown in Fig. 4.3.

4.1.2 Description of Convolutional Codes by Generator and Parity-Check Matrices with Rational Terms (Forney)

Thinking back to the usual description of digital filters by means of the z-transform, the following equations would represent the structure of the example of Fig. 4.1:

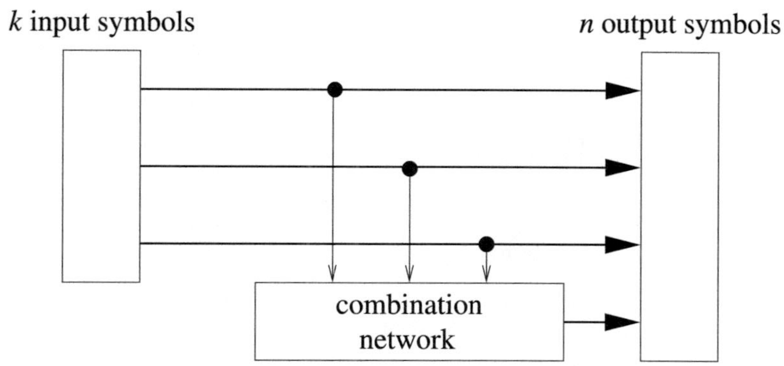

Fig. 4.3 The principle of systematic encoding for $k = 3$ and $n = 4$

$$\begin{aligned} C^{(1)}(z) &= I(z)\,(1 + \phantom{z^{-1} +}\ z^{-2} + z^{-3}) \\ C^{(2)}(z) &= I(z)\,(1 + z^{-1} + z^{-2} + z^{-3})\,. \end{aligned} \tag{4.9}$$

In coding theory and also elsewhere, we are used to the operator $D = z^{-1}$, instead. Then, the polynomial representation of the non-recursive convolutional encoder is given by

$$\begin{aligned} C^{(1)}(D) &= I(D)\,(1 + \ D^2 + D^3) \\ C^{(2)}(D) &= I(D)\,(1 + D + D^2 + D^3)\,. \end{aligned} \tag{4.10}$$

Polynomial multiplication corresponds to the convolution of the components of the sequences in (4.3) (multiplication in frequency domain ≡ convolution in time domain).

Writing this with a generator matrix:

$$\left(C^{(1)}(D)\,,\quad C^{(2)}(D)\right) = \mathrm{i}(D)\cdot\mathbf{G}(D)\,,\quad \mathbf{G} = (1 + D^2 + D^3\,,\ 1 + D + D^2 + D^3)\,. \tag{4.11}$$

As we already realized, the encoding is non-systematic. To be systematic , the generator matrix should contain the identity matrix, i.e., for $k = 1$ it should contain a one. We will now show, how a non-systematic encoder can be transformed into a systematic one, without modifying the code itself, i.e., without modifying the set of code sequences. We extend (4.11) as follows:

$$\left(C^{(1)}(D)\,,\ C^{(2)}(D)\right) = \mathrm{i}(D)\cdot(1 + D^2 + D^3)\cdot\left(1\,,\ \frac{1 + D + D^2 + D^3}{1 + D^2 + D^3}\right) = \mathrm{i}'(D)\cdot\mathbf{G}'(D)\,, \tag{4.12}$$

$$\mathbf{G}'(D) = \left(1\,,\ \frac{1 + D + D^2 + D^3}{1 + D^2 + D^3}\right)\,. \tag{4.13}$$

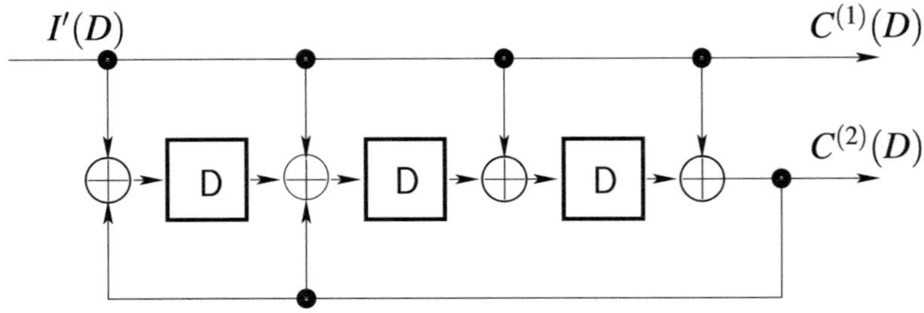

Fig. 4.4 Systematic convolutional encoder of rate 1/2

We will now concentrate a little on the right side of the matrix $\mathbf{G}'$.

$$C^{(2)}(D) = I'(D)\frac{1 + D + D^2 + D^3}{1 + D^2 + D^3} \tag{4.14}$$

$$C^{(2)}(D) \cdot (1 + D^2 + D^3) = I'(D) \cdot (1 + D + D^2 + D^3) \tag{4.15}$$

$$C^{(2)}(D) = I'(D) \cdot (1 + D + D^2 + D^3) + C^{(2)}(D) \cdot (D^2 + D^3) \tag{4.16}$$

With binary numbers, note that we have "+1" = "−1". Equation (4.16) leads to the encoder shown in Fig. 4.4.

We will now do the same conversion for the example with $k = 2$, which has the Forney generator matrix

$$\begin{array}{lll} \mathbf{g}_1^{(1)}(D) = 1 + D & \mathbf{g}_1^{(2)}(D) = D & \mathbf{g}_1^{(3)}(D) = 1 + D \\ \mathbf{g}_2^{(1)}(D) = D & \mathbf{g}_2^{(2)}(D) = 1 & \mathbf{g}_2^{(3)}(D) = 1\ , \end{array} \tag{4.17}$$

$$\mathbf{G}(D) = \begin{pmatrix} 1 + D & D & 1 + D \\ D & 1 & 1 \end{pmatrix} . \tag{4.18}$$

Gaussian elimination steps (linear combinations of rows, permutations of rows are also permitted) yield

$$\begin{pmatrix} D & 1 & 1 \\ 1 + D & D & 1 + D \end{pmatrix}$$

$$\begin{pmatrix} 1 & \frac{1}{D} & \frac{1}{D} \\ 1 + D & D & 1 + D \end{pmatrix}$$

$$\begin{pmatrix} 1 & \frac{1}{D} & \frac{1}{D} \\ 1 & \frac{D}{1+D} & 1 \end{pmatrix}$$

$$\begin{pmatrix} 1 & \frac{1}{D} & \frac{1}{D} \\ 0 & \frac{D}{1+D} - \frac{1}{D} & 1 - \frac{1}{D} \end{pmatrix}$$

$$\begin{pmatrix} 1 & \frac{1}{D} & \frac{1}{D} \\ 0 & \frac{D^2-1-D}{(1+D)D} & \frac{D-1}{D} \end{pmatrix}$$

$$\begin{pmatrix} 1 & \frac{1}{D} & \frac{1}{D} \\ 0 & 1 & \frac{(D-1)(1+D)}{D^2-1-D} \end{pmatrix}$$

$$\begin{pmatrix} 1 & 0 & \frac{1}{D}(1 - \frac{(D-1)(1+D)}{D^2-1-D}) \\ 0 & 1 & \frac{(D-1)(1+D)}{D^2-1-D} \end{pmatrix}$$

$$\begin{pmatrix} 1 & 0 & \frac{-1}{D^2-1-D} \\ 0 & 1 & \frac{D^2-1}{D^2-1-D} \end{pmatrix} .$$

We obtain the systematic generator matrix

$$\mathbf{G}'(D) = \begin{pmatrix} 1 & 0 & \frac{1}{1+D+D^2} \\ 0 & 1 & \frac{1+D^2}{1+D+D^2} \end{pmatrix} . \tag{4.19}$$

We could have obtained this result more directly by choosing a $k \times k$ submatrix of the generator matrix $\mathbf{M}_{k\times k}$ and extending the generator equation by $\mathbf{M}_{k\times k} \cdot \mathbf{M}_{k\times k}^{-1}$.

$$\mathbf{I}(D) \cdot \mathbf{G}(D) = \mathbf{I}(D) \cdot \begin{pmatrix} 1+D & D & 1+D \\ D & 1 & 1 \end{pmatrix} = \underbrace{\mathbf{I}(D) \cdot \mathbf{M}_{k\times k}}_{\mathrm{i}'(D)} \cdot \mathbf{M}_{k\times k}^{-1} \begin{pmatrix} 1+D & D & 1+D \\ D & 1 & 1 \end{pmatrix} \tag{4.20}$$

When determining the product of the inverse $\mathbf{M}_{k\times k}^{-1}$ and the generator matrix $\mathbf{G}(D)$, we obtain the equivalent systematic generator matrix $\mathbf{G}'(D)$.

$$\mathrm{i}'(D) \cdot \frac{1}{1+D+D^2} \begin{pmatrix} 1 & D \\ D & 1+D \end{pmatrix} \cdot \begin{pmatrix} 1+D & D & 1+D \\ D & 1 & 1 \end{pmatrix} = \mathrm{i}'(D) \cdot \begin{pmatrix} 1 & 0 & \frac{1}{1+D+D^2} \\ 0 & 1 & \frac{1+D^2}{1+D+D^2} \end{pmatrix} \tag{4.21}$$

We will now show the corresponding shift register. The two fractions in the rightmost column of $\mathbf{G}'(D)$ yield

$$C^{(3)}(D) = I_1(D) \cdot \frac{1}{1+D+D^2} + I_2(D) \cdot \frac{1+D^2}{1+D+D^2} , \tag{4.22}$$

$$C^{(3)}(D)(1+D+D^2) = I_1(D) \cdot 1 + I_2(D) \cdot (1+D^2) , \tag{4.23}$$

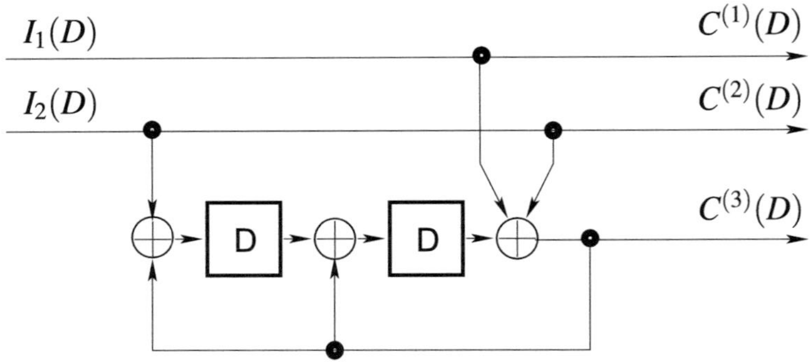

Fig. 4.5 Systematic encoder of rate 2/3

$$C^{(3)}(D) = I_1(D) \cdot 1 + I_2(D) \cdot (1 + D^2) + C^{(3)}(D)(D + D^2) . \tag{4.24}$$

Figure 4.5 shows the systematic encoder . Usually, such systematic encoders will be recursive.

Determining the H-Matrix — The Syndrome Former

Like in the block-coded case, the **H**-matrix follows from Theorem 3.5. From the systematic form of the generator matrix $\mathbf{G}'$, we obtain the parity-check matrix

$$\mathbf{H} = \left(\frac{1}{1 + D + D^2} , \frac{1 + D^2}{1 + D + D^2} , 1 \right) . \tag{4.25}$$

The parity-check matrix **H** can also be used to obtain a syndrome sequence, as we know it from block codes. Since we will later describe other more suitable decoding methods, we will not provide decoding algorithms based on the syndrome sequence in here.

4.1.3 The Two Canonical Forms to Realize Convolutional Encoders

The two equivalent canonical forms that we know from digital filters, may also be used as alternative canonical realizations of convolutional encoders. However, only one will appear to be suitable. The two canonical forms of a rational transmit function

$$g(D) = p(D)/q(D) = \frac{p_0 + p_1 D + \cdots + p_m D^m}{1 + q_1 D + \cdots + q_m D^m} \tag{4.26}$$

will thus be shortly described. Figures 4.6 and 4.7 depict the canonical forms in ‘Controller’ and ‘Observer’ structures, respectively. We show the equivalence of

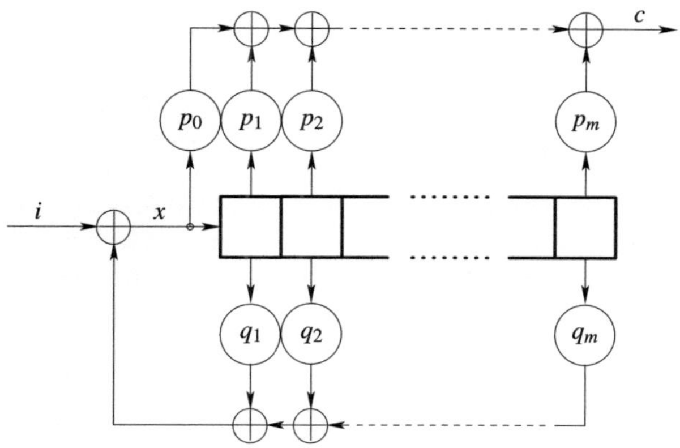

Fig. 4.6 Canonical 'controller' structure

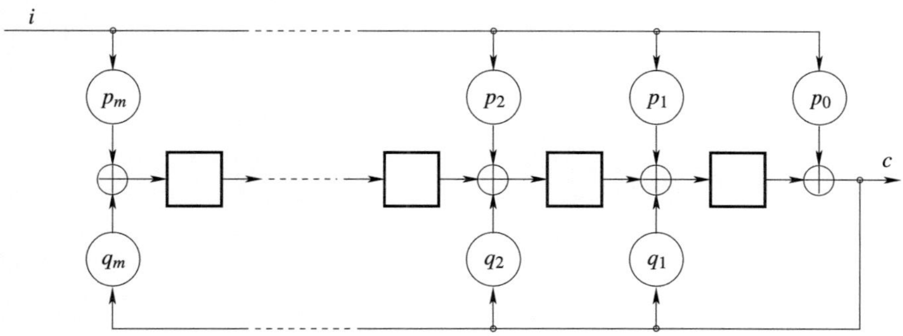

Fig. 4.7 Canonical 'observer' structure

both representations of the rational expression of Eq. (4.26). For the structure in Fig. 4.6, we have

$$c(D) = p(D) \cdot x(D) , \tag{4.27}$$

$$x(D) = i(D) + x(D) \cdot (q_1 D + \cdots + q_m D^m) \implies x(D) = \frac{i(D)}{1 - q_1 D - \cdots - q_m D^m} . \tag{4.28}$$

Since our arithmetic, in contrast to the filter application, is modulo 2, we replace the minus by a plus sign.

$$g(D) = c(D)/i(D) = p(D)/q(D) \tag{4.29}$$

For the structure in Fig. 4.7, we obtain

$$c(D) = i(D) \cdot (p_0 + p_1 D + \cdots + p_m D^m) + c(D)(q_1 D + \cdots + q_m D^m) , \tag{4.30}$$

from which we again obtain (4.26)

$$g(D) = c(D)/i(D) = p(D)/q(D) \ . \tag{4.31}$$

Only the controller structure of Fig. 4.6 leads to minimal realizations of convolutional encoders. In contrast to digital filters, a convolutional encoder has more outputs than inputs and the denominator determining the feedback for all generators will be the same. In a controller structure, only one shift register will then be required, whereas in case of an observer structure, separate shift registers for each output would be required.

4.2 Graphical Representations of Convolutional Codes

For simplicity, we select a code with a constraint length of $L = 3$ (octal code for the taps (5, 7)) according to Fig. 4.8.

4.2.1 Tree Diagram

You can't see the Wood for the tree!
Bath, England

Each input and the corresponding output sub-frame is represented as a branch of a tree. In the tree diagram of the $(5, 7)_8$ code in Fig. 4.9, an upward oriented branch ('edge' in graph-theory terms) corresponds to a '0' as an input and the downwards directed ones corresponds to a '1'. The points are denoted as states ('vertices' or 'nodes' in graph theory).

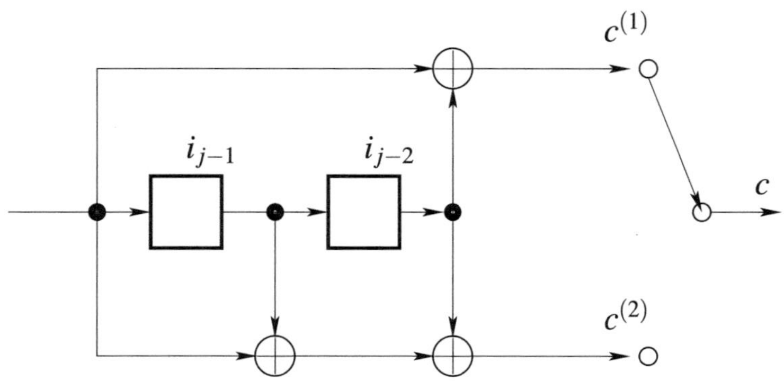

Fig. 4.8 Polynomial convolutional encoder of rate 1/2 with a constraint length of $L = 3$

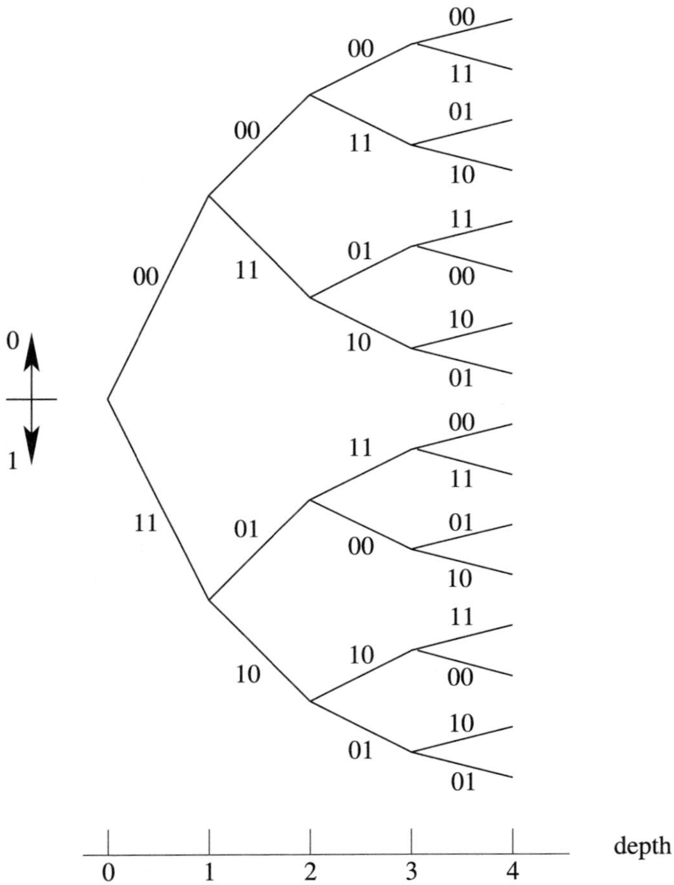

Fig. 4.9 Tree diagram

One parameter of the convolutional code can be observed in the tree diagram. On the right side of Fig. 4.9 one can see the same pattern, twice. Obviously, at this point, the original branching has no influence any more. Only the last two input bits have an influence, since the memory is only two.

Thus, the four states in the upper and lower parts at a depth of 3 could be combined without any loss of information. As the memory already implies, the convolutional code can be described by four, in general q^m (in the binary case 2^m) states.

By this combination of equivalent states, further representations are obtained: the trellis and the state diagrams. The tree diagram itself is the basis of so-called sequential decoding algorithms, e.g., the Fano and the stack algorithms. They will be described shortly in Chap. 6.

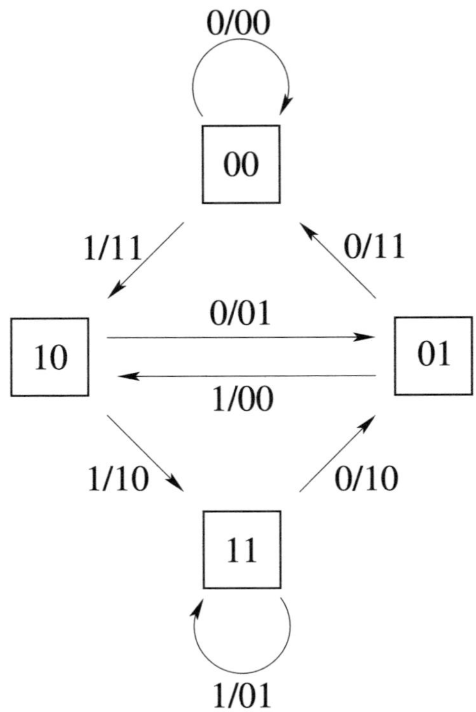

Fig. 4.10 State diagram

4.2.2 *State Diagram*

The state diagram is obtained by labeling the vertices of the tree graph with the (binary) state vector of the encoder and by combining equivalent (identical) states (vertices, nodes). One can, of course, also draw the state diagram directly from the encoder. For our example, we obtain the state diagram of Fig. 4.10.

When we will also have described the trellis diagram as a third graphical representation, we will especially use the state diagram to derive important properties of convolutional codes.

4.2.3 *Trellis Diagram*

> Give me the splendid silent sun, with all his beams full-dazzling
> Give me juicy autumnal fruit, ripe and red from the orchard
> Give me a field where the grass grows
> Give me an arbor, give me the **trellis**
>
> Walt Whitman

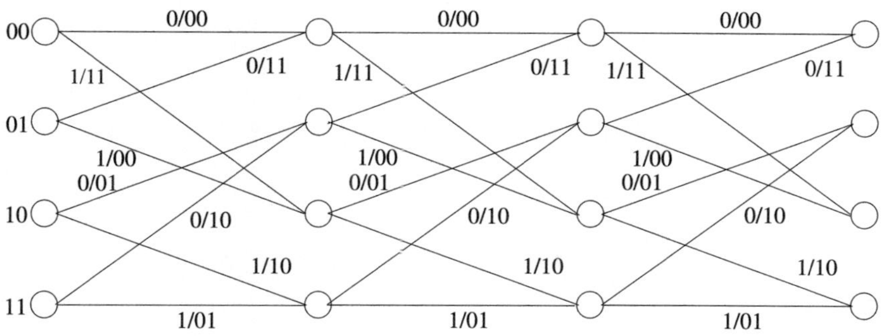

Fig. 4.11 Trellis diagram

The trellis diagram directly follows from the tree diagram by combining the equivalent states, but keeping the time sequential structure. An alternative would be to start from the state diagram and add the time scale by repeating the states for every time instant. We start the diagram from the zero state. In principle the sequence and with it the trellis can be infinitely long. However, measures have been developed to terminate the trellis by, e.g., forcing all paths to go back into the zero state at some time instant (Sect. 5.2.5). The Trellis diagram for our example code is shown in Fig. 4.11.

The trellis is the most common representation, especially, since it is the basis for the most important decoding algorithm, the Viterbi algorithm. Sometimes, convolutional codes are misleadingly denoted as trellis codes, although this term has much later been introduced for a means of coded modulation.

4.3 Distance Properties of Convolutional Codes

4.3.1 *Free Distance*

The most important characteristic of convolutional codes, apart from n,k, and m is the so-called **free distance**. It is the minimum Hamming distance between two arbitrary valid code sequences.

Definition 4.2

$$d_{free} = \min\{d_H(\mathbf{c}, \mathbf{c}'); \mathbf{c} \neq \mathbf{c}'\} \tag{4.32}$$

For linear codes, we additionally have

$$d_{\text{free}} = \min\{w_H(\mathbf{c}); \mathbf{c} \neq \mathbf{0}\} . \tag{4.33}$$

From the state diagram of our code example in Fig. 4.10, we can determine the free distance $d_{\text{free}} = 5$. Hereto, we start from state '00' and search for a path with the lowest number of ones in the code sequence, i.e., the lowest weight, to get back to state '00'. Since for a linear code, the minimum Hamming distance is equal to the minimum Hamming weight, we thus obtain the free distance by just checking the lowest weight code-sequence starting from the all-zeros state and returning to the all-zeros state.

4.3.2 Transfer Function of a Linear Convolutional Code

For error-probability calculations, not only the minimum distance or the free distance are needed, but also the number of possible sequences at certain distances, the so-called weight distribution. To this end, we again consider the all-zero state as the start and end point, but cut the graph in the middle of this state. Figure 4.12 shows the corresponding signal-flow graph that results from the state diagram in Fig. 4.10.

The number of ones in the code sequence will be specified by the powers of an operator D. From one state to another, one multiplies with the operator or its power that corresponds to a state transition (edge). A merger of two paths in one state is represented by an addition. One obtains a system of transition equations.

$$
\begin{aligned}
\Phi_{10} &= D^2 \cdot A(D) + \Phi_{01} \\
\Phi_{01} &= D \cdot \Phi_{10} + D \cdot \Phi_{11} \\
\Phi_{11} &= D \cdot \Phi_{10} + D \cdot \Phi_{11} \\
B(D) &= D^2 \cdot \Phi_{01}
\end{aligned}
\tag{4.34}
$$

The **transfer function** $T(D) = B(D)/A(D)$ summarizes all possible paths from state '00' and back. Solving for $T(D)$, we obtain

$$
T(D) = \frac{D^5}{1-2D} = D^5 + 2D^6 + 4D^7 + \cdots + 2^l D^{l+5} + \ldots . \tag{4.35}
$$

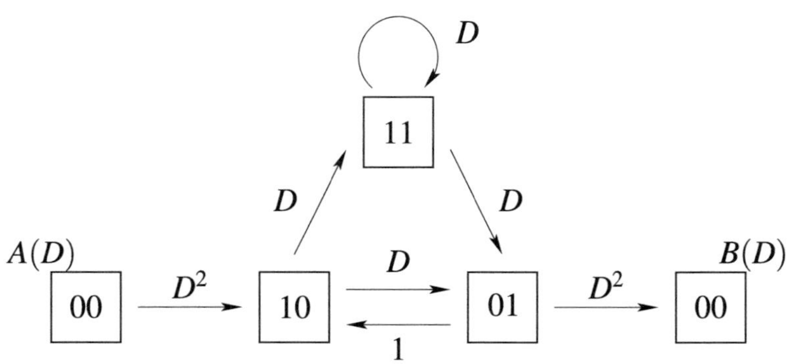

Fig. 4.12 Split state diagram for determining the transfer function of a linear convolutional code

The power series shows the distances (weights) together with the number of sequences at this distance (weight).

An alternative derivation is given in [2] that is also presented here. The time dependency is introduced there, making it possible to describe the accumulated weights as the transition formulas

$$\begin{aligned}
\varphi_{10}(t) &= D^2 \cdot a(t-1) + \varphi_{01}(t-1) \\
\varphi_{01}(t) &= D \cdot \varphi_{10}(t-1) + D \cdot \varphi_{11}(t-1) \\
\varphi_{11}(t) &= D \cdot \varphi_{10}(t-1) + D \cdot \varphi_{11}(t-1) \\
b(t) &= D^2 \cdot \varphi_{01}(t-1) \ ,
\end{aligned} \tag{4.36}$$

where the input and output is denoted by a and b, respectively. Applying the z-transform, we obtain

$$\begin{aligned}
\Phi_{10}(z) &= D^2 \cdot z^{-1} \cdot A(z) + z^{-1} \cdot \Phi_{01}(z) \\
\Phi_{01}(z) &= D \cdot z^{-1} \cdot \Phi_{10}(z) + D \cdot z^{-1} \cdot \Phi_{11}(z) \\
\Phi_{11}(z) &= D \cdot z^{-1} \cdot \Phi_{10}(z) + D \cdot z^{-1} \cdot \Phi_{11}(z) \\
B(z) &= D^2 \cdot z^{-1} \cdot \Phi_{01}(z) \ .
\end{aligned} \tag{4.37}$$

Solving this set of equations for $T(D, z) = B(z)/A(z)$ yields

$$\begin{aligned}
T(D, z) &= \frac{B(z)}{A(z)} = \frac{D^5 z^{-3}}{1 - Dz^{-1} - Dz^{-2}} \\
&= D^5 z^{-3} + D^6 z^{-4} + D^6 z^{-5} + D^7 z^{-5} + 2D^7 z^{-6} + \dots \ .
\end{aligned} \tag{4.38}$$

We are back to (4.35) when setting $z = 1$. Usually, instead of z^{-1}, the operator L is used for counting the length of the paths. Additionally, a further operator I may be introduced for the number of corresponding ones at the input of the encoder. The 'split' state diagram including all these operators is shown in Fig. 4.13.

From this, the transfer function can be determined as

$$\begin{aligned}
T(D, L, I) &= \frac{D^5 L^3 I}{1 - DL(1+L)I} \\
&= D^5 L^3 I + D^6 L^4 (1+L) I^2 + \cdots + D^{5+l} L^{3+l} (1+L)^l I^{1+l}
\end{aligned} \ . \tag{4.39}$$

Possible paths are now investigated in more detail. We obtain the distance, the length (number of edges passed through), the number of ones at the input of the encoder, and finally, the number such paths.

The path length is important for the correction capability for burst noise, whereas the number of input ones is necessary to determine the bit-error probability after decoding.

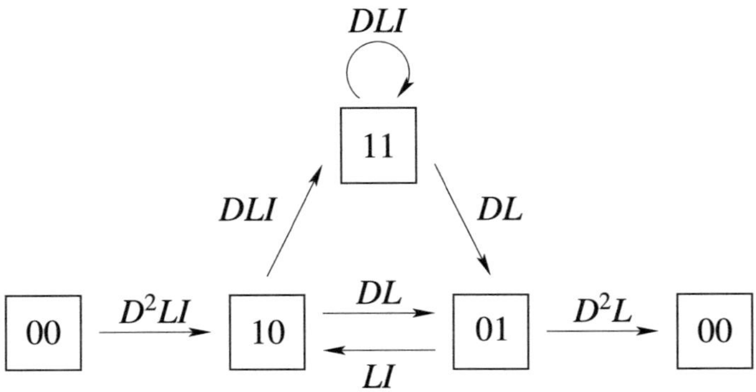

Fig. 4.13 Split state diagram for determining the extended transfer function of a linear convolutional code

4.3.3 Column Distance and Distance Profile

Definition 4.3 The **column distance** d_j of order j, $j = 0, 1, \ldots$ of a linear convolutional code is the minimum of the Hamming distances of all possible paths relative to the all-zeros path at step $j + 1$ after leaving the zero state.

The term 'column distance' is due to the structure of the generator matrix after $j + 1$ input frames of length k

$$\mathbf{G} = \begin{pmatrix} \mathbf{G}_0 & \mathbf{G}_1 & \mathbf{G}_2 & \cdots & \mathbf{G}_j \\ & \mathbf{G}_0 & \mathbf{G}_1 & \cdots & \mathbf{G}_{j-1} \\ & & & \ddots & \vdots \\ & & & & \mathbf{G}_0 \end{pmatrix}, \tag{4.40}$$

where with new input frames step-wise new columns are attached.

Definition 4.4 The **distance profile** is the vector of the column distances.

For our example, we obtain the distance profile of Fig. 4.14.

The limit of the column distance is

$$\lim_{j \to \infty} d_j = d_{\text{free}} \,. \tag{4.41}$$

The distance profile is useful for sequential decoding algorithms that are studied in Chap. 4.14. It is advantageous for such algorithms when the distance profile increases quickly. This ensures that wrong paths will not be proceeded very long.

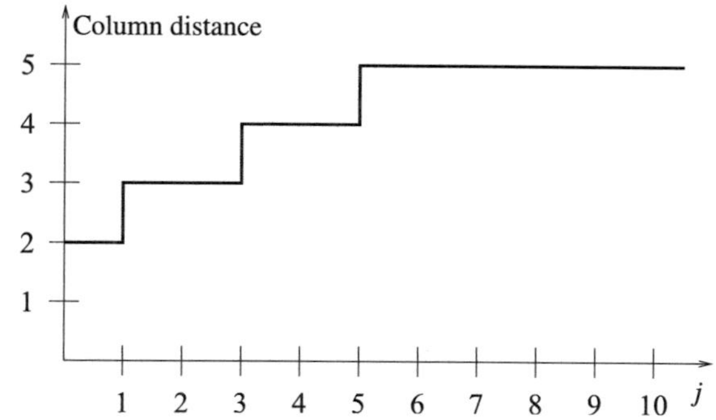

Fig. 4.14 Distance profile

4.3.4 Catastrophic Encoders

Definition 4.5 Catastrophic encoders have the undesired property that a limited number of modified code symbols correspond to an infinite number of modified information symbols.

A short disturbance would thus result in an infinitely long decoding error.

Theorem 4.1 *A linear convolutional encoder is only catastrophic, if there is a second loop in addition to the zero loop that does not establish a distance (weight) to the zero loop.*

In the nonlinear case without a zero loop, a catastrophic encoder means that there have to be two different loops in the state diagram with the same output sequence.

As a very simple example we consider the ($n = 2, k = 1, m = 2$) encoder with the generator matrix

$$\mathbf{G} = (1 + D\,,\; 1 + D^2)\,. \tag{4.42}$$

The state diagram is shown in Fig. 4.15.

The two loops at the states '00' and '11' lead to the same output sequence and thus, do not establish a distance.

In the example, we observe that catastrophic behavior is due to a common divisor (excluding pure delay D^1) in both generators.

$$\gcd\{1 + D, 1 + D^2\} = \gcd\{1 + D, (1 + D)^2\} = 1 + D \mod 2 \tag{4.43}$$

An infinite sequence given by the reciprocal value of the gcd, in this case $1/(1 + D) = \sum_{j=0}^{\infty} D^j$, would yield a finite length output sequence ($\neq 0$). Setting these few values to zero would mean an infinite impact on the input sequence. In this case a zero sequence would result.

A generator matrix can be shown to be non-catastrophic, if there is an $n \times k$ polynomial right inverse. If there is such an inverse, a finite error in the code sequence would also result in a finite error in the input sequence. (Since the matrices are not quadratic, there may be different right inverses.)

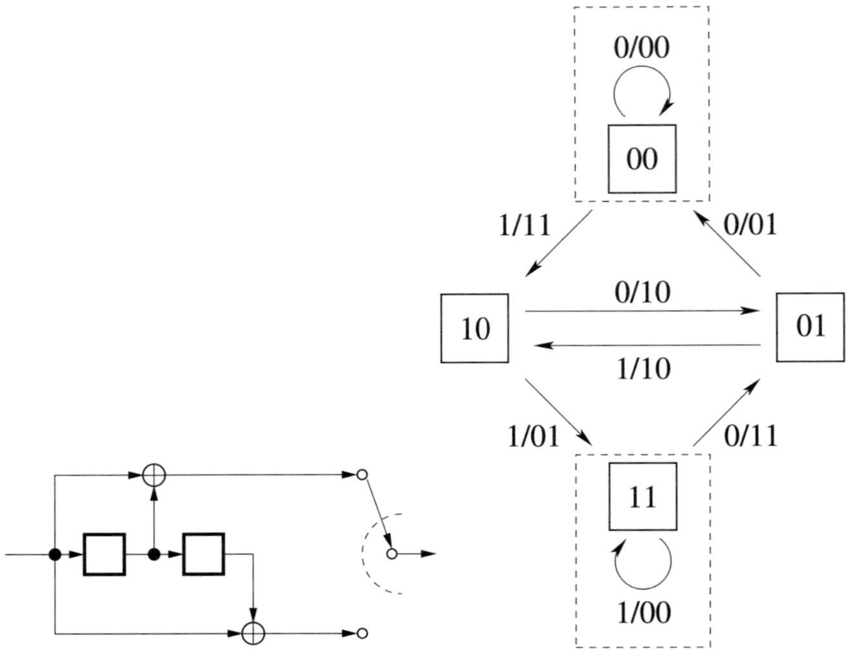

Fig. 4.15 State diagram of a catastrophic convolutional encoder

Systematic encoders have a trivial right inverse $\mathbf{G}^{-1} = \left[\mathrm{i}_{k\times k}|\mathbf{0}_{k\times(n-k)}\right]^T$ and are thus always non-catastrophic.

We give the following theorem without proof:

Theorem 4.2 ([3]) *A non-recursive linear (polynomial) convolutional encoder with k inputs and n outputs has a non-recursive inverse with or without a delay D^l, if*

$$gcd\left\{\Delta_j(D),\, j = 1, 2, \ldots, \binom{n}{k}\right\} = D^l\,, \tag{4.44}$$

where l is a non-negative integer; $\Delta_j(D)$ specifies the determinants of the $\binom{n}{k}$ different $k \times k$ sub-matrices of the generator matrix $\mathbf{G}(D)$.

Encoders with polynomial generator matrix and polynomial inverse generator matrix are called 'basic'.

An equivalent polynomial 'basic' encoder can be found by means of the invariant-factor theorem, also denoted as "$\mathbf{LDM}^T$" decomposition.

A decomposition in the form $\mathbf{G}_{k\times n}(D) = \mathbf{A}_{k\times k}(D)\mathbf{\Lambda}_{k\times n}(D)\mathbf{B}_{n\times n}(D)$ is calculated. $\mathbf{B}$ has a polynomial inverse. The diagonal matrix $\mathbf{\Lambda}$ can be obtained by trivial row and column operations onto $\mathbf{G}$, which are represented by $\mathbf{A}$ and $\mathbf{B}$. The equivalence follows from the fact that the product $\mathbf{A}(D)\mathbf{\Lambda}(D)$ times $\mathbf{B}(D)$ do only represent trivial (allowed) row operations on $\mathbf{B}(D)$. The polynomial right inverse is obtained from the first k rows of $\mathbf{B}^{-1}(D)$.

4.3.5 Minimum Encoders

Of theoretical interest would be the question of a minimum structure of an encoder for a given convolutional code. We especially think of the necessary shift-register cells. In practice, such a question is not very relevant for the encoder, because most of the implementation complexity lies in the decoder. The minimum encoder structure, however, is also relevant for the complexity of the trellis, since the number of states is determined by q^{km}. Landmark papers regarding the minimality of encoders are by Forney 1970 [4, 5], Johannesson, Wan 1993 [6], and McEliece, Lin 1996 [7]. Especially, the work of Johannesson is very suitable for a deeper understanding of convolutional codes. In this book, we can only give some aspects.

First we give a definition, when an encoder is called *non-degenerated.*

Definition 4.6 A linear polynomial convolutional encoder of rate $1/n$ with a constraint length L (memory $m = L - 1$) is called **non-degenerated**, if

1. $\exists_{j_1 \in \{1,\ldots,n\}} g_0^{(j_1)} = 1$,
2. $\exists_{j_2 \in \{1,\ldots,n\}} g_m^{(j_2)} = 1$,
3. $\exists_{j_1, j_2 \in \{1,\ldots,n\};\, j_1 \neq j_2} g^{(j_1)} \neq g^{(j_2)}$.

In cases where the first two points would not be fulfilled, the encoder could be described by shorter polynomials. If the last requirement would not be fulfilled, the encoder would represent a repetition code.

In the following, we gather some key definitions and results from [6] (partly relying on [4]).

We consider so-called (according to Forney) '*basic*' generator matrices of convolutional codes that are defined as follows:

Definition 4.7 A (realizable and delay-free) generator matrix of a convolutional codes is called 'basic', if the components are polynomials and there exists a polynomial right inverse.

Johannesson makes a distinction between generator and encoding matrix, where he requires that the encoding matrix should be realizable and delay-free. This is a general restriction in his paper and we will thus assume it throughout, when talking about a generator matrix, too.

Johannesson specifies convolutional codes with a $b \times c$ generator matrix somewhat differently as follows:

Constraint length: $\nu_i = \max_{1 \le j \le c} \{\text{degree } G_{ij}(D)\}$

Memory: $m = \max_{1 \le i \le b} \{\nu_i\}$

Overall constraint length: $\nu = \sum_{i=1}^{b} \nu_i$

In addition to states that we already know, Johannesson defines so-called *abstract states*. These are possible code sequences starting from time zero for information sequences that were unequal to zero only before time zero. The abstract state is given by an operator representation as follows:

$$s(D) = i(D) P\, G(D)\, Q\ , \tag{4.45}$$

where P limits the information sequence to the time before zero and Q extracts the output sequence from time zero on ($P + Q = 1$). The number of abstract states is always less or equal to the number of physical states.

Johannesson gives three different definitions of minimality: 'minimal-basic' generator matrix (minimum overall constraint length among all equivalent generator matrices), 'minimal' generator matrix[1] (minimum number of abstract states among all equivalent encoders), and 'minimal encoder' (realization with a minimum number of memory cells).

We provide the definitions together with some remarks.

Definition 4.8 A 'minimal basic' generator matrix is a basic generator matrix with a minimum overall constraint length ν among all equivalent generator matrices.

Generator matrices are equivalent, if they generate the same code. Especially, the known trivial row operations lead to an equivalent generator matrix. i.e., a left-sided matrix multiplication with a non-singular $b \times b$ matrix $\mathbf{T}(D)$ leads to an equivalent generator matrix

$$\mathbf{G}'(D) = \mathbf{T}(D)\mathbf{G}(D)\ . \tag{4.46}$$

In [6] the author shows that the generator matrix is only 'minimal-basic', if the maximum degree of all determinants of $b \times b$ sub-matrices of $\mathbf{G}(D)$ equals the overall constraint length. Each generator matrix is equivalent to a 'minimal-basic' generator matrix. The number of abstract states is 2^{ν}.

Definition 4.9 The generator matrix of a convolutional code is 'minimal', if the number of abstract states is minimal over all equivalent generator matrices.

The number of abstract states of a generator matrix that is equivalent to a 'minimal-basic' generator matrix is always greater or equal to the number of abstract states of a 'minimal-basic' generator matrix. Each 'minimal-basic' generator matrix is also a (basic) 'minimal' generator matrix. It is minimal if and only if the generator matrix $\mathbf{G}$ has a polynomial right inverse in D and a polynomial right inverse in D^{-1}. Each minimal generator matrix is non-catastrophic.

Now, we state the essential definition for a practical realization.

Definition 4.10 A 'minimal' encoder is a realization of a minimal generator matrix $\mathbf{G}(D)$ with a minimum number of memory cells over all realizations of $\mathbf{G}(D)$.

---

[1] Equals Forney's minimality definition in [4].

The canonical realization of a 'minimal-basic' generator matrix in 'controller' structure (see Sect. 4.1.3) is minimal. Since in principal, both canonical forms (controller, observer) lead to equivalent representations of a rational 'transfer function', one may assume, this should be valid for the observer structure, as well. When comparing both realizations, we realize that with a controller structure, however, multiple (n) outputs make use of the same memory cells. Note that with the controller realization, the input symbols itself are stored, independent of generator combinations. This is not the case in the observer realization with separate shift registers for each output.

Systematic generator matrices are always 'minimal'. This can be concluded from the existence of a polynomial right inverse in D and a polynomial right inverse in D^{-1}. A systematic generator matrix can be written as

$$\mathbf{G}(D) = (\mathbf{I}_{b\times b}\mathbf{A}(D)) \tag{4.47}$$

and has thus a right inverse

$$[\mathbf{G}(D)]^{-1} = \begin{pmatrix} \mathbf{I}_{b\times b} \\ \mathbf{A}(D) \end{pmatrix}, \tag{4.48}$$

which is polynomial in D and D^{-1}.

As we already know from Sect. 4.1.2 and Eq. (4.46), each generator matrix can be turned into a systematic one by trivial row operations. This will then be a minimal generator matrix that has a minimal encoder realization.

4.4 Tables of Convolutional Codes with Maximum Free Distance d_{free}

As examples, we provide two tables of good convolutional codes with rates 1/2 and 1/3 taken from [8–10] (see [10, 11] for other rates).

Maximum-d_{free} codes of rate 1/2			
	generators (octal)		
L	$g^{(1)}$	$g^{(2)}$	d_{free}
3	5	7	5
4	15	17	6
5	23	35	7
6	53	75	8
7	133	171	10
8	247	371	10
9	561	753	12
10	1167	1545	12
11	2335	3661	14
12	4335	5723	15
13	10533	17661	16
14	21675	27123	16

Maximum-d_{free} codes of rate 1/3				
	generators (octal)			
L	$g^{(1)}$	$g^{(2)}$	$g^{(3)}$	d_{free}
3	5	7	7	8
4	13	15	17	10
5	25	33	37	12
6	47	53	75	13
7	133	145	175	15
8	225	331	367	16
9	557	663	711	18
10	1117	1365	1633	20
11	2353	2671	3175	22
12	4767	5723	6265	24
13	10533	10675	17661	24
14	21645	35661	37133	26

To illustrate the use of those tables, we pick a rate-2/3 code from [10, 11]. It has a constraint length of $L = 2$ and free distance of $d_{free} = 3$. The octal representation of the generators is

$$17_8\,,\quad 06_8\,,\quad 15_8\;.$$

Written in binary form and as polynomials:

	0	0	1	1	1	1	0	0	0	1	1	0	0	0	1	1	0	1
i_1			1		D						D				1			
i_2				1		D				1						1		D

The generator matrix follows to be

$$\mathbf{G}(D) = \begin{pmatrix} 1+D & D & 1 \\ 1+D & 1 & 1+D \end{pmatrix}\;. \tag{4.49}$$

The shift register circuit is shown in Fig. 4.16.

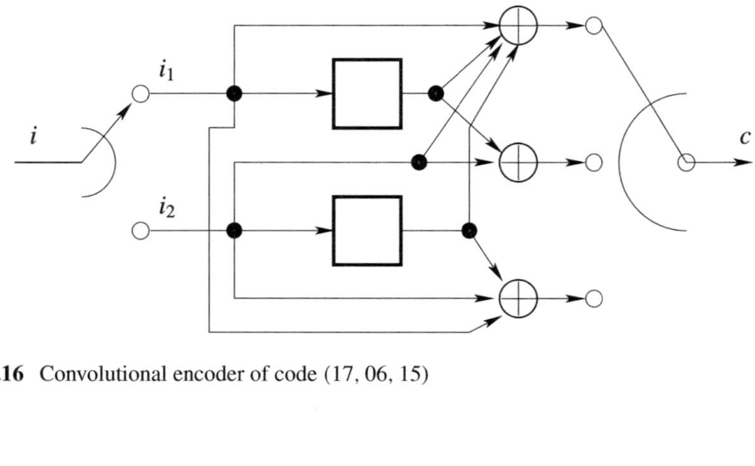

Fig. 4.16 Convolutional encoder of code (17, 06, 15)

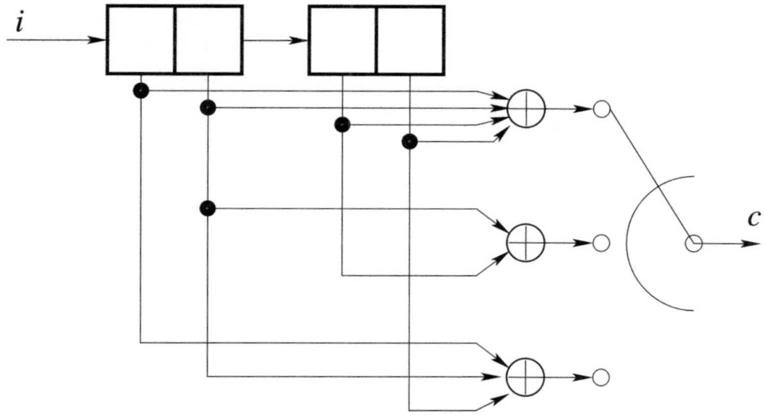

Fig. 4.17 Alternative shift-register constellation of the convolutional code (17, 06, 15)

When combining both inputs into a single shift register (see Fig. 4.17) and performing the shifts in double steps, one can directly read the taps from the binary representation.

Select a code, e.g., of rate 1/3, from the table (or the referenced sources) and draw the trellis. What is the special property that can be observed in the output pattern of path segments that emanate from or merge into a common state.

References

1. R. E. Blahut, *Theory and practice of error control codes*. Reading, MA: Addison-Wesley, 1983.
2. A. Michelson and A. Levesque, *Error-Control Techniques for Digital Communication*. Wiley, 1985.
3. J. L. Massey and M. K. Sain, "Inverses of linear sequential circuits," *IEEE Trans. Computers*, vol. 17, no. 4, pp. 330–337, 1968. [Online]. Available: https://doi.org/10.1109/TC.1968.229392
4. G. Forney, "Convolutional codes I: Algebraic structure," *IEEE Transactions on Information Theory*, vol. 16, no. 6, pp. 720–738, 1970.
5. G. Forney, "Correction to convolutional codes I: Algebraic structure," *IEEE Transactions on Information Theory*, vol. 17, p. 360, 1971.
6. R. Johannesson and Z. . Wan, "A linear algebra approach to minimal convolutional encoders," *IEEE Transactions on Information Theory*, vol. 39, no. 4, pp. 1219–1233, 1993.
7. R. J. McEliece and W. Lin, "The trellis complexity of convolutional codes," *IEEE Transactions on Information Theory*, vol. 42, no. 6, pp. 1855–1864, 1996.
8. J. P. Odenwalder, "Optimal decoding of convolutional codes," PhD thesis, University of California, Los Angeles, CA, 1970.
9. K. Larsen, "Short convolutional codes with maximal free distance for rates 1/2, 1/3, and 1/4 (corresp.)," *IEEE Transactions on Information Theory*, vol. 19, no. 3, pp. 371–372, 1973.

10. J. Proakis, *Digital Communications*, ser. Electrical engineering series. McGraw-Hill, 2001. [Online]. Available: https://books.google.de/books?id=sbr8QwAACAAJ
11. D. Daut, J. Modestino, and L. Wismer, "New short constraint length convolutional code constructions for selected rational rates (corresp.)," *IEEE Transactions on Information Theory*, vol. 28, no. 5, pp. 794–800, 1982.

Chapter 5
Convolutional Codes II—Viterbi and BCJR Decoders, Error Probabilities, Special Constructions

The path is the goal.

Confucius/Buddha

5.1 Viterbi Decoding of Convolutional Codes

Given a received sequence $\mathbf{r}$, decoding tries to find a corresponding code sequence $\mathbf{c}$ that differs least of all. Viterbi's algorithm is a so-called **maximum-likelihood decoder** or in the case of convolutional codes, a **maximum-likelihood sequence estimator** (MLSE). The focus in the name should, however, be on "sequence estimator", since one can easily move from Maximum-Likelihood (ML) to Maximum-A-Posteriori (MAP) probabilities, making the Viterbi algorithm a MAP sequence estimator. This will be highlighted more in Sect. 5.2.4. In the common formulation following the ML rule, the Viterbi algorithm searches for a solution $\mathbf{c}$ by maximizing the probability $P(\mathbf{r}|\mathbf{c})$.

As we will see in Sect. 5.2.4, this is an optimum decoding rule under the assumption that all input sequences occur with the same probability, which is often the case. The maximum-likelihood rule can easily be formulated by means of a metric.

For illustration purposes, we shortly discuss the case of a finite sequence. Let us consider a BSC (binary symmetric channel) with a bit-error probability p. The probability $P(\mathbf{r}|\mathbf{c})$ that a block $\mathbf{c}$ of length N is modified into a certain block $\mathbf{r}$ at Hamming distance d_H is given by

$$P(\mathbf{r}|\mathbf{c}) = p^{d_H}(1-p)^{N-d_H} = \left(\frac{p}{1-p}\right)^{d_H}(1-p)^N. \tag{5.1}$$

W. Henkel, *Channel Coding*, Signals and Communication Technology,
https://doi.org/10.1007/978-3-032-08236-7_5

Since the logarithm is a monotonically increasing function, one can minimize $-\log(P(\mathbf{r}|\mathbf{c}))$, instead:

$$-\log(P(\mathbf{r}|\mathbf{c})) = d_H \cdot \log\Bigg(\underbrace{\frac{1-p}{p}}_{\geq 1,\ \text{with} p \leq 0.5}\Bigg) - \underbrace{N \cdot \log(1-p)}_{\text{const.}}. \tag{5.2}$$

From this the very natural decoding rule follows to search for the codeword (code sequence) with the lowest Hamming distance to the received word (sequence).

In case of an **AWGN** channel, the alteration of a symbol is described by the conditional density

$$p(r_j|c_j) = \frac{1}{\sqrt{2\pi\sigma_n^2}} e^{-\frac{(r_j-c_j)^2}{2\sigma_n^2}}. \tag{5.3}$$

For N symbols, the probabilities multiply when assuming statistical independence.

$$P(\mathbf{r}|\mathbf{c}) = \prod_j \frac{1}{\sqrt{2\pi\sigma_n^2}} e^{-\frac{(r_j-c_j)^2}{2\sigma_n^2}} \tag{5.4}$$

Considering log-likelihoods again, it follows immediately that the Euclidean distances have to be minimized. The result is not unexpected, either.

A decoding in case of the AWGN using Euclidean distances or, in general, without hard quantization of the channel output, we talk about **soft-decision decoding**. If a quantization leads to, e.g., a BSC (binary symmetric channel) requiring to use Hamming distances in the decoding, this is called **hard-decision decoding**.

In case of a Gaussian channel, we obtain decoding areas in n-dimensional spaces around the codewords (code sequences) that are contained within $(n-1)$-dimensional surfaces. In two dimensions we obtain areas as given in Fig. 5.1.

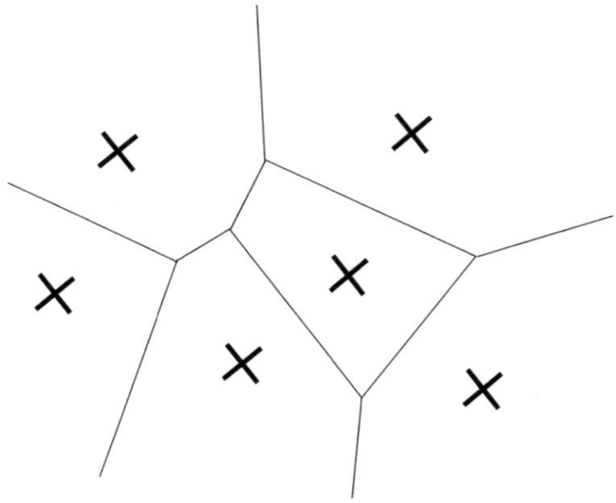

Fig. 5.1 Two-dimensional maximum-likelihood detection/decoding

Viterbi's algorithm is based on the trellis diagram of the code. At each transition in the trellis, new path metrics are computed, i.e., an incremental metric, the actual distance, is added to an accumulated metric at a certain node, which represents the total distance. At the end, the path (sequence) with the lowest distance (metric) is chosen as decoding result. From the paths that merge in a common state, only the single one with the best metric has to be stored. In turn, this means that only 2^m paths need to be processed in the Viterbi algorithm. This is achieved by selecting the best candidate of the merging paths at all states.

For infinite sequences of convolutional codes, the decoding time would also be infinite. Practically, however, proceeding further and further in the trellis, the surviving paths will merge on the left side. There is a rough rule of thumb that the decoding result can be output after a decoding delay of $5 \times L$ steps. One can additionally select the best of the 2^m paths having the best accumulated metric. Often, selecting an arbitrary path to put out the decoding result is good enough.

We decode a received sequence in the prepared trellis in Fig. 5.2 by hand. Figure 5.3 shows the solution.

Solution:

For a received sequence:	$11, 00, 11, 10, 00, 01, 11, 00, 11, \ldots$
Viterbi delivers:	
Transmitted sequence:	$11, 10, 01, 10, 00, 01, 11, 00, 11, \ldots$
Information sequence:	$1, 1, 1, 0, 1, 0, 0, 0, 1, \ldots$
Error sequence:	$00, 10, 10, 00, 00, 10, 00, 00, 00, \ldots$

Practical hard- and software realization
We present two typical solutions.

1. The typical solution utilizes two memory banks (A and B), illustrated in Fig. 5.4. Each bank has 2^m paths with a length of around $5Lk$ (info sequences) or alternatively, $5Ln$ (code sequences) are stored together with their actual accumulated metrics. After the add-compare-select operations at a new trellis segment (colored cells), the paths will be shifted, extended by a new segment, and stored in the other memory bank. With it, one symbol from the selected output path that is taken off the memory due to shifting is the output as the decoded symbol. Due to the alternating storage, paths can be eliminated completely and be replaced by duplicating others that will then only differ by the last (current) symbol.
2. The second method may especially be suited for software realizations. Instead of two storage banks, pointers are used to memorize the paths. The elimination of paths will then be realized by pointer changes. This is somehow similar to the manual decoding but may be more complicated than the method with the two storage banks.

There are also means of parallelizing the operations in the Viterbi algorithm. This is outside the scope of this book.

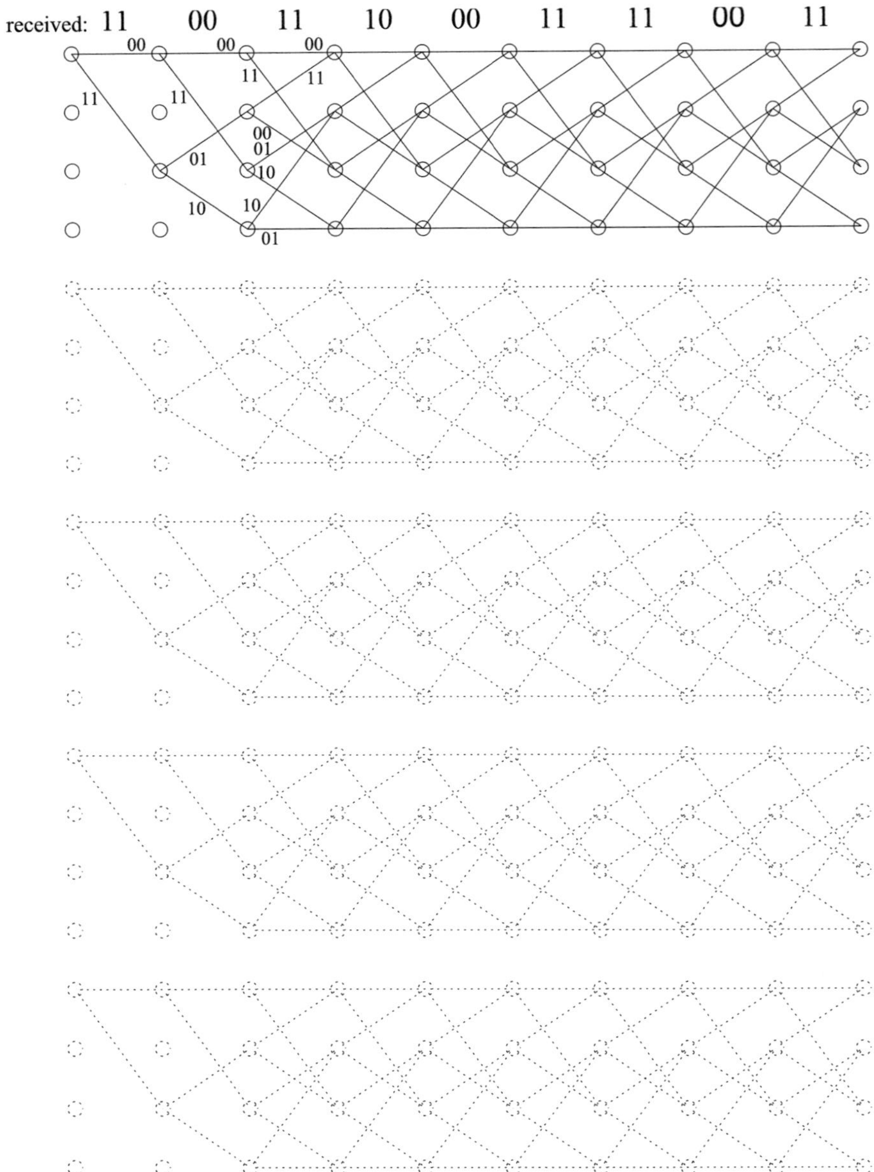

Fig. 5.2 Exercise trellis for decoding the (5, 7) code

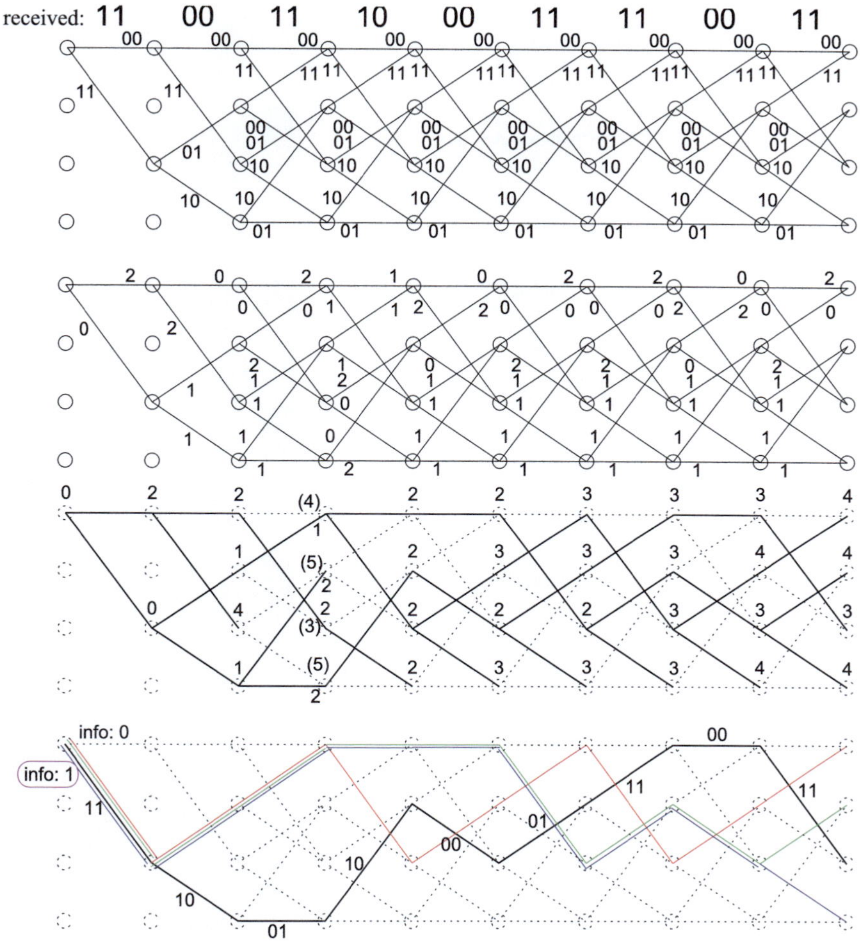

Fig. 5.3 Solution trellis for the decoding example with the (5, 7) code; at the trellises, subsequently, the valid code segments, the Hamming distances (metrics) relative to the received segments, the accumulated Hamming distances (accumulated metrics) at the states with non-continued paths due to worse metric at states shown with parentheses once, and finally, the decoding result are shown. All four possible backtraced paths merge at the leftmost segment. Hence, the information bit on the left is decoded to be 1, before the decoding window moves forward. When the decoding delay is less than $5L$, one might prefer to start from the best metric (black path)

Remark In Viterbi's algorithm, in principle, every non-negative and additive metric can be used to search for paths according to some criteria (not only distances). The triangular inequality needs not be fulfilled.

In the case of slow Fading, the metric of the AWGN (see (5.4)) may be extended by $1/\sigma_n^2$ ($\sigma_n = 1/\sqrt{2E_s/N_0}$, according to Sect. 1.3) to represent the variations of the received amplitude, i.e., of the signal-to-noise ratio E_s/N_0.

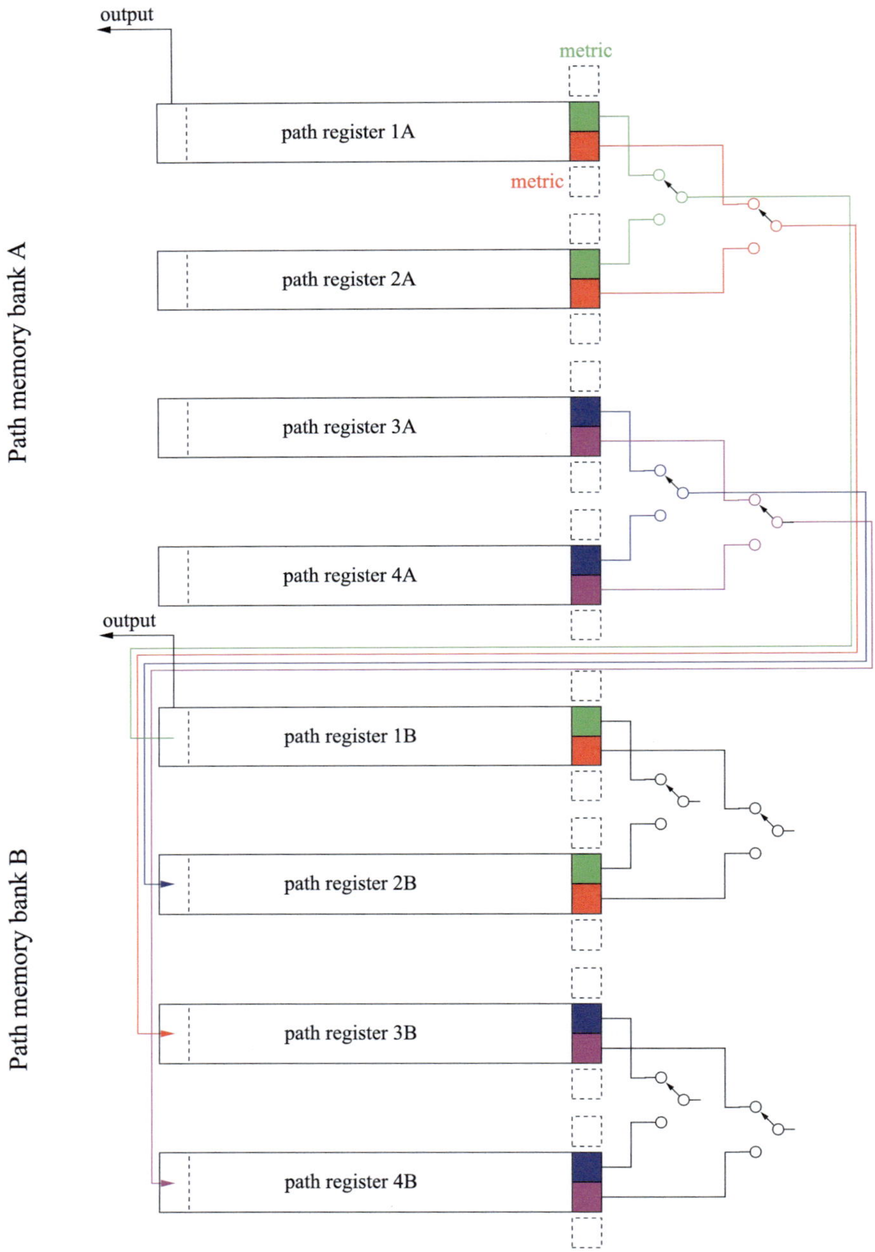

Fig. 5.4 Sketch of the two-bank solution of the Viterbi decoder

5.2 Error Probabilities

5.2.1 Error Probability after Decoding in Case of the BSC

For simplicity, we first consider the binary symmetric channel to obtain results for the error probability after decoding.

The probability that in the decoding a wrong path at a (Hamming) distance d in the trellis is chosen, is

$$P_d = \begin{cases} \sum_{e=(d+1)/2}^{d} \binom{d}{e} p^e (1-p)^{(d-e)}, & d \text{ odd}, \\ \frac{1}{2}\binom{d}{d/2} p^{d/2}(1-p)^{d/2} + \sum_{e=d/2+1}^{d} \binom{d}{e} p^e (1-p)^{(d-e)}, & d \text{ even}. \end{cases} \tag{5.5}$$

This is called the *pairwise error probability* .

The first term for d even is weighted by a factor of 1/2, since at a distance $d/2$, the wrong or the right path will be chosen with a probability of 1/2. The error-event probability to choose an arbitrary wrong path in the trellis can be estimated by ('Union Bound', see 14.2)

$$P_{\text{event}} \leq \sum_{d=d_{\text{free}}}^{\infty} A_d \cdot P_d, \tag{5.6}$$

where A_d denotes the weight distribution of the code (coefficients of $T(D)$). If we upper-bound P_d in (5.5) by $P_d < [2\sqrt{p(1-p)}]^d$ (considering the half-distance case and all possible weight-d pattern), we obtain

$$P_{\text{event}} \leq \sum_{d=d_{\text{free}}}^{\infty} A_d \cdot [2\sqrt{p(1-p)}]^d. \tag{5.7}$$

We rewrite this using the transfer function $T(D)$ as

$$P_{\text{event}} \leq T(D)|_{D=2\sqrt{p(1-p)}} \tag{5.8}$$

The term at the free distance contributes most. We can thus approximate (5.8) by

$$P_{\text{event}} \approx A_{d_{\text{free}}}[2\sqrt{p(1-p)}]^{d_{\text{free}}} \approx A_{d_{\text{free}}} 2^{d_{\text{free}}} p^{d_{\text{free}}/2}. \tag{5.9}$$

The transfer function $T(D, I) = T(D, I, L = 1)$ allows a weighting with the number of wrong information bits. The power of I represents the number of wrong bits on paths at a distance D. Since the lengths of the paths vary, a multiplication with the number of wrong bits provides at least an upper bound of the bit-error probability. For a code of rate $R = k/n$ we divide by k, the number of input bits per segment. Since k is a factor of the path length (in input bits), it should at least be introduced, even if the total path length is not. We obtain

$$P_b < \frac{1}{k} \left. \frac{\partial T(D, I)}{\partial I} \right|_{D=2\sqrt{p(1-p)}, I=1}, \tag{5.10}$$

$$\left. \frac{\partial T(D, I)}{\partial I} \right|_{I=1} = \frac{\partial}{\partial I} \sum_{d=d_{\text{free}}}^{\infty} \sum_{j=0}^{\infty} A_{d,j} D^d I^j |_{I=1} = \sum_{d=d_{\text{free}}}^{\infty} \underbrace{\sum_{j=0}^{\infty} j A_{d,j}}_{B_d} D^d = \sum_{d=d_{\text{free}}}^{\infty} B_d D^d. \tag{5.11}$$

B_d denotes the total number of erroneous information bits at all paths of distance (weight) d. We obtain the approximations

$$P_b \approx \frac{1}{k} B_{d_{\text{free}}} [2\sqrt{p(1-p)}]^{d_{\text{free}}} \approx \frac{1}{k} B_{d_{\text{free}}} 2^{d_{\text{free}}} p^{d_{\text{free}}/2}. \tag{5.12}$$

At this point, it is suitable to introduce the **coding gain**.

Definition 5.1 **Coding gain** is the power (energy) ratio between the power (energy) per transmitted bit without coding and the power (energy) per bit with coding at the same symbol- or bit-error probability.

The **asymptotic coding gain** is the coding gain at the limit of diminishing symbol- and bit-error ratios.

This also means that the coding gain is the ratio of the corresponding SNRs (signal-to-noise ratios) at the same error probability.

Exemplary bit-error ratio curves are shown in Fig. 5.5. We selected the curves of a Reed-Solomon code which has a diminishing probability for false decoding even at low SNR. Other codes may have worse performances at low SNRs and thus a visible cross-over point even for the curve with regards to the true SNR E_s/N_0.

When coding is applied, there is a relation between the energy per bit E_b and the energy per symbol E_s, which is the real signal energy. E_b may at first sight be seen as an abstract figure. It is, however, very useful to compare coding schemes with different rates. It thus, in a way, takes higher transmit rates into account that would be required for lower code rates (at the same data rates). A higher bandwidth would mean a higher noise power, or in energy terms, available energy has to be distributed among more transmitted bits for lower rate coding. The relation between E_b and E_s is given by

$$k \cdot E_b = n \cdot E_s \Longrightarrow E_b = \frac{1}{R} E_s. \tag{5.13}$$

For the SNR, this means

$$E_b/N_0 = 1/R \cdot E_s/N_0. \tag{5.14}$$

This would at first mean a higher required energy per bit in the coded case that would mean a loss if there would not be any coding gain due to error correction. This is the **rate loss** $10 \log_{10}(1/R)$. An E_b/N_0 BER curve and the rate loss are also incorporated in Fig. 5.5. Note that there are applications where the coding gain in E_s/N_0 should

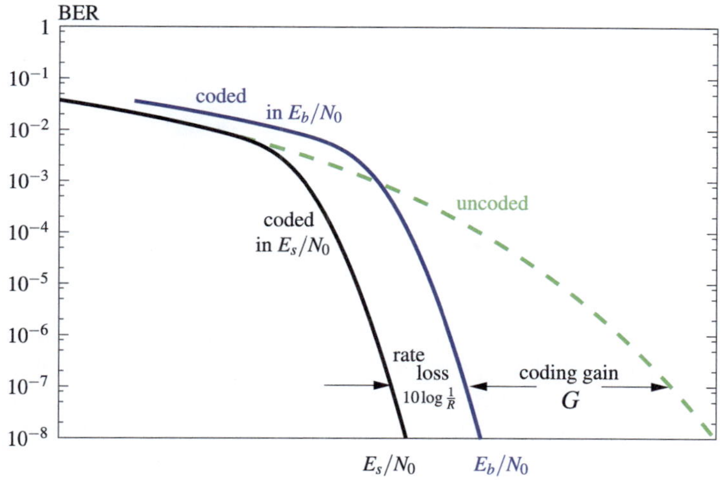

Fig. 5.5 Coding gain and rate loss

still be used (not reduced by the rate loss), especially when no additional redundancy has to be offered. This is, e.g., the case, when already available dummy bits in a protocol frame can be utilized for introducing the code redundancy.

Please also note that (see Fig. 5.5) the intersection between the uncoded and the coded E_b/N_0 curves is typically at BERs of around 10^{-3} to 10^{-2}. For lower SNRs uncoded transmission is to be preferred.

When considering modulation schemes with more than two signal points, Eq. (5.13) applies as well. The rate, however, will be $R > 1$. For example, an M-QAM has a rate $R = \mathrm{ld}(M)$.

In Sect. 1.3.3, Eq. (1.2), we derived the bit-error probability of the AWGN channel with hard quantization as

$$p = \frac{1}{2}\mathrm{erfc}\left(\sqrt{\frac{E_s}{N_0}}\right) = \frac{1}{2}\mathrm{erfc}\left(\sqrt{\frac{RE_b}{N_0}}\right) \approx \frac{1}{2}e^{-RE_b/N_0}, \tag{5.15}$$

where we used the so-called *Chernoff bound* for the approximation. If we insert (5.15) into (5.12), we obtain

$$P_{b\mathrm{coded}} \approx \frac{1}{k} B_{d_{\mathrm{free}}} 2^{d_{\mathrm{free}}/2} e^{-Rd_{\mathrm{free}} E_{b\mathrm{cod.}}/(2N_0)}. \tag{5.16}$$

Without coding, the rate would be $R = 1$ and thus, $E_b = E_s$. According to (5.15),

$$P_{b\mathrm{uncoded}} \approx \frac{1}{2}e^{-E_{b\mathrm{uncod.}}/N_0}. \tag{5.17}$$

For computing the asymptotic coding gain, the exponents in the coded and uncoded case should be the same. Hence,

$$\frac{E_{b\text{uncod.}}}{E_{b\text{cod.}}} = Rd_{\text{free}}/2. \tag{5.18}$$

The asymptotic coding gain is given by

$$G_0 = 10\log_{10}(Rd_{\text{free}}/2). \tag{5.19}$$

This is the asymptotic coding gain for hard decision. The possible gain with soft-decision decoding immediately becomes obvious when observing that the squared Euclidean distance is weighted by d_{free}, the number of positions where it occurs. Together with the rate loss, we obtain the asymptotic coding gain with soft decision

$$G_0 = 10\log_{10}(Rd_{\text{free}}). \tag{5.20}$$

When compared to hard decision, there is an improvement by 3 dB. Practically, a quantization with 3 bits is sufficient.

5.2.2 *The Error Probability after Soft-Decision Decoding for an AWGN Channel*

The probability to move from one path to another with binary transmission and a Hamming distance d between the paths is

$$P_d = \frac{1}{2}\text{erfc}\left(\sqrt{\frac{E_s}{N_0}\cdot d}\right). \tag{5.21}$$

As mentioned at the end of the previous section, we used the fact that the Euclidean distance with BPSK and d dimensions is given by $d_{E_d}^2 = d \cdot d_E^2$. Accordingly, in (1.2) E_s has to multiplied by d. From (5.21), we obtain the error event probability

$$P_{\text{event}} \leq \frac{1}{2}\sum_{d=d_{\text{free}}}^{\infty} A_d \cdot \text{erfc}\left(\sqrt{\frac{E_s}{N_0}\cdot d}\right) \tag{5.22}$$

in analogy with (5.7).

With the Chernoff bound $\frac{1}{2}\text{erfc}\left(\sqrt{\frac{E_s}{N_0}\cdot d}\right) \approx \frac{1}{2}\left(e^{-E_s/N_0}\right)^d$ and using the transfer function $T(D)$, the error-event probability can be approximated by

$$P_{\text{event}} < \frac{1}{2} T(D)|_{D=e^{-E_s/N_0}}. \tag{5.23}$$

Considering (5.10) and (5.11), the bit-error probability follows to be

$$P_b < \frac{1}{2} \frac{\partial T(D, I)}{\partial I}\bigg|_{D=e^{-E_s/N_0}, I=1} = \frac{1}{2} \sum_{d=d_{\text{free}}}^{\infty} B_d D^d \bigg|_{D=e^{-E_s/N_0}}. \tag{5.24}$$

The advantages of the Viterbi algorithm is the soft-decision maximum-likelihood decoding and the finite decoding delay. Its drawback is that the complexity, determined by the number of states, rises exponentially with the memory of the code. Practical realizations do usually not exceed 512 states.

Additionally to the capability to process analog input, especially with concatenated coding, it is important to also deliver analog information about the reliability of the decoding decision together with the decision, itself. We describe two different approaches, the so-called BCJR (Bahl, Cocke, Jelinek, Raviv) algorithm, sometimes referenced as MAP (maximum-a-posteriori probability)[1] decoder [1, 2] and the SOVA (soft-output Viterbi algorithm) by Huber [3] and Hagenauer [4]. We will first sketch Huber's proposal. Thereafter, we derive the BCJR algorithm which requires a blocking of the trellis. Practically, this will usually be the case, anyway. As has already been mentioned, the algorithm is no maximum-likelihood but a maximum-a-posteriori decoder, which is generally optimum. The differences between both approaches will be explained in advance.

5.2.3 Reliability Information of the Decoding Decision within the Viterbi Algorithm (SOVA, Soft-Output Viterbi Alg.)

No man, having put his hand to the plough
and looking back,
is fit for the kingdom of God.

Luke 9:62, King James version

From (5.4) we know that the maximum-likelihood metric $\lambda_{ij,t}$ between states i and j at discrete time t, which we use in the Viterbi algorithm, has the following form in case of an AWGN channel:

$$\lambda_{ij,t} = \text{const.} \cdot (r_t - c_{ij})^2. \tag{5.25}$$

[1] The term MAP decoder may be a somewhat misleading, since other algorithms can easily be reformulated to be MAP decoders, as well. The important property is that the BCJR algorithm determines probabilities of symbols or bits, in contrast to estimating a sequence in the Viterbi algorithm or SOVA. The latter, however, also relates to BCJR in determining probabilities.

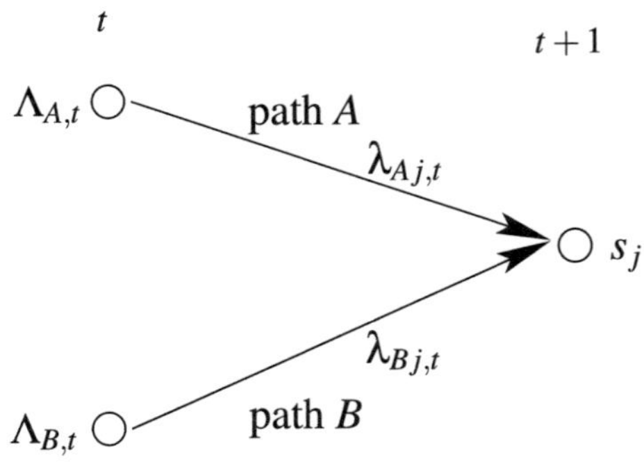

Fig. 5.6 Trellis section for explaining the SOVA algorithm

The two state numbers i and j specify a trellis transition.

Let us first consider the case $k = 1$, i.e., binary input. At each state there will then be two leaving branches and two ending branches.

Let branches A and B end in a common state as shown in Fig. 5.6. Let the time instant be t. For simplicity, we label the states and the paths that emerge from them with the same t.

We obtain conditional probabilities that a sequence $\mathbf{r}_t$ up to time instant t is received under the condition that the trellis path A or path B have been taken.

$$P(\mathbf{r}_t|\text{ path } A) = \text{const.} \cdot e^{-(\Lambda_{A,t}+\lambda_{Aj,t})} \tag{5.26}$$

$$P(\mathbf{r}_t|\text{ path } B) = \text{const.} \cdot e^{-(\Lambda_{B,t}+\lambda_{Bj,t})} \tag{5.27}$$

$\Lambda_{A,t}$ and $\Lambda_{B,t}$ are the accumulated metrics at states A and B, respectively, at time instant t and $\lambda_{Aj,t}$, $\lambda_{Bj,t}$ are the corresponding metric increments (Euclidean distances) of the path segments between t and $t+1$.

Without loss of generality, we assume A to be the path with the better metric, i.e., the one that would be chosen in the Viterbi algorithm.

$$\Lambda_{A,t} + \lambda_{Aj,t} < \Lambda_{B,t} + \lambda_{Bj,t} \tag{5.28}$$

We require the well-known.

Theorem 5.1 (Bayes)

$$P(a, b) = P(a|b) \cdot P(b) \tag{5.29}$$

With it, we express the probability that path A is the right path leading to state s_j under the condition of having received the sequence $\mathbf{r}_t$ up to time t (a-posteriori probability).

$$P(\text{Path } A, \mathbf{r}_t) = P(\text{Path } A|\mathbf{r}_t) \cdot P(\mathbf{r}_t) = P(\mathbf{r}_t|\text{Path } A) \cdot P(\text{Path } A). \tag{5.30}$$

Using the total-probability theorem, we write $P(\mathbf{r}_t)$ as

$$\begin{aligned} P(\mathbf{r}_t) &= P(\mathbf{r}_t, \text{Path } A) + P(\mathbf{r}_t, \text{Path } B) \\ &= P(\mathbf{r}_t|\text{Path } A) \cdot P(\text{Path } A) + P(\mathbf{r}_t|\text{Path } B) \cdot P(\text{Path } B). \end{aligned} \tag{5.31}$$

Inserted into (5.30), this yields

$$p_j := P(\text{Path } A|\mathbf{r}_t) = \frac{P(\mathbf{r}_t|\text{Path } A) \cdot P(\text{Path } A)}{P(\mathbf{r}_t|\text{Path } A) \cdot P(\text{Path } A) + P(\mathbf{r}_t|\text{Path } B) \cdot P(\text{Path } B)}. \tag{5.32}$$

Assuming equiprobable input sequences ($\longrightarrow P(\text{Path } A) = P(\text{Path } B)$), we obtain

$$p_j = 1/(1 + e^{-|\Delta\Lambda|}) \quad \text{with} \quad \Delta\Lambda = (\Lambda_{B,t} + \lambda_{Bj,t}) - (\Lambda_{A,t} + \lambda_{Aj,t}). \tag{5.33}$$

Additionally to the usual Viterbi operations (metric update, add-compare-select, alternating path storage), p_j is now used to update reliability measures at all path segments of path A. Like with the original Viterbi, this updating is only carried out within the finite path memory $t - \tau \le t' \le t$.

$$\chi_{A,t'}(l+1) = \begin{cases} \chi_{A,t'}(l) \cdot p_j & \text{for } i_{A,t'} \ne i_{B,t'} \text{ (or for } c_{A,t'} \ne c_{B,t'}) \\ \chi_{A,t'}(l) & \text{for } i_{A,t'} = i_{B,t'} \text{ (or for } c_{A,t'} = c_{B,t'}) \end{cases}. \tag{5.34}$$

l denotes the iteration counter. An update of the reliabilities $\chi_{A,t'}$ only takes place, if the input (or code) symbols i (or c) at both path segments A and B are different. If they are not, the decision between A and B does not give any further insight regarding these symbols and thus, the reliabilities are kept the same.

For the *non-binary case* (more than two paths merge into states), the procedure can be generalized. The time-dependent backward update value $p_A(t')$ (*cf.*, 5.34) for path A is then given by

$$p_A(t') = \sum_{H \in G_A(t')} w_H / \sum_{H \in G(t')} w_H. \tag{5.35}$$

with

$$G_A(t') = \left\{H \in G(t')|i_{H,t'} = i_{A,t'}\right\} \quad \text{or} \quad G_A(t') = \left\{H \in G(t')|c_{H,t'} = c_{A,t'}\right\},$$

where $G(t')$ is the set of all valid paths of a trellis segment at time t'. w_H denotes the path probability corresponding to the metric of the path H according to (5.26), (5.27). For determining $p_A(t')$, all paths are gathered in the numerator that have the same input (or code) pattern at the considered trellis segment. Equation (5.35) is a generalization of (5.32).

5.2.4 MAP Versus ML Decoding

Minimization of the bit-error probability

$$P(E|\mathbf{r}) = P(\hat{\mathbf{c}} \neq \mathbf{c}|\mathbf{r}) \tag{5.36}$$

is certainly the optimum decoding rule, where $\hat{\mathbf{c}}$ denotes the estimate of the transmitted codeword (code sequence) $\mathbf{c}$.

With the total-probability theorem and Bayes' theorem, we obtain

$$P(E) = \sum_{\mathbf{r}} P(E|\mathbf{r}) \cdot P(\mathbf{r}). \tag{5.37}$$

Only $P(E|\mathbf{r})$ can be influenced by the decoder, not $P(\mathbf{r})$, which depends on the probabilities of the transmit sequences and channel properties. Instead of minimizing $P(E|\mathbf{r}) = P(\hat{\mathbf{c}} \neq \mathbf{c}|\mathbf{r})$, one can also maximize $P(\hat{\mathbf{c}} = \mathbf{c}|\mathbf{r})$. $P(\hat{\mathbf{c}} = \mathbf{c}|\mathbf{r})$ is abbreviated by $P(\hat{\mathbf{c}}|\mathbf{r})$. Bayes' rule provides the relation between MAP (Maximum-A-Posteriori probability) and ML (Maximum Likelihood probability) decoding.

$$P(\mathbf{c}|\mathbf{r}) = P(\mathbf{r}|\mathbf{c}) \cdot \frac{P(\mathbf{c})}{P(\mathbf{r})}. \tag{5.38}$$

$P(\mathbf{c}|\mathbf{r})$ on the left represents the optimum MAP rule, whereas the ML rule $P(\mathbf{r}|\mathbf{c})$ is on the right. The ML rule is more often used and is easier to realize. In case of all transmitted codewords (sequences) occur with the same probability, both decoding rules are equivalent. Often this assumption holds, at least after using a scrambler.

We have described Viterbi's algorithm as a maximum-likelihood decoder. However, by just multiplying the likelihood-probabilities $P(\mathbf{r}|\mathbf{c})$ with the a-priori probabilities $P(\mathbf{c})$ according to (5.38), the corresponding MAP decoder is obtained. With the Euclidean distance being used as a metric, which results from taking the logarithm of the likelihood probability, an additive term would now represent $P(\mathbf{c})$.

Note that the Viterbi algorithm and also its MAP variant are sequence estimators. It is not an optimum estimator for single input symbols. The SOVA algorithm is a means of providing some relation to the single symbol. In Sect. 5.2.6, we will describe the BCJR algorithm providing a recursive computation for maximum-a-posteriori probabilities of symbols or bits. The BCJR algorithm is also often denoted as a MAP or APP (A-Posteriori-Probability) decoder, but it becomes an ML algorithm, when assuming equal probabilities for the code symbols. Hence, the Viterbi algorithm is a sequence estimator, the BCJR algorithm is an efficient probability calculation tool, no estimator.

5.2.5 Blocking of Convolutional Codes

As a basis for the symbol-/bit- oriented MAP algorithm by Bahl et al., which will be treated in the following section, a finite trellis will be required. This would mean a convolutional code of finite length. A finite trellis can be obtained by three means. The following listing goes back to the work of Ma and Wolf [5].

Direct Truncation:
No special measures are taken. The trellis and code sequence just ends at the desired block length nL. Each state can thus be assumed as an ending state. This simple solution has the drawback that the error probability will increase near the block end, since the decoding decision has to be made without a suitable decoding delay.

Termination, Zero Tail:
Appended input symbols ensure that a fixed state will be reached at the block end. In case of a non-recursive encoder it suffices to append zeros. With kM zeros the zero state will be reached after M steps. The disadvantage is the rate loss of $\frac{M}{M+L}$ with nL the block length.

Tail Biting:
For simplicity, let us again assume the encoder to be non-recursive. Then, pretransmitting Mk of the final information symbols, we achieve that the initial state at the beginning of the original block will be the same as at the end. With 'tail biting', however, the output symbols that correspond to the present information symbols are not transmitted. They are just used to define the initial state. Since all states can be selected and initial end states will be identical, the trellis can be illustrated as a closed ring. In principle, with tail biting a separate decoding should be carried out for every state, since at the receiver the end state (= initial state) is not known. In practice, however, one would apply some suboptimal procedure, like decoding on the ring and starting somewhat before the actual 'block' and also exceeding the end of the 'block'. Since it is ring structure, one can also decode iteratively around the ring. In contrast to the other means of blocking, tail biting does not lead to a rate loss.

Additionally to the paper by Ma and Wolf [5], maybe a more recent conference paper by Johannesson [6] should be referenced.

5.2.6 The BCJR Algorithm

Hindsight is easier than foresight.

The Bahl et al. algorithm [2] for computing maximum a-posteriori probabilities of symbols and bits is based on a blocked convolutional code, i.e., the trellis needs to be of finite length. We may think of a transversal (polynomial) convolutional encoder that is fed with zeros at the end of the block. This forces the trellis to merge in the zero state. Let the trellis segments be numbered by $0 \leq t \leq T$. Due to the finite trellis, it will be possible to formulate the MAP rule as a forward and a backward recursion.

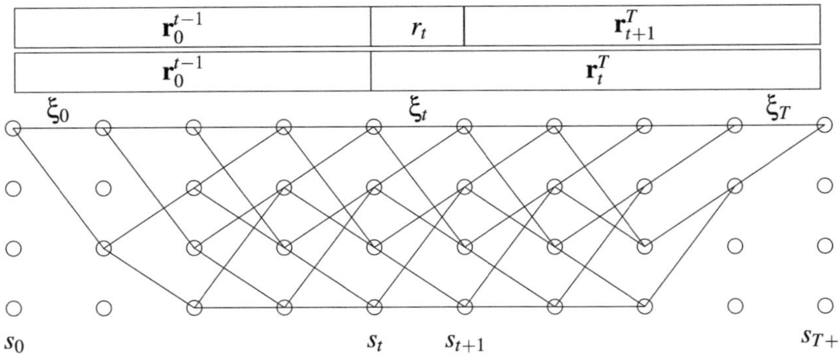

Fig. 5.7 Sample trellis for explaining the BCJR algorithm

Hereto, we consider the probability to have a (transmitter) state s_t and a corresponding received vector $\mathbf{r}$. Bayes' theorem will now be extensively used. The beginning and end of parts of a sequence will be shown as a subscript and superscript, respectively. See Fig. 5.7 for the time references.

$$\begin{aligned} P(s_t, \mathbf{r}) &= P(s_t, \mathbf{r}_0^{t-1}) \cdot P(\mathbf{r}_t^T | s_t, \mathbf{r}_0^{t-1}) = \\ &= P(s_t, \mathbf{r}_0^{t-1}) \cdot P(\mathbf{r}_t^T | s_t) \end{aligned} \tag{5.39}$$

There will not be any dependency of $\mathbf{r}_t^T$ from $\mathbf{r}_0^{t-1}$ due to the assumption of a memoryless channel. The left term of the product will be determined by a forward recursion, whereas the right term will lead to a backward recursion.

Considering the transitions ξ_t from one state s_t to another state s_{t+1} and using Bayes' theorem twice, we obtain

$$\begin{aligned} P(\xi_t, \mathbf{r}) &= P(s_t, s_{t+1}, \mathbf{r}) = \\ &= P(s_t, \mathbf{r}_0^{t-1}) \cdot P(s_{t+1}, r_t | s_t, \mathbf{r}_0^{t-1}) \cdot P(\mathbf{r}_{t+1}^T | s_{t+1}, s_t, \mathbf{r}_0^t) = \\ &= P(s_t, \mathbf{r}_0^{t-1}) \cdot P(s_{t+1}, r_t | s_t) \cdot P(\mathbf{r}_{t+1}^T | s_{t+1}). \end{aligned} \tag{5.40}$$

The last step uses the fact that the sequence part $\mathbf{r}_{t+1}^T$ does only depend on the initial state s_{t+1}, not on a previous state s_t or on $\mathbf{r}_0^t$, which can also be eliminated in the memoryless case, which we will only consider. Similarly, the dependence on $\mathbf{r}_0^{t-1}$ can be omitted in the argument of the factor in the middle, since s_t already sufficiently describes the history, because there is no channel memory.

When comparing (5.39) and (5.40) that refer to states and transitions between states, respectively, one recognizes that in (5.39), both sequence parts $\mathbf{r}_0^{t-1}$ and $\mathbf{r}_t^T$ directly follow each other, whereas there is a space left in the corresponding terms in (5.40), $\mathbf{r}_0^{t-1}$ and $\mathbf{r}_{t+1}^T$ (see Fig. 5.7). These terms will soon show up to represent the forward and backward recursions of the BCJR algorithm.

The intermediate term $P(s_{t+1}, r_t|s_t)$ provides the probability of valid trellis transitions. This value will be zero for non-valid transitions $\xi_t = (s_t, s_{t+1})$.

As has been mentioned, the left and right terms of the products in (5.39) and (5.40) will yield the forward and backward recursions.

$$\begin{aligned}\underline{P(s_t, \mathbf{r}_0^{t-1})} &= \sum_{s_{t-1}} P(s_t, s_{t-1}, \mathbf{r}_0^{t-1}) \\ &= \sum_{s_{t-1}} P(s_{t-1}, \mathbf{r}_0^{t-2}) \cdot P(s_t, r_{t-1}|s_{t-1}, \mathbf{r}_0^{t-2}) \\ &= \sum_{s_{t-1}} \underline{P(s_{t-1}, \mathbf{r}_0^{t-2})} \cdot P(s_t, r_{t-1}|s_{t-1})\end{aligned} \tag{5.41}$$

$$\begin{aligned}\underline{P(\mathbf{r}_t^T|s_t)} &= \sum_{s_{t+1}} P(\mathbf{r}_t^T, s_{t+1}|s_t) \\ &= \sum_{s_{t+1}} P(r_t, \mathbf{r}_{t+1}^T, s_{t+1}|s_t) \\ &= \sum_{s_{t+1}} P(\mathbf{r}_{t+1}^T|s_{t+1}s_t r_t) \cdot P(s_{t+1}, r_t|s_t) \\ &= \sum_{s_{t+1}} \underline{P(\mathbf{r}_{t+1}^T|s_{t+1})} \cdot P(s_{t+1}, r_t|s_t)\end{aligned} \tag{5.42}$$

In the recursions (5.41), (5.42), and also in (5.40), we find the term

$$P(s_t, r_{t-1}|s_{t-1}) = P(r_{t-1}|s_t, s_{t-1}) \cdot P(s_t|s_{t-1}) = P(r_{t-1}|\xi_{t-1}) \cdot P(s_t|s_{t-1}). \tag{5.43}$$

We again applied Bayes' theorem. We observe $P(s_t|s_{t-1}) = 1/2^k$ for valid transitions of a convolutional code of rate k/n when assuming equally probable input data and furthermore, $P(r_{t-1}|\xi_{t-1})$ corresponds to the Gaussian density in the case of AWGN. This represents the likelihood ($P(\mathbf{r}|\mathbf{c})$ according to Sect. 5.2.4).

$P(s_t|s_{t-1})$ in (5.43) expresses the **a-priori probability** of the information symbols. It will especially be important for iterative decoding (Sect. 12.6).

The probabilities in (5.41) are commonly denoted by "α", the ones in (5.42) by "β", and the ones in (5.43), which correspond to a trellis transition, by "γ". Using these conventions, Eqs. (5.39) and (5.40) would read

$$P(s_t^\nu, \mathbf{r}) = \alpha_t(s_t^\nu) \cdot \beta_t(s_t^\nu), \tag{5.44}$$

$$P(\xi_t^{\nu,\mu}, \mathbf{r}) = P(s_t^\nu, s_{t+1}^\mu, \mathbf{r}) = \alpha_t(s_t^\nu) \cdot \gamma_t(s_t^\nu, s_{t+1}^\mu) \cdot \beta_{t+1}(s_{t+1}^\mu), \tag{5.45}$$

respectively. Further variables have been introduced here, to specify certain states ν and μ at times t and $t+1$, respectively.

We are not so much interested in state or transition probabilities, but in the probabilities of information or code bits, instead. Information bits are either part of the state in the case of a non-recursive encoder or they are part of the code sequence, i.e., part of the code segment aligned to a state transition.

Studying the non-recursive encoder first, a state s_t is represented by the contents $i_{t,l}$, $l = 0, \dots, m-1$ of the encoder shift register. Let $\Gamma(i_{t,l})$ be the set of all states with a content $i_{t,l}$ at position l. The probability for this component follows to be

$$P(i_{t,l}, \mathbf{r}) = \sum_{s_t \in \Gamma(i_{t,l})} P(s_t, \mathbf{r}). \tag{5.46}$$

In the systematic case, we consider a component $c_{t,l}$ $l = 0, \dots, n-1$ of the code sequence and obtain

$$P(c_{t,l}, \mathbf{r}) = \sum_{\xi_t \in \Gamma(c_{t,l})} P(\xi_t, \mathbf{r}). \tag{5.47}$$

The reliability to be determined is $P(i_{t,l}|\mathbf{r})$, which relates to the joint probability in (5.47) by $P(i_{t,l}, \mathbf{r}) = P(i_{t,l}|\mathbf{r}) \cdot P(\mathbf{r})$. With precomputing and tabulating $P(\mathbf{r})$, the MAP probabilities can easily be obtained. However, one can as well use the quotient $P(i_{t,l}|\mathbf{r}) / \sum_{i' \neq i} P(i'_{t,l}|\mathbf{r})$ or its logarithm

$$\ln \frac{P(i_{t,l}|\mathbf{r})}{\sum_{i' \neq i} P(i'_{t,l}|\mathbf{r})} = \ln \frac{P(i_{t,l}, \mathbf{r})}{\sum_{i' \neq i} P(i'_{t,l}, \mathbf{r})}, \tag{5.48}$$

the so-called **log-likelihood ratio**, as a reliability measure, instead. In the binary case $(i = \pm 1)$, this would be

$$\ln \frac{P(i_{t,l} = +1|\mathbf{r})}{P(i'_{t,l} = -1|\mathbf{r})} = \ln \frac{P(i_{t,l} = +1, \mathbf{r})}{P(i'_{t,l} = -1, \mathbf{r})}. \tag{5.49}$$

For the components of the code sequence, the log-likelihood ratio would be

$$\ln \frac{P(c_{t,l}|\mathbf{r})}{\sum_{c' \neq c} P(c'_{t,l}|\mathbf{r})} = \ln \frac{P(c_{t,l}, \mathbf{r})}{\sum_{c' \neq c} P(c'_{t,l}, \mathbf{r})}, \tag{5.50}$$

in the binary case,

$$\ln \frac{P(c_{t,l} = +1|\mathbf{r})}{P(c'_{t,l} = -1|\mathbf{r})} = \ln \frac{P(c_{t,l} = +1, \mathbf{r})}{P(c'_{t,l} = -1, \mathbf{r})}. \tag{5.51}$$

The decoder decision based on the MAP values is an optimum decoding of the information or code symbols (bits) and leads to minimum symbol- or bit-error probabilities. Note, that the sequence of the resulting code symbols (bits) according to (5.47) needs not necessarily be a valid code sequence, although the trellis structure is considered in the algorithm. The algorithm operates on single symbols or bits in contrast to the Viterbi algorithm, which is a sequence estimator.

Although we assumed a blocked trellis by termination, there are also possibilities to formulate a windowed BCJR algorithm [7] by keeping the forward recursion unchanged and performing backward recursions inside a window initializing β by α. Performance is superior to the earlier described SOVA algorithm.

There are low-complexity realizations of the BCJR algorithm named **log-MAP** and **Max-log-MAP** algorithm, described in a separate subsequent subsection.

5.2.6.1 Log-MAP and Max-Log-MAP Algorithms

Since the calculations of the BCJR algorithm are still quite complex, alternative formulations have been proposed that use a logarithmic formulation, the so-called Log-MAP and Max-Log-MAP [8] algorithms. The first is just a reformulation, whereas the latter is an approximation thereof.

We use the description introduced in Eqs. (5.44) and (5.45). Instead of $\alpha_t(s_t^\nu)$, $\beta_{t+1}(s_{t+1}^\mu)$, and $\gamma_t(s_t^\nu, s_{t+1}^\mu)$, we are now using the log counterparts $\bar{\alpha}_t(s_t^\nu) = \ln(\alpha_t(s_t^\nu))$, $\bar{\beta}_{t+1}(s_{t+1}^\mu) = \ln(\beta_{t+1}(s_{t+1}^\mu))$, and $\bar{\gamma}_t(s_t^\nu, s_{t+1}^\mu) = \ln(\gamma_t(s_t^\nu, s_{t+1}^\mu))$. Within the following calculations, we make use of the so-called Jacobian logarithm [9]

$$\ln(e^a + e^b) = \max(a, b) + \ln(1 + e^{-|a-b|}) \tag{5.52}$$

for reducing the computational complexity.

Equation (5.52) follows from rephrasing

$$e^a + e^b = e^a\left(1 + e^{b-a}\right) = e^{a+\ln(1+e^{b-a})}, \tag{5.53}$$

leading to

$$e^a + e^b = \exp\left[\max(a, b) + \ln\left(1 + e^{-|a-b|}\right)\right]. \tag{5.54}$$

This can easily be checked for $a \geq b$ and $a < b$. For more than two terms, Eq. (5.52) can be applied recursively.

$$\begin{aligned} \ln(e^{a_1} + e^{a_2} + \cdots + e^{a_n}) &= \ln\left(\Phi + e^{a_n}\right), \quad \Phi = e^{a_1} + e^{a_2} + \cdots + e^{a_{n-1}} \\ &= \max(\ln(\Phi)), a_n) + \ln(1 + e^{-|\ln(\Phi)-a_n|}) \\ &= \max(\varphi, a_n) + \ln(1 + e^{-|\varphi-a_n|}) \end{aligned} \tag{5.55}$$

$\varphi = \ln(\Phi)$ can now iteratively be processed.

We now start from reformulating the forward and backward recursions in (5.41) and (5.42), respectively, into the α, β, γ-representation, leading to

$$\bar{\alpha}_t(s_t^{\mu}) = \ln\left(\alpha_r(s_t^{\mu})\right) = \ln\left(\sum_{s_{t-1}^{\nu}} \alpha_{t-1}(s_{t-1}^{\mu}) \cdot \gamma_{t-1}(s_{t-1}^{\nu}, s_t^{\mu})\right) \tag{5.56}$$

$$= \ln\left(\sum_{s_{t-1}^{\nu}} \exp\left(\ln(\alpha_{t-1}(s_{t-1}^{\nu}) \cdot \gamma_{t-1}(s_{t-1}^{\nu}, s_t^{\mu}))\right)\right) \tag{5.57}$$

$$= \ln\left(\sum_{s_{t-1}^{\nu}} \exp\left(\bar{\alpha}_{t-1}(s_{t-1}^{\nu}) + \bar{\gamma}_{t-1}(s_{t-1}^{\nu}, s_t^{\mu})\right)\right) \tag{5.58}$$

$$\overset{(5.52)}{=} \max_{s_{t-1}^{\nu}} \left(\bar{\alpha}_{l-1}(s_t^{\nu}) + \bar{\gamma}_l(s_t^{\nu}, s_{t+1}^{\mu})\right) + \ln\left(1 + e^{-|\Delta_{t-1}|}\right) \text{ and} \tag{5.59}$$

$$\bar{\beta}_t(s_t^{\nu}) = \ln\left(\beta_t(s_t^{\nu})\right) = \ln\left(\sum_{s_{t+1}^{\mu}} \exp\left(\ln(\beta_{t+1}(s_{t+1}^{\mu}) \cdot \gamma_t(s_t^{\nu}, s_{t+1}^{\mu}))\right)\right) \tag{5.60}$$

$$\overset{(5.52)}{=} \max_{s_{t+1}^{\nu}} \left(\bar{\beta}_{t+1}(s_{t+1}^{\mu}) + \bar{\gamma}_t(s_t^{\nu}, s_{t+1}^{\mu})\right) + \ln\left(1 + e^{-|\Delta_{t+1}|}\right), \tag{5.61}$$

where Δ_t represents the difference of the terms of the maximization. For $\bar{\gamma}_t(s_t^{\nu}, s_{t+1}^{\mu})$, we can write

$$\bar{\gamma}_t(s_t^{\nu}, s_{t+1}^{\mu}) = \ln\left(\gamma_t(s_t^{\nu}, s_{t+1}^{\mu})\right) \tag{5.62}$$

$$= \text{const.} - \frac{||\mathbf{r}(t) - \mathbf{c}_{\nu\mu}||^2}{2\sigma_N^2} + \ln\left(P(s_{t+1}^{\mu}|s_t^{\nu})\right) \tag{5.63}$$

$$= \text{const.} - \frac{||\mathbf{r}(t) - \mathbf{c}_{\nu\mu}||^2}{2\sigma_N^2} - \ln(\underset{\substack{\uparrow \\ e^0}}{1} + e^{\mp L_a(u)}) \tag{5.64}$$

$$\overset{(5.52)}{=} \text{const.} - \frac{||\mathbf{r}(t) - \mathbf{c}_{\nu\mu}||^2}{2\sigma_N^2} - \max(0, \mp L_a(i_t)) + \ln(1 + e^{-|L_a(i_t)|}), \tag{5.65}$$

using (5.43) and the Gaussian assumption for the channel noise (AWGN). We expressed $P(s_{t+1}^{\mu}|s_t^{\nu})$ by the a-priori information, the log-likelihood $L_a(i_t)$ of the corresponding information. For simplicity, we assumed the rate to be $1/n$, i.e., only one information bit per trellis segment.

Expressing the probabilities $P(+1)$ and $P(-1)$ or $P(0)$ and $P(1)$, respectively, in terms of the log-likelihood ratio directly follows from the definition

$$L = \ln \frac{P(+1)}{P(-1)} = \ln \frac{P(+1)}{1 - P(+1)}$$

$$\Longrightarrow e^L\,(1 - P(+1)) = P(+1) \Longrightarrow P(+1) = \frac{e^L}{1 + e^L} = \frac{1}{1 + e^{-L}}. \tag{5.66}$$

The $\mp$ sign in (5.64), i.e., in the substitution

$$P(s_t^{\nu}|s_{t+1}^{\mu}) = \frac{1}{1 + e^{\mp L_a(i_t)}} \tag{5.67}$$

is due to the fact that a certain state transition belongs to inputs $+1$ or -1 (0 or 1, respectively). The $-$ and $+$ relate to information values $+1$ (0) and -1 (1), respectively. The constant may be omitted. For further complexity reduction, the logarithmic correction terms in the above equations are usually stored in a look-up table instead of calculating the logarithm each time.

These equations lead to the Log-MAP algorithm. This algorithm has the same performance as the BCJR algorithm but less complexity. For the Max-Log-MAP algorithm, we omit the logarithmic correction terms in (5.59), (5.61), and (5.64). This is a further reduction in complexity but leads to small performance degradations. Links between the Max-Log-MAP algorithm and SOVA are discussed in [10].

5.3 Puncturing Convolutional Codes

Mut zur Lücke
The courage to bridge the gap

German student phrase for gaps in studying

With the given structure of convolutional codes, it appears to be difficult to have high-rate codes with a coderate near to one. One may think of rates $R = k/(k+1)$ with a big k. Such a code would have a trellis with 2^k branches emerging from a state and also merging into a state. This would require the Viterbi algorithm to search for the best metric among all these 2^k path metrics, which would mean a number of $2^k - 1$ comparisons.

It would also be nice to be able to modify the redundancy for a given fixed code structure according to varying channel properties or to be able to adapt to a source encoder, which typically delivers output bits of different significance. Thus, there should be a different code protection according to how important the bits are. This leads to so-called 'Unequal Error-Protection (UEP) Codes'. For block codes there exist different proposals that cannot be treated in here in detail.

With convolutional codes, there exists a very simple procedure to adapt the redundancy for a given code structure, i.e., a given trellis. Hereto, some output symbols (bits) are just not transmitted. This is called **puncturing**.

A puncturing scheme is usually described by means of a puncturing matrix $\boldsymbol{P}$. This matrix has dimensions $n \times P$ and consists of ones and zeros. The zeros determine the discarded output symbols (bits). The columns show the time sequence of the puncturing pattern. A column consisting of only ones means that all n output symbols (bits) of the convolutional encoder will be transmitted.

Example We again consider the simple example of a convolutional code with rate 1/2 and the generators 5_8 and 7_8, i.e., $1 + D^2$ and $1 + D + D^2$, respectively. We choose the puncturing matrix

$$\boldsymbol{P} = \begin{pmatrix} 1\,0 \\ 1\,1 \end{pmatrix}.$$

The punctured rate-1/2 encoder now transmits only 3 output bits instead of 4 for 2 input bits.

Another way to specify the puncturing pattern is by using the generators of the outputs. This has the form

$$\left\{P^{(1)}(D),\, P^{(2)}(D),\, P^{(3)}(D), \ldots,\, P^{(k+1)}(D)\right\} \tag{5.68}$$

for an intended code of rate $k/(k+1)$.

For our example code of rate 1/2, we obtain

$$\left\{1 + D^2, 1 + D + D^2, 1 + D + D^2\right\}.$$

The decoding of a punctured convolutional code with the Viterbi algorithm uses the trellis of the non-punctured code by just not including the non-transmitted bits (symbols) in the metric calculations. One could, of course, also compress P segments of a punctured trellis into one equivalent segment of a non-punctured trellis. This would, however, lead to the above-mentioned disadvantages in decoding complexity by requiring more comparisons. Figure 5.8 shows the trellis of the punctured code of original rate 1/2 (punctured to 2/3) together with the equivalent trellis of a non-punctured code of rate 2/3.

Note that we cannot conclude from a mother encoder to be non-catastrophic that the punctured encoder will also be non-catastrophic. On the contrary, a punctured catastrophic encoder will also be catastrophic.

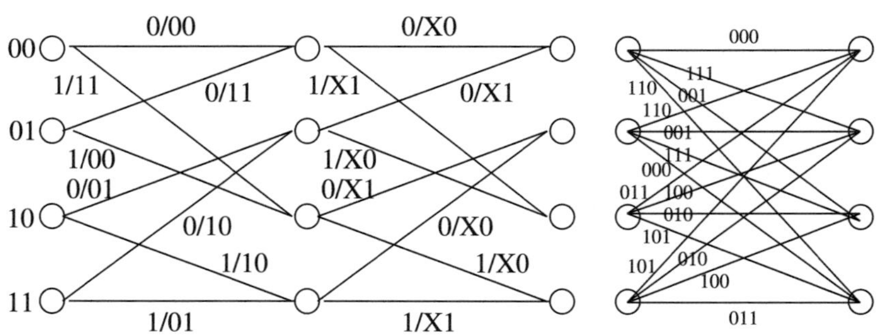

Fig. 5.8 Equivalent trellis representations of a punctured code

Table 5.1 Punctured codes

Original code		Punctured codes					
		$R = 2/3$		$R = 3/4$		$R = 4/5$	
m	$g^{(1)}, g^{(2)}$	$\boldsymbol{P}$	d_{free} $A_{d_{\text{free}}}, B_{d_{\text{free}}}$	$\boldsymbol{P}$	d_{free} $A_{d_{\text{free}}}, B_{d_{\text{free}}}$	$\boldsymbol{P}$	d_{free} $A_{d_{\text{free}}}, B_{d_{\text{free}}}$
2	5, 7	10	3	101	3	1011	2
		11	1, 1	110	6, 15	1100	1, 1
3	13, 17	11	4	110	4	1011	3
		10	3, 10	101	29, 124	1100	5, 14
4	23, 25	11	4	101	3	1010	3
		10	1, 1	110	1, 1	1101	3, 11
5	53, 75	10	6	100	4	1000	4
		11	19, 96	111	1, 3	1111	7, 40
6	133, 171	11	6	110	5	1111	4
		10	1, 3	101	8,42	1000	3, 12
7	247, 371	10	7	110	6	1010	5
		11	9,47	101	36, 239	1101	20, 168
8	561, 753	11	7	111	6	1101	5
		10	3, 11	100	10, 52	1010	7, 31

Original code		Punctured codes					
		$R = 5/6$		$R = 6/7$		$R = 7/8$	
m	$g^{(1)}, g^{(2)}$	$\boldsymbol{P}$	d_{free}	$\boldsymbol{P}$	d_{free}	$\boldsymbol{P}$	d_{free}
			$A_{d_{\text{free}}}, B_{d_{\text{free}}}$		$A_{d_{\text{free}}}, B_{d_{\text{free}}}$		$A_{d_{\text{free}}}, B_{d_{\text{free}}}$
2	5, 7	10111	2	101111	2	1011111	2
		11000	2, 2	110000	4, 5	1100000	6, 8
3	15, 17	10100	3	100011	2	1000010	2
		11011	15, 63	111100	1, 2	1111101	2, 4
4	23, 35	10111	3	101010	3	1010011	3
		11000	5, 20	110101	14, 69	1101100	13, 49
5	53, 75	10000	4	110110	3	1011101	3
		11111	19, 100	101001	5, 25	1100010	9, 60
6	133, 171	11010	4	111010	3	1111010	3
		10101	14, 92	100101	1, 5	1000101	2, 9
7	247, 371	11100	4	101001	4	1010100	4
		10011	2, 7	110110	11, 85	1101011	26, 258
8	561, 753	10110	5	110110	4	1101011	4
		11001	19, 168	101001	2, 9	1010100	6, 70

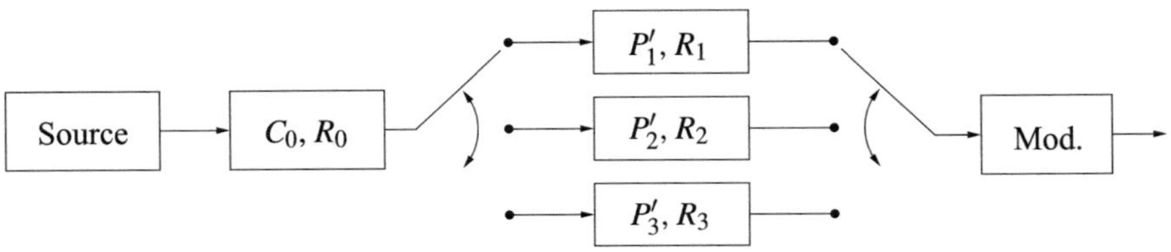

Fig. 5.9 A generalization of puncturing: a serial concatenation of a puncturing code of rate ≥ 1 with a mother code

In Table 5.1, we have gathered some puncturing schemes from [11–13]. Herein, $A_{d_{\text{free}}}$ denotes the number of sequences at the minimum distance, i.e., the first coefficient of the transfer function $T(D)$ used to express the error-event probability. Likewise, $B_{d_{\text{free}}}$ is the first coefficient of $\partial T(D, L, I)/\partial I|_{I=1,L=1}$ used for estimating the bit-error probability.

Generalizing the puncturing idea of simply omitting output bits and thereby increasing the rate of the code, one could also look at puncturing as a concatenation with a puncturing code of rate $R_{\text{punc}} \geq 1$. In Fig. 5.9 a mother code C_0 is followed by 'puncturing codes' P_i', which may be chosen according to protection requirements.

5.3.1 *Rate-Compatible Punctured Convolutional Codes (RCPC)*

In [14], Hagenauer introduced the so-called rate-compatibility criterion. This condition deals with the transition points when rates (puncturing pattern) are switched. In the transition, it has to be ensured that the free distance will not drop below the lower of the two neighboring distances that would be obtained in the regular case. Let $\mathbf{P}_{l_1}$ and $\mathbf{P}_{l_2}$ be puncturing matrices with rates $R_{l_1} < R_{l_2}$. Rate compatibility will be achieved when

$$\text{if } P_{l_1,ij} = 1 \text{ then } P_{l_2,ij} = 1 \text{ for all } l_2 \geq l_1 \tag{5.69}$$

or equivalently

$$\text{if } P_{l_1,ij} = 0 \text{ then } P_{l_2,ij} = 0 \text{ for all } l_2 \leq l_1. \tag{5.70}$$

This restriction means that a stronger code is obtained by additional placement of ones in the puncturing matrix of the weaker code. An example could be

$$\mathbf{P}_1 = \begin{bmatrix} 1\,1\,1\,0 \\ 1\,0\,0\,1 \end{bmatrix} \tag{5.71}$$

$$\mathbf{P}_2 = \begin{bmatrix} 1\,1\,1\,0 \\ 1\,1\,0\,1 \end{bmatrix}, \tag{5.72}$$

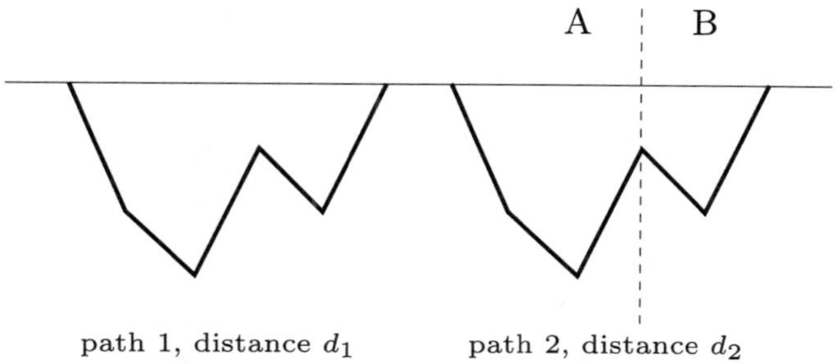

Fig. 5.10 Minimum-distance paths in a transition region

where the puncturing matrix $\mathbf{P}_2$ of the stronger code only contains an additional one where $\mathbf{P}_1$ has a zero. The ones of the weaker code are preserved.

Figure 5.10 sketches minimum distance trellis paths inside the weaker code segment A and, alternatively, when it would be continued in the other segment B. If in segment B, all ones will be preserved and only some more would be added, the minimum-distance path cannot deteriorate. The distance could stay the same or improve due to the rate change.

Starting from a convolutional code of rate $1/n$ and using an $n \times P$ puncturing matrix, the rates

$$R = \frac{P}{P+l}, \quad l = 1, \ldots, (n-1)P \tag{5.73}$$

can in principal be generated. $l = 1$ means only one parity component, whereas with $l = (n-1)P$, the whole puncturing matrix $\boldsymbol{P}$ is filled with ones.

Let us again consider the example of the (2,1,2) convolutional code with generators 5_8 and 7_8. Suitable puncturing matrices $\boldsymbol{P}_l, l = 1, \ldots, (n-1)$ with rates 4/5, 4/6, 4/7, 4/8 are

$$\boldsymbol{P}_1 = \begin{pmatrix} 1\,1\,1\,0 \\ 1\,0\,0\,1 \end{pmatrix} \boldsymbol{P}_2 = \begin{pmatrix} 1\,1\,1\,0 \\ 1\,1\,0\,1 \end{pmatrix} \boldsymbol{P}_3 = \begin{pmatrix} 1\,1\,1\,1 \\ 1\,1\,0\,1 \end{pmatrix} \boldsymbol{P}_4 = \begin{pmatrix} 1\,1\,1\,1 \\ 1\,1\,1\,1 \end{pmatrix}$$

In [14], a multiplicative description of the convolutional encoder was used, which we also show here to introduce this alternative presentation at least once (see Fig. 5.11). The following correspondences are commonly used:[2]

$$+1 = (-1)^0 \longleftrightarrow 0 \qquad -1 = (-1)^1 \longleftrightarrow 1 \tag{5.74}$$

As an example from [14], we list puncturing matrices for a convolutional code of rate 1/3 with $m = 6$ and the generators $g^{(1)} = (1011011)$, $g^{(2)} = (1111001)$, and

[2] As an alternative to $y = (-1)^x$, $x \in \{0, 1\}$, $y \in \{-1, 1\}$, one can as well use $y = 1 - 2x$

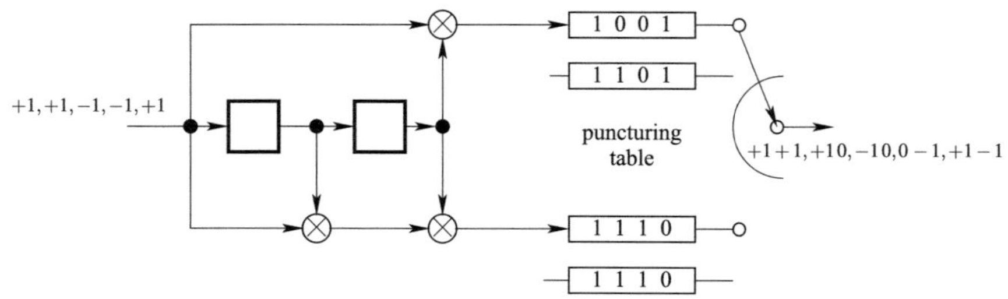

Fig. 5.11 Rate-compatible convolutional encoder with a puncturing according to $\boldsymbol{P}_1$ and $\boldsymbol{P}_2$

$g^{(3)} = (1100101)$ together with the corresponding free distances and the parameters $B_{d_{\text{free}}}$.

R	8/9	8/10	8/12	8/14	8/16	8/18	8/20	8/22	8/24
$\boldsymbol{P}$	1111 0111 1000 1000 0000 0000	1111 1111 1000 1000 0000 0000	1111 1111 1010 1010 0000 0000	1111 1111 1110 1110 0000 0000	1111 1111 1111 1111 0000 0000	1111 1111 1111 1111 1000 1000	1111 1111 1111 1111 1100 1100	1111 1111 1111 1111 1110 1110	1111 1111 1111 1111 1111 1111
d_{free}	3	4	6	7	10	10	11	12	14
$B_{d_{\text{free}}}$	24	24	12	12	288	14	8	2	8

Rate-compatible convolutional codes provide different rates and free distances with the same code structure.

5.4 Pruning Convolutional Codes

Less is more

Robert Browning, 1855

Figure 5.9 illustrated the structure of puncturing as a post-coding of a mother code with a puncturing code P_i'. Pruning is the opposite procedure [15, 16], precoding a mother code with codes P_i according to Fig. 5.12. The three shown pruning codes should illustrate a possible rate adaptation dependent on protection requirements.

Let us consider an example of two codes with generator matrices

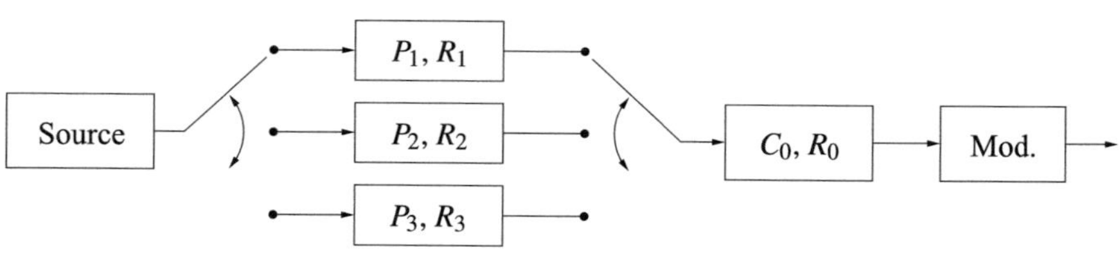

Fig. 5.12 Pruning as a serial concatenation of a pruning code P_i of rate ≤ 1 and a mother code

$$\mathbf{G}^{(0)}(D) = \begin{bmatrix} 1 & 1+D & 1+D \\ 1+D & D & 1+D \end{bmatrix} \text{ and} \tag{5.75}$$

$$\mathbf{G}^{(1)}(D) = \begin{bmatrix} 1+D+D^2 & 1+D+D^2 & 1+D^2 \end{bmatrix}, \tag{5.76}$$

where the second can be considered as a sub-code of the first. It is obvious that a pruning matrix

$$\mathbf{P}(D) = \begin{bmatrix} 1 & D \end{bmatrix} \tag{5.77}$$

multiplied with $\mathbf{G}^{(0)}(D)$ from the left leads to $\mathbf{G}^{(1)}(D)$.

The trellis segments of both codes $\mathbf{G}^{(0)}$ and $\mathbf{G}^{(1)}$ are shown in Fig. 5.13. It becomes visible what pruning means in a trellis representation: transitions are discarded from the trellis of $\mathbf{G}^{(0)}$ to realize the subcode $\mathbf{G}^{(1)}$.

Regarding the rates, we observe that the number of input bits is reduced from $k^{(0)}$ to $k^{(1)}$, i.e., the rate of the pruned code is given by

$$R^{(1)} = \frac{k^{(1)}}{n} = \frac{k^{(1)}}{k^{(0)}} \cdot \frac{k^{(0)}}{n} = R_P \cdot R^{(0)}, \tag{5.78}$$

with R_P and $R^{(0)}$ being the rates of the pruning and mother codes, respectively.

In a more strict sense, just like with puncturing understood as omitting output data, pruning can be seen as omitting input data, i.e., replacing input data by known values, e.g., by zeros according to some pruning scheme as shown in Fig. 5.14.

When just omitting p bits at the output (puncturing) or input (pruning), the rates are given in Table 5.2.

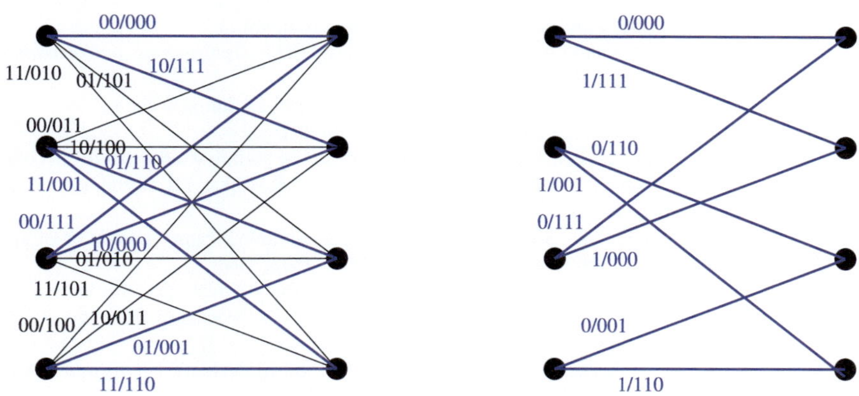

Fig. 5.13 Trellis segments of an unpruned (left) and a pruned (right) code

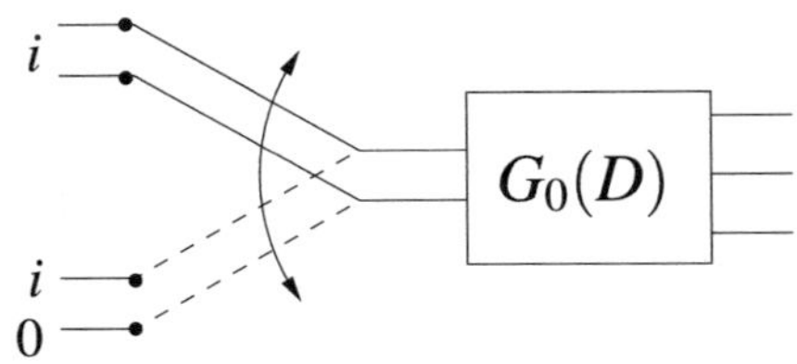

Fig. 5.14 Pruning by inserting known values, e.g., zeros instead of data according to some pruning pattern

Table 5.2 Puncturing and pruning rates

Puncturing	$R = \frac{k}{n-p}$
Pruning in case of non-systematic encoding	$R = \frac{k-p}{n}$
Pruning systematic bits	$R = \frac{k-p}{n-p}$

References

1. G. D. Forney, "The Viterbi algorithm," *Proceedings of the IEEE*, vol. 61, no. 3, pp. 268–278, 1973.
2. L. Bahl, J. Cocke, F. Jelinek, and J. Raviv, "Optimal decoding of linear codes for minimizing symbol error rate (corresp.)," *IEEE Transactions on Information Theory*, vol. 20, no. 2, pp. 284–287, 1974.
3. J. Huber and A. Rüppel, "Zuverlässigkeitsschätzung für die Ausgangssymbole von Trellis-Decodern (in German)," *AEÜ*, vol. 44, no. 1, pp. 8–..., 1990.
4. J. Hagenauer and P. Hoeher, "A Viterbi algorithm with soft-decision outputs and its applications," in *1989 IEEE Global Telecommunications Conference and Exhibition 'Communications Technology for the 1990s and Beyond'*, 1989, pp. 1680–1686 vol. 3.
5. H. Ma and J. Wolf, "On tail biting convolutional codes," *IEEE Transactions on Communications*, vol. 34, no. 2, pp. 104–111, 1986.
6. R. Johannesson, "Tailbiting: A bridge between block and convolutional codes," in *3rd ITG Conference Source and Channel Coding*, 2000, pp. 279–280.
7. J. Gwak, S. KimShin, and H.-M. Kim, "Reduced complexity sliding window BCJR decoding algorithms for Turbo codes," in *Cryptography and Coding*, M. Walker, Ed. Berlin, Heidelberg: Springer Berlin Heidelberg, 1999, pp. 179–184.
8. W. J. Gross and P. G. Gulak, "Simplified MAP algorithm suitable for implementation of turbo decoders," *Electronics Letters*, vol. 34, no. 16, pp. 1577–1578, 1998.
9. J. A. Erfanian, S. Pasupathy, and G. Gulak, "Reduced complexity symbol detectors with parallel structures," in *[Proceedings] GLOBECOM '90: IEEE Global Telecommunications Conference and Exhibition*, 1990, pp. 704–708 vol.2.
10. M. P. C. Fossorier, F. Burkert, , and J. Hagenauer, "On the equivalence between SOVA and max-log-MAP decodings," *IEEE Communications Letters*, vol. 2, no. 5, pp. 137–139, 1998.
11. J. Cain, G. Clark, and J. Geist, "Punctured convolutional codes of rate $(n-1/n)$ and simplified maximum likelihood decoding (corresp.)," *IEEE Transactions on Information Theory*, vol. 25, no. 1, pp. 97–100, 1979.
12. Y. Yasuda, K. Kashiki, and Y. Hirata, "High-rate punctured convolutional codes for soft decision viterbi decoding," *IEEE Transactions on Communications*, vol. 32, no. 3, pp. 315–319, 1984.
13. G. Begin and D. Haccoun, "High-rate punctured convolutional codes: structure properties and construction technique," *IEEE Transactions on Communications*, vol. 37, no. 12, pp. 1381–1385, 1989.

14. J. Hagenauer, "Rate-compatible punctured convolutional codes (RCPC codes) and their applications," *IEEE Transactions on Communications*, vol. 36, no. 4, pp. 389–400, 1988.
15. C.-H. Wang and C.-C. Chao, "Path-compatible pruned convolutional (PCPC) codes: a new scheme for unequal error protection," in *Proceedings. 1998 IEEE International Symposium on Information Theory (Cat. No.98CH36252)*, 1998, pp. 306–.
16. W. Henkel and N. von Deetzen, "Path pruning for unequal error protection turbo codes." Zurich: 2006 International Zurich Seminar on Communications, 2006. [Online]. Available: /wp-content/uploads/2014/01/izs06_vdeetzen.pdf

Chapter 6
Convolutional Codes III—Sequential Decoding: Fano Metric, Stack and Fano Algorithms

When you have exhausted all possibilities, remember this - you haven't.

Thomas Alva Edison

Sequential algorithms are tree-search algorithms, i.e., they search for the most probable transmit sequence in the code tree. The advantage compared to Viterbi's algorithm is that only a small part of the tree will usually be checked. Especially, when not many errors occur, the algorithm advances very quickly through the trellis. Sequential algorithms thus allow to decode codes with high memory. The disadvantage is that the decoding delay depends on the number of errors, i.e., the decoding time is a random variable. This is often undesirable and, hence, complexity-reduced forms of the Viterbi algorithm are preferred (M-, T-Alg.) [1, 2].

6.1 Fano-Metric

When comparing MAP and ML criteria in Sect. 5.2.4, we stated that in many cases, transmit sequences can be assumed to be equally probable. This would make MAP and ML identical. We will later see that this assumption cannot be made in iterative decoding. Already with sequential decoding this does not hold any more, since in there, sequences with different length are compared in their probability.

We use the MAP approach and derive the so-called Fano metric [3]. Let the received sequence be $\mathbf{r} = (\mathbf{r}_0, \mathbf{r}_1, \ldots, \mathbf{r}_T)$, where $\mathbf{r}_j,\ j = 0, \ldots, T$ denote the n output bits of a tree or trellis transition. If the decoder processes only t segments of length n, it compares with a shorter input sequence $\mathbf{c}_t = (\mathbf{c}_0, \mathbf{c}_2, \ldots, \mathbf{c}_{t-1})$, $t - 1 <$

W. Henkel, *Channel Coding*, Signals and Communication Technology,
https://doi.org/10.1007/978-3-032-08236-7_6

T, i.e., searches for the most probable, but shorter code sequence $\mathbf{c}_t$ when receiving the sequence $\mathbf{r}$. We again apply Bayes' theorem.

$$P(\mathbf{c}_t|\mathbf{r}) = \frac{P(\mathbf{r}|\mathbf{c}_t) \cdot P(\mathbf{c}_t)}{P(\mathbf{r})} \;. \tag{6.1}$$

As in the derivation of the ML rule, at least, we assume that the code sequences occur with the same probability if the length is the same. This probability is then given by

$$P(\mathbf{c}_t) = 2^{-k\cdot t} = 2^{-R\cdot t\cdot n} \;. \tag{6.2}$$

In case of a memoryless channel $\mathbf{r}_t \,\ldots\, \mathbf{r}_T$ does not provide any information about $\mathbf{c}_0 \,\ldots\, \mathbf{c}_{t-1}$. Equation (6.1) can thus be written as

$$P(\mathbf{c}_t|\mathbf{r}) = P(\mathbf{c}_t|\mathbf{r}_t) = \frac{P(\mathbf{r}_t|\mathbf{c}_t) \cdot P(\mathbf{c}_t)}{P(\mathbf{r}_t)} \;. \tag{6.3}$$

When modifying the Viterbi algorithm to a MAP decoder, we usually omit $P(\mathbf{r}_t)$, since this cannot be influenced by the decoder, anyway. In the case of sequential decoding, with it, the path length will be taken into account. This term will result in a portion n of the metric increment in (6.6).

Taking the logarithm of (6.3) leads to an additive metric. In the following, we will assume the code sequence to be i.i.d. (independent and identically distributed) which is actually not the case in a strict sense.

$$\log_2\left(2^{-R\cdot t\cdot n}\prod_{\tau=0}^{t-1}\prod_{\nu=0}^{n-1}\frac{P(r_{\tau\nu}|c_{\tau\nu})}{P(r_{\tau\nu})}\right) = -R\cdot t\cdot n + \sum_{\tau=0}^{t-1}\sum_{\nu=0}^{n-1}\log_2\left(\frac{P(r_{\tau\nu}|c_{\tau\nu})}{P(r_{\tau\nu})}\right) =$$

$$= \sum_{\tau=0}^{t-1}\sum_{\nu=0}^{n-1}\left(\log_2\left(\frac{P(r_{\tau\nu}|c_{\tau\nu})}{P(r_{\tau\nu})}\right) - R\right) \tag{6.4}$$

The so-called Fano metric is given as

$$\lambda_\tau = \sum_{\nu=0}^{n-1}\left(\log_2\left(\frac{P(r_{\tau\nu}|c_{\tau\nu})}{P(r_{\tau\nu})}\right) - R\right) \;. \tag{6.5}$$

In case of the binary symmetric channel (BSC), the metric can be simplified significantly. Assuming the channel input symbols (bits) to occur with equal probability ($P(c_{\tau\nu} = 0) = P(c_{\tau\nu} = 1) = 0.5$), we obtain from $P(r_{\tau\nu}) = \sum_{c_{\tau\nu}} P(r_{\tau\nu}|c_{\tau\nu})$ $P(c_{\tau\nu})$ that $P(r_{\tau\nu} = 0) = P(r_{\tau\nu} = 1) = 0.5$, as well. This allows to simplify (6.5) to

$$\lambda_\tau = n - k + \sum_{\nu=0}^{n-1} \log_2 \left(P(r_{\tau\nu}|c_{\tau\nu})\right) . \tag{6.6}$$

For use in examples, we compute the metrics for the case $p = 2^{-5}, n = 2, k = 1, R = 1/2$. We have to distinguish three cases:

$$\lambda_\tau = \begin{cases} 1 + 2 \cdot \log_2(1-p) & \approx \quad 1\,, \text{ if } r_\tau = c_\tau \\ 1 + \log_2(p) + \log_2(1-p) & \approx -4\,, \text{ if } r_\tau, c_\tau \text{ differ in one component} \\ 1 + 2 \cdot \log_2(p) & \approx -9\,, \text{ if } r_\tau, c_\tau \text{ differ in both components} \end{cases} \tag{6.7}$$

For channels with an analog output, one may quantize the output using intervals of width Δr. An interval Θ_l is given by $\{r \in \Theta_l : l\Delta r \leq r < (l+1)\Delta r\}$. The two probabilities of the Fano metric in (6.5) for binary, equally probable input symbols will then be

$$P(r_{\tau\nu} \in \Theta_l | c_{\tau\nu} = \pm 1) = 1/2 \cdot \text{erfc}\left(\frac{\mp 1 + l\Delta r}{\sqrt{2}\sigma}\right) - 1/2 \cdot \text{erfc}\left(\frac{\mp 1 + (l+1)\Delta r}{\sqrt{2}\sigma}\right) , \tag{6.8}$$

$$P(r_{\tau\nu} \in \Theta_l) = 1/2 \cdot P(r_{\tau\nu} \in \Theta_l | c_{\tau\nu} = +1) + 1/2 \cdot P(r_{\tau\nu} \in \Theta_l | c_{\tau\nu} = -1) . \tag{6.9}$$

6.2 Stack Decoder

As the name suggests, the stack decoder is a stack or list sorting procedure, where the sequences of different lengths are stored in a list according to their Fano metrics. The uppermost sequence with the best (highest) metric is extended by a segment of length n or k, if output or input symbols, respectively, are listed. After computing the new metrics, the 2^k extended sequences will again be sorted into the list. In case two sequences will have the same metric, one may, e.g., list the one first that ends with a zero.

As a decoding example, we choose:

Information sequence:	$(1, 1, 1, 0, 1, 0, 0, 0, 1, \ldots)$
Transmitted sequence:	$(11, 10, 01, 10, 00, 01, 11, 00, 11, \ldots)$
Received sequence:	$(11, 00, 11, 10, 00, 11, 11, 00, 11, \ldots)$.

The metric increments are given according to (6.7) and we start from the zero state. Step by step, the following lists will be created (cf., the tree diagram in Fig. 6.1):

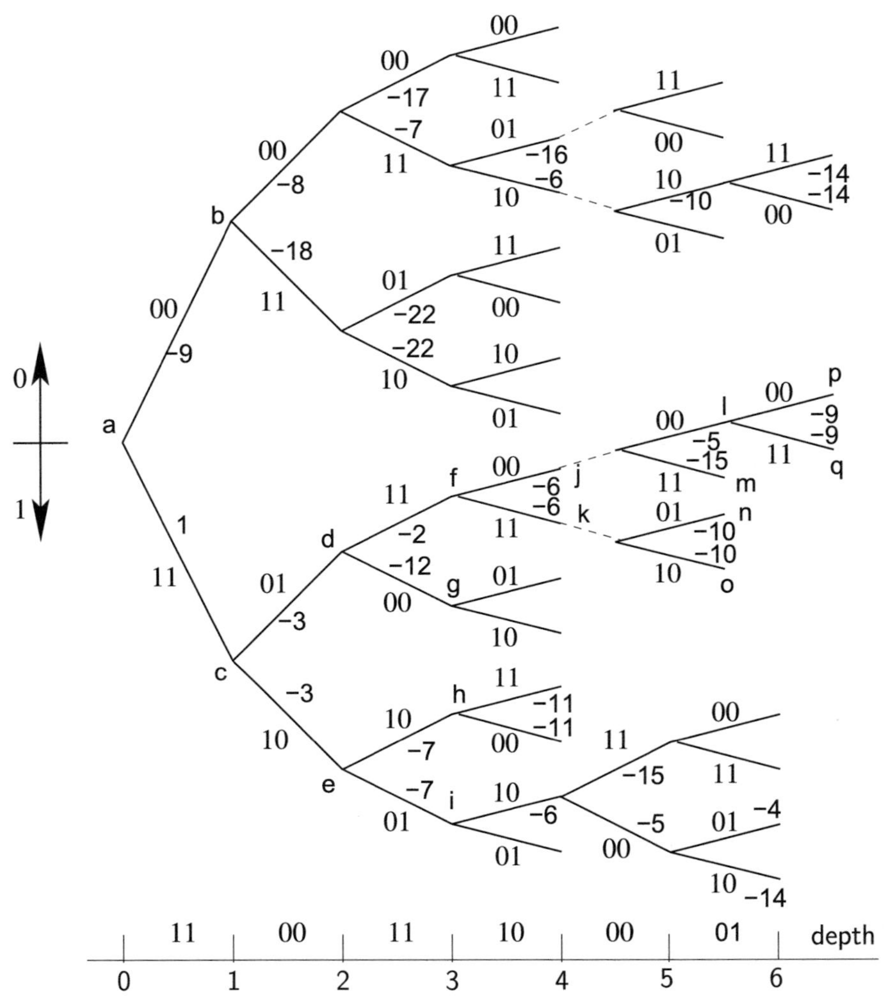

Fig. 6.1 Tree diagram for the correction of two errors with the stack and the Fano algorithm, to be described in the next section

i	c	λ
1	11	1
0	00	−9

i	c	λ
1, 0	11, 01	−3
1, 1	11, 10	−3
0	00	−9

i	c	λ
1, 0, 0	11, 01, 11	−2
1, 0, 1	11, 01, 00	−12
1, 1	11, 10	−3
0	00	−9

i	c	λ
1, 0, 0	11, 01, 11	−2
1, 1	11, 10	−3
0	00	−9
1, 0, 1	11, 01, 00	−12

i	c	λ
1, 0, 0, 0	11, 01, 11, 00	−6
1, 0, 0, 1	11, 01, 11, 11	−6
1, 1	11, 10	−3
0	00	−9
1, 0, 1	11, 01, 00	−12

i	c	λ
1, 1	11, 10	−3
1, 0, 0, 0	11, 01, 11, 00	−6
1, 0, 0, 1	11, 01, 11, 11	−6
0	00	−9
1, 0, 1	11, 01, 00	−12

i	c	λ
1, 1, 0	11, 10, 10	−7
1, 1, 1	11, 10, 01	−7
1, 0, 0, 0	11, 01, 11, 00	−6
1, 0, 0, 1	11, 01, 11, 11	−6
0	00	−9
1, 0, 1	11, 01, 00	−12

i	c	λ
1, 0, 0, 0	11, 01, 11, 00	−6
1, 0, 0, 1	11, 01, 11, 11	−6
1, 1, 0	11, 10, 10	−7
1, 1, 1	11, 10, 01	−7
0	00	−9
1, 0, 1	11, 01, 00	−12

i	c	λ
1, 0, 0, 0, 0	11, 01, 11, 00, 00	−5
1, 0, 0, 0, 1	11, 01, 11, 00, 11	−15
1, 0, 0, 1	11, 01, 11, 11	−6
1, 1, 0	11, 10, 10	−7
1, 1, 1	11, 10, 01	−7
0	00	−9
1, 0, 1	11, 01, 00	−12

i	c	λ
1, 0, 0, 0, 0	11, 01, 11, 00, 00	−5
1, 0, 0, 1	11, 01, 11, 11	−6
1, 1, 0	11, 10, 10	−7
1, 1, 1	11, 10, 01	−7
0	00	−9
1, 0, 1	11, 01, 00	−12
1, 0, 0, 0, 1	11, 01, 11, 00, 11	−15

i	c	λ
1, 0, 0, 0, 0, 0	11, 01, 11, 00, 00, 00	−9
1, 0, 0, 0, 0, 1	11, 01, 11, 00, 00, 11	−9
1, 0, 0, 1	11, 01, 11, 11	−6
1, 1, 0	11, 10, 10	−7
1, 1, 1	11, 10, 01	−7
0	00	−9
1, 0, 1	11, 01, 00	−12
1, 0, 0, 0, 1	11, 01, 11, 00, 11	−15

i	c	λ
1, 0, 0, 1	11, 01, 11, 11	−6
1, 1, 0	11, 10, 10	−7
1, 1, 1	11, 10, 01	−7
0	00	−9
1, 0, 0, 0, 0, 0	11, 01, 11, 00, 00, 00	−9
1, 0, 0, 0, 0, 1	11, 01, 11, 00, 00, 11	−9
1, 0, 1	11, 01, 00	−12
1, 0, 0, 0, 1	11, 01, 11, 00, 11	−15

i	c	λ
1, 0, 0, 1, 0	11, 01, 11, 11, 01	−10
1, 0, 0, 1, 1	11, 01, 11, 11, 10	−10
1, 1, 0	11, 10, 10	−7
1, 1, 1	11, 10, 01	−7
0	00	−9
1, 0, 0, 0, 0, 0	11, 01, 11, 00, 00, 00	−9
1, 0, 0, 0, 0, 1	11, 01, 11, 00, 00, 11	−9
1, 0, 1	11, 01, 00	−12
1, 0, 0, 0, 1	11, 01, 11, 00, 11	−15

i	c	λ
1, 1, 0	11, 10, 10	−7
1, 1, 1	11, 10, 01	−7
0	00	−9
1, 0, 0, 0, 0, 0	11, 01, 11, 00, 00, 00	−9
1, 0, 0, 0, 0, 1	11, 01, 11, 00, 00, 11	−9
1, 0, 0, 1, 0	11, 01, 11, 11, 01	−10
1, 0, 0, 1, 1	11, 01, 11, 11, 10	−10
1, 0, 1	11, 01, 00	−12
1, 0, 0, 0, 1	11, 01, 11, 00, 11	−15

i	c	λ
1, 1, 0, 0	11, 10, 10, 11	−11
1, 1, 0, 1	11, 10, 10, 00	−11
1, 1, 1	11, 10, 01	−7
0	00	−9
1, 0, 0, 0, 0, 0	11, 01, 11, 00, 00, 00	−9
1, 0, 0, 0, 0, 1	11, 01, 11, 00, 00, 11	−9
1, 0, 0, 1, 0	11, 01, 11, 11, 01	−10
1, 0, 0, 1, 1	11, 01, 11, 11, 10	−10
1, 0, 1	11, 01, 00	−12
1, 0, 0, 0, 1	11, 01, 11, 00, 11	−15

i	c	λ
1, 1, 1	11, 10, 01	−7
0	00	−9
1, 0, 0, 0, 0, 0	11, 01, 11, 00, 00, 00	−9
1, 0, 0, 0, 0, 1	11, 01, 11, 00, 00, 11	−9
1, 0, 0, 1, 0	11, 01, 11, 11, 01	−10
1, 0, 0, 1, 1	11, 01, 11, 11, 10	−10
1, 1, 0, 0	11, 10, 10, 11	−11
1, 1, 0, 1	11, 10, 10, 00	−11
1, 0, 1	11, 01, 00	−12
1, 0, 0, 0, 1	11, 01, 11, 00, 11	−15

i	c	λ
1, 1, 1, 0	11, 10, 01, 10	−6
1, 1, 1, 1	11, 10, 01, 01	−16
0	00	−9
1, 0, 0, 0, 0, 0	11, 01, 11, 00, 00, 00	−9
1, 0, 0, 0, 0, 1	11, 01, 11, 00, 00, 11	−9
1, 0, 0, 1, 0	11, 01, 11, 11, 01	−10
1, 0, 0, 1, 1	11, 01, 11, 11, 10	−10
1, 1, 0, 0	11, 10, 10, 11	−11
1, 1, 0, 1	11, 10, 10, 00	−11
1, 0, 1	11, 01, 00	−12
1, 0, 0, 0, 1	11, 01, 11, 00, 11	−15

i	c	λ
1, 1, 1, 0	11, 10, 01, 10	−6
0	00	−9
1, 0, 0, 0, 0, 0	11, 01, 11, 00, 00, 00	−9
1, 0, 0, 0, 0, 1	11, 01, 11, 00, 00, 11	−9
1, 0, 0, 1, 0	11, 01, 11, 11, 01	−10
1, 0, 0, 1, 1	11, 01, 11, 11, 10	−10
1, 1, 0, 0	11, 10, 10, 11	−11
1, 1, 0, 1	11, 10, 10, 00	−11
1, 0, 1	11, 01, 00	−12
1, 0, 0, 0, 1	11, 01, 11, 00, 11	−15

...

As in the Viterbi algorithm, the rows of the list will be realized by shift registers with finite length. When the maximum length is reached, first decoding results will be output, which may lead to wrong decoding results, even if this would not have been the case for longer registers. Sequences with the same metric will usually be grouped to reduce the sorting effort. Not only the length of the row registers, but also the depth of the stack, i.e., the number of rows, will be limited. Apart from such realization aspects, the decoding quality will usually be similar to the one of the Viterbi algorithm (assuming equally probable input sequences). However, one

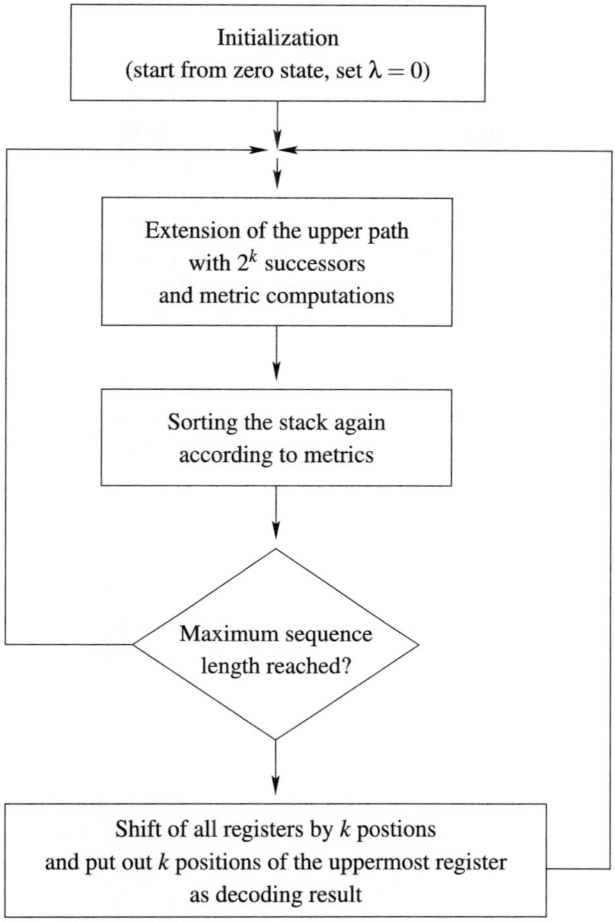

Fig. 6.2 Flow chart of the stack decoder

should note that, in contrast to the Viterbi algorithm, sequential decoding methods will never perform a full maximum-likelihood decoding, since not all relevant paths are processed (not even up to a maximum length).

The flow chart in Fig. 6.2 shows again the steps of the algorithm.

One might have realized some relation to the shortest path routing algorithm by Dijkstra [4, 5], when applying it to a tree and not including the stopping criterion when a desired end node is found.

6.3 Fano Decoder

The Fano algorithm is a tree-oriented method that only follows one branch of the tree. By moving forward (F), to the side (S), or backwards (R) in the tree it is tried to find the path with the best metric. The movements will be controlled by the exceeding or staying below a certain threshold T. When a correct path is pursued, the metric will increase in the long run. With channel errors the metric will decrease at once. The threshold will be adapted to the metric in certain steps. If a wrong path has been selected or in case of errors, the metric will fall below the threshold and will signal that another path should be chosen. Should this not be successful, as well, the threshold will be decreased in steps and it will be tried again to get across the critical position. Let $\Lambda_t = \sum_{\tau=0}^{\tau=t} \lambda_\tau$ be the accumulated Fano metric, initializing $\Lambda_{-1} = -\infty$ and $\Lambda_0 = 0$. The threshold T will be initialized with 0, the threshold increment Δ can be chosen to optimize the decoding. The algorithm can be best described by a table.

Rule	Condition			Operation	
	Previous movement	Compare Λ_{t-1}, Λ_t with threshold T		Threshold modification	Next movement
1	F or S	$\Lambda_{t-1} < T + \Delta$	$\Lambda_t \geq T$	$+j\Delta$	F
2	F or S	$\Lambda_{t-1} \geq T + \Delta$	$\Lambda_t \geq T$	0	F
3	F or S	Λ_{t-1} arbitrary	$\Lambda_t < T$	0	S or R
4	R	$\Lambda_{t-1} < T$	Λ_t arbitrary	$-\Delta$	F
5	R	$\Lambda_{t-1} \geq T$	Λ_t arbitrary	0	S or R

F: Forward movement to one of the following 2^k nodes with the best metric.

S or R: Movement to the side to the next node with the next best metric that differs from the actual path only in the last branch. If the actual node is the last of the 2^k nodes of a branching, a backward step is initiated.

j: $\Lambda_t - \Delta < T + j\Delta \leq \Lambda_t$, i.e., $j = \lfloor(\Lambda_t - T)/\Delta\rfloor$. Step-wise increment of the threshold T together with an increasing accumulated metric (of a long-term error-free path).

Investigated paths at a certain threshold that emanate from a node will be stored so that they will not checked again under the same conditions.

In the following, two examples are given. The first is a single error correction which does not require much effort. The corresponding tree diagram with the Fano metrics is given in Fig. 6.3. Figure 6.4 shows how the accumulated Fano metric develops. The decoding steps are listed in tabular form. The second example (tree diagram in Fig. 6.1) is similar to the one that we already studied with the Viterbi and stack algorithms. It becomes obvious that the decoding time will increase significantly. The decoding time does not only depend on the number of errors, but also on the threshold increment Δ. If it is chosen too big and errors accumulate, this can easily lead to a decoding error as can be seen from the example in Fig. 6.1.

It can be seen that in contrast to the stack decoder, Fano's algorithm does not require a lot of storage space, but the required number of computations may be

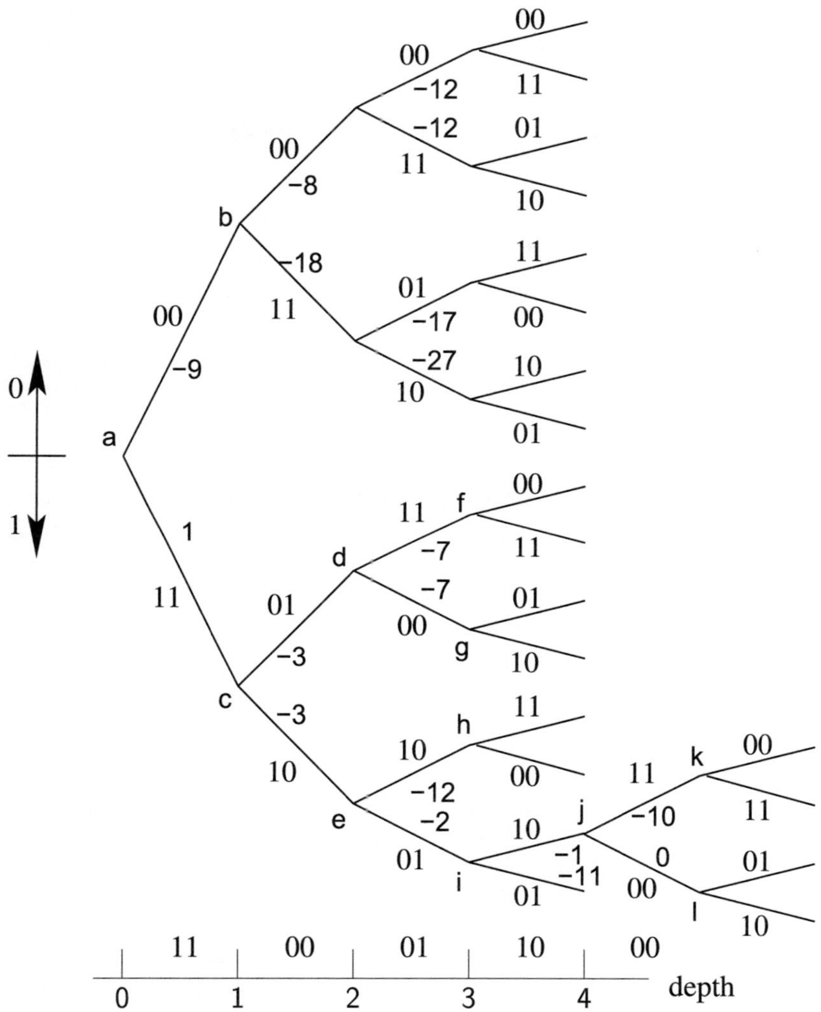

Fig. 6.3 Tree diagram of the correction of a single error with Fano's algorithm

significant. Similar to the Viterbi algorithm, the path length needs to be limited after which a decoding result is output to come to a finite decoding delay.

In general, the Viterbi decoder (or the BCJR algorithm) will be preferred if the number of states will allow. This is due to the more regular structure, but especially due to the constant number of operations required per time interval. In cases where a pure Viterbi algorithm is not feasible since the number of states is too high, the M algorithm [1], processing only the M best paths, can be an alternative.

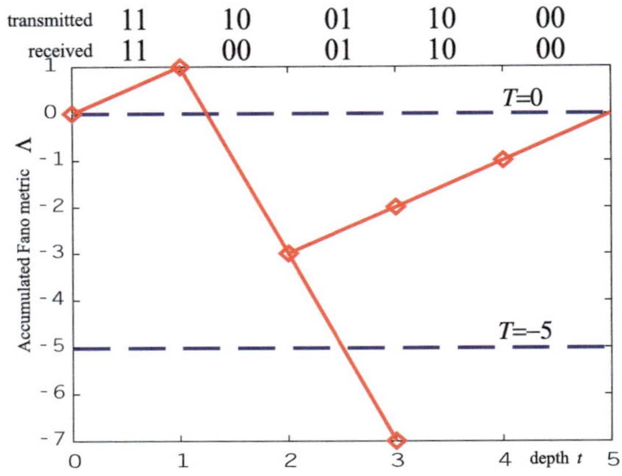

Fig. 6.4 Development of the Fano metric in the example of a single-error correction

The Viterbi algorithm is also applied for other tasks, e.g., in source encoding or when optimizing certain signal properties like in the so-called trellis shaping.

All algorithms (Viterbi, Fano, stack) have in common that they easily allow for soft-decision decoding which, as we already know, increases the coding gain by roughly 3 dB.

Transmitted: 11,10,01,10,00
Received: 11,00,01,10,00

Step	Node	Depth t	Prev. metric Λ_{t-1}	Act. metric Λ_t	T_{new}	Rule	Movement
		0	$-\infty$	0	0	1	F
1	c	1	0	1	0	1	F
2	d	2	1	−3	0	3	S
3	e	2	1	−3	0	3	R
4	c	1	0	1	0	5	R
5	a	0	$-\infty$	0	−5	4	F
6	c	1	0	1	−5	2	F
7	d	2	1	−3	−5	2	F
8	f	3	−3	−7	−5	3	S
9	g	3	−3	−7	−5	3	R
10	d	2	1	−3	−5	5	S
11	e	2	1	−3	−5	2	F
12	i	3	−3	−2	−5	1	F
13	j	4	−2	−1	−5	1	F
14	l	5	−1	0	0	1	F
⋮							

Transmitted: 11,10,01,10,00,01
Received: 11,00,11,10,00,01

Step	Node	Depth t	Prev. metric Λ_{t-1}	Act. metric Λ_t	T_{new}	Rule	Movement
		0	$-\infty$	0	0	1	F
1	c	1	0	1	0	1	F
2	d	2	1	−3	0	3	S
3	e	2	1	−3	0	3	R
4	c	1	0	1	0	5	R
5	a	0	$-\infty$	0	−5	4	F
6	c	1	0	1	−5	2	F
7	d	2	1	−3	−5	2	F
8	f	3	−3	−2	−5	1	F
9	j	4	−2	−6	−5	3	S
10	k	4	−2	−6	−5	3	R
11	f	3	−3	−2	−5	5	S
12	g	3	−3	−12	−5	5	R
13	d	2	1	−3	−5	5	S
14	e	2	1	−3	−5	2	F
15	h	3	−3	−7	−5	3	S
16	i	3	−3	−7	−5	3	R
17	e	2	1	−3	−5	5	R
18	c	1	0	1	−5	5	R
19	a	0	$-\infty$	0	−10	4	F
20	c	1	0	1	−10	2	F
21	d	2	1	−3	−10	2	F
22	f	3	−3	−2	−10	2	F
23	j	4	−2	−6	−10	2	F
24	l	5	−6	−5	−5	1	F
25	p	6	−5	−9	−5	3	S
26	q	6	−5	−9	−5	3	R
27	l	5	−6	−5	−10	4	F
28	p	6	−5	−9	−10	2	F
⋮							

References

1. J. Anderson, "Limited search trellis decoding of convolutional codes," *IEEE Transactions on Information Theory*, vol. 35, no. 5, pp. 944–955, 1989.
2. S. Simmons, "Breadth-first trellis decoding with adaptive effort," *IEEE Transactions on Communications*, vol. 38, no. 1, pp. 3–12, 1990.
3. J. Massey, "Variable-length codes and the Fano metric," *IEEE Transactions on Information Theory*, vol. 18, no. 1, pp. 196–198, 1972.

4. A. S. Tanenbaum and D. J. Wetherall, *Computer Networks*, 5th ed. USA: Prentice Hall Press, 2010.
5. E. W. Dijkstra, "A note on two problems in connexion with graphs," *Numer. Math.*, vol. 1, no. 1, p. 269–271, Dec. 1959. [Online]. Available: https://doi.org/10.1007/BF01386390

Chapter 7
Ungerböck's Trellis-Coded Modulation (TCM)

Divide et impera

Niccoló Machiavelli, 1532 and Ludwig XI

In Chap. 5, Eq. (5.13) and the subsequent paragraph, we introduced the rate loss that results from introducing redundancy sequentially into the data stream like it is done in channel coding. Redundancy could however also be provided by increasing the modulation signal set, e.g., by using a 2^{b+1}-QAM for transmitting only b bits of information per symbol. When combining modulation and coding in such a way, the aim is to increase the Euclidean distances between the encoded modulation sequences. This is not done in just 2 dimensions but in N or, in the limiting case, in infinitely many dimensions.

The error or Q-functions are determined by the minimum Euclidean distance, $Q(d_{E\,\min}/2\sigma_n)$. To be able to compare different modulation codes, the quadratic Euclidean distance is normalized by the mean power (or signal energy) of the modulation signal set. The coding gain relative to uncoded modulated transmission is

$$\gamma(C) = \frac{d^2_{E\,\text{coded}}}{P_{\text{coded}}} \cdot \frac{P_{\text{uncoded}}}{d^2_{E\,\text{uncoded}}} = \frac{d^2_{E\,\text{coded}}}{d^2_{E\,\text{uncoded}}} \cdot \frac{P_{\text{uncoded}}}{P_{\text{coded}}} = \frac{d^2_{E\,\text{coded}}}{d^2_{E\,\text{uncoded}}} \cdot \frac{E_{s\,\text{uncoded}}}{E_{s\,\text{coded}}} . \quad (7.1)$$

When coded modulation was developing, the intention was to replace an uncoded modulation scheme by a coded scheme with a larger signal set, still keeping the net data rate unchanged (no rate loss). A fair comparison at different rates can be achieved by using E_b in (7.1). This leads to

$$\gamma(C) = \frac{d^2_{E\,\text{coded}}}{d^2_{E\,\text{uncoded}}} \cdot \frac{E_{b\,\text{uncoded}}}{E_{b\,\text{coded}}} = \frac{d^2_{E\,\text{coded}}}{d^2_{E\,\text{uncoded}}} \cdot \frac{E_{s\,\text{uncoded}}}{E_{s\,\text{coded}}} \cdot \frac{R_{\text{coded}}}{R_{\text{uncoded}}} . \quad (7.2)$$

W. Henkel, *Channel Coding*, Signals and Communication Technology,
https://doi.org/10.1007/978-3-032-08236-7_7

7.1 Expected Coding Gain

In Sect. 2.4, we have derived the Capacity curves for different modulation alphabets. We show these curves again in Fig. 7.1. From the discussion in Eqs. (2.75) and (2.78), we conclude that one has to subtract 3 dB in E_s/N_0 in case of a one-sided noise PSD N_0.

For each modulation scheme, the SNR value has been marked that corresponds to a bit-error probability of 10^{-5}. The observation is now that it should be possible to transmit the same net data rate with the next bigger modulation signal set, i.e., with 8-PSK instead of 4-PSK, without any error (Channel Capacity curves!) at lower SNR. For example, when going left from the 10^{-5} marking on the 4-PSK curve to the next curve, one may be offered a coding gain G of around 7 dB. This argumentation gives an impression of the achievable coding gain. However, for $P_e \to 0 \Longrightarrow G \to \infty$, which is not too realistic.

7.2 Ungerböck's Code Construction

From the previous section, we concluded that one may double the cardinality of the signal set to obtain most of the possible coding gain. Practical coding schemes have to use the redundancy for an increase in Euclidean distance

$$d_{E\,\text{free}}^2 = \min_{c_j \neq c_j'} \sum_j d^2(c_j, c_j') \tag{7.3}$$

between code sequences.

The error-event probability follows from the free Euclidean distance using the Union-Bound approximation

$$P_{\text{event}} \gtrsim A_{d_{E\,\text{free}}} \cdot Q(d_{E\,\text{free}}/2\sigma_n)\ . \tag{7.4}$$

Most coded-modulation schemes – block-coded, as well – rely on the partitioning of the modulation alphabet in subsets with increasing Euclidean distance between points. This is called **set partitioning**. For symmetric point sets and symmetric partitioning, subsets with the same minimum Euclidean distance are obtained. A code can now be chosen such that he makes use of the different distances at different partition levels. Especially, $n = k + 1$ output bits of a rate-$k/(k + 1)$ code can be taken to address the first $k + 1$ binary partitions (*mapping by set partitioning*). Figure 7.2 shows the partitions of 8-PSK and 16-QAM.

Following Ungerböck's description [1–3], we are now considering simple trellis structures as given in Fig. 7.3 to observe the construction principles. We assume the case where a 4-PSK with 2 bits per symbol has to be replaced by a coded 8-PSK

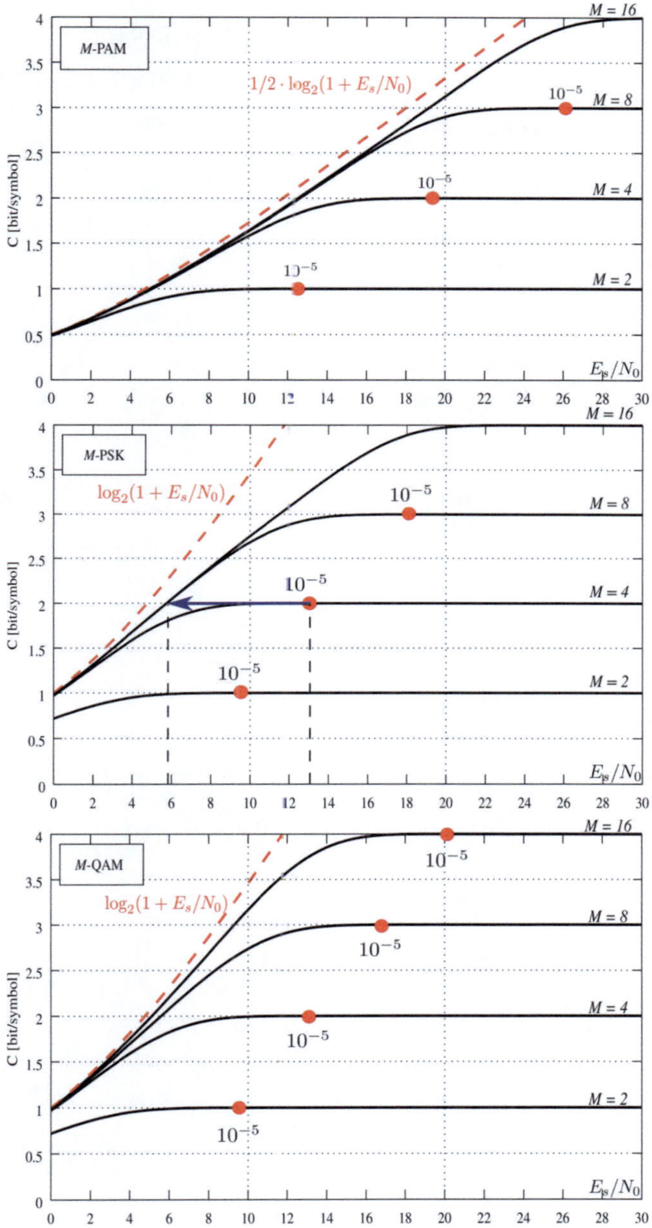

Fig. 7.1 The Channel Capacities for one-dimensional and two-dimensional modulation schemes dependent on the signal-to-noise ratio SNR=E_s/N_0 in dB

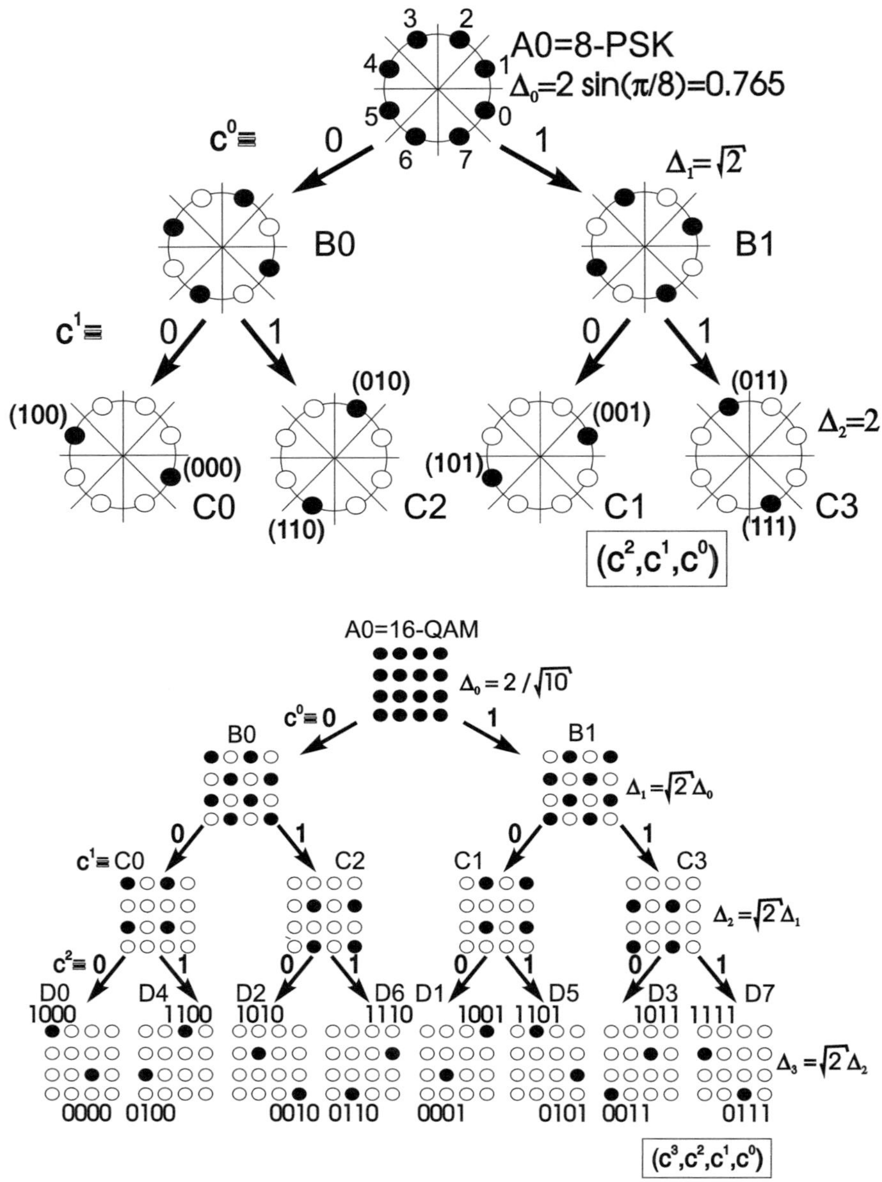

Fig. 7.2 Binary set partitioning of 8-PSK and 16-QAM

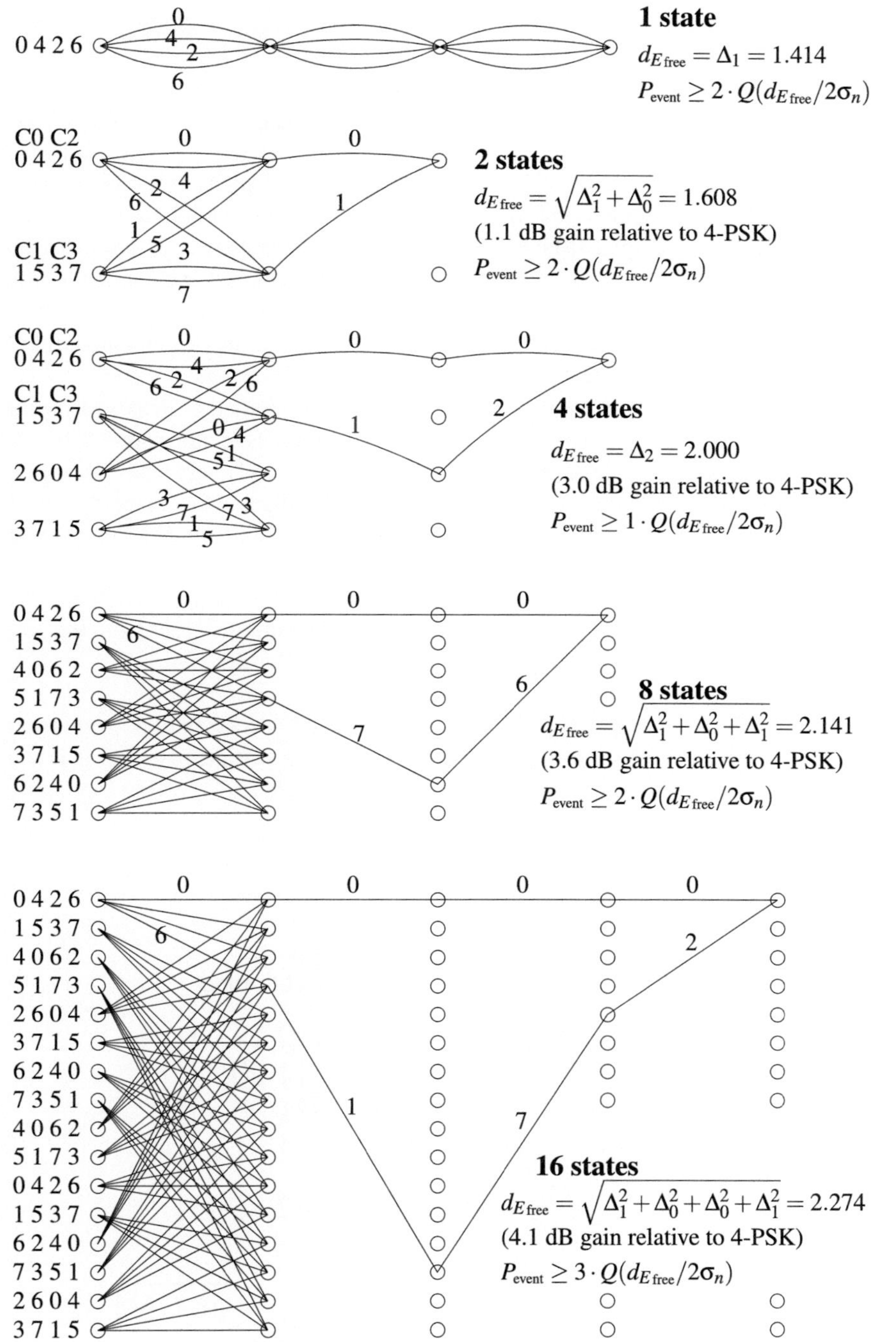

Fig. 7.3 Trellises for coded modulation (8-PSK) with 1, 2, 4, 8, and 16 states

with the same net rate of 2 bits per symbol. Step-wise, we will increase the number of trellis states:

1 state: This is a trivial case simply addressing the 4-PSK within the 8-PSK, i.e., the subsets $B0$ or $B1$. Four parallel transitions specify the four points of the 4-PSK. Coding gain: 0 dB

2 states: With two states, at least, we ensure that all paths emerging from a common state address only one PSK subset. This guarantees the minimum distance of the 4-PSK. For example, $B0$ has been allocated to the first state, whereas $B1$ has been chosen for the second state. Parallel transitions should represent signal points with the maximum possible Euclidean distances. Since there are only two states available, it is not possible to additionally fulfill the same rules when paths merge into a common state. Coding gain: 1.1 dB

4 states: With four states, it is now possible to ensure that all branches emerging from a state and merging into a common state do only address points from subsets $B0$ or $B1$. Thereby, the distance of the parallel transitions is already achieved. Additional distances that would accumulate between the first emerging and last merging branch do not have any effect on the free Euclidean distance, since it is limited by the parallel transitions. Coding gain: 3 dB.

8 and more states: Now it is possible to avoid parallel transitions completely and increasingly extend the length of the minimum-weight path (different from the zero path). Coding gain with 8 states: 3.6 dB, with 16 states: 4.1 dB

A 4-state encoded with mapper is shown in Fig. 7.4.

When partitioning bigger signal sets, it is usually not necessary to perform more than two or three partitioning steps to reach subsets with sufficiently big Euclidean distance (see the example of a trellis with 8 states for coded 16-QAM in Fig. 7.5).

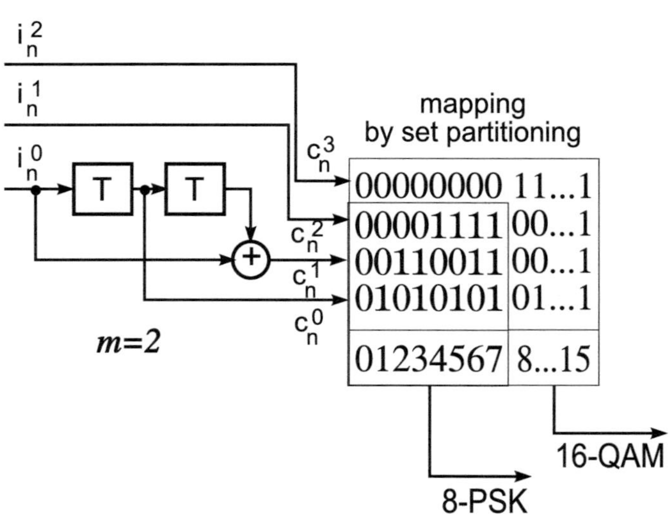

Fig. 7.4 Trellis encoder with 4 states

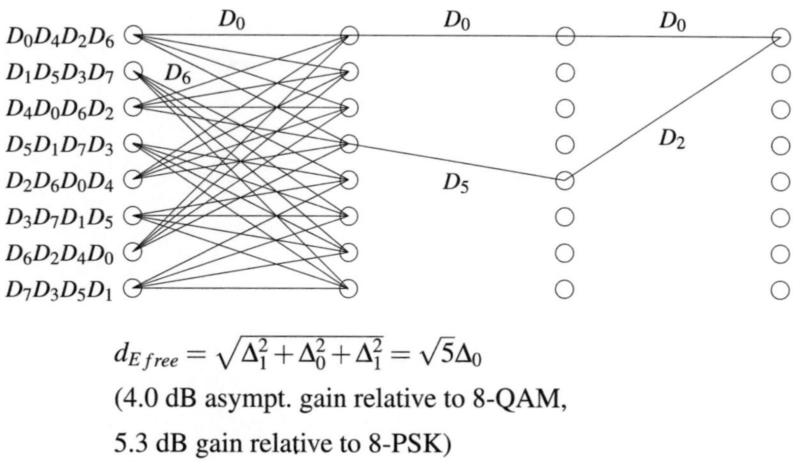

Fig. 7.5 Trellis with 8 states for trellis-coded 16-QAM

To conclude, the following rules should be followed to obtain a suitable trellis:

1. Every signal point should appear with the same probability which requires a certain symmetry and regularity.
2. Branches that emerge from a state shall address only points from the subsets $B0$ or $B1$.
3. Branches that merge into one state shall address only points from the subsets $B0$ or $B1$.
4. Parallel transitions, if they cannot be avoided, shall address signal points from the subsets $C0$ or $C1$ or $C2$ or $C3$.

When investigating some examples of trellis codes that are designed according to these rules, some common properties can be found that can be used to simplify a computer search.

When, e.g., viewing the parity-check matrices in Forney's representation

$$(H^k(D), \ldots, H^1(D), H^0(D)) \cdot \underbrace{(c^k(D), \ldots, c^1(D), c^0(D))^T}_{n=k+1} = \mathbf{0}$$

for some examples of coded 8-PSK:

$$\begin{array}{ll} m = 2 \; \mathbf{H}(D) = (\; 0 & D \quad\quad D^2 + 1 \quad) \\ m = 3 \; \mathbf{H}(D) = (\; D & D^2 \quad\quad D^3 + 1 \quad) \; , \\ m = 4 \; \mathbf{H}(D) = (\; D & D^3 + D^2 \;\; D^4 + D^3 + 1 \;) \end{array} \tag{7.5}$$

one may conclude that all components of the parity-check matrix have the structure

$$\begin{aligned}
&H^j(D) = 0 && k < j \le \log_2(M)\text{(parallel transitions)} \\
&H^j(D) = 0 + h^j_{m-1} D^{m-1} + \cdots + h^j_1 D^1 + 0, && 1 \le j \le k \\
&H^0(D) = D^m + h^0_{m-1} D^{m-1} + \cdots + h^0_1 D^1 + 1, \; j = 0\,. &&
\end{aligned} \tag{7.6}$$

We may note the property

$$h^j_0 = h^j_m = \begin{cases} 0, \; j \neq 0 \\ 1, \; j = 0 \end{cases}, \quad m \ge 2\ . \tag{7.7}$$

This property has relations to the given design rules.

Since the parity-check equations stay the same under multiplication by a common factor (maybe rational), one can modify them into

$$\begin{aligned}
&\mathbf{H}(D) = (\underbrace{0, \ldots, 0}_{\log_2(M)-k-1}, H^k(D), H^{k-1}(D), \ldots, H^0(D)) \\
\Longrightarrow\ &\mathbf{H}(D) = (\underbrace{0, \ldots, 0}_{\log_2(M)-k-1}, \frac{H^k(D)}{H^0(D)}, \frac{H^{k-1}(D)}{H^0(D)}, \ldots, 1)\,.
\end{aligned} \tag{7.8}$$

Theorem 3.5 then allows to directly write the corresponding generator matrix. We obtain

$$(c^k(D), \ldots, c^0(D)) = (i^{k-1}(D), \ldots, i^0(D)) \cdot \left(\mathbf{I}_k \left| \begin{matrix} 0 \\ \vdots \\ H^k(D)/H^0(D) \\ \vdots \\ H^1(D)/H^0(D) \end{matrix} \right. \right)\,. \tag{7.9}$$

The systematic recursive trellis encoder is shown in Fig. 7.6.

The special recursive structure follows from (7.7). The delay element on the right has the effect that error events that would lead to another valid code sequence, would appear delayed at position c^0. This means that the first error vector is of the form $\mathbf{e}_t = (e_t^{\log_2(M)-1}, \ldots, e_t^1, 0)$. Likewise, an error event ends with $\mathbf{e}_{t+\tau} = (e_{t+\tau}^{\log_2(M)-1}, \ldots, e_{t+\tau}^1, 0)$; otherwise, in the next step, an erroneous symbol would appear via the delayed feedback on the left. Since in Ungerböck's description, the upper partitioning is written on the right, this represents the rule that branches that emerge from a common node or merge into a common node should belong to the subsets $B0$ or $B1$.

We now study the *free Euclidean distance* of linear trellis codes. A transition between two valid code sequences $\mathbf{c}(D)$ and $\mathbf{c}'(D) = \mathbf{c}(D) + \mathbf{e}(D)$ is caused by an error sequence

$$\mathbf{e}(D) = \mathbf{e}_t D^t + \mathbf{e}_{t+1} D^{t+1} + \cdots + \mathbf{e}_{t+\tau} D^{t+\tau}\,, \quad \mathbf{e}_t, \mathbf{e}_{t+\tau} \neq 0\,, \quad \tau \ge 0\,,$$

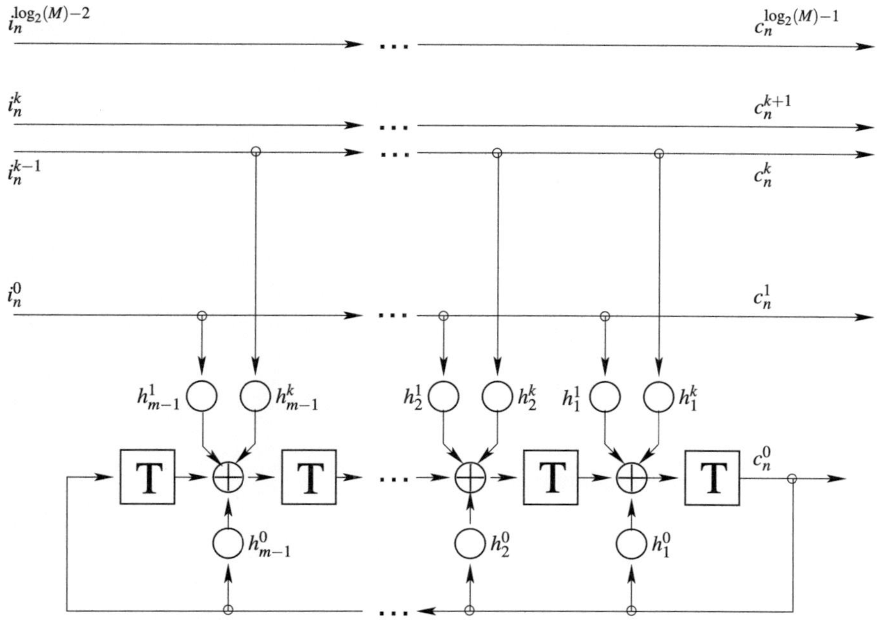

Fig. 7.6 Systematic TCM encoder

which is again a valid code sequence due to linearity.

For the Euclidean distance between the signal sequences that correspond to **c** and **c**′, we have

$$\sum_{j=t}^{j=t+\tau} d_E^2[a(\mathbf{c}_j), a(\mathbf{c}_j \oplus \mathbf{e}_j)] \geq \sum_{j=t}^{j=t+\tau} w^2(\mathbf{e}_j) =: w^2[\mathbf{e}(D)] \tag{7.10}$$

with $w^2(\mathbf{e}_j) = \min_{\mathbf{c}_j} d_E^2[a(\mathbf{c}_j), a(\mathbf{c}_j \oplus \mathbf{e}_j)]$.

Theorem 7.1 *For each sequence* $\mathbf{e}(D)$*, there exists a pair* $a(D)$ *and* $a'(D)$ *that fulfills (7.10) with equality.*

Proof Considering $w^2(\mathbf{e}_j) = \min_{\mathbf{c}_j} d_E^2[a(\mathbf{c}_j), a(\mathbf{c}_j \oplus \mathbf{e}_j)]$, due to the symmetry of the signal constellation, one can freely chose $\mathbf{c}_j^0$ to be zero or one. The remaining $\log_2(M) - 1$ elements are anyway information and can thus be chosen freely. Thus, equality is achieved for each term in Eq. (7.10). □

Similar to determining the free Hamming distance of convolutional codes, the free Euclidean distance has to be found by checking all code sequences different from the all-zeros sequence for its Euclidean weight, i.e.,

$$d_{E\,free}^2 = \min_{\mathbf{e}(D) \neq \mathbf{0}} w^2[\mathbf{e}(D)] \,. \tag{7.11}$$

When denoting the number of zeros on the right (first partitions) with $q(\mathbf{e}_j)$, we have

$$w(\mathbf{e}_j) \geq \Delta_{q(\mathbf{e}_j)} \,. \tag{7.12}$$

For example, for $\mathbf{e}_j = (e_j^{\log_2(M)-1}, \ldots, e_j^3, 1, 0, 0)$ we would have $q(\mathbf{e}_j) = 2$ and hence, $w(\mathbf{e}_j) \geq \Delta_2$.

The minimum distances $\Delta_{q(\mathbf{e}_j)}$ do not depend on the actually transmitted element of the code sequence $\mathbf{c}$. This justifies referencing to the all-zeros sequence.

The best trellis codes in terms of their free distance and with it, their *asymptotic* coding gain result from a computer search. According to a rule of thumb[1] (Codex, Motorola), the *effective* coding gain is reduced by $\log_2(A_{d_{E\text{free}}}) \cdot 0.2$ dB, i.e., each doubling of the number of nearest neighbors is said to lead to a gain reduction by 0.2 dB.

The following table provides codes for 8-PSK:

Codes for 8-PSK with 2 b/symbol

m	k	$H^0(D)$	$H^1(D)$	$H^2(D)$	$d_{E\,free}^2/\Delta_1^2$	$G_{8-PSK/4-PSK}^{\infty}$ / dB
2	1	5	2	–	2, 000	3.0
3	2	11	02	04	2, 293	3.6
4	2	23	04	16	2, 586	4.1
5	2	45	16	34	2, 879	4, 6
6	2	105	036	074	3.000	4.8
7	2	203	014	016	3, 172	5.0
8	2	405	250	176	3, 465	5.4
9	2	1007	0164	0260	3, 758	5.7
10	2	2003	0164	0770	3, 758	5.7

The parity-check polynomials are again given in octal form.

7.3 Multidimensional Partitioning According to Wei and Ungerböck

Up to now, we assumed that doubling the 2-dimensional modulation alphabet is essential for reaching the coding gain of coded modulation. This, first of all, leads to an initial loss of around 3 dB when doubling a QAM alphabet. This is due to the power increase when preserving the Euclidean minimum distance or, alternatively, reducing the distance when preserving the mean power. This loss has to be compensated by the code, before a real coding gain can be obtained. Multidimensional signal alphabets

[1] Should not be taken too serious.

lead to smaller losses when doubling. The two-dimensional loss when double in four dimensions is just 1.36 dB and less with even higher dimensions. Additionally, it is the boundaries in two dimensions, i.e., the boundaries of the so-called '**Constituent Constellation**' are shaped to minimize the average power. Packing the points into a sphere minimizes the average power. The drawback of multidimensional trellis codes is their higher number of nearest neighbors, i.e., the *effective* coding gain can be significantly lower than the asymptotic gain. Nevertheless, the achievable coding gains are quite good and, additionally, rotational invariance can be obtained. Otherwise, this would require nonlinear trellis codes (with *and* operations). Therefore, these codes that especially have been proposed by Wei, are widely used in telecommunications standards. We will especially describe the 16-state 4-dimensional Wei code [4] together with its set partitioning. A binary partitioning, as had been used by Ungerböck, will be shown subsequently.

7.3.1 Wei's 4-Dimensional Partitioning

The 4-dimensional signal alphabet consists of two 2-dimensional (constituent) QAM constellations as shown in Fig. 7.7.

Wei first considers subsets of the 4-dimensional constellation that he named **types**. They combine two subsequent 2-dimensional sublattices in the form $(A \times A)$, $(A \times B), \ldots, (D \times D)$. To better illustrate the 4-dimensional constellations, we show the two constituent 2-dimensional constellations in zoomed-in fashion in Fig. 7.8 The term lattice requires a definition.

Definition 7.1 An N-dimensional **lattice** Λ is an infinity regular structure of discrete points in $\mathbb{R}^{N'}$ that can be described by the linear combination

$$\Lambda = \left\{ \sum_{j=1}^{N} \lambda_j \mathbf{v}_j \mid \lambda_j \in \mathbb{Z},\ j = 1, \ldots, N \right\} \tag{7.13}$$

with the base vectors $\mathbf{v}_j$, $j = 1, \ldots, N$. Usually, we have $N' = N$.

To understand the 4-dimensional set partitioning, one should jointly consider Fig. 7.8 and Table 7.1 The $4 \cdot 4 = 16$ types have the same Euclidean distance as the constituent 2-dimensional lattices, namely $\Delta_3 = 2\Delta_0$. The description obviously starts from the other side of the partition tree. Two types are now combined to a **sublattice** in such a way that the Euclidean distance $\Delta_2 = 2\Delta_0$ is preserved. These combinations can be seen in the subsequent table. It is easy to see that the minimum distance stays the same. If we have a transition between A and B in the first two dimensions, there has to be the same transition between A and B in the other two dimensions. Hence, $\Delta_2^2 \geq 2 \cdot 2\Delta_0^2$. The union of the upper and lower four sublattices, Wei names **families**. They have the Euclidean minimum distance $\Delta_1 = \sqrt{2}\Delta_0$. From

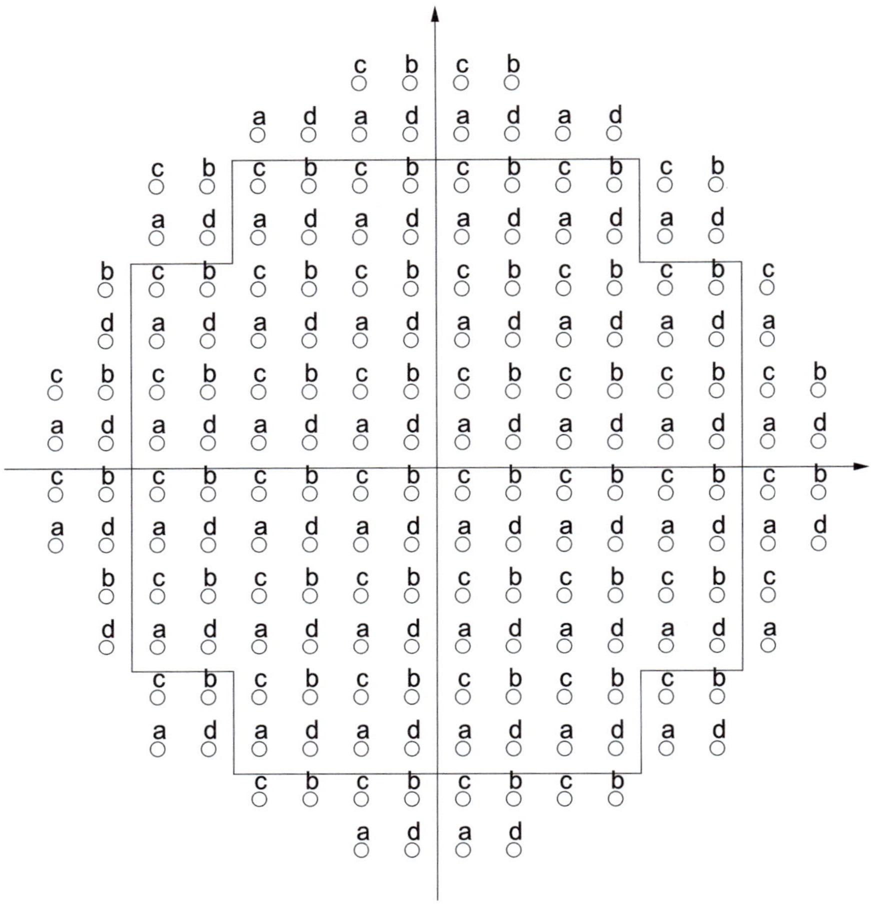

Fig. 7.7 192-point signal set and partitioning for Wei's rotationally invariant trellis-coded modulation

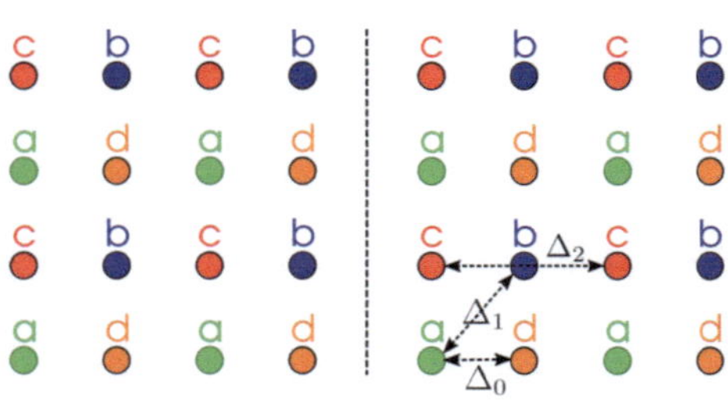

Fig. 7.8 Zoom-in of Fig. 7.7 to illustrate the two 2-dimensional constellations that make up the four dimensions

Table 7.1 Wei's 4D-partitioning

4D sublattices	y_t^0	i_t^0	$i_t^{1'}$	$i_t^{2'}$	4D types	c_t^0	c_t^1	c_{t+1}^0	c_{t+1}^1	
0	0	0	0	0	$(A \times A)$	0	0	0	0	Family 0
	0	0	0	1	$(B \times B)$	0	1	0	1	
1	0	0	1	0	$(C \times C)$	1	0	1	0	
	0	0	1	1	$(D \times D)$	1	1	1	1	
2	0	1	0	0	$(A \times B)$	0	0	0	1	
	0	1	0	1	$(B \times A)$	0	1	0	0	
3	0	1	1	0	$(C \times D)$	1	0	1	1	
	0	1	1	1	$(D \times C)$	1	1	1	0	
4	1	0	0	0	$(A \times C)$	0	0	1	0	Family 1
	1	0	0	1	$(B \times D)$	0	1	1	1	
5	1	0	1	0	$(C \times B)$	1	0	0	1	
	1	0	1	1	$(D \times A)$	1	1	0	0	
6	1	1	0	0	$(A \times D)$	0	0	1	1	
	1	1	0	1	$(B \times C)$	0	1	1	0	
7	1	1	1	0	$(C \times A)$	1	0	0	0	
	1	1	1	1	$(D \times B)$	1	1	0	1	

this example, we already see a typical property of a multidimensional partitioning. Sometimes, the minimum distance does not change.

The 1D and 2D partitions are again shown in Fig. 7.9.

7.3.2 4D Trellis Code with 16 States

The design rules for multidimensional trellis codes are almost the same as the ones for a two-dimensional signal sets.

1. Branches that leave from a common state or merge into one should belong to different sublattices and the same family.
2. The minimum distance between two different paths in the trellis should be bigger than the distances within a sublattice.
3. A so-called one-to-one function should exist that, in case of a rotation by the symmetry angle, would transform the states of a trellis transition that belong to a certain sublattice into other states that belong to a transition in the rotated sublattice.

The meaning of the three conditions is as follows:

(ad 1) This ensures the minimum Euclidean distance to be $d_{E\min}^2 \geq 2 \cdot \Delta_1^2 = 2 \cdot 2\Delta_0^2$.

(ad 2) This limits the number of nearest neighbors to the ones within a sublattice.

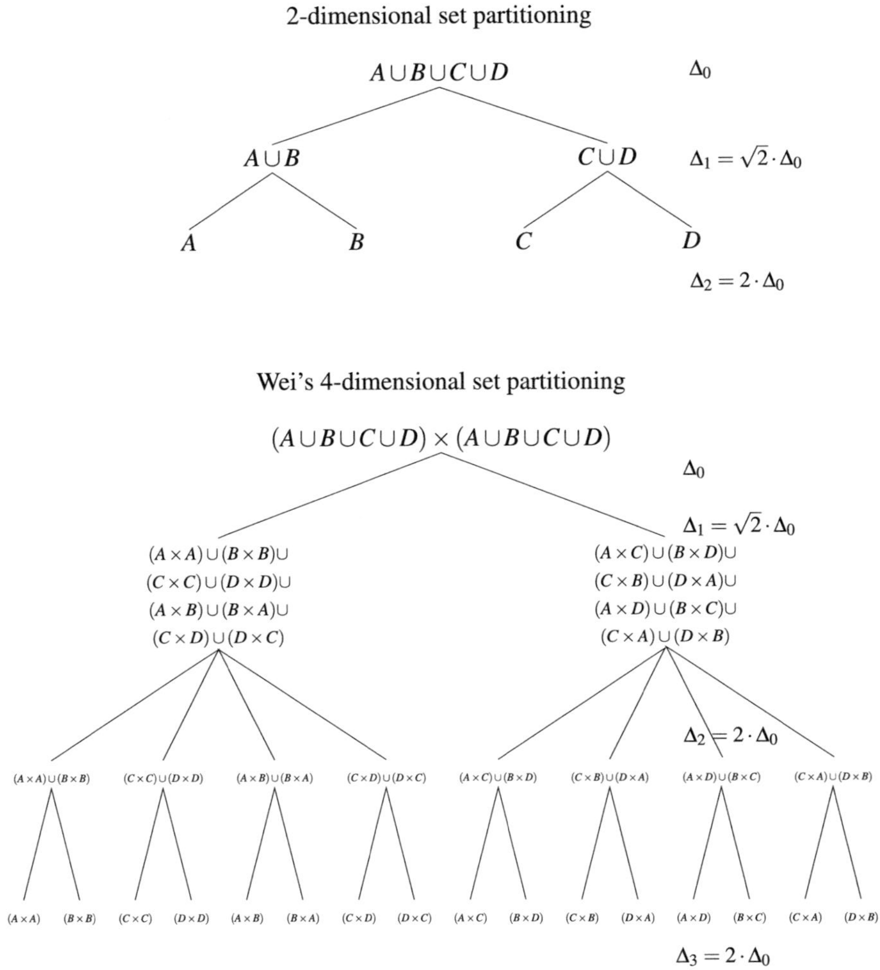

Fig. 7.9 Wei's 2- and 4-dimensional partitioning

(ad 3) This function ensures the rotational invariance of the code. Additionally, a differential en- and de-coding is required. Here, the one-to-one function F is

$$F;\,(W1,\,W2,\,W3,\,W4) \longrightarrow (\overline{W1},\,W2,\,\overline{W3},\,W4)\;.$$

A trellis and corresponding trellis encoder are shown in Figs. 7.10 and 7.11, respectively.

Two inputs that would be changed by a rotation of multiples of the symmetry angle of 90° ($00 \rightarrow 01 \rightarrow 10 \rightarrow 11 \rightarrow 00$) are differentially encoded modulo 4. All other bits besides the ones that are passed through the bit converter have to be rotationally

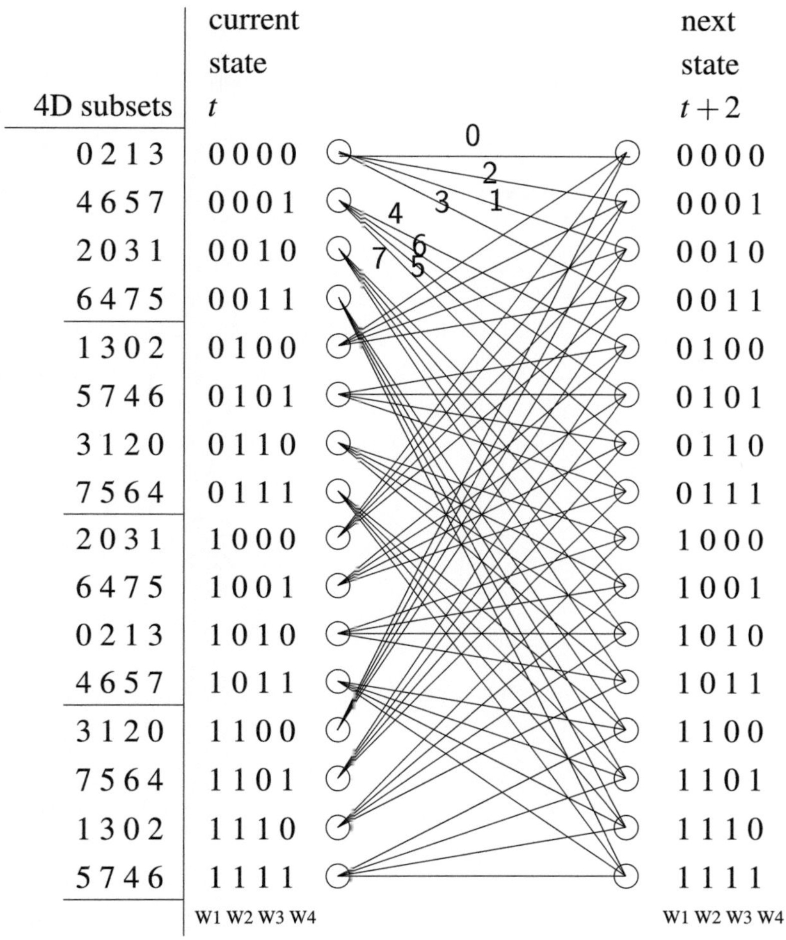

Fig. 7.10 Trellis of Wei's 4-dimensional code with 16 states

invariant. The function of the bit converter can be seen from the partitioning table and the following correspondences.

2D subsets	c_t^0, c_t^1
A	0, 0
B	0, 1
C	1, 0
D	1, 1

The 4D block encoder shown as Table 7.2 is used to select inner and outer areas of the 192-point signal set. Hereto, the inner area is divided in two. $(c_t^2, c_t^3) = (0, 0)$ or $(c_{t+1}^2, c_{t+1}^3) = (0, 0)$ select the first inner (half) area, $(0, 1)$ the other, and $(1, 0)$ the

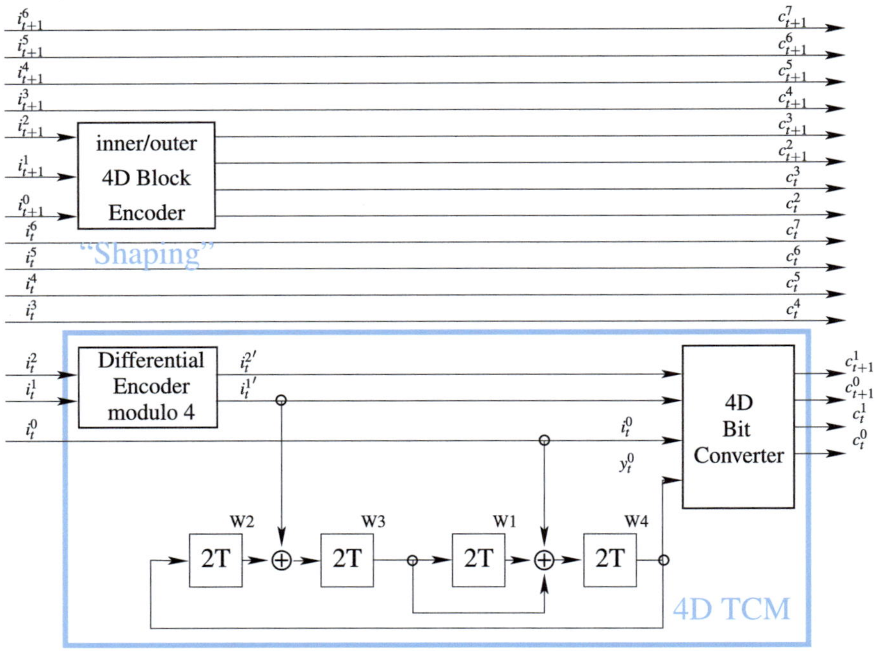

Fig. 7.11 Trellis encoder of Wei's 4-dimensional code with 16 states

Table 7.2 Block encoder

i^0_{t+1}	i^1_{t+1}	i^2_{t+1}	c^2_t	c^3_t	c^2_{t+1}	c^3_{t+1}
0	0	0	0	0	0	0
0	0	1	0	0	0	1
0	1	0	0	0	1	0
0	1	1	0	1	1	0
1	0	0	1	0	0	0
1	0	1	1	0	0	1
1	1	0	0	1	0	0
1	1	1	0	1	0	1

outer area. It is avoided to select the outer area by (c^2_t, c^3_t) and also by (c^2_{t+1}, c^3_{t+1}) thereby minimizing the average power.

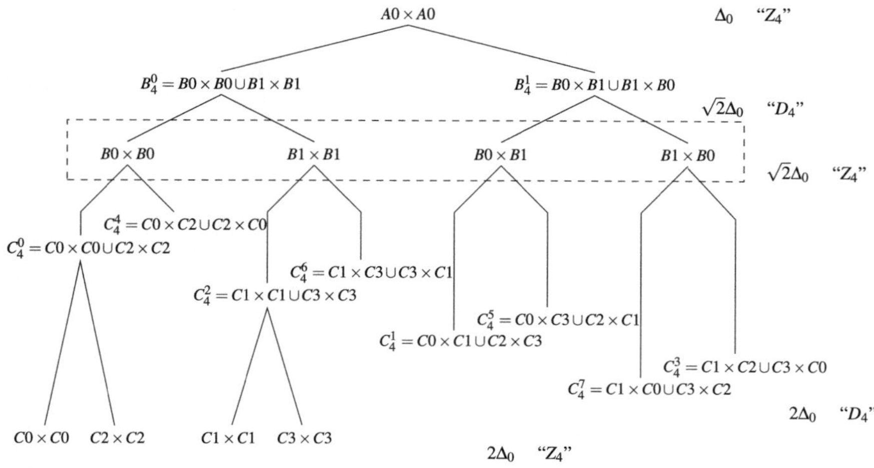

Fig. 7.12 Ungerböck's 4-dimensional partitioning

7.3.3 Ungerböck's 4-Dimensional Partitioning

Ungerböck's 4D codes make use of a binary partitioning shown in Fig. 7.12. The nomenclature is the one that we already used with the 2-dimensional QAM partitioning. Comparing the partitioning trees in Figs. 7.9 and 7.12, we recognize that they just differ in the intermediate partition of the Ungerböck scheme marked by a dashed frame. Nevertheless, we provide both variants since they are both used in literature together with their corresponding notations.

The border labels 'Z_4' and 'D_4' stand for scaled versions of the 4-dimensional integer lattice and the 4-dimensional Checkerboard Lattice (densest package in 4 dimensions).

Definition 7.2 The **Checkerboard lattice** D_N, $N \geq 3$ is given by those points with even coordinate sum, i.e.,

$$D_N = \left\{ (x_0, x_1, \ldots, x_{N-1}) \in \mathbb{Z}^N : \sum_{j=0}^{N-1} x_j \bmod 2 = 0 \right\} . \qquad (7.14)$$

References

1. G. Ungerboeck, "Channel coding with multilevel/phase signals," *IEEE Transactions on Information Theory*, vol. 28, no. 1, pp. 55–67, 1982.
2. G. Ungerboeck, "Trellis-coded modulation with redundant signal sets Part I: Introduction," *IEEE Communications Magazine*, vol. 25, no. 2, pp. 5–11, 1987.

3. G. Ungerboeck, "Trellis-coded modulation with redundant signal sets Part II: State of the art," *IEEE Communications Magazine*, vol. 25, no. 2, pp. 12–21, 1987.
4. L.-F. Wei, "Trellis-coded modulation with multidimensional constellations," *IEEE Transactions on Information Theory*, vol. 33, no. 4, pp. 483–501, 1987.

Chapter 8
Trellis Shaping

Das Runde muss ins Eckige.
The round must go into the square.

Sepp Herberger

In 1992 [1], trellis shaping was published by Forney. It uses a Viterbi algorithm in the transmitter to optimize certain parameters based on a chosen trellis structure. The paper concentrates on the reduction of the average power of an N-dimensional signal constellation. The achievable gains are small (around 1 dB), but the complexity is also very low. A similar gain increase in coded modulation, e.g., from 5 to 6 dB would require much more efforts. Even with iterative schemes (Turbo and LDPC codes), trellis shaping has to be used to close the final gap to Capacity. Before describing the procedure, the so-called '*ultimate shaping gain*' will be computed.

8.1 Maximum Gain of Power-Reducing Trellis Shaping

To see the influence of the shape of the signal constellation, we will first consider the coding gain in Eq. (7.1) under two conditions:

1. The probabilities of all points and the underlying lattices shall be the same in the coded and the uncoded cases.
2. The shape of the borders of the signal constellations shall be identical in the coded and uncoded cases (initially no shaping gain).

From the second condition, we get

W. Henkel, *Channel Coding*, Signals and Communication Technology,
https://doi.org/10.1007/978-3-032-08236-7_8

$$\frac{P_{\text{uncoded}}}{P_{\text{coded}}} = \left(\frac{V(\mathcal{R}_u)}{V(\mathcal{R}_c)}\right)^{2/N} . \tag{8.1}$$

$\mathcal{R}_u$ and $\mathcal{R}_c$ denote the regions that contain the signal sets Ω_u and Ω_c. $V(\mathcal{R}_u)$ and $V(\mathcal{R}_c)$ are the corresponding volumes.

With the first condition, we obtain[1]

$$\frac{P_{\text{uncoded}}}{P_{\text{coded}}} = \left(\frac{|\Omega_u|}{|\Omega_c|}\right)^{2/N} . \tag{8.2}$$

With the (relative) redundancy of a code,

$$\rho(C) = \left(\log_2 \frac{|\Omega_c|}{|\Omega_u|}\right) / N , \tag{8.3}$$

the coding gain $\gamma(C)$ can be written as

$$\gamma(C) = d_E^2(C) \cdot 4^{-\rho(C)} . \tag{8.4}$$

$d^2_{E\,\text{uncoded}}$ was assumed to be one. The definition of the relative redundancy is analogous to introducing the code rate in Definition 3.1. The steps towards (8.4) are the following:

$$(8.3) \Rightarrow \frac{|\Omega_u|}{|\Omega_c|} = 2^{-N\rho(C)}, \text{ together with (8.2) } \Rightarrow \frac{P_{\text{uncoded}}}{P_{\text{coded}}} = 2^{-2\rho(C)} = 4^{-\rho(C)} .$$

If we drop the second condition and choose different boundaries for the signal constellations, this has to be taken into account by the shaping gain, to be more exact, by the ratio of the shaping gains of both constellations.

$$\gamma = \frac{\gamma(\mathcal{R}_c)}{\gamma(\mathcal{R}_u)} \cdot d_E^2(C) \cdot 4^{-\rho(C)} = \frac{\gamma(\mathcal{R}_c)}{\gamma(\mathcal{R}_u)} \cdot \gamma(C) \left(= \frac{G(\mathcal{R}_u)}{G(\mathcal{R}_c)} \cdot \gamma(C) \right) \tag{8.5}$$

G is the so-called normalized second moment and will be studied later. If we consider the uncoded case to be an N-dimensional cube, we obtain

$$\gamma = \gamma(\mathcal{R}_c) \cdot \gamma(C) = \gamma_s \cdot \gamma_c . \tag{8.6}$$

The total gain is the product of the shaping and the coding gain.

The biggest shaping gain will result from choosing the boundary to be an N-dimensional sphere.

We compute the average power normalized to a single dimension of a cubic constellation $C_N = [-\frac{1}{2}, +\frac{1}{2}]^N$ with volume one as a reference.

[1] Vertical bars $|\ldots|$ denote the cardinality of a set, alternatively sometimes written as $\sharp\Omega = |\Omega|$).

$$P(C_N) = \frac{1}{N} \int_{-1/2}^{+1/2} \cdots \int_{-1/2}^{+1/2} (x_1^2 + \cdots + x_N^2) dx_1 \ldots dx_N = \frac{1}{12} \tag{8.7}$$

For the study of the spherical configuration $B_N(R)$, we first derive an expression for the volume to later be able to do a normalization. A spherical shell can surely be written as $\kappa \cdot r^{N-1} dr$ with some constant κ. The volume $V(B_N(R))$ then follows to be

$$V(B_N(R)) = \int_0^R \kappa r^{N-1} dr = \frac{\kappa}{N} R^N \tag{8.8}$$

We use a continuous approximation that is almost exact for big QAM constellations. The average power per single dimension is then given by

$$P(B_N(R)) = \frac{1}{N \cdot V(B_N(R))} \int_0^R r^2 \cdot \kappa r^{N-1} dr = \frac{1}{\kappa R^N} \cdot \frac{\kappa R^{N+2}}{N+2} = \frac{R^2}{N+2} \tag{8.9}$$

To obtain a dimensionless parameter and especially, to normalize to the two-dimensional size of the constellation, we introduce the **normalized** or **dimensionless second moment**

$$G(\mathcal{R}) = P(\mathcal{R}) / (V(\mathcal{R}))^{2/N} . \tag{8.10}$$

With the volume

$$V(B_N(R)) = \frac{R^N \pi^{N/2}}{\Gamma(N/2+1)} \tag{8.11}$$

(Γ: Gamma function) this normalized 2nd moment follows to be

$$\begin{aligned} G(B_N(R)) &= \frac{R^2/(N+2)}{(R^N \pi^{N/2} / \Gamma(N/2+1))^{2/N}} \\ &= \frac{(\Gamma(N/2+1))^{2/N}}{(N+2)\pi} . \end{aligned} \tag{8.12}$$

With Stirling's approximation $\Gamma(N/2+1) \approx (N/2e)^{N/2}$, the *ultimate shaping gain* becomes

$$\lim_{N\to\infty} \frac{G(C_N)}{G(B_N(R))} = \lim_{N\to\infty} \frac{\gamma(C_N)}{\gamma(B_N(R))} = \frac{1/12}{1/2\pi e} = \frac{\pi e}{6} = 1.53 \text{ dB} \tag{8.13}$$

The shaping gain as a function of the dimensionality N is given in the following table.

	Shaping gain	
N	$\gamma(B_N)$	dB
2	$\pi/3 = 1,047$	0,20
4	$\pi/2^{3/2} = 1,111$	0,46
8	1,183	0,73
12	1,224	0,88
16	1,252	0,98
24	1,287	1,10
32	1,309	1,17

A spherical constellation in N dimensions with $N \rightarrow \infty$ corresponds to a Gaussian density in two dimensions.

8.2 One- and Multidimensional Trellis Shaping

Forney's trellis shaping for minimizing the average power relies on a doubling of the signal set and modifies the probability distribution of the signal points in two dimensions. A gain of 0.95 dB is already achieved with a simple 4-state convolutional shaping code for a 16×16 signal constellation (256-QAM).

In the example of Fig. 8.1 eight bits are generated from seven for addressing the signal points. This added bit of redundancy leads to a doubling of the signal alphabet from 128 to 256 points. Only the MSB (**M**ost **S**ignificant **B**it) of the 128-point signal set is modified by the shaping code. When multiplying this MSB with the $(\mathbf{H}_s^T)^{-1}$

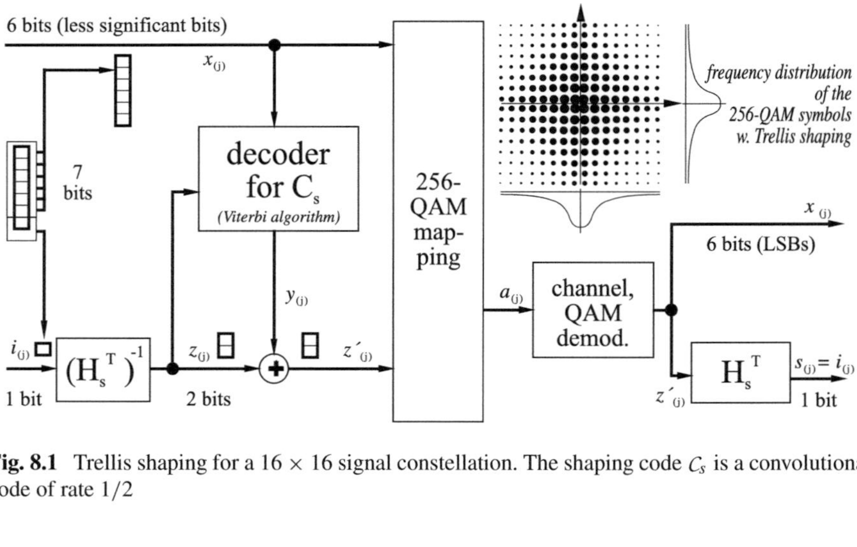

Fig. 8.1 Trellis shaping for a 16×16 signal constellation. The shaping code C_s is a convolutional code of rate $1/2$

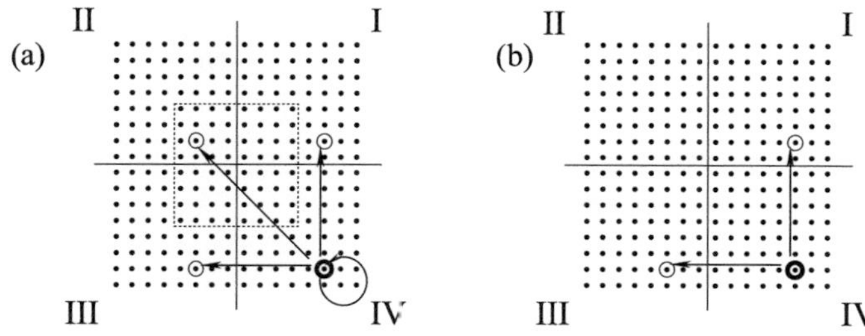

Fig. 8.2 Influence of the sign bits on the points of a 256-QAM: **a** with a free choice of the sign bits, **b** when applying trellis shaping

matrix, two bits are generated that are the sign bits of the QAM, i.e., they determine from which quadrant the points are taken. The six bits that are not modified are the lower significant bits of the QAM addressing. These LSBs (**L**ess **S**ignificant **B**its) select the points within a quadrant. The sign bits will be modified dependent on the signal power. This requires to take into account all of the eight bits of the symbol. This explains the arrows into the block 'Decoder for $\mathcal{C}_s$'.

In case the two sign bits could be chosen freely, i.e., not be generated by combining z and y, the point determined by the six lower significant bits within an 8×8-constellation could be moved arbitrarily into one of the four quadrants. Since the criterion is the minimum average energy, in Fig. 8.2, the point in quadrant II would be chosen. This kind of 'sign-bit shaping' would lead to the dashed equally distributed 8×8-constellation, unfortunately without any shaping gain. Only six information bits would then be transmitted in an equally distributed quadratic constellation.

Trellis shaping modifies the sign bits by a valid code sequence of the convolutional code $\mathcal{C}_s$ which can be generated by a Viterbi algorithm. In case of a shaping code of rate $1/2$, seven bits of information can still be transmitted together with obtaining a shaping gain. Although the shaping code does only allow to choose between two quadrants (see Fig. 8.2b), still a sufficient suppression of the outermost signal points is achieved leading to an almost Gaussian frequency distribution.

We are now going to study the signal path and the functions of the single components in some more detail.

When multiplying an arbitrary binary sequence $\mathbf{z}'$, i.e., the corresponding Laurent sequence (polynomial description) with the parity-check matrix $\mathbf{H}^T$ (syndrome former), we obtain the syndrome sequence $\mathbf{s}$:

$$\mathbf{s} = \mathbf{z}' \cdot \mathbf{H}^T . \tag{8.14}$$

We have $\mathbf{s} = \mathbf{0}$, if $\mathbf{z}'$ is a valid code sequence of the convolutional code $\mathcal{C}_s$. Since $\mathbf{z}' = \mathbf{z} \oplus \mathbf{y}$ results from a linear combination of $\mathbf{z}$ with a valid code sequence $\mathbf{y}$, $\mathbf{z}$ and $\mathbf{z}'$ lead to the same syndrome sequence:

$$\mathbf{z}' \cdot \mathbf{H}^T = (\mathbf{z} \oplus \mathbf{y}) \cdot \mathbf{H}^T = (\mathbf{z} \cdot \mathbf{H}^T) \oplus \underbrace{(\mathbf{y} \cdot \mathbf{H}^T)}_{=0} = \mathbf{z} \cdot \mathbf{H}^T = s\,. \tag{8.15}$$

If we apply the left inverse of the parity-check matrix to the information sequence **i** according to

$$\mathbf{i} \cdot \mathbf{H}^{T^{-1}} = \mathbf{z}\,, \tag{8.16}$$

we obtain for the sequence s generated by the parity-check matrix:

$$\mathbf{s} = \mathbf{z}' \cdot \mathbf{H}^T = \mathbf{z} \cdot \mathbf{H}^T = (\mathbf{i} \cdot \underbrace{\mathbf{H}^{T^{-1}}) \cdot \mathbf{H}^T}_{\mathrm{i}} = \mathbf{i}\,. \tag{8.17}$$

The information sequence is regenerated by the parity-check matrix. The inverse syndrome former $(\mathbf{H}^T)^{-1}$ ensures that the sequence **z** will never be part of a valid code sequence of the shaping code $\mathcal{C}_s$. Thus, only the superimposed code sequence **y** will be eliminated by the parity-check matrix.

Remark The parity-check matrix can be determined by applying $\mathbf{H} = [\mathbf{A}|\mathrm{i}_{n-k}] \Longleftrightarrow \mathbf{G} = [\mathrm{i}_k| - \mathbf{A}^T]$ according to Theorem 3.5.

Still, the syndrome former **H** should be non-recursive to avoid error propagation at the receiver.

In Forney's trellis shaping, a code sequence **y** of the shaping code is determined that minimizes the average power of the transmitted symbols when added to **z**. This is realized by means of the path search in the Viterbi algorithm, which is not used to decoding an information sequence but just generates a valid code sequence. The symbol energy $|a_{(j)}|^2$ of the output symbol $a_{(j)}$ that would result from the code sequence is used as metric. When passing through the trellis, the best sequence (the one that minimizes the averages power) is chosen according to this metric.

8.3 Multidimensional Trellis Shaping

For many applications, a doubling of the modulation signal set is not applicable. Power shaping for PAM constellations is such a case and also applications for line coding or for avoiding critical transitions near the origin in case of PSK over nonlinear channels.

What will be the increases of the mean power when doubling a QAM and a PAM signal set?

If a doubling of the signal set has to be avoided, the shaping redundancy has to be introduced sequentially. This will be done in the last partition according to Fig. 8.3 with, e.g., a redundancy share of 1/4.

The whole structure of the multidimensional trellis shaping is shown in Fig. 8.4. The inverse syndrome former has no small requirements, since it is located at the transmitter.

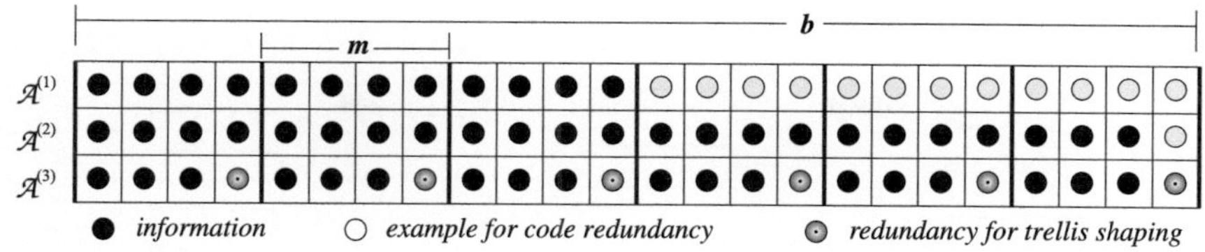

Fig. 8.3 Subdivision of a frame and introduction of redundancy in the last partition

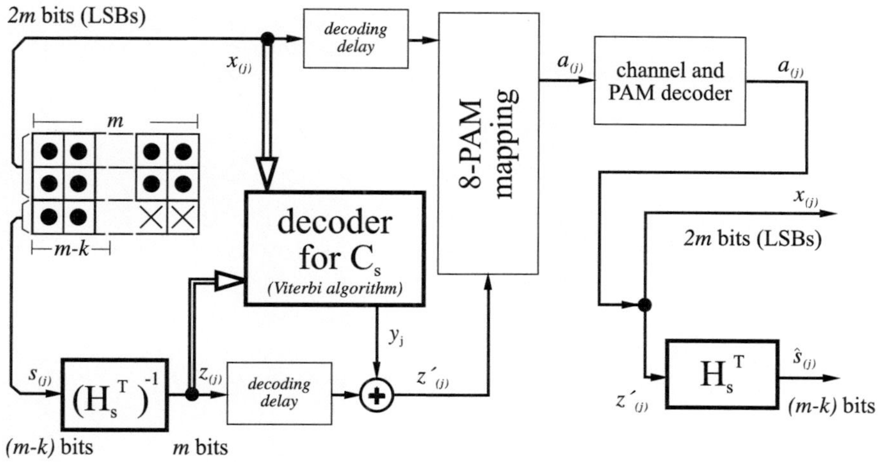

Fig. 8.4 Multidimensional trellis shaping (instead of PAM, QAM can be used, too)

We study an example with a shaping code of rate 1/4. The generator matrix of the shaping code is

$$\mathbf{G} = \begin{pmatrix} 1 + D^2 & 1 + D + D^2 & 1 + D + D^2 & 1 + D + D^2 \end{pmatrix} \ .$$

The parity-check matrix $\mathbf{H}^T$ follows to be

$$\mathbf{H}^T = \begin{pmatrix} 1 + D + D^2 & 1 + D + D^2 & 1 + D + D^2 \\ 1 + D^2 & 0 & 0 \\ 0 & 1 + D^2 & 0 \\ 0 & 0 & 1 + D^2 \end{pmatrix} \ .$$

The syndrome former should in general not be recursive to avoid error propagation. The syndrome former does not only have a single left inverse. The most simple form would be

$$\left(\mathbf{H}^T\right)^{-1} = \begin{pmatrix} 0 & \frac{1}{1+D^2} & 0 & 0 \\ 0 & 0 & \frac{1}{1+D^2} & 0 \\ 0 & 0 & 0 & \frac{1}{1+D^2} \end{pmatrix} .$$

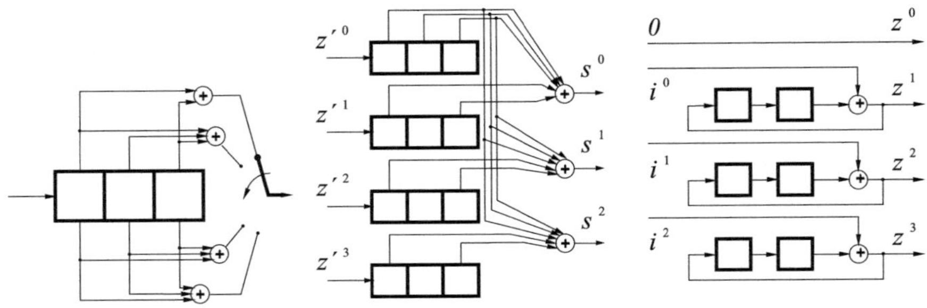

(a) Encoder of the convolutional code of rate 1/4. *(b) Shift register of the matrix* H^T *(c) Recursive shift register of the matrix* $(H^T)^{-1}$

Fig. 8.5 Shift register realizations of the matrices $\mathbf{G}$, $\mathbf{H}^T$, and $(\mathbf{H}^T)^{-1}$

In Fig. 8.5, the matrices $\mathbf{G}$, $\mathbf{H}^T$, and $(\mathbf{H}^T)^{-1}$ are realized by shift registers. The output sequence z of the inverse syndrome former $(\mathbf{H}^T)^{-1}$ is given by

$$(z^0, z^1, z^2, z^3) = (i^0, i^1, i^2) \cdot \begin{pmatrix} 0 & \frac{1}{1+D^2} & 0 & 0 \\ 0 & 0 & \frac{1}{1+D^2} & 0 \\ 0 & 0 & 0 & \frac{1}{1+D^2} \end{pmatrix}$$

$$\begin{aligned} z^0 &= 0 \,; & z^1 &= \tfrac{i^0}{1+D^2} = i^0 + z^1 D^2 \,; \\ z^2 &= \tfrac{i^1}{1+D^2} = i^1 + z^2 D^2 \,; & z^3 &= \tfrac{i^2}{1+D^2} = i^2 + z^3 D^2 \,. \end{aligned}$$

We show results for power shaping in Fig. 8.6 and for PAM line coding in Fig. 8.7. For line coding, the variance of the RDS[2] (Running Digital Sum) was used as the metric. Note that Viterbi's algorithm requires for an additive non-negative metric and the RDS can be negative. For comparison, additionally the power spectral density is plotted that would result when directly applying the RDS as a metric. Furthermore, a blocked line code due to Carter [3] with the same redundancy is shown as a reference.

The following tables show the power-shaping gain depending on the rate of the shaping code and the decoding delay for a shaping code with 4 states and 8-PAM. γ_{s1} is the shaping gain when comparing with an equally distributed 6-PAM, γ_{s2} is the gain compared to a time-variant 4/8-PAM with the same rate, and γ_{sF} follows the

[2] The variance of the RDS instead of the RDS had, e.g., already been applied by Justesen in 1982 [2].

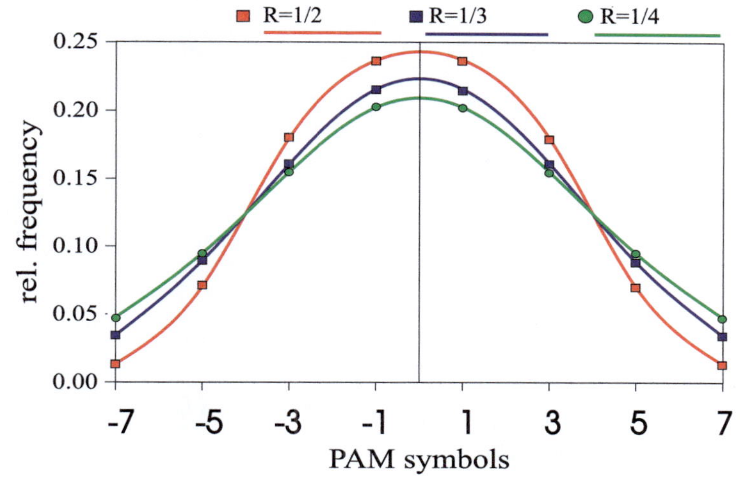

Fig. 8.6 Resulting histogram from power shaping for 8-PAM

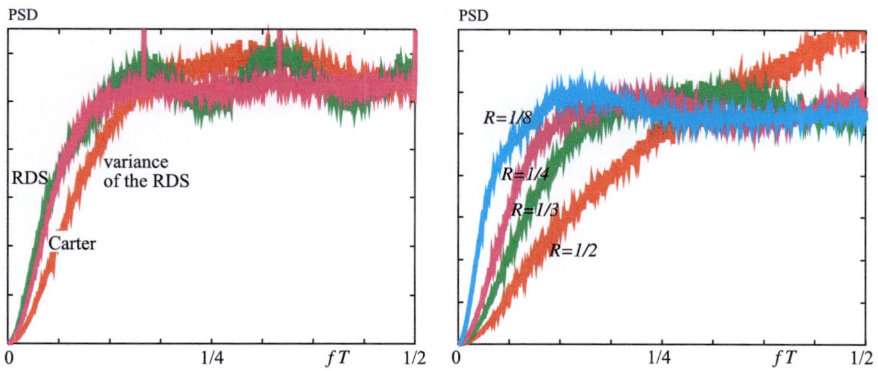

Fig. 8.7 Line-coding results with multidimensional trellis shaping; left: comparison when using the RDS, the variance of the RDS as metric, and Carter's line code; right: comparing different shaping code rates

above gain definition, i.e., when comparing with an equally distributed configuration with the same rate (although it does not exist in practice).

Gain as a function of the rate			
R	$\gamma_{s\,1}$/dB	$\gamma_{s\,2}$/dB	$\gamma_{s\,F}$/dB
1/2	3.910	1.828	0.830
1/3	2.753	1.481	0.705
1/4	2.214	1.297	0.680

Gain as a function of the decoding delay ($R = 1/3$)			
Delay	$\gamma_{s\,1}$/dB	$\gamma_{s\,2}$/dB	$\gamma_{s\,F}$/dB
5	2.500	1.228	0.452
10	2.648	1.375	0.599
20	2.725	1.453	0.677
60	2.753	1.481	0.705
200	2.753	1.481	0.705

8.3.1 Necessary Modifications in the Viterbi Algorithm when Used in Trellis Shaping

When discussing trellis shaping in literature, it is usually not mentioned that Viterbi's algorithm, due to the finite decoding delay, may produce invalid trellis transitions that do not correspond to a valid code sequence. This would cause systematic errors already on the transmitter side. The Viterbi algorithm has to be modified such that in case different paths appear μ positions before the output position in the path memories, the currently best path should be selected by worsening the metrics of all others. Henceforth, only this best path will be continued (see Fig. 8.8).

When the path is again spread out to all $2^{k \cdot M}$ states of the trellis, only one path will exist on the other end of the path registers. Since from one state, 2^k branches are emerging, the best path is distributed to $2^{k \cdot \mu}$ states after μ time intervals. Thus,

$$2^{k \cdot \mu} \geq 2^{k \cdot M} \Longleftrightarrow \mu \geq M \ .$$

The decoding delay should still not be chosen too small, e.g. $\geq 10 \cdot L$, in order not to reduce the shaping gain.

8.3.2 Constellation Expansion Ratio and Peak-to-Average Ratio

Up to now, we considered the intended outcome of trellis shaping, e.g., the reduction of the average power. However, it also comes with drawbacks. It increases the constellation, expressed by the so-called 'Constellation-Expansion Ratio'.

Definition 8.1 The **Constellation-Expansion Ratio** CER is the ratio of the cardinalities of the modulation signal sets with coding/shaping and without coding/shaping.

Additionally, the peak-to-average power ratio is increased which requires higher dynamics in the transmitter and receiver.

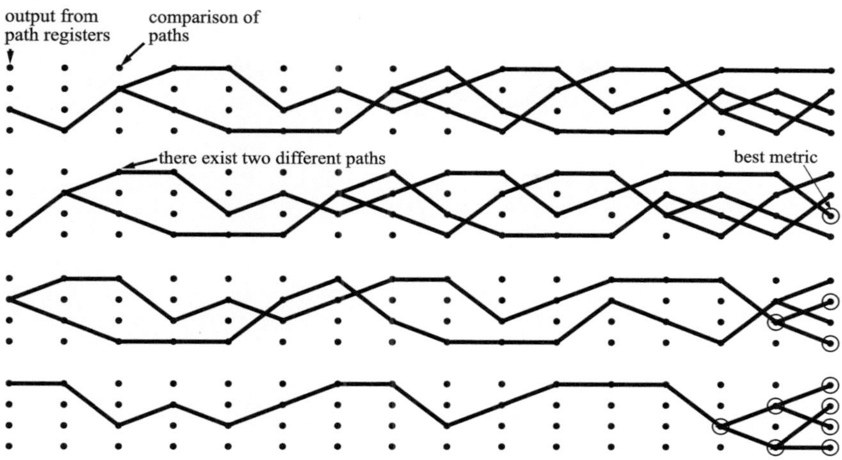

Fig. 8.8 Modification of the Viterbi algorithm; the circled states mark the path with the best metric

Definition 8.2 Peak-to-Average Ratio PAR is the ratio of peak and average powers. PAR is thus the square of the **Crest factor**.

Note that in the case of power shaping, we aim at a Gaussian frequency distribution, which has an infinite PAR! However, one can define combined metrics that also take into account the peak power.

References

1. G. D. Forney, "Trellis shaping," *IEEE Transactions on Information Theory*, vol. 38, no. 2, pp. 281–300, 1992.
2. J. Justesen, "Information rates and power spectra of digital codes," *IEEE Transactions on Information Theory*, vol. 28, no. 3, pp. 457–472, 1982.
3. R. O. Carter, "Low-disparity binary coding system," *Electronics Letters*, vol. 1, no. 3, pp. 67–68, 1965.

Chapter 9
Basics of Finite Fields (Galois Fields)

> The legend says that Galois wrote down his theory the night before he was killed in a duel on May 31, 1832 at the young age of only 20.

First we will discuss so-called prime fields. A special case we have already used, the binary number field.

9.1 Prime Fields

As the name suggests, a prime field is a finite field with a prime number of elements. The requirement to be prime will be explained after presenting the axioms for groups, rings, and fields. We start with the group $\mathcal{G}$.

Group axioms

1. *Closure*: $\forall_{a,b \in \mathcal{G}} : a + b \in \mathcal{G}$
2. *Associativity*: $\forall_{a,b,c \in \mathcal{G}} : (a + b) + c = a + (b + c) = a + b + c$
3. *Existence of an identity element*: $\forall_{a \in \mathcal{G}},\ 0 \in \mathcal{G} : a + 0 = a, \quad 0 + a = a$
4. *Existence of an inverse element*: $\forall_{a \in \mathcal{G}} \exists_{a' \in \mathcal{G}} : a + a' = 0, \quad a' + a = 0,$ $(a' = -a)$

   A **commutative (Abelian) group** additionally fulfills the commutative property:
5. *Commutative law*: $\forall_{a,b \in \mathcal{G}} : a + b = b + a$

Uniqueness: (follows from the previous axioms and is thus no axiom itself) $a + x = b$ has the unique solution $x = b + (-a) = b - a$

W. Henkel, *Channel Coding*, Signals and Communication Technology,
https://doi.org/10.1007/978-3-032-08236-7_9

A commutative group thus summarizes all properties that we know from the usual addition. A Ring additionally has rules for a second operation that we will write as multiplication.

Additional ring axioms

The first two group axioms (half group, module) shall be fulfilled for the multiplication as well and a distributive law is added.

1. *Closure:* $\forall_{a,b\in\mathcal{G}} : a \cdot b \in \mathcal{G}$
2. *Associativity:* $\forall_{a,b,c\in\mathcal{G}} : (a \cdot b) \cdot c = a \cdot (b \cdot c) = a \cdot b \cdot c$
3. *Distributive law:* $\forall_{a,b,c\in\mathcal{G}} : a \cdot (b + c) = (a \cdot b) + (a \cdot c)$

In a ring, we are now able to add and multiply as we are used to. Only the division requires at least an inverse element of the multiplication. Additional axioms follow for **fields**:

Additional field axioms

1. *Existence of an identity element:* $\forall_{a\in\mathcal{G}}\exists_{1\in\mathcal{G}} : a \cdot 1 = a, \quad 1 \cdot a = a$
2. *Existence of an inverse element:* $\forall_{a\in\mathcal{G},a\neq 0}\exists_{a'\in\mathcal{G}} : a \cdot a' = 1, \quad a' \cdot a = 1,$ $(a' = a^{-1})$
3. *Commutative law:* $\forall_{a,b\in\mathcal{G}} : a \cdot b = b \cdot a$

Uniqueness: (follows from the previous axioms and is thus no axiom itself) $a \cdot x = b$ has the unique solution $x = b \cdot a^{-1} = b/a$

To conclude, a field is a set $\mathcal{K}$ together with a commutative group describing an 'addition', a commutative group describing a 'multiplication' (not including the zero element '0' of the addition) and a single distributive law.

We will point out two properties that follow from the field axioms.

Theorem 9.1 No zero divisor: *$a \cdot b = 0$ is only fulfilled, if $a = 0$ or $b = 0$. If $a \neq 0$ and $b \neq 0$, we also require $a \cdot b \neq 0$. There are no zero divisors. In case a field has only P elements, with P a prime number, we always have*

$$\forall_{a,b\neq 0 mod\, P} : \quad a \cdot b \neq 0 \; mod \; P \tag{9.1}$$

Proof Let $0 < a, b < P$. Assuming that on the contrary $a \cdot b = j \cdot P = 0$ mod P. Since $a \not| P$ and $b \not| P$, we will conclude $a|j$ and $b|j$. Division by a or b leads to a contradiction to our assumption $0 < a, b < P$ because $a = \frac{j}{b} \cdot P > P$ or $b = \frac{j}{a} \cdot P > P$. □

Let us consider a set with 4 elements $\{0, 1, 2, 3\}$. Then we have $2 \cdot 2 = 4 \equiv 0$ mod 4, which contradicts the requirement not to have zero divisors.

Two finite fields, so called **Galois fields**, with the same number of elements are isomorphic, i.e., they have the same structure. Actually, they can be considered to be the same fields, only labeling the elements differently.

In the following, we present addition and multiplication tables of some prime fields. This means considering the field elements $0, 1, 2, \ldots, (P-1)$ and computing modulo (mod) P, i.e., we set $P \equiv 0$.

The simplest but for applications the most important field are the binary numbers $GF(P=2)$. The addition (XOR) and multiplication (AND) of the elements 0 and 1 are described by

+	0	1
0	0	1
1	1	0

·	0	1
0	0	0
1	0	1

Due to computing mod 2 in $GF(2)$, we have $(-1) = (+1)$!

For applications, $GF(2)$ itself is too small; one uses, as usual, words (bytes) of binary numbers. In the next section, these will be introduced as extension fields of characteristic P with $q = P^m$ elements (e.g., $q = 2^8$ for bytes). In our examples we will also use bigger prime fields, since this is easier to follow.

Subsequently, we also provide the addition and multiplication tables for $GF(3)$, $GF(5)$ and $GF(7)$.

+	0	1	2
0	0	1	2
1	1	2	0
2	2	0	1

·	0	1	2
0	0	0	0
1	0	1	2
2	0	2	1

+	0	1	2	3	4
0	0	1	2	3	4
1	1	2	3	4	0
2	2	3	4	0	1
3	3	4	0	1	2
4	4	0	1	2	3

·	0	1	2	3	4
0	0	0	0	0	0
1	0	1	2	3	4
2	0	2	4	1	3
3	0	3	1	4	2
4	0	4	3	2	1

+	0	1	2	3	4	5	6
0	0	1	2	3	4	5	6
1	1	2	3	4	5	6	0
2	2	3	4	5	6	0	1
3	3	4	5	6	0	1	2
4	4	5	6	0	1	2	3
5	5	6	0	1	2	3	4
6	6	0	1	2	3	4	5

·	0	1	2	3	4	5	6
0	0	0	0	0	0	0	0
1	0	1	2	3	4	5	6
2	0	2	4	6	1	3	5
3	0	3	6	2	5	1	4
4	0	4	1	5	2	6	3
5	0	5	3	1	6	4	2
6	0	6	5	4	3	2	1

We are now studying the multiplicative group of a prime field in some more detail. Equivalent statements can be made for extension fields that are discussed next. The multiplicative group has one element less than P, since the zero element is not contained. It consists of $\{1, 2, \ldots, P-1\}$ and has the order $N = P - 1$. As an example we consider the powers of elements of $GF(7)$.

z	z^0	z^1	z^2	z^3	z^4	z^5	z^6	
0	0	0	0	0	0	0	0	
1	1	1	1	1	1	1	1	
2	1	2	4	1	2	4	1	
3	1	3	2	6	4	5	1	⋆
4	1	4	2	1	4	2	1	
5	1	5	4	6	2	3	1	⋆
6	1	6	1	6	1	6	1	

The rows with $z = 5$ and $z = 3 = 5^5$ outline an important property of Galois fields, the existence of a **primitive element**.

Theorem 9.2 *Each Galois field $GF(q)$ has, at least, one element z with the property that by taking $(q-1)$ powers of $z = z^1$, i.e., $z, z \cdot z = z^2, \ldots, z^{q-1}$ all the $(q-1)$ elements $a \neq 0$ of $GF(q)$ are obtained.*

This theorem has been formulated for a general $GF(q)$, since this is not only the case for prime fields, but also for extension fields.
A primitive element is an element of the order N (N=number of elements of the multiplicative group), which means that $z^i \neq 1$ for $0 < i < N = (q-1)$ and $z^N = 1$. Other primitive elements z^i have the property that i is relative prime to N, otherwise we would have $(z^i)^j = 1$ for $j \cdot \gcd(i, N) = N$ and $j < N$. Thus, if i has a common divisor to N, the order of the element z^i will be $N/\gcd(i, N)$. A Galois field $GF(q)$ has so many primitive elements as it has numbers i, $0 < i < N$, that are relative prime to $N = q - 1$.

Let us again go back to our table of powers of $GF(7)$. There we have $N = P - 1 = 6$; relative prime is 5. Let us start from a primitive element $z = 5$. Then $5^5 = 3$ will also be primitive. If one starts from $z = 3$, $3^5 = 5$ will also be primitive. In case of 2 and 4, the gcd with respect to $N = 6$ equals 2, i.e., the order of $z^2 = 5^2 = 4 \bmod 7$ and $z^4 = 5^4 = 2 \bmod 7$ is equal to $N/2 = 6/2 = 3$.

Writing numbers in exponential form is especially suited for multiplications, since this turns into an addition of the exponents mod N. For the addition, of course, the exponential form is not suited. These are properties that we are already used to know from the infinite number fields $\mathbb{Z}$ and $\mathbb{R}$.

An element of order N is also known from complex numbers, especially used in the discrete Fourier transform . It is $z = e^{j\frac{2\pi}{N}}$, with j being the imaginary unit $j = \sqrt{-1}$. The similarity to the complex numbers will simplify the description of extension fields in the following section.

9.2 Extension Fields

If you don't have a solution, define one!

Let us first remember how complex number were once introduced. The equation $x^2 + 1 = 0$ did not have a solution in $\mathbb{R}$. Thus, an 'imaginary' element $j = \sqrt{-1}$

was defined as the solution. With it, operations with a vector consisting of two components $(\Re e, \Im m) \equiv \Re e + j\Im m$ were introduced. An extension field of the real numbers $\mathbb{C} \equiv \mathbb{R}^2$ was created. For arithmetic operations we are used to work with two different descriptions: the addition is done component-wise for real and imaginary parts, whereas the multiplication is performed in an exponential representation $|z|e^{j\phi_z}$ which proved to be better suited since exponents add when complex numbers are multiplied.

We will now describe the extension of the real numbers to the complex numbers and the prime field $GF(2)$ to the extension field $GF(2^2) \equiv (GF(2))^2$ in parallel. To make this even more obvious, we denote the imaginary element also by α.

Compare:

1. $\mathbb{R} \longrightarrow \mathbb{C} : x^2 + 1 = 0$ has no solution in $x \in \mathbb{R}$
   Defining equation for the field extension: $\alpha^2 + 1 \stackrel{!}{=} 0 \Longleftrightarrow \alpha^2 = -1 \Longleftrightarrow \alpha = \sqrt{-1}$
   Definition of the complex number field: $a = a_0 + a_1\alpha$, $a_0, a_1 \in \mathbb{R}$; we calculate mod $(\alpha^2 + 1)$
2. $GF(2) \longrightarrow GF(2^2) : x^2 + x + 1 = 0$ (coefficients from $GF(2)$) has no solution in $x \in GF(2)$
   Defining equation for the field extension: $\alpha^2 + \alpha + 1 \stackrel{!}{=} 0 \Longleftrightarrow \alpha^2 = \alpha + 1 \bmod 2$
   Definition of the elements of $GF(2^2)$: $a = a_0 + a_1\alpha$, $a_0, a_1 \in GF(2)$; we calculate mod $(\alpha^2 + \alpha + 1)$
3. $GF(P) \longrightarrow GF(q = P^m)$: $\quad p(x) = x^m + p_{m-1}x^{m-1} + \cdots + p_1x + p_0 = 0$ (coefficients $p_{m-1}, \ldots, p_1, p_0 \in GF(P)$) has no solution in $x \in GF(P)$ and also not in $x \in GF(P^n),\ n < m$
   Defining equation for the field extension: $p(\alpha) = 0 \Longleftrightarrow \alpha^m = -p_{m-1}\alpha^{m-1} - \cdots - p_1\alpha - p_0$
   Definition of the elements of $GF(P^m)$: $a = a_0 + a_1\alpha + \cdots + a_{m-1}\alpha^{m-1}$, $a_0, a_1, \ldots, a_{m-1} \in GF(P)$; we calculate mod $p(\alpha)$

9.2.1 Component Representation

From complex numbers, we are used to component-wise additions of real and imaginary parts. When multiplying, we have to note that $j^2 = \alpha^2 = -1$, i.e., we compute mod $(p(\alpha) = \alpha^2 + 1)$.

$$\begin{array}{l}
\textit{Addition in } \mathbb{C} \\
\hline
c = a + b \\
c = (a_0 + a_1\alpha) + (b_0 + b_1\alpha) \\
c = \underbrace{(a_0 + b_0)}_{c_0} + \underbrace{(a_1 + b_1)}_{c_1} \cdot \alpha
\end{array}$$

$$\begin{array}{l}
\textit{Multiplication in } \mathbb{C} \\
\hline
d = a \cdot b \\
d = (a_0 + a_1\alpha) \cdot (b_0 + b_1\alpha) \\
d = a_0 b_0 + (a_1 b_0 + a_0 b_1)\alpha + a_1 b_1 \underbrace{\alpha^2}_{=-1} \\
d = \underbrace{(a_0 b_0 - a_1 b_1)}_{d_0} + \underbrace{(a_0 b_1 + a_1 b_0)}_{d_1} \cdot \alpha
\end{array}$$

The only difference when computing in an extension of a prime field is that we do modulo operations based on another 'primitive' polynomial. Let us again consider the example $GF(2^2)$ with $p(\alpha) = \alpha^2 + \alpha + 1$. mod $p(\alpha)$ means that we set $\alpha^2 = 1 + \alpha$. We now add and multiply two numbers $a = a_0 + a_1\alpha$ and $b = b_0 + b_1\alpha$ from $GF(2^2)$ with $a_0, a_1, b_0, b_1 \in GF(2)$

$$\begin{array}{l}
\textit{Addition in } GF(2^2) \\
\hline
c = a + b \\
c = (a_0 + a_1\alpha) + (b_0 + b_1\alpha) \\
c = \underbrace{(a_0 + b_0)}_{c_0} + \underbrace{(a_1 + b_1)}_{c_1} \cdot \alpha
\end{array}$$

$$\begin{array}{l}
\textit{Multiplication in } GF(2^2) \\
\hline
d = a \cdot b \\
d = (a_0 + a_1\alpha) \cdot (b_0 + b_1\alpha) \\
d = a_0 b_0 + (a_1 b_0 + a_0 b_1)\alpha + a_1 b_1 \underbrace{\alpha^2}_{=1+\alpha} \\
d = \underbrace{(a_0 b_0 + a_1 b_1)}_{d_0} + \underbrace{(a_0 b_1 + a_1 b_0 + a_1 b_1)}_{d_1} \cdot \alpha
\end{array}$$

Like for the prime fields, we can provide addition and multiplication tables for $GF(2^2)$.

$+$	0	1	α	$1+\alpha$
0	0	1	α	$1+\alpha$
1	1	0	$1+\alpha$	α
α	α	$1+\alpha$	0	1
$1+\alpha$	$1+\alpha$	α	1	0

$\cdot$	0	1	α	$1+\alpha$
0	0	0	0	0
1	0	1	α	$1+\alpha$
α	0	α	$1+\alpha$	1
$1+\alpha$	0	$1+\alpha$	1	α

If we write the entries as vectors (a_0, a_1), we obtain

+	00	10	01	11
00	00	10	01	11
10	10	00	11	01
01	01	11	00	10
11	11	01	10	00

·	00	10	01	11
00	00	00	00	00
10	00	10	01	11
01	00	01	11	10
11	00	11	10	01

The dual representation can, of course, also be replaced by a decimal representation, e.g., by $a := a_0 \cdot 2^0 + a_1 \cdot 2^1$.

Remark 1 In the literature, often $GF(2^2)$ is misleadingly written as $GF(4)$. Note that then the extension field, i.e., $GF(2^2)$ is meant.

9.2.2 *Exponential Representation*

As we know from complex numbers and also already from prime fields, it is more convenient to use an exponential representation for the multiplication. Together with the 'primitive' polynomial we also define a **'primitive' element** α, which allows to write each element of the extension field in an exponential form. For $GF(2^2)$, this yields

$$\begin{array}{rl} 0 & = 0 \\ 1 & = \alpha^0 \\ \alpha & = \alpha^1 \\ 1+\alpha & = \alpha^2 \\ \hline 1 & = \alpha^3 \end{array}$$

When multiplying, the exponents have to be added. As with prime fields, we have to note that the cardinality of the multiplicative group is $q - 1 = P^m - 1$, i.e., $\alpha^{q-1} = \alpha^0 = 1$.

The multiplication table follows to be

$\cdot$	0	α^0	α^1	α^2
0	0	0	0	0
α^0	0	α^0	α^1	α^2
α^1	0	α^1	α^2	α^0
α^2	0	α^2	α^0	α^1

Since the exponential representation is not suited for the addition, we do not provide a corresponding table.

Following a few basic definitions and remarks, we will discuss a shift register structure that allows to compute the correspondence tables for component and exponential representations.

Finite fields are sometimes called 'circle-splitting fields', due to their property $\alpha^{q-1} = 1$ and $\alpha^j \neq 1$ for $0 < j < q - 1$. One may think of the similar property of the complex number $e^{\alpha \frac{2\pi}{N}}$ with $\alpha = j, \alpha^2 = -1, N = q - 1$ on the unit circle of the complex plane.

We have used the term 'primitive' polynomial, but have not yet formally defined it. This will now be done.

At the beginning of the chapter we realized that an important property of a field is to have no 'zero divisors'. This lead to prime fields with a prime number of elements. Now considering extensions of prime fields that are described by polynomials modulo a certain polynomial, we conclude that this polynomial should also not have any divisor polynomials. For simplicity, let us also assume that this polynomial has been normalized such that the coefficient of the term with the highest power equals one. The two properties are called *irreducible* and *monic*.

Definition 9.1 A polynomial $p(x)$ with coefficients from $GF(P)$ is called **irreducible** (over $GF(P)$) if it can only be divided by $\beta p(x)$ or β, with $\beta \in GF(P)$.[1]

Definition 9.2 A polynomial $p(x) = a_m x^m + \cdots + a_1 x^1 + a_0 x^0$ with coefficients a_j from $GF(P)$ is called **monic**, if $a_m = 1$.

Definition 9.3 A polynomial with the properties of both previous Theorems, 9.1 and 9.2, are called **prime**.

In order to generate all elements, it is necessary that the powers of the primitive element generate all elements of the extension field. If this is the case, the irreducible polynomial is called *primitive*.

Definition 9.4 An irreducible polynomial $p(x)$ with coefficients from $GF(P)$ and degree m that is used to define an element α by $p(\alpha) = 0$ is called **primitive** polynomial of $GF(P^m)$, if $\alpha^0 = \alpha^{P^m-1} = 1, \alpha^j \neq 1$ for $0 < j < P^m - 1$ and $\alpha^{j_1} \neq \alpha^{j_2}$ with $j_1 \neq j_2$ and $0 \leq j_1, j_2 < P^m - 1$.

For a later discussion of conjugates in $GF(P^m)$ and especially for introducing BCH codes, the following definition is required:

Definition 9.5 Let a monic polynomial $p(x)$ with coefficients from $GF(P)$ of degree m have a solution $x = \beta$ for $p(x) = 0$. If this polynomial has the lowest possible degree, it is called **minimal**.

---

[1] We do not consider multiple extensions. There we would have to start from $GF(P^{m_1})$ instead of $GF(P)$ to define $GF((P^{m_1})^{m_2}) = GF(P^{m_1 \cdot m_2})$.

Theorem 9.3 *A minimal polynomial $p(x)$ is irreducible.*

Proof If $p(x)$ can be factorized in $p(x) = p_1(x) \cdot p_2(x)$ and if the degrees of $p_1(x)$ and $p_2(x)$ are greater than zero, from $p(\beta) = p_1(\beta) \cdot p_2(\beta) = 0$ it follows that either $p_1(\beta) = 0$ or $p_2(\beta) = 0$. This is in contrast to the assumption that $p(x)$ should be the polynomial of lowest degree having the root β. □

The following theorem (without proof) ensures that there exists a suitable primitive polynomial with a corresponding primitive element for each field extension $GF(P^m)$.

Theorem 9.4 *For every prime field $GF(P)$ and every positive integer m, there exists at least one irreducible polynomial $p(x)$ with degree m over $GF(P)$ with the property that when defining $p(\alpha) = 0$, α will be a primitive element of $GF(P^m)$. This means that with $p(\alpha) = 0$, the $(P^m - 1)$ powers α^j mod $p(\alpha)$, $j = 1, \ldots (P^m - 1)$, (exponential representation) will be all $(P^m - 1)$ elements a unequal to zero of $GF(P^m)$ with $a = a_0 + a_1\alpha + \cdots + a_{m-1}\alpha^{m-1}$ (component representation), where $\alpha^{P^m-1} = \alpha^0 = 1$.*

If a primitive polynomial is found, also the one with mirrored coefficients will be primitive. We will state this in a more formal way, but will first require another definition.

Definition 9.6 Let $p(x) = p_0 + p_1x + \cdots + p_mx^m$ be a polynomial of degree m with coefficients from $GF(P)$. We denote

$$p'(x) = x^m \cdot p(1/x) = p_0x^m + p_1x^{m-1} + \cdots + p_{m-1}x + p_m$$

the corresponding **reciprocal** polynomial.

Theorem 9.5 *Let $p(x)$ be an irreducible polynomial in $GF(P)$. Then, the corresponding reciprocal polynomial will be irreducible, as well. If $p(x)$ is a primitive polynomial in $GF(P)$, the reciprocal polynomial will be primitive, too.*

In the following, we provide a table (entries taken from Table C.2 [1]) of some irreducible polynomials, where the complete and more detailed list can be found in [1]. The polynomials are given in octal representation and we indicate primitive polynomials by 'P', non-primitive ones by 'N'. Polynomials of lower degrees are without marking.

Let α denote the primitive element of the extension field. The first number then specifies the power α^j and then, the corresponding irreducible polynomial with the root α^j is given.

Table of irreducible polynomials [1]

Degree	j $p(x)$	j $p(x)$	j $p(x)$	j $p(x)$	j $p(x)$	j $p(x)$	j $p(x)$
2	1 7P						
3	1 13P						
4	1 23P	3 37N	5 07				
5	1 45P	3 75P	5 67P				
6	1 103P	3 127N	5 147P	7 111N	9 015	11 155P	21 007
7	1 211P	3 217P	5 235P	7 367P	9 277P	11 325P	13 203P
	19 313P	21 345P					
8	1 435P	3 567N	5 763N	7 551P	9 675N	11 747P	13 453P
	15 727N	17 023	19 545P	21 613N	23 543P	25 433N	27 477N
	37 537P	43 703P	45 471N	51 037	85 007		

Primitive polynomials of degrees 9 to 50 with minimum number of coefficients:

$$x^9+x^4+x^0$$
$$x^{10}+x^3+x^0$$
$$x^{11}+x^2+x^0$$
$$x^{12}+x^6+x^4+x^1+x^0$$
$$x^{13}+x^4+x^3+x^1+x^0$$
$$x^{14}+x^5+x^3+x^1+x^0$$
$$x^{15}+x^1+x^0$$
$$x^{16}+x^5+x^3+x^2+x^0$$
$$x^{17}+x^3+x^0$$
$$x^{18}+x^5+x^2+x^1+x^0$$
$$x^{19}+x^5+x^2+x^1+x^0$$
$$x^{20}+x^3+x^0$$
$$x^{21}+x^2+x^0$$
$$x^{22}+x^1+x^0$$
$$x^{23}+x^5+x^0$$
$$x^{24}+x^4+x^3+x^1+x^0$$
$$x^{25}+x^3+x^0$$
$$x^{26}+x^6+x^2+x^1+x^0$$
$$x^{27}+x^5+x^2+x^1+x^0$$
$$x^{28}+x^3+x^0$$
$$x^{29}+x^2+x^0$$
$$x^{30}+x^6+x^4+x^1+x^0$$
$$x^{31}+x^3+x^0$$
$$x^{32}+x^7+x^5+x^3+x^2+x^1+x^0$$
$$x^{33}+x^6+x^4+x^1+x^0$$
$$x^{34}+x^7+x^6+x^5+x^2+x^1+x^0$$
$$x^{35}+x^2+x^0$$
$$x^{36}+x^6+x^5+x^4+x^2+x^1+x^0$$
$$x^{37}+x^5+x^4+x^3+x^2+x^1+x^0$$
$$x^{38}+x^6+x^5+x^1+x^0$$
$$x^{39}+x^4+x^0$$
$$x^{40}+x^5+x^4+x^3+x^0$$
$$x^{41}+x^3+x^0$$
$$x^{42}+x^5+x^4+x^3+x^2+x^1+x^0$$
$$x^{43}+x^6+x^4+x^3+x^0$$
$$x^{44}+x^6+x^5+x^2+x^0$$
$$x^{45}+x^4+x^3+x^1+x^0$$
$$x^{46}+x^8+x^5+x^3+x^2+x^1+x^0$$
$$x^{47}+x^5+x^0$$
$$x^{48}+x^7+x^5+x^4+x^2+x^1+x^0$$
$$x^{49}+x^6+x^5+x^4+x^0$$
$$x^{50}+x^4+x^3+x^2+x^0$$

9.2.3 Log and Anti-Log Tables for Changing Between Exponential and Component Representation

In order to derive a simple means to determine the component from the exponential representation, we step-wise compute powers of α mod $p(\alpha)$. Starting from $\alpha^j = a_0 + a_1\alpha^1 + \cdots + a_{m-1}\alpha^{m-1}$, the computation mod $p(\alpha) = p_0 + p_1\alpha^1 + \cdots +$

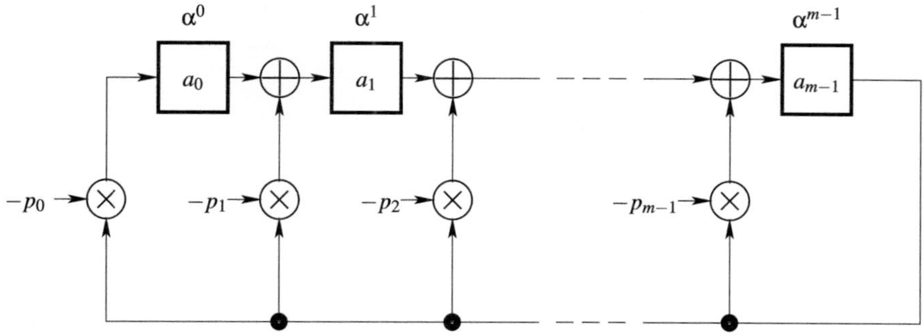

Fig. 9.1 Recursive shift register with a feedback given by the primitive polynomial to generate all elements of the multiplicative group of an extension field

$p_{m-1}\alpha^{m-1} + 1\alpha^m$, when increasing the power of α by one ($\alpha^{j+1} = \alpha^j \cdot \alpha$), leads to

$$\alpha^{j+1} = a_0\alpha^1 + a_1\alpha^2 + \cdots + a_{m-2}\alpha^{m-1} - a_{m-1}(p_0 + p_1\alpha^1 + \cdots + p_{m-1}\alpha^{m-1}).$$

We observe that this operation can be realized by the shift register in Fig. 9.1.

When starting from a shift register unequal to zero, e.g., with $\alpha^0 = 1$ (1 at leftmost position, otherwise zeros), all $P^m - 1$ elements of the multiplicative group of the extension field are run through.

We pick some of the primitive polynomials from the previous table, show the shift register, and provide the resulting correspondence tables for exponential/component representations (Figs. 9.2 to 9.4).

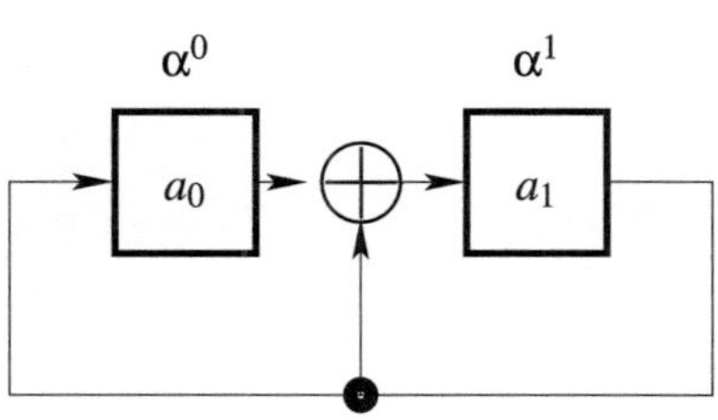

Fig. 9.2 Shift register to generate the correspondence table for $GF(2^2)$

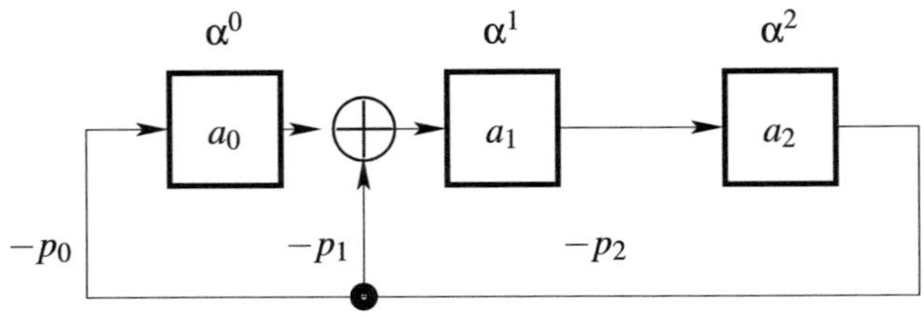

Fig. 9.3 Shift register to generate the correspondence table for $GF(2^3)$

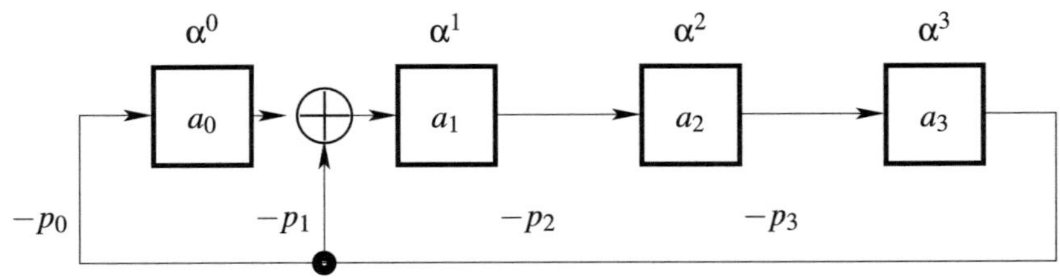

Fig. 9.4 Shift register to generate the correspondence table for $GF(2^4)$

Example 9.1 $GF(2^2)$ $p(x) \equiv 7_8 = 111_2 \Longrightarrow p(x) = 1 \cdot x^2 + 1 \cdot x^1 + 1 \cdot x^0 = x^2 + x + 1$ (Fig. 9.2)

Exponential representation α^j	*Component representation* a_0	a_1	*Decimal numbers* $a_0 \cdot 2^0 + a_1 \cdot 2^1$
	0	0	0
α^0	1	0	1
α^1	0	1	2
α^2	1	1	3

Example 9.2 $GF(2^3)$ $p(x) \equiv 13_8 = 001\,011_2 \Longrightarrow p(x) = 1 \cdot x^3 + 0 \cdot x^2 + 1 \cdot x^1 + 1 \cdot x^0 = x^3 + x + 1$ (Fig. 9.3)

Exponential representation α^j	*Component representation* a_0	a_1	a_2	*Decimal numbers* $a_0 \cdot 2^0 + a_1 \cdot 2^1 + a_2 \cdot 2^2$
	0	0	0	0
α^0	1	0	0	1
α^1	0	1	0	2
α^2	0	0	1	4
α^3	1	1	0	3
α^4	0	1	1	6
α^5	1	1	1	7
α^6	1	0	1	5

Example 9.3 $GF(2^4)$ $p(x) \equiv 23_8 = 010011_2 \Longrightarrow p(x) = 1 \cdot x^4 + 0 \cdot x^3 + 0 \cdot x^2 + 1 \cdot x^1 + 1 \cdot x^0 = x^4 + x + 1$ (Fig. 9.4)

Exponential representation α^j	*Component representation* a_0	a_1	a_2	a_3	*Decimal numbers* $a_0 \cdot 2^0 + a_1 \cdot 2^1 + a_2 \cdot 2^2 + a_3 \cdot 2^3$
	0	0	0	0	0
α^0	1	0	0	0	1
α^1					
α^2					
α^3					
α^4					
α^5					
α^6					
α^7					
α^8					
α^9					
α^{10}					
α^{11}					
α^{12}					
α^{13}					
α^{14}					

Note that in hardware or software implementations, the anti-log table may be chosen twice as large, including also the negative exponents. This avoids computations modulo $P^m - 1$ in the exponent, i.e., adding $P^m - 1$ in case of negative exponents before using the conversion table.

9.2.4 Synchronization Sequences m-Sequences, Barker Sequences

Since we have now seen how the extension field can be generated by a primitive polynomial, we are prepared to study the first application in form of the so-called m-sequences (also PN sequences that are, e.g., used for frame synchronization, noise generation, and as spreading sequences in CDMA (Code-Division Multiple Access). m-sequences are output sequences of shift register with taps given by primitive polynomials. Their length is thus $2^m - 1$ excluding the all-zeros state. The number of ones is 2^{m-1}, the number of zeros $2^{m-1} - 1$. If we again choose the symmetric 2-PSK signal set according to

$$+1 = (-1)^0 \longleftrightarrow 0 \qquad -1 = (-1)^1 \longleftrightarrow 1, \tag{9.2}$$

i.e.,

$$a_s = (-1)^{a_u} \quad \text{or} \quad a_s = 2 \cdot a_u - 1, \tag{9.3}$$

we obtain the cyclic autocorrelation function

$$R_0(j) = \begin{cases} 2^m - 1 & j = 0 \bmod 2^m - 1 \\ -1 & j \neq 0. \end{cases} \tag{9.4}$$

This results from the following considerations: first, the correlation equals the number of identical positions minus the number of different positions, i.e.,

$$R_0(j) = (N - d_H) - (d_H) = N - 2 \cdot d_H. \tag{9.5}$$

Regarding the set of cyclically shifted sequences as a linear and cyclic code, it has the parameters $(N = 2^m - 1, m, 2^{(m-1)})$. Since it is a linear code, the Hamming distance d_h between two codewords that differ by a cyclic shift equals the weight of another codeword (that can in this case also be obtained by a cyclic shift). We obtain

$$R_0(j) = N - 2 \cdot d_H = (2^m - 1) - 2 \cdot 2^{m-1} = -1, \quad j \neq 0 \tag{9.6}$$

The set of cyclically shifted m-sequences is also named *simplex code.*

The special property of the autocorrelation function is again depicted in Fig. 9.5.

Note that in order to see at least one period of this special correlation function when using a non-cyclic correlation, which would be used for frame-synchronization purposes, the m-sequence would have to be transmitted twice.

As further sequences with similar correlation properties, Barker and Barker-like sequences will be described. Barker sequences have either autocorrelations that are alternating between 0 and -1 outside of the maximum or have $-1, 0, +1$. Barker sequences do only exist up to a length of 13. However, Barker-like sequences (also non-binary ones) have been found up to lengths of around 50. Barker-like means that they were searched to have minimum further extrema in the autocorrelation function. Usually the absolute value of the further extrema is minimized. This is important in case of a phase uncertainty. If this should not be the case, negative maxima can be

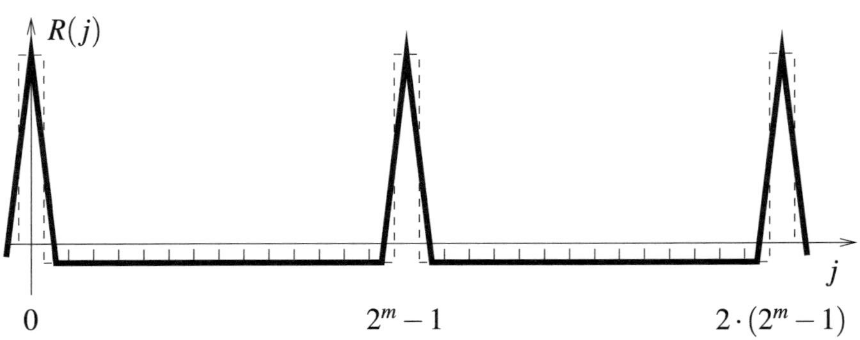

Fig. 9.5 Cyclic ACF of an m-sequence

tolerated. Note that for Barker sequences (and alike), a non-cyclic autocorrelation is computed, assuming zeros outside the sequence.

A table of the Barker sequences is given subsequently.

N	Barker sequences	Autocorrelation function $R_0(j)$
1	+	1
2	+ +	2 1
3	+ + −	3 0 −1
4	+ + + −	4 1 0 −1
5	+ + + − +	5 0 1 0 1
7	+ + + − − + −	7 0 −1 0 −1 0 −1
11	+ + + − − − + − − + −	11 0 −1 0 −1 0 −1 0 −1 0 −1
13	+ + + + + − − + + − + − +	13 0 1 0 1 0 1 0 1 0 1 0 1

All mirrored, inverse, and inverse/mirrored sequences are Barker sequences, too.

9.2.5 *Shift-Register Circuits for Multiplying and Dividing Polynomials*

After we have already described a shift-register structure to generate the elements of the extension field, we will now stud structures for the multiplication and division of polynomials. We will see that the already known shift register with the feedback given by the primitive polynomial is actually a division circuit.

At first, we will focus on the *multiplication* of two polynomials $i(x)$ and $g(x)$,

$$i(x) = i_{K-1}x^{K-1} + \cdots + i_1 x + i_0,$$
$$g(x) = g_M x^M + \cdots + g_1 x + g_0.$$

The coefficients of the product $c(x) = g(x) \cdot i(x)$ result from the convolution

$$c_j = \sum_{l=0}^{l=M} g_l \cdot i_{j-l}\,, \quad j = 0, \ldots, K + M - 1 \tag{9.7}$$

of the coefficients of the factor polynomials. The shift register in Fig. 9.6 realizes this convolution.

This structure is known as a transversal (FIR, Finite Impulse Response) filter. It is also known that there exist two canonical forms (see Sect. 4.1.3). Figure 9.7 shows these canonical realizations for the multiplication with $g(x) = x^8 + x^7 + x^4 + x^2 + x + 1$ over $GF(2)$.

The *division* of two polynomials $a(x)/g(x)$ can be written as follows, where we assumed $g(x)$ to be monic:

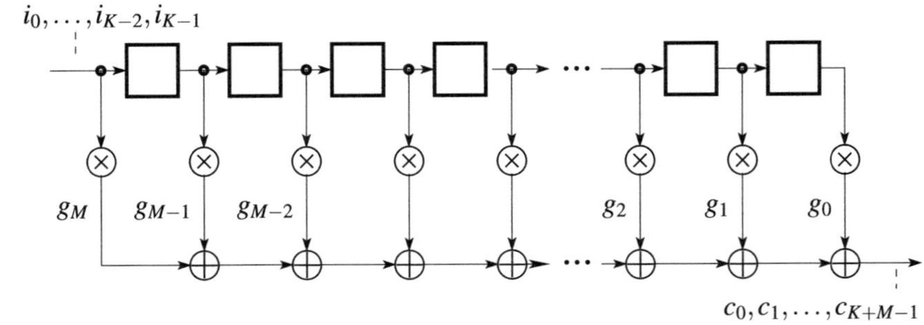

Fig. 9.6 Shift register for multiplying two polynomials $i(x)$ and $g(x)$

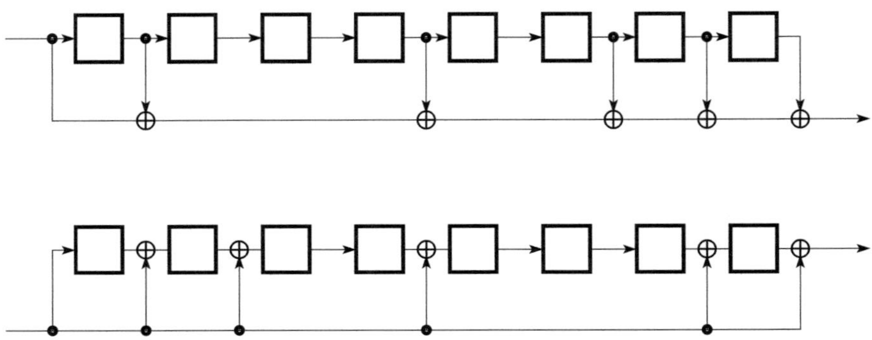

Fig. 9.7 Canonical shift registers for multiplying with $g(x) = x^8 + x^7 + x^4 + x^2 + x + 1$ over $GF(2)$

$$
\begin{array}{lll}
a_{N-1}x^{N-1} + & a_{N-2}x^{N-2} + \cdots + a_1 x + a_0 & : x^{N-K} + g_{N-K-1}x^{N-K-1} + \cdots + g_0 = \\
a_{N-1}x^{N-1} + & a_{N-1}g_{N-K-1}x^{N-2} + \cdots & \\
\hline
& (a_{N-2} - a_{N-1}g_{N-K-1})x^{N-2} + \cdots & \\
& (a_{N-2} - a_{N-1}g_{N-K-1})x^{N-2} + \cdots & \\
\hline
& \cdots &
\end{array}
$$

$$
= a_{N-1}x^{K-1} + (a_{N-2} - a_{N-1}g_{N-K-1})x^{K-2} + \cdots \tag{9.8}
$$

If we denote the iterative solutions, i.e., quotients as $Q^{(r)}(x)$ with $Q^{(0)}(x) = 0$ and the remainders as $R^{(r)}(x)$ with $R^{(0)}(x) = a(x)$, the division can be described by the recursions

$$
Q^{(r)}(x) = Q^{(r-1)}(x) + R^{(r-1)}_{N-r} \cdot x^{K-r} , \tag{9.9}
$$

$$
R^{(r)}(x) = R^{(r-1)}(x) - R^{(r-1)}_{N-r} \cdot x^{K-r} \cdot g(x) . \tag{9.10}
$$

After K iterations the quotient $Q^{(K)}(x)$ and the remainder $R^{(K)}(x)$ are obtained as the result of the division. The shift register structure in Fig. 9.8 realizes the recursions and is nothing else as the already known configuration for generating the elements

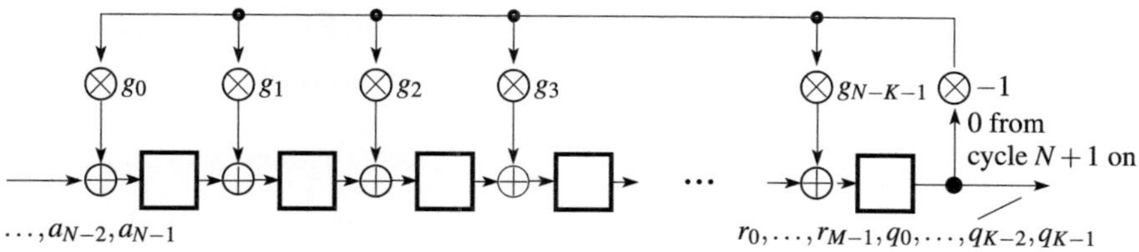

Fig. 9.8 Shift register to realize a division of polynomials $a(x)/g(x)$ ($g(x)$ monic)

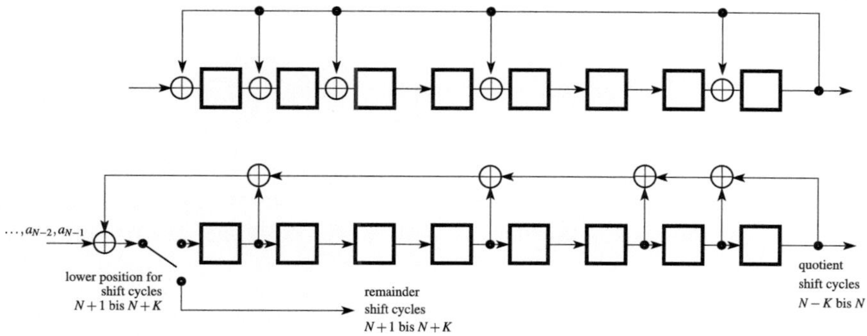

Fig. 9.9 Shift registers for dividing by $g(x) = x^8 + x^7 + x^4 + x^2 + x + 1$

(except zero) of an extension field. There we computed modulo a primitive polynomial, which is, of course, a division.

As an example, we consider the division by $g(x) = x^8 + x^7 + x^4 + x^2 + x + 1$ in Fig. 9.9. An alternative realization is obtained when performing the operations in the polynomial division (9.8) at equal powers.

The second realization is especially suited for generating m-sequences. In Sects. 9.2.3 and 9.2.4, we presented the first realization which is actually less suited because of the additions between shift-register cells.

9.2.6 Conjugates in $GF(P^m)$

We again make use of the analogy to the complex numbers. If a polynomial with *real* coefficients $f(x) = x^2 + f_1 x + f_0 = 0,\ f_0, f_1 \in \mathbb{R}$ has a complex root β_1, it also has its conjugate $\beta_2 = \beta_1^\star$ as root. We can thus factorize $f(x)$ as $f(x) = (x - \beta_1) \cdot (x - \beta_2) = (x - \beta_1) \cdot (x - \beta_1^\star)$. With $\beta_1 = b_0 + b_1\alpha$, we obtain $f(x) = (x - b_0 - b_1\alpha) \cdot (x - b_0 + b_1\alpha) = x^2 - 2b_0x + b_0^2 + b_1^2$. In the case of complex number, complex roots of polynomials with real coefficients will always be in conjugate pairs $\beta_1 = b_0 + b_1\alpha = |\beta_1|e^{+\alpha\phi}$ and $\beta_1^\star = b_0 - b_1\alpha = |\beta_1|e^{-\alpha\phi}$.

In extension fields of finite number fields there are also conjugates, however, not necessarily just two. For a more detailed treatment, we still require some properties of extension fields $GF(P^m)$.

We recall that powers of elements $\beta \in GF(P^m)$ have a maximum order of $P^m - 1$, i.e., they solve the equation[2]

$$x^{(P^m-1)} - 1 = 0. \tag{9.11}$$

Since each element of $GF(P^m)\backslash 0$ fulfills this equation, on the one hand, the factorization within the extension field will be

$$x^{(P^m-1)} - 1 = \prod_{\beta_j \in GF(P^m)\backslash 0} (x - \beta_j). \tag{9.12}$$

On the other hand, a unique factorization over $GF(P)$ with prime (irreducible and monic) polynomials is possible, as well (similar to prime factorization of an integer):

$$x^{(P^m-1)} - 1 = f_1(x) \cdots f_\nu(x). \tag{9.13}$$

Galois fields $GF(q = P^m)$ have the interesting property that powers P^μ of polynomials can be performed component-wise. This has no counterpart in complex algebra. This property we will then use to investigate the roots of polynomials $f_j(x)$.

Theorem 9.6 *Let P be the characteristic of a finite field $GF(q = P^m)$. For each polynomial $s(x)$ over $GF(q)$ and each number $\mu \in \mathbb{Z}$ we have*

$$\left[\sum_{j=0}^{l} s_j x^j\right]^{P^\mu} = \sum_{j=0}^{l} s_j^{(P^\mu)} x^{(j \cdot P^\mu)} \tag{9.14}$$

Proof First we consider $\mu = 1$ and separate the term s_0 from $s(x)$, i.e., $s(x) = s'(x) \cdot x + s_0$. A Pth power now yields

$$[s(x)]^P = \sum_{j=0}^{P} \binom{P}{j} [s'(x) \cdot x]^j s_0^{P-j}. \tag{9.15}$$

The binomial coefficient is equal to zero for $j \neq 0, P$.

$$\binom{P}{j} = \frac{P!}{j!(P-j)!} = \frac{P(P-1)!}{j!(P-j)!} \tag{9.16}$$

[2] The corresponding relation for complex numbers would be $x^N = 1$ with solutions $x = e^{j\frac{2\pi}{N}k}$, $k = 0..N-1$.

Since P is a prime number, the denominator has to divide $(P-1)!$. This means that the binomial coefficient has to be a multiple of P. Since our arithmetic is modulo P, $\binom{P}{j} = 0$ for $j \neq 0, P$. For $j = 0, P$ we have $\binom{P}{j} = 1$. Hence, we obtain

$$[s(x)]^P = [s'(x)]^P \cdot x^P + s_0^P \tag{9.17}$$

$s'(x)$ can be split in the same way, finally leading to

$$[s(x)]^P = \sum_{j=0}^{l} s_j^P x^{jP}. \tag{9.18}$$

For $\mu = 2$, we obtain

$$[s(x)]^{P^2} = [[s(x)]^P]^P = \left[\sum_{j=0}^{l} s_j^P x^{jP}\right]^P = \sum_{j=0}^{l} s_j^{(P^2)} x^{(jP^2)}. \tag{9.19}$$

It is now obvious that the theorem is valid for all $\mu \in \mathbb{Z}$ □

With the following theorem, we are approaching the investigation of zeros of a minimal polynomial with coefficients from $GF(P)$ and the conjugates.

Theorem 9.7 *Let $f(x)$ be a minimal polynomial over $GF(P)$ with a root $\beta \in GF(P^m)$. Then $f(x)$ is also a minimal polynomial of β^P.*

Proof To prove, let us consider the Pth power of the minimal polynomial $f(x)$

$$[f(x)]^P = \sum_{j=0}^{\text{degree } f(x)} f_j^P (x^P)^j. \tag{9.20}$$

$\gamma^P = \gamma$ for every element γ of a Galois field $GF(P)$, leading to

$$[f(x)]^P = \sum_{j=0}^{\text{degree } f(x)} f_j (x^P)^j = f(x^P). \tag{9.21}$$

From $f(\beta) = 0$, we then obtain

$$0 = [f(\beta)]^P = \sum_{j=0}^{\text{degree } f(x)} f_j (\beta^P)^j = f(\beta^P). \tag{9.22}$$

A minimal polynomial for β is at the same time also a minimal polynomial for β^P. □

Definition 9.7 Elements of $GF(P^m)$ that are zeros of the same minimal polynomial are called **conjugates**.

The conjugates can at once be listed when taking into account that $\beta^{(P^m)} = \beta$:

$$\left\{\beta, \beta^P, \beta^{(P^2)}, \beta^{(P^3)}, \ldots, \beta^{(P^{r-1})}\right\} \tag{9.23}$$

r is the degree of the minimal polynomial and the smallest integer with $\beta^{(P^r)} = \beta$.

Theorem 9.8 *The minimal polynomial of a field element $\beta \in GF(P^m)$ is given by*

$$f(x) = (x - \beta)(x - \beta^P)\ldots(x - \beta^{(P^{r-1})}) \tag{9.24}$$

At the same time this means $\beta \in GF(P^r)$. $GF(P^r)$ is the smallest extension field of $GF(P)$ that contains β.

Proof We already know that $f(x)$ has the given roots. We have to prove that $f(x)$ only has coefficients from the subfield $GF(P)$.
From Theorem 9.6, we know

$$[f(x)]^P = \left[\sum_j f_j x^j\right]^P = \sum_j f_j^P x^{jP}. \tag{9.25}$$

From the factorized representation, we obtain with $\beta^{(P^r)} = \beta$

$$[f(x)]^P = (x - \beta)^P (x - \beta^P)^P \ldots (x - \beta^{(P^{r-1})})^P = (x^P - \beta^P)(x^P - \beta^{(P^2)})\ldots(x^P - \beta) \tag{9.26}$$

$$\Longleftrightarrow [f(x)]^P = f(x^P) = \sum_j f_j x^{jP}. \tag{9.27}$$

When comparing with (9.25), we obtain $f_i^P = f_i$. Hence, the coefficients f_i are elements of the subfield $GF(P)$. □

We illustrate this with two examples.

Example 9.4 Let $p(x) = 1 + x + x^3$ be a primitive and thus also irreducible and minimal polynomial of degree $m = 3$ over $GF(P = 2)$. From it, we define the extension field $GF(2^3)$ by means of the primitive element α, the root of $p(\alpha)$, i.e., $\alpha^3 = 1 + \alpha$.

- With the root α, in total, $p(x)$ has $m = 3$ roots $\alpha, \alpha^2, \alpha^4$ that are conjugates (over $GF(2)$) ($\alpha^8 = \alpha^7 \cdot \alpha = 1 \cdot \alpha$, since $\alpha^{(2^m-1)} = \alpha^7 = 1$).
- If we would have started from $\beta = \alpha^2$, the same conjugated roots (over $GF(2)$) would have shown up, namely $\beta = \alpha^2$, $\beta^2 = \alpha^4$, $\beta^4 = \alpha^8 = \alpha$ ($\beta^8 = \alpha^2 = \beta$).

Proof: $p(x) \stackrel{?}{=} (x-\alpha)(x-\alpha^2)(x-\alpha^4) = (x+\alpha)(x+\alpha^2)(x+\alpha^4)$
$= \alpha \cdot \alpha^2 \cdot \alpha^4 + (\alpha\alpha^2 + \alpha\alpha^4 + \alpha^2\alpha^4) \cdot x + (\alpha + \alpha^2 + \alpha^4) \cdot x^2 + x^3$
$= \alpha^7 + ([1+\alpha] + [1+\alpha+\alpha^2] + \underbrace{[1+\alpha]^2}_{[1+\alpha^2]}) \cdot x + (\alpha + \alpha^2 + [\alpha+\alpha^2]) \cdot x^2 + x^3$
$= 1 + 1 \cdot x + 0 \cdot x^2 + x^3$

Example 9.5 A primitive polynomial over $GF(2)$ with degree $m = 4$ is $p(x) = 1 + x + x^4$. With it, we define a primitive element α for $GF(2^4)$ by $p(\alpha) = 0$ or $\alpha^4 = 1 + \alpha$. We have $\alpha^{(2^4-1)} = \alpha^{15} = 1$, but $\alpha^j \neq 1$ for $j = 1, 2, \ldots, 14$.

We are first sorting the 15 different elements α^j according to their conjugacy relations (over $GF(2)$).

$$\begin{array}{ll}
\alpha^1, \alpha^2, \alpha^4, \alpha^8 & (\alpha^{16} = \alpha^1)\ r = 4 \\
\alpha^3, \alpha^6, \alpha^{12}, \alpha^{24} = \alpha^9 & (\alpha^{18} = \alpha^3)\ r = 4 \\
\alpha^5, \alpha^{10} & (\alpha^{20} = \alpha^5)\ r = 2 \\
\alpha^7, \alpha^{14}, \alpha^{28} = \alpha^{13}, \alpha^{26} = \alpha^{11} & (\alpha^{22} = \alpha^7)\ r = 4 \\
\alpha^0 = 1 & r = 1
\end{array}$$

The set of conjugate roots is called **cyclotomic coset**.
The products of the corresponding linear factors will result in

$$\begin{array}{lll}
(x-\alpha)(x-\alpha^2)(x-\alpha^4)(x-\alpha^8) & = 1 + x + x^4 & =: m_1(x) \\
(x-\alpha^3)(x-\alpha^6)(x-\alpha^{12})(x-\alpha^9) & = 1 + x + x^2 + x^3 + x^4 & =: m_3(x) \\
(x-\alpha^5)(x-\alpha^{10}) & = 1 + x + x^2 & =: m_5(x) \\
(x-\alpha^7)(x-\alpha^{14})(x-\alpha^{13})(x-\alpha^{11}) & = 1 + x^3 + x^4 & =: m_7(x) \\
(x-\alpha^0) & = 1 + x & =: m_0(x)
\end{array}$$

The index j of the minimal polynomial m_j denotes that α^j is the root of $m_j(x)$. It is called **coset representative**.

Since the primitive element α is of order $N = 2^4 - 1 = 15$, the 15 roots of $x^{15} - 1$ are the α^j, $j = 0, 1, 2, \ldots, 14$ and we have

$$x^{15} - 1 = \prod_{j=0}^{14} (x - \alpha^j) = m_0(x) \cdot m_1(x) \cdot m_3(x) \cdot m_5(x) \cdot m_7(x) \tag{9.28}$$

Adding the zero element as an additional root, we obtain

$$x(x^{15} - 1) = x^{16} - x = (x - 0) \cdot (x - 1) \cdot m_1(x) \cdot m_3(x) \cdot m_5(x) \cdot m_7(x) \tag{9.29}$$

This is (without proof) the product of all irreducible polynomials of degrees $r = 1, 2,$ and 4 over $GF(P = 2)$.

At the end of this chapter, we gather some important further theorems.

Theorem 9.9 *Let* $n, r, s \in \mathbb{Z}$ *with* $n \geq 2, r \geq 1, s \geq 1$*; then we obtain*

$$n^s - 1 | n^r - 1 \Longleftrightarrow s | r. \tag{9.30}$$

Theorem 9.10 $x^{P^m} - x$ *is the product of all irreducible monic polynomials of degrees* r *over* $GF(P)$*, with* r *running through all divisors of* m *(incl.* $r = 1$ *and* $r = m$*).*

Theorem 9.11 $GF(P^m)$ *contains the subfields* $GF(P^r)$*, with* r *being a divisor of* m *(incl.* $r = 1$ *and* $r = m$*).*

Theorem 9.12 *Let* r *be the greatest common divisor of* m_1 *and* m_2*. Then,* $GF(P^r)$ *is the set of common elements from* $GF(P^{m_1})$ *and* $GF(P^{m_2})$*. In the case of different characteristics* $P_1 \neq P_2$*,* $GF(P_1^m)$ *and* $GF(P_2^m)$ *do only have the zero element in common.*

Theorem 9.13 *Let* n *and the characteristic* P *of an extension field* $GF(P^m)$ *be relative prime. Then, there exists an* m *for which* $x^n - 1$ *is a divisor of* $x^{(P^m - 1)} - 1$*.* $x^n - 1$ *has* n *different roots in* $GF(P^m)$*.*

Reference

1. W. Peterson and J. Weldon, E.J., *Error-Correcting Codes*, 6th ed. Cambridge, Massachusetts and London, England: MIT Press, 1981.

Chapter 10
Reed–Solomon Codes

Impulse strikes the low-pass wave,
Filters smooth what noise once gave.
Coding listens high to mend,
Both low and high, it helps defend.

ChatGPT-generated poem on Coding versus Signal Processing

Reed–Solomon codes are one of the most important codes in applications. They are applied in numerous modern transmission and storage system. One may just think of the CD player, ADSL, optical and wireless transmission. These block codes are not bit-, but symbol-oriented, a symbol consisting of some bits (over $GF(2^m)$, e.g., a byte). They are thus very suited for the correction of bursts. For practical applications, the existence of powerful en- and decoding algorithms are essential. RS codes fulfill the Singleton bound with equality. This property is also named *MDS (Maximum Distance Separable)*. It is also advantageous that the weight distribution can be computed easily. This simplifies error probability approximations. RS codes are based on the discrete Fourier transform. Before we will introduce it over finite fields, in the following section, we will illustrate encoding (and decoding) as a polynomial interpolation.

10.1 Encoding as a Polynomial Interpolation

A polynomial $a(x) = a_0 + a_1x + \cdots + a_{K-1}x^{K-1}$ of degree $K-1$ can be formulated dependent on given samples by means of so-called 'continuous' Kronecker delta functions $\delta_j(x)$. $a(x)$ is then given by the Lagrange interpolation

W. Henkel, *Channel Coding*, Signals and Communication Technology,
https://doi.org/10.1007/978-3-032-08236-7_10

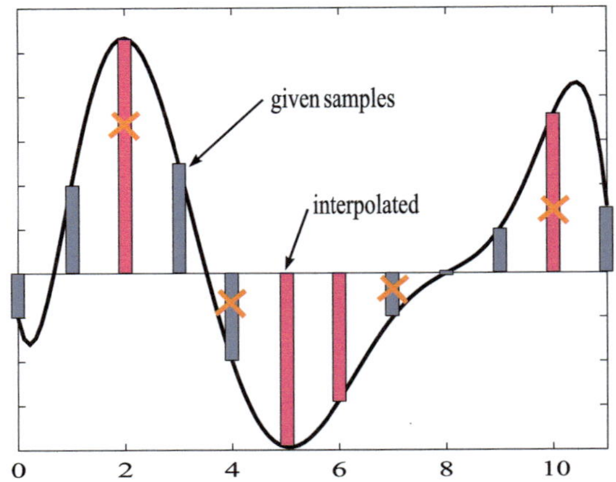

Fig. 10.1 Encoding as a polynomial interpolation

$$a(x) = \sum_{j=0}^{K-1} \delta_j(x) \cdot a(x_j) \tag{10.1}$$

$$\delta_j(x) = \frac{\prod\limits_{\substack{k=0,\dots,K-1\\ k\neq j}} (x - x_k)}{\prod\limits_{\substack{k=0,\dots,K-1\\ k\neq j}} (x_j - x_k)} = \frac{\prod_{k=0}^{K-1}(x - x_k)}{(x - x_j)\cdot\left[\frac{d}{dx}\prod_{k=0}^{K-1}(x - x_k)\right]_{x=x_j}} \tag{10.2}$$

For the delta function, we have

$$\delta_j(x) = \begin{cases} 1 & \text{if } x = x_j \\ 0 & \text{if } x = x_k\,,\ k = 0,\dots,K-1\,,\ x \neq x_j \end{cases} \tag{10.3}$$

With the delta functions, it is straight forward to compute further $N - K$ samples as a function of the K given samples assuming that the underlying polynomial is of limited degree $K - 1$. Figure 10.1 shows an interpolating polynomial of degree 7 with 8 predefined samples. Four further samples have been computed. These four samples are redundant, since the interpolating polynomial is already uniquely defined by 8 samples. Adding these four samples can be considered as an encoding. One may think of the 12 samples as a transmitted codeword. Let us imagine that four errors have occurred at known positions. Since the polynomial is uniquely defined by any arbitrary 8 samples, with 8 error-free samples, all 12 samples can again be recomputed. This procedure is called erasure decoding, the correction of errors at known positions.

In the following section, we will introduce the link between the polynomial interpolation and the DFT. To illustrate this already here, let us think of time-domain codeword samples to be located around the unit circle as shown in Fig. 10.2. For

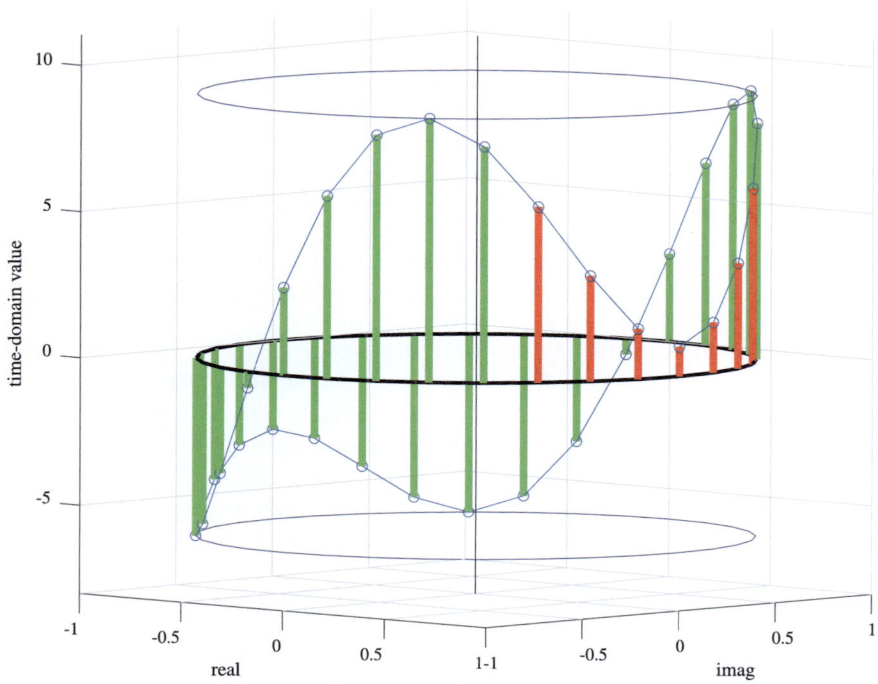

Fig. 10.2 Analog BCH code (RS code with conjugacy constraints)

drawing purposes, we are additionally forcing the time domain to be real by requiring DFT-domain components to be conjugate symmetric. This, the reader might later recognize as a complex BCH code after having read Chap. 11. In the figure, red bars stand for information symbols in time domain (original domain), while green ones represent redundant ones.

10.2 Reed–Solomon Codes and the Discrete Fourier Transform

In a finite field, only a finite number of samples can be used. This results from the powers of an *element of order* N. Let us, e.g., consider all the elements of an extension field $GF(P^m)$. Then there are $P^m - 1$ elements that can be generated as powers of the primitive element. This means that the possible code length would be $N = P^m - 1$. The values at these positions again result from a polynomial of degree $K - 1$. In an extension field, however, there are also elements of order N with $N|P^m - 1$.

From the limited degree of the polynomial $C(x)$, one can immediately make statements regarding the minimum distance = minimum weight of the resulting codes. At first, we recall the so-called **fundamental theorem of algebra**.

Theorem 10.1 *A polynomial* $C(x) = C_0 + C_1x + C_2x^2 + \ldots C_{K-1}x^{K-1}$ *of degree* $K-1$ *has at most* $K-1$ *different roots* x_j. *Hence, the polynomial can be factorized as* $C(x) = C_{K-1} \cdot (x - x_1) \cdot (x - x_2) \cdots (x - x_{K-1}) = C_{K-1} \cdot \prod_{j=1}^{K-1}(x - x_j)$.

With this, we can immediately provide a statement on the minimum weight and with it on the minimum distance of a code defined by a degree-limited polynomial.

Theorem 10.2 *Let* $C(x)$ *be a polynomial of degree* $K-1 = N-M-1$ *with arbitrary coefficients from a field* $\mathbb{F}$. *If we compute the values of the polynomial at* N *different positions* $x = x_j,\ x_j \in \mathbb{F},\ j = 0, \ldots, N-1$, *the vector of* N *samples* $(C(x_0), C(x_1), \ldots, C(x_{N-1}))$ *has minimum weight* $w_{Hm} = M + 1 = N - K + 1$. *Since the sum of two such vectors is equivalent to the sum of the corresponding polynomial coefficients, the sum of vectors fulfills the degree limitation, too. Thus, it is a linear code. The minimum distance is equal to the minimum weight.*

Proof The number of zeros cannot exceed $K-1 = N-M-1$. Hence, at least, $N-(K-1) = M+1$ positions have to be non-zero. □

This theorem also specifies an important property that is named as follows:

Definition 10.1 A **Maximum Distance Separable (MDS)** code fulfills the Singleton bound ($d_{Hm} \leq M+1 = N-K+1$) with equality.

According to the previous theorem this is the case. We will now formally define Reed–Solomon codes. (This definition will later be generalized.)

Definition 10.2 A **Reed–Solomon (RS) code** of length N and minimum Hamming distance d_{Hm} is the set of vectors, whose components are values of a polynomial $C(x)$ of degree $\leq K-1 = N-d_{Hm}$ at the positions z^j, with z being an element of order N from an arbitrary number field. We are, of course, especially interested in $z \in GF(P^m)$, $z^N = 1$, $z^j \neq 1$ for $0 < j < N$.

$$c = (c_0, \ldots, c_{N-1})\ , \quad c_j = C(x = z^j) \tag{10.4}$$

Example 10.1 $GF(P=7)$, primitive element: $z = 5$, order $N = P - 1 = 6$
We specify an RS code of length $N = 6$ with correction capability of $t = 2$ symbols. From $d_{Hm} \geq 2 \cdot t + 1$ follows the maximum degree of the polynomial $K - 1 = N - d_{Hm} = 6 - 5 = 1$. The degree-limited polynomial exists only of two components C_0, C_1. Since every component can assume $P = 7$ values, the code consists of $7 \cdot 7 = 49$ codewords.

Let the information be localized in the coefficients of the polynomial. With $C(x) = C_0 + C_1x = 3 + 1 \cdot x$, we obtain

$$
\begin{aligned}
c_0 &= C(x = z^0 = 1) = 3 + 1 \cdot 1 = 4 \\
c_1 &= C(x = z^1 = 5) = 3 + 1 \cdot 5 = 1 \\
c_2 &= C(x = z^2 = 4) = 3 + 1 \cdot 4 = 0 \\
&\vdots \\
c &= (c_0, \ldots, c_5) = (4, 1, 0, 2, 5, 6)
\end{aligned}
$$

The definition of RS codes by means of a polynomial at positions z^j with z being an element of order N reminds us to the well-known discrete Fourier transform that we will write in a maybe somewhat unusual form. Let us for a moment assume that the considered polynomial $C(x)$ has full degree $N-1$. Then we would have

$$
c_j = C(x = z^j) = \sum_{k=0}^{N-1} C_k z^{jk} \tag{10.5}
$$

This is nothing else than the IDFT from the DFT domain into the original domain. In the following, we again define forward and backward transforms of the DFT. We write the inverse transform first, since we have already introduced it. We could also have defined the first relation as the 'forward' transform; however, we would like to have a relation to time and frequency domain.

Definition 10.3 Let $C = (C_0, C_1, \ldots, C_{N-1})$ be the coefficient vector of a polynomial $C(x) = C_0 + C_1 x + \cdots + C_{N-1} x^{N-1}$ and let z be an element of order N (i.e., $z^N = 1$, but $z^j \neq 1$ for $0 < j < N$). The **discrete Fourier transform (DFT)** and its inverse transform (IDFT) are defined to be

IDFT:

$$
c_j = C(x = z^j) = \sum_{k=0}^{N-1} C_k z^{jk}\,, \quad j = 0, 1, \ldots, N-1\,, \tag{10.6}
$$

DFT:

$$
C_k = N^{-1} \cdot c(x = z^{-k}) = N^{-1} \cdot \sum_{j=0}^{N-1} c_j z^{-jk}\,, \quad k = 0, 1, \ldots, N-1\,, \tag{10.7}
$$

where we again have written the vector $\mathbf{c} = (c_0, c_1, \ldots, c_{N-1})$ as a polynomial $c(x) = c_0 + c_1 x + \cdots + c_{N-1} x^{N-1}$.

Note the alternative description of vectors as polynomials which is often used in coding theory.

We will provide the proof that the DFT transform is uniquely invertible.

Proof We start from (10.7):

$$\begin{aligned}
N^{-1} \cdot c(x = z^{-k}) &= N^{-1} \cdot \sum_{j=0}^{N-1} c_j z^{-jk} \\
&= N^{-1} \cdot \sum_{j=0}^{N-1} \left(\sum_{l=0}^{N-1} C_l z^{jl} \right) z^{-jk} \\
&= N^{-1} \cdot \sum_{l=0}^{N-1} C_l \sum_{j=0}^{N-1} z^{j(l-k)} \\
&= N^{-1} \cdot \sum_{l=0}^{N-1} C_l \sum_{j=0}^{N-1} \gamma^j \,, \quad \gamma = z^{l-k}
\end{aligned}$$

The geometric series $\sum_{j=0}^{N-1} \gamma^j$ is equal to

$$\sum_{j=0}^{N-1} \gamma^j = \begin{cases} N & \text{for } \gamma = z^{l-k} = 1, \text{ i.e., } l = k \\ \frac{\gamma^N - 1}{\gamma - 1} = 0 & \text{for } \gamma = z^{l-k} \neq 1, \text{ i.e., } l \neq k, \text{ but } \gamma^N = z^{N(l-k)} = 1\,. \end{cases}$$

Hence, in the transformation, only $N^{-1} \cdot c(x = z^{-k}) = N^{-1} \cdot C_k \cdot N$ is left, as required. □

In a prime field $GF(P)$, we have for $N = P - 1$: $N^{-1} = N = P - 1$, since $(P-1)(P-1) = P^2 - 2P + 1 = 1 \bmod P$. In an extension field of the binary numbers $GF(2^m)$, we even have $1/N = 1/(2^m - 1) = 1$.

In the following, we will recall some important properties of the discrete Fourier transform; especially, we are interested in the convolution and shift properties. Hereto, we note that in the polynomials we replace x by a power of an element of order N, i.e., x has the property $x^N = 1$. This allows to compute mod $(x^N - 1)$, i.e., x^N can be replaced by 1.

First, we will apply this property when multiplying two polynomials. Since we compute mod $(x^N - 1)$, the result will not have a degree higher than $N - 1$.

$$(a_0 + a_1 x + \cdots + a_{N-1} x^{N-1}) \cdot (b_0 + b_1 x + \cdots + b_{N-1} x^{N-1}) = c_0 + c_1 x + \cdots + c_{N-1} x^{N-1} \tag{10.8}$$

$$\begin{aligned}
c_0 &= b_0 \cdot a_0 + b_1 \cdot a_{N-1} + b_2 \cdot a_{N-2} + \cdots + b_{N-1} \cdot a_1 \\
c_1 &= b_0 \cdot a_1 + b_1 \cdot a_0 + b_2 \cdot a_{N-1} + \cdots + b_{N-1} \cdot a_2 \\
&\vdots \\
c_j &= \sum_{l=0}^{N-1} b_l \cdot a_{j-l \bmod N}
\end{aligned}$$

This is nothing else than the *cyclic convolution* of the coefficients of the vectors $\mathbf{a} = (a_0, a_1, \ldots, a_{N-1})$ and $\mathbf{b} = (b_0, b_1, \ldots, b_{N-1})$ that we are used to indicate with a '$\star$'.

$$\mathbf{a} \star \mathbf{b} \equiv a(x) \cdot b(x) \bmod (x^N - 1) \tag{10.9}$$

The following table (Eq. (10.10)) collects the convolution and shift properties of the DFT.

Original domain	DFT domain
$c_j = a_j \cdot b_j$	$C(x) = A(x) \cdot B(x)$, $C_k = \sum_{l=0}^{N-1} A_l \cdot B_{k-l \bmod N}$
$c(x) = N^{-1} a(x) \cdot b(x)$, $c_j = N^{-1} \cdot \sum_{l=0}^{N-1} a_l \cdot b_{j-l \bmod N}$	$A_k \cdot B_k$
$c_{j \bmod N} = a_{j-l \bmod N}$, $c(x) = a(x) \cdot x^l \bmod (x^N - 1)$	$C_k = A_k \cdot z^{-k \cdot l}$
$c_j = a_j \cdot z^{j \cdot l}$	$C_{k \bmod N} = A_{k-l \bmod N}$, $C(x) = A(x) \cdot x^l \bmod (x^N - 1)$

(10.10)

We shortly prove the two convolution theorems.

Proof 1*st* convolution theorem:

$$c_j = C(x = z^j) = A(x = z^j) \cdot B(x = z^j) = a_j \cdot b_j$$

2*nd* convolution theorem:

$$C_k = N^{-1} \cdot c(x = z^{-k}) = N^{-1} \cdot a(x = z^{-k}) \cdot N^{-1} \cdot b(x = z^{-k}) = A_k \cdot B_k$$

□

From the shift theorem in the DFT domain, we conclude an important property of RS codes allowing us to extend their definition. The shift theorem tells us that zeros stay unchanged and no new ones will be added when cyclically shifting the transform domain, i.e., the minimum distance is preserved.

Definition 10.4 (*extended version*) A **Reed–Solomon (RS) code** of length N and minimum Hamming distance d_{Hm} is a set of vectors, whose components are the values of a polynomial $C(x) = x^j \cdot C'(x)$ of degree$\{C'(x)\} \leq K - 1 = N - d_{Hm}$ at positions z^j, with z being an element of order N from an arbitrary number field.

$$c = (c_0, \ldots, c_{N-1}) \, , \quad c_j = C(x = z^j) \tag{10.11}$$

Before we will proceed to means of encoding, we will discuss some properties that will then be required.

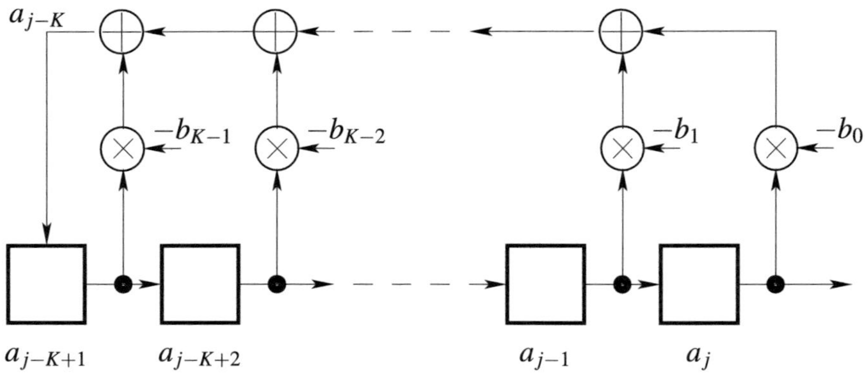

Fig. 10.3 Shift register of the convolution in Eq. (10.12)

First, we study the case when a product of two polynomials $a(x) \cdot b(x) = 0 \bmod (x^N - 1) = (\ldots) \cdot (x^N - 1)$. Since the product of two polynomials corresponds to the convolution of their coefficients, we obtain under the additional assumption that $b(x)$ is monic ($\text{degree}\{b(x)\} = K < N - 1, b_K = 1$)

$$0 = \sum_{l=0}^{N-1} b_l \cdot a_{j-l \bmod N} = 1 \cdot a_{j-K \bmod N} + \sum_{l=0}^{K-1} b_l \cdot a_{j-l \bmod N} \qquad (10.12)$$

This recursion can be realized by the shift register in Fig. 10.3.

Furthermore, we will require the fact that zeros in the original or transform domain will correspond to linear factors of the polynomial description in the transform or original domain, respectively.

$$c_j = 0 \Longleftrightarrow C(x) = (\ldots) \cdot (x - z^{+j}) \qquad (10.13)$$

$$C_{N-j} = 0 \Longleftrightarrow c(x) = (\ldots) \cdot (x - z^{+j}) \qquad (10.14)$$

All possible linear factors together yield

$$x^N - 1 = \prod_{j=0}^{N-1} (x - z^j) \qquad (10.15)$$

This follows from the fact that $(x^N - 1)$ can at most have N roots. Furthermore, since z is an element of order N, all N different powers z^j, $j = 0, 1, \ldots, N - 1$ are roots of $x^N - 1$ $((z^j)^N = (z^N)^j = 1)$.

10.3 Encoding

We have described RS codes by a degree-limited polynomial, i.e., requiring $M = 2t$ subsequent zeros from index K to $N-1$ of the DFT vector (not mentioning cylic shifts). How will we now choose the relation between K information symbols and the codewords? In principal, there are two possibilities. On one hand, the information can, of course, directly be chosen to be the K DFT-domain samples. An IDFT yields the code vector. On the other hand, the K samples can be specified in time domain and a polynomial interpolation would yield the other samples taking into account the limited degree of the polynomial. We thus distinguish between methods in DFT and in the original (time) domain. Usually, one of four different methods is applied. In the sequel, we will describe these four options.

10.3.1 Encoding in DFT Domain

As has been mentioned, the information can just be put into $K = N - 2t$ subsequent positions in DFT domain. We first write the IDFT as a matrix operation.

$$\mathbf{c} = \mathbf{C} \cdot \begin{pmatrix} 1 & 1 & 1 & 1 & \cdots \\ 1 & z^1 & z^2 & z^3 & \\ 1 & z^2 & z^4 & z^6 & \\ 1 & z^3 & z^6 & z^9 & \\ \vdots & & & & \ddots \end{pmatrix} \tag{10.16}$$

Let the information be $\mathbf{C} = (I_0, I_1, \ldots, I_{K-1}, \underbrace{0, \ldots, 0}_{2t=d_{Hm}-1})$. This yields the set of linear equations

$$\mathbf{c} = (I_0, I_1, \ldots, I_{K-1}) \cdot \begin{pmatrix} 1 & 1 & 1 & 1 & \cdots & 1 \\ 1 & z^1 & z^2 & z^3 & & \\ 1 & z^2 & z^4 & z^6 & & \\ \vdots & & & & & \\ 1 & z^{K-1} & z^{2(K-1)} & z^{3(K-1)} & \cdots & z^{(N-1)(K-1)} \end{pmatrix}. \tag{10.17}$$

In order to realize this as a shift register, we rewrite the equations, following the so-called Horner scheme, as

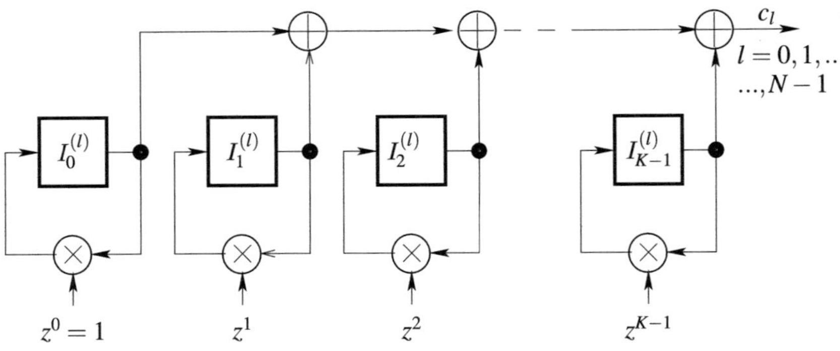

Fig. 10.4 IDFT shift register

$$\begin{array}{llllll} c_0 = C(z^0 = 1) & = I_0 & +I_1 & +I_2 & + \cdots + I_{K-1} \\ c_1 = C(z^1) & = I_0 & +I_1 \cdot z^1 & +I_2 \cdot z^2 & + \cdots + I_{K-1} \cdot z^{K-1} \\ c_2 = C(z^2) & = I_0 & +(I_1 \cdot z^1) \cdot z^1 & +(I_2 \cdot z^2) \cdot z^2 & + \cdots + (I_{K-1} \cdot z^{K-1}) \cdot z^{K-1} \, . \\ \vdots \end{array} \tag{10.18}$$

For the term of a sum denoted as $I_j^{(l)}$, we obtain the recursion $I_j^{(l+1)} = I_j^{(l)} \cdot z^j$ with $I_j^{(0)} = I_j$. This representation leads to the shift register shown in Fig. 10.4.

As an example, we study the code (6,2,5) over GF(7) with the primitive element $z = 5$ ($z^0 = 1$, $z^1 = 5$). With $(I_0, I_1) = (3, 1)$, we subsequently obtain

	$\cdot 1$	$\cdot 5$	
l	I_0^l	I_1^l	$\longrightarrow c_l = \sum_j I_j^l$
0	3	1	$\longrightarrow 4$
1	3	5	$\longrightarrow 1$
2	3	4	$\longrightarrow 0$
3	3	6	$\longrightarrow 2$
4	3	2	$\longrightarrow 5$
5	3	3	$\longrightarrow 6$

$$\mathbf{c} = (4, 1, 0, 2, 5, 6)$$

Since the DFT differs from the IDFT only in the factor N^{-1} and the sign of the powers of the element of order N, the same matrix description applies also to $C_j = N^{-1} \cdot c(x = z^{N-j})$, leading to the DFT shift register in Fig. 10.5.

As a check, one may compute the DFT vector $(C_0, C_1, \ldots, C_{N-1})$ from the time-domain vector $\mathbf{c} = (4, 1, 0, 2, 5, 6)$.

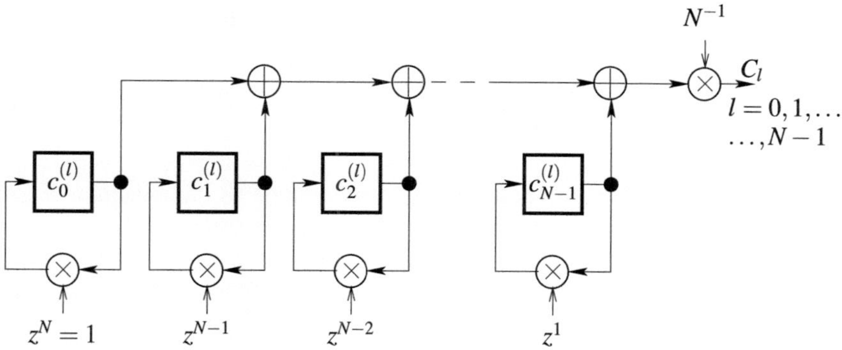

Fig. 10.5 DFT shift register

	$\cdot 1$	$\cdot 3$	$\cdot 2$	$\cdot 6$	$\cdot 4$	$\cdot 5$	
l	c_0^l	c_1^l	c_2^l	c_3^l	c_4^l	c_5^l	$\longrightarrow C_l = N^{-1} \cdot \sum_j c_j^{(l)}$
0							$\longrightarrow 3$
1							$\longrightarrow 1$
2							$\longrightarrow 0$
3							$\longrightarrow 0$
4							$\longrightarrow 0$
5							$\longrightarrow 0$

Since the encoding in DFT domain will not lead to a systematic codeword in time domain, i.e., the information will not be visible in the codeword, this encoding procedure will usually not be selected. The same applies for the non-systematic encoding directly in time domain, which will be described in the next section. However, this will be the basis for the next two encoding methods.

10.3.2 Non-systematic Encoding with the Generator Polynomial

The degree limitation of the polynomial $C(x)$ (degree$\{C(x)\} \leq K - 1 = N - d_{Hm}$) can be described by linear factors in time domain, since

$$C_{N-j} = N^{-1} \cdot c(x = z^{-(N-j)}) = N^{-1} \cdot c(x = z^j) = 0 \; , \; j = 1, ..., M \; . \quad (10.19)$$

$c(x)$ has to be a multiple of

$$g(x) = \prod_{j:C_{N-j}=0} (x - z^j) = g_0 + g_1 \cdot x + \cdots + 1 \cdot x^{2t} \; . \quad (10.20)$$

In the special case of zeros at the upper end, which we will mostly consider, this means

$$g(x) = \prod_{j=1}^{2t} (x - z^j) \,. \tag{10.21}$$

$g(x)$ is called **generator polynomial** due to its relation to the generator matrix. How the generator matrix is actually derived from the generator polynomial will be described later.

A codeword in polynomial representation $c(x)$ thus follows from the product

$$c(x) = \underbrace{i(x)}_{\text{degree: } K-1=N-2t-1} \cdot \underbrace{g(x)}_{\text{degree: } M=2t} \,. \tag{10.22}$$

The K coefficients of $i(x) = i_0 + i_1 \cdot x + \cdots + i_{K-1} \cdot x^{K-1}$ can be used as information. Clearly, $C_{N-j} = N^{-1} \cdot c(x) = N^{-1} \cdot i(x) \cdot g(x) = 0$ for the roots of $g(x)$, $x = z^{-(N-j)}$, $j = 1, \ldots, M$. The roots of the generator polynomial are hence in line with the zeros in DFT domain. The code, i.e., the set of codewords is the same as with encoding in DFT domain, having obeyed the degree limitation of the polynomial $C(x)$. However, the relation between information and codeword differs. Now, especially, the information is neither contained in the original, nor in the DFT domain. It is a non-systematic encoding.

In our example, we had four uppermost zeros in the DFT domain, which means

$$\begin{aligned} g(x) &= (x - z^1)(x - z^2)(x - z^3)(x - z^4) \\ &= (x - 5)(x - 4)(x - 6)(x - 2) \\ &= (x + 2)(x + 3)(x + 1)(x + 5) \\ &= 2 + 5x + 6x^2 + 4x^3 + x^4 \,. \end{aligned}$$

With the same information $i(x) = 3 + 1 \cdot x$, we obtain the codeword

$$c(x) = i(x) \cdot g(x) = 6 + 3x + 2x^2 + 4x^3 + x^5 \iff \mathbf{c} = (6, 3, 2, 4, 0, 1) \,,$$

which is not the same as the one that resulted from the DFT-domain encoding. We also determine the $i(x)$ that corresponds to the codeword that we obtained from the DFT-domain encoding.

$$i(x) = \frac{c(x)}{g(x)} =$$

$$
\begin{array}{lllllll}
(& 6x^5 & +5x^4 & +2x^3 & +0x^2 & +1x & +4 \quad):(x^4+4x^3+6x^2+5x+2)=6x+2 \\
 & -6x^5 & -3x^4 & -1x^3 & -2x^2 & -5x & \\
\hline
 & & 2x^4 & +1x^3 & +5x^2 & +3x & +4 \\
 & & -2x^4 & -1x^3 & -5x^2 & -3x & -4 \\
\hline
 & & 0 & & & &
\end{array}
$$

In this division, the K coefficients of $i(x)$ do only depend on the K highest coefficients of $c(x)$. The remaining $M = N - K$ coefficients of $c(x)$ have an influence on the remainder of the division, which has to be zero.

10.3.3 Systematic Encoding with the Generator Polynomial

From the previous section, we already know that the code polynomial can be described as a multiple of the generator polynomial.

$$c(x) = u(x) \cdot g(x) \ .$$

We now require to preserve the higher coefficients of the code polynomial $c(x)$ as a systematic part of the encoding. Therefore, we write

$$
\begin{aligned}
c(x) &= c_{N-1}x^{N-1} + \cdots + c_{N-K}x^{N-K} + c_{N-K-1}x^{N-K-1} + \cdots + c_0 \\
&= i_{K-1}x^{N-1} + \cdots + i_0x^{N-K} + c_{N-K-1}x^{N-K-1} + \cdots + c_0 \qquad (10.23)\\
&= u(x) \cdot g(x) \ . \qquad (10.24)
\end{aligned}
$$

The part of the code polynomial that does not carry information will now be moved to the right side.

$$
\begin{aligned}
c_{N-1}x^{N-1} + \cdots + c_{N-K}x^{N-K} &= u(x) \cdot g(x) - c_{N-K-1}x^{N-K-1} \cdots - c_1x - c_0 \\
&= u(x) \cdot g(x) + r(x) \qquad (10.25)
\end{aligned}
$$

This means that the remaining part of the codeword $-r(x)$ is equal to the remainder of the division of $c_{N-1}x^{N-1} + \cdots + c_{N-K}x^{N-K}$ by $g(x)$.

Example 10.2 In the example that we used to illustrate the DFT-domain encoding, we had the correspondence

$$\mathbf{c} = (4, 1, 0, 2, 5, 6) \qquad \mathbf{C} = (3, 1, 0, 0, 0, 0)$$

Let us use the two rightmost positions in the original domain as information, i.e., $c_5x^5 + c_4x^4 = 6x^5 + 5x^4$. With the generator polynomial $g(x) = x^4 + 4x^3 + 6x^2 + 5x + 2$, the remainder of the division is computed as follows.

$$
\begin{array}{lllllll}
(\; 6x^5 & +5x^4 &):(x^4{+}4x^3{+}6x^2{+}5x{+}2){=}6x{+}2 & & & & \\
-6x^5 & -3x^4 & -1x^3 & -2x^2 & -5x & & \\
\hline
 & 2x^4 & +6x^3 & +5x^2 & +2x & & \\
 & -2x^4 & -1x^3 & -5x^2 & -3x & -4 & \\
\hline
 & & 5x^3 & +0x^2 & +6x & +3 & = r(x)
\end{array}
$$

The parity positions of the codeword are obtained from the remainder $r(x)$ as $c_0 + c_1x + c_2x^2 + c_3x^3 = -r(x) = -(3 + 6x + 0x^2 + 5x^3) = 4 + 1x^1 + 0x^2 + 2x^3$.

When we determine the remainder, we actually compute modulo the polynomial $g(x)$. To come to a shift register structure, we formulate the division as an iterative computation mod $g(x)$. This yields a division circuit that we already know from Sect. 9.2.5. We write the part of $c(x)$ that carries the information as

$$
\begin{aligned}
c_{N-1}x^{N-1} + c_{N-2}x^{N-2} + \cdots + c_{N-K}x^{N-K} &= \\
c_{N-1}x^{N-1} + c_{N-2}x^{N-2} + \cdots + c_M x^M &= \\
(\ldots((0x + c_{N-1}x^M)x + c_{N-2}x^M)x + \ldots)x + c_M x^M \; . &
\end{aligned}
\tag{10.26}
$$

When starting in the inner brackets with the computation mod $g(x)$, the iteration for the remainder $r(x)$ will become

$$
r^{(j)}(x) = x \cdot r^{(j-1)}(x) + c_{N-j}x^M \bmod g(x) \; . \tag{10.27}
$$

Figure 10.6 shows the shift register for the example.

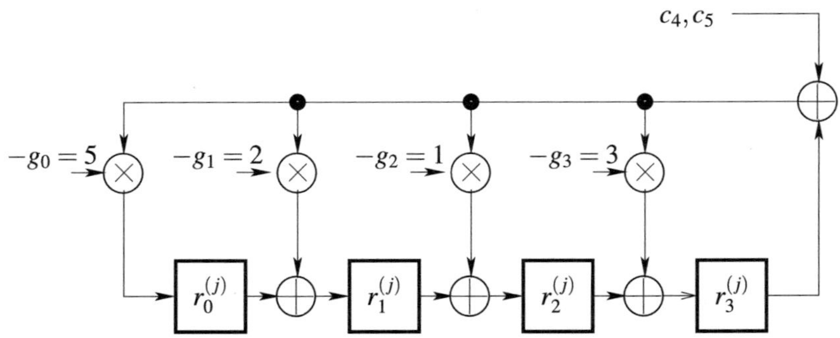

Fig. 10.6 Systematic encoder circuit based on the generator polynomial

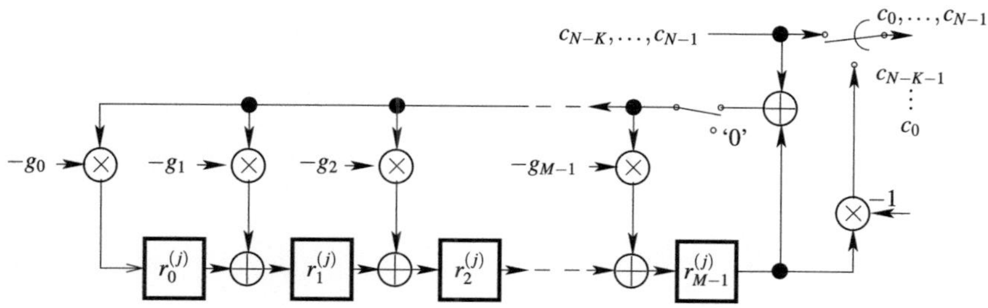

Fig. 10.7 Extended systematic encoder circuit based on the generator polynomial

The remainders that show up during the iterations are listed in the following table.

j	$r_0^{(j)}$	$r_1^{(j)}$	$r_2^{(j)}$	$r_3^{(j)}$	u_j
0	0	0	0	0	0
1	2	5	6	4	6
2	3	6	0	5	2

The result of the division is not too interesting. It is nevertheless computed and the coefficients will appear behind the (upper right) addition and are also listed in the rightmost column of the table. This column yields $u(x) = u_0 x + u_1 = 6x + 2$.

Noting that the parity positions result from the negative remainder, the shift register can be extended such that the complete codeword will be put out. Such an extension is shown in Fig. 10.7.

10.3.4 Systematic Encoding with the Parity-Check Polynomial

In (10.12) we provided a recursion formula and subsequently a shift register structure for the case when a product of two polynomials is a multiple of $(x^N - 1)$, i.e., $a(x) \cdot b(x) = 0 \bmod (x^N - 1) = (\ldots) \cdot (x^N - 1)$.

Let $a(x)$ be the code polynomial $c(x) = u(x) \cdot g(x)$, a multiple of $g(x)$. If we define a **parity-check polynomial**

$$h(x) := (x^N - 1)/g(x) = h_0 + h_1 x + \cdots + 1x^K \tag{10.28}$$

(degree $h(x) = N-$ degree $g(x) = N - M = K$),
we obtain

$$c(x) \cdot h(x) = 0 \bmod (x^N - 1) = (\ldots) \cdot (x^N - 1)\ . \tag{10.29}$$

Figure 10.8 shows the shift-register structure.

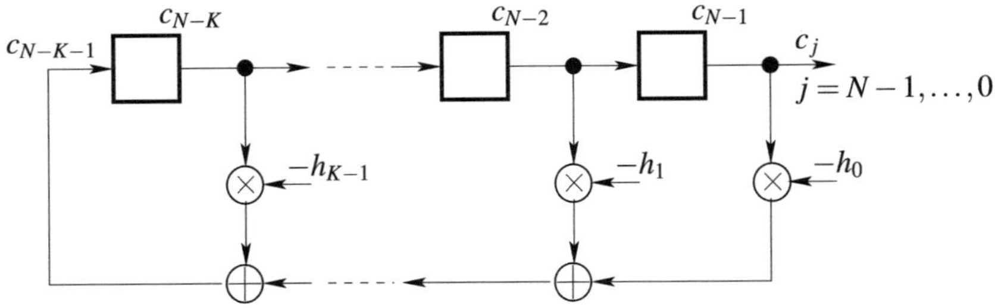

Fig. 10.8 Systematic encoding shift register based on the parity-check polynomial

Fig. 10.9 Systematic encoder using the parity-check polynomial of Example 10.3

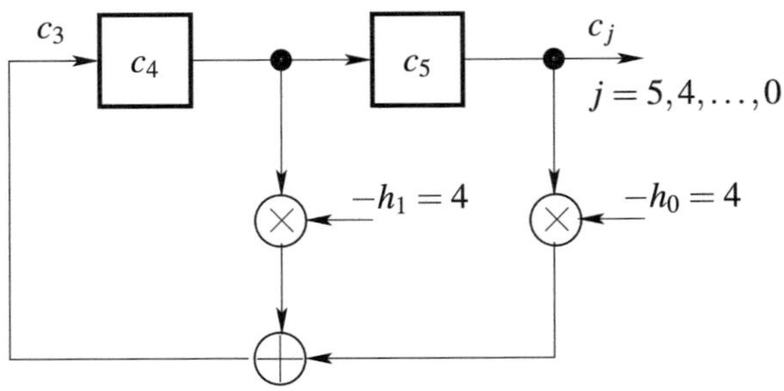

Example 10.3 In our example, we had $N = 6$ and $M = 4$ with $g(x) = (x - z^1)(x - z^2)(x - z^3)(x - z^4)$. $h(x)$ follows to be

$$h(x) = (x^6 - 1)/g(x) = (x - z^5)(x - z^0) = (x - 3)(x - 1) = 3 + 3x + x^2 \; .$$

The corresponding encoder circuit is shown in Fig. 10.9.
Note: An encoder on the basis of the generator polynomial in the previous section requires a shift register of length M, whereas the one using the parity-check polynomial needs a register of length K. Depending on the coderate, one or the other method will be preferred. When the number of parity positions is required to be variable, the circuit using the parity-check polynomial should be chosen. RS codes allow to adaptively change the number of parity positions, i.e., one can adaptively transmit more and more parities and always preserve the optimum error-correction properties ($t = \lfloor M/2 \rfloor$).

10.3.5 Generator and Parity-Check Matrices from Generator and Parity-Check Polynomials

We have currently described cyclic codes by polynomials. At the beginning, however, we specified linear block codes by their generator and parity-check matrices. We will now provide the connection between both representations. For simplicity, we only do this for the non-systematic encoding with the generator polynomial in Sect. 10.3.2 described by Eq. (10.22),

$$c(x) = i(x) \cdot g(x) \ .$$

We again arrange the coefficients of the polynomials as vectors in the form

$$\begin{aligned} c(x) &\Longleftrightarrow \mathbf{c} = (c_0, c_1, \ldots, c_{N-1}) \\ i(x) &\Longleftrightarrow \mathbf{i} = (i_0, i_1, \ldots, i_{K-1}) \ . \end{aligned}$$

The multiplication of two polynomials $i(x) \cdot g(x)$ corresponds to the convolution of their coefficients.

$$c_l = \sum_{j=0}^{K-1} i_j g_{l-j} \tag{10.30}$$

This can be rephrased by a set of linear equations with a Toeplitz matrix.

$$(c_0, c_1, \ldots, c_{N-1}) = (i_0, i_1, \ldots, i_{K-1}) \cdot \mathbf{G}$$

with

$$\mathbf{G} = \begin{pmatrix} g_0 & g_1 & g_2 & \cdot & \cdot & \cdot & \cdot & \cdot & g_{N-K} & 0 & 0 & 0 \cdot\cdot & 0 \\ 0 & g_0 & g_1 & g_2 & \cdot & \cdot & \cdot & \cdot & \cdot & g_{N-K} & 0 & 0 \cdot\cdot & 0 \\ 0 & 0 & g_0 & g_1 & g_2 & \cdot & \cdot & \cdot & \cdot & \cdot & g_{N-K} & 0 \cdot\cdot & 0 \\ \vdots & & & & & & & & & & & & \vdots \\ 0 & 0 & \cdot & \cdot & \cdot & 0 & g_0 & g_1 & g_2 & \cdot & \cdot & \cdots & g_{N-K} \end{pmatrix} \tag{10.31}$$

In order to determine a corresponding parity-check matrix, we consider the product

$$c(x) \cdot h(x) = i(x) \cdot g(x) \cdot h(x) = i(x)(x^N - 1) = -i(x) + x^N i(x) \ . \tag{10.32}$$

Since the maximum degree of $i(x)$ is $K - 1$, the coefficients of the powers K to $N - 1$ will be zero. Since the multiplication of polynomials means the convolution of their coefficients, we obtain

$$\sum_{j=0}^{K} h_j c_{l-j} = 0 \quad \text{for } l = K, \ldots, N-1 \ , \tag{10.33}$$

expanding it,

$$\begin{aligned} h_0c_K + h_1c_{K-1} + h_2c_{K-2} + \cdots + h_Kc_0 &= 0 \\ h_0c_{K+1} + h_1c_K + h_2c_{K-1} + \cdots + h_Kc_1 &= 0 \\ &\vdots \\ h_0c_{N-1} + h_1c_{N-2} + h_2c_{N-3} + \cdots + h_Kc_{N-K-1} &= 0\,. \end{aligned}$$

We obtain the parity-check equations

$$\underbrace{(0, 0, \ldots, 0)}_{N-K} = (c_0, c_1, \ldots, c_{N-1}) \cdot \mathbf{H}^T$$

with

$$\mathbf{H} = \begin{pmatrix} h_K & h_{K-1} & h_{K-2} & \cdot & \cdot & \cdot & \cdot & \cdot & h_0 & 0 & 0 & 0 \cdot \cdot 0 \\ 0 & h_K & h_{K-1} & h_{K-2} & \cdot & \cdot & \cdot & \cdot & \cdot & h_0 & 0 & 0 \cdot \cdot 0 \\ 0 & 0 & h_K & h_{K-1} & h_{K-2} \cdot & \cdot & \cdot & \cdot & \cdot & \cdot & h_0 & 0 \cdot \cdot \ 0 \\ \vdots & & & & & & & & & & & \vdots \\ 0 & 0 & \cdot & \cdot & \cdot & 0 & h_K & h_{K-1} & h_{K-2} & \cdot & \cdot & \cdot \cdot \cdot\ h_0 \end{pmatrix}. \tag{10.34}$$

This **H**-matrix is again the generator matrix $\mathbf{G}^\perp$ of the dual code with the generator polynomial $g^\perp(x) = x^K h(x^{-1})$, the reciprocal parity-check polynomial.

Taking advantage of the Euclidean division algorithm treated later, systematic generator and parity-check matrices can be derived, too. We do not provide this derivation.

10.4 The Decoding as an Interpolation Problem and the Derivation of the Key Equation for Error Localization

The decoding becomes very simple when the error positions are already given. This case is known as **erasure decoding**. Erased symbols are regenerated from the rest of the codeword. For RS codes, a possible procedure has already been described. The non-erased components determine the code polynomial of degree $\leq K - 1$ and replacing the erased components is then again a polynomial interpolation and is thus the same as the encoding. More problematic seems to find the location of errors. Hereto, first an error-indicator, called **syndrome** is required. The syndrome definition will be treated in the next section. The decoding, i.e., the error correction thus consists of three steps:

1. Computation of the syndrome,
2. Finding the error locations,
3. Determining the error values at the error locations and correction of the received word.

10.4.1 The Syndrome as an Error Indicator

The syndrome is usually defined as follows:

Definition 10.5 Terms computed from the received word $\mathbf{r}$ that are only dependent on the error vector $\mathbf{f}$ but not of the transmitted codeword $\mathbf{c}$, i.e., of the submitted information.

One possibility to define a syndrome would, e.g., be by means of the $\mathbf{H}$-matrix

$$\mathbf{s} = \mathbf{r}\,\mathbf{H}^T = (\mathbf{c}+\mathbf{f})\,\mathbf{H}^T = \mathbf{f}\,\mathbf{H}^T\ . \tag{10.35}$$

This syndrome vector could, e.g., be used to address the entries of a table of error pattern ordered by their syndromes (list decoding).

In the case of RS codes, however, it appears to be more suitable to define the M consecutive positions of the DFT vector as a syndrome that were required to be zero for all valid codewords.

$$\{\mathbf{c}|c_j = C(x=z^j), \text{degree } C(x) \le K-1 = N-M-1 = N-2t-1 = N-d_{Hm}\}\ . \tag{10.36}$$

Then, the syndrome $\mathbf{S}$ follows from

$$\mathbf{r} = \mathbf{c}+\mathbf{f} \;\circ\!\!-\!\!\bullet\; \mathbf{R} = \mathbf{C}+\mathbf{F} = (C_0+F_0,\ldots,C_{K-1}+F_{K-1},\underbrace{F_{N-2t},\ldots,F_{N-1}}_{\mathbf{S}})\ . \tag{10.37}$$

In polynomial representation this reads

$$R(x) = \underbrace{R_0 + R_1x + \cdots + R_{K-1}x^{K-1}}_{R^\star(x)(\text{unknown part of } F(x))} + \underbrace{R_{N-2t}x^{N-2t} + \cdots + R_{N-1}x^{N-1}}_{S(x)\cdot x^{N-2t}(\text{known part of } F(x))} \tag{10.38}$$

Since the correcting capability of RS codes does not change when cyclically shifting the zeros in the DFT vector, the syndrome can be located at every positions that are cyclically consecutive, i.e., also at the lower end.

$$\mathbf{r} = \mathbf{c}+\mathbf{f} \;\circ\!\!-\!\!\bullet\; \mathbf{R} = \mathbf{C}+\mathbf{F} = (\underbrace{F_0,\ldots,F_{2t-1}}_{\mathbf{S}},C_{2t}+F_{2t},\ldots,C_{N-1}+F_{N-1}) \tag{10.39}$$

In polynomial representation this reads

$$R(x) = \underbrace{R_0 + \cdots + R_{2t-1}x^{2t-1}}_{S(x)(\text{known part of } F(x))} + \underbrace{R_{2t}x^{2t} + \cdots + R_{N-1}x^{N-1}}_{R^\star(x)\cdot x^{2t}(\text{unknown part of } F(x))} \tag{10.40}$$

Note that the shift property of the DFT says that a cyclic shift in DFT domain corresponds to a multiplication with a factor in time domain, i.e., the error positions stay the same, whatever syndrome position was selected. Nevertheless, the error values are changed!

Example 10.4 We again consider our example over $GF(7)$ with $N = 6$ and $t = 2$:

$$\mathbf{c} = (4, 1, 0, 2, 5, 6) \circ\!\!-\!\!\bullet\ (3, 1, 0, 0, 0, 0)$$

Let the received vector be

$$\mathbf{r} = (4, 1, 0, 4, 5, 5)$$

We have the correspondence

$$\mathbf{r} = (\mathbf{4}, \mathbf{1}, \mathbf{0}, \mathbf{4}, \mathbf{5}, \mathbf{5}) \circ\!\!-\!\!\bullet\ (\mathbf{2}, \mathbf{1}, \underbrace{2, 1, 0, 5}_{\mathbf{S}})$$

This syndrome follows from the error vector $\mathbf{f} = (0, 0, 0, 2, 0, 6)$.

10.4.2 Prony's Curve-Fitting Method as a Decoding Algorithm

In Prony's approach [1], given samples are interpolated by a linear combination of exponential functions. The method is known for centuries (1795), but has been reinvented in the coding theory under the name *Gorenstein-Zierler* algorithm. Wolf [2] realized the equivalence in 1967.

Prony's method uses the following interpolation function:

$$y(x) = A_0 e^{a_0 x} + A_1 e^{a_1 x} + \cdots + A_{n-1} e^{a_{n-1} x} . \tag{10.41}$$

Abbreviating $\mu_j^x := e^{a_j x}$, this reads

$$y(x) = A_0 \mu_0^x + A_1 \mu_1^x + \cdots + A_{n-1} \mu_{n-1}^x . \tag{10.42}$$

In case of equidistant samples $x = 0, 1, \ldots, N_S - 1$, we obtain the set of equations

$$\begin{aligned} A_0 + A_1 + \cdots + A_{e-1} &= y_0 \\ A_0 \mu_0^1 + A_1 \mu_1^1 + \cdots + A_{e-1} \mu_{e-1}^1 &= y_1 \\ A_0 \mu_0^2 + A_1 \mu_1^2 + \cdots + A_{e-1} \mu_{e-1}^2 &= y_2 \\ &\vdots \\ A_0 \mu_0^e + A_1 \mu_1^e + \cdots + A_{e-1} \mu_{e-1}^e &= y_e \\ &\vdots \\ A_0 \mu_0^{N_S-1} + A_1 \mu_1^{N_S-1} + \cdots + A_{e-1} \mu_{e-1}^{N_S-1} &= y_{N_S-1} . \end{aligned} \tag{10.43}$$

With respect to the unknowns $A_0, \ldots, A_{e-1}$, the set of linear equations has a Vandermonde coefficient matrix, as we know it from the DFT/IDFT. Would all the μ_j be known, we would just have to solve the Vandermonde system for the A_j. With respect to the μ_j, however, the set of equation is nonlinear. The solution will be enabled by defining a polynomial

$$\mu^e + \alpha_1 \mu^{e-1} + \alpha_2 \mu^{e-2} + \cdots + \alpha_{e-1} \mu + \alpha_e = 0 \tag{10.44}$$

with the roots μ_j. Shortly, we will recognize that this polynomial is equivalent to the so-called *error-locator polynomial* in the decoding of RS codes, whose roots determine the error locations.

If we multiply the first equation from (10.43) with α_e, the second with α_{e-1}, ..., and the $(e+1)$st with 1 and sum up all these equations, we obtain the first equation of the following set of linear equations.

$$\begin{aligned} y_{e-1}\alpha_1 + y_{e-2}\alpha_2 + \cdots + y_0\alpha_e &= -y_e \\ y_e\alpha_1 + y_{e-1}\alpha_2 + \cdots + y_1\alpha_e &= -y_{e+1} \\ &\vdots \\ y_{N_S-2}\alpha_1 + y_{N_S-3}\alpha_2 + \cdots + y_{N_S-n-1}\alpha_e &= -y_{N_S-1} \end{aligned} \tag{10.45}$$

The further equations are obtained by successively starting from the second equation, third, and so forth. This set of equations can directly be solved for $N_S = 2e$ and has a **Toeplitz**[1] structure.

Equation (10.45) can be written as

$$(1, \alpha_1, \alpha_2, \ldots, \alpha_e) \begin{pmatrix} y_e & y_{e+1} & y_{e+2} & & y_{N_S-1} \\ y_{e-1} & y_e & y_{e+1} & \ddots & \\ y_{e-2} & y_{e-1} & y_e & \ddots & \\ & \ddots & \ddots & & \\ y_0 & & & & y_{N_S-e-1} \end{pmatrix} = (0, \ldots, 0)\,. \tag{10.46}$$

For such banded Toeplitz matrices exist efficient solution methods from which we will describe the most important two, the Berlekamp–Massey and the Euclidean division algorithm. In the area of signal processing (e.g., linear prediction, LPC), other algorithms have been introduced, namely the Levinson–Durbin and the Trench algorithms. The Levinson–Durbin algorithm, e.g., cannot be used in the decoding due to problems with singular submatrices. This is actually also known to be a problem in signal processing when submatrices become ill-conditioned. The Berlekamp–Massey and Euclidean algorithms, however, can easily be modified to be used in signal-processing applications.

[1] A **Hankel** matrix is an upside-down Toeplitz matrix.

The set of equations can be solved for $N_S = 2e$. Then the roots are to be determined and finally, the coefficients A_i are derived from the Vandermonde system.

The relation to the decoding problem can be seen at once when writing down the equations of the syndrome components dependent on the error positions and error values. For simplicity, we assume a syndrome at the lower end. We obtain

$$\begin{aligned} f_{l_0} + f_{l_1} + \cdots + f_{l_{e-1}} &= S_0 \\ f_{l_0}(z^{-l_0})^1 + f_{l_1}(z^{-l_1})^1 + \cdots + f_{l_{e-1}}(z^{-l_{e-1}})^1 &= S_1 \\ f_{l_0}(z^{-l_0})^2 + f_{l_1}(z^{-l_1})^2 + \cdots + f_{l_{e-1}}(z^{-l_{e-1}})^2 &= S_2 \\ &\vdots \\ f_{l_0}(z^{-l_0})^{2t-1} + f_{l_1}(z^{-l_1})^{2t-1} + \cdots + f_{l_{e-1}}(z^{-l_{e-1}})^{2t-1} &= S_{2t-1}\,. \end{aligned} \tag{10.47}$$

We observe the correspondences

$$\mu_j \equiv z^{-l_j} \qquad y_j \equiv S_j\,.$$

For $e \le t$, the set of equations can be uniquely solved. From the solutions $\mu_j = z^{-l_j}$ of the polynomial (10.44), the usage of the polynomial as an error-locator polynomial becomes obvious, since l_j are the error locations.

10.4.3 Derivation of the Key Equation

Slightly different from the previous section, the error-locator polynomial is usually defined as

Definition 10.6 The error-locator polynomial $\Gamma(x)$ is defined as

$$\Gamma(x) = \prod_{j\in\mathbb{F}}(x - z^j)\,,$$

where $\mathbb{F}$ is the set of indices of the error positions, i.e., ($\mathbb{F} = \{j | f_j \neq 0\}$).

Likewise, the non-error locator polynomial is defined as

$$\overline{\Gamma}(x) = \prod_{j\in\overline{\mathbb{F}}}(x - z^j)\,,$$

where $\overline{\mathbb{F}}$ is the set of indices of the error-free positions, i.e., ($\overline{\mathbb{F}} = \{j | f_j = 0\}$).

Due to $x^N - 1 = \prod_{j=0}^{N-1}(x - z^j)$, we have

$$\Gamma(x)\cdot\overline{\Gamma}(x) = (x^N - 1)\,. \tag{10.48}$$

Since $F(x)$ has zeros at the non-error positions ($j \in \overline{\mathsf{F}}:\ F(z^j) = 0$), we also have

$$F(x) = T(x) \cdot \overline{\Gamma}(x) = T(x) \cdot \prod_{j \in \overline{\mathsf{F}}} (x - z^j)\,. \tag{10.49}$$

$F(x)$ is also a multiple of $\overline{\Gamma}(x)$. The polynomial $T(x)$, the so-called *error-evaluator polynomial* will later be described when we will deal with the error values.

From the two previous equations, we obtain a relation, called the **key equation**:

$$\Gamma(x) \cdot F(x) = \Gamma(x) \cdot T(x) \cdot \overline{\Gamma}(x) = T(x) \cdot (x^N - 1) = 0 \mod (x^N - 1)\,. \tag{10.50}$$

The product of the polynomials $\Gamma(x)$ and $F(x)$ corresponds to the cyclic convolution of the coefficient vectors. Let e be the number of errors, we obtain

$$\sum_{l=0}^{N-1} \Gamma_l \cdot F_{j-l \bmod N} = \sum_{l=0}^{e} \Gamma_l \cdot F_{j-l \bmod N} = 0 \quad j = 0, \ldots, N-1\,. \tag{10.51}$$

The frequency components due to errors can only be directly read at the positions of the **syndrome S**. The decoding problem can now be formulated such that we have to find the error-locator polynomial with the least number of linear factors (roots) $(x - z^j)$, i.e., of lowest degree that fulfills the key equation (10.50) or (10.51). This is equivalent to searching for an error polynomial $F(x)$, from which we only know the syndrome positions, with as many linear factors $(x - z^j)$ as possible. The underlying assumption is that a smaller number of errors are more probable than a larger number of errors. This is usually the case (see, e.g., the binary symmetric channel). Furthermore, we assume that all codewords appear with the same probability and the error vector does not depend on the transmitted codeword.

In the following, we write the error-locator polynomial in a slightly different form in which the first coefficient is equal to one, i.e.,

$$\Gamma(x)|_{new} = \frac{1}{\prod_{j \in \mathsf{F}} z^j} \cdot \Gamma(x) = 1 + \Gamma_1 x + \Gamma_2 x^2 + \cdots + \Gamma_e x^e\,. \tag{10.52}$$

When starting the decoding, the actual number of errors is unknown. As we said, the natural assumption is that error pattern with lower weight are more probable. Thus, if the actual error number e is not known, the best we can do is to successively increase the degree of the error-locator polynomial and check, if Eq. (10.51) can be fulfilled. Hence, we work with an error-locator polynomial

$$\Gamma(x) = 1 + \Gamma_1 x + \Gamma_2 x^2 + \cdots + \Gamma_L x^L \tag{10.53}$$

of degree L and check

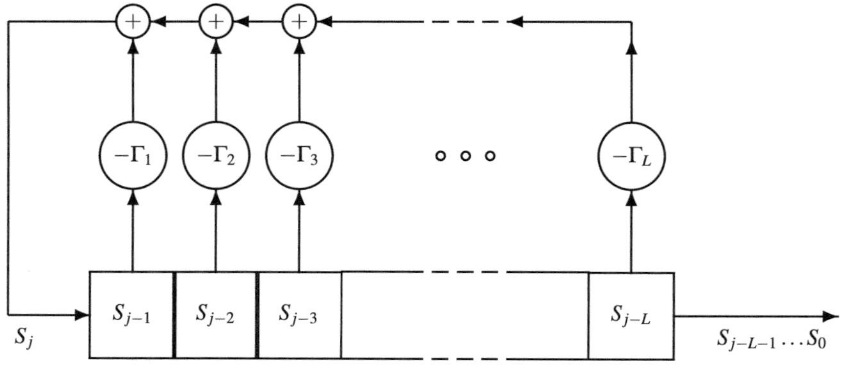

Fig. 10.10 Shift-register representation of the key equation

$$\sum_{l=0}^{L} \Gamma_l \cdot S_{j-l \bmod N} = 0\,, \quad S_{j-l \bmod N} = F_{j-l \bmod N}\,, \quad j_{S_0} + L \le j \le j_{S_{M-1}} \mod N$$

$$\iff \quad S_j = -\sum_{l=1}^{L} \Gamma_l \cdot S_{j-l \bmod N}\,, \quad j_{S_0} + L \le j \le j_{S_{M-1}} \mod N \qquad (10.54)$$

As long as $e \le t = \lfloor M/2 \rfloor$, a unique solution to Eq. (10.54) can be found. This solution can be represented by the linear shift register in Fig. 10.10.

10.5 The Berlekamp–Massey Algorithm for Solving the Key Equation

This Toeplitz algorithm was first described in Berlekamp's book [3] and further illustrated as shift-register synthesis by Massey [4]. In here, we will discuss Massey's description in parallel to a matrix-based illustration.

10.5.1 The Key Operations of the Algorithm

We are searching for a shift-register of shortest length according to Fig. 10.10, i.e., an error-locator polynomial of lowest degree L that fulfills the key equation (10.54). To this end, in the BMA we successively increase the length of the shift-register starting from $L = 0$ until L will be equal to the real error number e (assuming no decoding error).

A change in the coefficients Γ_j or additionally, a length change, will take place, if Eq. (10.54) is not fulfilled or in other words, if the *discrepancy*

$$d_n = S_n + \sum_{j=1}^{L_n} \Gamma_j S_{n-j} \tag{10.55}$$

is not equal to zero.

The new shift-register coefficients result from a previous one by adding an earlier coefficient set *before the last length change*. These coefficients will be shifted so far that they again meet the same syndrome positions that they once processed when leading to the discrepancy d_m. Accordingly, the shifted coefficient set yields the same discrepancy d_m that lead to the earlier length change. The recursion formula of the BMA for updating the coefficients of the error-locator polynomial,

$$\Gamma_{n+1}(x) = \Gamma_n(x) - \frac{d_n}{d_m} x^{n-m} \Gamma_m(x) , \tag{10.56}$$

$$\begin{aligned} n - m &: \text{ shift}, \\ d_n &: \text{ current discrepancy}, \\ d_m &: \text{ discrepancy before the last length change}, \end{aligned}$$

forces the discrepancy to zero.

A length change is only required, if $d_n \neq 0 \wedge 2L_n \leq n$.

A further illustration is given in Fig. 10.11, where the coefficient sets are shifted along the syndrome vector. There we see that $n - m$ leading zeros (right side) are added to the earlier coefficient set when the two coefficient sets are linearly combined at the position n to cancel out the current discrepancy. The prepending of the leading zeros is described by the multiplication by x^{n-m}.

The principal structure of the BMA will become more obvious when we look at the iteratively solved set of linear equations [5]. This leads to an alternative description to the more common shift-register synthesis that was once provided by Massey [4].

The key equation was

$$S_j = -\sum_{l=1}^{e} \Gamma_l S_{j-l} , \tag{10.57}$$

which corresponds to the set of linear equations

$$(1, \Gamma_1, \Gamma_2, \ldots, \Gamma_e) \begin{pmatrix} S_e & S_{e+1} & \cdot & \cdot & S_{2e} & \cdot & S_{M-1} \\ S_{e-1} & S_e & \ddots & & \cdot & & \cdot \\ \cdot & S_{e-1} & \ddots & \ddots & \cdot & & \cdot \\ \cdot & & \ddots & \ddots & S_{e+1} & & \cdot \\ S_0 & \cdot & \cdot & S_{e-1} & S_e & \cdot & S_{M-1-e} \end{pmatrix} = (0, \ldots, 0) \tag{10.58}$$

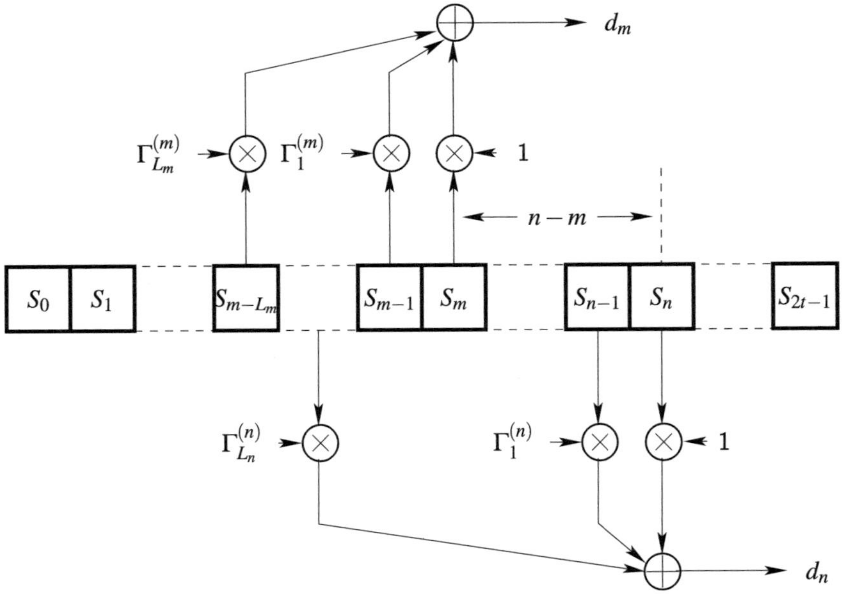

Fig. 10.11 Illustration of the recursion formula of the Berlekamp–Massey algorithm

with a Toeplitz coefficient matrix.

In the following, we describe the BMA as a logical consequence of the matrix structure and the requirement to find the error-locator polynomial of lowest possible degree. Note that this requirement results from the assumption that the probability of error pattern decreases with their weight.

The algorithm starts from $L = 0$ using the smallest possible sub-matrix

$$(1) \cdot (S_0) = (S_0) =: (d_0^I) . \tag{10.59}$$

The first discrepancy d_0^I is thus equal to S_0. Even if the discrepancy would be zero, it would be necessary to check the next bigger sub-system.

Since we are searching for the error-locator polynomial of lowest degree, it is natural to extend the vector $\mathbf{\Gamma}$ by appending a Zero to the right to investigate the next bigger sub-system. This does not yet increase the degree of the corresponding error-locator polynomial. We obtain the set of equations

$$(1, 0) \begin{pmatrix} S_1 & S_2 \\ S_0 & S_1 \end{pmatrix} = (d_0^{II}, d_1^{II}) . \tag{10.60}$$

We are looking for a solution leading to a zero right side. If d_0^{II} and d_1^{II} are not zero, the first position can be forced to zero, if also d_0^I was unequal zero.

If we use a vector (0, 1) together with a 2×2 matrix instead of (1) in Eq. (10.59), i.e., prepending a zero on the left, the first component on the right side will again be the earlier discrepancy $d_0^I = S_0$.

By linearly combining the two left and right zero-extended vectors, it is now possible to force the first component on the right side to zero.

$$[(1,0) - \frac{d_0^{II}}{d_0^I}(0,1)] \cdot \begin{pmatrix} S_1 & S_2 \\ S_0 & S_1 \end{pmatrix} = (0, d_1^{III}) \tag{10.61}$$

In case $d_1^{III} \neq 0$, the sub-matrix is non-singular ($\det \boldsymbol{S}_1 \neq 0$) and a length change together with using the next bigger sub-matrix is required. However, even if d_1^{III} should be zero, the next bigger sub-matrix would have to be checked if it is singular, too.

At this point, we like to mention that a length change in the sense of the usual BMA description [4] is performed, when the discrepancy was zero and the next operation extends the solution vector with non-zero components.

After the first steps of the algorithm and thus its initialization have been presented, we will now point out the main operations that rely on the Toeplitz structure.

It has already become visible that the extension of the solution vector with zeros on the left or right sides, together with considering the corresponding bigger Toeplitz sub-matrix represent the kernel of the algorithm. In the following we study the zero-extensions, i.e., its impact on the right side in some more detail.

Appending zeros on the right:

Extending the vector $\boldsymbol{\Gamma}$ by appending zeros on the right leads to a left shift of the right side by one position and two new components will show up on the right side.

$$(1, \Gamma_1, \Gamma_2, \ldots, \Gamma_l) \cdot \begin{pmatrix} S_l & & S_{2l} \\ & \ddots & \\ S_0 & & S_l \end{pmatrix} = (\rho_0, \rho_1, \rho_2, \ldots, \rho_l) \tag{10.62}$$

$$(1, \Gamma_1, \Gamma_2, \ldots, \Gamma_l, 0) \cdot \begin{pmatrix} S_{l+1} & & S_{2(l+1)} \\ & \ddots & \\ S_0 & & S_{l+1} \end{pmatrix} = (\rho_1, \rho_2, \ldots, \rho_l, \rho_{l+1}, \rho_{l+2}) \tag{10.63}$$

Prepending zeros on the left:

Extending the vector $\boldsymbol{\Gamma}$ by prepending zeros on the left preserves the right side and just adds one new component at the rightmost location.

$$(1, \Gamma_1, \Gamma_2, \ldots, \Gamma_l) \cdot \begin{pmatrix} S_l & & S_{2l} \\ & \ddots & \\ S_0 & & S_l \end{pmatrix} = (\rho_0, \rho_1, \rho_2, \ldots, \rho_l) \tag{10.64}$$

$$(0, 1, \Gamma_1, \Gamma_2, \ldots, \Gamma_l) \cdot \begin{pmatrix} S_{l+1} & & S_{2(l+1)} \\ & \ddots & \\ S_0 & & S_{l+1} \end{pmatrix} = (\rho_0, \rho_1, \rho_2, \ldots, \rho_l, \rho_{l+1}) \quad (10.65)$$

We use the property that an earlier solution vector (*before the last length change*) leads to zeros on the right side down from a certain component on. A prepending of zeros to the left preserves this right side except for new components on the right. Let the resulting vector be $\mathbf{\Gamma}_v$.

The current solution vector $\mathbf{\Gamma}$ will now be appended with zeros on the right end, shifting the right side of the set of equations to the left, until the first non-zero component exactly matches the position of the first non-zero component when using $\mathbf{\Gamma}_v$.

Both set of equations will then have the structure

$$(0, \ldots, 0, 1, \Gamma_{v1}, \Gamma_{v2}, \ldots) \cdot (\cdot) = (\underbrace{0, \ldots, 0}, d_{vj}, d_{vj+1}, d_{vj+2}, \ldots) \quad (10.66)$$

$$(1, \Gamma_1, \Gamma_2, \ldots, 0, \ldots, 0) \cdot (\cdot) = (\overbrace{0, \ldots, 0}, d_j, d_{j+1}, d_{j+2}, \ldots) \quad (10.67)$$

With a linear combination of both solution vectors, the first non-zero component d_j is forced to zero. The new solution vector will then be

$$\mathbf{\Gamma} := (1, \Gamma_1, \Gamma_2, \ldots, 0, \ldots, 0) - \underbrace{\frac{d_j}{d_{vj}}}_{=d_n/d_m} (0, \ldots, 0, 1, \Gamma_{v1}, \Gamma_{v2}, \ldots) \quad (10.68)$$

This is equivalent to the recursion (10.56).

The first non-zero component on the right side of the set of equations *before the last length change* acts like a marking that needs to be reached by the current solution vector by right-sided appending of zeros.

In the following, we illustrate the algorithm with two examples. The first one shows the basic procedure more clearly, whereas Example 10.6 treats the special case of singular sub-matrices. There, we will observe that it may even be necessary to extend the syndrome matrix by unknown components to proceed in the algorithm. These will however not be used in the following steps.

Both examples use an odd number of syndrome components, which may first appear to be unusual, since the correcting capability of an RS code is $t = \lfloor M/2 \rfloor$. When looking more carefully, one will realize that the last syndrome component is actually not required. It can only be used for an additional check, if all errors have been found.

From the example, we also observe that a length change in the sense of the BMA will only occur, when $d_n \neq 0 \wedge 2L_n \leq n$.

The last step of the second example shows the final result together with the original 4×4 matrix. The BMA solution, however, was already found in the previous step. This last step was only provided for illustration purposes. Note that it does not result from just eliminating the last row (and last column) of the 5×5 matrix which would correspond to the zero in the solution vector.

Example 10.5 GF(7), primitive element: 5, syndrome length: 5

Error vector: (1, 0, 0, 0, 1, 0) Syndrome: (5, 2, 4, 5, 2)

$$(1,\Gamma_1,\Gamma_2)\begin{pmatrix} 4 & 5 & 2 \\ 2 & 4 & 5 \\ 5 & 2 & 4 \end{pmatrix} \stackrel{!}{=} (0,0,0)$$

$$(1)\cdot(5) = (5)$$

$$(1,0)\begin{pmatrix} 2 & 4 \\ 5 & 2 \end{pmatrix} = (2,4)$$

$$(1,0) - \tfrac{2}{5}(0,1) = (1,1)$$

$$(1,1)\begin{pmatrix} 2 & 4 \\ 5 & 2 \end{pmatrix} = (0,6)$$

$$(1,1,0)\begin{pmatrix} 4 & 5 & 2 \\ 2 & 4 & 5 \\ 5 & 2 & 4 \end{pmatrix} = (6,2,0)$$

$$(1,1,0) - \tfrac{6}{5}(0,0,1) = (1,1,3)$$

$$(1,1,3)\begin{pmatrix} 4 & 5 & 2 \\ 2 & 4 & 5 \\ 5 & 2 & 4 \end{pmatrix} = (0,1,5)$$

$$(1,1,3) - \tfrac{1}{6}(0,1,1) = (1,2,4)$$

$$(1,2,4)\begin{pmatrix} 4 & 5 & 2 \\ 2 & 4 & 5 \\ 5 & 2 & 4 \end{pmatrix} = (0,0,0)$$

$$\Gamma(x) = 1 + 2x + 4x^2$$

$$\begin{aligned}
\Gamma(5^0) &= 1 + 2\cdot 1 + 4\cdot 1 = 0 \longleftarrow \\
\Gamma(5^1) &= 1 + 2\cdot 5 + 4\cdot 4 = 6 \\
\Gamma(5^2) &= 1 + 2\cdot 4 + 4\cdot 2 = 3 \\
\Gamma(5^3) &= 1 + 2\cdot 6 + 4\cdot 1 = 3 \\
\Gamma(5^4) &= 1 + 2\cdot 2 + 4\cdot 4 = 0 \longleftarrow \\
\Gamma(5^5) &= 1 + 2\cdot 3 + 4\cdot 2 = 1
\end{aligned}$$

Error positions: 0 and 4

Example 10.6 GF(11), primitive element: 6, syndrome length: 7

Error vector: (1, 0, 1, 0, 4, 0, 0, 0, 0, 0) Syndrome: (5, 8, 4, 7, 4, 5, 8)

$$(1,\Gamma_1,\Gamma_2,\Gamma_3)\begin{pmatrix} 7 & 4 & 5 & 8 \\ 4 & 7 & 4 & 5 \\ 8 & 4 & 7 & 4 \\ 5 & 8 & 4 & 7 \end{pmatrix} \stackrel{!}{=} (0,0,0,0)$$

$$(1)\cdot(5) = (5)$$

$$(1,0)\begin{pmatrix} 8 & 4 \\ 5 & 8 \end{pmatrix} = (8,4)$$

$$(1,0) - \tfrac{8}{5}(0,1) = (1,5)$$

$$(1,5)\begin{pmatrix} 8 & 4 \\ 5 & 8 \end{pmatrix} = (0,0)$$

$$(1,5,0)\begin{pmatrix} 4 & 7 & 4 \\ 8 & 4 & 7 \\ 5 & 8 & 4 \end{pmatrix} = (0,5,6)$$

$$(1,5,0,0)\begin{pmatrix} 7 & 4 & 5 & 8 \\ 4 & 7 & 4 & 5 \\ 8 & 4 & 7 & 4 \\ 5 & 8 & 4 & 7 \end{pmatrix} = (5,6,3,0)$$

$$(1,5,0,0) - \tfrac{5}{5}(0,0,0,1) = (1,5,0,10)$$

$$(1,5,0,10)\begin{pmatrix} 7 & 4 & 5 & 8 \\ 4 & 7 & 4 & 5 \\ 8 & 4 & 7 & 4 \\ 5 & 8 & 4 & 7 \end{pmatrix} = (0,9,10,4)$$

$$(1,5,0,10) - \tfrac{9}{5}(0,1,5,0) = (1,1,2,10)$$

$$(1,1,2,10)\begin{pmatrix} 7 & 4 & 5 & 8 \\ 4 & 7 & 4 & 5 \\ 8 & 4 & 7 & 4 \\ 5 & 8 & 4 & 7 \end{pmatrix} = (0,0,8,3)$$

$$(1,1,2,10,0)\begin{pmatrix} 4 & 5 & 8 & ? & ? \\ 7 & 4 & 5 & 8 & ? \\ 4 & 7 & 4 & 5 & 8 \\ 8 & 4 & 7 & 4 & 5 \\ 5 & 8 & 4 & 7 & 4 \end{pmatrix} = (0,8,3,?,?)$$

$$(1,1,2,10,0) - \tfrac{8}{5}(0,0,1,5,0) = (1,1,7,2,0)$$

$$(1,1,7,2,0)\begin{pmatrix} 4 & 5 & 8 & ? & ? \\ 7 & 4 & 5 & 8 & ? \\ 4 & 7 & 4 & 5 & 8 \\ 8 & 4 & 7 & 4 & 5 \\ 5 & 8 & 4 & 7 & 4 \end{pmatrix} = (0,0,0,?,?)$$

$$(1,1,7,2)\begin{pmatrix} 7 & 4 & 5 & 8 \\ 4 & 7 & 4 & 5 \\ 8 & 4 & 7 & 4 \\ 5 & 8 & 4 & 7 \end{pmatrix} = (0,0,0,0)$$

$$\Gamma(x) = 1 + x + 7x^2 + 2x^3$$

$$\begin{aligned}
\Gamma(6^0) &= \Gamma(1) = 0 \longleftarrow \\
\Gamma(6^1) &= \Gamma(6) = 9 \\
\Gamma(6^2) &= \Gamma(3) = 0 \longleftarrow \\
\Gamma(6^3) &= \Gamma(7) = 3 \\
\Gamma(6^4) &= \Gamma(9) = 0 \longleftarrow \\
\Gamma(6^5) &= \Gamma(10) = 5 \\
\Gamma(6^6) &= \Gamma(5) = 10 \\
\Gamma(6^7) &= \Gamma(8) = 7 \\
\Gamma(6^8) &= \Gamma(4) = 3 \\
\Gamma(6^9) &= \Gamma(2) = 3
\end{aligned}$$

Error positions: 0, 2, and 4

10.5.2 Massey's Description of the Berlekamp Algorithm

As was mentioned, the algorithm was originally described by Berlekamp in [3] and later illustrated as shift-register synthesis by Massey in [4]. In Massey's paper, all main proofs are given, especially the one showing that successively always the shift register of shortest length is found. Also the exact step size for length changes is derived there. In the following we provide the algorithm in Massey's formulation, which may directly be used for programming.

$$\begin{array}{l}
1)\ 1 \to \Gamma(x) \quad 1 \to \Gamma_v(x) \quad 1 \to \tau \\
\quad 0 \to L \quad 1 \to d_m \quad 0 \to n \\
2)\ \text{IF } n = M-1, \text{ STOP. OTHERWISE COMPUTE} \\
\quad d_n = S_n + \sum_{i=1}^{L} \Gamma_i S_{n-i}\,. \\
3)\ \text{IF } d_n = 0, \text{ THEN } \tau + 1 \to \tau, \text{ GO TO 6)}. \\
4)\ \text{IF } d_n \neq 0 \text{ AND } 2L > n, \text{ THEN} \\
\quad \Gamma(x) - d_n d_m^{-1} x^\tau \Gamma_v(x) \to \Gamma(x) \\
\quad \tau + 1 \to \tau \\
\quad \text{GO TO 6)}. \\
5)\ \text{IF } d_n \neq 0 \text{ AND } 2L \leq n, \text{ THEN} \\
\quad \Gamma(x) \to \Lambda(x) \\
\quad \Gamma(x) - d_n d_m^{-1} x^\tau \Gamma_v(x) \to \Gamma(x) \\
\quad n + 1 - L \to L \\
\quad \Lambda(x) \to \Gamma_v(x) \\
\quad d_n \to d_m \\
\quad 1 \to \tau. \\
6)\ n + 1 \to n \text{ RETURN TO 2)}.
\end{array} \tag{10.69}$$

(τ corresponds to the shift $n - m$.)

It is assumed that the operations become clear from the previous sections. In the following few paragraphs, some remarks for a deeper understanding of the BMA are provided.

10.5.3 Error and Erasure Decoding in the BMA

As we already know, erasures can be seen as errors at known positions. In analogy to the error-locator polynomial, we define an erasure polynomial

$$\Lambda(x) = \prod_{j \in \mathbb{E}} (x - z^j)\,, \tag{10.70}$$

where $\mathbb{E}$ denotes the index set of the erasure positions ($|\mathbb{E}| = a_E$).

With the matrix description, it is obvious that the algorithm should now start with the subset of equations

$$(1, \Lambda_1, \Lambda_2, \ldots, \Lambda_{a_E}) \cdot \begin{pmatrix} S_{a_E} & & S_{2a_E} \\ & \ddots & \\ S_0 & & S_{a_E} \end{pmatrix} = (\rho_0, \rho_1, \rho_2, \ldots, \rho_{a_E})\,, \tag{10.71}$$

i.e., the vector $\mathbf{\Gamma}$ will be initialized by $\mathbf{\Lambda}$. Then, the appending ($\to \Gamma(x)$) and prepending ($\to \Gamma_v(x)$) of zeros follows. The roots of the erasure polynomial $\Lambda(x)$ will be preserved when initializing the BMA with it. $\Lambda(x)$ will be a factor both in $\Gamma(x)$

and in $\Gamma_v(x)$, meaning that this factor will be preserved in all linear combinations of the two polynomials.

The first usable discrepancy in the above set of equations is ρ_0. Hence, the syndrome length that is left for determining the remaining errors is $M - a_E$. The number of correctable additional errors will then be $\lfloor \frac{M-a_E}{2} \rfloor$.

10.6 Euclidean Division Algorithm (EDA)

We know the Euclidean algorithm as a means of computing the gcd of two integers or polynomials (with integer coefficients). Divisions of two subsequent remainders are computed in a recursive fashion until finally the remainder will be zero and the gcd is found. Let the two numbers or polynomials be m and n or $m(x)$ and $n(x)$, respectively (not to be mistaken as code parameters). We will realize that the gcd(m, n) can be written as a linear combination of m and n. This relation is equivalent to the key equation, making the EDA a possible decoding method. In the next chapter we will further see that the EDA will also support the computation of the error values. However, there also exists a corresponding extension to the Berlekamp algorithm. The principal structure of the EDA will be discussed in the following section. Relations between the EDA and the BMA are discussed in [6, 7].

10.6.1 The Operations of the EDA

Let $r_{-2} = m$ or $m(x)$ and $r_{-1} = n$ or $n(x)$, where $m > n$ or degree$(m(x)) >$ degree$(n(x))$. Then, the recursions of the EDA are

$$
\begin{array}{rccl|l}
 & & & & r_{-2} = q_{-2} \cdot m + p_{-2} \cdot n \\
 & & & & \quad\;\; = 1 \cdot m + 0 \cdot n \\
 & & & & r_{-1} = q_{-1} \cdot m + p_{-1} \cdot n \\
 & & & & \quad\;\; = 0 \cdot m + 1 \cdot n \\
r_{-2} = a_0 \cdot r_{-1} + r_0 & a_0 = \left\lfloor \frac{r_{-2}}{r_{-1}} \right\rfloor & r_0 < r_{-1} < r_{-2} & & r_0 = q_0 \cdot m + p_0 \cdot n = 1 \cdot m - a_0 \cdot n \\
r_{-1} = a_1 \cdot r_0 + r_1 & a_1 = \left\lfloor \frac{r_{-1}}{r_0} \right\rfloor & r_1 < r_0 & & r_1 = q_1 \cdot m + p_1 \cdot n \\
\vdots & \vdots & \vdots & & \vdots \\
r_{j-2} = a_j \cdot r_{j-1} + r_j & a_j = \left\lfloor \frac{r_{j-2}}{r_{j-1}} \right\rfloor & r_j < r_{j-1} & & r_j = q_j \cdot m + p_j \cdot n \\
\vdots & \vdots & \vdots & & \vdots \\
r_{\tau-2} = a_\tau \cdot r_{\tau-1} + r_\tau & a_\tau = \left\lfloor \frac{r_{\tau-2}}{r_{\tau-1}} \right\rfloor & r_\tau < r_{\tau-1} & & r_\tau = q_\tau \cdot m + p_\tau \cdot n \\
r_{\tau-1} = a_{\tau+1} \cdot r_\tau + 0 & a_{\tau+1} = \left\lfloor \frac{r_{\tau-1}}{r_\tau} \right\rfloor & 0 < r_\tau & & 0 = q_{\tau+1} \cdot m + p_{\tau+1} \cdot n
\end{array}
\tag{10.72}
$$

The remainders are monotonically decreasing (in degree) until a remainder $r_{\tau+1}$ finally vanishes and the $\gcd(m, n) = r_\tau$ has been found.

The EDA delivers the gcd of two integers or polynomials follows from two considerations:

(1.) In reverse direction, the algorithms yields

$$r_\tau | r_{\tau-1} \Longrightarrow r_\tau | r_{\tau-2} \Longrightarrow r_\tau | r_{\tau-3} \Longrightarrow \ldots \Longrightarrow r_\tau | n \Longrightarrow r_\tau | m$$

(2.) In forward direction, we conclude that each common divisor of $r_{-2} = m$ and $r_{-1} = n$, also the gcd, will divide $r_{-2}, r_{-1}, r_0, r_1, \ldots r_\tau$. Expressed more formally,

$$\gcd(m,n)|m \text{ and } \gcd(m,n)|n \Longrightarrow \gcd(m,n)|r_0 \Longrightarrow \gcd(m,n)|r_1 \Longrightarrow \ldots \Longrightarrow \gcd(m,n)|r_\tau$$

From both considerations, we conclude that $r_\tau = \gcd(m, n)$ if $r_{\tau+1} = 0$.

With the steps of the EDA we have already shown, how the remainders follow as linear combinations of m and n. In the following theorem, we will state this again in a formal way and then proof it.

Theorem 10.3 *The remainders r_j of the EDA can be described as linear combinations of the integers m and n or the polynomials $m(x)$ and $n(x)$, whose gcd is determined. It can thus be written in the form*

$$r_j = q_j \cdot m + p_j \cdot n \,. \tag{10.73}$$

Proof We prove this by induction. The induction start is given by

$$\begin{aligned} r_{-2} &= 1 \cdot m + 0 \cdot n = q_{-2} \cdot m + p_{-2} \cdot n \\ r_{-1} &= 0 \cdot m + 1 \cdot n = q_{-1} \cdot m + p_{-1} \cdot n \,. \end{aligned} \tag{10.74}$$

Induction hypothesis: for every arbitrary $j - 2$ and $j - 1$, we assume

$$\begin{aligned} r_{j-2} &= q_{j-2} \cdot m + p_{j-2} \cdot n \,, \\ r_{j-1} &= q_{j-1} \cdot m + p_{j-1} \cdot n \,. \end{aligned} \tag{10.75}$$

Then, we obtain for j:

$$r_j = r_{j-2} - a_j \cdot r_{j-1} = (q_{j-2} - a_j \cdot q_{j-1}) \cdot m + (p_{j-2} - a_j \cdot p_{j-1}) \cdot n = q_j \cdot m + p_j \cdot n \tag{10.76}$$

with

$$\begin{aligned} q_j &= q_{j-2} - a_j \cdot q_{j-1} \\ p_j &= p_{j-2} - a_j \cdot p_{j-1} \,. \end{aligned} \tag{10.77}$$

□

The next two theorems give some further properties of the EDA.

Theorem 10.4 (without proof) *q_j and p_j are relative prime and the smallest integers or polynomials of lowest degrees that fulfill the equation*

$$r_j = q_j \cdot m + p_j \cdot n \, .$$

Theorem 10.5 *For the recursively appearing polynomials $r_j(x)$, $q_j(x)$, and $p_j(x)$, we have*

$$\textit{degree } r_{j-1} + \textit{degree } p_j = \textit{degree } m \tag{10.78}$$

$$\textit{degree } r_{j-1} + \textit{degree } q_j = \textit{degree } n \tag{10.79}$$

and thus, degree p_j − degree q_j = degree m − degree n

Proof First, we will prove (10.78). Hereto, we select the EDA iteration that leads to a_j. There, we have

$$\text{degree } r_{j-1} = \text{degree } r_{j-2} - \text{degree } a_j \tag{10.80}$$

$$\text{degree } p_j = \text{degree } p_{j-1} + \text{degree } a_j \tag{10.81}$$

Summing both equations yields

$$\text{degree } r_{j-1} + \text{degree } p_j = \text{degree } r_{j-2} + \text{degree } p_{j-1} \tag{10.82}$$

For $j = -1$, we obtain

$$\text{degree } r_{j-1} + \text{degree } p_j = \text{degree } r_{-2} + \text{degree } \underbrace{p_{-1}}_{=1} = \text{degree } m \tag{10.83}$$

For Eq. (10.79), there are similar arguments:

$$\text{degree } r_{j-1} = \text{degree } r_{j-2} - \text{degree } a_j \tag{10.84}$$

$$\text{degree } q_j = \text{degree } q_{j-1} + \text{degree } a_j \tag{10.85}$$

Summing both equations yields

$$\text{degree } r_{j-1} + \text{degree } q_j = \text{degree } r_{j-2} + \text{degree } q_{j-1} \tag{10.86}$$

For $j = 0$, we obtain

$$\text{degree } r_{j-1} + \text{degree } q_j = \text{degree } r_{-1} + \text{degree } \underbrace{q_0}_{=1} = \text{degree } n \tag{10.87}$$

□

In the sequel, we will describe two options to use the EDA as a decoding algorithm.

10.6.2 First EDA Approach for Solving the Key Equation

In Eq. (10.49), we have already quoted the relation between non-error locator polynomial and the DFT-domain polynomial of an error pattern.

$$F(x) = T(x) \cdot \overline{\Gamma}(x) = T(x) \cdot \prod_{j \in \overline{\mathsf{F}}} (x - z^j) \, .$$

In $\overline{\Gamma}(x)$, all linear factors from $x^N - 1$ are contained that do also belong to $F(x)$, namely such linear factors that generate zeros at the error-free positions. Hence,

$$\overline{\Gamma}(x) = \gcd\left(F(x), x^N - 1\right) \, . \tag{10.88}$$

Let us assume the syndrome to be located at the upper end. (We already know that the syndrome can be shifted cyclically without having any influence on the computation of the error locations.) By this, the upper $2t$ components of $F(x)$ are known and the EDA can be started. More known components will not be needed, since the algorithm can be terminated before reaching unknown components due to the expected degree of $\overline{\Gamma}(x)$. In order to set up the termination condition, we observe that with e errors, the degree is given by degree $\overline{\Gamma}(x) = N - e$. Due to $e \leq t$, we get degree $\overline{\Gamma}(x) \geq N - t$, which means that we pursue the steps of the EDA until the degree of $r_j(x)$ falls short of $N - t$. The last remainder before this happens will then be $\overline{\Gamma}(x) = \gcd\left(F(x), x^N - 1\right) = r_\tau(x)$. All following remainders should be zero.

If we do additionally compute the 'right' side, i.e., the linear combinations of m and n, the first vanishing remainder will represent the key equation (10.50).

$$\begin{aligned} r_{\tau+1}(x) = 0 &= q_{\tau+1}(x) \cdot (x^N - 1) + p_{\tau+1}(x) \cdot F(x) \\ 0 \qquad &= -T(x) \cdot (x^N - 1) + \quad \Gamma(x) \cdot F(x) \end{aligned} \tag{10.89}$$

The correspondence is valid up to a constant, which is especially of no concern for the error-locator polynomial.

We do not give a formal proof that the $2t$ known components of $F(x)$ suffice. It will anyway become obvious when studying an example.

Example 10.7 As an example we consider the transmitted codeword

$$\mathbf{c} = (4, 1, 0, 2, 5, 6) \;\circ\!\!-\!\!\bullet\; \mathbf{C} = (3, 1, 0, 0, 0, 0)$$

which will be erroneously received as

$$\mathbf{r} = (4, 1, 0, 4, 5, 5) \;\circ\!\!-\!\!\bullet\; \mathbf{R} = (2, 1, 2, 1, 0, 5) \, .$$

The error vector is

$$\mathbf{f} = (0, 0, 0, 2, 0, 6) \;\circ\!\!-\!\!\bullet\; \mathbf{F} = (6, 0, 2, 1, 0, 5)$$

However, from this, we only know the syndrome components $S = (2, 1, 0, 5)$. We now follow the iterations of the EDA.

$r_{j-2}(x) = a_j(x)r_{j-1}(x) + r_j(x)$	$q_j(x) = q_{j-2}(x) - a_j(x)q_{j-1}(x)$	$p_j(x) = p_{j-2}(x) - a_j(x)p_{j-1}(x)$
$r_{-2} = x^N - 1 = x^6 - 1$	$q_{-2} = 1$	$p_{-2} = 0$
$r_{-1} = F(x) = 5x^5 + 0x^4 + 1x^3 + 2x^2 + ?x^1 + ?x^0$	$q_{-1} = 0$	$p_{-1} = 1$
$(x^6 - 1) : (5x^5 + 0x^4 + 1x^3 + 2x^2 + ?x^1 + ?x^0) = 3x = a_0(x)$	$q_0 =$	$p_0 =$
$\underline{x^6 + 3x^4 + 6x^3 + ?x^2 + ?x^1}$	$q_{-2} - a_0 q_{-1} =$	$p_{-2} - a_0 p_{-1} =$
$4x^4 + 1x^3 + ?x^2 + ?x^1 - 1x^0$	1	$-3x$
$= r_0(x)$, degree $\geq N - t = 6 - 2 = 4$		
$(5x^5 + 0x^4 + 1x^3 + 2x^2 + ?) : (4x^4 + 1x^3 + ?) = 3x + 1 = a_1(x)$	$q_1 =$	$p_1 =$
$\underline{5x^5 + 3x^4 + ?x^3 + ?}$	$q_{-1} - a_1 q_0 =$	$p_{-1} - a_1 p_0 =$
$4x^4 + ?x^3 + ?$	$4x + 6$	$1 + (3x + 1)3x =$
$\underline{4x^4 + 1x^3 + ?}$		$2x^2 + 3x + 1$
$0x^4 + ?x^3 + ?$		
$= r_1(x)$, degree $< N - t = 4$	$= -T(x) \cdot const.$	$= \Gamma(x) \cdot const.$

As we know, a constant has no influence on the error locations. In the following chapter, we will show, that the computation of the error values is also not dependent on constants that show up both in $T(x)$ and in $\Gamma(x)$. Both polynomials can, of course, be normalized such that $\Gamma(x)$ becomes monic.

$$\Gamma(x) = (2x^2 + 3x + 1) \cdot 2^{-1} = x^2 + 5x + 4$$
$$T(x) = -(4x + 6) \cdot 2^{-1} = 5x + 4$$

The degree of the remainders is reduced by at least one at each step, i.e., degree $\{r_{-2}(x)\} = N$, degree $\{r_{-1}(x)\} \leq N - 1$, degree $\{r_0(x)\} \leq N - 2$, ..., degree $\{r_{t-1}(x)\} < N - t$. Hence, the termination criterion is reached latest at $r_{t-1}(x)$.

10.6.3 Second EDA Approach for Solving the Key Equation

Another EDA approach starts from a lower-ended syndrome. In the key equation (10.50), $F(x)$ is split into $S(x) + F^\star(x)$. Then, the equation reads

$$\Gamma(x) \cdot F(x) = \Gamma(x) \cdot S(x) + \Gamma(x) \cdot F^\star(x) = T(x) \cdot (x^N - 1) = -T(x) + x^N \cdot T(x) . \tag{10.90}$$

All coefficients on the right side vanish for powers from e to $N - 1$. On the left side, $F^\star(x)$ has powers starting from $2t$. This allows to rewrite the key equation into

$$\Gamma(x) \cdot S(x) = -T(x) + x^{2t} \cdot (\dots) . \tag{10.91}$$

We solve for $-T(x)$ and compare with a 'linear combination' from the EDA.

$$-T(x) = (\ldots) \cdot x^{2t} + \Gamma(x) \cdot S(x) \tag{10.92}$$
$$r_\tau(x) = q_\tau(x) \cdot x^{2t} + p_\tau(x) \cdot S(x) \tag{10.93}$$

In this, we have degree $T(x) =$ degree $r_\tau(x) < t$ and degree $r_{\tau-1} \geq t$. In Theorem 10.5, we have shown that

$$\text{degree}\, r_{\tau-1} + \text{degree}\, p_\tau = \text{degree}\, m = 2t\ . \tag{10.94}$$

This leads to degree $p_\tau \leq t$. $T(x)$ cannot have linear factors $(x - z^j)$ and has therefore no common linear factors with $\Gamma(x)$. Since $q_\tau(x)$ and $p_\tau(x)$ are relative prime, p_τ and r_τ do also not have common linear factors according to Eq. (10.93). Thus, the given correspondence holds. To summarize, this means starting from $m(x) = x^{2t}$ and $n(x) = S(x)$ the EDA is used to compute the first remainder $r_\tau(x)$ of degree less than t. Then follows $p_\tau = \Gamma(x)$ and $r_\tau = -T(x)$.
Use the second EDA approach for the example of the previous section!
What is the advantage of the second EDA approach compared to the first? (See Sect. 10.7.2*)*

10.7 Error Values

Up to now, our focus was on the localization of errors, with the argument that the remaining error correction is just an interpolation problem, i.e., the erroneous component will be replaced by polynomial interpolation. Nevertheless, it can mean a much lower complexity to directly determine the error values and subtract them from the received vector. Before showing this option in detail, we describe a very natural possibility to compute the error values. This makes sense, if the information is located in DFT domain.

10.7.1 Recursive Error-Value Computation

From the key equation (10.50) we derived a relation with a cyclic convolution (10.51) that now allows to recursively determine the whole error vector or error polynomial $F(x)$ in DFT domain after the error-locator polynomial $\Gamma(x)$ has been found. In turn, this means that the shift-register structure shown at the end of Sect. 10.4 can be used to successively compute the whole DFT-domain error vector. With this approach, we do not even need to know the error positions in time domain. However, if the information was encoded in time domain, it will be necessary to transform $F(x)$ into the time domain by an IDFT. Then, the error positions will become obvious. This transformation will not be required when computing the error values directly only at the error locations. This will be explained in the following section.

10.7.2 Forney's Direct Error-Value Computation

For only correcting errors at the error locations, first the roots z^j, $j \in \mathbb{F}$ of the error-locator polynomial have to be determined, since these specify the error positions j. This can simply be done by performing an inverse transform of the error-locator polynomial into the time domain. Zeros will then mark the error positions. The corresponding effort will be less than an inverse transform of $F(x)$, since the error-locator polynomial has only $e + 1$ coefficients unequal to zero.

For the error-value computation, we again make use of the key equation (10.50),

$$\Gamma(x) \cdot F(x) = T(x) \cdot (x^N - 1) \; .$$

From it, we obtain

$$f_j = F(x = z^j) = \left. \frac{T(x) \cdot (x^N - 1)}{\Gamma(x)} \right|_{x=z^j} . \tag{10.95}$$

Since numerator and denominator have a root for $x = z^j$ at the error locations j, we will formally derive numerator and denominator according to l'Hospital's rule. This yields

$$f_j = F(x = z^j) = \left. \frac{T'(x) \cdot (x^N - 1) + N \cdot x^{N-1} \cdot T(x)}{\Gamma'(x)} \right|_{x=z^j} \tag{10.96}$$

$$= N \cdot \left. \frac{T(x)}{x \cdot \Gamma'(x)} \right|_{x=z^j} . \tag{10.97}$$

Now, it is clear that also $T(x)$ out of the EDA is an important output and can be used for computing the error values.

From the Berlekamp algorithm, as we have described it, no $T(x)$ was computed. (However, there exists a corresponding modification.) $T(x)$ has then additionally to be computed to be able to use Forney's method.
We again use the key equation

$$\Gamma(x) \cdot F(x) = T(x) \cdot (x^N - 1) = -T(x) + x^N \cdot T(x) \; .$$

When comparing the higher powers from x^N on, they will result from

$$x^N \cdot T(x) \text{ and } \Gamma(x) \cdot (F_{N-e} \cdot x^{N-e} + \cdots + F_{N-1} \cdot x^{N-1}) \; .$$

When comparing coefficients having $T(x) = T_0 + T_1 x + \cdots + T_{e-1} x^{e-1}$, we obtain

$$
\begin{aligned}
x^N &: T_0 = \sum_{l=1}^{e} F_{N-l} \cdot \Gamma_l \\
x^{N+1} &: T_1 = \sum_{l=1}^{e-1} F_{N-l} \cdot \Gamma_{l+1} \\
&\vdots \\
x^{N+j} &: T_j = \sum_{l=1}^{e-j} F_{N-l} \cdot \Gamma_{l+j} \ , \quad j < e
\end{aligned}
\tag{10.98}
$$

Example 10.8 We use $\Gamma(x)$ out of the EDA to recompute $T(x)$. The received vector was

$$\mathbf{r} = (4, 1, 0, 4, 5, 5) \ \circ\!\!-\!\!\bullet \ \mathbf{R} = (2, 1, \underline{2, 1, 0, 5}) \ ,$$

having selected the upper four positions to be the syndrome. The error-locator polynomial was determined as

$$\Gamma(x) = x^2 + 5x + 4$$

Then, the coefficients of $T(x)$ follow to be

$$\left.\begin{aligned} T_0 &= F_5 \cdot \Gamma_1 + F_4 \cdot \Gamma_2 = 5 \cdot 5 + 0 = 4 \ , \\ T_1 &= F_5 \cdot \Gamma_2 \qquad\qquad\quad\ = 5 \end{aligned}\right\} T(x) = 4 + 5x \ ,$$

which is identical to the EDA output.

In the following two examples, the error values will be computed using the recursive DFT-domain approach and Forney's method.

Example 10.9 From $\mathbf{R} = (2, 1, \underline{2, 1, 0, 5})$ and $\Gamma(x) = x^2 + 5x + 4$ we determine the error vector in DFT domain by cyclic convolution (10.51) and the error vector in time domain then follows from an IDFT.

$$
\begin{aligned}
\Gamma_0 \cdot F_3 + \Gamma_1 \cdot F_2 + \Gamma_2 \cdot F_1 &= 0 \\
\Gamma_0 \cdot F_2 + \Gamma_1 \cdot F_1 + \Gamma_2 \cdot F_0 &= 0
\end{aligned}
$$

$$
\begin{aligned}
F_1 &= -\Gamma_0 \cdot F_3 - \Gamma_1 \cdot F_2 = -4 \cdot 1 - 5 \cdot 2 = 0 \\
F_0 &= -\Gamma_0 \cdot F_2 - \Gamma_1 \cdot F_1 = -4 \cdot 2 - 5 \cdot 0 = 6
\end{aligned}
$$

$$\Longrightarrow \mathbf{F} = (6, 0, 2, 1, 0, 5) \ \bullet\!\!-\!\!\circ \ \mathbf{f} = (0, 0, 0, 2, 0, 6)$$

Example 10.10 We now use Forney's approach to directly compute the error values at the two error locations. First we have to determine the locations itself. We apply the IDFT.

$$\gamma_j = \Gamma(x = z^j) \ , \quad z = 5 \ , \quad \boldsymbol{\gamma} = (3, 5, 5, 0, 4, 0)$$

For Forney's method we need $T(x) = 4 + 5x$ and $\Gamma'(x) = 5 + 2x$.

$$f_3 = N \cdot \frac{T(x)}{x \cdot \Gamma'(x)}\bigg|_{x=5^3} = 6 \cdot \frac{4+5 \cdot 5^3}{5^3 \cdot (5+2 \cdot 5^3)} = 6 \cdot 6 \cdot \frac{4+5 \cdot 6}{5+2 \cdot 6} = 2$$
$$f_5 = N \cdot \frac{T(x)}{x \cdot \Gamma'(x)}\bigg|_{x=5^5} = 6 \cdot \frac{4+5 \cdot 5^5}{5^5 \cdot (5+2 \cdot 5^5)} = 6 \cdot 5 \cdot \frac{4+5 \cdot 3}{5+2 \cdot 3} = 6$$

$$\Longrightarrow \mathbf{f} = (0, 0, 0, 2, 0, 6)$$

10.7.3 The Effect of a Cyclic Shift in DFT Domain

Up to now, we have only realized that for computing the error-locator polynomial, the syndrome can be cyclically shifted without having any effect, since a shift in DFT domain will only mean a multiplication with a factor (unequal to zero) in the original (time) domain. When we are computing error values, however, this has to be considered in more detail. Therefore, we again quote the shift property (10.10).

$$F^{\hookrightarrow}(x) = F(x) \cdot x^l \bmod (x^N - 1) \quad \bullet\!\!-\!\!\circ \quad f_j^{\hookrightarrow} = f_j \cdot z^{j \cdot l} \tag{10.99}$$

If we compute $f_j^{\hookrightarrow}$ by means of the Forney method as

$$f_j^{\hookrightarrow} = F^{\hookrightarrow}(x = z^j) = N \cdot \frac{T^{\hookrightarrow}(x)}{x \cdot \Gamma'(x)}\bigg|_{x=z^j}, \tag{10.100}$$

the desired error value f_j will be

$$f_j = f_j^{\hookrightarrow} \cdot z^{-j \cdot l} = N \cdot \frac{x^{-l} T^{\hookrightarrow}(x)}{x \cdot \Gamma'(x)}\bigg|_{x=z^j} = N \cdot \frac{T^{\hookrightarrow}(x)}{x^{l+1} \cdot \Gamma'(x)}\bigg|_{x=z^j}. \tag{10.101}$$

Thus, one can just replace the error-evaluator polynomial $T^{\hookrightarrow}(x)$ by $x^{-l}T^{\hookrightarrow}(x) = x^{N-l}T^{\hookrightarrow}(x)$ (since $x = z^j$) and apply Forney's method. $T(x) = x^{N-l}T^{\hookrightarrow}(x)$ does however not fulfill the usual degree limitation degree $T(x) < e$. This is achieved by reducing $T(x)$ modulo $\Gamma(x)$. This is possible, since anyway, all components of $T(x)$ that contain the error-locator polynomial are set to zero when setting $x = z^j$, $j \in \mathbb{F}$.

10.7.4 Error and Erasure Decoding

When describing the Berlekamp algorithm, we had already mentioned, how erasures could be taken into account by initializing the algorithm with the erasure polynomial

$$\Lambda(x) = \prod_{j \in \mathbb{E}} (x - z^j). \tag{10.102}$$

$\mathbb{E}$ denotes the set of indices of the erasure locations ($|\mathbb{E}| = a_E$). In this section, we present a general approach that is not related to a special decoding algorithm.

Let the received vector in the time domain be given by

$$\mathbf{r} = \mathbf{c} + \mathbf{f} + \mathbf{a},$$

where $\mathbf{c}$ is the transmitted codeword, $\mathbf{f}$ are the errors at unknown locations $j \in \mathbb{F}$, and $\mathbf{a}$ are the erasures at known locations $j \in \mathbb{E}$. Before using a decoding algorithm, we should eliminate the influence of the erasures. If we would multiply in DFT domain by the erasure polynomial $\Lambda(x)$, this would set the erased positions to zero in time domain.

$$\lambda_j = \Lambda(x = z^j) = \prod_{l \in \mathbb{E}} (x - z^l) \Bigg|_{x=z^j} = 0\,, \quad j \in \mathbb{E}$$

This will not mean any change for the error locations, since they are disjunct from the erasures. They will thus not be set to zero. Nevertheless, the syndrome range that is usable for determining the error-locator polynomial will be reduced. Due to the multiplication of the erasure polynomial

$$r_j^\diamond := r_j \cdot \lambda_j = \underbrace{c_j \cdot \lambda_j}_{c_j^\diamond} + \underbrace{f_j \cdot \lambda_j}_{f_j^\diamond} \;\circ\!\!-\!\!\bullet\; R^\diamond(x) := R(x) \cdot \Lambda(x) = \underbrace{C(x) \cdot \Lambda(x)}_{C^\diamond(x)} + \underbrace{F(x) \cdot \Lambda(x)}_{F^\diamond(x)} \tag{10.103}$$

with $C(x)$, the syndrome range will be reduced by the degree a_E of $\Lambda(x)$. Only $M - a_E$ syndrome components are left for computing $\Gamma^\diamond(x) = \Gamma(x)$ reducing the error-correcting capability to

$$e \leq \left\lfloor \frac{M - a_E}{2} \right\rfloor . \tag{10.104}$$

We already realized this when studying the erasure initialization in the BMA. Apart from the shortening of the usable syndrome, the decoding procedures stay the same. We summarize with

Theorem 10.6 *An RS code with M parities and the minimum Hamming distance $d_{Hm} = M + 1$ allows to correct a_E erasures and e errors, if $a_E + 2 \cdot e \leq M$.*

For the final error-value computations, the erasure and error-locator polynomial have to be combined as

$$\Gamma_{tot}(x) = \Gamma(x) \cdot \Lambda(x) . \tag{10.105}$$

Using the original syndrome out of $F(x)$, one can recursively compute the total error vector in DFT domain or, after determining the error value polynomial $T(x)$, Forney's method can be applied. This time, $T(x)$ does not result from the EDA when using the shortened syndrome.

We discussed possibilities of decoding of errors up to half the minimum Hamming distance, so-called bounded minimum-distance decoding (BMD) and we realized that knowing the error position (erasure decoding) we could improved the correction ability to twice the number of errors. There are, however, works to exceed half the Hamming distance. We will in here only mention some of the proposals. The first to mention is certainly the list decoding Guruswami-Sudan [8] algorithm based on polynomial interpolation, later improved in complexity by Vardy and Kötter in [9]. For low-rate RS codes, a multi-shift-register approach has been presented in [10]. Typically, however, RS codes are used with high code rates.

One may adjust the parameters K and M of an RS code easily. For reducing K, one can, of course, just fix information symbols to known values, not transmitting them any more. Reducing M can just be seen as setting erasures, thereby keeping the MDS property. This also allows for adaptively adding redundancy on request by the receiver starting from a minimum amount to be able to recognize decoding failure reliably up to its maximum. Already a small number of parity symbols ensures that false correction to another codeword will practically almost never occur, but instead decoding failure will be detected, which can be used to request more parity symbols (see Sect. 14.1).

References

1. R. de Prony, "Assai experimentale et analytique," *Ecole Polytech. (Paris)*, vol. 1, pp. 24–76, Dec 1795.
2. J. Wolf, "Decoding of Bose-Chaudhuri-Hocquenghem codes and Prony's method for curve fitting (corresp.)," *IEEE Transactions on Information Theory*, vol. 13, no. 4, pp. 608–608, 1967.
3. E. R. Berlekamp, *Algebraic Coding Theory*. St. Louis, San Francisco, Toronto, London, Sydney: McGraw-Hill, 1968.
4. J. Massey, "Shift-register synthesis and BCH decoding," *IEEE Transactions on Information Theory*, vol. 15, no. 1, pp. 122–127, 1969.
5. W. Henkel, "Another description of the Berlekamp-Massey algorithm," *IEE Proc. Part I*, vol. 136, no. 3, 1989.
6. J. Dornstetter, "On the equivalence between Berlekamp's and Euclid's algorithms (Corresp.)," *IEEE Transactions on Information Theory*, vol. 33, no. 3, pp. 428–431, 1987.
7. T. D. Mateer, "On the equivalence of the Berlekamp-Massey and the Euclidean algorithms for algebraic decoding," in *2011 12th Canadian Workshop on Information Theory*, 2011, pp. 139–142.
8. V. Guruswami and M. Sudan, "Improved decoding of Reed-Solomon and algebraic-geometry codes," *IEEE Transactions on Information Theory*, vol. 45, no. 6, pp. 1757–1767, 1999.
9. R. Koetter and A. Vardy, "Algebraic soft-decision decoding of Reed-Solomon codes," *IEEE Transactions on Information Theory*, vol. 49, no. 11, pp. 2809–2825, 2003.
10. G. Schmidt, V. Sidorenko, and M. Bossert, "Decoding Reed-Solomon codes beyond half the minimum distance using shift-register synthesis," in *2006 IEEE International Symposium on Information Theory*, July 2006, pp. 459–463.

Chapter 11
Bose-Chaudhuri-Hocqhenghem (BCH) Codes, Especially Binary BCH Codes

Two viewpoints:
BCH codes are subfield subcodes of RS codes,
... or ...
RS codes are a special case of BCH codes.

11.1 Definition and Examples

We defined RS codes by use of an element of order $N \mid (P^m - 1)$ for defining a DFT. M consecutive components had to vanish in DFT domain. The components in time and DFT domain were from the same number field $GF(P^m)$. We will now deviate from the requirement to have the same field in both domains. Instead, the components of the original (time) domain can now be from a sub-field $GF(P^{m_u})$ of $GF(P^m)$, $(m_u|m)$. Since we will not be considering multiple extensions, we will especially be interested in the case where $c_j \in GF(P)$ and $C_j \in GF(P^m)$. The components in the original domain are from the prime field of characteristic P, whereas in DFT domain the components are from an extension field.

We already know from the DFT over complex numbers that a real time-domain function requires the DFT components to fulfill conjugacy constraints. In the case of a complex DFT, letting all components $a_j \in \mathbb{R}$, leads to

$$\begin{aligned} A_j &= N^{-1} a(x = z^{-j}) \\ A_{N-j} &= N^{-1} a(x = z^{-(N-j)}) = N^{-1} a(x = z^{+j}) = A_j^\star \end{aligned} \tag{11.1}$$

Especially, for $j = 0$ and $j = N/2 \in \mathbb{N}$ we obtain

$$A_0 \in \mathbb{R} \quad \text{and} \quad A_{N/2} \in \mathbb{R}\,, \quad \text{if } N/2 \in \mathbb{N}. \tag{11.2}$$

W. Henkel, *Channel Coding*, Signals and Communication Technology,
https://doi.org/10.1007/978-3-032-08236-7_11

For finite fields, similar conjugacy constraints apply. However, there may be more than two conjugates. Let $c_j \in GF(P)$ and $C_j \in GF(P^m)$. Then, we have

$$\begin{aligned}
C_j &= N^{-1}c(x = z^{-j}) \\
C_{Pj} &= N^{-1}c(x = z^{-Pj}) = N^{-1}\left(c(x = z^{-j})\right)^P = N^{-1}(C_j \cdot N)^P \\
C_{P^2j} &= N^{-1}c(x = z^{-P^2j}) = N^{-1}\left(c(x = z^{-j})\right)^{P^2} = N^{-1}(C_j \cdot N)^{P^2} \\
&\vdots \\
C_{P^lj} &= N^{-1}c(x = z^{-P^lj}) = N^{-1}\left(c(x = z^{-j})\right)^{P^l} = N^{-1}(C_j \cdot N)^{P^l}
\end{aligned} \tag{11.3}$$

These relations will become a little simpler for fields of characteristics $P = 2$. If $z \in GF(2^m)$, we obtain: N is odd (*e.g.*, $N = 2^m - 1$) $\Longrightarrow N \bmod 2 = 1 \Longrightarrow N^{-1} = 1$, i.e., N^{-1} can be discarded from (11.3):

$$\begin{aligned}
C_j &= c(x = z^{-j}) \\
C_{2j} &= c(x = z^{-2j}) = \left(c(x = z^{-j})\right)^2 = C_j^2 \\
C_{2^2j} &= c(x = z^{-2^2j}) = \left(c(x = z^{-j})\right)^{2^2} = C_j^{2^2} \\
&\vdots \\
C_{2^lj} &= c(x = z^{-2^lj}) = \left(c(x = z^{-j})\right)^{2^l} = C_j^{2^l}
\end{aligned} \tag{11.4}$$

Before we come to examples of BCH codes, we give the following.

Definition 11.1 A BCH code of length $N = P^m - 1$ is a **primitive BCH code**, since the element of order N is also the primitive element of the underlying number field.

Example 11.1 In the following, we rederive the Hamming code as a primitive BCH code. It is a binary code, i.e., $c_j \in GF(2)$. The length is $N = 2^m - 1$. For $m = 3$ the length will be $N = 7$. From the table in Sect. 9.2.2 we grasp the primitive polynomial (13_8), i.e., $p(z) = z^3 + z + 1$. We first write the cyclotomic cosets representing the conjugates.

Cycl. coset	field	number of bits
$\{0\}$	$GF(2)$	1
$\{1, 2, 4\}$	$GF(2^3)$	3
$\{3, 6, 5\}$	$GF(2^3)$	3

(11.5)

We would like to correct one single error, i.e., the **designed** minimum Hamming **distance** is $d_{Hm} = 3$ and $M = 2$. From the coset $\{3, 6, 5\}$, we conclude that with zeros C_5 and C_6, also C_3 will vanish. The remaining positions in DFT domain are 0,1,2,4, where position 0 is just a binary number and the three conjugates are elements of the extension field $GF(2^3)$. In total, we have 4 bits information and 3 bits redundancy. Figure 11.1 depicts the code structure in DFT domain.

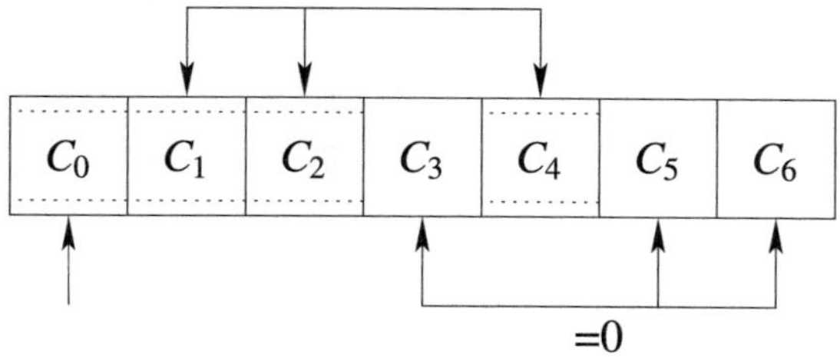

Fig. 11.1 DFT-domain structure of the Hamming code of length 7

Since the generator polynomial contains a linear factors of all conjugates (minimal polynomial), it also has only factors from the prime field $GF(2)$. We can also deduce this from the encoding methods in time domain where we multiply with $g(x)$. A codeword with components from $GF(P)$ can only be obtained, if also $g(x)$ has only coefficients from $GF(P)$.

$$
\begin{aligned}
g(x) &= (x - z^{-(N-1)}) \cdot (x - z^{-(N-2)}) \cdot (x - z^{-(N-4)}) \\
&= (x - z^1) \cdot (x - z^2) \cdot (x - z^4) = x^3 + x + 1
\end{aligned}
\tag{11.6}
$$

The generator matrix follows from (10.31).

$$
\mathbf{G} = \begin{pmatrix} 1\,1\,0\,1\,0\,0\,0 \\ 0\,1\,1\,0\,1\,0\,0 \\ 0\,0\,1\,1\,0\,1\,0 \\ 0\,0\,0\,1\,1\,0\,1 \end{pmatrix}
$$

Some trivial operations

$$
\mathbf{G} \equiv \begin{pmatrix} 1\,0\,1\,1\,1\,0\,0 \\ 0\,1\,1\,0\,1\,0\,0 \\ 0\,0\,1\,1\,0\,1\,0 \\ 0\,0\,0\,1\,1\,0\,1 \end{pmatrix} \equiv \begin{pmatrix} 1\,0\,0\,0\,1\,1\,0 \\ 0\,1\,0\,1\,1\,1\,0 \\ 0\,0\,1\,1\,0\,1\,0 \\ 0\,0\,0\,1\,1\,0\,1 \end{pmatrix} \equiv \left(\begin{array}{c|c} 1\,0\,0\,0 & 1\,1\,0 \\ 0\,1\,0\,0 & 0\,1\,1 \\ 0\,0\,1\,0 & 1\,1\,1 \\ 0\,0\,0\,1 & 1\,0\,1 \end{array}\right)
$$

lead to a systematic form, for which the **H** matrix can easily be derived following Theorem 3.5.

$$
\mathbf{H} = \left(\begin{array}{c|c} 1\,0\,1\,1 & 1\,0\,0 \\ 1\,1\,1\,0 & 0\,1\,0 \\ 0\,1\,1\,1 & 0\,0\,1 \end{array}\right)
$$

Obviously, this is the parity-check matrix of the Hamming code of length 7, although the columns are not sorted as a binary counter.

Example 11.2 We construct a primitive BCH code of length $N = 2^4 - 1 = 15$ with a designed distance of 5. Let z be the primitive element of $GF(2^4)$ with the primitive polynomial $p(z) = z^4 + z + 1 \equiv 0$. How are the 15 binary digits allocated to the components in DFT domain?

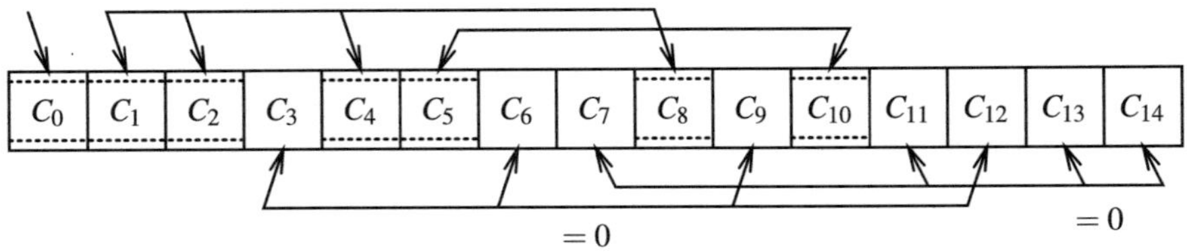

Fig. 11.2 Structure of a BCH code of length 15 and designed distance 5 in DFT domain

The cyclotomic cosets are

Cyclotomic coset	field	number of bits
$\{0\}$	$GF(2)$	1
$\{1, 2, 4, 8\}$	$GF(2^4)$	4
$\{3, 6, 12, 9\}$	$GF(2^4)$	4
$\{5, 10\}$	$GF(2^2)$	2
$\{7, 14, 13, 11\}$	$GF(2^4)$	4

(11.7)

In more detail:

$$\begin{array}{l} C_0 \in GF(2) \\ C_1,\ C_2 = C_1^2,\ C_4 = C_2^2 = C_1^4,\ C_8 = C_1^8,\ (C_{16} = C_1) \in GF(2^4) \\ C_3,\ C_6 = C_3^2,\ C_{12} = C_3^4,\ C_{24=9} = C_3^8,\ (C_{18} = C_3) \in GF(2^4) \\ C_5,\ C_{10} = C_5^2,\ (C_{20} = C_5) \in GF(2^2) \\ C_7,\ C_{14} = C_7^2,\ C_{28=13} = C_7^4,\ C_{26=11} = C_7^8,\ (C_{22} = C_7) \in GF(2^4)\ . \end{array}$$

When $t = 2$, the upper $2t = 4$ components are set to zero. Figure 11.2 depicts the structure in DFT domain.

Seven bits are left for data in C_0 (1), C_1 (4), and C_5 (2). This is the same number as we have components unequal to zero in DFT domain.

When constructing BCH code, the true distance can be significantly bigger than the 'designed distance'. This is caused by the multiple zeros due to the conjugacy constraints. In order to have many additionally (consecutive) zeros, the designed zeros should be placed from position 1 upwards or from $N - 1$ downwards. Note that position zero has no conjugates. Many decoding methods are only able to decode to (half) the designed distance. As an example, we discuss the perfect Golay code, derived as a non-primitive BCH code. Due to its symmetries, the (extended) Golay code offers a manifold of possible derivations that cannot all be studied in here (*e.g.*, MOD, Miracle Octad Generator). However, we will later describe the Turyn construction which is based on extended Hamming codes and allows to recognize code symmetries.

Example 11.3 Golay realized that the Hamming bound in Theorem 3.6 is just fulfilled for the parameters $N = 23$, $K = 12$, and $t = 3$. From this, he concluded the existence of such a binary perfect code.

For the construction, we require an element ξ of order $N = 23$. If we assume an upper zero at $N-1$ (or one at 1), and if we consider the cyclotomic coset

$$\{1, 2, 4, 8, 16, 9, 18, 13, 3, 6, 12\} , \tag{11.8}$$

we already obtain 4 consecutive zeros, which would mean a designed distance of 5. The true minimum distance is indeed 7. All cyclotomic cosets are

Cyclotomic coset	field	number of bits
$\{0\}$	$GF(2)$	1
$\{1, 2, 4, 8, 16, 9, 18, 13, 3, 6, 12\}$	$GF(2^{11})$	11
$\{5, 10, 20, 17, 11, 22, 21, 19, 15, 7, 14\}$	$GF(2^{11})$	11

(11.9)

The number field results to be $GF(2^{11})$. ξ should however have the order of 23. We observe that $2^{11} - 1 = 23 \cdot 89$. With $\xi = z^{89}$, we have $\xi^{23} = (z^{89})^{23} = z^{2^{11}-1} = 1$. Thus, we are about to design a non-primitive BCH code, since $N = 23|2^{11} - 1$ divides the primitive length. From both cyclotomic cosets, we obtain the generator polynomials

$$g_1(x) = x^{11} + x^9 + x^7 + x^6 + x^5 + x + 1 \tag{11.10}$$

$$g_2(x) = x^{11} + x^{10} + x^6 + x^5 + x^4 + x^2 + 1 \tag{11.11}$$

that both can be used to define the Golay code. 12 bits are left for information.

11.2 Specializing the RS Encoding Procedures for BCH Codes

In this section, we will present some simplifications for the encoding procedures of binary BCH codes when restricting the time-domain components to be elements of $GF(2)$. We discuss all four encoding methods again using the example of a BCH code of length $N = 15$ and $K = 7$ information bits.

11.2.1 Encoding in DFT Domain

In Sect. 10.3.1, we had reordered the transform into the original (time) domain as

$$\begin{aligned}
c_0 = C(z^0 = 1) &= I_0 + I_1 + I_2 + \cdots + I_{14} \\
c_1 = C(z^1) &= I_0 + I_1 \cdot z^1 + I_2 \cdot z^2 + \cdots + I_{14} \cdot z^{14} \\
c_2 = C(z^2) &= I_0 + (I_1 \cdot z^1) \cdot z^1 + (I_2 \cdot z^2) \cdot z^2 + \cdots + (I_{14} \cdot z^{14}) \cdot z^{14}. \\
&\vdots
\end{aligned}$$

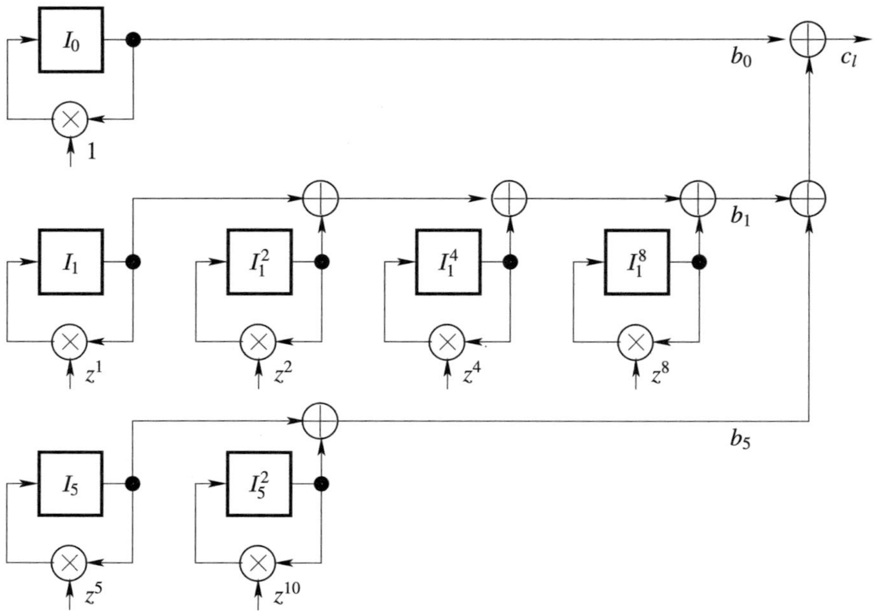

Fig. 11.3 Encoding in DFT domain for a BCH code with parameters ($N = 16$, $K = 7$)

The only components unequal to zero are

$$\begin{array}{ll} I_0 & \in GF(2) \\ I_1, I_2 = I_1^2, I_4 = I_1^4, I_8 = I_1^8 & \in GF(2^4) \\ I_5, I_{10} = I_5^2 & \in GF(2^2). \end{array}$$

Figure 11.3 shows the processing of components unequal to zero with the intermediate results b_0, b_1, and b_5.

It proves to be better to compute the intermediate results first, by representing I_1 as $I_1 = \zeta_0 + \zeta_1 z + \zeta_2 z^2 + \zeta_3 z^3$, $\zeta_j \in GF(2)$ and I_5 as $I_5 = \eta_0 + \eta_1 \xi^1$, $\eta_j \in GF(2)$:

$$\begin{aligned} I_1 &= \zeta_0 + \zeta_1 z + \zeta_2 z^2 + \zeta_3 z^3 \\ I_1^2 &= \zeta_0 + \zeta_1 z^2 + \zeta_2 z^4 + \zeta_3 z^6 \\ &= \zeta_0 + \zeta_1 z^2 + \zeta_2 (1 + z) + \zeta_3 (z^2 + z^3) \\ &= (\zeta_0 + \zeta_2) + \zeta_2 z + (\zeta_1 + \zeta_3) z^2 + \zeta_3 z^3 \\ I_1^4 &= (I_1^2)^2 \\ &= (\zeta_0 + \zeta_1 + \zeta_2 + \zeta_3) + (\zeta_1 + \zeta_3) z + (\zeta_2 + \zeta_3) z^2 + \zeta_3 z^3 \\ I_1^8 &= (\zeta_0 + \zeta_1) + (\zeta_2 + \zeta_3) z + (\zeta_1) z^2 + \zeta_3 z^3 \\ \hline \Sigma: &\quad I_1 + I_1^2 + I_1^4 + I_1^8 = \zeta_3 \end{aligned}$$

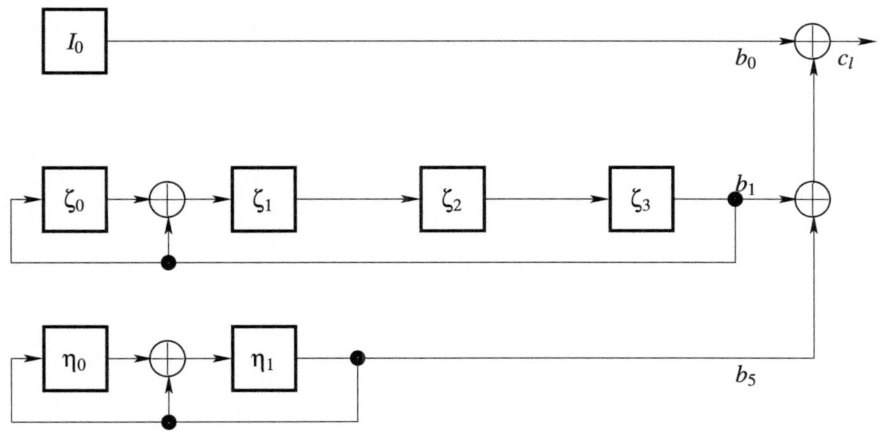

Fig. 11.4 Simplified DFT-domain encoder for a BCH code with parameters ($N = 16$, $K = 7$)

(We used the property that for a polynomial with coefficients from $GF(2)$ we have $(f(x))^2 = f(x^2)$. Note also the reduction modulo the primitive polynomial, which is $z^4 = 1 + z$.)

In the encoder, we iteratively multiply I_1 by z^1. Writing in components, this means

$$I_1 \cdot z = \zeta_0 z + \zeta_1 z^2 + \zeta_2 z^3 + \zeta_3(1+z) = \zeta_3 + (\zeta_0 + \zeta_3)z + \zeta_1 z^2 + \zeta_2 z^3.$$

Both results will now be used to simplify the block diagram and lead to the middle part (b_1) of Fig. 11.4.

For the lower part of the circuit, we should be aware that due to the two conjugates, I_5 is element of $GF(2^2)$. With $\xi = z^5$, we obtain an element of the multiplicative order 3, belonging to $GF(2^2)$. The corresponding irreducible polynomial is given as

$$m_5(x) = (x - \xi) \cdot (x - \xi^2) = x^2 + \underbrace{(\xi + \xi^2)}_{z^5+z^{10}=1} x + \underbrace{\xi^3}_{1} = x^2 + x + 1.$$

Hence, $m_5(x = \xi = z^5) = 0$, i.e., we do computations modulo $\xi^2 + \xi + 1$.
If we combine the components of b_5, we obtain

$$\begin{array}{rl} I_5 & = \eta_0 + \eta_1 z^5 \\ I_5^2 & = \eta_0 + \eta_1 z^{10} \\ & = (\eta_0 + \eta_1) + \eta_1 z^5 \\ \hline \Sigma: & I_5 + I_5^2 = \eta_1 \end{array}$$

In the circuit, we iteratively multiply I_5 with z^5, which means expressed with components

$$I_5 \cdot z^5 = (\eta_0 + \eta_1 \xi)\xi = \eta_1 + (\eta_0 + \eta_1)\xi.$$

Herewith, also the lower part of the encoder is described by computing modulo $\xi^2 + \xi + 1$.

In the following to short sections, we will now concentrate on the more important, systematic (in the original time domain) encoding methods. Like the non-systematic method that had been described in Sect. 10.3.2, these encoders rely on writing the codeword as a product

$$c(x) = u(x) \cdot g(x).$$

11.2.2 Systematic Encoding with the Generator Polynomial

When studying the systematic encoding in Sect. 10.3.3, we computed the redundancy of the codeword as the remainder of a division according to Eq. (10.25):

$$\begin{aligned} c_{N-1}x^{N-1} + \cdots + c_{N-K}x^{N-K} &= u(x) \cdot g(x) - c_{N-K-1}x^{N-K-1} \cdots - c_1 x - c_0 \\ &= u(x) \cdot g(x) + r(x). \end{aligned}$$

The minus signs can be ignored for binary BCH codes and additionally, the generator polynomial has only components from $GF(2)$, i.e., the generator polynomial

$$g(x) = \prod_j (x - z^{-j}) = \prod_l m_l(x), \quad l\text{: Indices of the cyclotomic cosets}$$

consists of minimal polynomials. Let us consider for example $C_{N-j} = N^{-1}c(x = z^{-(N-j)}) = 0$, we obtain $g(x) = (x - z^{-(N-j)}) \cdot (x - z^{-2(N-j)}) \cdots = (x - z^j) \cdot (x - z^{2j}) \cdot (x - z^{4j}) \cdots = (x + z^j) \cdot (x + z^{2j}) \cdot (x + z^{4j}) \ldots$, according to the size of the cyclotomic coset. Let us again consider an example with $N = 2^4 - 1 = 15$. Then, $C_{14} = 0$ means

$$g(x) = (x + z^1)(x + z^2)(x + z^4)(x + z^8) = m_1(x).$$

Automatically, two consecutive zeros are obtained in the DFT domain. Adding $C_{12} = 0$, we get

$$\begin{aligned} g(x) &= (x + z^1)(x + z^2)(x + z^4)(x + z^8) \cdot (x + z^3)(x + z^6)(x + z^{12})(x + z^9) \\ &= m_1(x) \cdot m_3(x) \\ &= 1 + x^4 + x^6 + x^7 + x^8. \end{aligned}$$

From the encoder presented in Sect. 10.3.3, we obtain a structure shown in Fig. 11.5. This differs only in not needing to negate the remainder to obtain the redundancy and the multiplications disappeared due to using binary numbers.

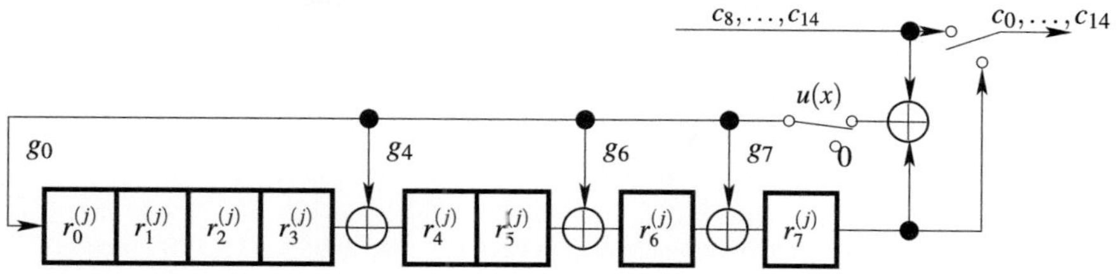

Fig. 11.5 Systematic encoder based on the generator polynomial of the (15,7) BCH code

11.2.3 Systematic Encoding with the Parity-Check Polynomial

In Sect. 10.3.4, we concluded from

$$c(x) = u(x) \cdot g(x)$$

that

$$c(x) \cdot h(x) = 0 \mod (x^N - 1).$$

Compared to our earlier description, the shift-register structure is simplified, since coefficients can only be 0 or 1. The parity-check polynomial, just as the generator polynomial, only has coefficients from $GF(2)$. It has the remaining linear factors not contained in the generator polynomial. These again constitute minimal polynomials, whose coefficients are elements of the prime field $GF(2)$. For our example with $g(x) = (x + z^1)(x + z^2)(x + z^4)(x + z^8) \cdot (x + z^3)(x + z^6)(x + z^{12})(x + z^9) = m_1(x) \cdot m_3(x)$, we obtain

$$\begin{aligned} h(x) &= (x^{15} - 1)/g(x) \\ &= \underbrace{(x + z^0)}_{m_0(x)} \cdot \underbrace{(x + z^5)(x + z^{10})}_{m_5(x)} \cdot \underbrace{(x + z^7)(x + z^{14})(x + z^{13})(x + z^{11})}_{m_7(x)} \\ &= (x + 1) \cdot (1 + x + x^2) \cdot (1 + x^3 + x^4) \\ &= (x + 1) \cdot (1 + x + x^2 + x^3 + x^6) \\ &= 1 + x^4 + x^6 + x^7 \end{aligned}$$

Following Sect. 10.3.4, the resulting encoder structure will be as shown in Fig. 11.6 and Table 11.1.

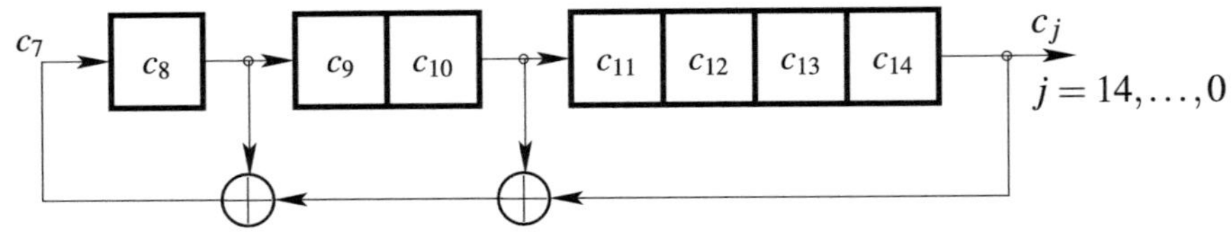

Fig. 11.6 Systematic encoder based on the parity-check polynomial of the (15,7) BCH code

11.2.4 The Decoding of Binary BCH Codes

The decoding is performed as with RS codes, but *error values* need not be determined. Since the components are just binary, in case of an error, the error value has to be 1.

When determining the syndrome in DFT domain, the conjugacy constraints can be used for complexity reduction. If S_j is known in DFT domain, together with it we obtain $S_{2j} = S_j^2$.

There is a manifold of specialized decoding methods for binary BCH codes that we are not able to discuss in here. We just mention a few:

- permutation decoding,
- Meggitt decoder,
- threshold decoding,
- majority-logic decoding,
- Kasami decoder, decoding with covering polynomials

Later we will present means of decoding short block codes based on their trellis, allowing for maximum-likelihood (ML, Viterbi) and maximum-a-posteriori probability (MAP, BCJR) decoding.

To conclude, we provide a list of primitive binary BCH codes as Table 11.1 taken from Stenbit [1].

Table 11.1 Generator polynomials of primitive binary BCH codes

N	K	t	$g(x)$	N	K	t	$g(x)$
7	4	1	13	255	171	11	15416214212342356077061630637
15	11	1	23		163	12	7500415510075602551574724514601
	7	2	721		155	13	3757513005407665015722506464677633
	5	3	2467		147	14	1642130173537165525304165305441011711
31	26	1	45		139	15	461401732060175561570722730247453567445
	21	2	3551		131	18	215713331471510151261250277442142024165471
	16	3	107657				
	11	5	5423325		123	19	120614052242066003717210326516141226272506267
	6	7	313365047				
63	57	1	103		115	21	60526665572100247263636404600276352556313472737
	51	2	12471				
	45	3	1701317		107	22	22205772322066256312417300235347420176574750154441
	39	4	166623567				
	36	5	1033500423		99	23	10656667253473174222741416201574332252411076432303431
	30	6	157464165547				
	24	7	17323260404441		91	25	6750265030327444172723631724732511075550762720724344561
	18	10	1363026512351725				
	16	11	6331141367235453		87	26	110136763414743236435231634307172046206722545273311721317
	10	13	472622305527250155				
	7	15	5231045543503271737		79	27	66700035637657500020270344207366174621015326711766541342355
127	120	1	211				
	113	2	41567		71	29	24024710520644321515554172112331163205444250362557643221706035
	106	3	11554743				
	99	4	3447023271		63	30	10754475055163544325315217357707003666111726455267613656702543301
	92	5	624730022327				
	85	6	130704476322273		55	31	7315425203501100133015275306032054325414326755010557044426035473617

(continued)

Table 11.1 (continued)

N	K	t	$g(x)$	N	K	t	$g(x)$
	78	7	26230002166130115				
	71	9	6255010713253127753		47	42	2533542017062646563033041377406233175123334145446045005066024552543173
	64	10	1206534025570773100045				
	57	11	335265252505705053517721		45	43	15202056055234161131101346376423701563670024470762373033202157025051541
	50	13	54446512523314012421501421				
	43	14	17721772213651227521220574343		37	45	5136330255067007414177447245437530420735706174323432347644354737403044003
	36	15	3146074666522075044764574721735				
	29	21	403114461367670603667530141176155		29	47	3025715536673071465527064012361377115342242324201174114060254757410403565037
	22	23	123376070404722522435445626637647043				
	15	27	22057042445604554770523013762217604353				
	8	31	7047264052751030651476224271567733130217		21	55	1256215257060332656001773153607612103227341405653074542521153121614466513473725
255	247	1	435				
	239	2	267543				
	231	3	156720665		13	59	464173200505256454442657371425006600433067744547656140317467721357026134460500547
	223	4	75626641375				
	215	5	23157564726421				
	207	6	16176560567636227		9	63	15726025217472463201031043255355134614162367212044074545112766115547705561677516057
	199	7	7633031270420722341				
	191	8	2663470176115333714567				
	187	9	52755313540001322236351				
	179	10	22624710717340432416300455				

Reference

1. J. Stenbit, "Table of generators for Bose-Chaudhuri codes (Corresp.)," *IEEE Transactions on Information Theory*, vol. 10, no. 4, pp. 390–391, 1964.

Chapter 12
Constructing Long Codes from Short Ones

Perfer et obdura: postmodo mitis erit.
Long last is finally good.

Publius Ovidius Naso (Ovid)

The longer codewords are, the more exactly matches the share of erroneous symbols the error-probability of the channel. If we assume that the number of correctable symbols is proportional to the number of redundancy components (no asymptotically bad codes), codewords should be as long as possible. In the case of RS codes, e.g., the codeword length $N = P^m - 1$ is practically limited by the size of the log and anti-log tables that are needed for fast computations in the discrete number field. Thus, there is a demand for constructing longer codewords from shorter ones.

Very often, there is also a requirement for concatenating at least two codes in order to eliminate errors by a second (outer) decoder that are left from the first (inner) decoding. Further advantages come from iterative decoding studied later in this chapter. A typical structure consists of an inner convolutional code and outer RS code. The Viterbi decoding typically leads to error burst when it fails. RS codes are very suited to correct bursty errors. Furthermore, the performance of RS codes can easily be computed and the probability for a decoding error, i.e., correction to a wrong codeword, is usually very small.

A further reason to construct longer codes from shorter ones is that the simpler decoding procedures for short codes can be used for the long code. Additionally, special correction properties, like burst-error correction, can be achieved. Currently, the most attractive reason for concatenation is that the ultimate coding gain promised by Channel Capacity computations can almost be reached.

In the following sections, we will describe different means of concatenation.

W. Henkel, *Channel Coding*, Signals and Communication Technology,
https://doi.org/10.1007/978-3-032-08236-7_12

12.1 (u, u + v) Construction and the Construction by Turyn

The $(\mathbf{u}, \mathbf{u}+\mathbf{v})$ construction generates codes of twice the length with good error correction capabilities. Especially Reed-Muller codes can be constructed like this.

Theorem 12.1 *Let two codes C_1 and C_2 be given with parameters $(N, \mathcal{K}_1, d_1)$ and $(N, \mathcal{K}_2, d_2)$, respectively, and the same length N. A code C_3 that consists of codewords from C_1 and C_2 according to*

$$(\mathbf{u}, \mathbf{u}+\mathbf{v}), \qquad \mathbf{u} \in C_1, \quad \mathbf{v} \in C_2 \tag{12.1}$$

will have the parameters $(2N, \mathcal{K}_1\mathcal{K}_2, \min\{2d_1, d_2\})$.
($\mathcal{K}$ is the cardinality of the code C.)

Proof Let $\mathbf{a} = (\mathbf{u}, \mathbf{u}+\mathbf{v})$ and $\mathbf{b} = (\mathbf{u}', \mathbf{u}'+\mathbf{v}')$ be two different codewords from C_3, where $\mathbf{u}, \mathbf{u}' \in C_1$ and $\mathbf{v}, \mathbf{v}' \in C_2$.

The first two parameters (codeword length and cardinality) are obvious and need not be proven. In order to prove the resulting minimum Hamming distance, we distinguish the cases $\mathbf{v} = \mathbf{v}'$ and $\mathbf{v} \neq \mathbf{v}'$.

$\mathbf{v} = \mathbf{v}'$:

$$d_H(\mathbf{a}, \mathbf{b}) = 2 \cdot d_H(\mathbf{u}, \mathbf{u}') \geq 2 \cdot d_1$$

$\mathbf{v} \neq \mathbf{v}'$:

$$\begin{aligned} d_H(\mathbf{a}, \mathbf{b}) &= w_H(\mathbf{u}-\mathbf{u}') + w_H(\mathbf{u}-\mathbf{u}'+\mathbf{v}-\mathbf{v}') \\ &\geq w_H(\mathbf{u}-\mathbf{u}') + w_H(\mathbf{v}-\mathbf{v}') - w_H(\mathbf{u}-\mathbf{u}') \\ &= w_H(\mathbf{v}-\mathbf{v}') \geq d_2 \end{aligned}$$

□

For linear codes, the product $\mathcal{K}_3 = \mathcal{K}_1 \cdot \mathcal{K}_2$ means also $K_3 = K_1 + K_2$.

Example 12.1 From a parity code $(4, 3, 2)$ and a repetition code $(4, 1, 4)$, we obtain a code with parameters $(8, 4, 4)$. This is the extended Hamming codes or first order Reed-Muller code. If we further combine this code with the repetition code $(8, 1, 8)$, this again leads to a first order Reed-Muller code with parameters $(16, 5, 8)$. The second order RM code $(16, 11, 4)$ follows from the parity-check code $(8, 7, 2)$ and the first order RM code $(8, 4, 4)$. All RM codes can be generated in this way.

Figure 12.1 shows, how the RM codes can be recursively defined.

A threefold length can be achieved using **Turyn's construction**. This is especially suited for a simple representation of the extended Golay code (24,12,8).

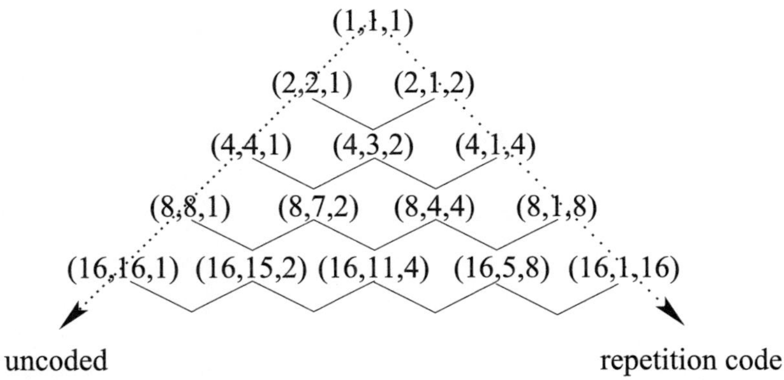

Fig. 12.1 The recursive structure of Reed-Muller codes resulting from the ($\mathbf{u}, \mathbf{u}+\mathbf{v}$) construction

Theorem 12.2 *Let the codes C_1 and C_2 with parameters $(N, \mathcal{K}_1, d_1)$ and $(N, \mathcal{K}_2, d_2)$, respectively, be given. A code C_3 will now be constructed according to*

$$(\mathbf{a}+\mathbf{x}, \mathbf{b}+\mathbf{x}, \mathbf{a}+\mathbf{b}+\mathbf{x}), \qquad \mathbf{a}, \mathbf{b} \in C_1, \quad \mathbf{x} \in C_2.$$

C_3 now has the parameters $(3N, \mathcal{K}_1^2\mathcal{K}_2, d_3)$. In the linear case (if the component codes are linear, so will be C_3), a lower bound for d_3 is given by

$$w_H(\mathbf{a}+\mathbf{x}, \mathbf{b}+\mathbf{x}, \mathbf{a}+\mathbf{b}+\mathbf{x}) = 2w_H(\mathbf{a} \vee \mathbf{b}) \\ - w_H(\mathbf{x}) + 4s \geq 2w_H(\mathbf{a} \vee \mathbf{b}) - w_H(\mathbf{x}). \quad (12.2)$$

s is the number of positions where $a_j = 0$, $b_j = 0$, and $x_j = 1$.

Proof A proof is only required for the lower bound of $w_H(C_3)$. First we will assume $\mathbf{x}$ to be the all-zeros word. Then, we obtain

$$w_H(\mathbf{a}, \mathbf{b}, \mathbf{a}+\mathbf{b}) = \underbrace{w_H(\mathbf{a}) + w_H(\mathbf{b})}_{w_H(\mathbf{a}\vee\mathbf{b})+w_H(\mathbf{a}\wedge\mathbf{b})} + \underbrace{w_H(\mathbf{a}+\mathbf{b})}_{w_H(\mathbf{a}\vee\mathbf{b})-w_H(\mathbf{a}\wedge\mathbf{b})} \quad (12.3)$$

For $x_j \neq 0$ terms will additionally appear that we will denote by $s|_{cond.}$. We hereby specify the number of ones in x at positions that are given by the condition $(cond.)$. The modifications in the weights of $\mathbf{a}$, $\mathbf{b}$, $\mathbf{a}+\mathbf{b}$ are given by

$$\begin{aligned} &-s|_{a_j=1} + s|_{a_j=0} \\ &-s|_{b_j=1} + s|_{b_j=0} \\ &-s|_{a_j+b_j=1} + s|_{a_j+b_j=0} \end{aligned} \quad (12.4)$$

$$= -s|_{a_j+b_j=1} + 3 \cdot s|_{a_j=0,b_j=0} - s|_{a_j=1,b_j=1} \quad (12.5)$$

The first and last term together yield $-s|_{a_j \vee b_j=1} = -(s|_{a_j,b_j\ arb.} - s|_{a_j=0,b_j=0})$, and we obtain

$$- s|_{a_j,b_j\ arb.} + 4 \cdot s|_{a_j=0,b_j=0} = -w_H(\mathbf{x}) + 4 \cdot s. \tag{12.6}$$

□

The following theorem will describe how the Golay code can be derived from the Hamming code.

Theorem 12.3 *Let C_1' be a (7,4,3) Hamming code and let C_2' be formed by mirroring the codeword of the Hamming code. C_1 and C_2 are (8,4,4) codes that are obtained by appending a parity bit to C_1' and C_2', respectively. C_3 will then be the extended Golay code with parameters (24,12,8).*

Proof We only need to prove that the minimum Hamming distance is 8. Then this is necessarily the extended Golay code, since this is the only code with these parameters.

Let $\mathbf{u} = (\mathbf{a} + \mathbf{x}, \mathbf{b} + \mathbf{x}, \mathbf{a} + \mathbf{b} + \mathbf{x})$ be a word different from the all-zeros word. Each of the components **a**, **b**, and **x** have weights 0, 4, or 8. We distinguish three cases:

1. If only one component **a**, **b**, or **x** is unequal to zero, we have $w_H(\mathbf{u}) \geq 8$.
2. Two of the three components have the weight 4. Again, this means $w_H(\mathbf{u}) \geq 8$. If, e.g., $w_H(\mathbf{a}) = 4$ and $w_H(\mathbf{x}) = 4$, then $w_H(\mathbf{a} + \mathbf{x}) \geq 2$.
3. Let $w_H(\mathbf{a}) = w_H(\mathbf{b}) = w_H(\mathbf{x}) = 4$. Only the case $\mathbf{a} \neq \mathbf{b}$ is of interest. Then, $w_H(a \vee b) \geq 6$ and Theorem 12.2 yields again $w_H(\mathbf{u}) \geq 8$.

We write down the generator matrices C_1 and C_2 of the two codes to see its properties.

	1 0 0 0 0 1 1	1
$\mathbf{G}_{C_1}$	0 1 0 0 1 0 1	1
	0 0 1 0 1 1 0	1
	0 0 0 1 1 1 1	0
	1 1 0 0 0 0 1	1
	1 0 1 0 0 1 0	1
$\mathbf{G}_{C_2}$	0 1 1 0 1 0 0	1
	1 1 1 1 0 0 0	0

□

Since some means of code concatenation is also suited for the correction of bursty errors, we devote the next section to some remarks on burst-error correction.

12.2 Burst-Error Correction

Fire the Fire code!

Definition 12.1 An error burst of length t denotes all possible error pattern within a section of length t (within a codeword). An error burst has to start and end with an error.

Usually only a certain maximum number of error-free symbols are allowed within a burst. If this is exceeded, the next erroneous symbol is considered to belong to another burst.

The most important found for burst-error correction is the so-called **Reiger bound** [1] which corresponds to the Singleton bound for the corrections of random errors.

Theorem 12.4 (Reiger bound) *A linear block code which is able to correct all single error bursts of length t needs to have at least* 2t *parity symbols.*

Proof Let us assume that all bursts of length t could be corrected. Then there can be no codeword that would itself represent a burst of length $2t$, i.e., that would only have components unequal to zero within a segment of length $2t$. Note that otherwise, two such codewords that are modified by bursts of length t could lead to the same word.

Two vectors belong to the same coset, if their difference is a valid codeword. We choose two vectors that are unequal to zero in only the first $2t$ components. If they would belong to the same coset, their difference would be codeword which in turn would be a burst of length $2t$. We have already realized that such codewords do not exist. Therefore, two such vectors have to belong to different cosets and the number of such cosets is as big as the number of such vectors. The number of vectors that differ from zero only in the first $2t$ positions is q^{2t} ($q = P^m$). This means at least q^{2t} cosets and thus, at least, $2t$ parity symbols. □

In earlier times, typical the so-called **Fire code** was used for burst-error correction. We shortly provide the definition.

Definition 12.2 A Fire code is cyclic with a generator polynomial

$$g(x) = (x^{2t-1} - 1) \cdot p(x),$$

where $p(x)$ is an irreducible polynomial of degree m, $m \geq t$, which does not divide $(x^{2t-1} - 1)$. The block length of the fire code is the smallest integer N, such that $g(x)$ divides $x^N - 1$.

We recall that RS codes fulfill the Singleton bound with equality (MDS). This is also the case for the Reiger bound. This means, as has already been mentioned, that RS codes are especially suited for burst-error correction. Nevertheless, in special cases other codes may still be preferred, e.g., if they can be realized more easily. In such cases, one may even accept if the Reiger bound is not fulfilled. Fire codes allow for a special decoding method, called '*error trapping*'. Later, we will describe *array codes* that also can be decoded in a simple fashion.

In the following section, we will present the simplest, but very effective and almost always applied method to obtain a longer code length and improve the burst-error correcting capability: **interleaving**.

12.3 Interleaving

In this section, we describe the two main interleaver structures: the block and the convolutional interleavers. The block interleaver appears to be more illustrative and is very suited for a quick realization in simulation programs. However, in practical implementations, one will usually apply a convolutional interleaver, since it has only half the delay. The block interleaver is described first.

For **block interleaving**, we have to think of matrices of dimensions *interleaver depth* $\times N = D_i \times N$ that are installed in the transmitter and the receiver. N needs not necessarily be the codeword length, but for simplicity, we assume this in Fig. 12.2.

At the transmitter, the information will be input in rows and the corresponding code redundancy will be computed. Transmission will be in columns. At the receiver the matrix will again be filled in columns and the be decoded in rows. Thereby, the burst-error correcting capability is increased to $D_i \cdot t$. The disadvantage is that it comes with a delay of twice the matrix size, since the matrices have to be filled at the transmitter and the receiver. The memory requirements also correspond to the matrix sizes.

An interleaver thus allows to increase the burst-error correction capability significantly or also, it allows to use codes for burst-error correction that were originally only suited for randomly distributed errors. The size of the interleaver/de-interleaver matrices is limited by the inter-arrival times of the bursts. Many bursts inside an interleaver matrix may easily exceed the correction capability.

A possible realization of a **convolutional interleaver** is depicted in Fig. 12.3, which follows the principle structure of [2]. A thorough treatment of different forms of convolutional interleavers can be found in [3].

$r_{0,0}$	$r_{0,1}$	$r_{0,2}$		$\cdots$	$\cdots$		$r_{0,N-2}$	$r_{0,N-1}$
$r_{1,0}$	$r_{1,1}$	$r_{1,2}$		$\cdots$	$\cdots$		$r_{1,N-2}$	$r_{1,N-1}$
$r_{2,0}$	$r_{2,1}$	$r_{2,2}$		$\cdots$	$\cdots$		$r_{2,N-2}$	$r_{2,N-1}$
$r_{3,0}$	$r_{3,1}$	$r_{3,2}$					$r_{3,N-2}$	$r_{3,N-1}$
$\vdots$	$\vdots$	$\vdots$					$\vdots$	$\vdots$
$r_{D_i-1,0}$	$r_{D_i-1,1}$	$r_{D_i-1,2}$		$\cdots$	$\cdots$		$r_{D_i-1,N-2}$	$r_{D_i-1,N-1}$

Fig. 12.2 Block interleaver

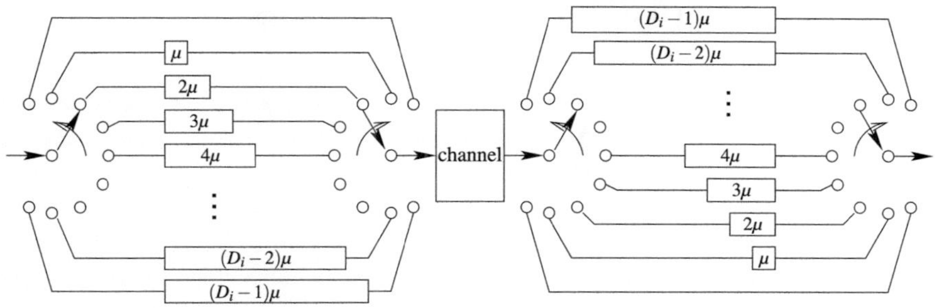

Fig. 12.3 Possible realization of a convolutional interleaver

When considering a single path on the receiver side, this will be reached again after D_i symbols, i.e., a burst that is longer than D_i symbols leads to more than one error in the same codeword. We study the sequence resulting from the de-interleaver in some more detail. The time instants will be modified as follows (we assume $D_i = 3$):

$$\begin{aligned} 1 &\longrightarrow 1 \\ 2 &\longrightarrow 2 + \mu D_i \\ 3 &\longrightarrow 3 + 2\mu D_i \\ 4 &\longrightarrow 4 \\ 5 &\longrightarrow 5 + \mu D_i \\ 6 &\longrightarrow 6 + 2\mu D_i \\ &\vdots \end{aligned}$$

For $D_i = 3$ and $\mu = 2$, the following sequence results:

1			4			7	2		10	5		13	8	3	16	11	6	19	14	9	22	...

For the convolutional interleaver, we conclude $N = \mu \cdot D_i \pm 1$ depending on the orientation of the switch rotation (+1 with the shown orientation). In the given sequence, possible starting instants of blocks of length $\mu \cdot D_i + 1$ (=7) are $1, 2, 3, 22, \ldots$.

The total delay is $(D_i - 1)\mu D_i \approx D_i^2 \mu$, which is roughly half the delay of a block interleaver. The required memory is also only half as much. Additionally, the synchronization has only to be search in D_i possible positions, not in $N \cdot D_i$ as in the case of block interleavers.

12.4 Product and Array Codes

A natural extension of a block interleaver is to provide not only code redundancy in rows, but also use error correcting codes in columns. This is called product code or array code. Figure 12.4 shows the structure.

In its simplest form, a parity code (binary or also over an arbitrary extension field) can be used in rows and columns. Violating the parities in rows and columns mark the error positions. Herewith, a parity-check code is now also able to correct errors at unknown positions, not just detect them.

These array codes with parity-check codes in rows and columns may be used for burst-error correction. Hereto, the transmission, i.e., the reading from the transmitter matrix is done in diagonal fashion (see [4, 5]). These array codes are specified by the parameters $(N_1, N_2; s)$, where N_1 is the number of rows, N_2 is the number of columns and s is the step size when going from diagonal to diagonal. For $s = 1$ the reading cycle can be formulated as

$$f(i, j) = (j - i)N_1 + i \mod (N_1 N_2) \tag{12.7}$$

$$i = 0, 1, \ldots, N_1 - 1 \quad j = 0, 1, \ldots, N_2 - 1.$$

One can show that with such an array code, all error bursts up to a length of $N_1 - 1$ can be corrected, if $N_2 \geq 2N_1 - 3$. When considering an example with $N_1 = 5$ and $N_2 = 2N_1 - 3 = 7$, is is obvious, that an error burst of length $N_1 - 1 = 4$ leads to parity violations in $N_1 - 1$ subsequent rows and columns starting with the first row and column that corresponds to the first error in the burst. In case of an error burst with N_1 errors, however, errors could compensate each other in the parity sum (if the error burst does not start in the first row.

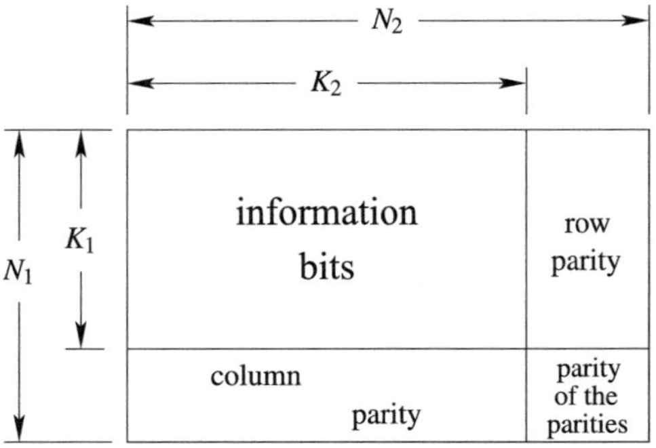

Fig. 12.4 Product code

0	5	10	15	20	25	30
31	1	6	11	16	21	26
27	32	2	7	12	17	22
23	28	33	3	8	13	18
19	24	29	34	4	9	14

(12.8)

The starting point of an error burst can only be determined by the violations of the column parities, if a possible error-free range G_{in} inside the bundle cannot be as long as the remaining error-free range G_{out} outside the bundle. This means

$$G_{out} = N_2 - (N_1 - 1) > (N_1 - 1) - 2 = G_{in} \tag{12.9}$$

$$\Longrightarrow N_2 > 2N_1 - 4 \Longrightarrow N_2 \geq 2N_1 - 3$$

The decoding algorithm determines the longest error free range of the column parities. The error burst starts right after it (continuing in a cyclic fashion). The error positions follow when combining the column and row parity violations and proceeding from top to bottom.

A disadvantage is that usually only one error burst can be corrected. The decoding complexity is very low and the decoding delay is twice the matrix size like with block interleaving. However, it is possible to reduce the transmitter-sided delay by around 30%, when a special filling scheme is applied [6].

12.5 Serially Concatenated Codes

A widely used combination of codes the concatenation according to Fig. 12.5. Two encoders and decoders are serially concatenated. One can consider the inner encoder, channel, and inner decoder as a new channel ('super channel'), since this is the one that the outer code will actually see as its channel.

One may, e.g., think of an RS code with parameters (N_a, K_a, d_a) over $GF(2^{K_i})$ as an outer code. For the inner code, each symbol of the outer code (binary vector of length K_i) is the information part of the inner codeword of length N_i. The inner code

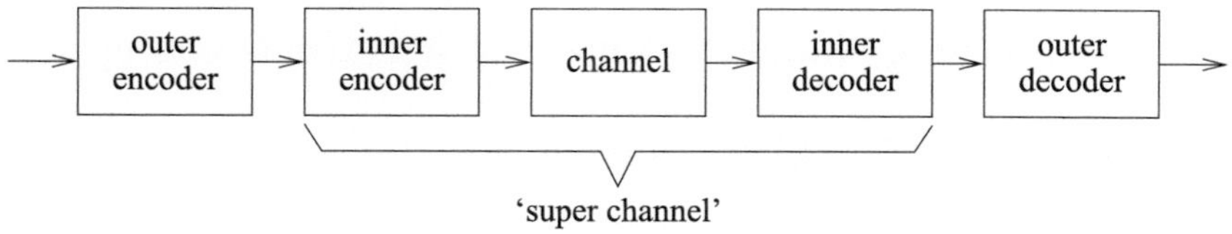

Fig. 12.5 Serial concatenation

thus has the parameters (N_i, K_i, d_i). The overall code parameters of the concatenated code are then $(N_a N_i, K_a K_i, d_{Hm} \geq d_a d_i)$. The coderate is $R = \frac{K_a K_i}{N_a N_i} = R_a R_i$.

Not always will the parameters be adjusted like this. At least, it should be ensured that inner erroneous codewords cannot affect multiple symbols of the outer code.

A traditional concatenation consists of inner convolutional or trellis code (TCM) together with an outer RS code with a byte-interleaver in between. An interleaving keeping bytes together is chosen, since an RS code is byte-correcting. Erroneous bits should not be distributed to different bytes. Typically, a Viterbi algorithm as an inner decoder leads to bursty errors which should be kept together in bytes when an outer RS decoder follows. Due to the availability of the hardware originally developed for deep-space missions, these schemes became a quasi-standard for some time. The convolutional code was of rate $1/n$, usually 1/2 or 1/3 with 64 states (meanwhile up to 512 states are implemented) and the RS code used $GF(2^8)$. Up to a correction capability of $t = 32$, RS chips are readily available. The convolutional code, since it was already implemented, was also once proposed to be used for coded modulation. Hereto, I and Q components of a QAM had to be encoded separately (no set partitioning). This proposal was named **pragmatic trellis code** [7, 8]. However, usually, instead of the serial concatenation of convolutional and RS codes, later a concatenation of trellis-coded modulation was replacing the convolutional code using coded 8-PSK instead of 4-PSK. The CCSDS standard [9] with 4-PSK used a convolutional code of memory 6 and rate 1/2 and an RS code with parameters (255,223,31) over GF(8). The interleaver between is a block interleaver, whereas otherwise, in most applications convolutional interleavers are used, e.g., in DSL. Later satellite systems use concatenations of trellis coded modulation, e.g., 64-state Ungerböck-type TCM or 4-dimensional TCM (Ungerböck/Wei), the latter together with an RS code (255,239,17) [10]. Currently, also Turbo and LDPC codes are used in Satellite systems. Nevertheless, also partly short block codes are used (expurgated Hamming code (63,56,4) derived from (63,57,3) Hamming code restricting to only even parities [11]).

Generally, concatenated codes lead to steeper error-probability curves (over E_b/N_0) and thus to higher coding gains at low error probabilities. At high error rates, concatenated codes may be inferior. We will see very steep BER curves when decoding concatenated codes iteratively. The following sections will give some details, but first, the information theoretic limits will be outlined.

12.6 Approaching Shannon's Limits by Iterative Decoding

12.6.1 Information-Theoretic Limits

Turbo codes, Low-Density Parity-Check codes, and alike allow to approach the Shannon limit(s). In this section, we will now derive these information-theoretic limits.

For the Capacity in the AWGN case, one typically finds results relating to one- or two-sided power spectral densities. To avoid confusion, in the following, we will provide results for both assumptions. On the left, we assume N_0 to be the double-sided PSD, on the right, the one-sided, distinguished as C_{N_0} and $C_{N_0/2}$, respectively. The AWGN Channel Capacity in bit/symbol is given by

$$\begin{aligned} C_{N_0} &= \frac{1}{2}\cdot\log_2\left(1+\frac{E_s}{N_0}\right), C_{N_0/2} = \frac{1}{2}\cdot\log_2\left(1+\frac{E_s}{N_0/2}\right) \quad \text{for the one-dimensional case,} \\ C_{N_0} &= \log_2\left(1+\frac{E_s}{N_0}\right),\quad C_{N_0/2} = \log_2\left(1+\frac{E_s}{N_0/2}\right) \quad \text{for the two-dimensional case.} \end{aligned} \tag{12.10}$$

This means the rate will be less than (replacing C by R)

$$\begin{aligned} R_{N_0} &\le \tfrac{1}{2}\cdot\log_2\left(1+R_{N_0}\cdot\tfrac{E_b}{N_0}\right),\ R_{N_0/2} \le \tfrac{1}{2}\cdot\log_2\left(1+2R_{N_0/2}\cdot\tfrac{E_b}{N_0}\right) \quad \text{1D,} \\ R_{N_0} &\le \log_2\left(1+R_{N_0}\cdot\tfrac{E_b}{N_0}\right),\quad R_{N_0/2} \le \log_2\left(1+2R_{N_0/2}\cdot\tfrac{E_b}{N_0}\right) \quad \text{2D,} \end{aligned} \tag{12.11}$$

where we have also introduced the rate loss, i.e., using E_b/N_0 instead of E_s/N_0. Solving for E_b/N_0 yields (omitting the index for R)

$$\begin{aligned} \frac{E_b}{N_0} &\ge \frac{2^{2R}-1}{R},\quad \frac{E_b}{N_0} \ge \frac{2^{2R}-1}{2R} \quad \text{1D,} \\ \frac{E_b}{N_0} &\ge \frac{2^{R}-1}{R},\quad \frac{E_b}{N_0} \ge \frac{2^{R}-1}{2R} \quad \text{2D.} \end{aligned} \tag{12.12}$$

For $R \to 0$, we obtain the lowest SNR limit from which on in principal error-free communication should be possible. The limits obtained by applying l'Hospital's rule are

$$\begin{aligned} \lim_{R\to 0}\frac{E_b}{N_0} &\ge 2\cdot\ln(2) = 1.386 \equiv 1.42\,\text{dB}, \quad -1.58\,\text{dB} \quad \text{1D,} \\ \lim_{R\to 0}\frac{E_b}{N_0} &\ge \ln(2) = 0.693 \equiv -1.592\,\text{dB} \approx -1.6\,\text{dB},\ -4.6\,\text{dB} \quad \text{2D.} \end{aligned} \tag{12.13}$$

For a fixed rate of $R = 1/2$, we obtain for 1D: 3 dB and 0 dB for two-sided and one-sided power spectral densities, respectively; for 2D: -0.817 dB and -3.817 dB, respectively.

These values are based on the requirement of having no errors at all. If we tolerate some error probability p_b (which we will denote D for a moment to avoid confusion), we can make use of a result of rate-distortion theory[1] (see Sect. 2.8), which is quite obvious. The rate of a binary source to be transmitted when tolerating a distortion D is

[1] Fano's Lemma 2.1 and the converse to the coding theorem also allow to derive a lower bound for the error probability. From $P_s \ge 1 - C/R = 1 - \frac{\log_2(1+RE_b/N_0)}{R}$ and the limit $R \to 0$, we obtain $P_s \ge 1 - \frac{1}{\ln(2)}\cdot\frac{E_b}{N_0}$. However, P_s denotes a symbol-error ratio.

$$R(D) = \begin{cases} h(p) - h(D), & 0 \leq D \leq \min\{p, 1-p\} \\ 0, & D > \min\{p, 1-p\}, \end{cases} \tag{12.14}$$

Assuming an original binary source with the binary entropy function $h(p) = -p\log_2(p) - (1-p)\log_2(1-p))$ with a maximum of 1 bit, $1 - h(D)$ would determine the rate required to represent the source data when accepting a distortion D, where likewise $h(D) = -D\log_2(D) - (1-D)\log_2(1-D)$. The actual bit rate that has to be related to the Capacity is then only $R \cdot (1 - h(D))$. This changes Eq. (12.11) into

$$\begin{aligned} &R\cdot(1-h(D)) \leq \tfrac{1}{2}\cdot\log_2\left(1+R\cdot\tfrac{E_b}{N_0}\right),\; R\cdot(1-h(D)) \leq \tfrac{1}{2}\cdot\log_2\left(1+2R\cdot\tfrac{E_b}{N_0}\right) && \text{1D},\\ &R\cdot(1-h(D)) \leq \log_2\left(1+R\cdot\tfrac{E_b}{N_0}\right),\quad R\cdot(1-h(D)) \leq \log_2\left(1+2R\cdot\tfrac{E_b}{N_0}\right) && \text{2D}. \end{aligned} \tag{12.15}$$

$$\begin{aligned} &\frac{E_b}{N_0} \geq \frac{2^{2R(1-h(D))}-1}{R},\; \frac{E_b}{N_0} \geq \frac{2^{2R(1-h(D))}-1}{2R} && \text{1D},\\ &\frac{E_b}{N_0} \geq \frac{2^{R(1-h(D))}-1}{R},\; \frac{E_b}{N_0} \geq \frac{2^{R(1-h(D))}-1}{2R} && \text{2D}. \end{aligned} \tag{12.16}$$

The limit for $R \to 0$ is again determined applying l'Hospital's rule.

$$\begin{aligned} &\frac{E_b}{N_0} \geq 2\cdot\ln(2)\cdot(1-h(D)),\; \frac{E_b}{N_0} \geq \ln(2)\cdot(1-h(D)) && \text{1D},\\ &\frac{E_b}{N_0} \geq \ln(2)\cdot(1-h(D)),\quad \frac{E_b}{N_0} \geq \frac{1}{2}\cdot\ln(2)\cdot(1-h(D)) && \text{2D}. \end{aligned} \tag{12.17}$$

The parametric plot[2] of the pairs $(E_b/N_0,\ p_b = D)$ for $R \to 0$ in Fig. 12.6 provides the ultimate limits for error-ratio curves that are approached by iterative-decoding schemes. Likewise, curves for rates greater than zero can be computed.

Note that we computed lower limits in E_b/N_0. There is no such limit in E_s/N_0!

12.6.2 Iterative Decoding of Product Codes

One could imagine that the product codes introduced in Sect. 12.4 that are decoded in rows and columns could be decoded iteratively many times alternating between rows and columns and making use of earlier decoding (soft) outputs. This is actually the underlying principle of **parallel concatenated codes** with **Turbo decoding**. They have been first published under the name 'Turbo' codes [12] but based on convolutional codes. However, the principle can more easily be described with block product

[2] Note that the parametric plot is limited to $p_b \leq 0.5$. Exceeding this value would mean an improvement again, which would lead to two values of p_b for a given E_b/N_0.

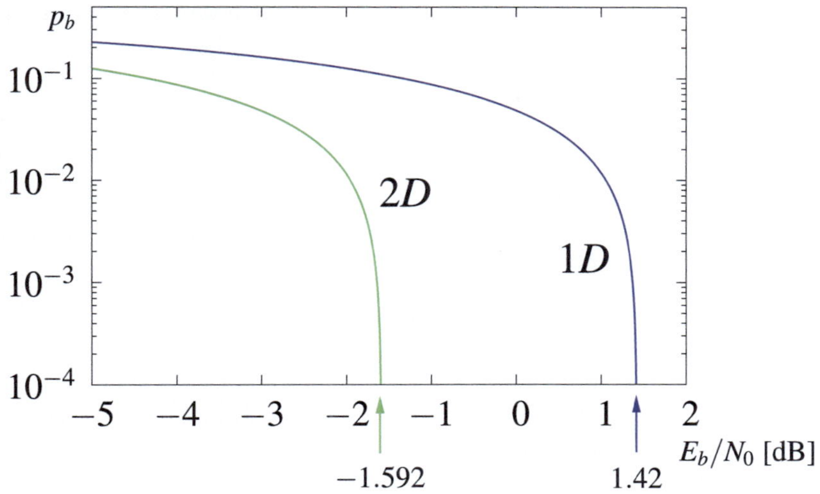

Fig. 12.6 Shannon limits for $p_b(E_b/N_0)$ assuming a two-sided noise PSD N_0; for a one-sided noise PSD, a shift according to (12.13) has to be applied

Fig. 12.7 Parallel concatenated block code

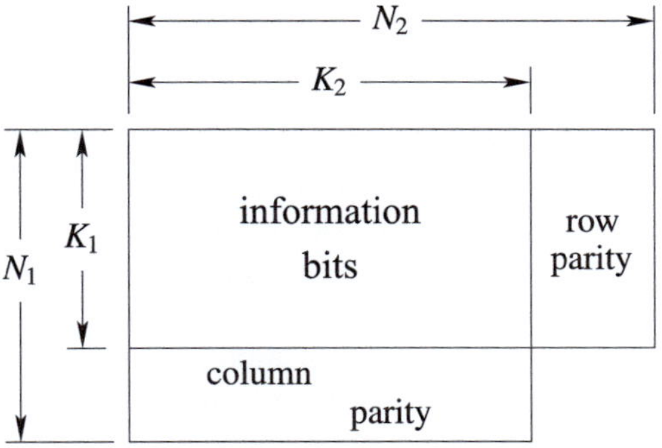

codes. We deviate from the usual product code in omitting the parity-of-parities. The structure that we base our introductory treatment on is shown in Fig. 12.7, a parallel concatenated code. The serial concatenation was already shown as the original product code in Fig. 12.4. There, rows and and column parities can only be computed serially due to the parity-of-the-parities component.

Before we describe the iterative decoding of parallel concatenated codes, we introduce the so-called **log-likelihood algebra** which has the advantage that multiplications of probabilities turn into additions of log-likelihoods.

We refer to a binary alphabet, where we will write $\{+1, -1\}$ as the representations of $\{0, 1\}$. The modulo-2 addition over $\{0, 1\}$ then corresponds to the multiplication over $\{+1, -1\}$. To make it more visible, we will in the following write the multiplication as '$\times$'.

The log-likelihood ratio is defined as follows.

Definition 12.3 Let $P_{\mathbf{u}}(u)$ be the probability that a random variable $\mathbf{u}$ will be equal to u. Then the log-likelihood ratio for $u \in \{-1, 1\}$ is defined as

$$L_{\mathbf{u}}(u) = \log \frac{P_{\mathbf{u}}(u = +1)}{P_{\mathbf{u}}(u = -1)}. \qquad (12.18)$$

$L_{\mathbf{u}}(u)$ is thus a 'soft' value, whose sign represents the quantized decision. The absolute value of the log-likelihood ratio $|L_{\mathbf{u}}(u)|$ is a measure for the reliability. Usually, the natural logarithm is chosen, i.e.,

$$L_{\mathbf{u}}(u) = \ln \frac{P_{\mathbf{u}}(u = +1)}{P_{\mathbf{u}}(u = -1)}.$$

As we can write conditional probabilities, we can also transfer this into log-likelihood ratios. The conditional log-likelihood ratio is thus

$$\begin{aligned} L_{\mathbf{u}|\mathbf{y}}(u|y) = & \log \frac{P_{\mathbf{u}}(u = +1|y)}{P_{\mathbf{u}}(u = -1|y)} \\ = & \log \frac{P_{\mathbf{u}}(u = +1)}{P_{\mathbf{u}}(u = -1)} + \log \frac{P_{\mathbf{y}|\mathbf{u}}(y|u = +1)}{P_{\mathbf{y}|\mathbf{u}}(y|u = -1)} \\ = & L_{\mathbf{u}}(u) + L_{\mathbf{y}|\mathbf{u}}(y|u), \end{aligned} \qquad (12.19)$$

where we again made use of Bayes' rule. Note that the joint log-likelihood ratio $L_{\mathbf{u},\mathbf{y}}(u, y)$ equals the conditional ratio $L_{\mathbf{u}|\mathbf{y}}(u|y)$, since after applying Bayes' rule the term with $P_{\mathbf{y}}(y)$ cancels out.

For convenience, we will omit the indices from now on.

Since for binary codes, the modulo-2 addition is the central operation and is equivalent to the multiplication $(\times)$ over $\{+1, -1\}$, we determine the log-likelihood ratio of the product of two random variables from $\{+1, -1\}$. The result will be required for our first simple example of the decoding of a parallel concatenated code.

For $L(u_1 \times u_2)$, Hagenauer [13] introduced an own operator

$$L(u_1) \boxplus L(u_2) := L(u_1 \times u_2). \qquad (12.20)$$

In the sequel, we will show that

$$L(u_1) \boxplus L(u_2) = L(u_1 \times u_2) = \ln \left(\frac{1 + e^{L(u_1)} e^{L(u_2)}}{e^{L(u_1)} + e^{L(u_2)}} \right). \qquad (12.21)$$

We start with reformulating the log-likelihood ratio

$$L(u) = \ln\left(\frac{P(u=+1)}{P(u=-1)}\right) = \ln\left(\frac{P(u=+1)}{1-P(u=+1)}\right) \tag{12.22}$$

$$e^{L(u)} = \left(\frac{P(u=+1)}{1-P(u=+1)}\right). \tag{12.23}$$

This yields

$$e^{L(u)} - e^{L(u)} \cdot P(u=+1) = P(u=+1), \tag{12.24}$$

$$e^{L(u)} = P(u=+1)\cdot(1+e^{L(u)}), \tag{12.25}$$

$$P(u=+1) = \frac{e^{L(u)}}{1+e^{L(u)}}, \tag{12.26}$$

$$P(u=-1) = 1-P(u=+1) = 1-\frac{e^{L(u)}}{1+e^{L(u)}} = \frac{1}{1+e^{L(u)}}. \tag{12.27}$$

These relations allow us to provide the log-likelihood ratio for multiplied random variables over $\{+1, -1\}$ (XOR over $\{0, 1\}$) in Eq. (12.21).

$$L(u_1) \boxplus L(u_2) = L(u_1 \times u_2) \tag{12.28}$$

$$= \ln\frac{P(u_1 \times u_2 = +1)}{P(u_1 \times u_2 = -1)} \tag{12.29}$$

$$= \ln\frac{P(u_1=+1)\cdot P(u_2=+1) + P(u_1=-1)\cdot P(u_2=-1)}{P(u_1=+1)\cdot P(u_2=-1) + P(u_1=-1)\cdot P(u_2=+1)} \tag{12.30}$$

$$= \ln\frac{\frac{e^{L(u_1)}}{1+e^{L(u_1)}}\cdot\frac{e^{L(u_2)}}{1+e^{L(u_2)}} + \frac{1}{1+e^{L(u_1)}}\cdot\frac{1}{1+e^{L(u_2)}}}{\frac{e^{L(u_1)}}{1+e^{L(u_1)}}\cdot\frac{1}{1+e^{L(u_2)}} + \frac{e^{L(u_2)}}{1+e^{L(u_2)}}\cdot\frac{1}{1+e^{L(u_1)}}} \tag{12.31}$$

$$= \ln\frac{1+e^{L(u_1)}\cdot e^{L(u_2)}}{e^{L(u_1)}+e^{L(u_2)}} \tag{12.32}$$

Usually, for this the approximation

$$L(u_1) \boxplus L(u_2) = \ln\frac{1+e^{L(u_1)}\cdot e^{L(u_2)}}{e^{L(u_1)}+e^{L(u_2)}}$$
$$\approx \text{sign}\,(L(u_1))\cdot\ \text{sign}\ (L(u_2))\cdot\min\,(|L(u_1)|, |L(u_2)|) \tag{12.33}$$

is used. We observe the following properties:

$$L(u) \boxplus \infty = L(u) \tag{12.34}$$

$$L(u) \boxplus -\infty = -L(u) \tag{12.35}$$

$$L(u) \boxplus 0 = 0. \tag{12.36}$$

Induction shows that

$$\sum_{j=1}^{J}\boxplus\, L(u_j) = L\left(\prod_{j=1}^{J} u_j\right) = \ln \frac{\prod_{j=1}^{J}\left(e^{L(u_j)}+1\right)+\prod_{j=1}^{J}\left(e^{L(u_j)}-1\right)}{\prod_{j=1}^{J}\left(e^{L(u_j)}+1\right)-\prod_{j=1}^{J}\left(e^{L(u_j)}-1\right)}. \quad (12.37)$$

Abbreviating $\tanh(u/2) = (e^u - 1)/(e^u + 1)$, we obtain

$$\sum_{j=1}^{J}\boxplus\, L(u_j) = \ln \frac{1+\prod_{j=1}^{J}\tanh\left(L(u_j)/2\right)}{1-\prod_{j=1}^{J}\tanh\left(L(u_j)/2\right)} = 2\,\mathrm{artanh}\left(\prod_{j=1}^{J}\tanh\left(L(u_j)/2\right)\right). \quad (12.38)$$

Like in (12.33), this can be approximated by

$$\sum_{j=1}^{J}\boxplus\, L(u_j) \approx \left(\prod_{j=1}^{J}\mathrm{sign}\left(L(u_j)\right)\right)\cdot \min_{j=1..J}|L(u_j)| \quad (12.39)$$

In the following, we assume an AWGN channel. When transmitting a value $u \in \{+1, -1\}$, let y be the output of the receiver matched filter. We already formulated the conditional log-likelihood ratio in Eq. (12.19). We will now specialize it for the AWGN case.

$$\begin{aligned} L(u|y) &= \ln \frac{P(y|u=+1)}{P(y|u=-1)} + \ln \frac{P(u=+1)}{P(u=-1)} \\ &= \ln \frac{e^{-(y-a)^2/(2\sigma_n^2)}}{e^{-(y+a)^2/(2\sigma_n^2)}} + \ln \frac{P(u=+1)}{P(u=-1)} \\ &= L_c \cdot y + L(u) \end{aligned} \quad (12.40)$$

We abbreviated $L_c = 2a/\sigma_n^2 = 4a \cdot E_s/N_0$, with an amplitude a.[3] We also use the even shorter form $L_c(y) := L_c \cdot y$. For the following derivations, we will require the log-likelihood ratio when receiving two statistically independent disturbed signals. One may think, e.g., of two different independent transmission paths ('dual diversity') or of a repetition code . Let the outputs be y_1 and y_2. The conditional log-likelihood ratio will then be

[3] In case of a fading channel , σ and also the amplitude a are time-variant.

$$\begin{aligned} L(u|y_1, y_2) &= \log \frac{P(u=+1|y_1, y_2)}{P(u=-1|y_1, y_2)} \\ &= \log \frac{P(y_1, y_2|u=+1)}{P(y_1, y_2|u=-1)} + \log \frac{P(u=+1)}{P(u=-1)} \\ &= \log \frac{P(y_1|u=+1)}{P(y_1|u=-1)} + \log \frac{P(y_2|u=+1)}{P(y_2|u=-1)} \\ &\quad + \log \frac{P(u=+1)}{P(u=-1)} \qquad (12.41) \\ &= L_{c1} \cdot y_1 + L_{c2} \cdot y_2 + L(u). \qquad (12.42) \end{aligned}$$

Now, we study the example of decoding a parallel concatenated codes with (3,2,2) parity-check codes as component codes. Let the received signal be $L_c \cdot y$. The received word is given in matrix form:

$$\begin{array}{|c|c|c|} \hline L_c(y_{11}) & L_c(y_{12}) & L_c(p_1^-) \\ \hline L_c(y_{21}) & L_c(y_{22}) & L_c(p_2^-) \\ \hline L_c(p_1^|) & L_c(p_2^|) & \\ \hline \end{array} = \begin{array}{|c|c|c|} \hline 0.8 & 0.7 & -1.0 \\ \hline 0.2 & 1.5 & -1.2 \\ \hline -2.0 & -0.5 & \\ \hline \end{array}$$

Starting with the horizontal decoding, we observe that for determining u_{11}, there will be an indirect information provided by $u_{12} \times p_1^-$ besides the directly received component. When assuming statistically independence, we already know from (12.42) that the corresponding log-likelihood ratios are to be added to obtain the total reliability. However, we will not do this now, but in a later step together with the result from the vertical decoding. As an intermediate step, we define the so-called *extrinsic* information in horizontal direction, thereafter in vertical direction.

The horizontal extrinsic values are given by[4]

$$\begin{aligned} L_{eh}(\hat{u}_{11}) &= [L_c(y_{12}) + L(u_{12})] \boxplus L_c(p_1^-) \\ L_{eh}(\hat{u}_{12}) &= [L_c(y_{11}) + L(u_{11})] \boxplus L_c(p_1^-) \\ L_{eh}(\hat{u}_{21}) &= [L_c(y_{22}) + L(u_{22})] \boxplus L_c(p_2^-) \\ L_{eh}(\hat{u}_{22}) &= [L_c(y_{21}) + L(u_{21})] \boxplus L_c(p_2^-). \qquad (12.43) \end{aligned}$$

In our example, let us assume that at the beginning, all log-likelihood ratios for the probabilities of transmit symbols are the same, i.e., the transmit symbols are considered to be equally probable. For the subsequent iterations, however, we utilize the results of previous iterations as a-priori information $L(u_{ij})$.

Thus, the relations for the vertical extrinsic values will be

[4] The '^' labels estimates.

$$
\begin{aligned}
L_{ev}(\hat{u}_{11}) &= [L_c(y_{21}) + L(u_{21})] \boxplus L_c(p_1^|) \\
L_{ev}(\hat{u}_{12}) &= [L_c(y_{22}) + L(u_{22})] \boxplus L_c(p_2^|) \\
L_{ev}(\hat{u}_{21}) &= [L_c(y_{11}) + L(u_{11})] \boxplus L_c(p_1^|) \\
L_{ev}(\hat{u}_{22}) &= [L_c(y_{12}) + L(u_{12})] \boxplus L_c(p_2^|).
\end{aligned}
\tag{12.44}
$$

We will now browse through the steps of our example. The first horizontal iteration is given by

$$
\begin{aligned}
L_{eh}(\hat{u}_{11}) &= [0.7 + 0] \boxplus - 1.0 = -0.7 \\
L_{eh}(\hat{u}_{12}) &= [0.8 + 0] \boxplus - 1.0 = -0.8 \\
L_{eh}(\hat{u}_{21}) &= [1.5 + 0] \boxplus - 1.2 = -1.2 \\
L_{eh}(\hat{u}_{22}) &= [0.2 + 0] \boxplus - 1.2 = -0.2,
\end{aligned}
$$

afterwards the vertical iteration

$$
\begin{aligned}
L_{ev}(\hat{u}_{11}) &= [0.2 - 1.2] \boxplus - 2.0) = 1.0 \\
L_{ev}(\hat{u}_{12}) &= [1.5 - 0.2] \boxplus - 0.5 = -0.5 \\
L_{ev}(\hat{u}_{21}) &= [0.8 - 0.7] \boxplus - 2.0 = -0.1 \\
L_{ev}(\hat{u}_{22}) &= [0.7 - 0.8] \boxplus - 0.5 = 0.1.
\end{aligned}
$$

In the following, we list the intermediate results for some iterations.

$L_{eh}(\hat{u}_{ij})$		$L_{ev}(\hat{u}_{ij})$		$L(\hat{u}_{ij})$		$L_{eh}(\hat{u}_{ij})$		$L_{ev}(\hat{u}_{ij})$		$L(\hat{u}_{ij})$	
−0.7	−0.8	1.0	−0.5	1.1	−0.6	−0.2	−1.0	1.0	−0.5	1.6	−0.8
−1.2	−0.2	−0.1	0.1	−1.1	1.4	−1.2	−0.1	−0.6	0.3	−1.6	1.7

$L_{eh}(\hat{u}_{ij})$		$L_{ev}(\hat{u}_{ij})$		$L(\hat{u}_{ij})$		$L_{eh}(\hat{u}_{ij})$		$L_{ev}(\hat{u}_{ij})$		$L(\hat{u}_{ij})$	
−0.2	−1.0	1.0	−0.5	1.6	−0.8	−0.2	−1.0	1.0	−0.5	1.6	−0.8
−1.2	0.4	−0.6	0.3	−1.6	2.2	−1.2	0.4	−0.6	0.3	−1.6	2.2

$L(\hat{u}_{ij})$ is the required analog information that follows from the sum

$$
L(\hat{u}_{ij}) = L_c(y_{ij}) + L_{eh}(\hat{u}_{ij}) + L_{ev}(\hat{u}_{ij}) \tag{12.45}
$$

of the log-likelihood ratios, assumed to be statistically independent, which is actually not the case, especially not for higher iteration numbers.

12.6.3 A-priori, Intrinsic, and Extrinsic Information

We have already realized in (12.42) that log-likelihood ratios add up, if the information comes along independent paths. Also the a-priori log-likelihood is added. We are now considering a code vector $\mathbf{x}$ being transmitted and determine the logarithmic MAP ratio $L(x_i|\mathbf{y})$, where x_i is a dedicated component of the codeword and $\mathbf{y}$ is the received word.

$$\begin{aligned} L(x_i|\mathbf{y}) = & \ln \frac{P(x_i=+1|\mathbf{y})}{P(x_i=-1|\mathbf{y})} = \ln \frac{P(\mathbf{y}|x_i=+1)}{P(\mathbf{y}|x_i=-1)} + \ln \frac{P(x_i=+1)}{P(x_i=-1)} \\ = & \underbrace{\ln \frac{P(y_i|x_i=+1)}{P(y_i|x_i=-1)}}_{\text{intrinsic}} + \underbrace{\ln \frac{P(\mathbf{y}_{\setminus i}|x_i=+1)}{P(\mathbf{y}_{\setminus i}|x_i=-1)}}_{\text{extrinsic}} + \underbrace{\ln \frac{P(x_i=+1)}{P(x_i=-1)}}_{\text{a priori}} \end{aligned} \tag{12.46}$$

The split in y_i and $\mathbf{y}_{\setminus i}$ ($\mathbf{y}$ without the ith component) terms is due to a memoryless channel assumption (independence). The extrinsic information is often labeled $L_E(x_i|\mathbf{y}_{\setminus i})$, although it somehow turns the arguments around. The a-priori log-likelihood function, we just label $L(x_i)$ or $L_A(x_i)$.

As an example, as in [14], we show the split in (12.46) again for the exemplary case of two information and two parity bits, where the u_i are the information bits.

According to the MAP rule, let us decide on u_0 using the log-likelihood (MAP) ratio

$$\begin{aligned} L(u_0|\mathbf{y}) = & \ln \frac{p(\mathbf{y}|u_0=+1, u_1=+1)\cdot P(u_0=+1)\cdot P(u_1=+1)+\cdots}{p(\mathbf{y}|u_0=-1, u_1=+1)\cdot P(u_0=-1)\cdot P(u_1=+1)+\cdots} \\ & \frac{\cdots + p(\mathbf{y}|u_0=+1, u_1=-1)\cdot P(u_0=+1)\cdot P(u_1=-1)}{\cdots + p(\mathbf{y}|u_0=-1, u_1=-1)\cdot P(u_0=-1)\cdot P(u_1=-1)} \\ = & \ln \frac{P(u_0=+1)}{P(u_0=-1)} \\ & + \ln \frac{p(\mathbf{y}|u_0=+1, u_1=+1)\cdot \frac{P(u_1=+1)}{P(u_1=-1)} + p(\mathbf{y}|u_0=+1, u_1=-1)}{p(\mathbf{y}|u_0=-1, u_1=+1)\cdot \frac{P(u_1=+1)}{P(u_1=-1)} + p(\mathbf{y}|u_0=-1, u_1=-1)} \\ = & L(u_0) + \ln \frac{p(\mathbf{y}|u_0=+1, u_1=+1)\cdot e^{L(u_1)} + p(\mathbf{y}|u_0=+1, u_1=-1)}{p(\mathbf{y}|u_0=-1, u_1=+1)\cdot e^{L(u_1)} + p(\mathbf{y}|u_0=-1, u_1=-1)} \\ = & \underbrace{L(u_0)}_{\text{a priori}} + \underbrace{\ln \frac{p(y_0|u_0=+1)}{p(y_0|u_0=-1)}}_{\text{intrinsic } L(y_0|u_0)} + \\ & \underbrace{\ln \frac{p(\mathbf{y}_{\setminus 0}|u_0=+1, u_1=+1)\cdot e^{L(u_1)} + p(\mathbf{y}_{\setminus 0}|u_0=+1, u_1=-1)}{p(\mathbf{y}_{\setminus 0}|u_0=-1, u_1=+1)\cdot e^{L(u_1)} + p(\mathbf{y}_{\setminus 0}|u_0=-1, u_1=-1)}}_{\text{extrinsic } L_E(u_0|\mathbf{y}_{\setminus 0})} \end{aligned} \tag{12.47}$$

$$L(u_0|\mathbf{y}) = L(u_0) + L(y_0|u_0) + L_E(u_0|\mathbf{y}_{\setminus 0}). \tag{12.48}$$

Although formulated out in (12.47) and later equations, the actual expression for the extrinsic information is not required, since it indirectly results from the other terms in (12.48), i.e., after subtracting a-priori and intrinsic information from the MAP LLR $L(u_i|\mathbf{y})$, which is delivered from, e.g., a BCJR algorithm that we had described in Sect. 5.2.6. Figures 12.8, 12.9, 12.10, 12.11, and 12.13 show those subtractions around the decoders.

The general formulation of equations (12.47) and (12.48) for K message bits is given by

$$L(u_i|\mathbf{y}) = L(u_i) + \ln \frac{\sum_{\mathbf{u}:u_i=+1} p(\mathbf{y}|\mathbf{u}) \cdot \exp\left[\sum_{j:j\neq i,u_j=+1} L(u_j)\right]}{\sum_{\mathbf{u}:u_i=-1} p(\mathbf{y}|\mathbf{u}) \cdot \exp\left[\sum_{j:j\neq i,u_j=+1} L(u_j)\right]} \quad \text{and} \quad (12.49)$$

$$= L(u_i) + L(y_i|u_i) + \ln \frac{\sum_{\mathbf{u}:u_i=+1} p(\mathbf{y}_{\setminus i}|\mathbf{u}) \cdot \exp\left[\sum_{j:j\neq i,u_j=+1} L(u_j)\right]}{\sum_{\mathbf{u}:u_i=-1} p(\mathbf{y}_{\setminus i}|\mathbf{u}) \cdot \exp\left[\sum_{j:j\neq i,u_j=+1} L(u_j)\right]}, \quad (12.50)$$

respectively. The specifier $u_j = +1$ in the sum of log-likelihood ratios means only including the terms that had the probability condition with $u_j = +1$, since one divides through the negative counterparts just as in (12.47), i.e., all terms are only existing with all positive ones and then the last one with all negative ones would not have the exponential term at all. Multiplying numerators and denominators by $\exp\left(-1/2 \cdot \sum_{j=0}^{K-1} L(u_j)\right)$, would symmetrize the expression leading to

$$L(u_i|\mathbf{y}) = L(u_i) + \ln \frac{\sum_{\mathbf{u}:u_i=+1} p(\mathbf{y}|\mathbf{u}) \cdot \exp\left[\frac{1}{2}\mathbf{u} \cdot \mathbf{L}^T\right]}{\sum_{\mathbf{u}:u_i=-1} p(\mathbf{y}|\mathbf{u}) \cdot \exp\left[\frac{1}{2}\mathbf{u} \cdot \mathbf{L}^T\right]} \quad \text{and} \quad (12.51)$$

$$= L(u_i) + L(y_i|u_i) + \ln \frac{\sum_{\mathbf{u}:u_i=+1} p(\mathbf{y}_{\setminus i}|\mathbf{u}) \cdot \exp\left[\frac{1}{2}\mathbf{u} \cdot \mathbf{L}^T\right]}{\sum_{\mathbf{u}:u_i=-1} p(\mathbf{y}_{\setminus i}|\mathbf{u}) \cdot \exp\left[\frac{1}{2}\mathbf{u} \cdot \mathbf{L}^T\right]}, \quad (12.52)$$

Boldface **u** and **L** denote row vectors with components u_j and $L(u_j)$.

Figure 12.8 shows the information flow of L-values at the decoder. It obtains a-priori information $L(u)$ and intrinsic information $L(y_i|u_i)$ which represents the channel. It outputs a log-likelihood ratio that can be used for a final decision and from which an extrinsic information can be derived by subtracting the input L-values. The figure represents the processing unit for decoding a parallel concatenated code.

There will be cases where a direct channel output is not available and just an a-priori L-value will be provided. This leads to a unit shown in Fig. 12.9. Typically it is a decoder component for serially concatenated codes, where an inner decoder delivers an L-value to the outer code, but the outer code has no access to the channel output. Both, the inner and outer code will have the codeword of the outer code as a coupling element. Thus, an iterative procedure has to process this codeword, not the

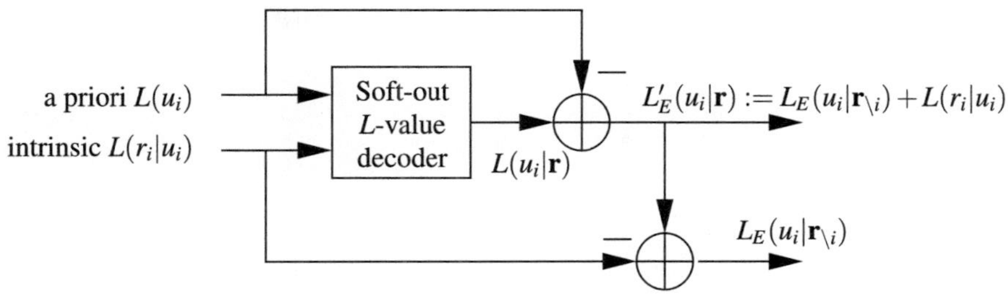

Fig. 12.8 L-value flow of a soft-output decoder unit

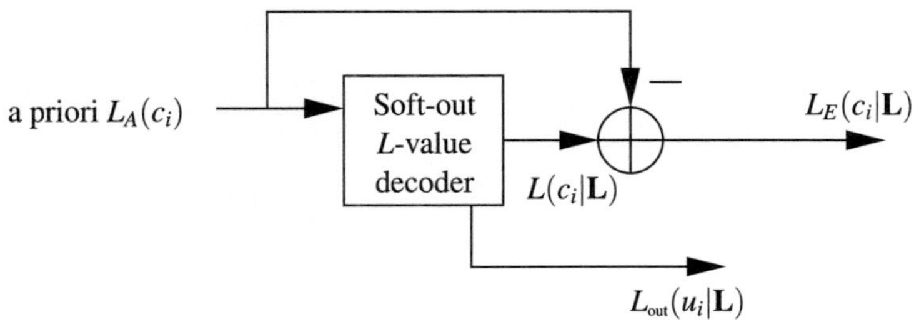

Fig. 12.9 L-value flow of a soft-output decoder unit in case no channel output is available

final information in the first place. The corresponding L-value that is correspondingly defined for these codeword positions c_i (also in ± 1 notation) will be

$$L(c_i|\mathbf{y}) = L(c_i) + \underbrace{\ln \frac{\sum_{\mathbf{c}:c_i=+1} \exp\left[\frac{1}{2} \cdot \mathbf{c} \cdot \mathbf{L}^T\right]}{\sum_{\mathbf{c}:c_i=-1} \exp\left[\frac{1}{2} \cdot \mathbf{c} \cdot \mathbf{L}^T\right]}}_{L_E(c_i|\mathbf{L})}. \tag{12.53}$$

Note that due to the lack of a direct channel input, the weighting with the conditional channel probabilities is missing.

Equation (12.53) does not yet provide a final output, since the iterations will work on the outer codewords. The final output will be

$$L_{\text{out}}(u_i|\mathbf{L}) = \ln \frac{\sum_{\mathbf{u}:u_i=+1} \exp\left[\frac{1}{2} \cdot \mathbf{c}(\mathbf{u}) \cdot \mathbf{L}^T\right]}{\sum_{\mathbf{u}:u_i=-1} \exp\left[\frac{1}{2} \cdot \mathbf{c}(\mathbf{u}) \cdot \mathbf{L}^T\right]}. \tag{12.54}$$

This result may require some more derivation. First, we need to discuss the **statistical properties of log-likelihood ratios**.

Let us first assume an AWGN channel with

$$z = c + n, \tag{12.55}$$

c being the discrete ± 1 input, n the noise, and z the output.

The Gaussian density

$$p(z|C=c) = \frac{1}{\sqrt{2\pi}\sigma_n} \cdot e^{-(z-c)^2/2\sigma_n^2} \tag{12.56}$$

leads to the log-likelihood ratio

$$L(z|c) = \ln \frac{p(z|c=+1)}{p(z|c=-1)} = \ln \frac{e^{+2z/2\sigma_n^2}}{e^{-2z/2\sigma_n^2}} = \frac{2}{\sigma_n^2} \cdot z = \frac{2}{\sigma_n^2} \cdot (c+n) \tag{12.57}$$

Taking into account the statistics of z, we see that the mean and variance of $L(z|c)$ will be

$$\mu_L = 2/\sigma_n^2 \cdot c \quad \text{and} \quad \sigma_L^2 = \left(\frac{2}{\sigma_n^2}\right)^2 \sigma_n^2 = 4/\sigma_n^2, \tag{12.58}$$

respectively. Letting $c=+1$, this means that there is a relation between mean and variance according to

$$\mu_L = \sigma_L^2/2. \tag{12.59}$$

This relation, i.e., the possibility to describe the density by only a single parameter, μ_L or σ_L, is a property of *consistent* densities.

Definition 12.4 A density of probability $f(x)$ is said to be consistent (i.e. with exponential symmetry) iff

$$f(x) = e^x f(-x), \quad \forall x \in \mathbb{R}$$

Having L_i as an input to the decoder and comparing with $2/\sigma_n^2 \cdot c$, $c = \pm 1$, we obtain the log-likelihood ratio of a single bit

$$\ln \frac{p(L_i|+1)}{p(L_i|-1)} = \ln \frac{\exp\left[-\frac{\left(L_i - \frac{2}{\sigma_n^2}(+1)\right)^2}{2\cdot\frac{4}{\sigma_n^2}}\right]}{\exp\left[-\frac{\left(L_i - \frac{2}{\sigma_n^2}(-1)\right)^2}{2\cdot\frac{4}{\sigma_n^2}}\right]} = \ln \frac{\exp\left[\frac{+2\cdot\frac{2}{\sigma_n^2}\cdot L_i\cdot(+1)}{2\cdot\frac{4}{\sigma_n^2}}\right]}{\exp\left[\frac{+2\cdot\frac{2}{\sigma_n^2}\cdot L_i\cdot(-1)}{2\cdot\frac{4}{\sigma_n^2}}\right]}$$

$$= \ln \frac{\exp\left[+\frac{1}{2}\cdot L_i \cdot (+1)\right]}{\exp\left[+\frac{1}{2}\cdot L_i \cdot (-1)\right]}. \tag{12.60}$$

We adopted a Gaussian assumption for L_i.

Now, we are prepared to return to (12.54). Assuming the input vectors u_i to appear with the same probability, due to Bayes' rule, the conditional MAP probabilities $p(u_i|L_i)$ can be turned into the conditional likelihood probabilities $p(L_i|u_i)$.

Together with our intermediate discussion leading to (12.60), Eq. (12.54) becomes obvious.

We have now described the decoder blocks and its functions. As already mentioned, the Soft-out L-value decoders will mostly be realized by the BCJR algorithm. described in Sect. 5.2.6. There one observes, how the a-priori and intrinsic information are processed to obtain the output log-likelihood ratios. The BCJR algorithm yields L-values for the code and information components, hence, does not require any further computation of the extrinsic information apart from the ones shown in Figs. 12.8 and 12.9 In the following section, we will now describe the complete iterative structures of "Turbo" decoders for parallel and serial concatenated codes.

12.6.4 Iterative "Turbo" Decoding of Parallel and Serially Concatenated Codes

We will start from the first proposal of **parallel concatenated codes** in [12] which coined the name "Turbo" codes. The encoder is shown in Fig. 12.10. Two recursive systematic convolutional encoders are used, where the information reaches the second encoder through an interleaver. As in our earlier example with the parallel concatenated parity-check codes, the parities are derived from different information, making it possible to obtain from received information and parities 'almost' independent estimates of the information.

The puncturing at the end may be used to not reduce the coderate by having redundancy added from two encoders.

Why have recursive systematic codes been chosen? The choice of systematic codes is not essential but convenient. First, the reliability information given by the log-likelihood ratios does not differ between code and information symbols, since the information is part of the code sequence. Furthermore, we have seen in (12.47) and (12.50), (12.52), that the intrinsic information can be separated very easily and a real extrinsic information is left. More important is the fact that the equivalent systematic encoders that can be determined from convolutional codes given in the typical tables like the ones provided at the end of Chap. 4 will be recursive (see Sect. 4.1.2). Recursive codes are essential to obtain good distance properties which determine the asymptotic performance of concatenated codes with iterative decoding. This area in the bit-error ratio curves (see Fig. 12.12) is often called *error-floor region*, which is a little misleading. The curves just flatten out to asymptotically approach the performance predicted by the minimum Hamming distance (of the constituent codes). The performance at low signal-to-noise ratios does not simply depend on the minimum distance. This area is called *water-fall region* and will come near to the limits predicted in Sect. 12.6.1. A separate Sect. 12.7 will be devoted to study the convergence of iterative decoding giving some insight regarding the water-fall region, as well.

Especially good distance properties will be achieved when a low-weight output sequence of one encoder is compensated by a high-weight output from the second encoder. It is obvious that a non-recursive encoder will not be suited, since a low-weight input will also yield a low-weight output and after interleaving, the second encoder will have a low-weight output, as well. A recursive encoder, however, will produce an infinite sequence (without taking blocking into consideration) after being triggered by a single one at the input. For recursive encoders, short input sequences with, e.g., 2 or 3 input ones may be critical and lead to low-weight output sequences. The interleaver has to ensure that the second encoder will not lead to a low-weight output at the same time. Thus, a quick test of interleavers consists of trying out input pattern of weights 2 and 3. Parallel concatenated codes with almost *random* interleavers obtain good weight distributions with very low complex codes. Actually, the codes should be simple and have not too high memory, since otherwise the decoding iterations will stop very early due to cycles in the information flow contradicting the independence assumption mentioned before. Due to the low minimum distance determined by the weak constituent codes, at some point, the bit-error ratio curves of Turbo codes (typical between 10^{-7} and 10^{-5}) will flatten out. This means, a further concatenation with, e.g., an RS code may be required to ensure really low bit-error ratios at low SNR.

Interleaver sizes that are proposed range from typically a few thousands to several 10,000 bits. In Berrou's paper, they used to work with 65,000 bits. However, if it is not required to approach Channel Capacity too tightly, the iterative procedures

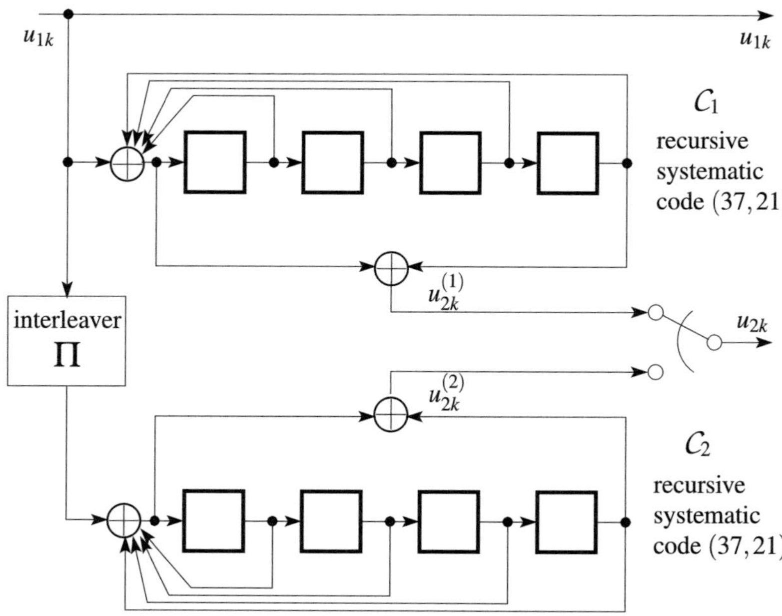

Fig. 12.10 Encoder of a “Turbo” code

works also with suitable interleavers of sizes of around 200 bits. Some possible interleaver types are, e.g., random, S-random, convolutional with random switching. S-random [15] specifies an interleaver with a guaranteed spread. In [15], it is defined as "a random permutation generating random integers i, $1 \leq i \leq N$", where each "randomly selected integer is compared to S previously selected integers. If the current selection is equal to any S previous selections within a distance $\pm S$, then the current selection is rejected. This process is repeated until all N integers are selected." There are also combinatorial analytical designs, but typically the performance is worse than with "S"-random interleavers.

Let us now discuss the decoder structure. The essential building blocks, the L-value soft-out APP decoders, we have already studied in the previous section (see Fig. 12.8), so that we can now just focus on the interaction of these units. The way they interact will, of course, be the counterpart of the encoding. The principle of the parallel concatenated encoder together with the corresponding decoder is shown in Fig. 12.11.

Π and Π^{-1} specify the interleaver and deinterleaver, respectively. They reorder the sequences for a decoder such that they are according to the information sequence that the corresponding encoder was operating on.

The extrinsic information from the decoder obtained after subtracting intrinsic $L(y_i^{(\dots)}|u_i)$ and a-priori $L_A^{(\dots)} = L(u_i)$ will be the a-priori information for the following decoder. Thus, $L_A^{(1)}$ and $L_A^{(2)}$ will be reordered versions of $L_E^{(2)}$ and $L_E^{(1)}$, respectively.

The number of iterations needed depends on the codes. This will be studied later. The convergence will furthermore strongly depend on the quality of the interleavers. It gets stuck as soon as the same information is fed back in cycles.

A sample BER versus E_b/N_0 performance curve of a parallel concatenated curves with iterative decoding is shown in Fig. 12.12. This can simply be generated using a ready-built Matlab routine [16]. However, note that the performance is by far not optimum, neither code nor interleaver, but it nicely outlines the characteristics.

We distinguish three areas: the pinch-off, waterfall, and error-floor regions. Better schemes show a flooring at significantly lower error ratios, e.g., at 10^{-5} and a waterfall close to the Shannon limit, which we added to the plot for diminishing BER according to Eq. (12.12). One may compare the much better performance already in the original publication by Berrou et al. [12].

A more detailed reasoning for the first two regions will be postponed to Sect. 12.7. Here, we only realize that from a certain SNR on, which is near the Shannnon limit, the BER drops. Note that the Turbo scheme consisting of two encoders and an interleaving appear like encoding a very long code. The requirement of the codeword to be long was an early result of information theory. The channel coding theorem by Shannon was assuming the codeword length to go to infinity. The actual constituent codes, however, are actually weak and with some low probability bit-error pattern appear that exceed the small minimum distance. This causes the error-floor region, which is no strict floor, but a region where the curve approaches the performance bound predicted by the minimum-distance term in the Union Bound approximation. Since the

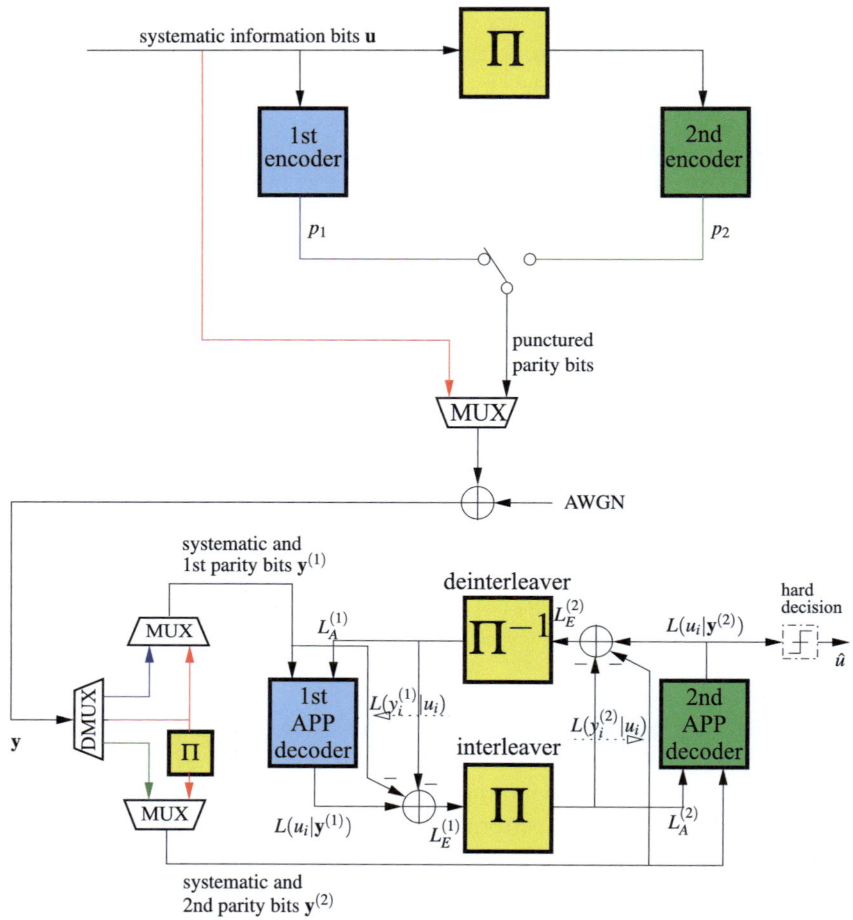

Fig. 12.11 Encoder and iterative decoder for a parallel concatenated code (APP decoder: A-Posteriori Probability, e.g., BCJR dec.)

constituent codes have relatively low minimum distance, the minimum distance of a parallel concatenated code is actually low, too. For example, a non-punctured parallel concatenated code code based on identical binary systematic recursive constituent codes has a minimum distance d_{free}^{pc} of

$$d_{free}^{pc} = 2 \cdot d_{free}^{c} - 1, \tag{12.61}$$

where d_{free}^{c} is the free distance of the constituent codes.

This can easily be seen from the block-coded case where the minimum distance appears in a single row and single columns. As earlier when deriving the Singleton bound in Theorem 3.3, we assume one single non-zero entry in the information part.

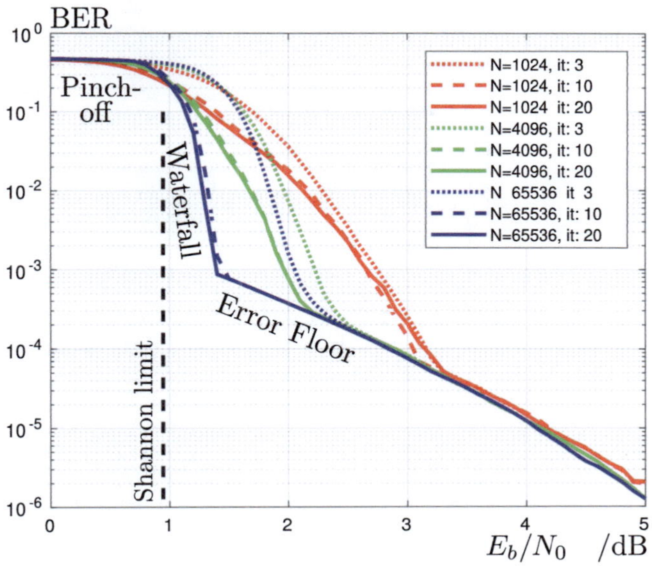

Fig. 12.12 Sample BER curve of a parallel concatenated code with iterative decoding, $R = 1/3$, different interleaver sizes and different numbers of iterations [16]

Then the row and column weights are ${d_H}_{min}^{row}$ and ${d_H}_{min}^{col}$, respectively. Since the single non-zero information bit is not transmitted twice, we obtain

$$d_{H\,min} = {d_H}_{min}^{row} + {d_H}_{min}^{col} - 1.$$

In the case of parallel concatenated convolutional codes, we require at least one single information bit to be nonzero to make a path leave the all-zero sequence. Then, both codes will at least lead to a d_{free} distance. Since the information bit is only transmitted once, Eq. (12.61) follows.

The iterative decoding of the **serial concatenated scheme** as shown in Fig. 12.13 differs from the parallel concatenated case in having to operate on the code sequence $\mathbf{c}^{(2)}$ of the outer code, which is the input sequence $\mathbf{u}^{(1)}$ to the inner encoder after reordering by the interleaver. The inner APP (e.g., BCJR) decoder block has the same functionality as in the parallel concatenated case and is realized as shown in Fig. 12.8. Similar to the parallel concatenated case, encoder (1) is provided with the channel input $L(r_i^{(1)}|u_i^{(1)})$ and the a-priori L-value $L_A(u_i^{(1)})$. The output is $L(u_i^{(1)}|\mathbf{r}^{(1)})$. We then subtract the a-priori information, but the intrinsic information is not subtracted and is thus forwarded to the outer decoder which has no direct access to the channel. Note that in the parallel concatenated case, the subtraction was necessary, since otherwise, the intrinsic information would have been taken twice. We call the mixed extrinsic/intrinsic information $L'_E(u_i^{(1)}|\mathbf{r}^{(1)})$. After reshuffling $L'_E(...)$ in the deinterleaver, the outer decoder follows Fig. 12.9. The only input is the a-priori value $L_A^{(2)}$, being the interleaved $L'_E(u_i^{(1)}|\mathbf{r}^{(1)})$. As already shown in Fig. 12.9, we will have

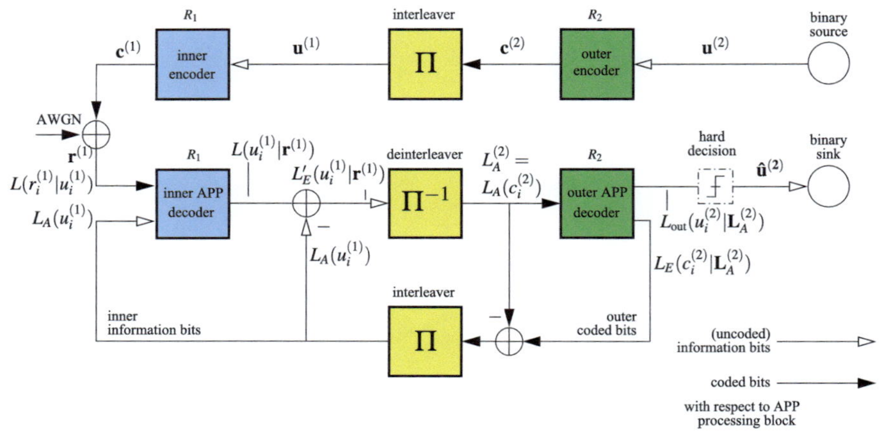

Fig. 12.13 Encoder and iterative decoder for a serially concatenated code

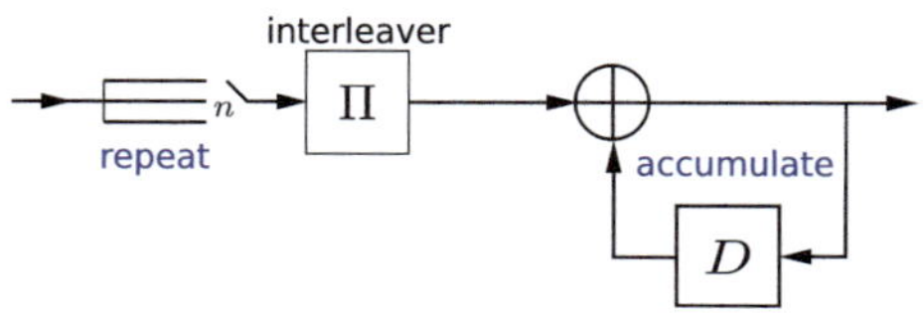

Fig. 12.14 Repeat-Accumulate code

two outputs at the outer decoder: one needed for the iterations and operating on $\mathbf{c}_2$ and another, providing the data output. They are $L_E(c_i^{(2)}|\mathbf{L}_A^{(2)})$ and $L_{\text{out}}(u_i^{(2)}|\mathbf{L}_A^{(2)})$, respectively.

A very simple serially concatenated Turbo coding scheme with good performance is the Repeat-Accumulate (RA) code [17] shown in Fig. 12.14. The accumulator is rate-1 code and hence, the overall rate is determined by the repetition code to be $1/n$.

Starting from the original paper by Berrou, Glavieux, Thitimajshima [12], meanwhile, there is a manifold of publications on parallel and serial concatenation together with iterative (Turbo) decoding. In here, we followed Hagenauer [13], Sklar [18], and Kramer, Ten Brink [14]. Books specializing on the topic are by Vucetic and Yuan [19], Heegard and Wicker [20], Soleymani et al. [21], Jezequel et al. [22], Hanzo et al. [23], Giulietti et al. [24], Barbulescu [25]. There are also special issues from IEEE JSAC [26–28], IEEE Trans. on Inf. Theory [29], IEEE Communications Magazine [30], IEEE Signal Processing Magazine [31], and Turbo-coding conference meanwhile renamed "International Symposium on Topics in Coding (ISTC)," originating from ENST (now IMT Atlantique) in Brest, France [32].

12.7 The Convergence Behavior of Turbo Codes — the EXIT Chart

EXIT (extrinsic information transfer) charts have been proposed in [33] and provide an information-theoretic tool to investigate the convergence behavior of iterative decoding schemes. They use the transfer characteristic from the (input) Mutual Information between transmitted data (bit) and a-priori information at the input of a decoder to the (output) Mutual Information between transmitted data (bit) and extrinsic information at the output of a decoder. Thus, EXIT curves describe the influence of one single decoding operation onto the Mutual Information.

Using the relation between mean and standard deviation of the log-likelihood ratio of the a-priori information according to (12.59), i.e.,

$$\mu_A = \sigma_A^2/2 \tag{12.62}$$

and applying a Gaussian assumption for a-priori and extrinsic informations, we obtain

$$p_A(\xi|X=x) = \frac{e^{-\frac{(\xi-\frac{\sigma_A^2}{2}\cdot x)^2}{2\sigma_A^2}}}{\sqrt{2\pi}\,\sigma_A}\,. \tag{12.63}$$

Observation shows that p_A and p_E actually approach a Gaussian density with growing number of iterations. Furthermore, we make use of the assumption of infinitely big interleavers in a turbo scheme, thereby avoiding correlations between the a-priori information and the channel observation. We will later see that finite interleavers will lead to deviations from the EXIT curves.

In the binary case with equally distributed X, the Mutual Information $I_A = I(X;A)$ follows to be

$$\begin{aligned} I_A &= \frac{1}{2}\cdot\sum_{x=-1,1}\int_{-\infty}^{+\infty} p_A(\xi|X=x)\cdot\log_2\frac{2\cdot p_A(\xi|X=x)}{p_A(\xi|X=-1)+p_A(\xi|X=+1)}\,d\xi \\ &= 1-\int_{-\infty}^{\infty}\frac{e^{-\frac{\left(\xi-\sigma_A^2/2\right)^2}{2\sigma_A^2}}}{\sqrt{2\pi}\,\sigma_A}\cdot\log_2\left[1+e^{-\xi}\right]d\xi\,. \end{aligned} \tag{12.64}$$

The second step was possible since the integral for $X=+1$ and -1 is the same.

Likewise, the Mutual Information $I_E = I(X;E)$ is described by

$$I_E = \frac{1}{2}\sum_{x=-1,1}\int_{-\infty}^{+\infty} p_E(\xi|X=x)\cdot\log_2\frac{2\cdot p_E(\xi|X=x)}{p_E(\xi|X=-1)+p_E(\xi|X=+1)}\,d\xi. \tag{12.65}$$

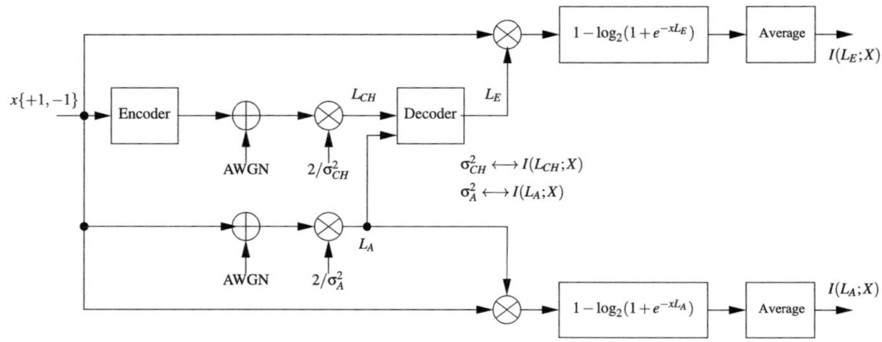

Fig. 12.15 Procedure for determining the EXIT curve (from [34])

These function can only be computed numerically. Nevertheless, I_A is monotonically increasing and thus invertible in $\sigma := \sigma_A = 2/\sigma_n$ according to (12.58). Let us define

$$J(\sigma) = I_A(\sigma_A = \sigma). \tag{12.66}$$

A Mutual Information transfer characteristic $I_E = T(I_A, E_b/N_0)$, i.e., $I_E = T(I_A)$ for a fixed E_b/N_0, can now be obtained by first determining σ_A from a given I_A inverting (12.66). Then, p_E in (12.65) results from a Monte-Carlo simulation with histogram measurement. Finally, the extrinsic Mutual Information I_E results from inserting it into (12.65). There is actually not even a requirement for p_E to be Gaussian. Figure 12.16 shows such EXIT curves for different signal-to-noise ratios.[5] The underlying code is $(023, 037)_8$, where the two octal numbers specify the feedback and feed-forward polynomials, respectively, with low degrees on the right, i.e.,

$$(023, 037)_8 \equiv (010011, 011111) \equiv \left(1, \frac{1 + D + D^2 + D^3 + D^4}{1 + D + D^4}\right).$$

Note that in earlier chapters on convolutional codes, we defined the lower degrees to be on the left. However, here we decided to follow [33].

An equivalent way to determine EXIT curves not requiring the inversion of (12.66) may be more suited for computing. This procedure is depicted in Fig. 12.15. The derivation of this scheme starts from rephrasing (12.64) into an expectation

$$I_A = 1 - \int_{-\infty}^{\infty} p_A(\xi|X = +1) \cdot \log_2\left[1 + e^{-\xi}\right] d\xi = 1 - E_\xi\left\{\log_2\left[1 + e^{-\xi}\right]\right\}. \tag{12.67}$$

The nonlinear function can be expressed as

[5] Figures and some text is taken from [33] with permission from the author.

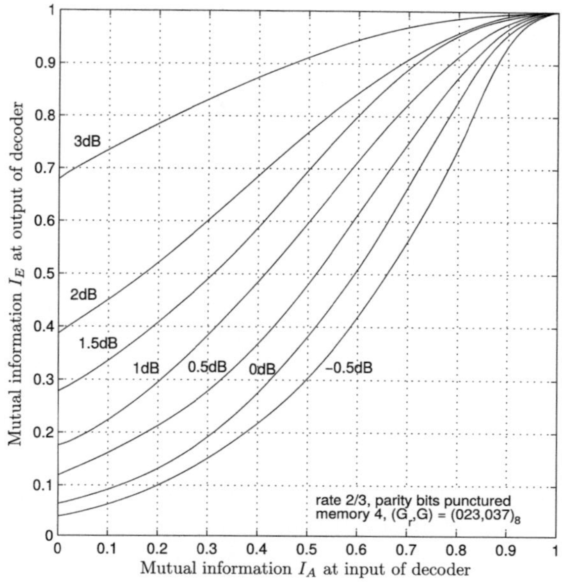

Fig. 12.16 EXIT characteristic for a rate-2/3 convolutional code with E_b/N_0 as a parameter

$$
\begin{aligned}
1 - E_\xi \left\{\log_2\left[1+e^{-\xi}\right]\right\} &= E_\xi \left\{\log_2\left[\frac{2}{1+e^{-\xi}}\right]\right\} = E_\xi \left\{\log_2\left[1+\tanh(\xi/2)\right]\right\} \\
&= E_\xi \left\{\log_2\left[1+\lambda\right]\right\}, \qquad (12.68)
\end{aligned}
$$

where we introduced the '*soft bit*'

$$
\begin{aligned}
\lambda(\xi) = \; & E_x\{x\} = (+1)\cdot P(X=+1) + (-1)\cdot P(X=-1) \\
= \; & \frac{e^\xi}{1+e^\xi} - \frac{1}{1+e^\xi} = \frac{e^\xi - 1}{1+e^\xi} = \frac{e^{\xi/2} - e^{-\xi/2}}{e^{\xi/2} + e^{-\xi/2}} = \tanh\left(\xi/2\right) \qquad (12.69)
\end{aligned}
$$

as the average of x. This average relates log-likelihood ratios and analog values. For the derivation, we used (12.26) and (12.27).

If the input values x are not equally likely ($P(x) \neq 1/2$, $L(x) \neq 0$), (12.67) will generalize to

$$I_A = h(P(x)) - E\left\{\log_2\left[1+e^{-\xi}\right]\right\}, \qquad (12.70)$$

where $h(p) = -p\log_2 p - (1-p)\log_2(1-p)$ is the binary entropy function.

Assuming ergodicity, one can replace the ensemble average by the time average, leading to

$$I_A = 1 - E\left\{\log_2\left[1+e^{-\xi}\right]\right\} \approx 1 - \frac{1}{N}\sum_{n=1}^{N} \log_2\left[1+e^{-x_n\cdot\xi_n}\right]. \qquad (12.71)$$

x_n has been added to take into account both possible values for x and correct the sign of ξ.

The a-priori and intrinsic log-likelihood ratios L_A and $L_{CH} = L(u_i|\mathbf{y})$, respectively, are obtained following Eq. (12.57) by multiplying the binary data and (0,1)-distributed AWGN with $2/\sigma_A$ or $2/\sigma_{CH}$. Note that equations (12.64), (12.66), (12.67), and (12.71) provide the relation between Mutual Information I and σ, The lower path just uses the relation (12.71) to compute the Mutual Information $I(L_A; X)$ from the given standard deviation σ_A, whereas the upper part uses the same relation after passing L_A and L_{CH} through the decoder.

The described process only requires the simulation of one decoder, thereby reducing the simulation time significantly. EXIT charts offer performance evaluations in a very short time and thereby simplify the search for good Turbo codes (and also other iteratively decodable schemes).

The EXIT Chart

In an iterative decoding scheme for Turbo codes, we have learned that the extrinsic information of one decoder is used as a-priori information of the other (see, e.g., Fig. 12.11). If we would like to draw both decoder EXIT characteristics into one graph, we would just have to swap the axis for one decoder. We do this for the second decoder.

The two curves now allow to visualize the iterations. Let n be the iteration index and we consider E_b/N_0 to be fixed. The iteration starts from the origin with zero a-priori knowledge $I_{A_1,0} = 0$. At iteration n, the extrinsic output of the first decoder is $I_{E_1,n} = T_1(I_{A_1,n})$. $I_{E_1,n}$ is forwarded to the second decoder to become $I_{A_2,n} = I_{E_1,n}$ (ordinate). The extrinsic output of the second decoder is $I_{E_2,n} = T_2(I_{A_2,n})$, which is fed back to the first decoder to become the a-priori knowledge $I_{A_1,n+1} = I_{E_2,n}$ (abscissa) of the next iteration. Note that interleaving does not change Mutual Information.

The iteration proceeds as long as $I_{E_2,n+1} > I_{E_2,n}$. With $I_{E_2,n+1} = T_2(T_1(I_{E_2,n}))$ this can be formulated as $T_1(I_{E_2,n}) > T_2^{-1}(I_{E_2,n})$. The iteration stops if $I_{E_2,n+1} = I_{E_2,n}$, or equivalently, $T_1(I_{E_2,n}) = T_2^{-1}(I_{E_2,n})$, which corresponds to an intersection of both characteristics in the EXIT chart.

Simulated **trajectories** for two different SNRs are shown in Figs. 12.17 and 12.18.

Figure 12.18 shows results with a bigger interleaver of 10^6 bits. The stronger deviation of the trajectories in Fig. 12.17 is due to the shorter interleaver which earlier causes statistical dependencies. In Fig. 12.18, we clearly see the opening of the convergence channel at about 0.7 dB.

Trajectories can be computed in different ways, showing either the snapshot behavior, i.e., the block-wise forwarding of Mutual Informations (log-likelihood ratios) or an average over many blocks. The individual trajectories will, of course, show variations. Practically, they can, e.g., be computed using the approach in Fig. 12.15. Hereto, we have to implement it twice for both decoders and information to the second decoder and also the extrinsic information has to be fed through an interleaver. The latter will be the a-priori input to the second decoder. This means the a-priori log-likelihood ratio of the first decoder is initialized with zero and the

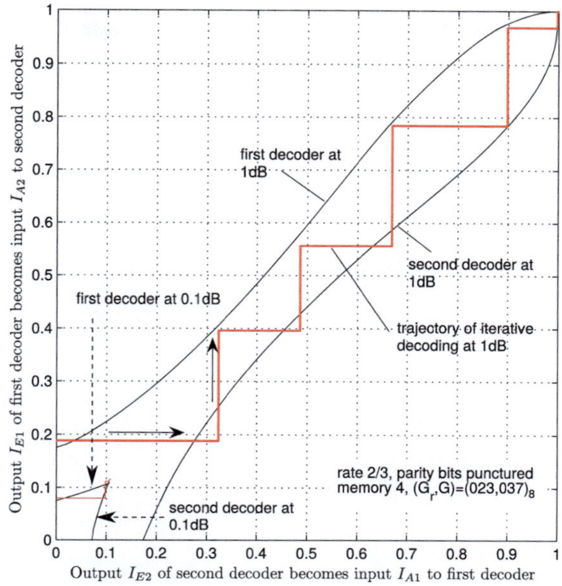

Fig. 12.17 Simulated trajectories of iterative decoding at $E_b/N_0 = 0.1$ dB and 1 dB for a symmetric parallel concatenated code and a random interleaver of 60,000 bits

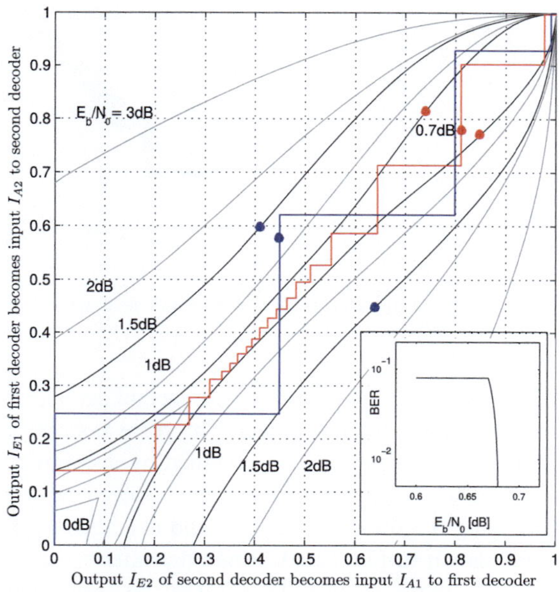

Fig. 12.18 EXIT charts for different SNR values. Two trajectories are shown at 0.7 and 1.5 dB for a symmetric parallel concatenated code and a random interleaver of 10^6 bits

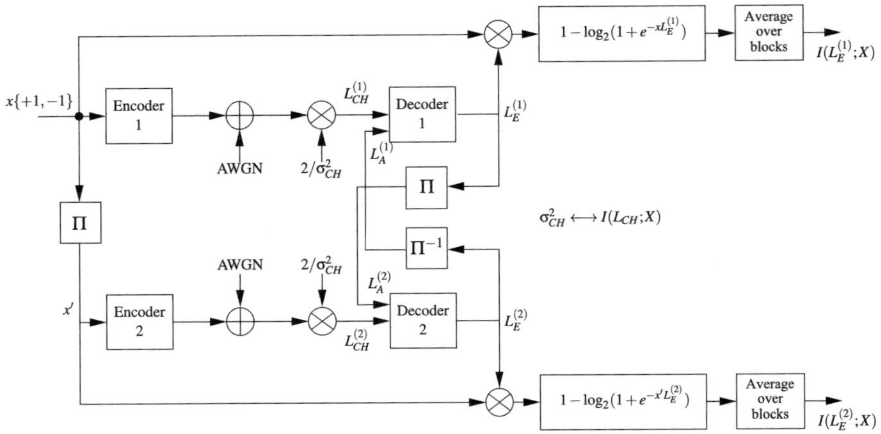

Fig. 12.19 Procedure for determining EXIT trajectories

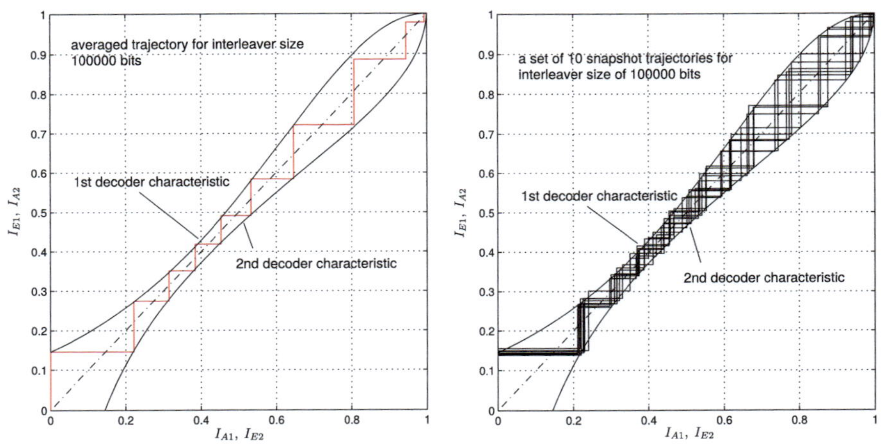

Fig. 12.20 Averaged and snapshot trajectories for a large interleaver size of 100000 bits

extrinsic log-likelihood ratio is handed over to the second decoder as a-priori information after passing it through the interleaver. The corresponding circuit is shown in Fig. 12.19. The averaged trajectories are obtained by averaging the output over more than one block. Thus, snapshot and averaged trajectories just differ by the duration of the averaging. Figures for snapshot and averaged trajectories for very long interleavers are shown in Fig. 12.20. When the interleaver is shorter, due to statistical dependencies, the iterations will not follow the ideal EXIT characteristics any more, but die out earlier as can be seen in Fig. 12.21. Deviations from the EXIT curves for longer interleavers are due to terminating one trellis and leaving the other unterminated. This shifts the reliability slightly towards the one with the terminated trellis.

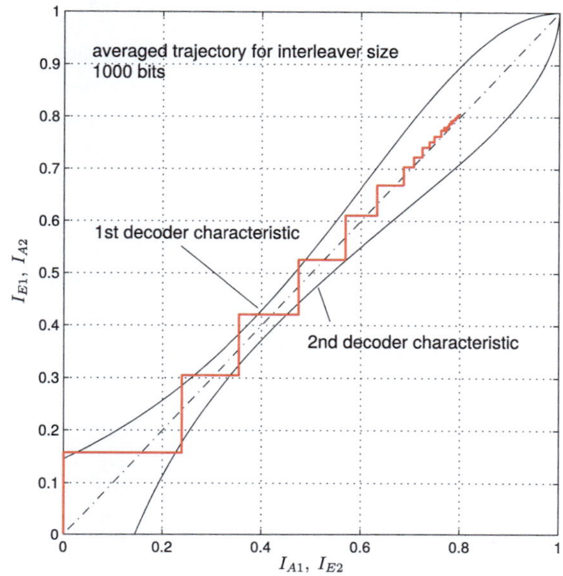

Fig. 12.21 Averaged trajectories for an interleaver of size 1000 bits

Let us interpret the EXIT charts in relation to a bit-error ratio versus SNR plot as given in Fig. 12.12. When two curves intersect, the decoding process will stop at high error rates. This will be the case at very low signal-to-noise ratios. This was referred to as the *pinch-off region* in BER versus SNR plots. The *waterfall region* with convergence to high Mutual Informations (usually one, although there are codes and applications where one cannot be reached) is achieved when the convergence channel opens and the trajectories can sneak through. The third region in bit-error ratio curves is called *error-floor region*, which is actually no error floor, but a flattening out to finally approach the performance determined by the actual minimum distance, which is in turn determined by the small minimum distances of the constituent codes. In the error-floor region, the channel in the EXIT chart will already be wide open, but details on the error-floor region cannot be seen from the EXIT chart.

In [35, 36], the area of the gap between EXIT curves have been related to the performance gap of the rate to capacity. The derivation there was based on the BEC (binary erasure channel), but the principle results were expected to hold for other channels, as well. The conclusion is that the two EXIT curves should be as close as possible, without any intersection. This will, of course, require a large number of iterations. In [35], it is furthermore shown that the best serial concatenation requires the inner code to be of rate 1, which is realized by the Repeat-Accumulate codes that we had shown in Fig. 12.14.

Bit-error ratios can be introduced into the EXIT chart as a contour plot. In order to obtain a simple derivation of error-probabilities, we assume all log-likelihood ratios in the iterative decoding (intrinsic L_I, extrinsic L_E, and a priori L_A) to be statistically independent and Gaussian distributed. Since these L-values are added to obtain the final decision (sign) and reliability (absolute value), the corresponding variances add up, too.

$$\sigma_D^2 = \sigma_I^2 + \sigma_E^2 + \sigma_A^2 \tag{12.72}$$

From (1.2), we know that the hard-decision error ratio of a Gaussian-distributed variable is given by

$$\frac{1}{2}\mathrm{erfc}\left(\frac{\mu_D}{\sqrt{2}\sigma_D}\right) = Q\left(\frac{\mu_D}{\sigma_D}\right), \tag{12.73}$$

not normalizing the mean μ_D to unity. Using the relations between mean μ_D and variance σ_D of the log-likelihood ratios described in (12.59), (12.62), we obtain

$$\frac{1}{2}\mathrm{erfc}\left(\frac{\sigma}{2\sqrt{2}}\right) = Q\left(\frac{\sigma}{2}\right), \tag{12.74}$$

From (12.58) and $\sigma_n = 1/\sqrt{2E_s/N_0}$ (see Sect. 1.3.1), we obtain

$$\sigma_I^2 = 4/\sigma_n^2 = 8 \cdot \frac{E_s}{N_0} = 8 \cdot R \cdot \frac{E_b}{N_0} \tag{12.75}$$

The other variances of L_A and L_E follow from (12.66) as

$$\sigma_A = J^{-1}(I_A), \quad \sigma_E = J^{-1}(I_E) \tag{12.76}$$

Inserting (12.75) and (12.76) into (12.74) using (12.72), we finally obtain

$$\begin{aligned} &\frac{1}{2}\mathrm{erfc}\left(\frac{\sqrt{8R \cdot E_s/N_0 + \left(J^{-1}(I_A)\right)^2 + \left(J^{-1}(I_E)\right)^2}}{2\sqrt{2}}\right) \\ &= Q\left(\frac{\sqrt{8R \cdot E_s/N_0 + \left(J^{-1}(I_A)\right)^2 + \left(J^{-1}(I_E)\right)^2}}{2}\right), \end{aligned} \tag{12.77}$$

An exemplary contour plot added to an EXIT chart is shown in Fig. 12.22.

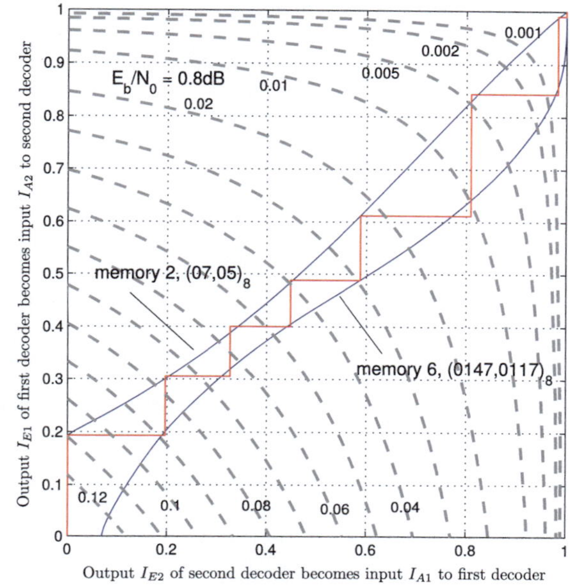

Fig. 12.22 Contour plot of bit-error probabilities inside an EXIT chart

12.8 Low-Density Parity-Check (LDPC) Codes

12.8.1 Basic Definitions

In this subsection, we introduce the basic definitions of LDPC codes originally proposed by Gallager in his Ph.D. thesis 1963 [37], which was rediscovered after the appearance of Turbo codes in 1993 [12] by MacKay [38, 39].

An LDPC code is usually illustrated by use of the bipartite Tanner graph [40], showing the codeword symbols as circles and the checks as boxes. The Tanner graph of the Hamming code with the check matrix introduced in (3.7) as

$$\mathbf{H} = \begin{pmatrix} 0001111 \\ 0110011 \\ 1010101 \end{pmatrix} \tag{12.78}$$

is shown in Fig. 12.23.

Subdividing the MAP LLR for an outgoing edge message from a variable node in the Tanner graph into its information components following (12.46), the other edges emanating from check nodes are extrinsic information components. The intrinsic information is indicated by the vertical lines into the variable nodes. A-priori information components are not shown in the graph, but would have to be added as further inputs to the variable nodes. Typically, the a-priori share is omitted in the literature assuming equally probable binary data meaning zero log-likelihood ratios.

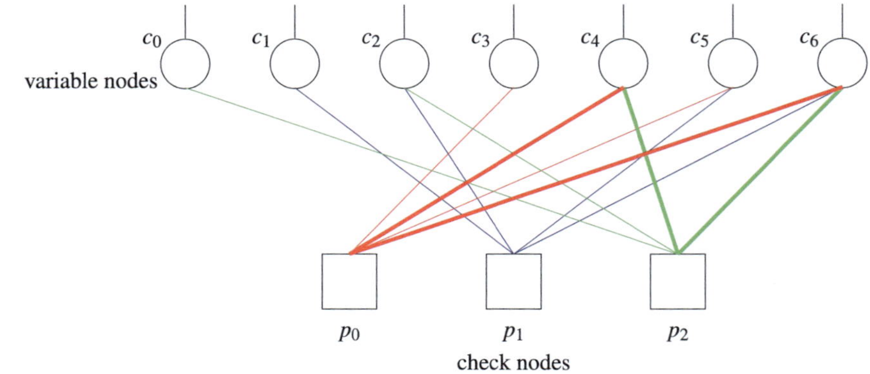

Fig. 12.23 Tanner graph of the Hamming code (cycle of length 4 highlighted)

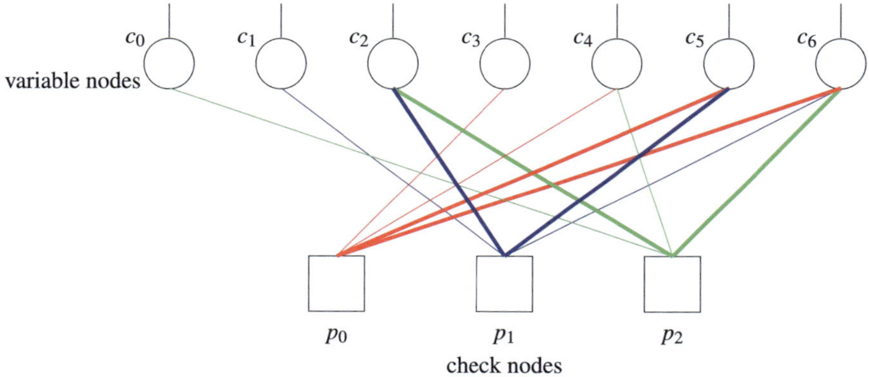

Fig. 12.24 Tanner graph of the Hamming code (cycle of length 6 highlighted)

The Hamming code is only used for illustration purposes and is, of course, no LDPC code. An LDPC code should have a sparse parity-check matrix and they typically have codeword lengths of more than 2000. In Fig. 12.23, a **cycle** of length 4 is shown in bold, which is also the smallest cycle one can think of. In Eq. (12.78) the corresponding nodes are also shown in the same color and make up a rectangle, which can easily be recognized. Likewise, a length-6 cycle are marked in (12.79).

$$\mathbf{H} = \begin{pmatrix} 0001111 \\ 0110011 \\ 1010101 \end{pmatrix} \tag{12.79}$$

The corresponding marking in the Tanner graph is shown in Fig. 12.24.

Due to statistical dependencies in the decoding algorithms due to short cycles, especially those of length four shall be avoided and the *girth* should be maximized, which we define formally.

Definition 12.5 The **Girth** of a graph is the length of the shortest cycle.

The graph in Fig. 12.23 showed an irregular variable-node profile. In general, we distinguish regular and irregular LDPC codes, whereas the latter leads to better performances.

12.8.1.1 Regular LDPC Codes

Definition 12.6 A regular LDPC code with its three parameters (N, t_c, t_r) is defined by a matrix with exactly t_c and t_r ones per column and row, respectively.

The code rate is $R = K/N \geq 1 - t_c/t_r$, with equality if $\mathbf{H}$ is full rank. This follows easily from

$$t_c N = t_r M \Longrightarrow \frac{M}{N} = \frac{t_c}{t_r} \Longrightarrow R = \frac{K}{N} = \frac{N-M}{N} = 1 - \frac{t_c}{t_r}. \tag{12.80}$$

Those three parameters define a family of regular codes, and one code among this family is given by a particular realization of the parity-check matrix. In an equivalent way, an LDPC code can be represented by a bipartite graph, called factor graph [41–43], or Tanner graph [40], made of two kinds of nodes: variable nodes representing bits of codeword, and check nodes associated with parity-check functions. Those two kinds of vertices are linked with each other by edges indicating to which parity equation variable nodes, i.e., the associated bits, take part in.

$$\mathbf{H} = \begin{bmatrix} 1\,1\,1\,1\,0\,0\,0\,0\,0\,0 \\ 1\,0\,0\,0\,1\,1\,1\,0\,0\,0 \\ 0\,1\,0\,0\,1\,0\,0\,1\,1\,0 \\ 0\,0\,1\,0\,0\,1\,0\,1\,0\,1 \\ 0\,0\,0\,1\,0\,0\,1\,0\,1\,1 \end{bmatrix}$$

The ith bit node and the lth check node are connected if $H_{l,i} = 1$. The degree of connection of a bit node (the same for a check node) is the number of edges linked to this node. A node is said i connected or of degree i if it is connected to i edges. Figure 12.25 shows the representation of a regular code parameterized by $(N = 8, t_c = 2, t_r = 4)$. One code corresponds to one particular realization of the interleaver.

12.8.1.2 Irregular LDPC Codes

A code is irregular if it is not regular. The usual parameterization of irregular LDPC codes is done by means of polynomials:

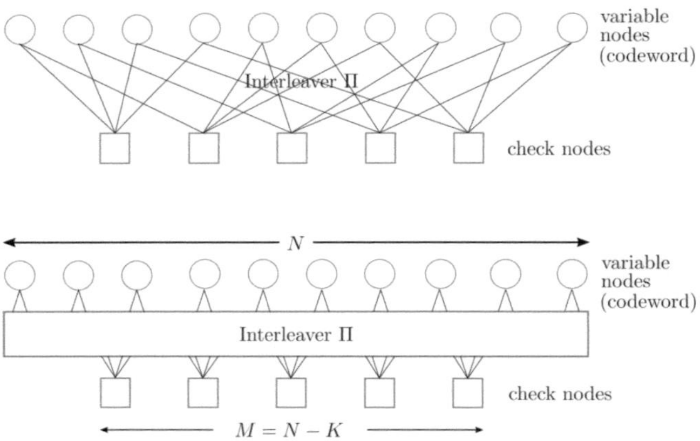

Fig. 12.25 Representation of a regular code ($N = 10$, $t_c = 2$, $t_r = 4$): the upper Tanner graph is a realization of the code, the bottom drawing symbolizes the family of such codes

- Polynomial associated with variable nodes:

$$\lambda(x) = \sum_{i=2}^{t_{cmax}} \lambda_i x^{i-1}, \tag{12.81}$$

  where λ_i is the proportion of edges of the graph connected to bit nodes of degree i, and t_{cmax} is the maximum number of edges linked to a bit node.
- Polynomial associated with check nodes:

$$\rho(x) = \sum_{j=2}^{t_{rmax}} \rho_j x^{j-1}, \tag{12.82}$$

  where ρ_j is the proportion of edges of the graph connected to check nodes of degree j, and t_{rmax} is the maximum number of edges linked to a check node.

Those two quantities are linked by the code rate

$$R = 1 - \frac{M}{N} = 1 - \frac{M/E}{N/E} = 1 - \frac{\sum_{j=2}^{t_{rmax}} \rho_j/j}{\sum_{i=2}^{t_{cmax}} \lambda_i/i}, \tag{12.83}$$

where E is the total number of edges. Note that the sums compute the average over $1/j$ and $1/i$, where i and j denote the check and variable node degrees, respectively. These averages are, of course, equal to M/E and N/E, respectively.

There is also a dual parameterization of the previous one:

- Polynomial associated with variable nodes:

$$\tilde{\lambda}(x) = \sum_{i=2}^{t_{cmax}} \tilde{\lambda}_i x^{i-1}, \tag{12.84}$$

where $\tilde{\lambda}_i$ is the proportion of bit nodes of degree i.

- Polynomial associated with check nodes:

$$\tilde{\rho}(x) = \sum_{j=2}^{t_{rmax}} \tilde{\rho}_j x^{j-1}, \tag{12.85}$$

where $\tilde{\rho}_j$ is the proportion of check nodes of degree j.

The transition from one parameterization to another is done by:

$$\begin{aligned} \tilde{\lambda}_i &= \frac{\lambda_i/i}{\sum_k \lambda_k/k}, \quad \tilde{\rho}_j = \frac{\rho_j/j}{\sum_k \rho_k/k}, \\ \lambda_i &= \frac{i\tilde{\lambda}_i}{\sum_k k\tilde{\lambda}_k}, \quad \rho_j = \frac{j\tilde{\rho}_j}{\sum_k k\tilde{\rho}_k}. \end{aligned} \tag{12.86}$$

Thus, a family of irregular codes is parameterized by $(N, \lambda(x), \rho(x))$. The regular case is a particular case of this parameterization where $\lambda(x)$ and $\rho(x)$ are monomials. Figure 12.26 is a graphical representation for this kind of code. $(\lambda(x), \rho(x))$ defines the irregularity profile of the code according to columns and rows.

12.8.2 Systematic Encoding of LDPC Codes

For practical reasons, encoding should be systematic: information bits are directly copied into the codeword, as introduced in Sect. 3.3. There we used a strict definition of the systematic form of the generator and parity-check matrices with an identity matrix. In Theorem 3.5, we showed the resulting easy transition between the two matrices. Determining the generator matrix $\mathbf{G}$ for encoding as shown there is still possibly. However, using elementary row operations to come up with an identity matrix inside the check matrix $\mathbf{H}$ will possibly lead to a non-sparse rest of the matrix. However, note, one will not use that H-matrix for the decoding of the LDPC code. It is just an intermediate step to come to a valid G-matrix. Elementary row operations on the H-matrix will not change the code, just lead to a quick path to a generator matrix.

We now describe a systematic representation of the parity-check matrix containing a triangular part. This is often used with LDPC codes, since then, the H-matrix allows for encoding and decoding, and no G-matrix is additionally needed. The sparsity of the matrix is more or less preserved and performance is usually not degraded visibly.

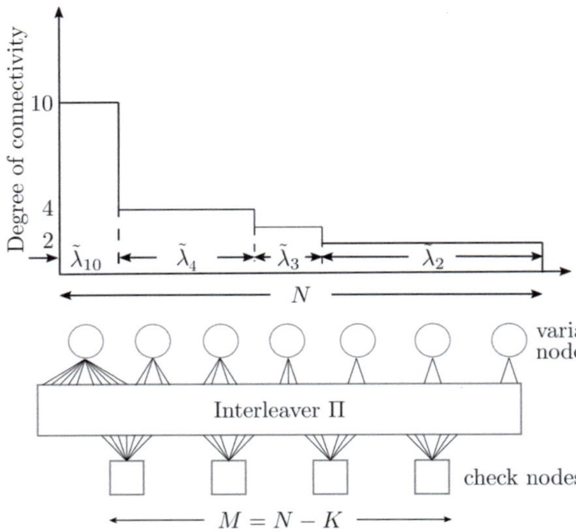

Fig. 12.26 Representation of a family of irregular codes

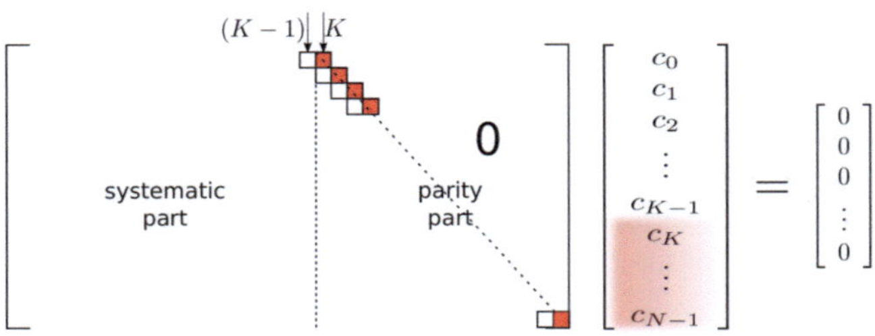

Fig. 12.27 Systematic encoding with a triangular H matrix

As shown in Fig. 12.27, the information bits are then associated with the non-triangular portion, and redundancy bits are computed recursively from parity equations starting from the first row, which addresses the first parity component at position K. The redundancy is associated with the triangular part.

12.8.3 Decoding LDPC Codes by Belief Propagation

Although a maximum likelihood decoding of LDPC codes is possible, the complexity increases too much as soon as we consider sufficiently long codes, which is important to obtain decent performances. A sub-optimum decoding algorithm, known as Sum-Product algorithm or Belief Propagation (BP) algorithm is used instead. It spreads along edges messages forwarding probabilities or logarithmic likelihood ratios (LLR). To each branch two messages are associated, one for each direction. The principle of BP is Bayes rule applied locally (on every bit of the codeword) and iteratively to estimate a posteriori probabilities (APP) of every bit. It has been shown that over a cycle-free graph (tree case), local factorization of Bayes rules leads to exact computation of APP of bit nodes. In this case, messages over the whole graph are independent from each other. However, in a non cycle free graph (which is the case for any finite length LDPC code), messages are not independent, and then APP are not computed exactly, that says that the algorithm is not optimal anymore. The sparser the graph, that says H, will be, the less numerous cycles will be, and the less important the dependency between messages will be.

Definition 12.7 The messages over edges are one dimensional and called *LLR*, for logarithm likelihood ratio. *LLR* of a message coming from a variable node will be denoted by v, and u will denote a message coming from a variable node. They are respectively defined by

$$v = \log \frac{p(y|c=0)}{p(y|c=1)} \tag{12.87}$$

$$u = \log \frac{p(y^{'}|c^{'}=0)}{p(y^{'}|c^{'}=1)} \tag{12.88}$$

where c is the bit value of the node and y denotes all the information available to the node up to the present iteration obtained from edges other than the one carrying v. $c^{'}$ is the bit value of the variable node that gets the message from the check node up to the present iteration obtained from edges other than the one carrying u.

Let us now present the BP algorithm, where messages over edges are one dimensional (LLR), with $v = \log \frac{p(y|c=0)}{p(y|c=1)}$, the outgoing message from a bit node and $u = \log \frac{p(y^{'}|c^{'}=0)}{p(y^{'}|c^{'}=1)}$ the out-coming message from a check node. Each decoding iteration is consists of two stages:

- Update of a bit node of degree i (notations on Fig. 12.28a)

$$v_m^{(l)} = u_0 + \sum_{k=1,k\neq m}^{i} u_k^{(l-1)}, \quad \forall m = 1...i \tag{12.89}$$

  v_m is the message (LLR) along the mth edge coming out of a bit node. The messages u_k are the LLR coming out of a check node and u_0 is the LLR of the channel observation. At the first iteration, every messages u_k are equal to zero.
- Update of a check node of degree j (notations on Fig. 12.28b)

$$\tanh \frac{u_k^{(l)}}{2} = \prod_{m=1,m\neq k}^{j} \tanh \frac{v_m^{(l)}}{2}, \quad \forall k = 1...j \tag{12.90}$$

  u_k is the message (LLR) along the kth edge coming out of a check node. The messages v_m are the LLR coming out of a bit node.

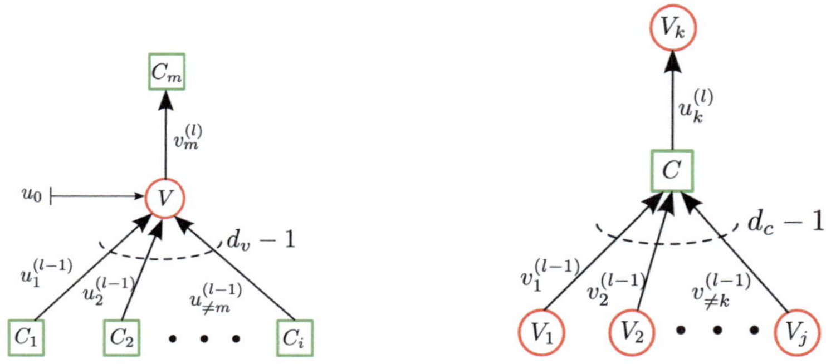

(a) Update of variable nodes. (b) Update of check nodes.

Fig. 12.28 Node operations of the message-passing algorithm

One iteration of the BP algorithm is accomplished when all messages of the graph have been computed once by the previous equations. After L iterations, we can compute the a-posteriori ratio for each bit node given by

$$v_{app,n} = u_0 + \sum_{k=1}^{i} u_k^{(L)}, \forall n = 1, ..., N, \tag{12.91}$$

and the final decision on binary values of data nodes is taken by

$$\hat{m}_n = \frac{1 - \text{sign}(v_{app,n})}{2}, \forall n = 1, ..., N. \tag{12.92}$$

For studying the asymptotic performance, i.e., the error-floor region, so-called stopping sets and trapping sets need to be introduced. Hereto, we follow [44–46], respectively.

Definition 12.8 [44, 45] A **stopping set** $\mathcal{S}$ is a subset of $\mathcal{V}$, the set of variable nodes, such that all neighbors of $\mathcal{S}$, i.e., all check nodes which are connected to $\mathcal{S}$, are connected, at least, twice. The support set of any codeword is a stopping set and, in particular, so is the empty set.

Figure 12.29 shows such a stopping set.

Lemma 12.1 [44, 45] *(Basic Properties of Stopping Sets)*

1. *Let $\mathcal{S}_1$ and $\mathcal{S}_2$ be two stopping sets. Then $\mathcal{S}_1 \cup \mathcal{S}_2$ is a stopping set.*
2. *Each subset of $\mathcal{V}$ contains a maximum stopping set (which might be the empty set).*

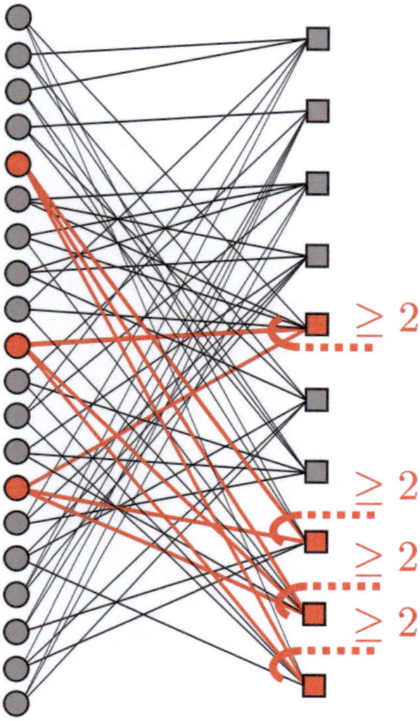

Fig. 12.29 Stopping set [44]

3. *Let C be a binary linear code. Assume that we use C to transmit over the BEC (Binary Erasure Channel) and that we employ a Belief-Propagation (BP) decoder until either the codeword has been recovered or until the decoder fails to progress further. Let $\mathcal{E}$ denote the subset of $\mathcal{V}$ that is erased by the channel. Then the set of erasures that remains when the decoder stops is equal to the maximum stopping set contained in $\mathcal{E}$.*

Proof To see the first claim, note that if c is a neighbor of $\mathcal{S}_1 \cup \mathcal{S}_2$ then it must be a neighbor of at least one of $\mathcal{S}_1$ or $\mathcal{S}_2$. Without loss of generality assume that c is neighbor of $\mathcal{S}_1$. Since $\mathcal{S}_1$ is a stopping set, c has at least two connections to $\mathcal{S}_1$ and therefore, at least two connections to $\mathcal{S}_1 \cup \mathcal{S}_2$. Each subset of $\mathcal{V}$ thus contains a maximum—the union of all stopping sets contained in $\mathcal{V}$ (which might be the empty set). It remains verify the third claim. Let $\mathcal{S}$ be a stopping set contained in $\mathcal{E}$. We claim that the BP decoder cannot determine the variable nodes contained in $\mathcal{S}$. This is true since, even if all other bits were known, every neighbor of $\mathcal{S}$ has at least two connections to the set $\mathcal{S}$ and so all messages to $\mathcal{S}$ are erasure messages. It follows that the decoder cannot determine the variables contained in the maximum stopping set contained in $\mathcal{E}$. Conversely, if the decoder terminates at a set $\mathcal{S}$, then all messages entering this subset must be erasure messages, which happens only if all neighbors of $\mathcal{S}$ have at least two connections to $\mathcal{S}$. In other words, $\mathcal{S}$ must be a stopping set and, since no erasure contained a stopping set can be determined by the BP decoder, it must be the maximum such stopping set. □

Stopping sets denote pattern at which a BP decoder gets stuck in contrast to a MAP decoder, which only fails if the set of erasures include the support set of a codeword. Hence, the set of pattern that a BP decoder fails is bigger than the one of MAP decoder. The error floor of a BP decoder is not defined by the minimum distance of the code, but by the stopping set (in case of a binary erasure channel). Erroneous decoding results due to stopping sets are typically called *pseudo-codewords*.

The stopping sets are well-defined for the binary erasure channel. For more general channels (binary symmetric or Gaussian) and the error floor behavior of message-passing decoders, so-called *trapping sets* have been defined. According to [47], "near codewords" determine failures in the error-floor region, which are named trapping sets. These sets are comprised of a small number of variable nodes and the induced sub-graph has also only a small number of odd degree check nodes. To be more precise, an (a, b) trapping set has a variable nodes and b odd degree check nodes neighbors in the sub-graph induced by the trapping set. For more details, the reader is referred to [46, 47]. Pseudo-codewords are further analyzed in [48] and so-called *Absorbing Sets* are studied in [49].

12.8.4 Factor Graph

A very related graphical representation of a Tanner graph (see Fig. 12.23) was proposed by Forney [50] following a paper by Frey et al. [41]. The factor graph description was further applied to all kinds of coding, signal-processing, and estimation algorithms by Löliger [42, 43], thereby obtaining a common graphical description and putting them into a message passing or sum-product framework. We may remind of the variable- and check-node update equations in (12.89) and (12.90), which discloses the sum-product structure and excluding the current edge in the summation (and product) shows the relation to how one computes marginals of multi-dimensional probabilities summing or integrating out all other variables. For general graphs, Löliger shows that the sum-product formulation boils down to the distributive law. Here, we will limit ourselves to just redraw the Tanner graph of the Hamming code of Fig. 12.23 with factor-graph symbols in Fig. 12.30. However, one may also redraw Markov models, convolutional codes with Viterbi or BCJR and many more. We do not go into further details since the slightly different graphical representation does not change algorithms as such, but offers a common framework.

12.8.5 EXIT Chart for LDPC Codes

We now present the asymptotic study of LDPC codes over the AWGN channel, which we are going to use from now on. Since the previous introduced density evolution method is too complex to be easily applied, a simpler version has been introduced by Chung [51] for the particular case of the transmission over Gaussian channel. Densi-

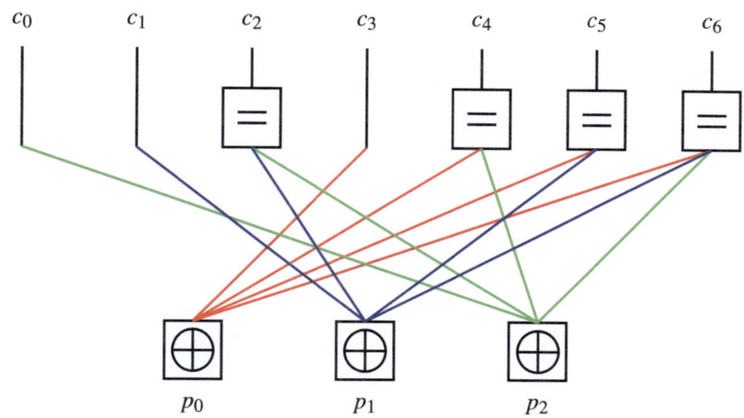

Fig. 12.30 Forney factor graph of the Hamming code, cf. Fig. 12.23

ties of messages are modeled by Gaussian density or mixture of Gaussian densities for a regular and irregular codes, respectively. The messages are log-likelihood ratios and follow the consistency property of Definition 12.4.

Thanks to the consistency of messages along stages of BP decoding, the Gaussian approximation allows to boil down the asymptotic decoding study to study of only one parameter along the iterations, representing the Gaussian $N(m, 2m)$ distribution. In contrast to the EXIT charts of Turbo codes, the huge advantage of LDPC codes is that their parameters and parameters of the channel allow to find an analytical relation between the value of the study parameter (which can be m for example) between iteration l and $l + 1$. In [51], densities of messages u coming from check nodes and v from bit nodes are modeled by consistent Gaussian densities. This seems realistic for messages v, but debatable for messages u (Figs. 4 and 5 in [51]). We assume transmission using BPSK modulation over an AWGN channel whose noise variance is σ^2. The zero codeword is transmitted (since for a channel and the BP decoder fulfilling symmetry condition, error probabilities at the lth iteration do not depend on the transmitted codeword). Therefore, u_0 is Gaussian $N(2/\sigma^2, 4/\sigma^2)$ which is consistent according to Definition 12.4. Theorem 3 of [52] (p. 628) asserts that consistency is kept along iterations for a given binary-input memoryless output-symmetric channel. Then, in order to be able to model message densities to be Gaussian, they must fulfill the consistency condition: $N(m, \sigma^2)$ is consistent if and only if $\sigma^2 = 2m$. That is the reason why the density evolution can be expressed as a one parameter evolution. Chung et al. [51] chose the mean of messages, but we can choose, still under the Gaussian approximation of the message densities, to follow the Mutual Informations of a virtual AWGN channel, whose output would be messages v or u coming out from bit nodes or check node, respectively.

Mutual Information for a Gaussian Consistent Channel

We are redoing the derivation from Eqs. (12.64) to (12.71) with slightly different annotations. Let v be a message such that $v \sim N(\pm m, 2m)$ that is the output of a binary-input Gaussian channel. The Mutual Information (now named x_v) between v and input c of the virtual channel is given by[6]

$$x_v = I(v,c) = H(v) - H(v|c) \tag{12.93}$$

$$\begin{aligned} x_v = &-\int_{\mathbf{R}} (\sum_{c=\pm1} P_c(c) p_{v|c}(v|c)) \log_2 (\sum_{c=\pm1} P_c(c) p_{v|c}(v|c)) dv + \\ &+ \int_{\mathbf{R}} \left(\sum_{c=\pm1} P_c(c) p_{v|c}(v|c) \log_2 (p_{v|c}(v|c)) \right) dv \end{aligned} \tag{12.94}$$

$$\begin{aligned} x_v = &-\frac{1}{2} \sum_{c=\pm1} \int_{\mathbf{R}} p_{v|c}(v|c) \log_2 \left(\frac{1}{2} (p_{v|c}(v|c=1) + p_{v|c}(v|c=-1)) \right) dv + \\ &+ \frac{1}{2} \sum_{c=\pm1} \int_{\mathbf{R}} p_{v|c}(v|c) \log_2 (p_{v|c}(v|c))\, dv \end{aligned} \tag{12.95}$$

$$x_v = \frac{1}{2} \sum_{c=\pm1} \int_{\mathbf{R}} p_{v|c}(v|c) \log_2 \left(\frac{2 p_{v|c}(v|c)}{p_{v|c}(v|c=+1) + p_{v|c}(v|c=-1)} \right) dv. \tag{12.96}$$

We now abbreviate $p_{v|c}(v|c)$ by $p(v|c)$. Since the channel is symmetric, we have $p(v|c=-1) = p(-v|c=+1)$, and by consistency $p(-v|c=1) = p(v|c=1) \cdot e^{-v}$, this implies

$$x_v = \int_{\mathbf{R}} p(v|c=+1) \log_2 \left(\frac{2p(v|c=+1)}{p(v|c=+1) + p(v|c=-1)} \right) dv \tag{12.97}$$

$$= \int_{\mathbf{R}} p(v|c=+1) \log_2 \left(\frac{2p(v|c=+1)}{p(v|c=+1)(1+e^{-v})} \right) dv \tag{12.98}$$

$$= 1 - \int_{\mathbf{R}} p(v|c=+1) \log_2 (1+e^{-v}) dv \tag{12.99}$$

$$= 1 - \frac{1}{\sqrt{4\pi m}} \int_{\mathbf{R}} \log_2(1+e^{-v}) \exp\left(-\frac{(v-m)^2}{4m} \right) dv = J(m) \tag{12.100}$$

J is called the Mutual Information function, linking Mutual Information of a Gaussian consistent channel to the mean of messages whose density is $N(m, 2m)$. Equation (12.100) is rewritten as

$$J(m) = 1 - E_x(\log_2(1+e^{-x})), \quad x \sim N(m, 2m). \tag{12.101}$$

[6] Capital P stands for a probability mass function, whereas lower-case p denotes a probability density function.

J is continuous and a strictly monotonous function, so J^{-1} exists and permits to compute the mean of messages from the Mutual Information.

Evolution Equations

Let $x_{cv}^{(l)}$ and $x_{vc}^{(l)}$ be the Mutual Information associated with messages coming from check nodes to variable nodes and from variable nodes to check nodes, respectively. From [53], we have the following update relation:

- Update at variable nodes

$$x_{vc}^{(l)} = \sum_{i=2}^{t_{cmax}} \lambda_i J(\frac{2}{\sigma^2} + (i-1)J^{-1}(x_{cv}^{(l-1)})) \tag{12.102}$$

- Update at check nodes

$$x_{cv}^{(l)} = 1 - \sum_{j=2}^{t_{rmax}} \rho_j J((j-1)J^{-1}(1 - x_{vc}^{(l)})) \tag{12.103}$$

Proof Let α denote a bit node, and $\overline{m}$ the mean of message m. From Eq. (12.89) we have

$$\overline{m}_{0,\alpha}^{(l)} = \overline{u}_\alpha + \overline{m}_1^{(l-1)} + \cdots + \overline{m}_{i-1}^{(l-1)}. \tag{12.104}$$

Assuming that $\overline{m}$ is $\overline{m_{cv}}$ the average over the whole graph of messages coming from check nodes, and by symmetry of the channel,

$$\overline{m}_{0,\alpha}^{(l)} = \frac{2}{\sigma^2} + (\text{degree of } \alpha - 1) \cdot \overline{m}_{cv}^{(l-1)}. \tag{12.105}$$

Using the J function, we have $\overline{m_{cv}} = J^{-1}(x_{cv})$. In the same way as for general density evolution, averaging over the whole graph of messages coming from variable nodes leads to Eq. (12.102).

Proof of Eq. (12.103):
Now let β denote a check node. We can rewrite

$$-\ln\left(\tanh(\frac{m_{0,\alpha}}{2})\right) = -\ln\left(\frac{e^{m_{0,\alpha}} - 1}{e^{m_{0,\alpha}} + 1}\right). \tag{12.106}$$

Now, by Bayes rule and assuming $P(x = -1) = P(x = +1)$, we obtain

$$m_{0,\alpha} = \ln\left(\frac{P(x=+1|y)}{P(x=-1|y)}\right) = \ln\left(\frac{P(y|x=+1)}{P(y|x=-1)}\right), \tag{12.107}$$

where x is the random variable describing the codeword bit value associated with the variable node α, and y is the random variable describing all the information incorporated into this message. Let $v[0] = P(y|x = +1)$ and $v[1] = P(y|x = -1)$. A message going out of a check node will be called u.

$$-\ln\left(\tanh(\frac{m_{0,\alpha}}{2})\right) = -\ln\left(\frac{v[0]/v[1]-1}{v[0]/v[1]+1}\right) \tag{12.108}$$

$$-\ln\left(\tanh(\frac{m_{0,\alpha}}{2})\right) = -\ln\left(\frac{v[0]-v[1]}{v[0]+v[1]}\right) \tag{12.109}$$

Using the Discrete Fourier Transform, we have

$$\begin{bmatrix} DFTv[0] \\ DFTv[1] \end{bmatrix} = \begin{bmatrix} 1 & 1 \\ 1 & -1 \end{bmatrix} \cdot \begin{bmatrix} v[0] \\ v[1] \end{bmatrix} = \begin{bmatrix} v[0]+v[1] \\ v[0]-v[1] \end{bmatrix} \tag{12.110}$$

Finally, we have

$$-\ln\left(\tanh(\frac{m_{0,\alpha}}{2})\right) = DFTv, \tag{12.111}$$

defining $DFTv = \ln\left[\frac{DFTv[0]}{DFTv[1]}\right]$. This means that a check node sums up the messages, but in the DFT domain. Moreover, according to Eq. (12.101) and also defining $v = \ln\left[\frac{v[0]}{v[1]}\right]$, we express the Mutual Information of $DFTv$ by

$$\begin{aligned} x_{DFTv} &= 1 - E\left\{\log_2(1+e^{-DFTv})\right\} \\ &= 1 - E\left\{\log_2(1+\frac{e^v-1}{e^v+1})\right\} = 1 - E\left\{\log_2(\frac{2e^v}{e^v+1})\right\} \\ &= 1 - E\left\{1-\log_2(1+e^{-v})\right\} = E\left\{\log_2(1+e^{-v})\right\}, \end{aligned} \tag{12.112}$$

which from (12.101) is found to be

$$x_{DFTv} = 1 - x_v. \tag{12.113}$$

We can then describe the evolution of x_{DFTu} exactly in the same way as x_{vc}, since the update of $DFTu$ is exactly the same as for $m_{0,\alpha}$,

$$DFT\overline{m}_{0,\beta}^{(l)} = DFT\overline{m}_1^{(l)} + \cdots + DFT\overline{m}_{j-1}^{(l)}, \tag{12.114}$$

which means,

$$DFT\overline{m}_{0,\beta}^{(l)} = (j-1)DFT\overline{m}_{vc}^{(l)}. \tag{12.115}$$

With $DFT\overline{m}_{vc}^{(l)} = J^{-1}(DFTx_{vc}) = J^{-1}(1-x_{vc})$, we obtain

$$x_{DFTu} = J\left((j-1)J^{-1}(1-x_{vc})\right), \tag{12.116}$$

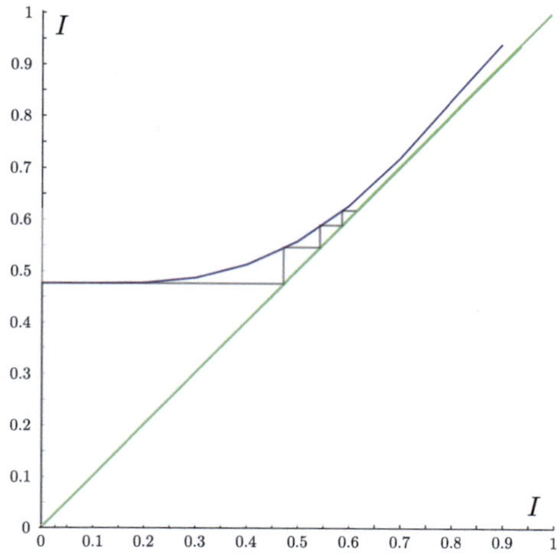

Fig. 12.31 EXIT curve example for an LDPC code

finally, over the whole graph,

$$x_{DFTu} = \sum_j \rho_j J\left((j-1)J^{-1}(1-x_{vc})\right). \tag{12.117}$$

Applying Eq. (12.113), we prove Eq. (12.103):

$$x_{cv}^{(l)} = 1 - \sum_{j=2}^{t_{rmax}} \rho_j J((j-1)J^{-1}(1-x_{vc}^{(l)})). \tag{12.118}$$

□

The combination of equations (12.102) and (12.103) yields the EXIT chart of the code defined by $(\lambda(x), \rho(x))$ shown in Fig. 12.31. It is an explicit nonlinear function of $(\lambda(x), \rho(x))$ and of parameters of the channel (σ^2 in our case):

$$x_{vc}^{(l)} = F(\underline{\lambda}, \underline{\rho}, x_{vc}^{(l-1)}, \sigma^2), \tag{12.119}$$

where $\underline{\lambda} = [\lambda_2, \ldots, \lambda_{t_{cmax}}]^T$ and $\underline{\rho} = [\rho_2, \ldots, \rho_{t_{rmax}}]^T$. In the figure, the 45° straight line mirrors the results back expressing that the same code is used again. Alternatively, one may draw the two updates separately (as in [36]), resulting in steps between two corresponding EXIT curves. Several optimization methods exist, which can consider $\rho(x)$ as fixed in order to make F linear in $\underline{\lambda}$. The convergence threshold is defined by the smallest E_b/N_0 beyond which $x_{vc}^{(l)} \to 1$ when $l \to \infty$.

The iterative steps in EXIT charts provide the most essential ingredients of Density Evolution, which we will describe in the following section.

12.8.6 Density Evolution

The first step in the design of irregular LDPC codes is to determine the degree distributions $\lambda(x)$ and $\rho(x)$ for the variable and check node sides, respectively. This is a design relating to the ensemble of possible code relations, assuming no cycles and infinite length. After having determined the degree distributions, the next step will be to establish an H-matrix following the degree distributions as closely as possible and avoiding short cycles (and stopping or trapping sets). This section is devoted to the first step, whereas the actual H-matrix design is described in the following Sect. 12.8.7.

12.8.6.1 Full Density Evolution

Typically, the densities of Log-Likelihood ratios (LLRs) are assumed to be consistent Gaussians during the decoding process. This is an approximation and not necessarily true for the incoming intrinsic information from the channel. To be exact, one would have to follow the iteration steps (12.89) and (12.90) and process the densities exactly, which is the actual meaning of "Density Evolution". Mostly, the term is however used for the simplification assuming Gaussian LLRs with the relation between mean and variance as given in (12.59) and (12.101). We will also describe this simplification in the optimization of the degree distributions, since it allows for convex optimization routines, i.e., linear programming (Simplex alg.), which is much less complex than full density evolution, which we will sketch shortly, first.

At the variable nodes, when considering LLR densities of the intrinsic information from the channel and the ones coming from the connected check nodes (except for the outgoing edge), Eq. (12.89) is just a sum of random variables. This means the convolution of the corresponding densities, or likewise, the product of its characteristic functions.

The check-node operations are much more involved. Equation (12.90) can first be simplified in log domain, where typically, a minus sign is added, resulting in

$$-\ln\tanh\frac{u_k^{(l)}}{2} = \sum_{m=1,m\neq k}^{j} -\ln\tanh\frac{v_m^{(l)}}{2}, \quad \forall k=1,\ldots,j \tag{12.120}$$

$$\Longleftrightarrow \frac{u_k^{(l)}}{2} = -\tanh^{-1}\left[\exp\left[\sum_{m=1,m\neq k}^{j} -\ln\tanh\frac{v_m^{(l)}}{2}\right]\right], \quad \forall k=1,\ldots,j$$

$$\Longleftrightarrow \frac{u_k^{(l)}}{2} = [\ln\tanh]^{-1}\left[-\sum_{m=1,m\neq k}^{j} -\ln\tanh\frac{v_m^{(l)}}{2}\right], \quad \forall k=1,\ldots,j \tag{12.121}$$

Having a summation would also here now mean a convolution of densities or the product of the corresponding characteristic functions. The $-\ln\tanh(x)$ and $[\ln\tanh]^{-1}(x)$

functions change densities by dividing through their derivatives. This leads to numerical issues, where necessarily ranges have to be limited. One will have to represent large values by border spikes in the distributions. One may intermediately also work with probability mass functions instead of densities and hence, instead of dividing through derivatives, change range boundaries according to the given function.

tanh preserves the sign and the following logarithm will lead to complex values. Densities will be two-dimensional, where the imaginary values are 0 and π. This means, one has 2D densities on lines through these two imaginary values. Hence, convolutions would be two-dimensional and one could define characteristic functions using a 2D DFT of $2 \times N$ size. The later exponentiation will then recover the sign, making the density one-dimensional again.

In Gallager's thesis [37] (p. 43) and, e.g., in Ryan/Lin [54] (p. 221) LLRs are split into the sign (hard decision) and the amplitude (reliability), thereby avoiding the 2D convolution or 2D DFT. Equation (12.90) is then rephrased rewriting the LLR $v_m(l)$ omitting the iteration counter (l) as

$$\begin{aligned} v_m &= \alpha_m \beta_m, \\ \alpha_m &= \operatorname{sign}(v_m), \\ \beta_m &= |v_m|. \end{aligned} \tag{12.122}$$

This leads to

$$\tanh \frac{u_k^{(l)}}{2} = \prod_{m=1,m\neq k}^{j} \alpha_m^{(l)} \cdot \prod_{m=1,m\neq k}^{j} \tanh \frac{\beta_m^{(l)}}{2}, \quad \forall k = 1 \ldots j \tag{12.123}$$

and

$$\begin{aligned} u_k^{(l)} &= \prod_{m=1,m\neq k}^{j} \alpha_m^{(l)} \cdot 2 \cdot \tanh^{-1} \prod_{m=1,m\neq k}^{j} \tanh \frac{\beta_m^{(l)}}{2} \\ &= \prod_{m=1,m\neq k}^{j} \alpha_m^{(l)} \cdot 2 \cdot \tanh^{-1} \left[\exp \left[\ln \left[\prod_{m=1,m\neq k}^{j} \tanh \frac{\beta_m^{(l)}}{2} \right] \right] \right] \\ &= \prod_{m=1,m\neq k}^{j} \alpha_m^{(l)} \cdot 2 \cdot [\ln \tanh]^{-1} \left[- \sum_{m=1,m\neq k}^{j} - \ln \tanh \frac{\beta_m^{(l)}}{2} \right]. \end{aligned} \tag{12.124}$$

Formulating $y = \phi(x) := -\ln \tanh(x/2)$ yields

$$u_k^{(l)} = \left[\prod_{m=1,m\neq k}^{j} \alpha_m^{(l)} \right] \cdot \phi^{-1} \left[\sum_{m=1,m\neq k}^{j} \phi(\beta_m^{(l)}) \right]. \tag{12.125}$$

$\phi(x)$ is a positive function for positive argument and interestingly,

$$\phi^{-1}(x) = \phi(x). \tag{12.126}$$

For the density after a transform with $\phi(x)$, we need the absolute value of the slope

$$\left|\frac{d\phi(x)}{dx}\right| = \left|\frac{d\phi^{-1}(x)}{dx}\right| = \frac{1}{|\sinh(x)|}, \tag{12.127}$$

hence,

$$\left|\frac{d\phi(x)}{dx}\right|_{x=\phi^{-1}(y)} = \frac{1}{|\sinh(\phi(y))|} = \frac{1}{|\sinh(-\ln(\tanh(y/2))|} = |\sinh(y)| \tag{12.128}$$

and finally, the density $p(y) = p(\phi(x))$ after the transformation with ϕ is obtained as

$$p_Y(y) = \frac{1}{|\sinh(y)|} \cdot p_X(\phi^{-1}(y)) = \frac{1}{|\sinh(y)|} \cdot p_X(\phi(y)). \tag{12.129}$$

Finally, one can also rephrase the product $\prod_m \alpha_m^{(l)}$ in (12.123) over $\{\pm 1\}$ as a modulo-2 sum (XOR) over $\{0, 1\}$.

This was to sketch the operations required to compute the full density evolution. We are now simplifying this expressing the evolution of the mean or variance of Gaussian density as an idealization, which is often meant when talking about density evolution.

12.8.6.2 Density Evolution under Consistency Assumption

We are now describing the essential components of a linear program that is able to deliver one of the degree distributions given the other one, where we start from the check degree polynomial and optimize the rate given the SNR. Good check-node degree distributions are known to only exist of a few (two or three) neighboring degrees [52]. One can, of course, determine both distributions, obeying that "concentration" of the check degrees. For convergence, Eqs. (12.102) and (12.103) should show an increase in Mutual Information. Those two relations will then also be central to the convex optimization to be formulated. First, however, we may define constraints that have to be met in the linear program. One of them is the so-called "**stability condition**".

The erasure channel treatment is a convenient starting point. Hereto, we follow [44], Sect. 3.9 and [52], III.E. Let us first consider a check node of degree i and an erasure probability of x_{l-1} at the $(l-1)$th iteration. An outgoing message from this check node will be no erasure, if all other $(j-1)$ connections are available, i.e., no erasures. This means the probability for an erasure at the outgoing edge is

$$1 - (1 - x_l)^{j-1}. \tag{12.130}$$

Taking into account the degree distribution represented by $\rho(x)$, this will yield

$$\sum_j \rho_j (1 - (1 - x_{l-1})^{j-1}) = 1 - \rho(1 - x_{l-1}). \tag{12.131}$$

Moving on to the variable-node side, there, an erasure will result at an outgoing edge, if all incoming ones are erased, which one can express as

$$\varepsilon \cdot (1 - \rho(1 - x_{l-1}))^{i-1}, \tag{12.132}$$

where $\varepsilon = x_0$ stands for the erasure probability from the channel input link. Considering the variable node degree distribution $\lambda(x)$, we obtain

$$x_l = \varepsilon \cdot \lambda\left(1 - \rho(1 - x_{l-1})\right) = x_0 \cdot \lambda\left(1 - \rho(1 - x_{l-1})\right). \tag{12.133}$$

For investigating the convergence behavior, x_l should converge to zero and we would like to know the supremum for $\varepsilon = x_0$ that would still ensure convergence. From Taylor expansion around zero, i.e., for small erasure probability in the course of the iterations, we could write

$$x_l = x_0 \cdot \lambda'(0)\rho'(1)x_{l-1} + O(x_{l-1}^2). \tag{12.134}$$

Here, $\rho'(1)$ results from the inner derivative at zero and the outer one yields $\lambda'(0)$, since $\rho(1) = 1$. For convergence, we require

$$\varepsilon = x_0 < \frac{1}{\lambda'(0)\rho'(1)}, \tag{12.135}$$

which provides a bound for the convergence threshold.

For the more general binary input symmetric output channel (especially, BSC — binary symmetric channel and BIAWGN — binary input additive white Gaussian noise channel), Richardson and Urbanke [44] reformulate such a channel as a degraded BEC (binary erasure channel). This is a typical approach for the "degraded broadcast channel". It is drawn as a cascade of the BEC and another channel using the ternary output of the BEC as an input. We sketch the reasoning of the approach. For the BEC, assuming an erasure probability of 2ε, the resulting error probability will be $P_e = \varepsilon$, since with a chance of 1/2, we obtain the right value in case of an erasure. The considered degraded BEC is shown in Fig. 12.32, where $a(y)$ stands for the density of the LLR y.

From Fig. 12.32, we note that only the erasures of the left BEC channel will later lead to errors. Hence, the first term of Eq. (12.134) describes the probability of considered the LLR density from the input, which is named p_0 in [52]. Hence, with an erasure probability of 2ε (instead of ε in Eq. (12.134)), we obtain a term

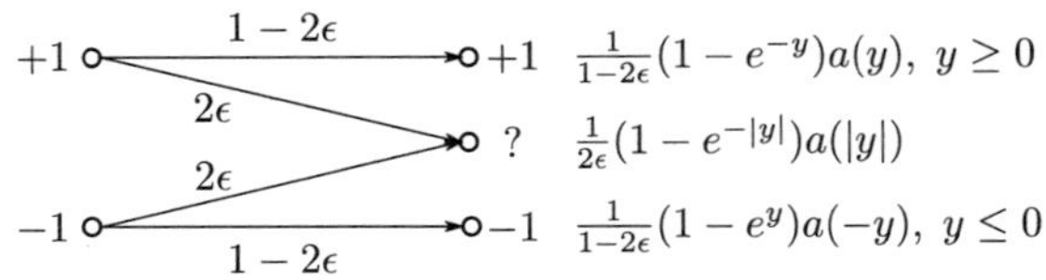

Fig. 12.32 Degraded BEC to describe a general binary-input symmetric output channel

$2\varepsilon\lambda'(0)\rho'(1)p_0$ for an iteration, leading to $2\varepsilon(\lambda'(0)\rho'(1))^n p_0^{\otimes n}$, where "$\otimes n$" stands for n-fold convolution. Note that every time at a variable node, the intrinsic information is added, which means a convolution of the corresponding LLR densities p_0. For the error probability, we obtain

$$\text{BER} = 2\varepsilon(\lambda'(0)\rho'(1))^n P_e(p_0^{\otimes n}) + O(\varepsilon^2). \tag{12.136}$$

For $n \to \infty$, Richardson et al. [52] define

$$r := \lim_{n\to\infty} \frac{1}{n} \ln P_e(p_0^{\otimes n}), \tag{12.137}$$

which allows to rewrite (12.136) as

$$\text{BER} = 2\varepsilon(\lambda'(0)\rho'(1))^n e^{-nr} \text{ for } n \to \infty. \tag{12.138}$$

Rephrasing this for one iteration only, this could be formulated as

$$r^1 := \ln P_e(p_0) \text{ and } \text{BER}^1 = 2\varepsilon(\lambda'(0)\rho'(1))e^{-r}. \tag{12.139}$$

Then the so-called Bhattacharyya constant is used to relate to the error probability (according to Lemma 4.63 in [52]) and then r is rephrased as

$$r^1 := -\ln \int p_0(x)e^{-x/2}dx. \tag{12.140}$$

Without going through proper necessity and sufficiency proofs as provided in [44, 52], for convergence, we require

$$\int p_0(x)e^{-x/2}dx < \frac{1}{\lambda'(0)\rho'(1)}. \tag{12.141}$$

The actual optimization for the code ensemble, i.e., not yet the finite length H-matrix design for an actual code realization, is typically performed via a linear program (Simplex alg.). The essential steps are sketched in the following.

One may optimize $\sum_{i=2}^{d_{vmax}} \frac{\lambda_i}{i}$ instead of the rate as given in Eq. (12.83), when assuming the check-node degree distribution $\rho(x)$ to be given.

One constraint is $\boxed{\sum_{i=2}^{d_{vmax}} \lambda_i = 1}$.

Further constraints are, e.g., $\boxed{\text{proportion constraints}}$ in case of multi-edge-type LDPC codes [55].

The main one is the convergence constraint of Eq. (12.119),

$$\boxed{F\left(\boldsymbol{\lambda}, \boldsymbol{\rho}, \sigma^2, x_{vc}^{(l-1)}\right) > x_{vc}^{(l-1)}}$$

and finally, one may add the described $\boxed{\text{stability condition}}$.

12.8.7 Construction Algorithms for the Check Matrix

In this section[7], we will describe the basic concepts of several well-known construction algorithms, such as random construction, the progressive edge-growth (PEG) algorithm, zigzag construction, the approximate cycle extrinsic message degree (ACE) algorithm, and an ACE-constrained PEG algorithm. We do not discuss algorithms based on combinatorics, namely designs and Steiner systems, projective or Euclidean geometry. Such constructions are treated in, e.g., [54].

Random Construction

The random construction algorithm places the edges randomly in the graph, according to the given variable node and check node degree distributions. Length-4 cycles between degree-2 variable nodes shall be avoided. The resulting Tanner graph will have a girth of only 4.

Progressive Edge-Growth (PEG) Construction

The PEG algorithm is an efficient algorithm for the construction of parity-check matrices with large girth by progressively connecting variable nodes and check nodes [54, 58–60]. The original PEG algorithm starts from the set of variable nodes and check nodes and provides empty sockets to the variable nodes according to the degree distribution (or approximating the degree distribution). One may, however, also add sockets to the check nodes to match or approximate the distribution there, as well. In the following, we describe the original PEG first, i.e., without checking fulfillment of the check-node degree distribution. Nevertheless, the resulting check-node degree distribution is known to be close to uniform, i.e., a concentrated form is obtained that was found to lead to good results in [52].

Starting from the variable nodes with the smallest number of sockets, edges are chosen according to an edge selection procedure. The selection procedure aims at minimizing the impact of each new edge on the girth. This is done by expanding a local tree from the current variable node down to a certain depth. Expanding does not mean going back from check node to other variable nodes. It is just checking the

[7] Description partly taken from [56].

local tree that is currently obtained from the processed variable node. If possible, the algorithm connects the variable node to a check node that is not yet reached at this depth of the tree. If all check nodes are reached, the check node that will create the largest cycle through the current variable node is selected. If several possible choices exist, a check node with the lowest check node degree under the current graph setting is chosen. Finally, if there is more than one possible lowest-degree check node left, one of them is chosen randomly. With these operations, the check node degree distribution of the resulting Tanner graph is automatically as concentrated as possible.

To support the choices to some extent, one should note that variable nodes are better supported with a higher number of edges to it, whereas the connected check nodes should have a lower degree to improve their performance. PEG starts from a low degree variable node that will not see short cycles, since no further connections were there. The first edge from a variable node is connected to a low-degree check node. This improves performance and levels out the effect of low-degree variable and low-degree check nodes. In the decoding, unequal error protection properties will then also be leveled out quickly.

Before summarizing the algorithm, we define $\mathcal{N}_{v_i}^l$ to be the set of check nodes which have been reached by a tree of depth l, rooted at v_i. Accordingly, $\bar{\mathcal{N}}_{v_i}^l$ is the complementary set and contains all check nodes which have not been reached by the tree.

Algorithms 1 and 2 show the pseudo-code of the two PEG variants.

Algorithm 1: PEG variant for a given variable-node degree distribution

---

Provide the variable nodes with a number of sockets according to its degree distribution.
Sort the variable nodes with decreasing number of sockets.
for $i = N$ **to** 1 **do**
  for $k = 1$ **to** d_{v_i} **do**
    if $k == 1$ **then**
      Connect the first edge randomly to a check node with the lowest degree under the current graph setting;
    else
      (any edge other than the first)
      Expand a tree from variable node v_i up to depth l under the current graph setting such that the cardinality of $\mathcal{N}_{v_i}^l$ stops increasing but is less than $N - K$, or $\bar{\mathcal{N}}_{v_i}^l \neq \emptyset$ but $\bar{\mathcal{N}}_{v_i}^{l+1} = \emptyset$;
      In the first situation, choose a check-node with the smallest degree and connect it to v_i, in the second situation, choose a check node with the largest distance on the tree before closing the cycle with the new edge;
    end
  end
end

Algorithm 2: PEG variant for given variable- and check-node degree distributions

Provide all nodes with a number of sockets according to the degree distributions;
Sort the variable nodes with decreasing number of sockets;
for $i = N$ **to** 1 **do**
  for $k = 1$ **to** d_{v_i} **do**
    if $k == 1$ **then**
      Connect the first edge randomly to a check node with the lowest degree under the current graph setting;
    else
      (any edge other than the first)
      Expand a tree from variable node v_i up to depth l under the current graph setting such that the cardinality of $\mathcal{N}_{v_i}^l$ stops increasing but is less than $N - K$, or $\bar{\mathcal{N}}_{v_i}^l \neq \emptyset$ but $\bar{\mathcal{N}}_{v_i}^{l+1} = \emptyset$;
      Mark those check nodes from the set $\bar{\mathcal{N}}_{v_i}^l$ as candidates which do not violate the intended check node degree distribution $\tilde{\rho}(x)$;
      Randomly pick a check node from the candidate list;
    end
  end
end

Zigzag Construction

The zigzag construction algorithm connects the edges of degree-two variable nodes in a zigzag manner, according to [59]. In principle, the part of the parity-check matrix corresponding to the degree-two variable nodes will be bi-diagonal. This algorithm avoids all cycles involving only variable nodes of degree two, assuming that the number N_2 of degree-two variable nodes is smaller than the number of check nodes, i.e., $N_2 < N - K$. The remaining edges may be connected randomly in the same way as described for the random algorithm (zigzag-random) or according to the PEG algorithm (zigzag-PEG). The zigzag construction is of interest both due to the easy encoding, that is the result of the almost diagonal shape of the part of the parity-check matrix that corresponds to the parity bits, and the avoidance of cycles involving only degree-two variable nodes, which have been shown to degrade the BER performance, see [61].

Approximate Cycle Extrinsic Message Degree (ACE) Construction

For finite block lengths, Tian et al. [61] proposed an efficient graph conditioning algorithm called the approximate cycle extrinsic message degree (ACE) algorithm. The aim of the ACE construction is to lower the error floor by emphasizing both the connectivity as well as the length of cycles. The ACE algorithm avoids small cycle clusters that are isolated from the rest of the graph and is shown to significantly lower the error-floors of irregular LDPC codes, while only slightly degrading the performance in the waterfall region. The algorithm is based on the extrinsic message degree (EMD) of a variable node set.

Definition 12.9 (*Extrinsic Message Degree (EMD)*) An extrinsic check node of a variable node set $\mathcal{V}$ is a check node that is connected to $\mathcal{V}$ by a single edge. The EMD of a variable node set is the number of extrinsic check nodes of $\mathcal{V}$.

In order to statistically increase the smallest stopping set size in the graph, the algorithm ensures that all cycles with less than a given length have an EMD greater than a given value. If there are no variable nodes in a cycle that share common check nodes outside the cycle, the EMD of this cycle is $\sum_i (d_i - 2)$, where d_i is the degree of the ith variable node in the cycle. In order to keep the EMD calculable, check node sharing is neglected for all cycles.

Definition 12.10 (*Approximate Cycle EMD (ACE)*) The approximate cycle EMD (ACE) of a cycle is defined by $\sum_i (d_i - 2)$, where d_i is the degree of the ith variable node in the cycle.

Therewith, an LDPC code with parameters (d_{ACE}, η) can be constructed, where all cycles whose lengths are $2d_{ACE}$ or less have an ACE of at least η. The ACE algorithm is an efficient Viterbi-like algorithm with linear complexity proposed to detect and avoid harmful short cycles during code construction.

Given the variable node degree distribution $\lambda(x)$, columns of the parity-check matrix are generated one at a time starting from low-weight columns. The edges of every new column are generated randomly and the ACE algorithm checks whether the (d_{ACE}, η) requirement is met. If not, this column is generated again. This procedure is repeated until the whole parity check matrix is generated. Also here, similar to the modified PEG Alg. 2, we have added extra constraints to construct a graph according to the given check node degree distribution $\rho(x)$.

The performance of highly irregular LDPC codes is of great interest when considering irregular unequal error protecting (UEP) LDPC codes, since the UEP properties are obtained by assigning variable nodes with high degree to the best protected class. However, with highly irregular codes it is difficult to ensure a high girth. The ACE algorithm is a suitable algorithm for such codes.

The pseudo-code of ACE is shown as Algorithm 3.

Algorithm 3: ACE algorithm

Provide all nodes with a number of sockets according to the degree distributions.
Sort the variable nodes with decreasing number of sockets.
Define (d_{ACE}, η)
for $i = N$ **to** 1 **do**
  do
    Mark those check nodes as candidates which do not violate the intended check node degree distribution $\tilde{\rho}(x)$;
    Randomly connect the d_{v_i} edges to check nodes from the candidate list;
    Check if constraint (d_{ACE}, η) is fulfilled under the current graph setting;
  while *ACE constraint* (d_{ACE}, η) *is not fulfilled*;
end

PEG-ACE Construction

The PEG-ACE algorithm is a generalization of the popular PEG algorithm, which is shown to generate good LDPC codes with short and moderate block lengths having large girth. In the PEG-ACE algorithm [62], the sequential methodology of the PEG algorithm is employed with a modified check node selection procedure. If the creation of cycles cannot be avoided while adding an edge, the PEG-ACE construction algorithm chooses an edge that creates the longest possible cycle with the largest possible ACE value. The algorithm constructs a code with the largest possible ACE constraints, which is assumed to reduce the number of stopping sets significantly. As the PEG algorithm, the PEG-ACE construction algorithm usually picks a check node among its candidates which has the lowest check node degree. In the depicted Algorithm 4, we have again only allowed for those check nodes as candidates which do not violate the intended check node profile.

Algorithm 4: PEG-ACE algorithm

```
Provide all nodes with a number of sockets according to the degree distributions;
Sort the variable nodes with decreasing number of sockets;
for i = N to 1 do
    for k = 1 to d_{v_i} do
        if k == 1 then
            Connect the first edge randomly to a check node with the lowest degree under the
              current graph setting;
        else
            Expand a tree from variable node v_i up to depth l under the current graph setting
              such that the cardinality of N^l_{v_i} stops increasing but is less than N − K, or
              N̄^l_{v_i} ≠ ∅ but N̄^{l+1}_{v_i} = ∅;
            Mark those check nodes from the set N̄^l_{v_i} as candidates which do not violate the
              intended check node degree distribution ρ̃(x);
            If the candidate list contains more than one survivor, choose the one with the
              maximum d_{ACE} value;
        end
    end
end
```

12.8.8 *Protograph Construction and Quasi-Cyclic LDPC Codes*

A compressed description of the structure of an LDPC code and its H-matrix is possible through so-called Protographs. This starts from a small Tanner graph with the desired degree distribution, typically called the base graph. This has a few nodes only, just as in Fig. 12.33. A so-called *lifting* leads to copying the graph a certain number of times to reach the intended overall length of the codeword. A permutation between the subgraphs leads to the final Tanner graph as also shown in Fig. 12.33, where, for illustration, we only copied the graph twice and permuted the edges between the two copies. The lifting (copy and permutation) can also easily be represented by starting

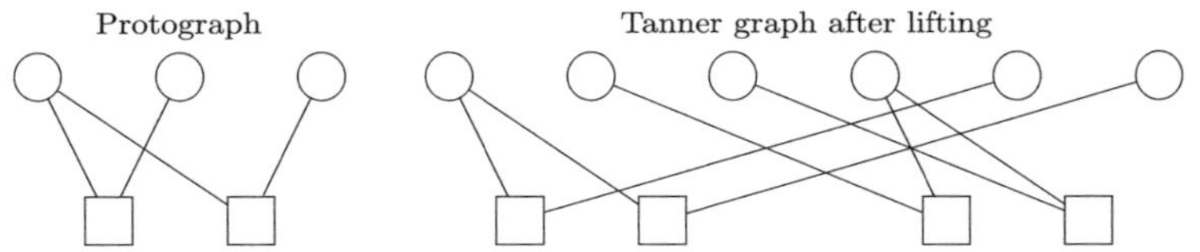

Fig. 12.33 Protograph and Tanner graph after lifting

from the H-matrix of the protograph and replacing every 1-entry by a permutation matrix. The following example illustrates this.

Example 12.2 Let us start from the base H-matrix

$$\mathbf{H} = \begin{bmatrix} 1\,1\,0 \\ 1\,0\,1 \end{bmatrix}. \tag{12.142}$$

The corresponding Tanner graph is the one shown on the left side of Fig. 12.33.

For the lifting by 2, we replace the 1-entries by the 2×2 permutation matrices

$$\begin{bmatrix} 1\,0 \\ 0\,1 \end{bmatrix}, \begin{bmatrix} 0\,1 \\ 1\,0 \end{bmatrix}, \tag{12.143}$$

leading to the final H-matrix

$$\mathbf{H}_{lift} = \begin{bmatrix} 1\,0 & 0\,1 & 0\,0 \\ 0\,1 & 1\,0 & 0\,0 \\ & & \\ 1\,0 & 0\,0 & 0\,1 \\ 0\,1 & 0\,0 & 1\,0 \end{bmatrix}. \tag{12.144}$$

We obtain the Tanner graph on the right of Fig. 12.33. Note that the odd and even rows and columns belong to the left and right half of the duplicated variable and check-node arrangement. This means, one may number the columns as 1, 4, 2, 5, 3, 6 and the rows as 1, 3, 2, 4. Note that the degrees at the variable and check-node sides are preserved.

When replacing the ones by cyclic permutation matrices, a quasi-cycle LDPC code is obtained. Cyclic permutations can be chosen such that the girth is maximized.

A quasi-cyclic code is defined as follows.

Definition 12.11 [54] Let B, K, and t be positive integers such that $K < tB$. A (tB, K) linear block code C_{qc} over GF(2) is called a quasi-cyclic (QC) code, if the following conditions hold: (1) each codeword in C_{qc} consists of t sections of B bits each; and (2) every t-sectionized cyclic-shift of a codeword in C_{qc} is also a codeword in C_{qc}. Such a QC code is called a t-section QC code.

Many protograph codes adopted in different standardized systems are linked to LDPC variants of repeat-accumulate (RA) codes shown earlier in Fig. 12.33 for the Turbo-coded case. We consider the H matrix of a systematic RA code which can be described as split into two sub-matrices

$$\mathbf{H} = [\mathbf{H}_R \mathbf{H}_A]. \tag{12.145}$$

The systematic part is on the right providing the lower triangular structure just as in Fig. 12.27. To represent the repetition, $\mathbf{H}_R$ contains a number of ν ones in every column, but without with row weight 1. This means a certain bit in that range is protected by ν independent checks. This is realizing "diversity" like a repetition code. The accumulator properties are realized by XOR-ing neighboring components in $\mathbf{H}_A$. The structure of the overall H-matrix is then

$$\mathbf{H} = \left[\begin{array}{ccc|ccccccc}
1 & & & 1 & & & & & & (1) \\
1 & & & 1 & 1 & & & & & \\
1 & & & & 1 & 1 & & & & \\
 & 1 & \uparrow & & & 1 & 1 & & & \\
 & 1 & \nu & & & & 1 & 1 & & \\
 & 1 & \downarrow & & & & & 1 & 1 & \\
 & \vdots & & & & & & \ddots & \ddots &
\end{array}\right]. \tag{12.146}$$

The one in parentheses in the right upper corner is the tailbiting variant. For illustration purposes, we chose the μ ones to be consecutive, which is usually not the case.

When choosing an irregular $\mathbf{H}_R$, the codes will be denoted IRA (Irregular Repeat Accumulate). In the following, we give a few examples of codes with repeat and accumulation operations in different arrangements. We start showing the protograph of the simple RA code of Fig. 12.14. Figure 12.34 shows the serial concatenation again and its protograph counterpart. This and further protographs can be found in [63, 64].

Figure 12.34 shows the non-systematic case. Non-filled circles are not transmitted (punctured). Filled circles are transmitted. For the systematic case, one would have to fill the circle on the left, as well. The right side of the graph shows the accumulation function with the XOR functions. Here, they are wrapping around, i.e., it is the

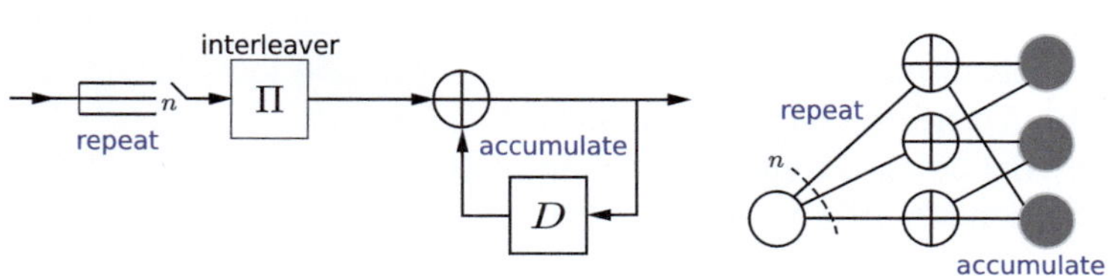

Fig. 12.34 Repeat-Accumulate code and its protograph

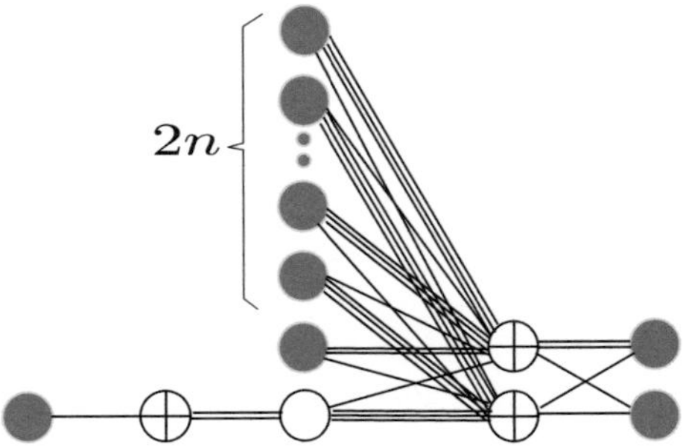

Fig. 12.35 AR4JA protograph

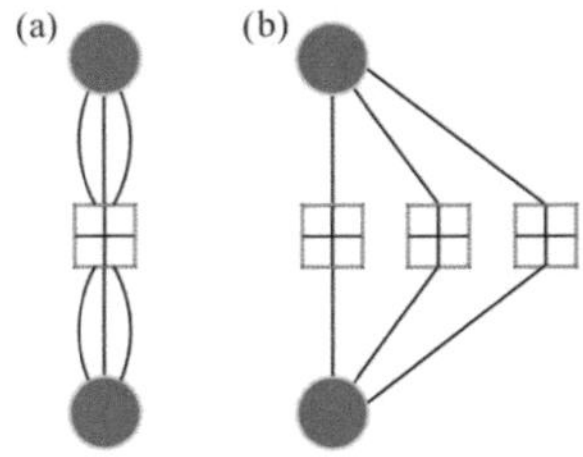

Fig. 12.36 Protograph with a single check node and its threefold representation according to Eq. (12.147)

"tailbiting" variant. As with all protographs, replacing each edge with a permutation in a lifting operation will lead to the final code. In later shown protographs, parallel lines will be likewise permuted individually.

We show some examples of protograph codes used in applications. Figure 12.35 shows the AR4JA (Accumulate-Repeat-4-Jagged-Accumulate) protograph from [65] adopted by CCSDS [66] for near-earth and deep-space applications. The rate is $R = \frac{2n+2}{2n+4} = \frac{n+1}{n+2}$, where the numerator follows from all filled and empty circles minus the XOR nodes, and the denominator is the number of all filled (transmitted) nodes. $n = 0$ results in $R = 1/2$ and $n = 1$ yields $R = 2/3$.

For further reading on protograph constructions, see, e.g., [54, 67].

12.8.9 Spatially Coupled LDPC Codes

A convolution structure of LDPC codes can be obtained by spreading a protograph over time.[8] The idea goes back to works of Felström and Zigangirov [68] for convolutional LDPC codes and terminated variants described by Lentmaier, Costello, Kudekar, Richardson, Urbanke et al. [69, 70]. For a short introduction, we use an example from a presentation by Costello [71].

The description starts from a very simple protograph with two variable nodes and a single check node, shown in Fig. 12.36a).

[8] This could, of course, also be spreading over frequency in a multi-carrier system.

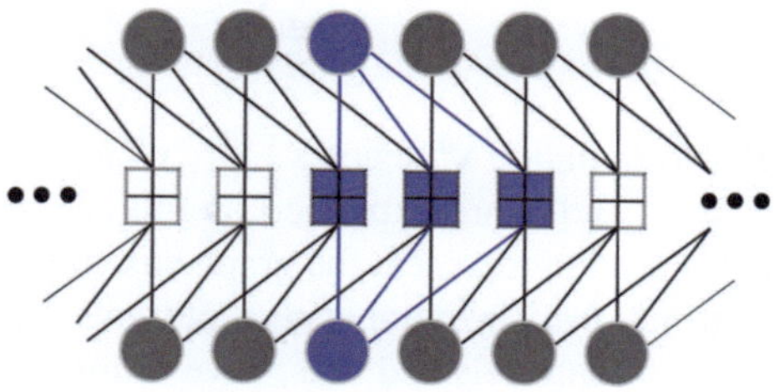
Fig. 12.37 Convolutional, spatially coupled Protograph

The parity check base matrix is

$$\mathbf{B} = [3 \quad 3] \quad \Longrightarrow \quad \begin{bmatrix} \mathbf{B}_0 \\ \mathbf{B}_1 \\ \mathbf{B}_2 \end{bmatrix} = \begin{bmatrix} 1\,1 \\ 1\,1 \\ 1\,1 \end{bmatrix} \tag{12.147}$$

This has 3 parallel edges, which would be distributed in the lifting process. We draw them as 3 checks in Fig. 12.36b). This protograph is now not seen isolated but spread in time to realize the spatially coupled (SC) LDPC protograph, i.e., a *convolutional* protograph shown in Fig. 12.37.

The corresponding infinite base matrix $\mathbf{B}_\infty$ unveils the convolutional structure of the parity-check matrix which we had discussed in Sect. 4.1.1 for G and H matrices of convolutional codes.

$$\mathbf{B}_\infty = \begin{bmatrix} \ddots & \ddots & \ddots & & & \\ & \mathbf{B}_2 & \mathbf{B}_1 & \mathbf{B}_0 & & \\ & & \mathbf{B}_2 & \mathbf{B}_1 & \mathbf{B}_0 & \\ & & & \mathbf{B}_2 & \mathbf{B}_1 & \mathbf{B}_0 \\ & & & \ddots & \ddots & \ddots \end{bmatrix}. \tag{12.148}$$

12.8.10 Multi-edge-Type LDPC Codes

Multi-edge-type LDPC codes[9] [44, 73] are a generalization of irregular and regular LDPC codes. Diverting from standard LDPC ensembles where the graph connectivity is constrained only by the node degrees, in the multi-edge setting, several edge classes can be defined, and every node is characterized by the number of connections to edges of each class. Within this framework, the code ensemble can be specified through two node-perspective multinomials associated with variable and check nodes, which are defined in [44] as

[9] This section on multi-edge-type LDPC codes is taken from the thesis of a former Ph.D. student [72].

$$\nu(\mathbf{r}, \mathbf{x}) = \sum \nu_{\mathbf{b},\mathbf{d}} \mathbf{r}^{\mathbf{b}} \mathbf{x}^{\mathbf{d}} \text{ and } \mu(\mathbf{x}) = \sum \mu_{\mathbf{d}} \mathbf{x}^{\mathbf{d}}. \tag{12.149}$$

The formulation $\mathbf{x}^{\mathbf{d}}$ denotes $\prod_{i=1}^{m_e} x_i^{d_i}$ and likewise, $\mathbf{r}^{\mathbf{b}}$ denotes $\prod_{i=0}^{m_r} r_i^{b_i}$. The vectors **b**, **d**, **r**, and **x** are explained as follows. First, let m_e denote the number of edge types used to represent the graph ensemble and m_r the number of different received distributions. The number m_r represents the fact that the different bits can go through different channels and thus, have different received distributions. Each node in the ensemble graph has associated with it a vector $\mathbf{x} = (x_1, \ldots, x_{m_e})$ that indicates the different types of edges connected to it and a vector $\mathbf{d} = (d_1, \ldots, d_{m_e})$ referred to as *edge degree vector* which denotes the number of connections of a node to edges of type i, where $i \in (1, \ldots, m_e)$.

For the variable nodes, there is additionally the vector $\mathbf{r} = (r_0, \ldots, r_{m_r})$, which represents the different received distributions and the vector $\mathbf{b} = (b_0, \ldots, b_{m_r})$, which indicates the number of connections to the different received distributions. We assume that **b** has exactly one entry set to 1 and the rest set to zero. This simply indicates that each variable node has access to only one channel observation at a time. In other words, per edge type, we assume a certain received channel distribution. Finally, the coefficients $\nu_{\mathbf{b},\mathbf{d}}$ and $\mu_{\mathbf{d}}$ are non-negative reals such that if n is the total number of variable nodes, $\nu_{\mathbf{b},\mathbf{d}} n$ and $\mu_{\mathbf{d}} n$ represent the number of variable nodes of type (**b**,**d**) and check nodes of type **d**, respectively. Furthermore, Richardson and Urbanke [44] define

$$\nu_{x_j}(\mathbf{r}, \mathbf{x}) = \frac{\partial \nu(\mathbf{r}, \mathbf{x})}{\partial x_j} \text{ and } \mu_{x_j}(\mathbf{x}) = \frac{\partial \mu(\mathbf{x})}{\partial x_j}. \tag{12.150}$$

In a valid multi-edge ensemble, the number of connections of each edge type should be the same at both variable and check nodes sides. This gives rise to the *socket count equality* constraint, which can be written as

$$\nu_{x_j}(\mathbf{1}, \mathbf{1}) = \mu_{x_j}(\mathbf{1}), \quad j = 1, \ldots, m_e, \tag{12.151}$$

where **1** denotes a vector with all entries equal to 1, with length being clear from the context.

Figure 12.38 sketches a multi-edge-type Tanner Graph.

To mention some exemplary applications, Slepian-Wolf coding asks for a multi-edge-type description, where the parities or syndromes are typically experiencing a different channel than given by the source relations [74]; other typical applications are joint source-channel coding and unequal error protection codes.

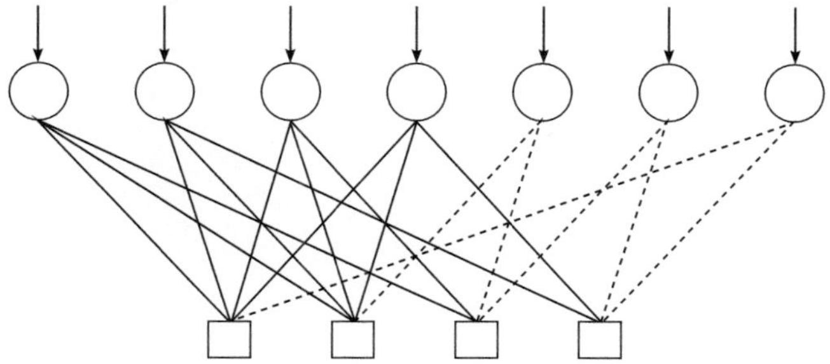

Fig. 12.38 Multi-edge-type graph with two different edge types and one received distribution

12.8.11 Non-binary LDPC Codes

Non-binary LDPC codes have originally been proposed by Davey and MacKay [75]. Later, major works especially on decoding algorithms were conducted by Declercq, Fossorier et al. [76, 77]. In here, we use examples and roughly follow the descriptions in [78].

A non-binary LDPC code over GF(2^m) has to distinguish 2^m elements a and hence, the intrinsic input to the Tanner graph will already be

$$u_{0,j}^{a} = P(x_j = a|r_j) = \prod_{\mu=1}^{m} P_{j,\mu}^{a_\mu} \quad \forall_{a \in \mathrm{GF}(2^m)}. \tag{12.152}$$

Hence, we should think of a vector of length 2^m with probabilities for every possibly realization of a.

In contrast to (12.46), we used the a-posteriori (AP) probability, not the likelihood ratio. Considering AP or Likelihood does not make a difference, when the a-priori LLR is zero, i.e., when we assume equally likely symbols and their binary components.

The Tanner graph itself now has Galois field elements on its edges, which act as permutations. We show an example from [78] with a check-matrix

$$\mathbf{H} = \begin{bmatrix} 3\,1\,0\,1\,0\,4\,0\,0\,0\,0 \\ 0\,0\,1\,3\,0\,0\,0\,0\,5\,1 \\ 0\,0\,2\,0\,7\,7\,0\,1\,0\,0 \\ 1\,0\,0\,0\,0\,0\,5\,6\,0\,7 \\ 0\,6\,0\,0\,7\,0\,6\,0\,6\,0 \end{bmatrix}$$

The underlying Galois field is assumed to be GF(2^3) with a primitive polynomial $p(\alpha) = \alpha^3 + \alpha + 1$ and the elements are just numbered from 0 to 7, according to the binary coefficients in the number representation $a_0 + a_1\alpha + a_2\alpha^2$.

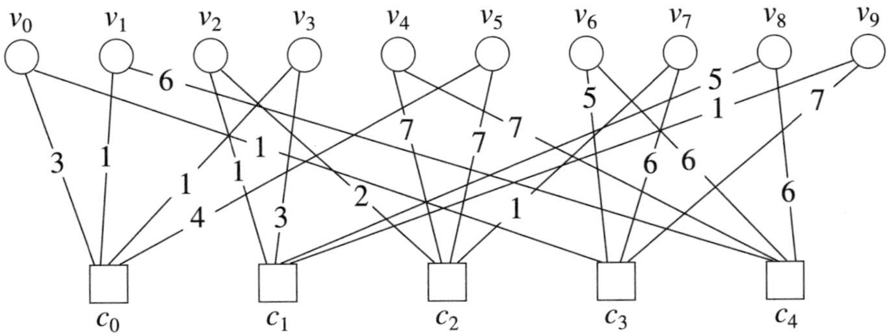

Fig. 12.39 Tanner graph of non-binary LDPC code

The Tanner graph is shown in Fig. 12.39. The permutations due to the GF(2^3) elements on the edge have similar effects as the lifting of protograph codes when replacing ones in the protograph H-matrix by permutation matrices. The performance of non-binary codes is said to be superior in the error-floor region. Their drawback, as we will see, lies in the decoding complexity.

For decoding, we define a vector message from check node C_i to variable node V_j by[10] $\mathbf{u}_{ij} = [u_{ij}(a)]_{a \in \mathrm{GF}(2^m)}$. Likewise, a vector message from a variable node $V_{j'}$ to a check node C_i is defined as $\mathbf{v}_{j'i} = [v_{j'i}(v_{j'})]_{v_{j'} \in \mathrm{GF}(2^m)}$.

We start with the processing at the variable node. The variable node probability $v_{ji}(a)$ from variable node V_j to check node C_i is given by

$$v_{ji}(a) = \underbrace{\varepsilon_{ji}}_{\text{const.}} \cdot \underbrace{u_{0,j}^{a}}_{\text{intrinsic}} \cdot \underbrace{\prod_{i' \in \mathcal{N}(j) \setminus \{i\}} u_{i'j}(a)}_{\text{extrinsic}} \qquad \forall a \in \mathrm{GF}(2^m), \tag{12.153}$$

where $u_{i'j}(a)$ are the probability inputs from check node i' to variable node j, $\mathcal{N}(j)$ denotes the check-node neighborhood[11] of the jth variable node. ε_{ji} is a normalization constant ensuring that $\sum_{a \in \mathrm{GF}(2^m)} v_{ji}(a) = 1$.

At the end of the iterations, the exclusion in the product of Eq. (12.153) will be removed, i.e., leading to the final variable node probability

$$v_j(a) = \underbrace{\varepsilon_j}_{\text{const.}} \cdot \underbrace{u_{0,j}^{a}}_{\text{intrinsic}} \cdot \underbrace{\prod_{i \in \mathcal{N}(j)} u_{ij}(a)}_{\text{extrinsic}}. \tag{12.154}$$

From this one, the actual hard decision would follow from

$$\hat{v}_j(a) = \arg \max_{a \in \mathrm{GF}(2^m)} v_j(a). \tag{12.155}$$

[10] [...] means vector of ...

[11] Neighborhood means connected through edges.

The check-node computations are more involved. The non-binary check equations have to be fulfilled, which is expressed by the so-called "configuration set" $\mathrm{Conf}_{ij}(a)$ for a $\nu_j = a$. This is written as

$$\mathrm{Conf}_{ij}(a) = \left\{ [\nu_{j'}]_{j' \in \mathcal{M}\setminus\{j\}} : \sum_{j' \in \mathcal{M}\setminus\{j\}} h_{ij'}\nu_{j'} = h_{ij}a \right\}. \tag{12.156}$$

The vector message component from C_i to V_j is then expressed as

$$v_{ij}(a) = \sum_{\boldsymbol{\nu}_{ij} \in \mathrm{Conf}_{ij}(a)} \prod_{j' \in \mathcal{M}(i)\setminus\{j\}} u_{j'i}(\nu_{j'}), \tag{12.157}$$

where $\boldsymbol{\nu}_{ij} = [\nu_{j'}]_{j' \in \mathcal{M}(i)\setminus\{j\}}$ and $\mathcal{M}(i)$ is the variable node neighborhood of check node C_i.

The product with $h_{ij'}$ in (12.156) is a permutation and hence, the probability for $\tilde{\nu}_{j'} = h_{ij'}\nu_{j'}$ can be determined by

$$\tilde{u}_{j'i}(v'_j) = u_{j'i}(h_{ij'}^{-1} \cdot v'_j). \tag{12.158}$$

Additional to $\tilde{\nu}_{j'} = h_{ij'}\nu_{j'}$, we introduce $\tilde{\boldsymbol{\nu}}_{ij} = [\nu_{j'}]_{j' \in \mathcal{M}(i)\setminus\{j\}}$, $\tilde{a} = h_{ij}a$, $\tilde{\mathbf{u}}_{ij} = [\tilde{u}_{ij}(\tilde{\nu}_{j'})]_{\tilde{\nu}_{j'} \in \mathrm{GF}(2^m)}$, $\tilde{\mathbf{v}}_{ij} = [\tilde{v}_{ij}(\tilde{a})]_{\tilde{a} \in \mathrm{GF}(2^m)}$, with $\tilde{u}_{j'i}(\tilde{v}_{j'i}) = u_{ij}(v_{j'})$, $\tilde{v}_{ij}(\tilde{a}) = v_{ij}(a)$.

This allows to rewrite (12.157) as

$$\tilde{v}_{ij}(\tilde{a}) = \sum_{\mathbf{v}_{ij} \in \mathrm{Conf}^{\star}_{ij}(a)} \prod_{j' \in \mathcal{M}(i)\setminus\{j\}} \tilde{u}_{j'i}(\tilde{\nu}_{j'})$$

with

$$\mathrm{Conf}^{\star}_{ij}(a) = \left\{ [\tilde{\nu}_{j'}]_{j' \in \mathcal{M}\setminus\{j\}} : \sum_{j' \in \mathcal{M}\setminus\{j\}} \tilde{\nu}_{j'} = \tilde{a} \right\}. \tag{12.159}$$

Equations (12.158) and (12.159) express a convolution-like structure, which can be made use of by an FFT-like or Hadamard-transform approach, where the latter is proven in [79] for a simplified expression $y = x_1 + x_2 + \cdots + x_L$ similar to the sum in (12.159). One would then do the Hadamard transform (or DFT/FFT) of the probabilities $\tilde{u}_{j'i}(\tilde{\nu}_{j'})$ over the field elements and multiply those transforms. An inverse Hadamard transform then delivers the probability mass function $\tilde{v}_{ij}(\tilde{a})$. For the complete proof, we refer to [79]. A 2×2 Hadamard matrix is, of course, also a 2×2 DFT matrix. [54, 77, 78] denote this as an m-dimensional 2×2 DFT (using an outer tensor product annotation).[12]

[12] We thank David Declercq for pointing us to the Hadamard-related proof in [79].

12.9 Polar Codes

For to everyone who has will more be given,
and he will have an abundance.
But from the one who has not,
even what he has will be taken away.

Matthew 25:29

Polar coding has been introduced by Arıkan in 2009 [80] for channel polarization, followed by a paper on source polarization in 2010 [81]. It seems, however, more convenient to start from the source coding aspect, although we are not focusing on source coding otherwise. This approach is also later followed by Arıkan's presentation series at UC Berkeley in 2015 [82–84]. Our presentation is closely connected to Arıkan's lectures and draws additionally on his papers and [85].

12.9.1 Source Polarization

We start from considering a binary memoryless source X with a given probability mass function P_X and $x \in \{0, 1\}$. Let us first consider a pair of such i.i.d. random variables (X_1, X_2) and transform them to a new pair of random variables, named (U_1, U_2) by

$$(U_1, U_2) = (X_1, X_2)\mathbf{F} = (X_1, X_2)\begin{bmatrix} 1 & 0 \\ 1 & 1 \end{bmatrix}. \tag{12.160}$$

This transformation step is also shown in Fig. 12.40 and is actually known from the $(\mathbf{u}, \mathbf{u} + \mathbf{v})$ construction introduced in Sect. 12.1, where Arıkan's formulation is more like $(\mathbf{u} + \mathbf{v}, \mathbf{v})$. Likewise, the matrix in the transform reminds also of a Hadamard matrix with

$$\mathbf{H}_2 = \begin{bmatrix} 1 & 1 \\ 1 & -1 \end{bmatrix}. \tag{12.161}$$

When mapping -1 to zero and $+1$ to one, this would lead to a similar formulation.
The transformation preserves the overall entropy, i.e.,

$$H(X_1, X_2) = 2\,H(X) = H(U_1, U_2). \tag{12.162}$$

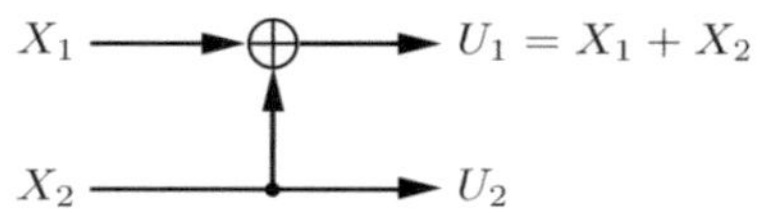

Fig. 12.40 Polarization with **F**.

We also remember the Chain Rule (2.6) for the entropy, derived from Bayes' theorem, namely

$$H(U_1, U_2) = H(U_1) + H(U_2|U_1). \tag{12.163}$$

U_2 is equal to X_2, allowing to rewrite this as

$$H(U_1, U_2) = H(U_1) + H(X_2|U_1) \leq H(U_1) + H(X_2). \tag{12.164}$$

Together with (12.162), this yields

$$\begin{aligned} 2H(X) \leq H(U_1) + H(X_2) \Longrightarrow\ & H(U_1) \geq H(X) \text{ and} \\ & H(U_2|U_1) = H(X_2|U_1) \leq H(X) \end{aligned} \tag{12.165}$$

Putting this into a sequence as

$$H(U_1) \geq H(X) \geq H(U_2|U_1) \tag{12.166}$$

creates polarized sources U_1 and $U_2|U_1$. Equality only holds if $H(X)$ equals zero or one.

We now apply the same step recursively, using the Kronecker product $\mathbf{F} \otimes \mathbf{F}$, which leads to

$$\begin{bmatrix} 1 & 0 \\ 1 & 1 \end{bmatrix} \otimes \begin{bmatrix} 1 & 0 \\ 1 & 1 \end{bmatrix} = \begin{bmatrix} 1 & 0 & 0 & 0 \\ 1 & 1 & 0 & 0 \\ 1 & 0 & 1 & 0 \\ 1 & 1 & 1 & 1 \end{bmatrix}. \tag{12.167}$$

In general, the Kronecker product is defined as

$$\mathbf{A} \otimes \mathbf{B} = \begin{bmatrix} a_{11}\mathbf{B} & \cdots & a_{12}\mathbf{B} \\ \vdots & \ddots & \vdots \\ a_{21}\mathbf{B} & \cdots & a_{21}\mathbf{B} \end{bmatrix}, \tag{12.168}$$

leading to

$$\mathbf{F}^{\otimes n} = \mathbf{F} \otimes \mathbf{F}^{\otimes n-1} = \begin{bmatrix} \mathbf{F}^{\otimes n-1} & \mathbf{0} \\ \mathbf{F}^{\otimes n-1} & \mathbf{F}^{\otimes n-1} \end{bmatrix}. \tag{12.169}$$

Spelling out relations based on (12.167) reads

$$\begin{aligned} U_1 &= X_1 + X_2 + X_3 + X_4 \\ U_2 &= X_2 + X_4 \\ U_3 &= X_3 + X_4 \\ U_4 &= X_4. \end{aligned}$$

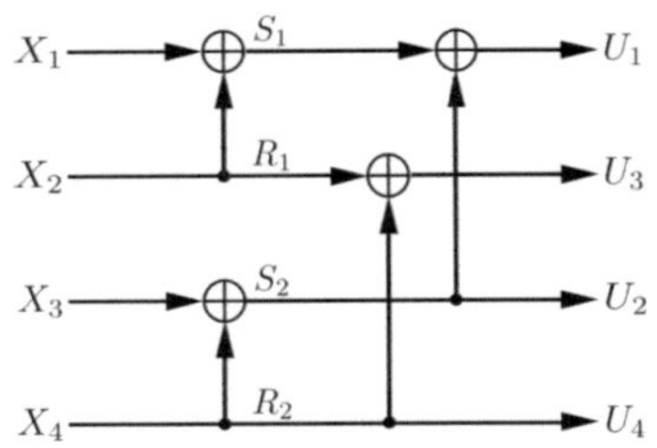

Fig. 12.41 Polarization with $\mathbf{F}^{\otimes 2} \cdot \mathbf{B}_4$

The corresponding Fig. 12.41 as shown in [81] has a slight modification exchanging U_2 and U_3. This is expressed with an additional permutation matrix $\mathbf{B}_N$, leading to

$$\mathbf{G}_N = \mathbf{F}^{\otimes n} \cdot \mathbf{B}_N, \tag{12.170}$$

for $N = 4$,

$$\mathbf{G}_4 = \begin{bmatrix} 1\,0\,0\,0 \\ 1\,1\,0\,0 \\ 1\,0\,1\,0 \\ 1\,1\,1\,1 \end{bmatrix} \cdot \begin{bmatrix} 1\,0\,0\,0 \\ 0\,0\,1\,0 \\ 0\,1\,0\,0 \\ 0\,0\,0\,1 \end{bmatrix}. \tag{12.171}$$

This is the 'bit-reversal' permutation known from the FFT, where dependent on decimation in time or frequency one has a permutation at the input or output, respectively. In a matrix description of the DFT, one would first use odd columns (or rows) thereafter even ones, then again recursively apply the same kind of permutation for half the size again. The polarization leads to "butterfly" structures similar to the ones in a Cooley-Tukey FFT. Multiplying with the bit-reversal permutation could then be seen as recovering the "original" structure just as one would return from the FFT permuted matrix back to the original DFT matrix. The permutation is, of course, just a different labeling of outputs.

The entropies in Fig. 12.41 are ordered as

$$H(U_1) \geq H(S_1) = H(S_2) \geq H(U_2|U_1), \tag{12.172}$$

$$H(U_3|\mathbf{U}^2) \geq H(R_1|S_1) = H(R_2|S_2) \geq H(U_4|\mathbf{U}^3). \tag{12.173}$$

We use a notation similar to Arıkan's with $\mathbf{U}^i = (U_1, ..., U_i)$. The first equation is equivalently derived from (12.166) and the second follows from the entropy preservation and the multivariate Chain Rule

$$H(\mathbf{U}^N) = \sum_{i=1}^{N} H(U_i|U_{i-1}, ..., U_1). \tag{12.174}$$

For $N = 4$ this means

$$
\begin{aligned}
4H(X) &= H(\mathbf{U}^4) = H(U_1) + H(U_2|U_1) + H(U_3|\mathbf{U}^2) + H(U_4|\mathbf{U}^3) && (12.175)\\
&= H(S_1) + H(R_1|S_1) + H(S_2) + H(R_2|S_2) && (12.176)\\
&= 2H(S_1) + 2H(R_1|S_1), && (12.177)\\
2H(R_1|S_1) &= H(U_3|\mathbf{U}^2) + H(U_4|\mathbf{U}^3). && (12.178)
\end{aligned}
$$

Comparing to (12.164) and (12.165), we now obtain (12.173).

Each polarization step splits into high- and low-entropy versions. Iteratively, the high and low entropy sources are again split. This also explains the permutation carried out in Fig. 12.41 and Eqs. (12.170) and (12.171). Thereby one obtains a concentration on the both ends of the entropy scale, meaning zero or one and with growing N diminishing share in between those values. Arıkan proves this introducing a random process defined by martingales using Bhattacharyya parameters, where in [81], he refers to his first publication [80].

The behavior is summarized in [81] in a theorem that we quote here.

Theorem 12.5 *Let X be a Bernoulli(p) source with $P_X(1) = p$, $P_X(0) = 1 - p$ with an entropy $H(p) = h(p) = -p\log_2(p) - (1-p)\log_2(1-p)$. For any $N = 2^n$, $n \geq 1$, let $\mathbf{U}^N = \mathbf{X}^N\mathbf{G}_N$. Then for any $\delta \in (0, 1)$,*

$$\lim_{N\to\infty} \frac{|\{i \in [1, N] : H(U_i|\mathbf{U}^{i-1}) \in (1-\delta, 1]\}|}{N} = H(X)$$

and

$$\lim_{N\to\infty} \frac{|\{i \in [1, N] : H(U_i|\mathbf{U}^{i-1}) \in [0, \delta)\}|}{N} = 1 - H(X).$$

In other words,

$$\lim_{N\to\infty} \frac{|\{i \in [1, N] : \delta < H(U_i|\mathbf{U}^{i-1}) < 1-\delta|}{N} = 0, \tag{12.179}$$

which holds for $\delta = 2^{-N^\beta}$, $\beta < 1/2$, i.e., up to $\delta \approx 2^{-\sqrt{N}}$.

This means, the higher N, the more conditional entropies are concentrated (polarized) close to the limits 0 or 1 and the intermediate range is less and less populated. Hence, one could perform lossless source coding by only considering those virtual source signals U_i that have a conditional entropy close to one, i.e., bigger than $1-\delta$ or to be on the safe side, those that have bigger entropy than δ. For large N, the difference can be neglected, since the range in between is not populated much. We understand that an i.i.d. source X is modified into a virtual one with memory, U, where bits have high conditional entropy and are then put out as they are and the others, since their conditional entropy is essentially zero, they are deterministic and can be recovered from the high entropy ones.

The split into high and low entropy sets reminds us of the Asymptotic Equipartition Property (AEP) splitting source sequences into typical and untypical sets, where only the typical one need to be encoded, thereby leading to Shannon's source coding theorem.

The recovery error of the given source coding scheme is of the order of $O(2^{-N^{\beta}})$, $\beta < 1/2$.

Figure 12.41, even more so for larger polarization structures, shows a similarity to the Cooley-Tukey FFT structure or the Fast Walsh-Hadamard transform with its butterflies and the known complexity of $O(N \log_2 N)$, which is the same here, likewise having $n = \log_2 N$ stages.

12.9.2 Channel Polarization

12.9.2.1 Polarization of Capacities

We consider a symmetric channel with discrete input alphabet and arbitrary output alphabet, but will limit ourselves in this section to binary input and discrete output. This means, we are considering a symmetrical discrete memoryless channel with binary input. The channel, we denote with W. We express N channel uses, expressed as N parallel channels W. We apply a generator $\mathbf{G}_N$ to feed the independent channel realizations according to Fig. 12.42. This $\mathbf{G}_N$ is not arbitrary, but is chosen to polarize the channel. Arıkan proposed the same operation that we have already introduced in the previous section, but also other choices (even random ones) would lead to a polarization effect, but may come with higher complexity.

The Channel Capacity of that N channels shall not be changed by $\mathbf{G}_N$, which means the uniform input to W shall be provided by uniform inputs U_i. The Capacity is given by

$$C(\mathbf{W}_N) = \sup_{P(\mathbf{U})} I(\mathbf{U}^N; \mathbf{Y}^N) = \sup_{P(\mathbf{X})} I(\mathbf{X}^N; \mathbf{Y}^N) = N \cdot C(W) \tag{12.180}$$

and the Chain Rule for the Mutual Information similar to the one for entropies in (12.174) is given by

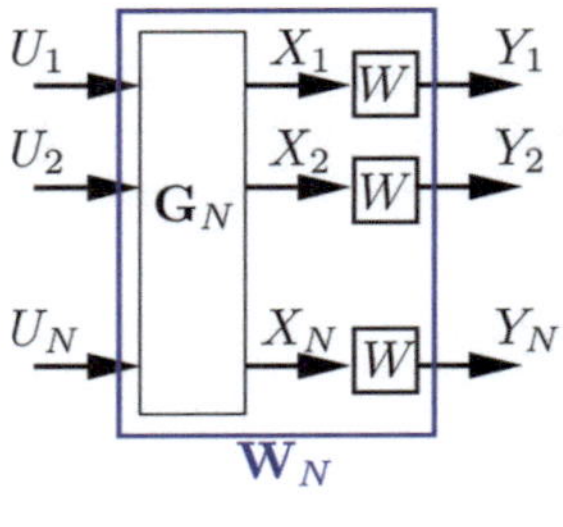

Fig. 12.42 Preprocessing of N combined independent channels with $\mathbf{G}_N$

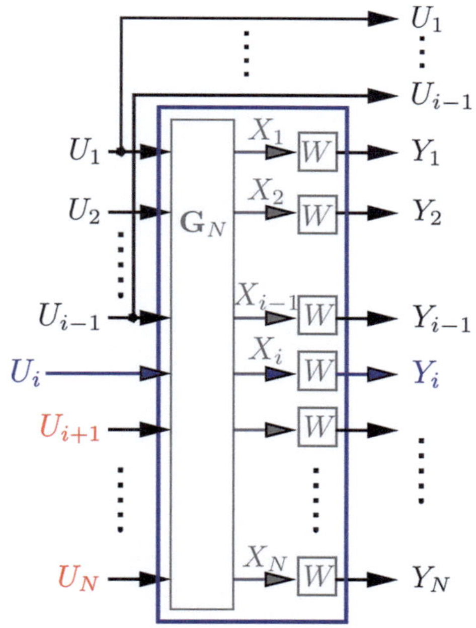

Fig. 12.43 Channel split according to Chain Rule

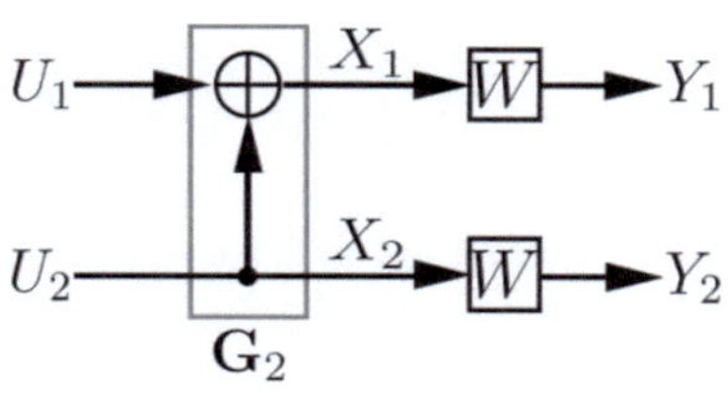

Fig. 12.44 Polarization with two component channels/channel uses

$$C(\mathbf{W}_N) = \sup_{P(\mathbf{U})} I(\mathbf{U}^N; \mathbf{Y}^N) = \sum_{i=1}^{N} I(U_i; \mathbf{Y}^N, \mathbf{U}^{i-1}) = \sum_{i=1}^{N} C(W_i). \qquad (12.181)$$

Here, we defined the terms in the Chain Rule as individual channels, also interpreting $\mathbf{U}^{i-1}$ as an additional output to the ith input U_i as shown in Fig. 12.43. The inputs $U_{i+1}...U_N$, shown in red, are then interpreted as unknown interfering components.

To describe the function of the generator $\mathbf{G}_N$, let us begin with an example of only two inputs and two outputs, i.e., consider $\mathbf{G}_2$ in Fig. 12.44 following the approach already shown in the previous section in Fig. 12.40.

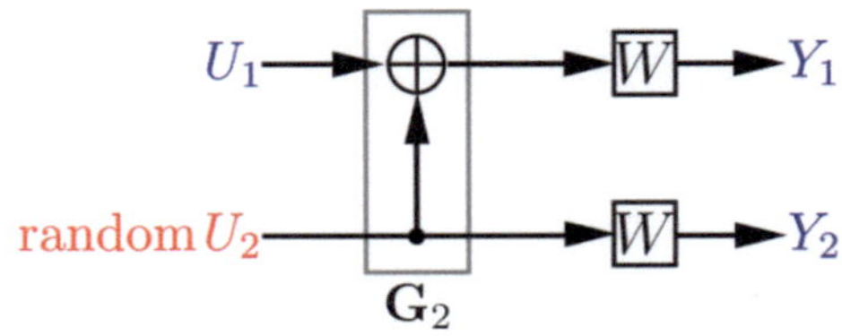

Fig. 12.45 Channel W_1

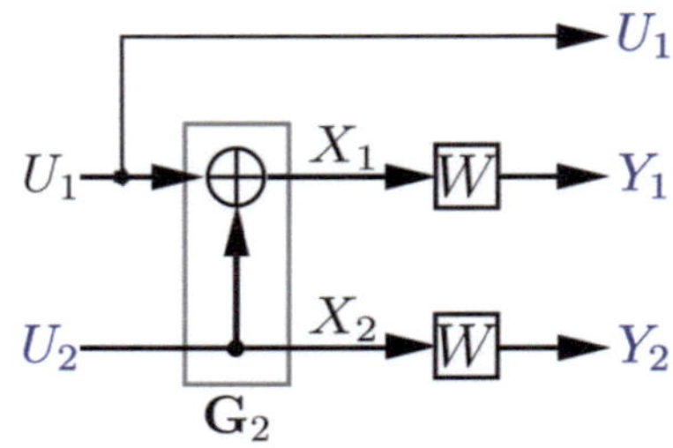

Fig. 12.46 Channel W_2

$\mathbf{G}_2$ together with the two individual channels W lead to new channels

$$W_1 : U_1 \longrightarrow (Y_1, Y_2), \tag{12.182}$$

$$W_2 : U_2 \longrightarrow (Y_1, Y_2, U_1). \tag{12.183}$$

For W_1, highlighted in Fig. 12.45, we consider U_2 as random interference. Y_1 alone would then not allow to recover U_1, since a Bernoulli(1/2) sequence at U_2 would make the Capacity of $U_1 \to Y_1$ vanish. However, the second output Y_2 allows for estimating U_2 thereby providing some information about U_1 considering both outputs Y_1 and Y_2. In Fig. 12.46 for W_2, considering U_1 as a known "output" looks strange at first sight. However, as the process of polarization is continued recursively with such arrangements, the channels will be polarized to either be non-existent, i.e., having no Capacity or be ideal with a diminishing share in between. The zero Capacity channels are provided with a fixed and known value (could be zeros or ones or ideally uniformly distributed zeros or ones). Those bits are called "frozen". The Capacity-one channels are error free and hence, in both cases, U_1 can be considered to be known, ignoring the diminishing group in between the extremes. However, those could also be frozen. An error in a non-frozen bit will, of course, cause error propagation.

We observe channel polarization expressed by

$$C(W_1) \leq C(W) \leq C(W_2). \tag{12.184}$$

The right inequality is obvious, since omitting variables from the second argument will reduce Mutual Information or leave it unchanged, i.e.,

$$C(W_2) = \sup I(U_2; Y_1 Y_2 U_1) = \sup I(X_2; Y_1 Y_2 U_1) \geq \sup I(X_2; Y_2).$$

The left inequality in (12.184) then follows from the preservation of the overall Capacity.

$$C(W_1) + C(W_2) = 2C(W) = \sup I(U_1; Y_1Y_2) + \sup I(U_2; Y_1Y_2U_1),$$

with equality iff $C(W)$ is zero or one. One case follows intuitively from letting U_1 be perfectly known, which would mean repeating U_2 and sending it through two independent channels W. This would then lead to twice the Capacity, hence, can only be equal to $C(W)$, if the Capacity is zero.

From (12.184), we observe that we created two new channels, one better, one worse than W. Arıkan labeled them as

$$W^- = W_1 \quad \text{and} \quad W^+ = W_2,$$

the minus and plus signs labeling the worse and better channels, respectively.

Now, the scheme is recursively applied after duplicating the W^+ channels and the W^- channels, thereby splitting them again into worse and better ones, which are then labeled as

$$\begin{aligned} &W^{--}, W^{-+}, \text{ resulting from two } W^- \text{ channels,} \\ &W^{+-}, W^{++}, \text{ resulting from two } W^+ \text{ channels,} \end{aligned}$$

thereby leading to channels with (usually at that initial step) increasing Capacities, W^{--}, W^{-+}, W^{+-}, W^{++}. That 2nd recursive step is illustrated in Fig. 12.47. Likewise, we show the next recursive step splitting $\mathbf{W}^8$ in Fig. 12.48. For the further explanation, we will stick to length 8, but the treatment will, of course, likewise be valid for bigger lengths.

For increasing recursive steps, the Capacities are concentrating around the limits zero and one. This is typically illustrated drawing so-called martingales. We also draw them in Fig. 12.49, but without going into the corresponding theory

Fig. 12.47 Channel W_4 split into W^{--},W^{-+},W^{+-},W^{++}

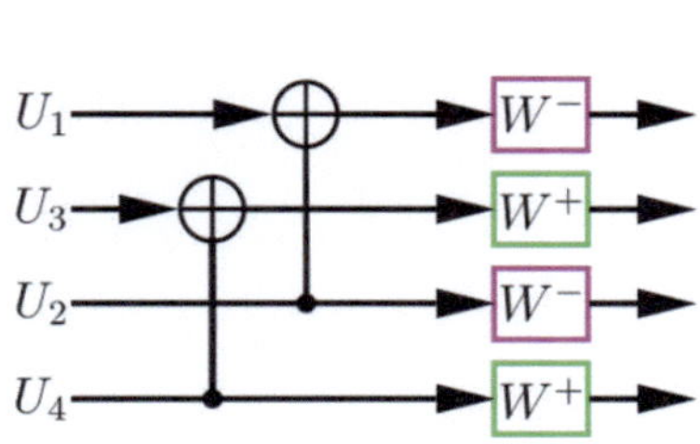

around bounded martingales.[13] We show the derivation for an erasure channel with erasure probability ε. The Capacity of an erasure channel W_ε is known to be $C_\varepsilon = 1 - \varepsilon$. Combining two such channels leads to a Capacity of $2C_\varepsilon$. Considering the first polarized channel W_1 in Fig. 12.45, this requires to have both W_ε to be non-erased, i.e., $C(W_1) = C(W^-) = C_\varepsilon^2 = (1-\varepsilon)^2$. Due to Capacity preservation, $C(W_2) = C(W^+) = 2C_\varepsilon - C_\varepsilon^2 = 2(1-\varepsilon) - (1-\varepsilon)^2 = 1 - \varepsilon^2$. Recursively, $C(W^{--})$ and $C(W^{-+})$ will be computed as $[C(W^-)]^2$ and $2C(W^-) - [C(W^-)]^2$, respectively. Likewise, $C(W^{+-})$ and $C(W^{++})$ will be computed as $[C(W^+)]^2$ and $2C(W^+) - [C(W^+)]^2$. Continuing this recursion leads to the Capacity martingales in Fig. 12.49.

The concentration to the extreme Capacities zero and one are already visible, but even more so in a histogram for the values at the rightmost stage shown in Fig. 12.50. In Fig. 12.51, the channels are sorted according to their Capacities.

When now comparing the numbering on the left input side of Fig. 12.48, which evolved from the recursive doubling of the number of involved channels, we recognize that it does not comply with the matrix

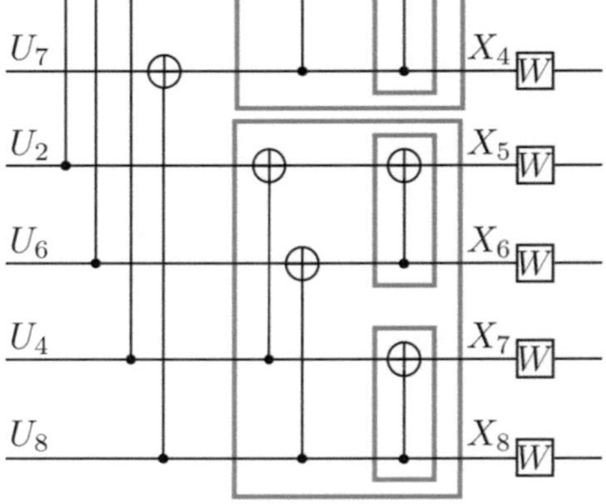

Fig. 12.48 W_8 polarization split

[13] Doob's martingale convergence theorems.

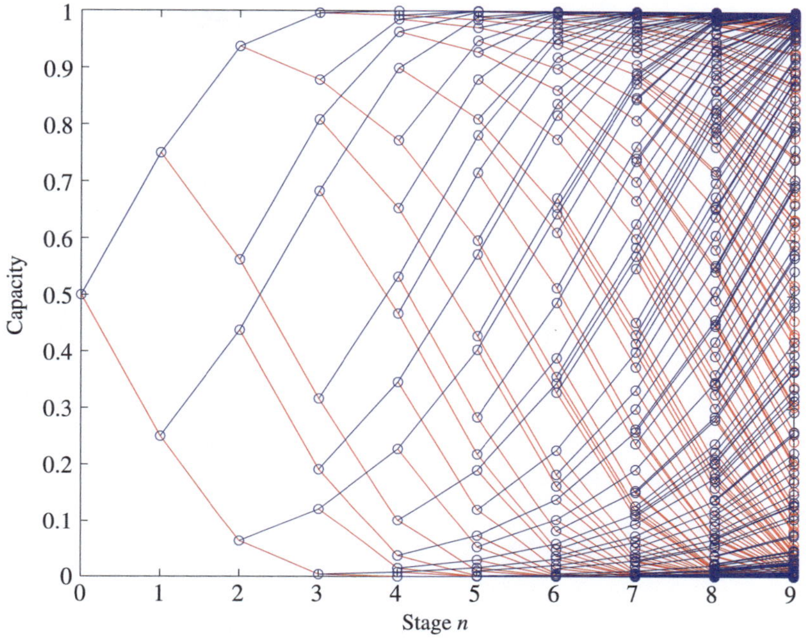

Fig. 12.49 Martingales for polarizing an erasure channel with an erasure probability of $\varepsilon = 1/2$

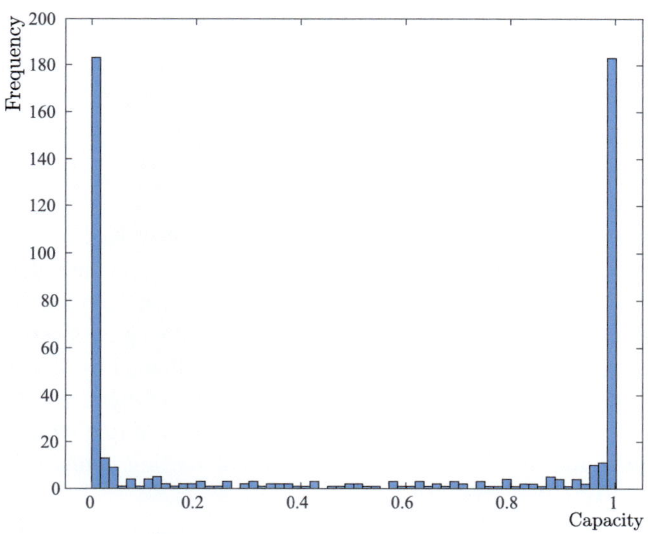

Fig. 12.50 Histogram for capacities at the rightmost stage of Fig. 12.50

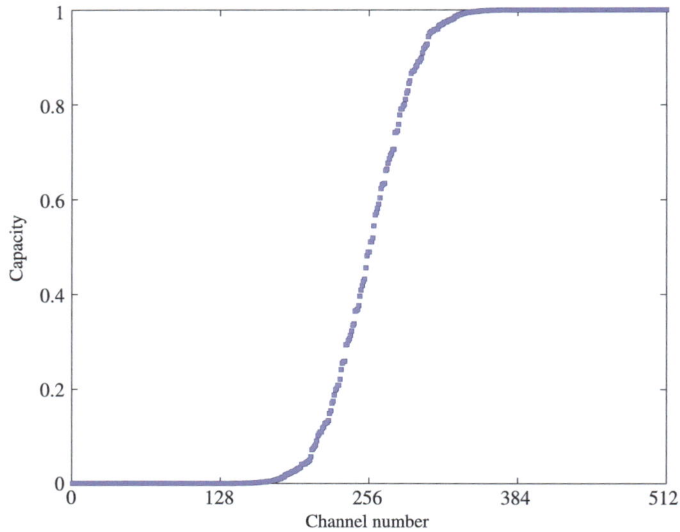

Fig. 12.51 Channels sorted according to their capacities

$$\mathbf{F}^{\otimes 3} = \left[\begin{array}{cccc|cccc} 1&0&0&0&0&0&0&0 \\ 1&1&0&0&0&0&0&0 \\ 1&0&1&0&0&0&0&0 \\ 1&1&1&1&0&0&0&0 \\ \hline 1&0&0&0&1&0&0&0 \\ 1&1&0&0&1&1&0&0 \\ 1&0&1&0&1&0&1&0 \\ 1&1&1&1&1&1&1&1 \end{array}\right], \tag{12.185}$$

but rather to a version after applying a permutation matrix $\mathbf{B}_8$ from the left to the operations of Fig. 12.48, the so-called bit-reversal permutation, the order in line with $\mathbf{F}^{\otimes 3}$ is obtained. This bit-reversal permutation is also known from the Cooley-Tukey FFT and results from resorting odd/even rows (or columns) recursively. This means in our example, first writing out the rows 1, 3, 5, 7, followed by 2, 4, 6, 8. This is recursively reshuffled as 1, 5, 3, 7 and 2, 6, 4, 8, respectively. This will realize an interchange of positions $2 \leftrightarrow 5$ and $4 \leftrightarrow 7$. This again is in line with reversing the LSB-MSB direction in a binary representation, but starting counting from 0, i.e., 000, 001, 010, 011, 100, 101, 110, 111.

Adding this bit-reversal permutation to Fig. 12.48 leads to Fig. 12.52, where we also marked the frozen bits with zeros and the remaining inputs are for non-systematic encoding. The frozen bit positions correspond to the lower Capacity values at $n = 3$ in Fig. 12.49.

We found that the "butterfly" structure in Fig. 12.52 without the bit-reversal input permutation can be expressed as $\mathbf{B}_8\mathbf{F}^{\otimes 3}$. We recall that with the transpose form of the FFT, where when moving from decimation in time to decimation in frequency or vice

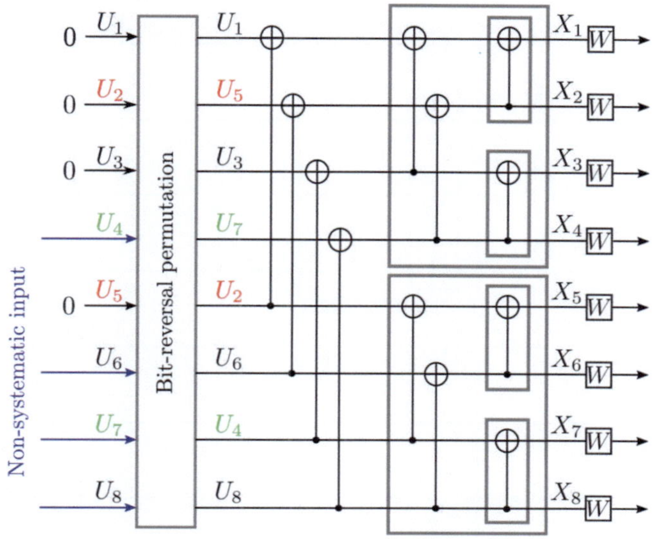

Fig. 12.52 W_8 polarization split together with bit-reversal input permutation

versa, the permutation is also moving to the opposite side, where row permutation becomes a column permutation or vice versa. We recognize that

$$\mathbf{B}_8 \mathbf{F}^{\otimes 3} \mathbf{B}_8^T = \mathbf{F}^{\otimes 3}. \tag{12.186}$$

We however note that a permutation towards the independent channels will not have any effect on the Capacities. We may turn the butterfly sequence around obtaining another equivalent encoder structure depicted in Fig. 12.53, which will later be simplified as a trellis-like graph for decoding.

12.9.2.2 Systematic Encoding of Polar Codes

So far the encoding that we described (see Figs. 12.52 and 12.53) is non-systematic. In [86], it is shown that taking the same bit positions on the channel side as we had for the non-frozen positions, a systematic encoding can be realized.

Let $\mathbf{F}_N = \mathbf{F}^{\otimes n}$ be the overall generator matrix, $\mathbf{u}_{\mathcal{A}}$ the non-frozen non-systematic input bits, $\mathbf{u}_{\mathcal{A}^c}$ the frozen non-systematic input bits, $\mathbf{x}_{\mathcal{B}}$ the systematic input bits, and $\mathbf{x}_{\mathcal{B}^c}$ the remaining parity bits at the output. In [86], the following relations are given.

$$\mathbf{x}_{\mathcal{B}} = \mathbf{u}_{\mathcal{A}} \mathbf{F}_{\mathcal{A}\mathcal{B}} + \mathbf{u}_{\mathcal{A}^c} \mathbf{F}_{\mathcal{A}^c\mathcal{B}} \tag{12.187}$$
$$\mathbf{x}_{\mathcal{B}^c} = \mathbf{u}_{\mathcal{A}} \mathbf{F}_{\mathcal{A}\mathcal{B}^c} + \mathbf{u}_{\mathcal{A}^c} \mathbf{F}_{\mathcal{A}^c\mathcal{B}^c} \tag{12.188}$$

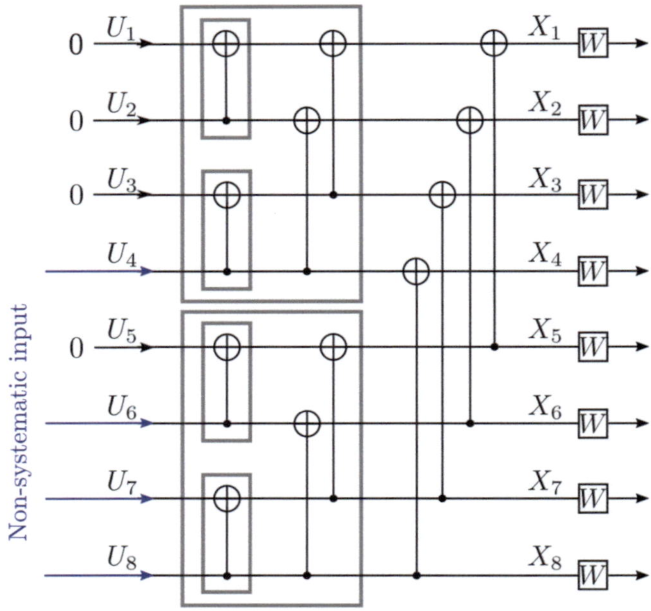

Fig. 12.53 W_8 polarization in transposed structure

$\mathbf{F}_{\mathcal{AB}}$ denotes the submatrix of $\mathbf{F}$ at the rows and columns specified by the sets $\mathcal{A}$ and $\mathcal{B}$, respectively. For a systematic encoding to exist, we need to be able to start from $\mathbf{x}_{\mathcal{B}}$ and obtain the non-frozen bits $\mathbf{u}_{\mathcal{A}}$ given the frozen ones $\mathbf{u}_{\mathcal{A}^c}$. From this, the parities $\mathbf{x}_{\mathcal{B}^c}$ would, of course, follow, too. From (12.187), we can solve for $\mathbf{u}_{\mathcal{A}}$ by

$$\mathbf{u}_{\mathcal{A}} = (\mathbf{x}_{\mathcal{B}} - \mathbf{u}_{\mathcal{A}^c}\mathbf{F}_{\mathcal{A}^c\mathcal{B}})(\mathbf{F}_{\mathcal{AB}})^{-1}. \tag{12.189}$$

Equation (12.188) will then deliver the parity $\mathbf{x}_{\mathcal{B}^c}$. This means, the matrix $\mathbf{F}_{\mathcal{AB}}$ has to have an inverse. Fortunately, $\mathbf{F}$ and all submatrices using the same selection set for rows and columns $\mathbf{F}_{\mathcal{AA}}$, i.e., $\mathcal{B} = \mathcal{A}$, are lower triangular matrices with ones on the main diagonal. This means, choosing the same positions for the non-frozen and systematic bits allows for systematic encoding. In [86], a recursive procedure with a complexity of $O(N \log N)$ is also outlined.

12.9.2.3 Successive Cancellation Decoding

We restrict ourselves to describe what Arıkan called successive cancellation decoding. This is not the best performing algorithm, but comes with the lowest complexity of $O(N \log N)$.

In Fig. 12.54, we start backward processing the upper part. The colored XOR operation would be expressed in Log-Likelihoods as in Eq. (12.38) or likewise (12.90),

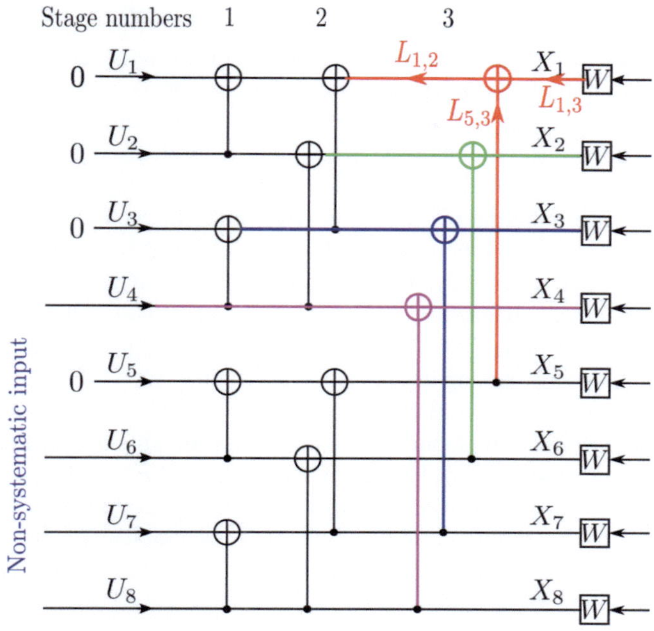

Fig. 12.54 Decoding along the polar code of length 8

i.e., in the form of

$$L_{1,2} = \tanh^{-1}\left[\tanh(L_{1,3}/2) \cdot \tanh(L_{5,3}/2)\right], \tag{12.190}$$

for the uppermost red XOR in LLR domain. All other colored parts follow likewise. Recursively, the resulting LLR values are now the input of the next stage to the left, continuing the process until ending up at U_1. This can now be hard decided according to the sign of the LLR. A hard decision would in LLR terms then be replaced by $\pm\infty$, i.e., assumed as perfectly known ± 1. This hard decision would, of course, not be carried out, if the bit was frozen. Then, instead, the frozen value would be inserted, which, when assumed to be zero would be equivalent to an LLR of $+\infty$. After having decided U_1 as $\hat{U}_1$, the leftmost upper XOR would now mean combining $\pm\infty$ with the LLR coming from the right to determine U_2. This combination is according to (12.38) formulated as

$$L_{U_2} = \text{sign}(L_{\hat{U}_1}) \cdot L_{1,1}. \tag{12.191}$$

Thereafter, U_2 is hard decided to become $\hat{U}_2$. Then, $\hat{U}_1$ and $\hat{U}_2$ are combined at the 1st stage XOR as a product of the corresponding ± 1 representation. Now, the 2nd stage XORs deliver hard decision/LLR combinations to process U_3 and U_4 in the same way.

Summarizing, left oriented operations at the beginning are the typical check-node or $\boxplus$ operations in combining LLRs. Decisions are taken on the left according to the sign of the incoming LLRs. Downward oriented processing combines hard decisions from the left with continuous LLRs from the right. Right oriented processing is forwarding hard decisions through the XORs, which are products in ± 1 representation.

In, e.g., Niu et al. [85], Fig. 12.54 is redrawn in a trellis fashion with added variable nodes also labeling the decoding steps with corresponding arrows. Also, tree representations are common, especially for introducing the so-called Simplified SC decoding [87] and Successive Cancellation List/Stack (SCL/SCS) decoding [88, 89]. List decoders are supported by additional CRC codes to select the corresponding decoding result from the list [90, 91]. Since the operations are the same as in an LDPC Tanner graph, message passing can be applied, as well.

To conclude the treatment of Polar codes, they are the first class of codes that can show with information theoretic means that they are able to reach Capacity by generating virtual good and bad channels. The complexity for encoding and decoding is of $O(N \log N)$. Turbo and LDPC coding come with a decoding complexity linear in N, however, the latter might lead to a higher $O(N^2)$ complexity at the transmitter, if the recursive encoding with a triangular H-matrix (Sect. 12.8.2) is not used.

12.10 Generalized Concatenated Codes (GCC)

Similar to set partitioning, where we partitioned a signal set into subsets, a code can be partitioned into sub-codes. Each partitioning can then be protected by some other codes. Such a partitioning scheme is shown in Fig. 12.55.[14]

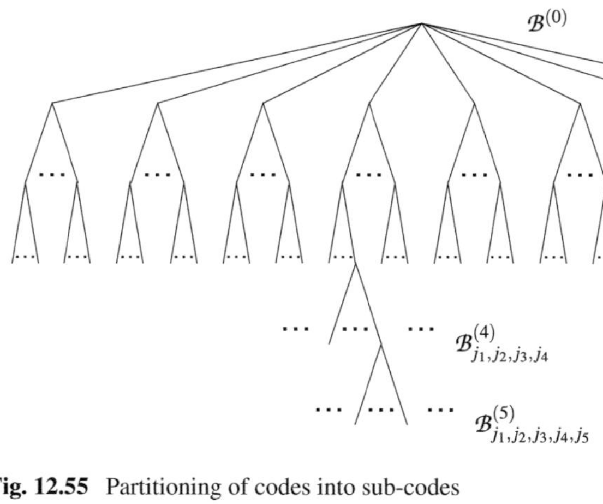

Fig. 12.55 Partitioning of codes into sub-codes

[14] The description of GC codes follows [92].

We have partitioned a code $\mathcal{B}^{(0)}$ into codes $\mathcal{B}^{(1)}_{j_1}$, $j_1 = 0, \ldots, \rho_1 - 1$ and also every code $\mathcal{B}^{(1)}_{j_1}$ into codes $\mathcal{B}^{(2)}_{j_1, j_2}$, $j_2 = 0, \ldots, \rho_2 - 1$, etc. Formally, we can write

$$\mathcal{B}^{(0)} = \cup_{j_1=0}^{\rho_1-1} \mathcal{B}^{(1)}_{j_1}, \qquad \mathcal{B}^{(1)}_{j_1} = \cup_{j_2=0}^{\rho_2-1} \mathcal{B}^{(2)}_{j_1, j_2} \cdots \tag{12.192}$$

The cardinality of the lth inner code is

$$\mathcal{K}_i^{(l)} = \prod_{\nu=l+1}^{r} \rho_\nu, \tag{12.193}$$

where r denotes the number of partitions. ρ_r is the number of code words in the last partition. The parameters of the codes $\mathcal{B}^{(l)}_{j_1, \ldots, j_l}$ are thus $(N_i, \prod_{j=l+1}^{r} \rho_j, d_l)$, with the minimum Hamming distances $d_0 \leq d_1 \leq d_2 \leq \cdots \leq d_r$. A codeword in $\mathcal{B}^{(0)}$ is specified by the partition indices $b_{j_1, j_2, \ldots, j_r}$, $j_1 = 0, \ldots, \rho_1 - 1$, $\ldots$, $j_r = 0, \ldots, \rho_r - 1$ according to the sub-codes $\mathcal{B}^{(1)}_{j_1}$, $\mathcal{B}^{(2)}_{j_1, j_2}$, etc.

Each partitioning is protected by an outer code $\mathcal{A}^{(l)}$ over the alphabet $GF(\rho_l)$ with parameters $(N_a, \mathcal{K}_a^{(l)}, \delta_l)$. If we write the codewords of the outer codes as rows of a matrix

$$\begin{bmatrix} a_1^{(1)} & a_2^{(1)} & a_3^{(1)} & \ldots & a_{N_a}^{(1)} \\ a_1^{(2)} & a_2^{(2)} & a_3^{(2)} & \ldots & a_{N_a}^{(2)} \\ a_1^{(3)} & a_2^{(3)} & a_3^{(3)} & \ldots & a_{N_a}^{(3)} \\ \vdots & \vdots & \vdots & & \vdots \\ a_1^{(r)} & a_2^{(r)} & a_3^{(r)} & \ldots & a_{N_a}^{(r)} \end{bmatrix}, \tag{12.194}$$

the columns select the codewords from the inner code $\mathcal{B}^{(0)}$ according to the given partitioning. **Generalized Concatenated Codes** as we described them with the $N_i \times N_a$ matrix, have once been proposed by Blokh, Zyablov, and Zinoviev [93–95].

Theorem 12.6 *A generalized concatenated code with outer codes $\mathcal{A}^{(l)}$ and inner codes $\mathcal{B}^{(l)}_{j_1, \ldots, j_l}$, $l = 0, \ldots, r$ has the parameters*

$$(N_a N_i, \prod_{l=1}^{r} \mathcal{K}_a^{(l)}, d_{Hm} \geq \min_l \{\delta_l d_l\})$$

Proof We only need to prove the minimum distance. Let us assume that two code matrices (12.194) $\mathbf{A}$ and $\mathbf{\Lambda}$ differ from the μth row on. Due to the minimum distance of the outer codes, this would then be the case at least δ_μ positions in the μth row. The codewords of the inner codes that correspond to the numbers $b_{j_1, j_2, \ldots, j_{\mu-1}, \alpha}$ and $b_{j_1, j_2, \ldots, j_{\mu-1}, \beta}$ $(\alpha \neq \beta)$, both belong to the sub-code $\mathcal{B}^{(\mu-1)}_{j_1, j_2, \ldots, j_{\mu-1}}$ with the minimum distance d_μ. Hence, the binary codewords of the GC code differ at $d_\mu \delta_\mu$ positions. □

Example 12.3 [92] Let $\mathcal{B}^{(0)}$ represent all binary vectors of length 4, i.e., we have code parameters (4,16,1). $\mathcal{B}^{(0)}$ can be partitioned into two (4,8,2) 'even' ($\mathcal{B}_0^{(1)}$) and 'odd' ($\mathcal{B}_1^{(1)}$) parity-check codes, which can in turn be represented as the 4 cosets of the (4,2,4) repetition code {(0000), (1111)}:

'Even' (4,8,2)	'Odd' (4,8,2)
0000	0001
1111	1110
0011	0010
1100	1101
0110	0100
1001	1011
1010	1000
0101	0111

The partition parameters are

$$r = 3, \quad \rho_1 = 2, \quad \rho_2 = 4, \quad \rho_3 = 2.$$

As outer codes, we use

$$\begin{aligned} \mathcal{A}^{(1)} &= (8, 2, 8)\text{-}code\ over\ GF(2), \\ \mathcal{A}^{(2)} &= (8, 4^4, 4)\text{-}code\ over\ GF(2^2), \\ \mathcal{A}^{(3)} &= (8, 2^7, 2)\text{-}code\ over\ GF(2). \end{aligned}$$

The resulting GC code has parameters $(32, 2^{16}, 8)$, where we again specified the cardinality instead of the number of information symbols.

For quite some time before the introduction of iterative decoding, code constructions based on GC codes belonged to the best known codes. The construction is not restricted only to the concatenation of codes. An 'inner code' can be an arbitrary set that can be partitioned into subsets, e.g., also a modulation alphabet is a suitable choice. In this special case, the so-called multilevel codes are obtained. They are described in some detail in Chap. 17. Multilevel codes may ease the understanding of GC codes.

References

1. S. Reiger, "Codes for the correction of 'clustered' errors," *IRE Transactions on Information Theory*, vol. 6, no. 1, pp. 16–21, March 1960.
2. G. Forney, "Burst-correcting codes for the classic bursty channel," *IEEE Transactions on Communication Technology*, vol. 19, no. 5, pp. 772–781, October 1971.
3. J. Ramsey, "Realization of optimum interleavers," *IEEE Transactions on Information Theory*, vol. 16, no. 3, pp. 338–345, May 1970.

4. M. Blaum, H. van Tilborg, and P. Farrell, "A class of burst error-correcting array codes (corresp.)," *IEEE Transactions on Information Theory*, vol. 32, no. 6, pp. 836–839, November 1986.
5. H. C. A. van Tilborg, "An overview of recent results in the theory of burst-correcting codes," in *Coding Theory and Applications, 3rd International Colloquium, Toulon, France, November 2–4, 1988, Proceedings*, 1988, pp. 164–184. [Online]. Available: https://doi.org/10.1007/BFb0019855
6. W. Henkel and H. Y. Chung, "New filling procedure to reduce delay of burst-error correcting array codes," *Electronics Letters*, vol. 30, no. 6, pp. 465–466, March 1994.
7. A. J. Viterbi, J. K. Wolf, E. Zehavi, and R. Padovani, "A pragmatic approach to trellis-coded modulation," *IEEE Communications Magazine*, vol. 27, no. 7, pp. 11–19, 1989.
8. J. K. Wolf and E. Zehavi, "p^2 codes: pragmatic trellis codes utilizing punctured convolutional codes," *IEEE Communications Magazine*, vol. 33, no. 2, pp. 94–99, 1995.
9. CCSDS, "Historical document telemetry channel coding, CCSDS 101.0-B-4, Blue Book, Issue 4," May 1999, https://public.ccsds.org/Pubs/101x0b4s.pdf.
10. CCSDS, "Historical document tm channel coding profiles, CCSDS 131.4-M-1, Magenta Book," July 2011, https://public.ccsds.org/Pubs/131x4m1s.pdf.
11. CCSDS, "TC synchronization and channel coding – summary of concept and rationale, CCSDS 230.1-G-2, Green Book," July 2012, https://public.ccsds.org/Pubs/230x1g2e1.pdf.
12. C. Berrou, A. Glavieux, and P. Thitimajshima, "Near Shannon limit error-correcting coding and decoding: Turbo-codes. 1," in *Proceedings of ICC '93 - IEEE International Conference on Communications*, vol. 2, May 1993, pp. 1064–1070 vol. 2.
13. J. Hagenauer, E. Offer, and L. Papke, "Iterative decoding of binary block and convolutional codes," *IEEE Transactions on Information Theory*, vol. 42, no. 2, pp. 429–445, March 1996.
14. G. Kramer and S. ten Brink, "Turbo codes and iterative decoding (course notes)," May 2003.
15. D. Divsalar and F. Pollara, "Turbo codes for PCS applications," in *Proceedings IEEE International Conference on Communications ICC '95*, vol. 1, June 1995, pp. 54–59 vol.1.
16. Matlab, "High rate convolutions codes for turbo coding," https://de.mathworks.com/help/comm/ug/high-rate-convolutional-codes-for-turbo-coding.html, R2023a.
17. D. Divsalar, H. Jin, and R. McEliece, "Coding theorems for 'turbo-like' codes," in *Allerton Conf. on Communication, Control, and Computing*, 1998, pp. 201–210.
18. B. Sklar, "A primer on turbo code concepts," *IEEE Communications Magazine*, vol. 35, no. 12, pp. 94–102, 1997.
19. B. Vucetic and J. Yuan, *Turbo Codes: Principles and Applications*. Norwell, MA, USA: Kluwer Academic Publishers, 2000.
20. C. Heegard and S. B. Wicker, *Turbo Coding*. Norwell, MA, USA: Kluwer Academic Publishers, 1999.
21. M. R. Soleymani, Y. Gao, and U. Vilaipornsawai, *Turbo Coding for Satellite and Wireless Communications*. Springer Publishing Company, Incorporated, 2013.
22. M. Jezequel and R. Pyndiah, *Turbo Codes: Error-Correcting Codes of Widening Application (Innovative Technology Series: Information Systems and Networks)*. Kogan Page, 2003.
23. L. Hanzo, T. H. Liew, and B. L. Yeap, *Turbo Coding, Turbo Equalisation and Space-Time Coding for Transmission over Fading Channels*. Wiley, 2002.
24. A. Giulietti, B. Bougard, and L. van der Perre, *Turbo Codes: Desirable and Designable*. Kluwer, 2004.
25. S. A. Barbulescu, "What a wonderfol turbo world – CD," http://people.myoffice.net.au/~abarbulescu/. [Online]. Available: http://people.myoffice.net.au/~abarbulescu/
26. S. Benedetto, D. Divsalar, and J. Hagenauer, "Guest editorial concatenated coding techniques and iterative decoding: Sailing toward channel capacity," *IEEE Journal on Selected Areas in Communications*, vol. 16, no. 2, pp. 137–139, 1998.
27. P. H. Siegel, D. Divsalar, E. Eleftheriou, J. Hagenauer, D. Rowitch, and W. H. Tranter, "Guest editorial the turbo principle: from theory to practice," *IEEE Journal on Selected Areas in Communications*, vol. 19, no. 5, pp. 793–799, May 2001.
28. P. H. Siegel, D. Divsalar, E. Elepftheriou, J. Hagenauer, and D. Rowitch, "Guest editorial - the turbo principle: from theory to practice II," *IEEE Journal on Selected Areas in Communications*, vol. 19, no. 9, pp. 1657–1661, Sep. 2001.

29. B. J. Frey, R. Koetter, G. D. Forney, F. R. Kschischang, R. J. McEliece, and D. A. Spielman, "Introduction to the special issue on codes on graphs and iterative algorithms," *IEEE Transactions on Information Theory*, vol. 47, no. 2, pp. 493–497, 2001.
30. M. Fossorier and S. Olcer, "Guest editorial - capacity approaching codes, iterative decoding algorithms, and their applications," *IEEE Communications Magazine*, vol. 41, no. 8, pp. 100–101, 2003.
31. A. Kavcic, J. M. F. Moura, and V. Bhagavatula, "Iterative, soft signal processing for digital communications - from the guest editors," *IEEE Signal Processing Magazine*, vol. 21, no. 1, pp. 26–108, 2004.
32. ENST (IMT Atlantique), International Symposium on Turbo Codes & Related Topics, renamed as International Symposium on Topics in Coding, (ISTC), http://conferences.telecom-bretagne.eu/turbocodes/.
33. S. ten Brink, "Convergence behavior of iteratively decoded parallel concatenated codes," *IEEE Transactions on Communications*, vol. 49, no. 10, pp. 1727–1737, 2001.
34. J. Hagenauer, "The EXIT chart - introduction to extrinsic information transfer in iterative processing," in *2004 12th European Signal Processing Conference*, Sep. 2004, pp. 1541–1548.
35. A. Ashikhmin, G. Kramer, and S. ten Brink, "Code rate and the area under extrinsic information transfer curves," in *Proceedings IEEE International Symposium on Information Theory,*, June 2002, p. 115.
36. A. Ashikhmin, G. Kramer, and S. ten Brink, "Extrinsic information transfer functions: model and erasure channel properties," *IEEE Transactions on Information Theory*, vol. 50, no. 11, pp. 2657–2673, 2004.
37. R. G. Gallager, *Low-Density Parity-Check Codes*. M.I.T. Press, 1963. [Online]. Available: http://justice.mit.edu/people/pubs/ldpc.ps
38. D. J. C. MacKay and R. M. Neal, "Good codes based on very sparse matrices," in *Cryptography and Coding*, C. Boyd, Ed. Berlin, Heidelberg: Springer Berlin Heidelberg, 1995, pp. 100–111.
39. D. MacKay, "Good error-correcting codes based on very sparse matrices," *IEEE Transactions on Information Theory*, vol. 45, no. 2, pp. 399–431, 1999.
40. R. Tanner, "A recursive approach to low complexity codes," *IEEE Transactions on Information Theory*, vol. 27, no. 5, pp. 533–547, Sep. 1981.
41. B. J. Frey, F. R. Kschischang, H. andrea Loeliger, and N. Wiberg, "Factor graphs and algorithms," in *Proc. 35th Allerton Conf. on Communications, Control, and Computing, (Allerton*, 1998, pp. 666–680.
42. H. A. Loeliger, "An introduction to factor graphs," *IEEE Signal Processing Magazine*, vol. 21, no. 1, pp. 28–41, 2004.
43. H.-A. Loeliger, "An introduction to factor graphs," http://people.binf.ku.dk/~thamelry/MLSB08/hal.pdf, Copenhagen, 2008.
44. T. Richardson and R. Urbanke, *Modern Coding Theory*. New York, NY, USA: Cambridge University Press, 2008. [Online]. Available: https://documents.epfl.ch/groups/i/ip/ipg/www/2010-2011/Statistical_Physics_for_Communication_and_Computer_Science/mct-new.pdf
45. Changyan Di, D. Proietti, I. E. Telatar, T. J. Richardson, and R. L. Urbanke, "Finite-length analysis of low-density parity-check codes on the binary erasure channel," *IEEE Transactions on Information Theory*, vol. 48, no. 6, pp. 1570–1579, 2002.
46. B. Vasić, S. K. Chilappagari, D. V. Nguyen, and S. K. Planjery, "Trapping set ontology," in *Proceedings of the 47th annual Allerton conference on Communication, control, and computing*, ser. Allerton'09. Piscataway, NJ, USA: IEEE Press, 2009, pp. 1–7. [Online]. Available: http://dl.acm.org/citation.cfm?id=1793974.1793976
47. T. Richardson, "Error-floors of LDPC codes," in *Proceedings of the 41st Allerton Conference on Communication, Control and Computing*, 2003, pp. 1426–1435.
48. P. O. Vontobel and R. Koetter, "Graph-cover decoding and finite-length analysis of message-passing iterative decoding of LDPC codes," 2005.
49. L. Dolecek, Z. Zhang, V. Anantharam, M. J. Wainwright, and B. Nikolic, "Analysis of absorbing sets and fully absorbing sets of array-based LDPC codes," *IEEE Transactions on Information Theory*, vol. 56, no. 1, pp. 181–201, 2010.
50. G. Forney, "Codes on graphs: normal realizations," *IEEE Transactions on Information Theory*, vol. 47, no. 2, pp. 520–548, 2001.

51. S.-Y. Chung, T. J. Richardson, and R. L. Urbanke, "Analysis of sum-product decoding of low-density parity-check codes using a gaussian approximation," *IEEE Transactions on Information Theory*, vol. 47, no. 2, pp. 657–670, 2001.
52. T. Richardson, M. Shokrollahi, and R. Urbanke, "Design of capacity-approaching irregular low-density parity-check codes," *IEEE Transactions on Information Theory*, vol. 47, no. 2, pp. 619–637, 2001.
53. D. Declercq, *Optimisation et performances des codes LDPC pour des canaux non-standards (in French)*. Habilitation à diriger des recherches: Université de Cergy-Pontoise, 2003.
54. W. Ryan and S. Lin, *Channel Codes: Classical and Modern*. Cambridge University Press, 2009. [Online]. Available: https://books.google.de/books?id=0gwqxBU_t-QC
55. J. Etesami and W. Henkel, "LDPC code construction for wireless physical-layer key reconciliation," in *2012 1st IEEE International Conference on Communications in China (ICCC)*, 2012, pp. 208–213.
56. N. von Deetzen, *Modern Coding Schemes for Unequal Error Protection*, ser. Communications and coding series. (PhD Thesis), 2009. [Online]. Available: https://books.google.de/books?id=N-9SPgAACAAJ
57. S. Lin and D. J. Costello, *Error control coding: fundamentals and applications*. Upper Saddle River, NJ: Pearson/Prentice Hall, 2004.
58. X.-Y. Hu, E. Eleftheriou, and D. M. Arnold, "Regular and irregular progressive edge-growth Tanner graphs," *IEEE Transactions on Information Theory*, vol. 51, no. 1, pp. 386–398, 2005.
59. X.-Y. Hu, E. Eleftheriou, and D. M. Arnold, "Progressive edge-growth Tanner graphs," in *GLOBECOM'01. IEEE Global Telecommunications Conference (Cat. No.01CH37270)*, vol. 2, 2001, pp. 995–1001.
60. H. Xiao and A. Banihashemi, "Improved progressive-edge-growth (PEG) construction of irregular LDPC codes," in *IEEE Global Telecommunications Conference, 2004. GLOBECOM '04.*, vol. 1, 2004, pp. 489–492 Vol. 1.
61. T. Tian, C. R. Jones, J. D. Villasenor, and R. D. Wesel, "Selective avoidance of cycles in irregular LDPC code construction," *IEEE Transactions on Communications*, vol. 52, no. 8, pp. 1242–1247, 2004.
62. D. Vukobratovic and V. Senk, "Generalized ACE constrained progressive edge-growth LDPC code design," *IEEE Communications Letters*, vol. 12, no. 1, pp. 32–34, 2008.
63. A. Abbasfar, D. Divsalar, and K. Yao, "Accumulate-repeat-accumulate codes," *IEEE Transactions on Communications*, vol. 55, no. 4, pp. 692–702, 2007.
64. D. Divsalar et al., "ARA type protograph codes," https://ntrs.nasa.gov/archive/nasa/casi.ntrs.nasa.gov/20080020436.pdf, 2008, uS Patent 7,343,539 B2.
65. D. Divsalar, S. Dolinar, and C. Jones, "Construction of protograph LDPC codes with linear minimum distance," in *2006 IEEE International Symposium on Information Theory*, 2006, pp. 664–668.
66. CCSDS, "Low density parity check codes for use in near-earth and deep space applications," The Consultative Committee for Space Data Systems, Orange book, Issue 2, Tech. Rep. 131.1-0-2, 2007.
67. Y. Fang, G. Bi, Y. L. Guan, and F. C. M. Lau, "A survey on protograph LDPC codes and their applications," *IEEE Communications Surveys Tutorials*, vol. 17, no. 4, pp. 1989–2016, 2015.
68. A. Jimenez Felstrom and K. Zigangirov, "Time-varying periodic convolutional codes with low-density parity-check matrix," *IEEE Transactions on Information Theory*, vol. 45, no. 6, pp. 2181–2191, 1999.
69. M. Lentmaier, A. Sridharan, D. J. Costello, and K. S. Zigangirov, "Iterative decoding threshold analysis for LDPC convolutional codes," *IEEE Transactions on Information Theory*, vol. 56, no. 10, pp. 5274–5289, 2010.
70. S. Kudekar, T. Richardson, and R. Urbanke, "Threshold saturation via spatial coupling: Why convolutional LDPC ensembles perform so well over the BEC," in *2010 IEEE International Symposium on Information Theory*, 2010, pp. 684–688.
71. D. J. Costello, Jr., "Spatially coupled LDPC codes," European School of Information Theory (ESIT), https://www.itsoc.org/conferences/schools/past-schools/european-school-2017/program-1/esit17costelloslides.pdf, 2017.

72. H. V. B. Neto, "Analysis and design of modern coding schemes for unequal error protection and joint source-channel coding," Ph.D. dissertation, Jacobs University, Shaker, 2012. [Online]. Available: https://nbn-resolving.org/urn:nbn:de:101:1-201503013317
73. T. Richardson and R. Urbanke, "*Multi-Edge Type LDPC Codes*," http://infoscience.epfl.ch/record/95821, https://www.researchgate.net/publication/37439748_Multi-edge_type_LDPC_codes, EPFL, 2004.
74. D. Slepian and J. Wolf, "Noiseless coding of correlated information sources," *IEEE Transactions on Information Theory*, vol. 19, no. 4, pp. 471–480, 1973.
75. M. C. Davey and D. MacKay, "Low-density parity check codes over GF(q)," *IEEE Communications Letters*, vol. 2, no. 6, pp. 165–167, 1998.
76. L. Barnault and D. Declercq, "Fast decoding algorithm for LDPC over GF($2q$)," in *Proceedings 2003 IEEE Information Theory Workshop (Cat. No.03EX674)*, 2003, pp. 70–73.
77. D. Declercq and M. Fossorier, "Decoding algorithms for nonbinary LDPC codes over GF(q)," *IEEE Transactions on Communications*, vol. 55, no. 4, pp. 633–643, 2007.
78. K. Deka, "*Investigations on binary and non-binary LDPC codes*," Ph.D. dissertation, IIT Guwahati, Guwahati - 781039, Assam, India, 2016.
79. Xiangming Li and M. R. Soleymani, "A proof of the Hadamard transform decoding of the belief propagation algorithm for LDPCC over GF(q)," in *IEEE 60th Vehicular Technology Conference, 2004. VTC2004-Fall. 2004*, vol. 4, 2004, pp. 2518–2519 Vol. 4.
80. E. Arıkan, "Channel polarization: A method for constructing capacity-achieving codes for symmetric binary-input memoryless channels," *IEEE Transactions on Information Theory*, vol. 55, no. 7, pp. 3051–3073, 2009.
81. E. Arıkan, "Source polarization," in *2010 IEEE International Symposium on Information Theory*, 2010, pp. 899–903.
82. E. Arıkan, "Polar Codes I," https://www.youtube.com/watch?v=PNBFUV-ZetY, Simons Institute, UC Berkeley, 2015.
83. E. Arıkan, "Polar Codes II," https://www.youtube.com/watch?v=ODCOzvPIAUw, Simons Institute, UC Berkeley, 2015.
84. E. Arıkan, "Polar Codes III," https://www.youtube.com/watch?v=Xqn-iQ259J0, Simons Institute, UC Berkeley, 2015.
85. K. Niu, K. Chen, J. Lin, and Q. T. Zhang, "Polar codes: Primary concepts and practical decoding algorithms," *IEEE Communications Magazine*, vol. 52, no. 7, pp. 192–203, 2014.
86. E. Arıkan, "Systematic polar coding," *IEEE Communications Letters*, vol. 15, no. 8, pp. 860–862, 2011.
87. A. Alamdar-Yazdi and F. R. Kschischang, "A simplified successive-cancellation decoder for polar codes," *IEEE Communications Letters*, vol. 15, no. 12, pp. 1378–1380, 2011.
88. I. Tal and A. Vardy, "List decoding of polar codes," *IEEE Transactions on Information Theory*, vol. 61, no. 5, pp. 2213–2226, 2015.
89. K. Niu and K. Chen, "Stack decoding of polar codes," *Electronics Letters*, vol. 48, pp. 695–697(2), 2012. [Online]. Available: https://digital-library.theiet.org/content/journals/10.1049/el.2012.1459
90. K. Niu and K. Chen, "CRC-aided decoding of polar codes," *IEEE Communications Letters*, vol. 16, no. 10, pp. 1668–1671, 2012.
91. B. Li, H. Shen, and D. Tse, "An adaptive successive cancellation list decoder for polar codes with cyclic redundancy check," *IEEE Communications Letters*, vol. 16, no. 12, pp. 2044–2047, 2012.
92. F. MacWilliams and N. Sloane, *The Theory of Error-Correcting Codes*, 5th ed. Amsterdam: North-holland Publishing Company, 1986.
93. E. L. Blokh and V. Zyablov, "Generalized concatenated codes," *Problemy Peredachi Informatsii*, vol. 10, 07 1974.
94. V. A. Zinoviev, "Generalized concatenated codes for channels with error bursts and independent errors," *Problemy Peredachi Informatsii*, vol. 17, no. 4, pp. 53–56, 1981.
95. V. A. Zinoviev, V. V. Zyablov, and S. L. Portnoy, "Concatenated methods for construction and decoding of codes in Euclidean space," *USSR Academy of Science, IPPI (preprint)*, pp. 53–56, 1987.

Chapter 13
Network and Rateless Codes

> Networking is more about farming than it is about hunting.
> It's about cultivating relationships.
>
> Ivan Misner

13.1 Deterministic and Random Network Coding

This section will only give a glimpse of network coding and some references. Network coding replaces standard routing by applying more elaborate functions than simple packet forwarding at network nodes. Nevertheless, we are starting from point-to-point routing in networks, especially, regarding the maximum information flow in networks. The maximum flow can be determined by the Ford-Fulkerson algorithm [1], which is a greedy method choosing paths along edges reserving the bottleneck Capacity, but also introducing a reverse edge for such selected flow to be able to later modify them on edges again to finally find the optimum maximum flow. Since there is a manifold of descriptions of the algorithm available online, we will not explain the algorithm in detail in here.

An important theorem is the so-called Max-Flow Min-Cut Theorem [2].

Theorem 13.1 (Max-Flow Min-Cut Theorem) *The maximum value of a flow from source to sink is equal to the minimum Capacity over all cuts between source and sink.*

For multicast situations, where multiple users are supposed to receive a set of messages, in 2000, Ahlswede, Cai, Li, and Yeung initiated the work on network coding [3] with general operations at network nodes. This was specialized to linear network coding by Li et al. [4]. There, especially the proof is provided that linear

W. Henkel, *Channel Coding*, Signals and Communication Technology,
https://doi.org/10.1007/978-3-032-08236-7_13

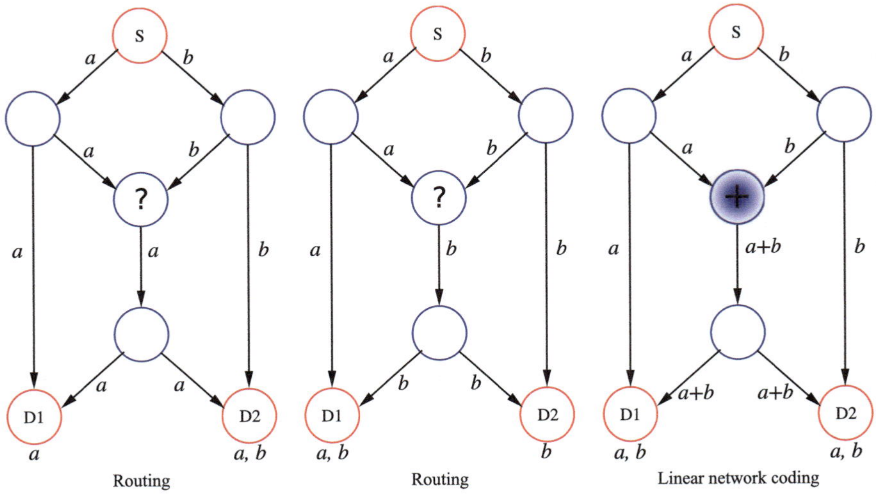

Fig. 13.1 The butterfly network

Fig. 13.2 Linear network coding at a relay

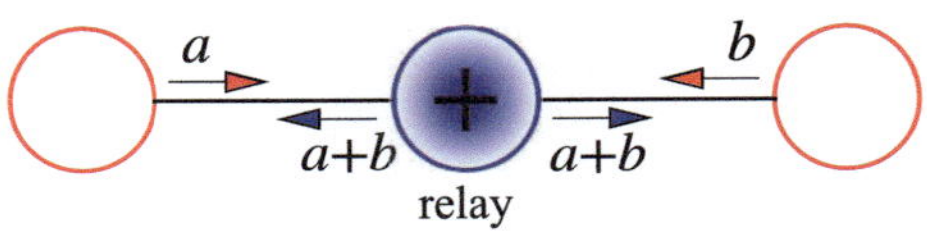

combinations of packets at nodes can provide the max flow to all destinations. Linear network coding was initially thought to be deterministic, i.e., chosen to be constant for a certain network topology and multicast situation. It reduced the load on the network while providing the maximum flow to the end nodes.

The typical example shown for the efficient use of network coding is the butterfly network in Fig. 13.1. Here we first show routing options not fulfilling the maximum flow to the end nodes, whereas a simple XOR at one node provides the maximum flow to both destinations D1 and D2. Both these destination nodes have to apply linear operations again (XOR) to solve for the individual messages.

Another simple is certainly a relay in the middle as shown in Fig. 13.2, which should forward two packages at the same time. This is realized by XOR-ing them and sending them to both end nodes simultaneously, allowing to XOR the own data packet out again. Instead of an XOR, i.e., a modulo-2 sum, one can, of course, apply a usual sum and apply this scheme over real or complex numbers, requiring to subtract own messages at the end nodes.

The key to network coding is to provide a global encoding leading to a system of equations that is non-singular and hence one can solve for the original data packages. The given examples were based summations over GF(2), i.e., simple binary operations. However, bigger Galois fields offer more possibilities to ensure that the system of equations is not singular. Typically, one uses an extension field of the binaries. Kötter and Médard moved to algebraic framework for a more thorough treatment of

Capacity issues, also discussing robustness in case of missing packets to a node and also delay issues, while many works had assumed "delay-free" networks.

Deterministic network coding requires a centralized or local algorithm to determine the coding nodes, which will not be required when just doing linear combinations with random factors (random linear network coding, RLNC) using some bigger Galois field. This, however, requires to keep track of the coefficients on certain packets to know the final set of equations. Ho, Médard et al. proposed random linear network coding in 2006 [5], which does not need a central infrastructure, but a packet header needs to additionally provide a field for factors that also need to be updated at every processing node. This can be realized by initializing some vector as unit vectors prepended (or attached) to the data packet. At the receiving nodes, individual factors will then show up in those fields. The overhead needed may be significant and header compression techniques may be applied.

Network coding comes with an inherent security against eavesdropping (wiretapping). Already the middle edge containing $a + b$ in Fig. 13.1 is secured by not showing a or b individually. Cai and Yeung address security issues already in 2002 in [6]. Feldman et al. continued the work in 2004 in [7] proposing a matrix operation on a vector concatenating an information and a random part where the number of components of the latter has to exceed the number of wiretapped edges. The matrix is essentially mixing information and random components additionally to the network coding operations.

Probably, Cai and Young [8–10] started looking into error correction first focusing on the input alphabet size deriving network coding Hamming and Gilbert-Varshamov bounds. An interesting and simple approach comes with random linear network coding proposed by Lun et al. [11] for links with erasures, i.e., packet loss. Here, redundancy is not just added at the source as a point-to-point solution, just as known from standard error correcting codes. Instead, more random linear combinations of stored packages are produced and forwarded at intermediate nodes, adjusting the required redundancy to the individual link qualities. As long as sufficient linear combinations arrive at the destinations, Gaussian elimination can then obtain the original messages.

Applying random linear combinations at the source, only, leads to rateless codes discussed in the following section.

For some tutorials on network coding, the reader is referred to [12–15].

13.2 Rateless Codes

Erasure-correcting rateless codes[1] first appeared under the name Tornado codes in 1997/1998 [17, 18], later followed by a more commonly known paper by Luby in 2002 which termed the name Luby Transform (LT) codes [19]. An extension were so-called Raptor codes [20–22]. Together with Online codes in [23] those codes are

[1] This section on rateless codes is to a large extent taken from the thesis of a former PhD student [16].

summarized under the class of so-called rateless codes. Rateless codes are particularly suitable for the transmission of data through channels that can be represented by the binary erasure channel (packet loss) with unknown erasure probabilities, a situation where traditional erasure correcting codes turn out to be suboptimal. These codes are termed "rateless", since the source will, in principle, continue sending random combinations of bits of packets, thereby increasing the codeword length to infinity for a certain fixed number of information bits (packets). Practically, one will, of course, set some limit. Rateless codes are also very interesting for multicast transmission, since they eliminate the requirement for retransmission.

13.2.1 LT Codes

The **encoding algorithm** for LT codes [19] can be described as follows. Suppose we like to encode a message composed of k input symbols. Each output symbol is formed by first determining its degree i according to a degree distribution $\rho(x) = \sum_{i=1}^{k} \rho_i x^i$, where ρ_i denotes the probability of i being chosen. The output symbol is then formed choosing i input symbols uniformly and at random and performing an XOR operation on them. The process is repeated until a sufficient number of output symbols $n = \gamma k$ arrives at the receiver. The quantity $\gamma \geq 1$ is called the overhead. We can describe the formation of an output symbol following the LT encoding in a step by step manner as follows:

1. Randomly choose the output symbol degree i from the degree distribution $\rho(x)$.
2. Choose uniformly and at random i symbols among the original k input symbols.
3. Form the output symbol performing the bit-wise exclusive-or of the chosen i symbols.

The encoding procedure can be depicted as a bipartite graph with k variable nodes and n check nodes. Figure 13.3 shows the bipartite graph resulting from the encoding of $k = 8$ input symbols into $n = 10$ output symbols ($\gamma = 10/8$). To be applied degree distributions for optimizing data recover are introduced in [19], under the names "Ideal/Robust Soliton Distribution."

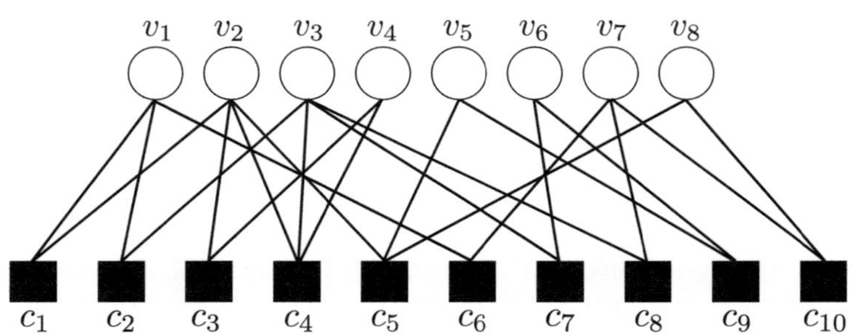

Fig. 13.3 Factor graph representing the result of LT encoding for a code with $k = 8$ and $\gamma = 10/8$

The **decoding algorithm** of LT codes can easily be described with the help of the graph induced by the encoding as follows

1. Find an output symbol c_j, for $j = 1, \ldots, n$, that is connected to only one input symbol v_i. In case there is no output symbol fulfilling this condition, the decoding is halted and more output symbols will be required for successful decoding.
   a. Determine v_i as $v_i = c_j$,
   b. Add the value of v_i to all its neighboring output symbols,
   c. Remove v_i together with all edges emanating from it from the graph.
2. Repeat (1) until every v_i, for $i = 1, \ldots, k$, is recovered.

Note that it is supposed here that the decoder knows the degree and the set of neighbors of each output symbol. Strategies to accomplish this can be found in [19].

Raptor codes add a precoder to improve the successful recovery probability. RaptorQ codes denote a systematic Raptor code. They are used in standards like IETF RFC 5053 [24] and IETF RFC 6330 [25], respectively. DVB-H IPDC, DVB-IPTV are further standards where such codes were adopted.

References

1. L. R. Ford and D. R. Fulkerson, "Maximal flow through a network," *Canadian Journal of Mathematics*, vol. 8, p. 399–404, 1956.
2. G. B. Dantzig and D. R. Fulkerson, "On the max flow min cut theorem of networks," 1955.
3. R. Ahlswede, Ning Cai, S. . R. Li, and R. W. Yeung, "Network information flow," *IEEE Transactions on Information Theory*, vol. 46, no. 4, pp. 1204–1216, 2000.
4. S.-Y. R. Li, R. W. Yeung, and Ning Cai, "Linear network coding," *IEEE Transactions on Information Theory*, vol. 49, no. 2, pp. 371–381, 2003.
5. T. Ho, M. Médard, R. Koetter, D. R. Karger, M. Effros, J. Shi, and B. Leong, "A random linear network coding approach to multicast," *IEEE Transactions on Information Theory*, vol. 52, no. 10, pp. 4413–4430, 2006.
6. Ning Cai and R. W. Yeung, "Secure network coding," in *Proceedings IEEE International Symposium on Information Theory,*, 2002, pp. 323–.
7. J. Feldman, T. Malkin, R. Servedio, and C. Stein, "On the capacity of secure network coding," 01 2004.
8. Ning Cai and R. W. Yeung, "Network coding and error correction," in *Proceedings of the IEEE Information Theory Workshop*, 2002, pp. 119–122.
9. R. W. Yeung and N. Cai, "Network error correction, I: Basic concepts and upper bounds," *Commun. Inf. Syst.*, vol. 6, no. 1, pp. 19–35, 2006. [Online]. Available: https://projecteuclid.org:443/euclid.cis/1175791040
10. N. Cai and R. W. Yeung, "Network error correction, II: Lower bounds," *Commun. Inf. Syst.*, vol. 6, no. 1, pp. 37–54, 2006. [Online]. Available: https://projecteuclid.org:443/euclid.cis/1175791041
11. D. S. Lun, M. Médard, R. Koetter, and M. Effros, "On coding for reliable communication over packet networks," *Physical Communication*, vol. 1, no. 1, pp. 3 – 20, 2008. [Online]. Available: http://www.sciencedirect.com/science/article/pii/S1874490708000086
12. M. Médard and A. Sprintson, *Network Coding: Fundamentals and Applications*. Elsevier Science, 2012. [Online]. Available: https://books.google.de/books?id=yGqtA9Mv_TgC

13. C. Fragouli and E. Soljanin, *Network Coding Fundamentals*, ser. Foundations and trends in networking. Now Publishers, 2007. [Online]. Available: https://books.google.de/books?id=jFCAn8My7SYC
14. R. W. Yeaung, S.-Y. R. Li, N. Cai, and Z. Zhang, *Network Coding Theory*. Boston - Delft: now, 2006.
15. M. Sanna and E. Izquierdo, "A survey of linear network coding and network error correction code constructions and algorithms," *Int. J. Digital Multimedia Broadcasting*, vol. 2011, 07 2011.
16. H. V. B. Neto, "Analysis and design of modern coding schemes for unequal error protection and joint source-channel coding," Ph.D. dissertation, Jacobs University, Shaker, 2012. [Online]. Available: https://nbn-resolving.org/urn:nbn:de:101:1-201503013317
17. M. G. Luby, M. Mitzenmacher, M. A. Shokrollahi, and D. A. Spielman, "Efficient erasure correcting codes," *IEEE Transactions on Information Theory*, vol. 47, no. 2, pp. 569–584, 2001.
18. J. W. Byers, M. Luby, M. Mitzenmacher, and A. Rege, "A digital fountain approach to reliable distribution of bulk data," Digital Equipment Corporation, Tech. Rep. SRC Technical Note 1998-003, 1998.
19. M. Luby, "LT codes," in *The 43rd Annual IEEE Symposium on Foundations of Computer Science, 2002. Proceedings.*, 2002, pp. 271–280.
20. A. Shokrollahi, "Raptor codes," in *2007 IEEE Information Theory Workshop on Information Theory for Wireless Networks*, 2007, pp. 1–1.
21. A. Shokrollahi, "Raptor codes," *IEEE Transactions on Information Theory*, vol. 52, no. 6, pp. 2551–2567, 2006.
22. A. Shokrollahi and M. Luby, "Raptor codes," *now, Foundations and Trends® in Communications and Information Theory*, vol. 6, no. 3–4, pp. 213–322, 2011. [Online]. Available: http://dx.doi.org/10.1561/0100000060
23. P. Maymounkov, "Online codes," NYU, Tech. Rep. TR2003-883, Nov. 2002.
24. M. Luby, A. Shokrollahi, and M. Watson, "Raptor forward error correction scheme for object delivery," IETF, Standard, Oct. 2007.
25. M. Luby, A. Shokrollahi, and M. Watson, "RaptorQ forward error correction scheme for object delivery," IETF, Standard, Aug. 2011.

Chapter 14
Decoding Error Probabilities for Block Codes

Failure is success in progress.

Albert Einstein

14.1 Exact Computation of the Probabilities of Non-correction, Decoding Error, and Decoding Failure

There are three cases, already stated in the title of this section, to be distinguished. An error vector that causes a transmitted word to lie outside the correction sphere[1] of the transmitted (correct) codeword does not allow a correction to the right codeword. We compute a probability for **non-correction**, where the received word can either lie outside of every decoding sphere or in a decoding sphere of another codeword. We speak of **decoding failure** or **decoding error**, respectively. Figure 14.1 shows the corresponding areas.

Before we can determine the three probabilities, we have to distinguish between binary and symbol-oriented codes, i.e., if they are defined over $GF(2)$ or $GF(2^m)$ (in general, $GF(q)$). With a bit-error probability $p_{b\times}$ of a binary symmetric channel (BSC) the **symbol-error probability** $p_{s\times}$ for symbols from $GF(2^m)$ follows as

$$p_{s\times} = 1 - (1 - p_{b\times})^m . \tag{14.1}$$

[1] In here, we discuss so-called bounded minimum distance decoding, i.e., decoding within a sphere of radius $t = \lfloor d - 1/2 \rfloor$.

W. Henkel, *Channel Coding*, Signals and Communication Technology,
https://doi.org/10.1007/978-3-032-08236-7_14

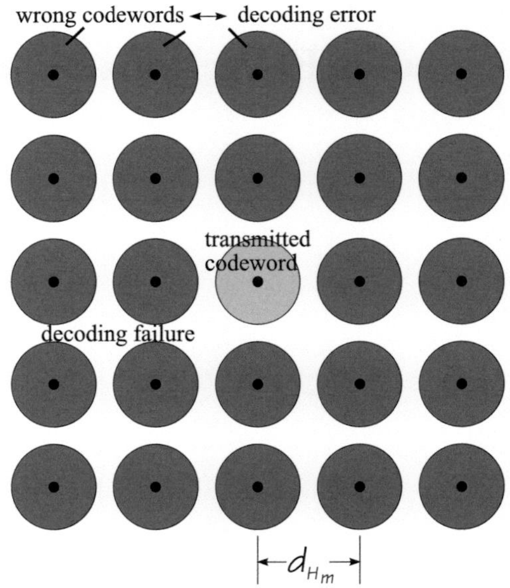

Fig. 14.1 Areas of correct decoding, decoding failure, and decoding error

$(1 - p_{b\times})^m$ is the probability that all m binary components will be error-free. In the following, we sometimes just write "p". Dependent on the code, this stands for $p_{b\times}$ or $p_{s\times}$.

The relation for correct decoding is easily obtained:

$$p_c = \sum_{\nu=0}^{t} \binom{N}{\nu} p^\nu (1-p)^{N-\nu}. \tag{14.2}$$

It is nothing else than the probability for error pattern of weight smaller or equal to the correction capability t of the code. The probability for **non-correction** is thus

$$p_n = 1 - p_c = 1 - \sum_{\nu=0}^{t} \binom{N}{\nu} p^\nu (1-p)^{N-\nu} = \sum_{\nu=t+1}^{N} \binom{N}{\nu} p^\nu (1-p)^{N-\nu}. \tag{14.3}$$

For our further derivations, we will need the probability $p(h)$ of a certain error pattern of Hamming weight h inside a codeword with symbols from $GF(q)$, which is

$$p(h) = \left(\frac{p}{q-1}\right)^h (1-p)^{N-h}. \tag{14.4}$$

We first derive the probability for a decoding error p_e; the probability for a decoding failure p_f will immediately follow from

$$p_f = p_n - p_e. \tag{14.5}$$

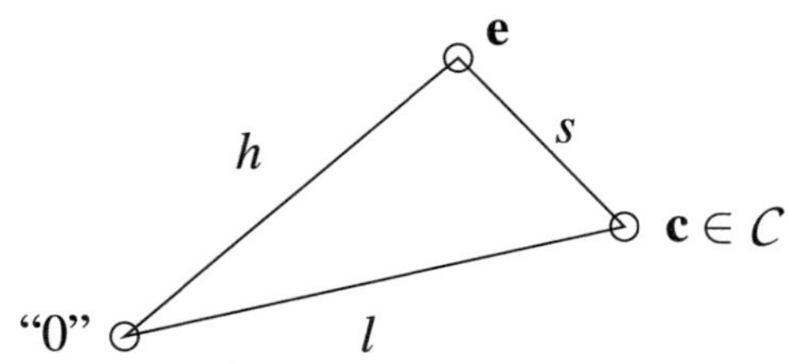

Fig. 14.2 Illustration of the parameters $(l, h; s)$; since we assume linearity, the zero word has been chosen as the reference point

For determining the probability of erroneous decoding, on the one hand we need the weight distribution[2] A_j of the code and a value $\Theta(l, h; s)$, specifying the number of error pattern **e** of weight h at a distance s from another codeword of weight l (see Fig. 14.2). The probability of a **decoding error** follows to be[3]

$$\begin{aligned} p_e &= \sum_{h=0}^{N} p(h) \cdot \sum_{s=0}^{t} \sum_{l=1}^{N} A_l \cdot \Theta(l, h; s) \\ &= \sum_{h=0}^{N} \left(\frac{p}{q-1}\right)^h (1-p)^{N-h} \cdot \sum_{s=0}^{t} \sum_{l=1}^{N} A_l \cdot \Theta(l, h; s), \end{aligned} \tag{14.6}$$

where

$$\Theta(l, h; s) = \sum_{\substack{i,j,k \\ i+j+k=s \\ l+k-j=h}} \left[\binom{N-l}{k}(q-1)^k\right]\left[\binom{l}{i}(q-2)^i\right]\left[\binom{l-i}{j}\right]. \tag{14.7}$$

The factors in (14.7) can be illustrated by Fig. 14.3. For simplification, ranges have been shown to be connected.

Let first $N - l$ components to be zero. $\binom{N-l}{k}(q-1)^k$ then specifies all possibilities, to change k components of these to a non-zero value. The second term stands for parts of the error vectors that have no influence on the Hamming distance, since non-zero components will be modified to $q - 2$ other non-zero components. There are $\binom{l}{i}(q-2)^i$ possibilities. The last term, finally, describes the possibilities, to set j of the remaining $l - i$ non-zero components to zero. The weight of the error vector is $h = l + k - j$, <weight of the erroneous codeword> + <additional non-zero components by modifying k of the $N - l$ from zero to some non-zero value> – <zeroed components>. All modifications together result in the Hamming distance $s = i + j + k$ to the considered erroneous codeword.

[2] For RS codes the weight distribution can be given closed form. In other codes, the so-called MacWilliams Identity may be helpful, which provides a relation between the weight distributions of dual codes.

[3] The presentation in (14.6) and (14.7) follows the one in [1]. We assume the codes to be linear.

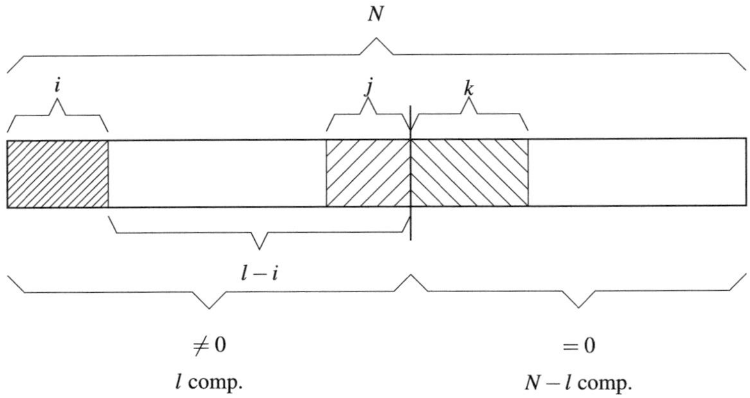

Fig. 14.3 Illustration of the factors of $\Theta(l, h; s)$

In the binary case with $q = P = 2$, Eq. (14.6) is simplified. Since we need only consider $i = 0$, we obtain

$$p_e = \sum_{h=0}^{N} p^h (1-p)^{N-h} \cdot \sum_{s=0}^{t} \sum_{l=1}^{N} A_l \cdot \sum_{\substack{j,k \\ j+k=s \\ l+k-j=h}} \binom{N-l}{k} \binom{l}{j}. \tag{14.8}$$

Substituting $s - j = k$ yields[4]

$$\begin{aligned} p_e &= \sum_{h=0}^{N} p^h (1-p)^{N-h} \cdot \sum_{s=0}^{t} \sum_{l=1}^{N} A_l \cdot \sum_{\substack{k \\ h=l-s+2k}} \binom{N-l}{k} \binom{l}{s-k} \\ &= \sum_{l=1}^{N} A_l \cdot \sum_{s=0}^{t} \sum_{k=0}^{s} \binom{N-l}{k} \binom{l}{s-k} \cdot \underbrace{p^{l-s+2k} \cdot (1-p)^{N-l+s-2k}}_{p^k (1-p)^{N-l-k} \cdot p^{l-(s-k)} (1-p)^{s-k}} \end{aligned} \tag{14.9}$$

k specifies the share of s components that leads to changes within the $N - l$ zeros. $s - k$ components in the range of l non-zero components will then be set to zero and $l - (s - k)$ components stay non-zero. This relation could also have been found directly without the lengthy derivation from the general case.

All decoding error probabilities are related to the whole codeword, i.e., they are word-error probabilities. Often, however, we are interested in symbol- or bit-error probabilities. In order to formulate the symbol-error probability for symbol-based codes or for the bit-error probability of binary codes, in (14.6) and (14.9), only A_l has to be replaced by $\frac{\delta_l}{K} \cdot A_l$; δ_l is the number of symbol errors within the K

[4] For the summation limits, note that $A_l = 0$ for $l = 1, \ldots, d_{Hm} - 1$ and $d_{Hm} \geq 2t + 1$.

information components in case of a decoding error to a codeword at distance l. For linear codes, δ_l/K can be approximated by l/N. The probability of decoding failure will be weighted by an average symbol-error probability and the summation of both portions yields the symbol-error probability (bit-error probability for binary codes) after the decoding. From the symbol-error probability of symbol-oriented codes, in turn, the bit-error probability can be approximated as $p_b \approx p_s/2$.

An approximation of the symbol-error probability p_s from the probability p_n of not being able to correct follows from the assumption, the most probable error pattern for erroneous decoding would have the weight $d_{Hm} = 2t + 1$.

$$p_s \approx \frac{d_{Hm}}{N} \cdot p_n \tag{14.10}$$

Somewhat more exact would be the approximation

$$p_s \approx \sum_{\nu=t+1}^{N} \frac{\nu}{N} \binom{N}{\nu} p_{s\times}^{\nu} (1 - p_{s\times})^{N-\nu}. \tag{14.11}$$

For binary codes we have $p_b = p_s$.

The approximation (14.11) is especially suitable, when the probability for a decoding error can be neglected. This can especially be done in the case of RS codes with reasonable parameter choices. For RS codes, McEliece and Swanson [2] provide the rough approximation for the probability of a decoding error under the condition that more than t errors have occurred:

$$p_e|_{e>t} \leq 1/t!\,. \tag{14.12}$$

The steps for computing the residual error probability after decoding will be pointed out again in the case of RS codes. We assume a binary symmetric channel.

1. Computation of the symbol-error probability before the decoding $p_{s\times}$ from the bit-error probability $p_{b\times}$ according to (14.1):

$$p_{s\times} = 1 - (1 - p_{b\times})^m.$$

2. Computation of the symbol-error probability p_s after decoding according to (14.11):

$$p_s \approx \sum_{\nu=t+1}^{N} \frac{\nu}{N} \binom{N}{\nu} p_{s\times}^{\nu} (1 - p_{s\times})^{N-\nu}.$$

3. In case the bit-error probability instead of the symbol-error probability is required after the decoding, it will lie between the pessimistic approximation $p_b \leq p_s/2$ and the optimistic one $p_b \geq p_s/m$ (only one bit of the RS symbol of length m is assumed to be wrong). More exact will be the approximation $p_b \leq p_s \cdot \frac{p_{b\times}}{p_{s\times}}$,

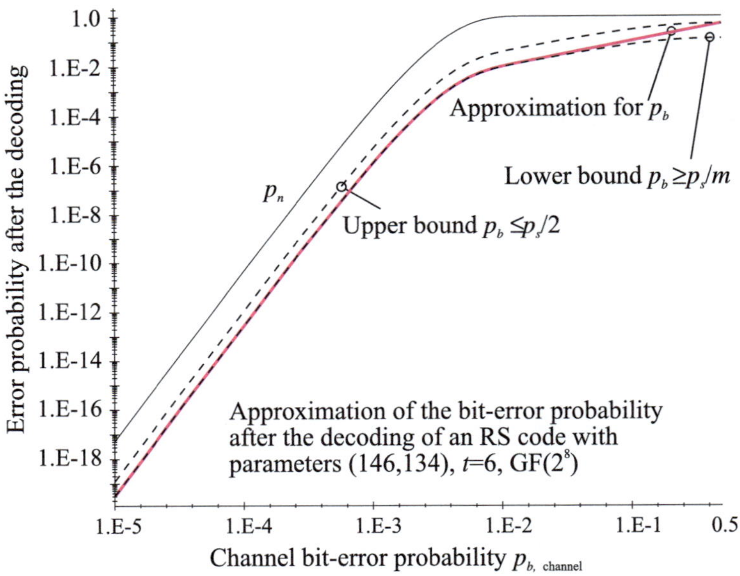

Fig. 14.4 Approximation of the bit-error probability after the decoding of an RS code with parameters (146,134), $t = 6$, GF(2^8)

assuming that the probability of symbol-error pattern of length m stay the same also after the decoding. This is a worst-case approximation, since the RS decoding especially eliminates errors that are concentrated in bursts.

Figure 14.4 shows the results for a shortened[5] RS code with parameters ($N = 146$, $K = 134$, $t = 6$) over $GF(2^8)$ together with the probability of non-correction p_n.

14.1.1 Error-Detection Probability

If we use a code for error detection, only, i.e., not correcting errors at all, we immediately obtain the probability of having at least one error from (14.3). It is

$$p_n = 1 - p_c = 1 - (1 - p)^N. \tag{14.13}$$

The probability that an error vector will lead to another codeword, results from (14.9) as

[5] RS codes can be shortened in information or redundancy without loosing their MDS properties. Omitting information symbols does not influence the correction capabilities (just means zeroing information), whereas shortening of the redundancy is equivalent to erasures and thus, reduces the Hamming distance accordingly.

$$p_e = \sum_{l=1}^{N} A_l \cdot p^l \cdot (1-p)^{N-l}. \tag{14.14}$$

The probability to be able to detect an error (decoding failure) is

$$p_f = p_n - p_e = 1 - \sum_{l=0}^{N} A_l \cdot p^l \cdot (1-p)^{N-l}. \tag{14.15}$$

14.2 Union-Bound Approximation

We have already used the *Union Bound* in Sect. 5.2.1 without calling it by this name. We repeat Eq. (5.5) and interpret it for block codes.

$$p_\infty(l) = \begin{cases} \sum\limits_{e=(l+1)/2}^{l} \binom{l}{e} p^e (1-p)^{(l-e)}, & l \text{ odd} \\ \frac{1}{2}\binom{l}{l/2} p^{l/2}(1-p^{l/2}) + \sum\limits_{e=l/2+1}^{l} \binom{l}{e} p^e (1-p)^{(l-e)}, & l \text{ even} \end{cases} \tag{14.16}$$

It computes the probability, to decide for the wrong codeword from half the distance on. In a two-dimensional Euclidean space, a graphical representation could be given as in Fig. 14.5a. This would be suitable, e.g., for an AWGN channel and points in Euclidean space. It can just give an intuition in the case of a finite field. It shows clearly, at least, an overlap of areas when drawing border lines at half the distances between neighboring points ('codewords'). From this we obtain the upper bound

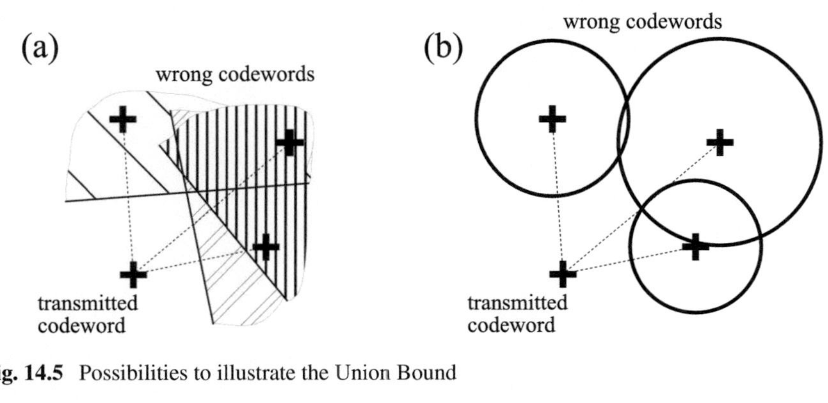

Fig. 14.5 Possibilities to illustrate the Union Bound

$$p_n \leq \sum_{l=1}^{N} A_l \cdot p_{\infty}(l) \tag{14.17}$$

One can also draw another picture when substituting $l - e = e'$ and $(1 - p) = p'$. Then a representation with correction spheres around all other wrong codewords can be drawn with radii of half the distances between the right and the considered wrong codewords. Figure 14.5b shows such an illustration.

Both possibilities show that a two-dimensional illustration in Euclidean space necessarily has its weaknesses.

References

1. R. E. Blahut, *Theory and practice of error control codes*. Reading, MA: Addison-Wesley, 1983.
2. R. McEliece and L. Swanson, "On the decoder error probability for Reed-Solomon codes (Corresp.)," *IEEE Transactions on Information Theory*, vol. 32, no. 5, pp. 701–703, Sep. 1986.

Chapter 15
Coding Bounds

True wisdom is a matter among other things
of discovering and accepting our limits ...

In this section, we will derive the most important coding bounds that relate the parameters N, K, and d_{Hm}. The resulting error probability is not an issue in here. We already know the **Singleton bound** [1] from Theorem 3.3,

$$d_{Hm} = w_{Hm} \leq 1 + N - K \tag{15.1}$$

and the **Hamming or Sphere-Packing bound** [2] from Theorem 3.6,

binary case:

$$\sum_{j=0}^{t} \binom{n}{j} \leq 2^{N-K}, \tag{15.2}$$

non-binary case:

$$\sum_{j=0}^{t} \binom{n}{j} (q-1)^j \leq q^{N-K}. \tag{15.3}$$

In the following we will describe some more bounds, without being able to give a thorough treatment.

W. Henkel, *Channel Coding*, Signals and Communication Technology,
https://doi.org/10.1007/978-3-032-08236-7_15

Theorem 15.1 (Plotkin bound) *The minimum Hamming distance d_{Hm} of a binary code is related to the codeword length N and the cardinality $\mathcal{K} = 2^K$ according to*

$$d_{Hm} \leq \frac{N \cdot \mathcal{K}}{2 \cdot (\mathcal{K} - 1)} = \frac{N \cdot 2^K}{2 \cdot (2^K - 1)}; \tag{15.4}$$

in the non-binary case,

$$d_{Hm} \leq \frac{N \cdot (q-1) \cdot q^{K-1}}{q^K - 1}. \tag{15.5}$$

Proof We only proof the binary case.

Let us imagine the codewords $\mathbf{c}_j$, $j = 1, \ldots, \mathcal{K}$ to be written as rows of a $\mathcal{K} \times N$ matrix. Summing all the Hamming distances between all possible pairs of codewords yields

$$\sum_{j_1=1}^{\mathcal{K}} \sum_{j_2=1}^{\mathcal{K}} d_H(\mathbf{c}_{j_1}, \mathbf{c}_{j_2}) = \sum_{n=1}^{N} \sum_{j_1=1}^{\mathcal{K}} \sum_{j_2=1}^{\mathcal{K}} d_H(c_{j_1,n}, c_{j_2,n}). \tag{15.6}$$

Let $Z(n)$ be the number of zeros in the nth column of the matrix. Let us first assume that $c_{j_1,n}$ is equal to 1. With $Z(n)$ possibilities for j_2 with a zero in this column, we obtain

$$\sum_{j_2=1}^{\mathcal{K}} d_H(c_{j_1,n}, c_{j_2,n}) = Z(n). \tag{15.7}$$

There are $\mathcal{K} - Z(n)$ positions j_1 with $c_{j_1,n} = 1$; therefore,

$$\sum_{j_1:c_{j_1,n}=1} \sum_{j_2=1}^{\mathcal{K}} d_H(c_{j_1,n}, c_{j_2,n}) = (\mathcal{K} - Z(n)) \cdot Z(n). \tag{15.8}$$

On the contrary, there are also $Z(n)$ positions for j_1 with $c_{j_1,n} = 0$ and $\mathcal{K} - Z(n)$ positions for j_2 with $c_{j_2,n} = 1$, from which

$$\sum_{j_1=1}^{\mathcal{K}} \sum_{j_2=1}^{\mathcal{K}} d_H(c_{j_1,n}, c_{j_2,n}) = 2 \cdot (\mathcal{K} - Z(n)) \cdot Z(n) \tag{15.9}$$

is obtained. For $Z(n) = \mathcal{K}/2$ the maximum is achieved on the right side. We obtain the inequality

$$\sum_{j_1=1}^{\mathcal{K}} \sum_{j_2=1}^{\mathcal{K}} d_H(\mathbf{c}_{j_1}, \mathbf{c}_{j_2}) \leq N \cdot \mathcal{K}^2/2, \tag{15.10}$$

where all N codeword positions have been taken into account.

Alternatively, we could only consider that $d_H(\mathbf{c}_{j_1}, \mathbf{c}_{j_2=j_1}) = 0$ in the distance summation. All other codewords have to differ at least at so many positions as given by the minimum distance d_{Hm}. This yields

$$\sum_{j_1=1}^{\mathcal{K}} \sum_{j_2=1}^{\mathcal{K}} d_H(\mathbf{c}_{j_1}, \mathbf{c}_{j_2}) = \sum_{j_1=1}^{\mathcal{K}} \sum_{j_2 \neq j_1} d_H(\mathbf{c}_{j_1}, \mathbf{c}_{j_2}) \geq \mathcal{K} \cdot (\mathcal{K} - 1) \cdot d_{Hm}. \tag{15.11}$$

From both inequalities together we obtain the Plotkin bound (15.4). □

In Plotkin's original publication [3] from the year 1960, only the binary case of Theorem 15.1 was treated. Later, the Plotkin bound has often been reformulated. Some codes were then excluded without notion. Mostly, also only the limiting case $N \to \infty$ is shown, not allowing to illustrate, in which ranges the bound will be valid. Additionally, the derivation is often missing so that special conditions do not become visible. In the sequel, we will describe a representation out of [4], together with the underlying assumptions.

First, instead of N, let the length be $\nu \leq N$. From (15.5), we obtain

$$d_{Hm}(q^K - 1) \leq \nu q^{K-1}(q - 1), \tag{15.12}$$

$$q^{K-1}(q d_{Hm} + \nu - \nu q) \leq d_{Hm}. \tag{15.13}$$

Assuming that $(q d_{Hm} + \nu - \nu q) > 0$, we get

$$q^K \leq \frac{q d_{Hm}}{q d_{Hm} + \nu - \nu q}. \tag{15.14}$$

Now, we choose $\nu \in \mathbb{N}$ such[1] that $(q d_{Hm} - 1)/(q - 1) = \nu + \varepsilon$ with $0 \leq \varepsilon < 1$, which yields

$$q^K \leq \frac{q d_{Hm}}{q d_{Hm} - (q - 1)\nu} = \frac{q d_{Hm}}{1 + (q - 1)\varepsilon}. \tag{15.15}$$

For a bigger codeword length $N > \nu$, each addition component could be an information component, which would mean a multiplicity of the cardinality by at most $q^{N-\nu}$, i.e.,

$$q^K \leq q^{N-\nu} \frac{q d_{Hm}}{1 + (q - 1)\varepsilon} = \frac{q^{N-[(q d_{Hm}-1)/(q-1)]+\varepsilon} q d_{Hm}}{1 + (q - 1)\varepsilon} \tag{15.16}$$

With $q^\varepsilon \leq 1 + (q - 1)\varepsilon$, we obtain

$$q^K \leq q^{N-[(q d_{Hm}-1)/(q-1)]} q d_{Hm}, \tag{15.17}$$

---

[1] In the binary case, this choice means $\nu = 2d_{Hm} - 1$, and in turn $N \geq 2d_{Hm} - 1 \Leftrightarrow d_{Hm}/N \leq 1/2 + 1/N$. The dashed curve in Fig. 15.1 shows the bound for this range. The repetition code will only be treated right with the original representation of the Plotkin bound in Theorem 15.1.

and taking the log yields the result

$$K \leq N - \frac{q d_{Hm} - 1}{q - 1} + 1 + \log_q d_{Hm}. \tag{15.18}$$

Most of the bounds like Hamming, Plotkin, Elias, Hartmann-Tzeng, ... are upper bounds for the reachable coderate at a given minimum distance. A lower bound is the one by **Varshamov** and **Gilbert**.

The Varshamov-Gilbert bound[2] relies on a property of the **H** matrix of linear codes that we have already described in Sect. 3.2. The **H**-matrix of a linear code with a minimum Hamming distance d_{Hm} has to have $d_{Hm} - 1$ linearly independent columns. This allows to construct the matrix by adding columns. One starts from a column of length M and adds a second that cannot be expressed as a multiple of the first. A further column should not be expressible as a linear combination of the first two. Finally, the jth column should not be expressible by a linear combination of arbitrary $d_{Hm} - 2$ already available columns. This procedure ensures that $d_{Hm} - 1$ columns of the **H**-matrix will be linearly independent.

With $j - 1$ columns, there are

$$\binom{j-1}{1}(q-1) + \binom{j-1}{2}(q-1)^2 + \cdots + \binom{j-1}{d_{Hm}-2}(q-1)^{d_{Hm}-2} \tag{15.19}$$

possibilities for linear combinations. For another column to be added that will not be equal to one of the linear combinations, the total number of nonzero columns $q^M - 1$ that can be constructed should be greater than the number of linear combinations. We assume that all linear combinations lead to different results. This assumption leads to the smallest possible K. Note that we search for a lower bound.

$$\binom{j-1}{1}(q-1) + \binom{j-1}{2}(q-1)^2 + \cdots + \binom{j-1}{d_{Hm}-2}(q-1)^{d_{Hm}-2} < q^M - 1 \tag{15.20}$$

With this, we can define a code with $K = j - M$ information symbols and a distance d_{Hm}. Let N be the highest value for j, where (15.20) is still fulfilled. This yields

$$\binom{N}{1}(q-1) + \binom{N}{2}(q-1)^2 + \cdots + \binom{N}{d_{Hm}-2}(q-1)^{d_{Hm}-2} \geq q^M - 1 \tag{15.21}$$

and we obtain the

Theorem 15.2 (Varshamov-Gilbert bound)

$$\sum_{l=0}^{d_{Hm}-2} \binom{N}{l}(q-1)^l \geq q^{N-K}. \tag{15.22}$$

---

[2] This presentation follows [4].

The one has been included in the summation.

This result can be formulated in another way by using a special case of the *Chernoff bound*, namely

$$\sum_{l=\lambda N}^{N} \binom{N}{l} \leq \lambda^{-\lambda N} \mu^{-\mu N} , \quad \mu = 1 - \lambda , \quad \lambda > \frac{1}{2}. \tag{15.23}$$

Using the entropy for abbreviation,

$$H(\lambda) = -\lambda \log_2 \lambda - \mu \log_2 \mu = \frac{1}{N} \log_2 \left(\lambda^{-\lambda N} \mu^{-\mu N}\right). \tag{15.24}$$

For the binary case with $q = 2$, we obtain

$$2^{N-K} \leq \sum_{l=0}^{d_{Hm}-2} \binom{N}{l} \leq \left(\frac{N - d_{Hm} + 2}{N}\right)^{-(N-d_{Hm}+2)} \left(\frac{d_{Hm} - 2}{N}\right)^{-(d_{Hm}-2)}$$
$$= 2^{NH[(d_{Hm}-2)/N]} \tag{15.25}$$

and furthermore,

$$N - K \leq NH\left(\frac{d_{Hm} - 2}{N}\right). \tag{15.26}$$

The coding bounds derived in here are illustrated again in Fig. 15.1 for $N = 256$. Note the support of the Plotkin-bound formulation according to (15.18) (dashed).

Remark In the two previous chapters, often binomial terms have appeared. These can be difficult to treat numerically. An approximation may be used, instead, that is known as **Stirling formula**. It is given by

$$\nu! = \sqrt{2\pi\nu}\left(\frac{\nu}{e}\right)^{\nu} \cdot e^{\left[\frac{1}{12\nu} - \frac{1}{360\nu^3} + \ldots\right]} = \sqrt{2\pi\nu}\left(\frac{\nu}{e}\right)^{\nu} \cdot \left[1 + \frac{1}{12\nu} + \frac{1}{(12\nu)^2} + \cdots\right]$$
$$\approx \sqrt{2\pi\nu}\left(\frac{\nu}{e}\right)^{\nu} \tag{15.27}$$

and allows the approximation for big ν. As an example, we apply the approximation to (14.3), i.e.,

$$p_n = \sum_{\nu=t+1}^{N} \binom{N}{\nu} p^{\nu}(1-p)^{N-\nu} = \sum_{\nu=t+1}^{N} \mathcal{P}_{\nu}$$

with

$$\mathcal{P}_{\nu} = \binom{N}{\nu} p^{\nu}(1-p)^{N-\nu}.$$

We have

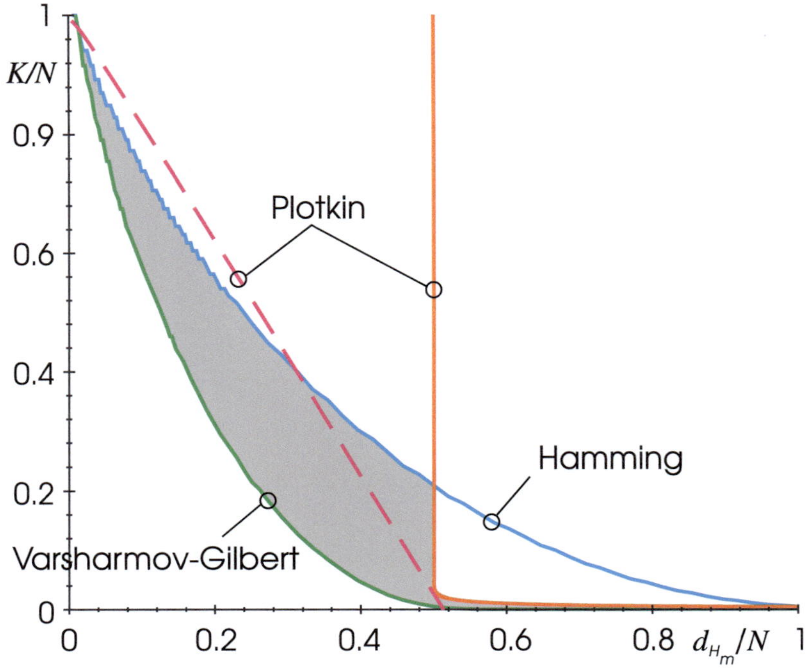

Fig. 15.1 Comparison of coding bounds ($N = 256$, Plotkin: solid orange: Eq. (15.4), dashed pink: Eq. (15.18))

$$\mathcal{P}_{\nu+1} = \mathcal{P}_\nu \cdot \frac{N-\nu}{\nu+1} \cdot \frac{p}{1-p} < \mathcal{P}_\nu \cdot \underbrace{\frac{(N-\nu)\cdot p}{\nu\cdot(1-p)}}_{=:\, u_\nu},$$

where $u_\nu > u_{\nu+1}$ for $\nu > Np$. Under this condition, the following bounds apply for p_n.

$$\mathcal{P}_{t+1} < p_n < \mathcal{P}_{t+1} \cdot (1 + u_{t+1} + u_{t+1}^2 + \ldots u_{t+1}^{N-t-1}) < \mathcal{P}_{t+1} \cdot \sum_{l=0}^{\infty} u_{t+1}^l$$
$$= \mathcal{P}_{t+1} \cdot \frac{1}{1-u_{t+1}} = \mathcal{P}_{t+1} \cdot \frac{(t+1)(1-p)}{(t+1)-pN}$$

with

$$\mathcal{P}_{t+1} \approx \frac{1}{\sqrt{2\pi \frac{(t+1)(N-(t+1))}{N}}} \cdot \left(\frac{p\cdot N}{t+1}\right)^{(t+1)} \cdot \left(\frac{(1-p)\cdot N}{N-(t+1)}\right)^{N-(t+1)}.$$

References

1. R. Singleton, "Maximum distance q-nary codes," *IEEE Transactions on Information Theory*, vol. 10, no. 2, pp. 116–118, April 1964.
2. R. W. Hamming, "Error detecting and error correcting codes," *The Bell System Technical Journal*, vol. 29, no. 2, pp. 147–160, April 1950.
3. M. Plotkin, "Binary codes with specified minimum distance," *IRE Transactions on Information Theory*, vol. 6, no. 4, pp. 445–450, Sep. 1960.
4. W. Peterson and J. Weldon, E.J., *Error-Correcting Codes*, 6th ed. Cambridge, Massachusetts and London, England: MIT Press, 1981.

Chapter 16
Trellis Structures of Block Codes

> There is a one-to-one correspondence between each codeword in the code and ... any path from the all-zero node at depth 0 to the all-zero node at depth n.
>
> Jack Wolf, 1978

Up to now, we have not discussed algorithms that would allow soft-decision decoding of block codes. Only, erasures could be treated, which is a kind of introducing channel-state information in the decoding process. A refinement is Forney's **Generalized-Minimum-Distance Decoding** [1] which allows a maximum-likelihood decoding of block codes. In the **Chase Algorithms** [2] for binary codes, different groups of unreliable bits are inverted and every time, the decoding is repeated. The most probable codes (with the smallest Euclidean distance to the received word) will then be chosen. In case of a parity-check code, the Chase algorithm would just invert the least reliable bit, if the parity would not be fulfilled. This is also named **Wagner Decoding**. All these algorithms cannot be treated in details. Instead, we show procedures, how to draw a trellis for a given block code. This allows for maximum-likelihood soft-decision decoding with the Viterbi algorithm (or SOVA, BCJR, ...), if the trellis will not be too big.

In the following sections, we will first show a general construction method which leads to a minimal trellis. This will usually not unveil symmetries of the code. Other means, based on the $(\mathbf{u}, \mathbf{u}+\mathbf{v})$ and Turyn constructions, are described afterwards and give some more insights.

W. Henkel, *Channel Coding*, Signals and Communication Technology,
https://doi.org/10.1007/978-3-032-08236-7_16

16.1 Wolf Trellis

16.1.1 Trellis Construction from the Parity-Check Matrix

This trellis construction [3, 4] relies on the **H**-matrix of a linear code. For a valid codeword we have

$$\mathbf{H}\mathbf{c}^T = \mathbf{0} \tag{16.1}$$

Writing the **H**-matrix as a succession of column vectors,

$$\mathbf{H} = (\mathbf{h}_0, \mathbf{h}_1, \ldots, \mathbf{h}_{N-1}), \tag{16.2}$$

we can write

$$\sum_{j=0}^{N-1} c_j \mathbf{h}_j = \mathbf{0}. \tag{16.3}$$

This leads to a trellis construction by defining all possible $q^M = q^{N-K}$ intermediate results as states that are reached by each new added term. Of course, not necessarily, every such state is really used. The trellis starts from state 0 and ends there, again, since the syndrome of all valid codewords has to be zero. This means that all paths have to be eliminated that do not go through the final zero state. Each trellis path goes through $N+1$ states and each of the q^K codewords (trellis paths) consists of N state transitions.

As a first example, we determine the trellis of a (4, 3, 2) parity-check code with

$$\mathbf{H} = (1, 1, 1, 1)$$

in Fig. 16.1.

A repetition code (4, 1, 4) has a parity-check matrix

$$\mathbf{H} = \begin{pmatrix} 1 & 1 & & \\ 1 & & 1 & \\ 1 & & & 1 \end{pmatrix}$$

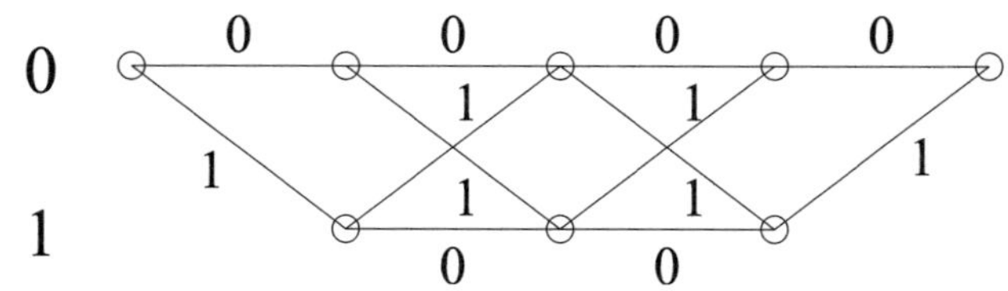

Fig. 16.1 Trellis of a (4, 3, 2) parity-check code

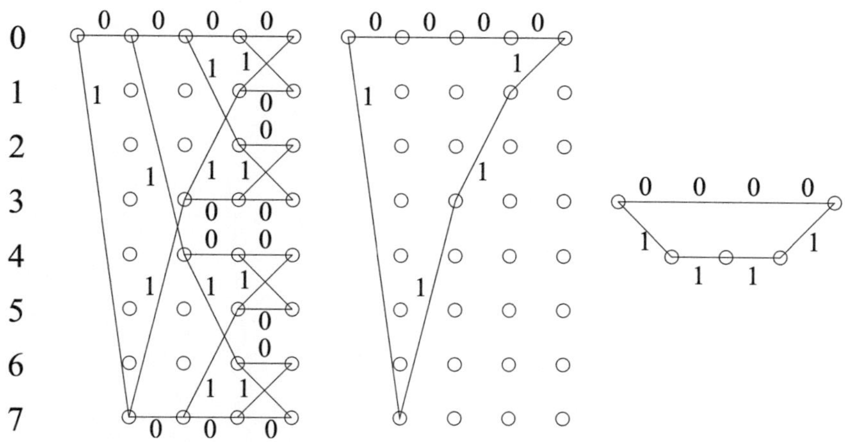

Fig. 16.2 Trellis of the (4, 1, 4) repetition code

and the corresponding trellis is shown in Fig. 16.2, leading to a very intuitive solution after eliminating invalid paths.

As a final example for Wolf's approach, the extended Hamming code with the parameters (8, 4, 4) is studied. In the inner part, state transitions have been drawn that will have no connection to the final zero state and are thus invalid.

As a parity-check matrix of the extended Hamming code we take

$$\mathbf{H} = \begin{pmatrix} 11111111 \\ 00001111 \\ 00110011 \\ 01010101 \end{pmatrix},$$

from which we can draw the trellis in Fig. 16.3.

A trellis construction based on the generator matrix is described in [5].

16.1.2 Trellis Construction from the Shift Registers for Systematic Encoding

In Sect. 11.2.2, we have specialized the shift register circuits for systematic encoding with the generator polynomial for binary BCH codes. Also in here, let us concentrate on binary cyclic codes. The content of the shift register can be seen as state of a trellis as we are used from convolutional codes. For illustration, we determine the trellis of the (7, 4, 3) Hamming code. According to Eq. (11.6), the generator polynomial is

$$g(x) = x^3 + x + 1,$$

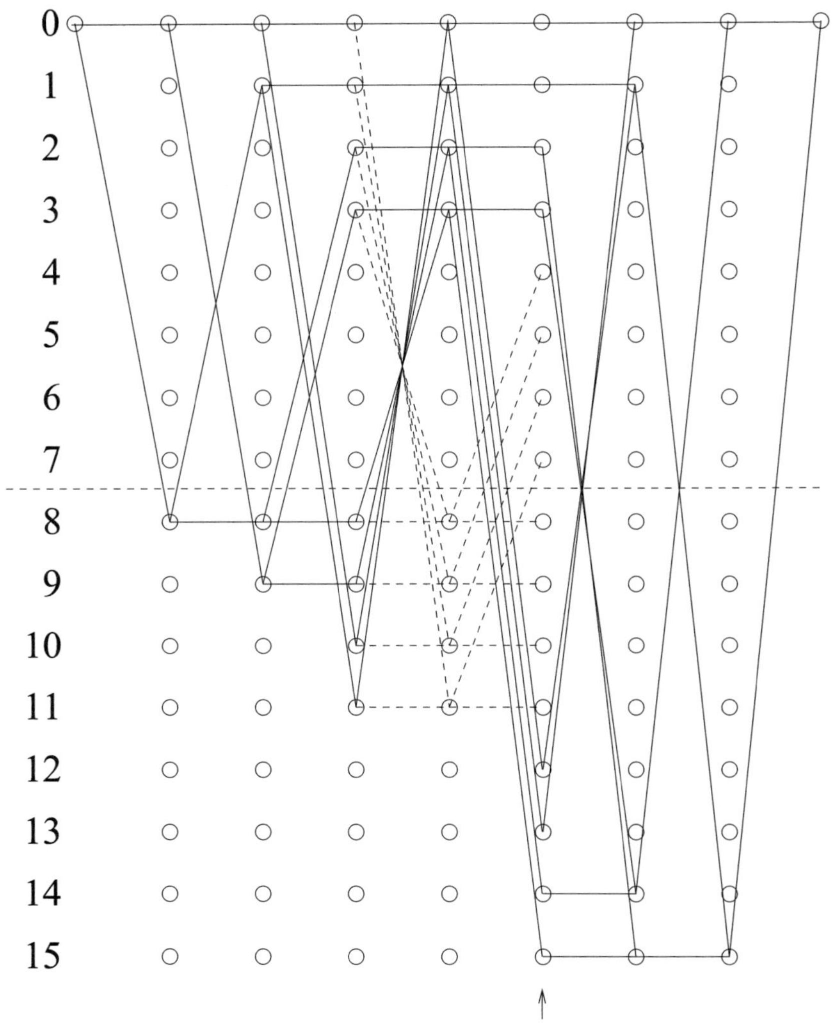

Fig. 16.3 Trellis of the extended Hamming code with the parameters (8, 4, 4)

from which we obtain the encoding shift register in Fig. 16.4. The corresponding trellis is depicted in Fig. 16.5.

The paths are labeled with the components of the codeword, the first four components $(c_6, \ldots, c_3)$ being identical to the information bits. Note the three different ranges of the trellis. In general, the number of used states dependent on the depth τ is given by

$$\begin{array}{ll} I\; q^{\tau} & 0 \leq \tau \leq M \\ II\; q^{M} & M \leq \tau \leq N - M = K \\ III\; q^{N-\tau} & N - M = K \leq \tau \leq N \end{array} \tag{16.4}$$

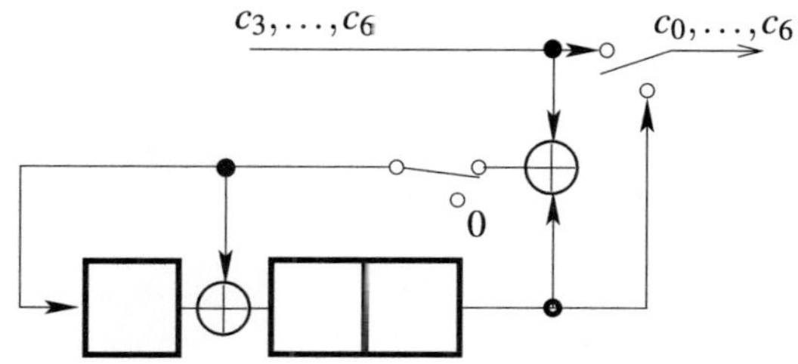

Fig. 16.4 Encoder circuit based on the generator polynomial $g(x) = x^3 + x + 1$

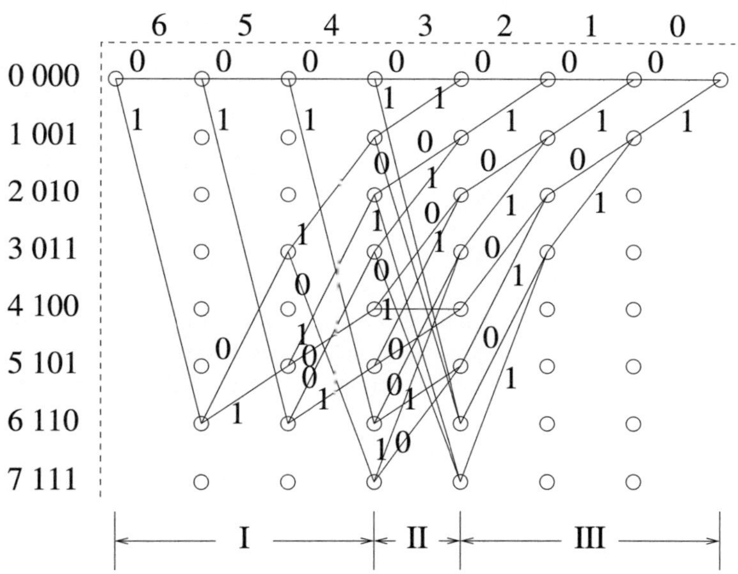

Fig. 16.5 Trellis of the encoder circuit in the previous figure

The maximum number of states is $2^M = 2^{N-K}$. A similar construction can also be described based on the parity-check polynomial as given in Sect. 11.2.3. Hereto, only a switch has to be introduced in the left connection that allows first to fill the shift register and to zero the feedback at the end, as soon as c_0 is at the left position of the shift register. Such a trellis has 2^K states. One may prefer this method when $K < M$.

16.2 A Trellis Based on the (u, u + v) Construction

In Example 12.1 of Sect. 12.1, we showed how all Reed-Muller codes can be recursively derived by means of the (**u**, **u** + **v**)-construction. In this section, we will now use this construction to draw the trellises of first-order RM codes. To this end, we put the codeword components in the order

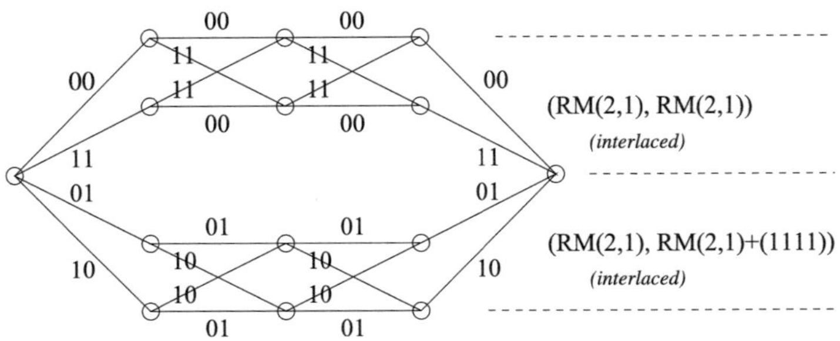

Fig. 16.6 Trellis of the (8, 4, 4)-RM(3, 1) code (extended Hamming code)

$$(u_0, u_0 + v_0, u_1, u_1 + v_1, \ldots, u_{N-1}, u_{N-1} + v_{N-1}), \tag{16.5}$$

i.e., pairwise interlaced. From the mentioned example, we already know that all RM$(m, 1)$ codes follow from the recursion

$$\text{RM}(m, 1) = (\text{RM}(m-1, 1), \text{RM}(m-1, 1) + \mathbf{1})\,. \tag{16.6}$$

1 is the repetition code of length 2^{m-1}. Starting from the RM(2, 1) code with the parameters (4, 3, 2), the parity-check code, the trellis of the (8, 4, 4)-RM(3, 1) code (extended Hamming code) can be drawn as in Fig. 16.6. (Note the interlacing of components!)

Using the construction once more, we obtain the (16, 5, 8)-RM(4, 1) code with a trellis depicted in Fig. 16.7. Likewise, the trellises of all RM codes can be developed.

16.3 Trellis Construction for the Binary Extended Golay Code Using the Turyn Construction

In Sect. 12.1, we have already seen a simple construction of the (24, 12, 8) extended Golay code. This construction due to Turyn, is based on two component codes that are both equivalent to the extended Hamming code. Let us denote the two codes as (8, 4) and $(8, 4)^\star$. The Golay code then follows from

$$(\mathbf{a} + \mathbf{x}, \mathbf{b} + \mathbf{x}, \mathbf{a} + \mathbf{b} + \mathbf{x}) \quad \mathbf{a},\ \mathbf{b} \in (8, 4), \quad \mathbf{x} \in (8, 4)^\star. \tag{16.7}$$

As a basis, we use a subdivision of the code (8, 8) (uncoded 8-bit words) as a partition chain.

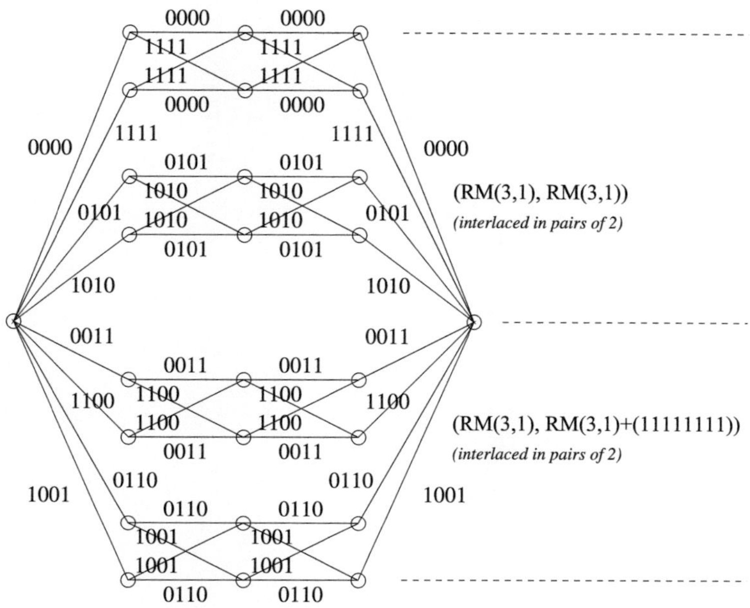

Fig. 16.7 Trellis of the (16, 5, 8)-RM(4, 1) code

$$\begin{aligned}
\mathbf{G}^{\star}_{(8,8)/(8,7)} &= \begin{pmatrix} 1111\ 1110 \end{pmatrix} \\
\mathbf{G}^{\star}_{(8,7)/(8,4)} &= \begin{pmatrix} 0111\ 1000 \\ 1001\ 1100 \\ 0101\ 0110 \end{pmatrix} \\
\mathbf{G}_{(8,4)/(8,1)} &= \begin{pmatrix} 1111\ 0000 \\ 1100\ 1100 \\ 1010\ 1010 \end{pmatrix} \\
\mathbf{G}_{(8,1)} &= \begin{pmatrix} 1111\ 1111 \end{pmatrix}
\end{aligned} \tag{16.8}$$

The code (8, 4) is constructed by $\mathbf{G}_{(8,1)}$ and $\mathbf{G}_{(8,4)/(8,1)}$, the code $(8,4)^{\star}$ by $\mathbf{G}_{(8,1)}$ and $\mathbf{G}^{\star}_{(8,7)/(8,4)}$. This means also that $\mathbf{G}^{\star}_{(8,7)/(8,4)} = \mathbf{G}_{(8,4)^{\star}/(8,1)}$. The generator matrix of the Golay code can now be formulated as[1]

$$\mathbf{G}_{(24,12)} = \mathbf{G}_{(3,3)} \otimes \mathbf{G}_{(8,1)} + \mathbf{G}_{(3,2)} \otimes \mathbf{G}_{(8,4)/(8,1)} + \mathbf{G}_{(3,1)} \otimes \mathbf{G}_{(8,4)^{\star}/(8,1)}, \tag{16.9}$$

where '⊗' denotes the Kronecker product. The last sum term is the threefold repetition $(x^{\star}, x^{\star}, x^{\star})$ of a word resulting from the generator matrix $\mathbf{G}_{(8,4)^{\star}/(8,1)}$. Since there are $2^3 = 8$ such words, the trellis consists of 8 sub-divisions that follow from the 8 cosets. The sum term in the middle is a parity-check code, whose components result from the generator matrix $\mathbf{G}_{(8,4)/(8,1)}$. This means that 6 information bits can be arbitrarily chosen and the 16 code bits determine the remaining 8 bits. The first

[1] This representation is taken from [6, 7].

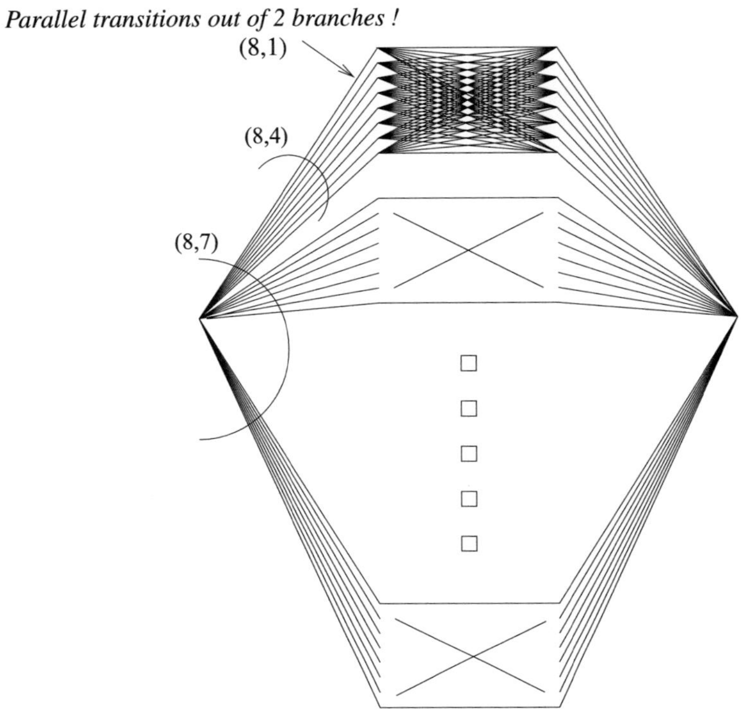

Fig. 16.8 Trellis of the (24, 12, 8) extended Golay code

sum term finally means that the trellis consists of parallel branches of cosets of the repetition code (8, 1). Figure 16.8 sketches the trellis.

In [8], the Golay code is shown to be represented with a less complex so-called tail-biting trellis with only 16 sates. The structure of this trellis is the one that one obtains also from terminating a convolutional code by 'Tail Biting' (cf., Sect. 5.2.5 and [9]). In [9], a tail-biting trellis is represented as cosets of a code with a single start and end state. The coset leaders have zeros in the middle segment. The tail-biting trellis structure consists of a header, a common middle segment, and a tail as shown in Fig. 16.9.

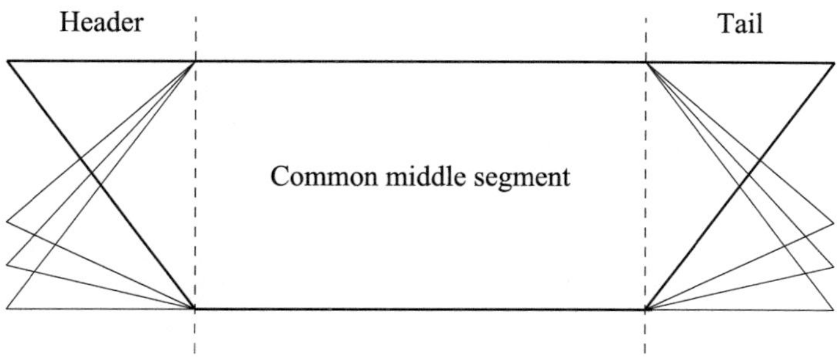

Fig. 16.9 Structure of a tail-biting trellis

References

1. G. Forney, "Generalized minimum distance decoding," *IEEE Transactions on Information Theory*, vol. 12, no. 2, pp. 125–131, 1966.
2. D. Chase, "A class of algorithms for decoding block codes with channel measurement information," *IEEE Transactions on Information Theory*, vol. 18, no. 1, pp. 170–182, 1972.
3. J. Wolf, "Efficient maximum likelihood decoding of linear block codes using a trellis," *IEEE Transactions on Information Theory*, vol. 24, no. 1, pp. 76–80, 1978.
4. L. Bahl, J. Cocke, F. Jelinek, and J. Raviv, "Optimal decoding of linear codes for minimizing symbol error rate (corresp.)," *IEEE Transactions on Information Theory*, vol. 20, no. 2, pp. 284–287, 1974.
5. R. J. McEliece, "On the BCJR trellis for linear block codes," *IEEE Transactions on Information Theory*, vol. 42, no. 4, pp. 1072–1092, 1996.
6. G. D. Forney, "Coset codes. I. introduction and geometrical classification," *IEEE Transactions on Information Theory*, vol. 34, no. 5, pp. 1123–1151, 1988.
7. G. D. Forney, "Coset codes. II. binary lattices and related codes," *IEEE Transactions on Information Theory*, vol. 34, no. 5, pp. 1152–1187, 1988.
8. A. R. Calderbank, G. D. Forney, and A. Vardy, "Minimal tail-biting trellises: the Golay code and more," *IEEE Transactions on Information Theory*, vol. 45, no. 5, pp. 1435–1455, 1999.
9. S. Lin and R. Y. Shao, "General structure and construction of tail biting trellises for linear block codes," in *2000 IEEE International Symposium on Information Theory (Cat. No.00CH37060)*, June 2000, pp. 117–.

Chapter 17
Multilevel Coded Modulation

Life is lived on levels and arrived at in stages.
Edwin Louis Cole

Multilevel codes have been proposed by Imai and Hirakawa in 1977 [1] (see also the description in [2]). The construction follows the one of generalized concatenated codes of Sect. 12.10. In multilevel coding, the inner code $\mathcal{B}^{(0)}$ is a signal set of a modulation alphabet. This signal set is partitioned as we know this from Sect. 7.2, where we described trellis-coded modulation. As an example, we show the partitioning of an 8-PAM in Fig. 17.1.

Following the GC-coding scheme, the points of the 8-PAM is considered as an inner code. It has been partitioned in three steps. Accordingly, the outer codes $\mathcal{A}^{(l)}$, $l = 1, 2, 3$ will be required for error protection. The outer codewords $a^{(1)}$, $a^{(2}$, and $a^{(3)}$ can be written as the rows of a matrix

$$\mathcal{A} \ni A = \begin{pmatrix} a^{(1)} \\ a^{(2)} \\ a^{(3)} \end{pmatrix} = \begin{pmatrix} a_1^{(1)}, a_2^{(1)}, \ldots, a_N^{(1)} \\ a_1^{(2)}, a_2^{(2)}, \ldots, a_N^{(2)} \\ a_1^{(3)}, a_2^{(3)}, \ldots, a_N^{(3)} \end{pmatrix} \begin{matrix} \longleftarrow \in \mathcal{A}^{(1)} \\ \longleftarrow \in \mathcal{A}^{(2)} \\ \longleftarrow \in \mathcal{A}^{(3)} \end{matrix} \tag{17.1}$$

We assumed block codes, but convolutional codes can as well be used in the multilevel scheme. Such solutions especially have low complexity. The columns of the matrix are the numbers of the corresponding signal points of the 8-PAM according to the set partitioning. The first component defines a 4-PAM subset, the second a 2-PAM subset of the already chosen 4-PAM subset. Finally, the third component specifies the single point within the 2-PAM subset.

A multilevel code can in principal be decoded by two means: by using the overall trellis or by using the so-called *multi-stage decoding*, where the decoding is performed step-wise through the outer component codes. The multi-stage decoding is

W. Henkel, *Channel Coding*, Signals and Communication Technology,
https://doi.org/10.1007/978-3-032-08236-7_17

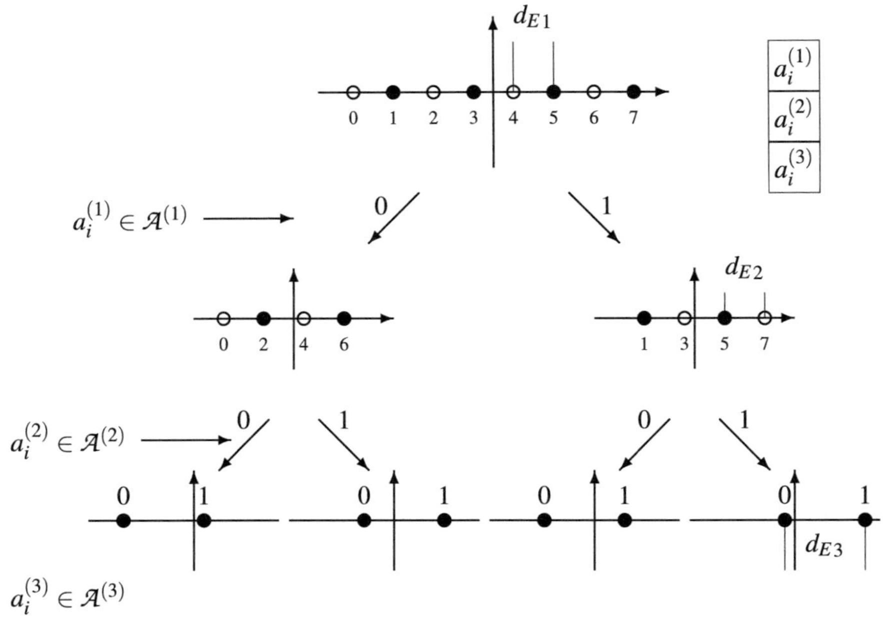

Fig. 17.1 Binary partitioning of 8-PAM

much less complex and the performance is only slightly inferior to the full maximum-likelihood decoder based on the overall trellis. We draw the overall trellis for a simple example given by

$$\begin{aligned} \mathcal{A}^{(1)} &= (8, 1, 8) \text{ repetition code} \\ \mathcal{A}^{(2)} &= (8, 7, 2) \text{ parity-check code} \\ \mathcal{A}^{(3)} &= (8, 8, 1) \text{ uncoded} \end{aligned} \tag{17.2}$$

The *product trellis* is shown in Fig. 17.2. Since the last level is uncoded, only two codes have to be considered. First note that the trellis is subdivided in two by the repetition code. When the first component of the repetition code is 0 or 1, of course, all component are the same. The parity of the second code can change with every component or just stay constant. This is represented by cross structures. The number of states that are a measure for the complexity of the decoding follows from the product of the number of states of the component trellises (in our example $2 \cdot 2 = 4$).

In general a *multi-stage decoding* is less complex, although this is not too obvious from our simple example. The complexity in case of multi-stage decoding is not given by the product of state numbers but by the sum, since the codes are decoded one after another. Decoding starts from the first code to find the 4-PAM subsets within the 8-PAM. After this decision is made, the 2-PAM subsets will be specified by decoding the second code, etc.. Figure 17.3 outlines the procedure.

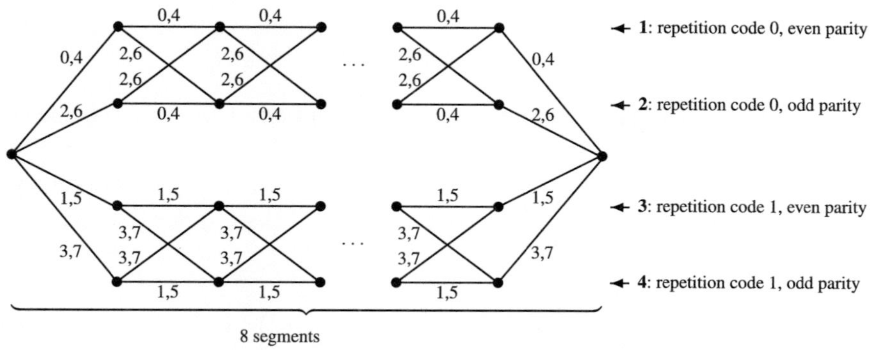

Fig. 17.2 Product trellis of a multilevel code with the component codes (8, 1, 8), (8, 7, 2), and (8, 8, 1)

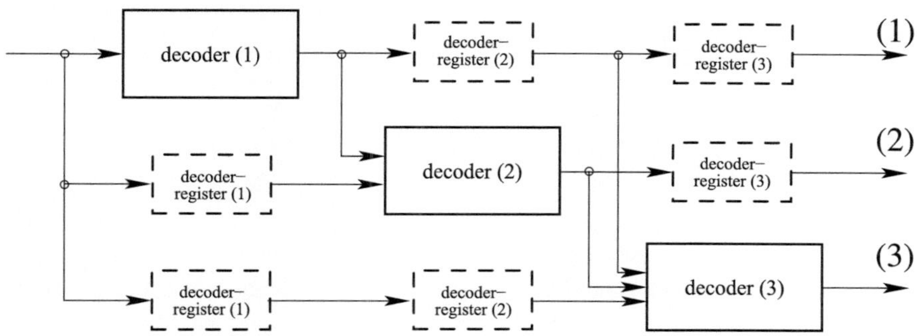

Fig. 17.3 Multi-stage decoding

Multi-stage decoding has only a slightly smaller coding gain (usually just a fraction of a dB) compared to full maximum-likelihood decoding of the product trellis. The difference results from the fact that later decoded codewords cannot have any effect on the earlier decoded ones. However, the effect is not so strong, since, as will be described later, the minimum Hamming distance of the component codes decreases from level to level. Thus, the code protection will not be so strong at the last levels. Thus, the last levels cannot do much to reduce the number of nearest neighbors that are already resulting from multiple representations in the first levels.

17.1 Rules for Multi-level Code Design

When we studied generalized concatenated codes in Sect. 12.10, in Theorem 12.6, we stated that the resulting distance of a GC code is $d_{Hm} \geq \min_l\{\delta_l d_l\}$. Since a multilevel code is a special case of a GC code, we can just take over this result with the same arguments in the proof. Only, the inner code is a modulation alphabet, meaning that the distance d_l is the squared Euclidean distance. We formulate

Theorem 17.1 *A multilevel code, consisting of outer codewords* $\mathcal{A}^{(l)}$ *with parameters* $(N_a^{(l)}, K_a^{(l)}, \delta_{Hl})$, $l = 1, \ldots, r$, *over the finite field* $GF(q_l)$ *and the partitions of a modulation alphabet* $\mathcal{B}^{(l)}_{j_1,\ldots,j_l}$, $l = 0, \ldots, r$, $j_l \in [0, q_l - 1]$, *with the squared Euclidean minimum distance* $d_{E\,l}^2$ *between the sub-alphabets at the same partition level has the parameters*

$$\left(N_a, \prod_{l=1}^{r} \mathcal{K}_a^{(l)}, d_{E\,m}^2 \geq \min_l\{\delta_l d_{E\,l}^2\}\right). \tag{17.3}$$

In case of a regular, e.g., *binary partitioning and linear outer codes, the parameters can instead be given using the number of information components instead of the cardinality, yielding*

$$\left(N_a, \sum_{l=1}^{r} K_a^{(l)}, d_{E\,m}^2 \geq \min_l\{\delta_l d_{E\,l}^2\}\right). \tag{17.4}$$

Since the total minimum distance is the minimal product of outer Hamming distances times inner squared Euclidean distances, it may appear to be optimum to choose the codes such that the **distance products are the same at every partition level**. This approach only aims at the Euclidean distance and thus the asymptotic coding gain. When computing error probabilities, not only the minimum distance has to be considered, but also the distance spectrum (weight distribution in the case of linear codes). Hereto, see the union-bound approximation in Eq. (14.17)

$$p_n \leq \sum_{l=d_{H\,m}}^{N} A_l \cdot p_{\infty}(l)\,, \tag{17.5}$$

with $p_{\infty}(l)$ in the case of AWGN being

$$p_{\infty}(l) = 1/2 \cdot \mathrm{erfc}\left(\frac{l/2}{\sqrt{2}\sigma}\right). \tag{17.6}$$

An alternative construction principle had been described in [3, 4]. There, the multiple representation of information components by signal points is implicitly taken into account. In a binary set partitioning of an 8-PAM, e.g., in the first subdivision, 4 signal points correspond to a zero and the other 4 signal points correspond to one. This means that there is not only one nearest neighbor but two (in general two per dimension), if the point is not located at the border. The number of nearest neighbors at the minimum Euclidean distance $\sqrt{\delta_l \cdot d_{E\,l}^2}$ is $(2D)^{\delta_l}$ at D dimensions.

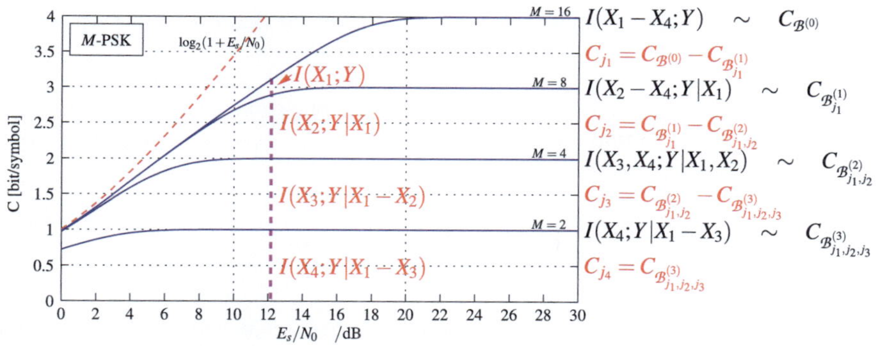

Fig. 17.4 Mutual informations/capacities in multi-lever coded modulation, here for M-PSK

More detailed considerations regarding the weight distribution of multilevel codes will be postponed to the following section.

Huber's construction principle [3, 4] relies on computing the Channel Capacities at every level of a multilevel code. These determine the maximum rates of the outer codes. They follow from the *Chain Rule for the Mutual Information* that we had derived in Theorem 2.5. We are redrawing the Capacity curves from Fig. 2.7 as Fig. 17.4, where we label the curves with the Mutual Information of the bits $X_1, \ldots, X_4$ (for 16-PSK) addressing the points of the modulation alphabet in a set-partitioning manner. $I(X_1 - X_4; Y)$ means the Mutual Information using the complete 16-PSK, $I(X_2 - X_4; Y|X_1)$ stands for a 8-PSK subset with X_1 being 0 or 1, etc.. For simplicity, let us consider the lowest two curves standing for 4- and 2-PSK. The Chain Rule then states

$$I(X_3, X_4; Y|X_1, X_2) = I(X_3; Y|X_1, X_2) + I(X_4; Y|X_1, X_2, X_3) \tag{17.7}$$

which can be rewritten as

$$I(X_3, X_4; Y|X_1, X_2) - I(X_4; Y|X_1, X_2, X_3) = I(X_3; Y|X_1, X_2) \tag{17.8}$$

We clearly see that the level Capacities for the multi-level coded modulation are given be the differences between the Capacity curves.

In the figure, we also additionally entered our annotations with the inner alphabets $\mathcal{B}^{(l)}$. In this formulation, we can write the Capacity differences as

$$C_{\{j_1\}} = C_{\mathcal{B}^{(0)}} - C_{\mathcal{B}^{(1)}_{j_1}}. \tag{17.9}$$

for the first level and in general, as

$$C_{\{j_l\}} = C_{\mathcal{B}^{(l-1)}_{j_1,\ldots,j_{l-1}}} - C_{\mathcal{B}^{(l)}_{j_1,\ldots,j_{l-1},j_l}}. \tag{17.10}$$

As an example, we compute the Capacity shares for the three binary partition levels of an 8-PAM.

Example 17.1 As an example, let us consider the one-dimension constellation 8-PAM given in Fig. 17.1 with the signal points $\{\pm 1, \pm 3, \pm 5, \pm 7\}$. Let the channel be AWGN. First, we abbreviate the Gaussian density as

$$g(r, \mu, \sigma) = \frac{1}{\sqrt{2\pi}\sigma} e^{(-(r-\mu)^2/(2\sigma^2))}.$$

We now compute all Capacities of the signal subsets starting from the two-point constellation, e.g., $\{-1, +7\}$. The Capacities of the partition levels follow from (17.10).

$$c_{\{-1,+7\}} = \frac{1}{2}\left[g(r, -1, \sigma)\log_2\left(\frac{g(r, -1, \sigma)}{p_{\{-1,+7\}}(r)}\right) + g(r, +7, \sigma)\log_2\left(\frac{g(r, +7, \sigma)}{p_{\{-1,+7\}}(r)}\right)\right]$$

with

$$p_{\{-1,+7\}}(r) = \frac{1}{2}\left[g(r, -1, \sigma) + g(r, +7, \sigma)\right]$$

$$\begin{aligned} c_{\{-5,-1,+3,+7\}} = \frac{1}{4}\Bigg[& g(r, -5, \sigma)\log_2\left(\frac{g(r, -5, \sigma)}{p_{\{-5,-1,+3,+7\}}(r)}\right) + \\ & g(r, -1, \sigma)\log_2\left(\frac{g(r, -1, \sigma)}{p_{\{-5,-1,+3,+7\}}(r)}\right) + \\ & g(r, +3, \sigma)\log_2\left(\frac{g(r, +3, \sigma)}{p_{\{-5,-1,+3,+7\}}(r)}\right) + \\ & g(r, +7, \sigma)\log_2\left(\frac{g(r, +7, \sigma)}{p_{\{-5,-1,+3,+7\}}(r)}\right)\Bigg] \end{aligned}$$

with

$$p_{\{-5,-1,+3,+7\}}(r) = \frac{1}{4}\left[g(r, -5, \sigma) + g(r, -1, \sigma) + g(r, +3, \sigma) + g(r, +7, \sigma)\right].$$

The Capacity $c_{\{\pm 1, \pm 3, \pm 5, \pm 7\}}$ follows correspondingly. The level Capacities are

$$\begin{aligned} c_{\{j_1\}} &= c_{\{\pm 1, \pm 3, \pm 5, \pm 7\}} - c_{\{-5,-1,+3,+7\}}, \\ c_{\{j_2\}} &= c_{\{-5,-1,+3,+7\}} - c_{\{-1,+7\}}, \\ c_{\{j_3\}} &= c_{\{-1,+7\}}. \end{aligned}$$

Figure 17.5 shows all the Capacities.

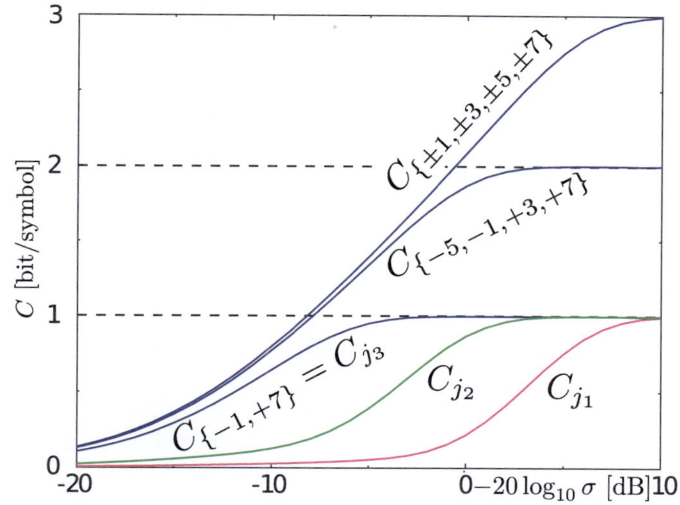

Fig. 17.5 Capacities of the signal sub-constellations of 8-PAM and its differences, the level capacities

17.2 The Weight Distribution of Multilevel Codes

In [4], the weight distribution of multilevel codes has been derived. We describe the case of a regular binary partitioning. The weight distribution allows to determine an approximation of the bit-error ratios after decoding by use of the Union Bound. For the AWGN channel, we have already given the Union Bound in (17.5) and (17.6).

For deriving the weight distribution, let us consider an element $b \in \mathcal{B}_{j_1, j_2, \ldots, j_q, 0}$. The opposite binary symbol 1 in the $(q+1)$st partition is realized by $\sigma = 2^{r-q-1}$ different points. Let the squared Euclidean distances between b and the σ representatives of the opposite binary symbol be $d_1, d_2, \ldots, d_\sigma$. An outer codeword of weight $\delta \geq \delta_q$ can be realized by $\sigma^\delta = 2^{(r-q-1)\cdot\delta}$ different words or sequences of signal points. In case the squared Euclidean distances d_i occur $j_i \in \{0, 1, \ldots, \delta\}$ times, where $\sum_{i=1}^{\sigma} j_i = \delta$, we have

$$\frac{\delta!}{j_1! j_2! \cdots j_\sigma!} \tag{17.11}$$

different combinations, for which the squared Euclidean distances d_i, $i \in \{1, 2, \ldots, \sigma\}$ to point b occur j_i times, each. The weight distribution follows to be

$$\underbrace{\sum_{j_1}\sum_{j_2}\cdots\sum_{j_\sigma}}_{\sum_{i=1}^{\sigma}=\delta} \frac{\delta!}{j_1!j_2!\cdots j_\sigma!} D^{d_1\cdot j_1}\cdot D^{d_2\cdot j_2}\cdots D^{d_\sigma\cdot j_\sigma} = (D^{d_1}+D^{d_2}+D^{d_\sigma})^{\delta} \tag{17.12}$$

Inside the parentheses on the right side, the Euclidean weight distribution of the signal alphabet

$$T_E^q(D) = \sum_{i=1}^{\sigma} D^{d_i} = \sum_{i'} A_{E\,i'}^q D^{d_{i'}} \tag{17.13}$$

is given, where terms with the same squared Euclidean distance have been gathered in the factor $A_{E\,i'}^q$.

In case of a regular partitioning the reference point $b \in \mathcal{B}_{j_1,j_2,\ldots,j_q,0}$ has no influence. The weight distribution for a Hamming distance of δ positions is then given by

$$[T_E^q(D)]^{\delta}. \tag{17.14}$$

For a given weight distribution $T_H(\mathcal{D}) = 1\cdot\mathcal{D}^0 + \mathcal{A}_{H\,min}\cdot\mathcal{D}^{\delta_{min}} + \mathcal{A}_{H\,2}\cdot\mathcal{D}^{\delta_2} + \ldots\ (\delta_i > \delta_{min},\ i = 2, 3, \ldots)$ of the linear (outer) code at level $q+1$, the total weight distribution regarding squared Euclidean distances is

$$T_E^q(D)^{tot} = T_H(\mathcal{D} = T_E^q(D)) = \sum_{i'} \mathcal{A}_{H\,i'}^q (T_E^q(D))^{\delta_{i'}}. \tag{17.15}$$

Example 17.2 We study the binary partitioning of an 8-PAM shown in Fig. 17.1. Let us consider the sub-division of the whole signal set into two subsets, i.e., we start from $q = 0$. The worst case is referring to one of the two inner points. The possible Euclidean distances to points representing the opposite binary number are

$$d_1^2 = d_2^2 = 1 \quad d_3^2 = d_4^2 = 9$$

The worst Euclidean weight distribution of an 8-PAM is then given by

$$[T_E^0(D)] = 2\cdot D^1 + 2\cdot D^9$$

Together with the (Hamming) weight distribution of an outer code, Eq. (17.15) yields the overall weight distribution. Inserting it into (17.5), an approximation of the error probability after decoding is obtained.

Besides almost reaching the Channel Capacity with suitably chosen component codes, multilevel codes allow easy implementation of additional properties. For example, frame synchronization sequences or line codes for spectral shaping can be implemented in component codes or rotationally invariant multilevel codes can easily be constructed. We devote the following section to this topic.

17.3 Multilevel Rotationally Invariant Encoding for PSK and QAM

Rotationally invariant codes do not require to dissolve phase ambiguities, a very convenient property. Besides having design criteria regarding the Euclidean distance, additional code constraints have to be fulfilled. In the case of trellis-coded modulation, nonlinear [5, 6] or multidimensional constructions (see Sect. 7.3) with certain symmetries are required. One may compare the corresponding complexity in Sect. 7.3 with the solution based on multilevel codes described in here.

First, we consider the pure rotational invariance of the code. This does not yet mean rotational invariance for the information symbols. Hereto, a further step is required, which we will study thereafter. The presentation follows [7, 8], but parts of the results can also be found in [9]. We will first discuss PSK.

17.3.1 Rotational Invariance Conditions for Multilevel Encoded PSK

Figure 17.6 again shows the binary partitioning of 8-PSK, as we already know it from the treatment of trellis-coded modulation. To ensure rotational invariance by multiples of the symmetry angle, $l \cdot \pi/4$, $l = 0, 1, \ldots, 7$ in the case of 8-PSK, it suffices to prove it for the smallest possible symmetry angle, which is $\pi/4$ for 8-PSK.

The following table shows modifications at the different levels caused by phase shifts by the symmetry angle of M-PSK up to $M = 16$. The upper (or lower) half without the first column describes the behavior of 8-PSK.

Rotation by $+\pi/8$ equivalent to adding $(0, 0, 0, 1)$								
0	0	0	0	$\longrightarrow$	0	0	0	1
0	0	$\boxed{0}$	1	$\longrightarrow$	0	0	$\boxed{1}$	0
0	0	1	0	$\longrightarrow$	0	0	1	1
0	$\boxed{0}$	$\boxed{1}$	1	$\longrightarrow$	0	$\boxed{1}$	$\boxed{0}$	0
0	1	0	0	$\longrightarrow$	0	1	0	1
0	1	$\boxed{0}$	1	$\longrightarrow$	0	1	$\boxed{1}$	0
0	1	1	0	$\longrightarrow$	0	1	1	1
$\boxed{0}$	$\boxed{1}$	$\boxed{1}$	1	$\longrightarrow$	$\boxed{1}$	$\boxed{0}$	$\boxed{0}$	0
1	0	0	0	$\longrightarrow$	1	0	0	1
1	0	$\boxed{0}$	1	$\longrightarrow$	1	0	$\boxed{1}$	0
1	0	1	0	$\longrightarrow$	1	0	1	1
1	$\boxed{0}$	$\boxed{1}$	1	$\longrightarrow$	1	$\boxed{1}$	$\boxed{0}$	0
1	1	0	0	$\longrightarrow$	1	1	0	1
1	1	$\boxed{0}$	1	$\longrightarrow$	1	1	$\boxed{1}$	0
1	1	1	0	$\longrightarrow$	1	1	1	1
$\boxed{1}$	$\boxed{1}$	$\boxed{1}$	1	$\longrightarrow$	$\boxed{0}$	$\boxed{0}$	$\boxed{0}$	0

We observe that bits at the first level (left) will all be inverted. At higher levels, this is only the case when all lower components, i.e., all those listed further to the

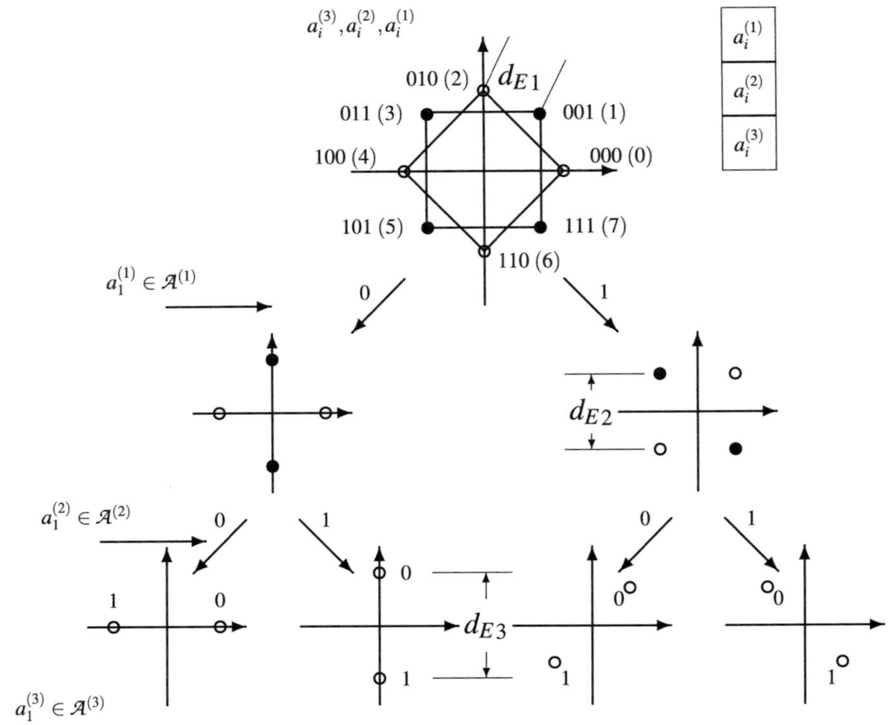

Fig. 17.6 Binary partitioning of 8-PSK

right, are equal to one. This can be formulated as an AND or multiplication. Thus, a rotation by the symmetry angle means

$$a_i^{(1)}|_{+2\pi/M} = a_i^{(1)} + 1 \mod 2 \tag{17.16}$$

$$a_i^{(j)}|_{+2\pi/M} = a_i^{(j)} + \prod_{\eta=1}^{j-1} a_i^{(\eta)} \mod 2\,, \quad j = 2, \ldots, k. \tag{17.17}$$

We conclude that the component codes have to fulfill the following conditions to ensure rotational invariance of the overall multilevel code:

$$\begin{aligned} (1, 1, \ldots, 1) &\in \mathcal{A}^{(1)}, \\ \prod_{m=1}^{j-1} a^{(m)} &\in \mathcal{A}^{(j)}, \quad j = 2, \ldots, k\,. \end{aligned} \tag{17.18}$$

We recall the special property of Reed-Muller codes in (3.20):
$\mathrm{RM}(0, m) \subset \mathrm{RM}(1, m) \subset \mathrm{RM}(2, m) \subset \ldots \subset \mathrm{RM}(m, m)$ and

$$(1, 1, \ldots, 1) \in \mathrm{RM}(r, m),$$

$$a_{r^{(\eta)}} \in \mathrm{RM}(r^{(\eta)}, m) \Longrightarrow \prod_{\sum_{\eta=1}^{j-1} r^{(\eta)} \leq r^{(j)}} a_{r^{(\eta)}} \in \mathrm{RM}(r^{(j)}, m). \tag{17.19}$$

Hence, rotational invariance can be achieved by choosing the component codes to be Reed-Muller codes with

$$\begin{gathered}\mathcal{A}^{(1)} = \mathrm{RM}(r^{(1)}, m),\ \mathcal{A}^{(2)} = \mathrm{RM}(r^{(2)}, m), \ldots, \ \mathcal{A}^{(k)} = \mathrm{RM}(r^{(k)}, m),\\ r^{(1)} < r^{(2)} < \ldots < r^{(k)},\\ \sum_{\eta=1}^{j-1} r^{(\eta)} \leq r^{(j)} \vee r^{(j)} = m, \quad j = 2, \ldots, k.\end{gathered} \tag{17.20}$$

This means $\mathcal{A}^{(1)} \subset \mathcal{A}^{(2)} \subset \cdots \subset \mathcal{A}^{(k)}$, excluding equality.

For multilevel QAM, the conditions simplify, as will be shown in the following section.

17.3.2 *Rotational Invariance Conditions for Multilevel Encoded QAM*

As an example, let us consider the binary partitioning of a 16-QAM according to Fig. 17.7. We observe that in case of an M-QAM it is possible to achieve rotational invariance for all bits from the third on by choosing a rotational invariant numbering without any further conditions on the component codes. Only for the first two component codes requirements apply that are the same as for M-PSK.

According to the binary partitioning of 16-QAM, a multilevel code with four outer codes can be used. The code matrix is given by

$$\mathcal{A} \ni A = \begin{pmatrix} a^{(1)} \\ a^{(2)} \\ a^{(3)} \\ a^{(4)} \end{pmatrix} = \begin{pmatrix} a_1^{(1)}, a_2^{(1)}, \ldots, a_n^{(1)} \\ a_1^{(2)}, a_2^{(2)}, \ldots, a_n^{(2)} \\ a_1^{(3)}, a_2^{(3)}, \ldots, a_n^{(3)} \\ a_1^{(4)}, a_2^{(4)}, \ldots, a_n^{(4)} \end{pmatrix} \begin{matrix} \longleftarrow \in \mathcal{A}^{(1)} \\ \longleftarrow \in \mathcal{A}^{(2)} \\ \longleftarrow \in \mathcal{A}^{(3)} \\ \longleftarrow \in \mathcal{A}^{(4)}. \end{matrix} \tag{17.21}$$

A rotation by the symmetry angle of 90° ($\pi/2$) leads to the following changes:

$$\begin{aligned} a_s^{(1)} &= (1, \ldots, 1) + a^{(1)} \\ a_s^{(2)} &= a^{(1)} + a^{(2)} \\ a_s^{(j)} &= a^{(j)} \quad j = 3, \ldots, i, \end{aligned} \tag{17.22}$$

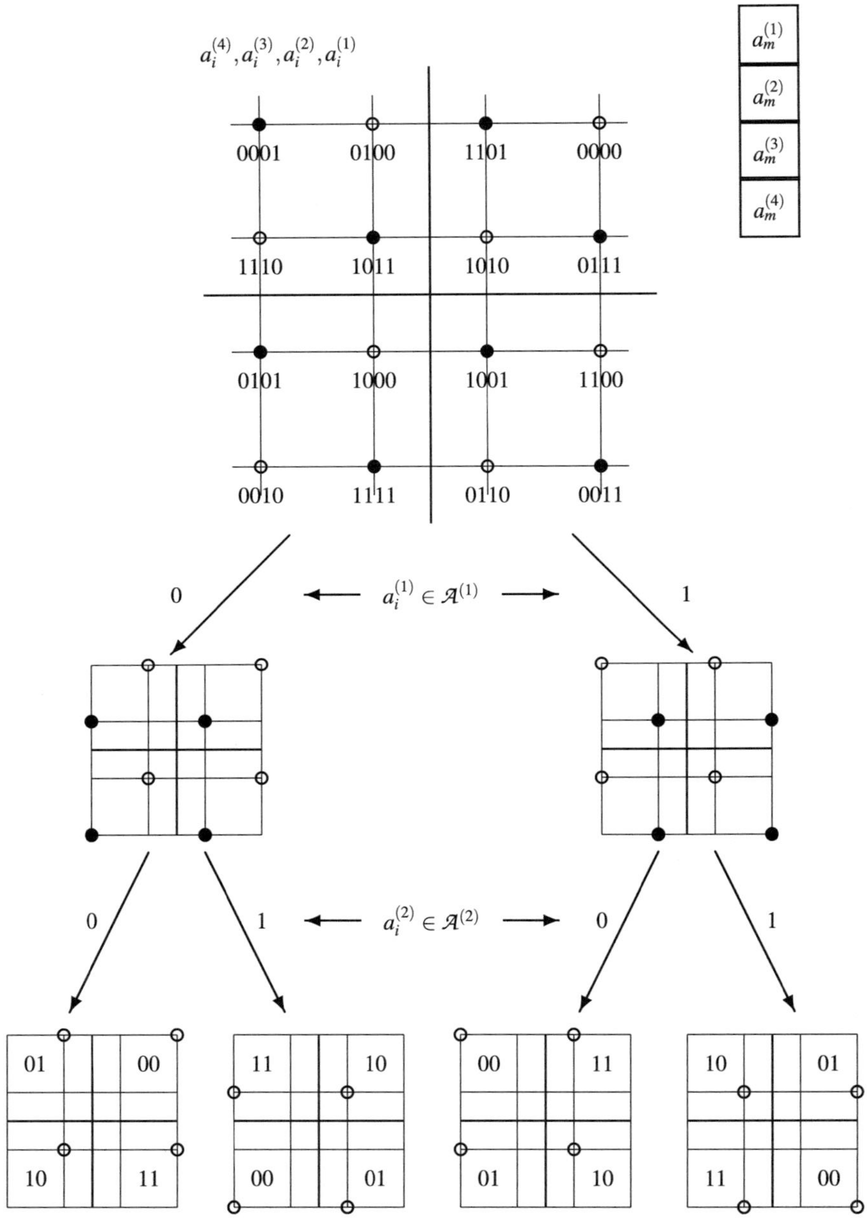

Fig. 17.7 Binary partitioning of 16-QAM

as can be seem from the following table.

Rotation by $+\pi/2$ equivalent to adding (0, 0, 0, 1) without carry to the two leftmost positions								
0	0	0	0	$\longrightarrow$	0	0	0	1
0	0	0	1	$\longrightarrow$	0	0	1	0
0	0	1	0	$\longrightarrow$	0	0	1	1
0	0	1	1	$\longrightarrow$	0	0	0	0
0	1	0	0	$\longrightarrow$	0	1	0	1
0	1	0	1	$\longrightarrow$	0	1	1	0
0	1	1	0	$\longrightarrow$	0	1	1	1
0	1	1	1	$\longrightarrow$	0	1	0	0
1	0	0	0	$\longrightarrow$	1	0	0	1
1	0	0	1	$\longrightarrow$	1	0	1	0
1	0	1	0	$\longrightarrow$	1	0	1	1
1	0	1	1	$\longrightarrow$	1	0	0	0
1	1	0	0	$\longrightarrow$	1	1	0	1
1	1	0	1	$\longrightarrow$	1	1	1	0
1	1	1	0	$\longrightarrow$	1	1	1	1
1	1	1	1	$\longrightarrow$	1	1	0	0

This leads to the conditions

$$(1, 1, \ldots, 1) \in \mathcal{A}^{(1)} \text{ and } \mathcal{A}^{(1)} \subset \mathcal{A}^{(2)} \tag{17.23}$$

for the rotational invariance of multilevel encoded M-QAM.

How can conditions (17.23) *be formulated for Reed-Muller codes of orders $r^{(j)}$ and length $N = 2^m$?*

Up to now, we have derived conditions for the rotational invariance of codes, i.e., we have ensured that a rotation by multiples of the symmetry angle will transfer one valid codeword into another valid codeword. This does not yet mean that the information will not be changed. To ensure this too, we recall that even in uncoded transmission, a differential encoding is used. The following section describes differential en- and decoding in the binary case. Thereafter, the principle will be applied to rotational invariant multilevel codes.

17.4 Differential Encoding and Decoding for Binary Transmission

Long before error-correcting codes have been applied, the problem of receiver-sided phase uncertainties and the corresponding solution was well known. A differential encoding of the data is applied which transforms the information into phase differences between neighboring symbols. A possible phase offset has no effect.

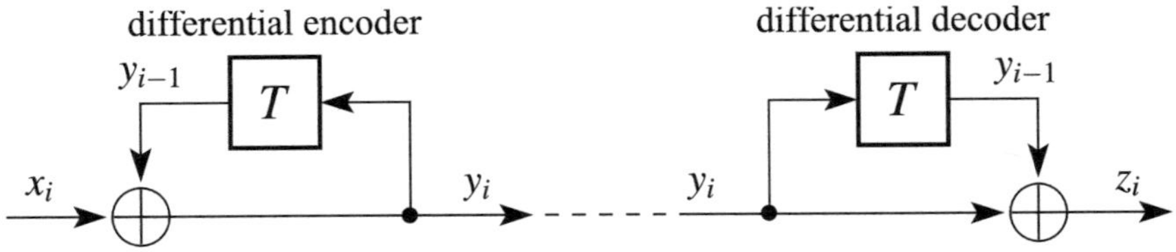

Fig. 17.8 Binary differential en- and decoding

Figure 17.8 shows the differential en- and decoding in the binary case. We assume here that still a coherent demodulation with hard decision is preceding the differential decoder. An incoherent demodulation would be possible as well, determining phase differences between neighboring symbols as differential receiver-sided operation.[1] As far as the noise is concerned, however, two noise samples would then be added (to be exact, they are subtracted, but this does not make any difference). If we assume statistical independence, this would mean a doubling of the noise variance and thus, a 3-dB loss in signal-to-noise ratio. This is the loss between incoherent and coherent demodulation.

Formally, differential en- and decoding are described by

$$x_i + y_{i-1} = y_i \quad \text{and} \quad y_i + y_{i-1} = z_i \pmod 2 \quad \Longrightarrow z_i = x_i \,. \tag{17.24}$$

Differential decoding should be a difference between neighboring symbols or their angles. In the binary case, however, a subtraction is the same as an addition, allowing to draw an XOR (mod-2 sum) in Fig. 17.8.

In the next section, we will generalize the differential encoding in order to apply it to M-PSK and M-QAM.

17.5 Differential Encoding and Decoding for Rotationally Invariant Multilevel Codes

17.5.1 Differential Encoding for M-PSK

We first consider 8-PSK. The signal points that we numbered from 0 to 7 in Fig. 17.6 are located on a circle. It is then obvious to perform a differential en- and decoding by addition and subtraction modulo 8, i.e., in general modulo M, M being the number of signal points. Figure 17.9 shows the block diagrams for differential en- and decoding for rotationally invariant multilevel encoded 8-PSK. The modulo addition and subtraction is block-wise according to the codeword length of the corresponding block codes.

[1] We again use the correspondences $0 \equiv +1$ and $1 \equiv -1$ between binary 0/1 alphabet and the antipodal signal points of a 2-PSK.

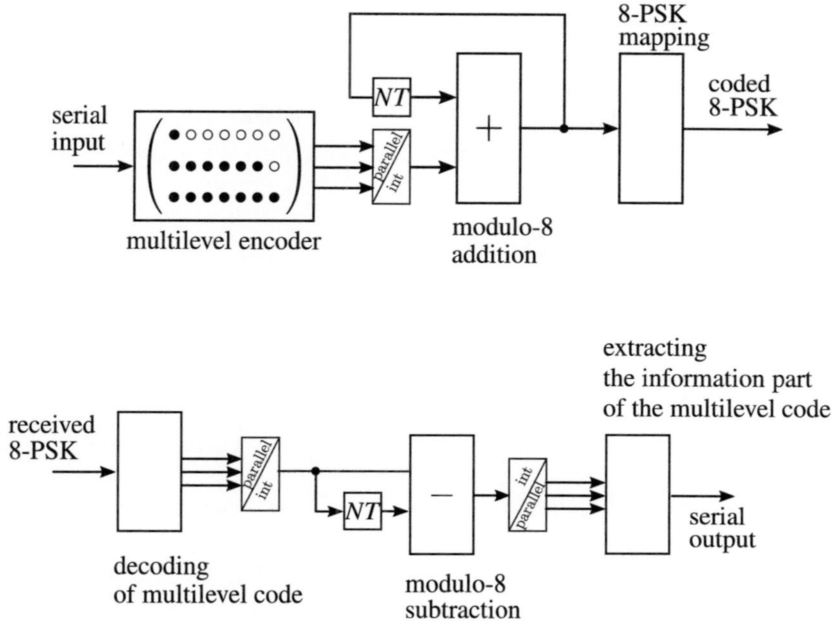

Fig. 17.9 Differential encoder (top) and decoder (bottom) for rotationally invariant multilevel encoded 8-PSK

The non-symmetric arrangement of differential encoder and decoder has the advantage that no incoherent detection is necessary (no loss of 3 dB). After the modulo-8 addition of two neighboring multilevel codewords (and the channel) directly the multilevel decoder is positioned. This leads to an additional code constraint, namely that the modulo-8 sum of two multilevel codewords has to lead to a valid multilevel codeword, again.

We will study this in some more detail. The addition of two multilevel codewords has to be performed with carry. We write the sum of $A_1 \in \mathcal{A}$ and $A_2 \in \mathcal{A}$, $A_1 \neq A_2$ with their components $A_k^{(j)}$ (octal representation) as

$$4 \cdot (A_1^{(3)} + A_2^{(3)}) + 2 \cdot (A_1^{(2)} + A_2^{(2)}) + (A_1^{(1)} + A_2^{(1)}). \tag{17.25}$$

The first condition is $(A_1^{(1)} + A_2^{(1)}) \in \mathcal{A}^{(1)} \bmod 2$, which is anyway fulfilled in the case of linear component codes. A carry has to be considered, when $A_1^{(1)}$ and $A_2^{(1)}$ have a one at the same position, i.e., when the component-wise product $A_1^{(1)} \cdot A_2^{(1)}$ equals one. We conclude that the product of two codewords of the code $\mathcal{A}^{(1)}$ have to be valid codewords of $\mathcal{A}^{(2)}$.

We abbreviate the carry by $A_3^{(2)} := A_1^{(1)} \cdot A_2^{(1)}$. A further carry to the third component of the octal representation follows when $A_1^{(2)} + A_2^{(2)} + A_3^{(2)}$ is greater than one. In other words, a carry to the third component occurs, when at least two of the three components $A_1^{(2)}, A_2^{(2)}, A_3^{(2)}$ have ones at the same position. $A_1^{(2)} \cdot A_2^{(2)} \vee A_1^{(2)} \cdot A_3^{(2)} \vee A_2^{(2)} \cdot A_3^{(2)}$ have to be contained in $\mathcal{A}^{(3)}$. With $a \vee b = a + b + a \cdot b$, we obtain

$$A_1^{(2)} \cdot A_2^{(2)} \vee A_1^{(2)} \cdot A_3^{(2)} \vee A_2^{(2)} \cdot A_3^{(2)} = A_1^{(2)} \cdot A_2^{(2)} + A_1^{(2)} \cdot A_3^{(2)} + A_2^{(2)} \cdot A_3^{(2)}. \tag{17.26}$$

The additional constraint for the component codes of a rotationally invariant multilevel code for M-PSK for the proposed differential en- and decoding now follows as

$$A_1^{(j)} \in \mathcal{A}^{(j)},\ A_2^{(j)} \in \mathcal{A}^{(j)} \Longrightarrow A_1^{(j)} \cdot A_2^{(j)} \in \mathcal{A}^{(j+1)}, \quad j = 1, \ldots, k-1 \tag{17.27}$$

Check that for Reed-Muller codes RM(r, m) as component codes, this can be expressed as:

$$2 \cdot r^{(j)} \leq r^{(j+1)} \quad \vee \quad r^{(j+1)} = m \tag{17.28}$$

The code choice is simplified, if the differential encoding is slightly modified according to Fig. 17.10. In this case, the additional constraint for the third component code is avoided. This modification is only possible if a systematic encoding is used. Due to the modification, the differential decoding yields wrong results in the parity positions. However, since we do only extract information symbols, this is not an issue.

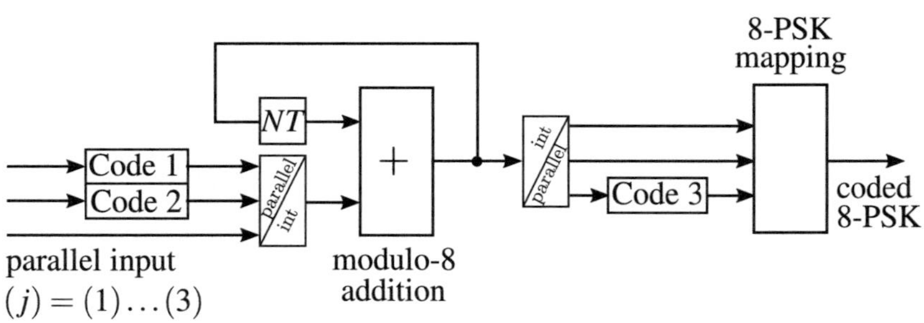

Fig. 17.10 Modified differential encoder

Example 17.3 The simplest example of a multilevel code that fulfills the rotational invariance conditions and also the additional constraints due to differential en- and decoding is

(j)	(N, K, d_H)	$\mathrm{RM}(r, m)$
1	(8, 1, 8)	(0, 3)
2	(8, 7, 2)	(2, 3)
3	(8, 8, 1)	(3, 3)

Determine the asymptotic coding gain from the products of Hamming and Euclidean distances!

Search for other examples with longer Reed-Muller codes and higher coding gain. Amongst those there are UEP (unequal error protection) codes with different minimum-distance products at the code levels.

17.5.2 *Differential Encoding for M-QAM*

M-QAM has only 90° symmetries. The differential encoding needs only be modulo 4. Figure 17.11 shows the differential en- and decoders for QAM which correspond to Figs. 17.9 and 17.10 (bottom) for PSK.

For modulo-4 differential encoded QAM, (17.27) simplifies to one single additional constraint:

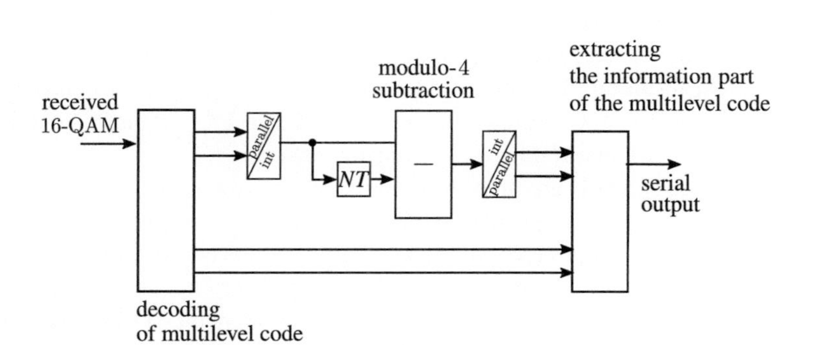

Fig. 17.11 Differential encoding (top) and decoding (bottom) for 90° rotationally invariant (block-) coded 16-QAM

$$A_1^{(1)} \in \mathcal{A}^{(1)},\ A_2^{(1)} \in \mathcal{A}^{(1)} \Longrightarrow A_1^{(1)} \cdot A_2^{(1)} \in \mathcal{A}^{(2)} \tag{17.29}$$

How can conditions (17.29) be formulated for Reed-Muller codes of orders $r^{(j)}$ and lengths $N = 2^m$?

Example 17.4 An example of a multilevel scheme that fulfills the rotational invariance conditions and also the additional constraint due to differential en-/decoding, is subsequently shown.

(j)	(N, K, d_H)	RM(r, m)
1	(32, 16, 8)	(2, 5)
2	(32, 26, 4)	(3, 5)
3	(32, 31, 2)	(4, 5)
4	(32, 32, 1)	(5, 5)

Determine the asymptotic coding gain from the products of Hamming and Euclidean distances!

Search for other examples with Reed-Muller codes, e.g., with lengths 8 and 16.

In our treatment of rotationally invariant codes we always assumed to have block codes as component codes. Nevertheless, convolutional codes can be used as well. Sub-frames of length n will then be used in a similar way as code blocks of length N. The conditions for rotational invariance have to be reformulated into conditions for the generators. This is easier for QAM, since only conditions for the first two levels have to be fulfilled. For a detailed treatment, see [10].

17.6 Other Forms of Coded Modulation

One may, of course, just map code bits directly to modulation alphabets, then, however, using a Gray-code mapping, where neighboring points will only differ by a single bit. Gray-code mapping results from a mirroring procedure, where points and mappings are mirrored according to used dimensions and more labels are added to distinguish the mirrored subsets, also according to a Gray code. Figure 17.12 shows this for 16-QAM resulting from mirrored Gray-coded 4-QAM. A Gray code exists only for 2^{2m}-QAM, i.e., not for cross constellations of size 2^{2m+1}. One can obtain a Gray code for M-PAM and M-PSK signal sets by mirroring.

If, e.g., RS code symbols are mapped to modulation symbols, one would prefer the RS symbol size to be a multiple of the QAM symbol size (or vice versa). In case of an RS code over GF(2^8) the 8 bits of a symbol should encode two 16-QAM symbols in an aligned fashion. In a non-aligned mapping, a single erroneous QAM symbol could lead to two erroneous RS symbols. To improve RS decoding performance, one may use guard bands instead of decision thresholds for the QAM signal set and set erasures, if received values fall into such a guard band.

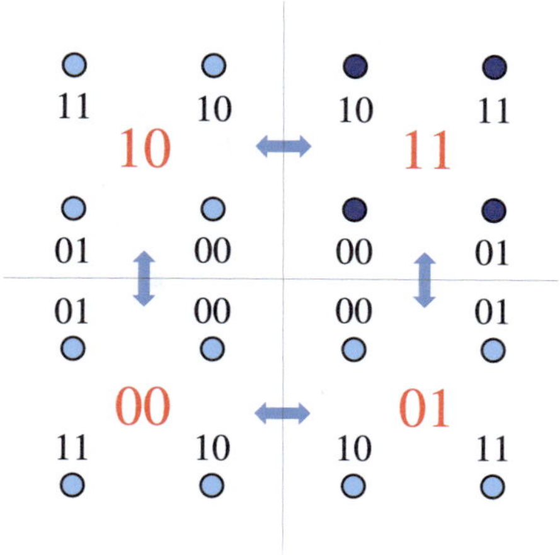

Fig. 17.12 Gray-coded 16-QAM

A comparable performance to TCM and multilevel codes is achieved by bit-interleaved coded modulation (BICM) [11, 12]. Here, a binary code is followed by a bit interleaver and Gray mapping for the modulation. The deinterleaver processes analog information, e.g., LLRs, followed by a decoder. The binary code could also be Turbo or LDPC codes.

References

1. H. Imai and S. Hirakawa, "A new multilevel coding method using error-correcting codes," *IEEE Transactions on Information Theory*, vol. 23, no. 3, pp. 371–377, 1977.
2. A. R. Calderbank, "Multilevel codes and multistage decoding," *IEEE Transactions on Communications*, vol. 37, no. 3, pp. 222–229, 1989.
3. J. Huber, "Multilevel codes: Distance profiles and channel capacity," in *ITG-Fachtagung 'Codierung für Quelle, Kanal und Übertragung'*, Oct 1994, pp. 305–319.
4. J. Huber and U. Wachsmann, "Capacities of equivalent channels in multilevel coding schemes," *Electronics Letters*, vol. 30, no. 7, pp. 557–558, 1994.
5. M. Oerder and H. Meyr, "Rotationally invariant trellis codes for MPSK modulation," *Archiv für Elektronik und Übertragungstechnik (AEÜ)*, vol. 41, no. 1, pp. 28–32, feb 1987.
6. G. Ungerboeck, "Trellis-coded modulation with redundant signal sets Part II: State of the art," *IEEE Communications Magazine*, vol. 25, no. 2, pp. 12–21, 1987.
7. W. Henkel, "Phase-invariant coded phase shift keying using Reed-Muller codes," *AEÜ*, vol. 46, no. 3, pp. 125–130, 1992. [Online]. Available: www.wp-content/uploads/2014/01/aeu_rm.pdf
8. W. Henkel, "Conditions for 90 degrees phase-invariant block-coded QAM," *IEEE Transactions on Communications*, vol. 41, no. 4, pp. 524–527, 1993.
9. T. Kasami, T. Takata, T. Fujiwara, and S. Lin, "On linear structure and phase rotation invariant properties of block M-PSK modulation codes," *IEEE Transactions on Information Theory*, vol. 37, no. 1, pp. 164–167, 1991.
10. W. Henkel and M. Koch, "90°-Rotationally invariant multilevel convolutionally encoded QAM," *European Transactions on Telecommunications*, vol. 4, no. 2, pp. 141–147, 1993. [Online]. Available: https://onlinelibrary.wiley.com/doi/abs/10.1002/ett.4460040209

11. G. Caire, G. Taricco, and E. Biglieri, "Bit-interleaved coded modulation," *IEEE Transactions on Information Theory*, vol. 44, no. 3, pp. 927–946, 1998.
12. E. Zehavi, "8-PSK trellis codes for a Rayleigh channel," *IEEE Transactions on Communications*, vol. 40, no. 5, pp. 873–884, 1992.

Chapter 18
An Introduction to Lattices

... for the comb of the hive-bee, as far as we can see,
is absolutely perfect in economizing labor and wax.

Charles Darwin

In the previous chapter, we have already designed lattices without having introduced this term. Lattices can be described by multilevel codes or, in general, by generalized concatenated codes. Nevertheless, in here, we will introduce the Lattice terminology. We already introduced them formally in Definition 7.1 as a linear combination of basis vectors $\mathbf{v}_j$, $j = 1, \ldots, N$:

$$\Lambda = \left\{ \sum_{j=1}^{N} \lambda_j \mathbf{v}_j \mid \lambda_j \in \mathbb{Z},\ j = 1, \ldots, N \right\} . \tag{18.1}$$

(For simplicity, we have assumed that all dimensions of $\mathbb{R}^N$ are used.) In the N-dimensional space, a regular grid is defined, whose fundamental unit is called **Fundamental Region** or **Voronoi Cell**, where the latter is a special case of the first, if different ways of incorporating the boundaries is ignored. Subsequently, we give the definitions of these divisions.

Definition 18.1 A **Fundamental Region** $\mathcal{R}$ is a region from $\mathbb{R}^N$ of a lattice Λ that contains exactly one point from the equivalence class modulo Λ. In other words, $\mathcal{R}$ is a complete system of coset representatives for Λ in $\mathbb{R}^N$.

Definition 18.2 Let $\mathcal{P} = \{P_0, P_1, P_2, \ldots\}$, $P_j \in \mathbb{R}^N$ be the set of lattice points. A **Voronoi Cell** $V(P_j)$ of a lattice point P_j is the set of all points $x \in \mathbb{R}^N$ that are at least as near to P_j (in Euclidean sense) as to every other lattice point.

$$V(P_j) = \left\{ x \in \mathbb{R}^N :\ \forall_{l \neq j}\ ||x - P_j||_2 \leq ||x - P_l||_2 \right\} \tag{18.2}$$

W. Henkel, *Channel Coding*, Signals and Communication Technology,
https://doi.org/10.1007/978-3-032-08236-7_18

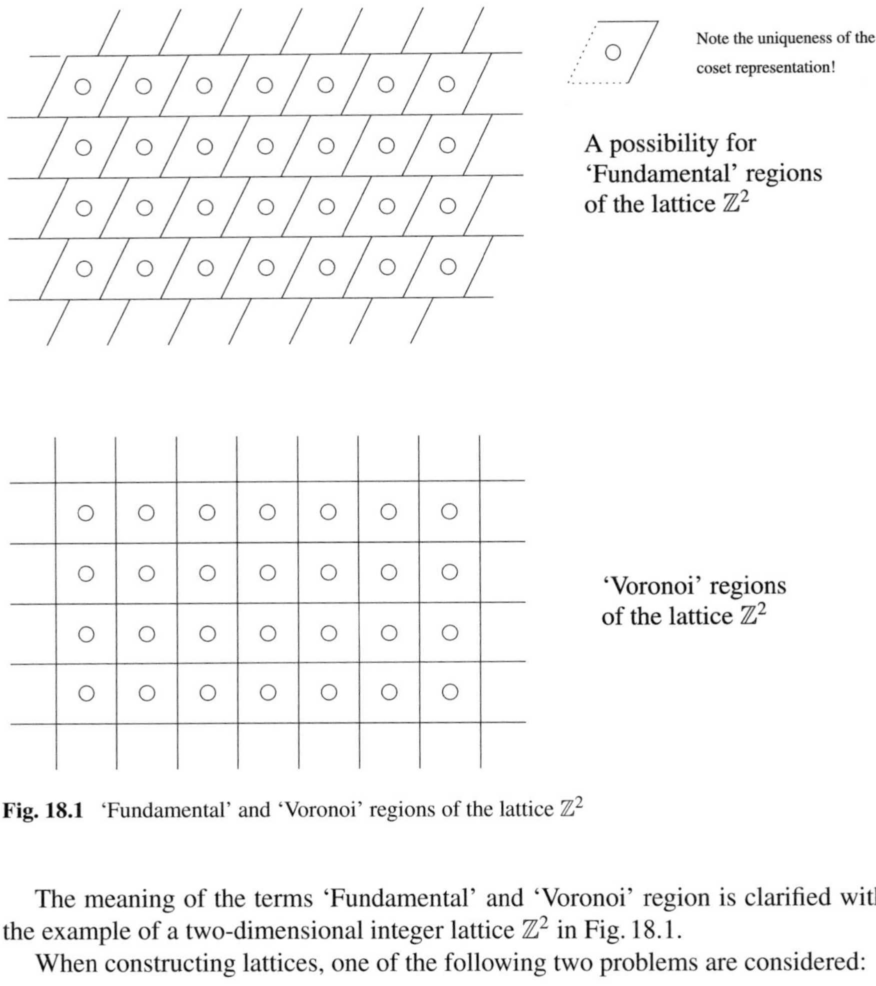

Fig. 18.1 'Fundamental' and 'Voronoi' regions of the lattice $\mathbb{Z}^2$

The meaning of the terms 'Fundamental' and 'Voronoi' region is clarified with the example of a two-dimensional integer lattice $\mathbb{Z}^2$ in Fig. 18.1.

When constructing lattices, one of the following two problems are considered:

- packing problem,
- covering problem.

The first problem is treated in coded modulation, where a maximum number of points at a given Euclidean distance are placed. This maximizes the rate. The quantization problem is opposite to that. Here, one tries to cover the available spaces with a minimum number of points. For both orientations, we define the **Packing Radius** and the **Covering Radius**, respectively.

Definition 18.3 The **Packing Radius** ρ_p is half the minimum Euclidean distance.

Definition 18.4 The **Covering Radius** ρ_c denotes the smallest upper bound on the distance of every arbitrary point of the $\mathbb{R}^N$ to the nearest point $P_j \in \mathcal{P}$.

$$\rho_c = \sup_{x \in \mathbb{R}^N} \inf_{P \in \mathcal{P}} ||x - P||_2 \tag{18.3}$$

As a two-dimensional example, Fig. 18.2 shows the hexagonal grid, which is the densest packing in two dimensions (a fact that bees have known for long).

From the basis vectors

$$\begin{aligned}\mathbf{v}_1 &= (v_{11}, v_{12}, v_{13}, \ldots, v_{1\mu})\\ \mathbf{v}_2 &= (v_{21}, v_{22}, v_{13}, \ldots, v_{2\mu})\\ &\vdots\\ \mathbf{v}_N &= (v_{N1}, v_{N2}, v_{N3}, \ldots, v_{N\mu})\end{aligned}$$

of a lattice, the so-called **generator matrix**

$$\mathbf{M} = \begin{pmatrix} v_{11} & v_{12} & v_{13} & \ldots & v_{1\mu} \\ v_{21} & v_{22} & v_{13} & \ldots & v_{2\mu} \\ \vdots & \vdots & \vdots & & \vdots \\ v_{N1} & v_{N2} & v_{N3} & \ldots & v_{N\mu} \end{pmatrix} \tag{18.4}$$

is constructed. The product

$$\mathbf{A} = \mathbf{M}\mathbf{M}^T \tag{18.5}$$

is named the **Gram matrix** of the lattice. The volume of the Fundamental (Voronoi) region V_R is given by

$$V_R = \sqrt{\det A}. \tag{18.6}$$

This volume is often called $\sqrt{\det \Lambda}$.

In case of the packing problem of coded modulation, one tries to maximize the share of the spheres with packing radius ρ_p and volume $V_{\circ,N}$ of the total space, *i.e.*, the **density** Δ of the lattice

$$\Delta = \frac{V_{\circ,N}}{V_R} \tag{18.7}$$

is to be maximized.

In case of the hexagonal lattices, the volume (area) of the comprised circles is $\pi \cdot \rho_p^2$ and the volume (area) of the hexagons is $6/\sqrt{3} \cdot \rho_p^2$. The density follows to be $\Delta = \pi/6 \cdot \sqrt{3} = 0,9069$. Then densest three-dimensional packing has a density of $\Delta = \pi/\sqrt{18} = 0,7405$.

The volume of an N-dimensional sphere is

$$V_{\circ,N} = V_{\circ,N,\rho_p=1} \cdot \rho_p^N \tag{18.8}$$

with

$$V_{\circ,N,\rho_p=1} = \frac{\pi^{N/2}}{\Gamma(N/2+1)} = \frac{2^N \pi^{(N-1)/2}((N-1)/2)!}{N!} \tag{18.9}$$

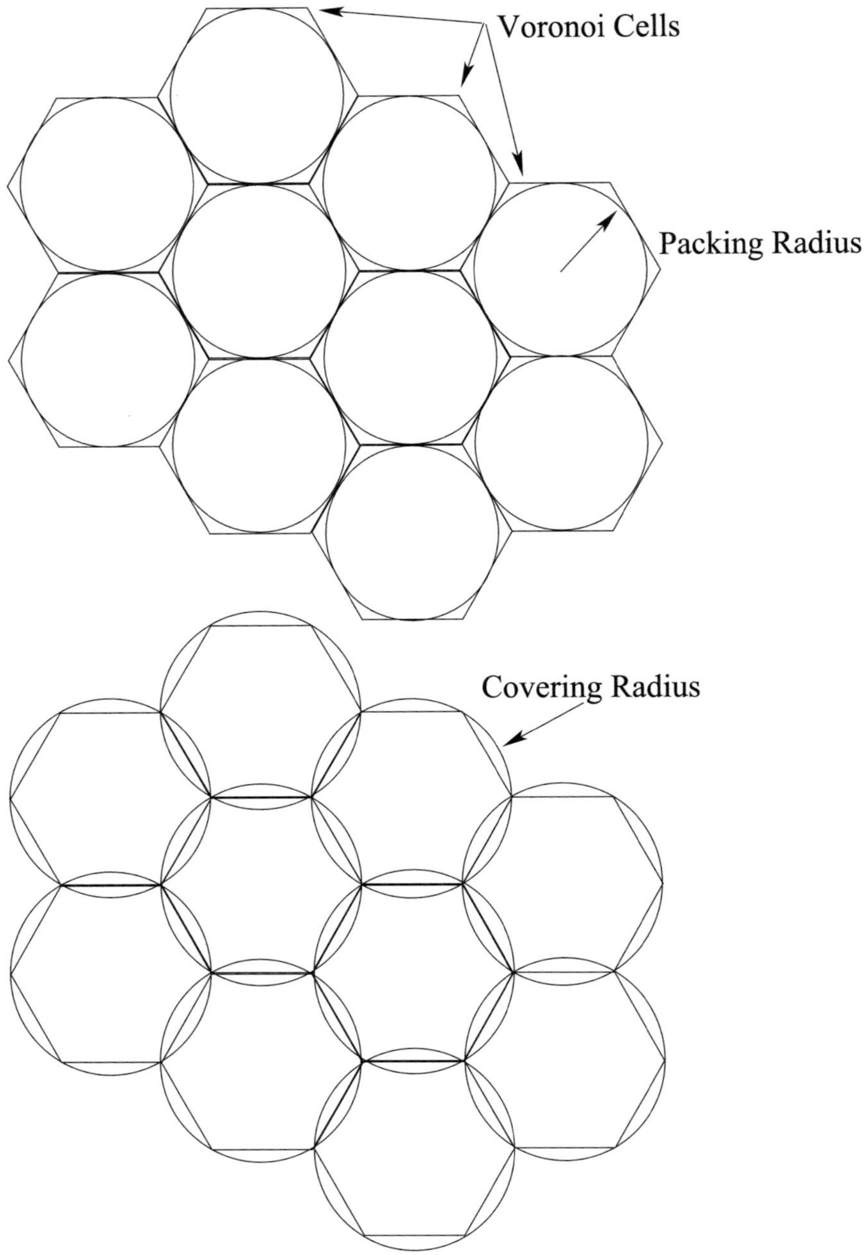

Fig. 18.2 Covering and packing radius for the hexagonal lattice

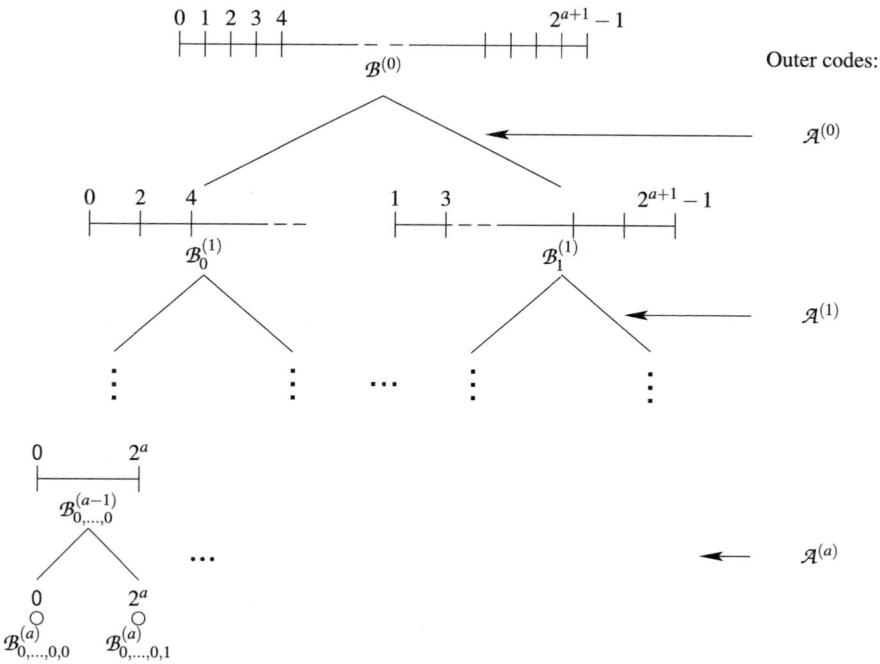

Fig. 18.3 Binary partitioning of a segment of $\mathbb{Z}$

In the following, we will present four lattice constructions following Conway and Sloane in [1], named 'A', 'B', 'C', 'D'. These are based on a binary partitioning of a one-dimensional alphabet (a segment of $\mathbb{Z}$) according to Fig. 18.3. Thereafter, we will discuss the choices for outer codes $\mathcal{A}^{(j)}$, $j = 0, 1, \ldots, a$, of a multilevel code (generalized concatenated code) and the resulting densities. In lattice theory, the multilevel scheme is usually named *Leech Coordinate Array*.

As we already know, the packing radius ρ_p equals half the Euclidean minimum distance δ_E. The volume $V_\square$ of the (cubic) N-dimensional space that embraces $0, 1, \ldots, 2^{a+1}-1$ in each dimension is

$$V_\square = (2^{a+1})^N \,. \tag{18.10}$$

If $\mathcal{K}$ lattice points lie inside the considered region, the density is given by

$$\Delta = \frac{\mathcal{K}}{2^{(a+1)N}} \cdot V_{\circ,N,\rho_p=1} \cdot \left(\frac{\delta_E}{2}\right)^N \,. \tag{18.11}$$

In case of a multilevel code which we base our description on, we have

$$\mathcal{K} = 2^{\sum_{j=0}^{a} K^{(j)}} \tag{18.12}$$

$$\delta_E^2 = \min_{j=0,\ldots,a} \left\{ d^{(j)} \cdot (2^j)^2 \right\}. \tag{18.13}$$

Subsequently, we discuss the four lattices constructions.

A: $\mathcal{A}^{(0)} : (N, \mathcal{K}^{(0)}, d),\ \mathcal{A}^{(1)} : (N, N, 1),\ \ \delta_E^2 \geq \min\{d \cdot 1, 1 \cdot 4\}$,

$$\Delta \geq \frac{\mathcal{K}^{(0)} \cdot 2^{Na}}{2^{(a+1)N}} \cdot V_{\circ,N,\rho_p=1} \cdot (\delta_E/2)^N = \frac{\mathcal{K}^{(0)}}{2^N} \cdot V_{\circ,N,\rho_p=1} \cdot \min\left\{ \left(\frac{\sqrt{d}}{2} \right)^N, 1 \right\}$$

B: $\mathcal{A}^{(0)} : (N, \mathcal{K}^{(0)}, d),\ \mathcal{A}^{(1)} : (N, N-1, 2),\ \ \delta_E^2 \geq \min\{d \cdot 1, 2 \cdot 4\}$,

$$\Delta \geq \frac{\mathcal{K}^{(0)} \cdot 2^{Na-1}}{2^{(a+1)N}} \cdot V_{\circ,N,\rho_p=1} \cdot (\delta_E/2)^N = \frac{\mathcal{K}^{(0)}}{2^{N+1}} \cdot V_{\circ,N,\rho_p=1} \cdot \min\left\{ \left(\frac{\sqrt{d}}{2} \right)^N, 2^{N/2} \right\}$$

C: $d^{(j)} = \gamma \cdot 4^{a-j},\ \gamma = 1, 2,\ \ \delta_E^2 \geq \min_{j=0,\ldots,a} \{d^{(j)} \cdot (2^j)^2\} = \min_{j=0,\ldots,a} \{\gamma \cdot 4^{a-j} \cdot 4^j\} = \gamma \cdot 4^a$,

$$\Delta \geq \frac{\mathcal{K}}{4^N} \cdot \gamma^{N/2} \cdot V_{\circ,N,\rho_p=1}$$

D: $\mathcal{A}^{(0)} \subseteq \mathcal{A}^{(1)} \subseteq \cdots \subseteq \mathcal{A}^{(a)},\ \ \mathcal{A}^{(a)} : (N, N, 1)$ (uncoded), $\ d^{(j)} \geq 4^{a-j}/\gamma,\ \gamma = 1, 2$, $\delta_E^2 \geq \min_{j=0,\ldots,a} \{4^{a-j}/\gamma \cdot 4^j\} = 4^a/\gamma$

$$\Delta \geq \frac{2^{\sum_{j=0}^{a-1} K^{(j)} + N}}{2^{2N} \cdot \gamma^{N/2}} \cdot V_{\circ,N,\rho_p=1} = \frac{2^{\sum_{j=0}^{a-1} K^{(j)}}}{2^N \cdot \gamma^{N/2}} \cdot V_{\circ,N,\rho_p=1}$$

We now provide some know lattices of every group.

to A: Let $\mathcal{A}^{(0)}$ be a parity-check code $(N, N-1, 2)$. We obtain the so-called **Checkerboard Lattice** D_N in $\mathbb{R}^N$.

to B: Let $\mathcal{A}^{(0)}$ be the repetition code (8, 1, 8). We obtain the **Gosset-Lattice** E_8. With a first-order Reed-Muller code with parameters (16, 5, 8) as $\mathcal{A}^{(0)}$ we obtain the **Laminated Lattice** Λ_{16}.
With the extended Golay code (24, 12, 8), we obtain a lattice known as $h\Lambda_{24}$ or H_{24}. It contains half the lattice points of the densest Lattice in 24 dimensions, the **Leech Lattice** Λ_{24}. The Leech lattice Λ_{24} is obtained by adding a translated version of $h\Lambda_{24}$, shifted by $(-3/2, \underbrace{1/2, 1/2, \ldots, 1/2}_{23})$ to $h\Lambda_{24}$, itself.

to C: With this construction, also non-lattices packings are obtained. With the $(2r)$th order Reed-Muller code for $C^{(r)}$, *e.g.*, a packing with the name P_{Nr} in $\mathbb{R}^N$ results.

to D: With Reed-Muller codes, the so-called **Barnes-Wall Lattices** BW_N over $\mathbb{R}^N$ are obtained. For example, $C^{(0)}$: (16, 5, 8) and $C^{(1)}$: (16, 15, 2) lead to $\Lambda_{16} = BW_{16}$. This special choice we know already from construction B.

Although we described lattices using multi-level coded modulation based on partitioning the one-dimensional integers, one should mention that not all multi-level coding constructions will lead to lattices in a strict sense according to Eq. (18.1). Further details on Lattice A can be found in the book by Ram Zamir [2], whereas C and D were treated in [3].

References

1. J. H. Conway, N. J. A. Sloane, and E. Bannai, *Sphere-packings, Lattices, and Groups*. Berlin, Heidelberg: Springer-Verlag, 1987.
2. R. Zamir, B. Nazer, I. Bistritz, and Y. Kochman, *Lattice Coding for Signals and Networks: A Structured Coding Approach to Quantization, Modulation, and Multiuser Information Theory*, ser. Lattice Coding for Signals and Networks: A Structured Coding Approach to Quantization, Modulation, and Multi-user Information Theory. Cambridge University Press, 2014. [Online]. Available: https://books.google.de/books?id=0ysDBAAAQBAJ
3. R. Zamir, "Nested lattice / non-lattice constructions," in *2016 9th International Symposium on Turbo Codes and Iterative Information Processing (ISTC)*, Sept 2016, p. w/o paper.

Chapter 19
Block Shaping with Shell Mapping

In cooking onions it is well to first know your onion.

Seattle Post, 1900

We learned in Chap. 8 that the so-called 'ultimate shaping gain', the maximum gain achievable by shaping the probability distribution of the signal points, can be achieved by going for infinitely many dimensions $N \rightarrow \infty$. We computed it in (8.13) to be $\frac{\pi e}{6} = 1,53$ dB. The idea of infinitely many dimensions lead to Forney's trellis shaping, which we described in Sect. 8.2. The trellis of the transmitter-sided Viterbi algorithm allowed for infinitely long sequences.
Following our parallel description of block and convolutional codes, we now describe a block-oriented shaping approach. Especially, we will see that also a finite number of dimensions, e.g., just two, allow to obtain the 'ultimate shaping gain'. Hereto, the signal space is divided in infinitely many shells. Thus, again, there is a transition to infinity. It is intuitively clear that a Gaussian distribution in one or two dimensions can also be obtained by a increasingly finer sub-division of the signal space with corresponding probabilities.

To derive the shaping gain from the shell perspective, we will first follow the formal steps from [1] and will thereafter show how a so-called lexicographic order of shells can be obtained as used in the V.34 voice-band modem standards [2].

The division of the signal spaces starts from a basis region that we name $\mathcal{R}$. We now use a sequence of growing copies of this basis region that are contained in one another.

$$\mathcal{R} = \alpha_0\mathcal{R},\ \alpha_1\mathcal{R},\ \alpha_2\mathcal{R},\ \ldots,\ \alpha_{T-1}\mathcal{R}$$

We subdivide the constellation Ω with the boundary $\alpha_{T-1}\mathcal{R}$ into the sub-constellations $\Omega_0, \ldots, \Omega_{T-1}$ with $\Omega_0 = \Omega \cap \mathcal{R}$ and

W. Henkel, *Channel Coding*, Signals and Communication Technology,
https://doi.org/10.1007/978-3-032-08236-7_19

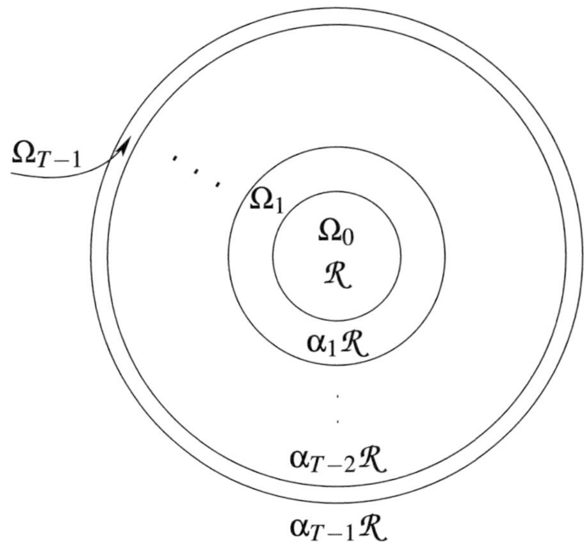

Fig. 19.1 A two-dimensional subdivision in concentrically comprised subconstellations

$$\Omega_i = \Omega \cap (\alpha_i \mathcal{R} \backslash \alpha_{i-1}\mathcal{R}),\ i = 1, 2, \ldots, T-1\ . \tag{19.1}$$

Figure 19.1 illustrates the subdivision for the two-dimensional case.

Let us assume that the signal subconstellations of a lattice in $\mathbb{R}^N$ have all the same size. Then, the volume of a region $\alpha_i \mathcal{R}$ is given by

$$V(\alpha_i \mathcal{R}) = (i+1)V(\mathcal{R})\ , \tag{19.2}$$

i.e., the scaling factor α_i equals $\alpha_i = (i+1)^{1/N}$. Let us assume that the points within a subconstellation will appear with the same probability and a subconstellation Ω_i is chosen with a probability f_i. If P_i is the average power of a subconstellation Ω_i, the average power of the shells chosen with different probabilities is

$$P = \sum_{i=0}^{T-1} f_i P_i\ . \tag{19.3}$$

We show that this power can be expressed as

Lemma 19.1

$$P = \sum_{i=0}^{T-1} \left((i+1)^{2/N+1} - i^{2/N-1}\right) f_i P_0\ , \tag{19.4}$$

with P_0 being the average power of the subconstellation Ω_0

Proof We prove this lemma using a continuous approximation, where we assume the probability density function to be constant (equally distributed) within a region and zero outside. Using the representation in (8.10), $G(\mathcal{R}) = P(\mathcal{R})/(V(\mathcal{R}))^{2/N}$, we observe that a scaling of a region $\mathcal{R}$ by the volume factor a increases the average power by a factor $a^{2/N}$. Letting $P_i = t_i * P_0$, we get

$$\frac{1}{i+1}\sum_{j=0}^{i} t_j P_0 = (i+1)^{2/N} P_0 \,. \tag{19.5}$$

For $t_0 = 1$, we instantly obtain $t_1 = 2^{2/N+1} - 1 = 2^{2/N+1} - 1^{2/N+1}$ and for $i \geq 2$, the proof is provided by the computation

$$\begin{aligned} t_i &= (i+1)^{2/N+1} - \sum_{j=0}^{i} t_j = (i+1)^{2/N+1} - t_{i-1}\sum_{j=0}^{i-2} t_j = \\ &= (i+1)^{2/N+1} - \left(i^{2/N+1} - \sum_{j=0}^{i-2} t_j\right) - \sum_{j=0}^{i-2} t_j \\ &= (i+1)^{2/N+1} - i^{2/N+1}. \end{aligned} \tag{19.6}$$

□

We will now compute the shaping gain resulting from using the N-dimensional shells with different probabilities. This part of the shaping gain is called *biasing gain*. Using a sphere instead of a cube leads to some further shaping gain, which we already listed in Sect. 8.1 for different numbers of dimensions.

To be able to do a fair comparison with a constellation with a constant probability distribution, it is important to know, how big this constellation should be. The unequal probability distribution corresponds to an information content. This binary entropy is given by

$$H(f_0, \ldots, f_{T-1}) = -\sum_{i=0}^{T-1} f_i \log_2(f_i) \tag{19.7}$$

with the probabilities $f_0, \ldots, f_{T-1}$ of the sub-constellations (shells) $\Omega_0, \ldots, \Omega_{T-1}$. To be able to transmit this additional information, a equal-frequency constellation of the size

$$\Omega' = 2^{H(f_0,\ldots,f_{T-1})} \cdot \Omega_0 \tag{19.8}$$

would be required. Assuming that the region $\mathcal{R}$ is achieved by scaling, i.e., has the same principal shape and the same underlying lattice (actually, a continuous approximation will be used), the average power P' of the constellation Ω' will be

$$P' = 2^{2\,H(f_0,\ldots,f_{T-1})/N} \cdot P_0 \,. \tag{19.9}$$

Together with (19.4), we can define the *biasing gain.*

Definition 19.1 The **biasing gain** $\gamma_N(f_0, \ldots, f_{T-1})$ is the ratio between P' and P, given by

$$\gamma_N(f_0, \ldots, f_{T-1}) = \frac{2^{2\,H(f_0,\ldots,f_{T-1})/N}}{\sum_{i=0}^{T-1}\left((i+1)^{2/N+1} - i^{2/N-1}\right) f_i} \,. \tag{19.10}$$

The **biasing gain** is the possible reduction of the average power due to unequal probabilities $f_0, \ldots, f_{T-1}$. We assume that the constellations for equal and non-equal probabilities rely on the same lattice (for the derivation, a continuous approximation is used) and their boundaries have the same shape.

Since the *biasing gain* is due to unequal probabilities, letting the probabilities $f_0 = f_1 = \cdots = f_{T-1} = 1/T$ to be the same, yields $\gamma_N(f_0, \ldots, f_{T-1}) = 1$, i.e., 0 dB.

Definition 19.2 For a given shaping code C_s with a rate $R(C_s)$ and probabilities $f_0, \ldots, f_{T-1}$ for the sub-constellations $\Omega_0, \ldots, \Omega_{T-1}$, we define the **biasing gain** $\gamma_N(C_s)$ as

$$\gamma_N(C_s) = \frac{2^{2R(f_0,\ldots,f_{T-1})/N}}{\sum_{i=0}^{T-1}\left((i+1)^{2/N+1} - i^{2/N-1}\right) f_i} \,. \tag{19.11}$$

Since the rate $R(C_s)$ is less or equal to the entropy $H(f_0, \ldots, f_{T-1})$, we have

$$\gamma_N(C_s) \leq \gamma_N(f_0, \ldots, f_{T-1}) \,. \tag{19.12}$$

The biasing gain $\gamma_N(C_s)$ will approach the maximum possible value $\gamma_N(f_0, \ldots, f_{T-1})$ with increasing complexity of the shaping code C_s.

In (8.13), we computed the ultimate shaping gain of an N-dimensional sphere B_N relative to an N-dimensional cube to be $\frac{\pi e}{6} \approx 1,53$ dB for $N \to \infty$. The ultimate shaping gain takes into account the shape of the region as well as the frequency distribution. The following theorem states that this ultimate gain can also be obtained at finite number of dimensions, if the number of sub-constellations will be infinite.

Theorem 19.1 *Let us consider an N-dimensional signal constellation with a sub-division into T concentric shells as sub-constellations. With a maximum possible biasing gain of*

$$\gamma(T, N) := \max_{f_0,\ldots,f_{T-1}} (f_0, \ldots, f_{T-1}) \tag{19.13}$$

the maximum overall gain for $T \to \infty$ will be

$$\gamma(B_N) \cdot \lim_{T\to\infty} \gamma(T, N) = \pi e/6 \,, \tag{19.14}$$

where $\gamma(B_N)$ is the shaping gain of the N-dimensional sphere relative to the N-dimensional cube.

Proof We proof this for the two-dimensional case ($N = 2$). We have already listed $\gamma(B_N)$ for different numbers of dimensions in Chap. 8. For $N = 2$ we had $\gamma(B_2) = \pi/3$. Hence, we have to prove that $\lim_{T\to\infty} \gamma(T, 2) = e/2$. From (19.10) for $N = 2$ we conclude that in order to compute the maximum biasing gain $\gamma(T, 2)$, we have to maximize

$$J = H(f_0, \ldots, f_{T-1}) - \ln\left(\sum_{i=0}^{T-1}(2i+1)f_i\right) \tag{19.15}$$

under the condition $\sum_{i=0}^{T-1} f_i = 1$.
With the assumption

$$f_i = \frac{(1-x)}{(1-x^T)}x^i, \quad i = 0, 1, \ldots, T-1, \tag{19.16}$$

resulting from a Lagrangian and thus fulfilling the condition, J can be easily maximized. For $\lim\limits_{T\to\infty} \gamma(T, 2)$, we obtain

$$f_i = (1-x)x^i\,, \quad i = 0, 1, \ldots, \infty, \tag{19.17}$$

allowing to write J as

$$\begin{aligned} J &= -\sum_{i=0}^{\infty}(1-x)x^i[\ln(1-x) + i\ln x] - \ln\left(\sum_{i=0}^{\infty}(2i+1)(1-x)x^i\right) \\ &= -(1-x)\ln(1-x)\sum_{i=0}^{\infty}x^i - x(1-x)\ln x\sum_{i=1}^{\infty}ix^{i-1} \\ &\quad - \ln\left(1 + 2x(1-x)\sum_{i=0}^{\infty}ix^{i-1}\right). \end{aligned} \tag{19.18}$$

With

$$\sum_{i=1}^{\infty}ix^{i-1} = \frac{d}{dx}\left(\frac{1}{(1-x)}\right) = \frac{1}{(1-x)^2}\,, \tag{19.19}$$

we can again simplify J as

$$\begin{aligned} J &= -\ln(1-x) - \frac{x\ln x}{1-x} - \ln\left(1 + \frac{2x}{(1-x)}\right) \\ &= -\frac{x\ln x}{1-x} - \ln(1+x)\,. \end{aligned} \tag{19.20}$$

Differentiating J after x leads to

$$(\ln 2)\frac{dJ}{dx} = -\frac{1}{(1-x)} - \frac{\ln x}{(1-x)^2} - \frac{1}{(1+x)} = \frac{1}{(1-x)^2}\left(-\ln x + \frac{2(x-1)}{(x+1)}\right), \tag{19.21}$$

and we can show that $dJ/dx > 0$ inside the interval (0,1). The maximum is achieved at the border. If we determine the limit for $x \to 1$, we obtain

$$\ln\left(\lim_{T\to\infty}\gamma(T,2)\right) = \lim_{x\to 1}\left(-\frac{x\ln x}{1-x} - \ln(1+x)\right) = \lim_{x\to 1}\frac{1}{\ln 2}\left(-\frac{x\ln x}{1-x} - \ln(1+x)\right). \tag{19.22}$$

Finally, l'Hospital yields the desired result

$$\lim_{T\to\infty}\gamma(T,2) = 2^{\frac{1-\ln(2)}{\ln(2)}} = 2^{-1}\cdot 2^{\frac{1}{\ln(2)}} = e/2. \tag{19.23}$$

□

19.1 Lexicographic Order in Shell Mapping

We will now establish the list of used shells in the so-called lexicographic order. For the description, we will follow [3]. Further references are [4–6] and the corresponding V.34 voice-band standard [2]. The treatment in [3] is linked to the Wei code (see Sect. 7.3), which is natural, since this is also part of the V.34 standard.

Let us assume M rings in a 2-dimensional (2D) point constellation. Then the total number of points L would be

$$L = 4M2^u = M2^{u+2}, \tag{19.24}$$

where u are uncoded bits (parallel transitions in the trellis) and one has 4 alternative points selected by the Wei code. Let us note again that the Gaussian distribution can either be (approximately) obtained by confining points from a lattice by an N-dimensional sphere, wither a large N, ideally to infinity, or by choosing the probabilities of rings to approximate the Gaussian. In a shell setting in N dimensions, we choose them equally probable which represents the flat distribution confined by a sphere.

Shell mapping needs to allocate frames (vectors) of indices of length N to a vector of K data bits. The N frame components refer to 2D symbol intervals. According to the K bits, one would have to tabulate 2^K frames. Maximum M^N ring arrangements, i.e., frames, are sorted according to their weight, which was coined "lexicographic" order. The list from 0 to $M^N - 1$ has increasing weight and the 2^K smallest weight frames are actually used. Encoding and decoding appears then, in principle, easy, since one would map the K bits to shell frames and likewise, when points are inside a certain shell, one would also map it back to the K bits. With the practically chosen parameters, however, the lists would be very large and recursive algorithms are applied. For such algorithms we refer to the given references.

As a weight, one could take the Euclidean squared weight of the ring as a energy/power measure. Motorola had selected 0 to $M - 1$ as a reasonable choice, since in 2D with QAM signaling, the energy/power is proportional to the area in 2D [5] as can be seen from Eq. (8.1). The weight of a frame should, of course, be the sum of the component weights, as one would determine the squared Euclidean distance of a vector to the origin (squared Euclidean weight).

We are now determining the number of ring frames, i.e., p-tuples of ring indices $\mathbf{r} = (r_1, \ldots, r_p)$ with weight $j = w_1(r) + \cdots + w_1(r_p)$, which we denote $M_p(j)$. Introducing a generating function, which one could regard as a z-transform, we write

$$G_p(z) = \sum_k M_p(k) z^k \,. \tag{19.25}$$

Since the Motorola weight function is $w_1(i) = i$, the number of 1-tuples (single) is $M_1(j) = 1$ for all rings. We obtain the finite geometric series

$$G_1(z) = \sum_{k=0}^{M-1} z^k = \frac{1 - z^M}{1 - z} \,. \tag{19.26}$$

When considering a 2-tuple, i.e., a pair of rings, to obtain weight j, we obtain the combinations expressed by the convolution

$$M_2(j) = \sum_{k=0}^{j} M_1(k) M_1(j - k) \tag{19.27}$$

or equivalently by the product of z-transforms

$$G_2(z) = G_1^2(z) \,. \tag{19.28}$$

In general, we have

$$M_{2p}(j) = \sum_{k=0}^{j} M_p(k) M_p(j - k) \quad \text{and} \quad G_{2p}(z) = G_p^2(z) \,. \tag{19.29}$$

The number of ring frames with eight less or equal to j is given by

$$C_N(j) = \sum_{k=0}^{j} M_N(k). \quad (19.30)$$

Overall, we need 2^K ring frames according to the number of bits K. To be able to be sufficient for a mapping the number of ring frames available should be bigger than what is required, i.e., $C_N(j) \geq 2^K$. The smallest j just fulfilling this requirement is denoted by J.

To come to the desired lexicographical ordering, we define an i-tuple of scalar ring indices as

$$\mathbf{r}^{[i]} = [r_1, \ldots, r_k, \ldots, r_i] \text{ with } r_k \in \{0, 1, \ldots, M-1\},\ k = 1, \ldots, i. \quad (19.31)$$

The ordering in the V.34 standard is based on separating in halves. According, the first and second halves of $\mathbf{r}^{[i]}$ is denoted as

$$\mathbf{r}_1^{[i]} = \left[r_1, \ldots, r_{i/2}\right] \text{ and } \mathbf{r}_2^{[i]} = \left[r_{i/2+1}, \ldots, r_i\right]. \quad (19.32)$$

$D_i(\mathbf{r}^{[i]})$ denotes the index of the ring i-tuple $\mathbf{r}^{[i]}$ and is also equal to the number of elements on the list below $\mathbf{r}^{[i]}$. A doubling procedure is defined starting from the ring index function

$$D_1(\mathbf{r}) = r \text{ for } r = 0, \ldots, M-1 \quad (19.33)$$

and following the subsequently listed rules to arrange for all ring i-tuples. We directly cite from [3].

Case 1: Different weight i-tuples $\mathbf{u}^{[i]}$ and $\mathbf{v}^{[i]}$

List an i-tuple $\mathbf{u}^{[i]}$ below $\mathbf{v}^{[i]}$ if $w_i(\mathbf{u}^{[i]}) < w_i(\mathbf{v}^{[i]})$, where $w_i(.)$ is the i-dimensional weight function.

Case 2: Equal weight i-tuples, but first halves have different $i/2$-dimensional indices.

In this case, $w_i(\mathbf{u}^{[i]}) = w_i(\mathbf{v}^{[i]})$, but the first halves of $\mathbf{u}^{[i]}$ and $\mathbf{v}^{[i]}$ are different. List $\mathbf{u}^{[i]}$ below $\mathbf{v}^{[i]}$, if

$$D_{i/2}(\mathbf{u}^{[i]}) < D_{i/2}(\mathbf{v}^{[i]}).$$

Case 3: Equal weight i-tuples, indices of first halves are the same

In this case, $w_i(\mathbf{u}^{[i]}) = w_i(\mathbf{v}^{[i]})$ and $\mathbf{u}_1^{[i]} = \mathbf{v}_1^{[i]}$. List $\mathbf{u}^{[i]}$ below $\mathbf{v}^{[i]}$, if

$$D_{i/2}(\mathbf{u}_2^{[i]}) < D_{i/2}(\mathbf{v}_2^{[i]}).$$

Reference [3] also provides the CER (Constellation Expansion Ratio), which we had defined earlier in Definition 8.1. Given K bits to be mapped to N rings, where the number of rings was M, we require

$$2^K \leq M^N \quad \Leftrightarrow \quad 2^{K/N} \leq M. \quad (19.34)$$

The total number of bits B allocated to a frame is given by

$$B = Nu + K + 4(N/2) = N(u+2) + K2^K \leq M^N. \tag{19.35}$$

u had been the uncoded bits, K the number of bits into shell mapping and 4 bits are coming from the Wei code per 2 dimensions. In the unshaped case, this would require a 2D constellation of size

$$\left[2^{N(u+2)+K}\right]^{1/N} = 2^{u+2+K/N}. \tag{19.36}$$

Together with $L = M2^{u+2}$ from Eq. (19.24), the CER follows to be

$$\text{CER} = \frac{M2^{u+2}}{2^{u+2+K/N}} = M2^{-K/N}. \tag{19.37}$$

References

1. A. R. Calderbank, *Bandwidth Efficient Communication*. Lecture Notes, Princeton University, 1993.
2. "V.34: A modem operating at data signalling rates of up to 33 600 bit/s for use on the general switched telephone network and on leased point-to-point 2-wire telephone-type circuits," ITU-T, Standard, Aug. 1998.
3. S. A. Tretter, *Constellation Shaping, Nonlinear Precoding, and Trellis Coding for Voiceband Telephone Channel Modems with Emphasis on ITU-T Recommendation V.34*. New York: Kluwer / Springer Science+Business Media, 2002.
4. R. Laroia, N. Farvardin, and S. A. Tretter, "On optimal shaping of multidimensional constellations," *IEEE Transactions on Information Theory*, vol. 40, no. 4, pp. 1044–1056, Jul 1994.
5. R. F. H. Fischer, "Calculation of shell frequency distributions obtained with shell-mapping schemes," *IEEE Transactions on Information Theory*, vol. 45, no. 5, pp. 1631–1639, Jul 1999.
6. R. F. H. Fischer, *Precoding and Signal Shaping for Digital Transmission*. John Wiley & Sons, 2002.

Chapter 20
Exercises

Tis early practice only makes the master.

Friedrich Schiller, Wilhelm Tell

20.1 Questions

20.1.1 Information Theory

Exercise 20.1 Let us consider a binary source with probabilities $P(0) = p$ and $P(1) = (1 - p)$. A symbol consists of two such bits which are considered to be statistically independent. Determine the entropy of such a combined source directly and use logarithm rules to simplify the result such that it appears as a function of the entropy of single binary digits.

Exercise 20.2 Let (X_1, X_2, X_3) be a vector-valued random variable that can only assume the values (000), (011), (101), and (110) with the same probability of 1/4. Determine the entropies

1. $H(X_1)$	4. $H(X_1, X_2, X_3)$
2. $H(X_1, X_2)$	5. $H(X_3\|X_1, X_2)$
3. $H(X_2\|X_1)$	6. $H(X_3)$

Exercise 20.3 Simplify $H(X, Y) = H(X|Y) + H(Y|X)$ such that you will be able to observe the relation between X and Y.

W. Henkel, *Channel Coding*, Signals and Communication Technology,
https://doi.org/10.1007/978-3-032-08236-7_20

Exercise 20.4 When would Fano's lemma tend to a linear relation for the error probability?

Exercise 20.5

(a) The following 4ary channel is given. Compute the Mutual Information and the Channel Capacity of such a channel.

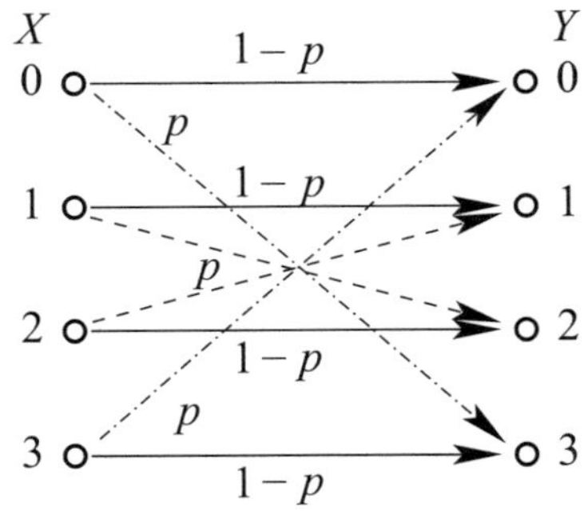

(b) Modify the channel to be 4ary symmetric with identical transition probabilities to other values. Determine the corresponding Mutual Information and Channel Capacity, again.

Exercise 20.6 Imagine a binary non-symmetric channel with transition probabilities p_1 and p_2 from input value 0 to output value 1 and from input value 1 to output value 0, respectively. Determine the Mutual Information and an equation that has to be fulfilled to determine the Capacity of this channel.

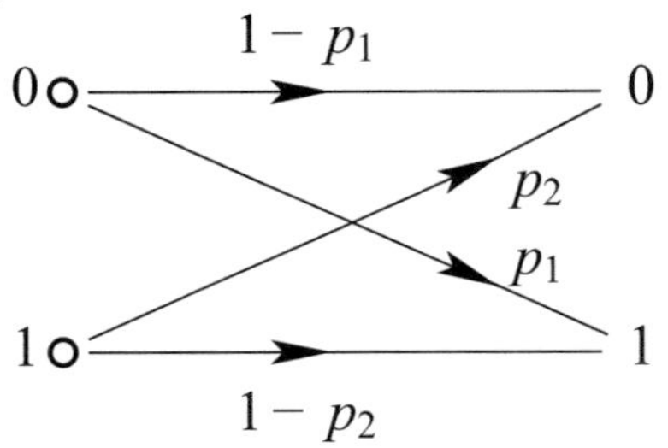

Exercise 20.7 Discrete memoryless channels are described by the following diagrams. Determine their Capacities. Derivations or reasonings are required.

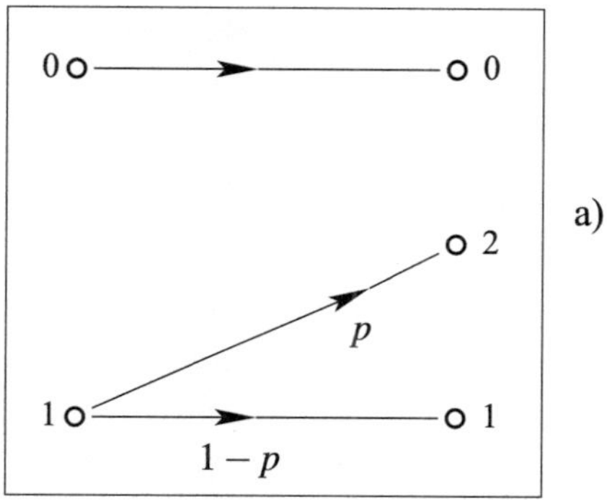

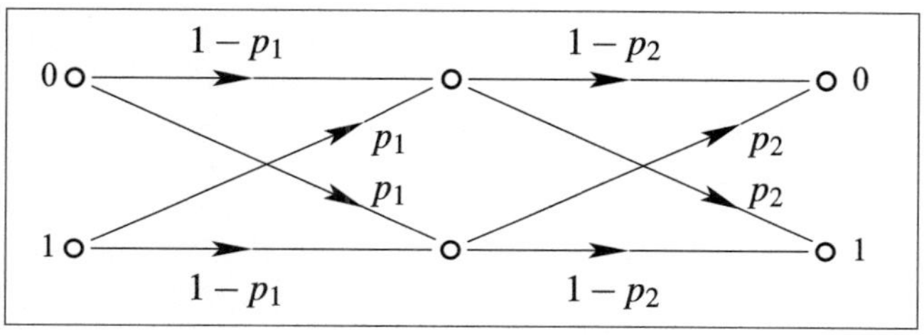

Exercise 20.8 Evaluate the differential entropy $H(X)$, where X is a sum of two independent normal random variables with means μ_1, μ_2 and variances σ_1^2, σ_2^2.

Exercise 20.9

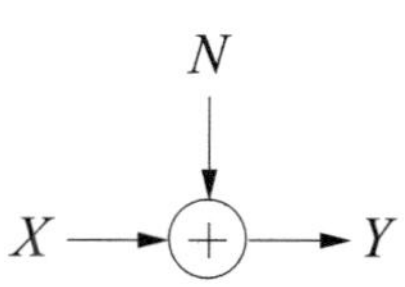

Let N follow an arbitrary distribution with known variance σ_N^2 and Entropy $H(N)$. Let the input variance be σ_X^2. X and N are assumed to be statistically independent. What will be the desired distribution of Y to maximize the Mutual Information $I(X;Y)$ and what will be this maximum?

Exercise 20.10 Prove that the geometric mean of the signal-to-noise ratios of statistically independent Gaussian channels (AWGN) determines the sum Capacity at high signal-to-noise ratios.

<u>***Note:***</u> The geometric mean of $x_1, \ldots, x_N$ is defined as $\sqrt[N]{\prod_{i=1}^{N} x_i}$.

Exercise 20.11 Does an increase in bandwidth to infinity lead to an unlimited increase in Capacity or will the Capacity be limited. Derivation required!

Exercise 20.12 Let us consider a ternary source with probabilities p_1, p_2, and $p_3 = 1 - p_1 - p_2$. Let the distortion model be given by

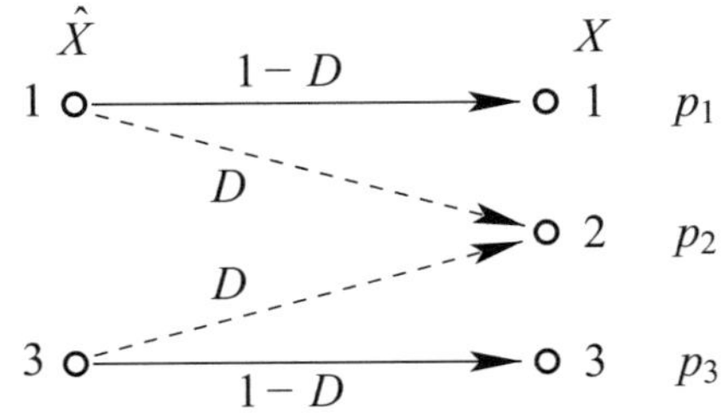

where $\hat{X}$ is the distorted value, and X is the original undistorted source value. What will be the Mutual Information $I(X; \hat{X})$?

Describe, what the given distortion model means (one or two sentences).

Exercise 20.13 $R(D)$ is the rate-distortion function. Assume the binary case with equal distribution of both values (0, 1). You are willing to accept a distortion (bit-error ratio) of 10^{-3}. What would be the ratio that you could increase the original data rate on the channel.

20.1.2 Linear Block Codes

Exercise 20.14 What is the relation between repetition and parity-check codes.

Exercise 20.15 Assume a binary code vector (GF(2)) with an even number of ones. Compute the scalar product with itself. What will be the result? If you would obtain this result in the case of real or complex numbers, what would you conclude? Does this conclusion hold in GF(2)?

Exercise 20.16 Why is it so easy to determine the single error in a Hamming code directly from the syndrome?

Exercise 20.17 What is the dual code to a single parity-check code? Sketch the G and H matrices for both codes.

Exercise 20.18 What is the property of a row vector $\mathbf{a}$ fulfilling $\mathbf{a} \cdot \mathbf{a}^T = 0$ over GF(2)?

Exercise 20.19 In the case of self-duality, how can you choose the H matrix given a certain G matrix. Assuming that you have $N = 24$. What are necessarily the parameters K and M? For self-duality, what would you know about the number of ones per row in the G and H matrices?

20.1.3 Convolutional Codes I Representation and Formal Description

Exercise 20.20 A rate-1/3 convolutional code is given in octal representation as (4, 7, 7).

(a) Show the corresponding shift-register circuit.
(b) Draw the state diagram.
(c) Determine the free (minimum) Hamming distance.
(d) Draw the trellis starting from the initial state 00 and decode the received sequence 101, 111, 010, 000 with Viterbi's algorithm. Make clear, which intermediate steps are necessary and make a final decision after all four segments have been received. What is the most probable information sequence?

Exercise 20.21 The generators of a convolutional code of rate 1/2 are specified as (15, 17) in octal representation.

(a) Draw the encoder after writing the octal numbers as binaries which would then specify the shift register taps.
(b) Write the Forney generator matrix (the matrix of polynomials in D)
(c) Draw the state diagram and the trellis.
(d) Is the code systematic/non-systematic, recursive/non-recursive?
(e) When you look at the trellis, what is the essential construction rule for branches emerging from a common state or joining again at a common state.

Exercise 20.22 Assume a non-recursive convolutional code with the octal representation (3, 5). Draw the state and the trellis diagrams. You may observe loops that produce identical output. Mark them! This behavior is called catastrophic. What would be the effect when you have a limited number of transmission errors on the channel?

Exercise 20.23

(a) What is the property that guarantees that you can take the all-zero sequence as the reference to determine the minimum distance and the distance profile of a convolutional code?
(b) What is the property of good convolutional codes when paths are entering a common state or they are emerging from a common state?

20.1.4 Convolutional Codes II, Viterbi and BCJR Decoders

Exercise 20.24

(a) Relate the detection rules ML and MAP.

(b) Compare the Viterbi and BCJR algorithms. Is MAP/ML the means to distinguish the two or can both be MAP or ML?
(c) Assume a vector **x** to be transmitted and **y** be received. Determine $P(x_i|\mathbf{y})$ after first telling, if this is a ML or a MAP expression. Break it up in three components using Bayes' rule.

Exercise 20.25

(a) What is the operation at a state in the Viterbi algorithm?
(b) Why can one read out any path from the path register after a certain decoding delay?
(c) Why can we choose the all-zero sequence as a valid reference for determining the minimum distance and also the distance spectrum? What is the underlying code property?

Exercise 20.26 The Viterbi algorithm is known as a Maximum-Likelihood Sequence Estimator (MLSE). When you look at individual bit estimates, does the Viterbi algorithm achieve the best estimate in a ML sense?

20.1.5 Ungerböck's Trellis-Coded Modulation (TCM)

Exercise 20.27 Imagine the four points of a one-dimensional 4-PAM signal set. Let them be labeled as a, b, c, d. Subdivide this set into two cosets (subsets) which look the same apart from a shift. Let us consider the trellis structure given below. Having in mind the construction principles of a binary convolutional code, it should be obvious, what the construction principle for an Euclidean-space code should be. Here, maximization of the minimum (free) Euclidean distance is the goal. How should the trellis be labeled with a, b, c, d, noting that the sub-constellations already ensure a certain Euclidean distance.

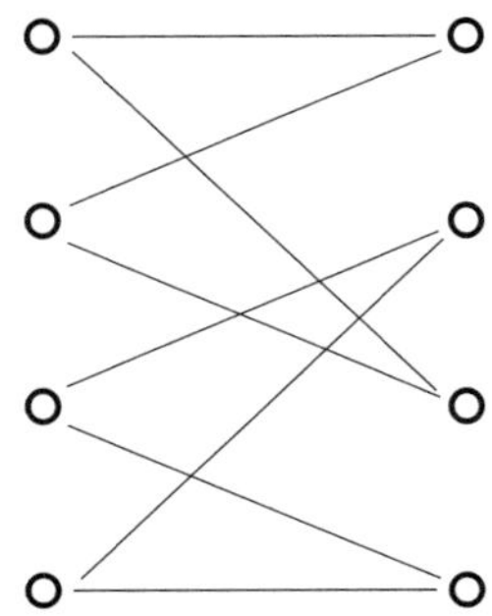

Exercise 20.28 Assume we use mapping in an 8-PSK according to set-partitioning. Let the received point in the complex plane be $y = y_r + jy_i$. Write the log-likelihood ratio $\ln \frac{p(0)}{p(1)}$ for the first bit of the set-partitioning tree, taking into account all signal points that belong to the corresponding subset. Do this in a Union-bound fashion. Assume that all points in the constellation are occurring with the same probability. Let us assume a rotation offset φ to a point mapped to zero.

20.1.6 Trellis Shaping, Shell Mapping

Exercise 20.29 Assume a uniform distribution inside a two-dimensional sphere. Determine the one-dimensional marginal density.

20.1.7 Basics of Finite Fields (Galois Fields)

Exercise 20.30

(a) Compute $(1+\alpha)^4$ in GF(2^m) with a primitive polynomial $p(\alpha) = 1 + \alpha + \alpha^4$. First determine m!
(b) Compute $(1+\alpha)^{20}$.
(c) List the conjugates of α in the given Galois field. Also rephrase them all in component representation making use of the primitive polynomial.

Exercise 20.31

(a) Imagine to have a function with some sample pairs (x_i, y_i). You are thinking of doing a polynomial interpolation or approximation, where the first one is required to go through the points, the latter is a curve fitting according to some smallest average distance. Both are well-known for real and complex numbers. Are they possible over a finite field, as well? Explain!
(b) Assume some Galois field GF(2^4). What is the maximum order of an element of that field? Let us call this element α. What other orders could you find for other elements? How do they relate to α?
(c) An element of order N allows to define a DFT? What is the element of order N that you are used to from the conventional DFT over complex numbers?
What is the maximum length of the DFT for GF(2^4)? Could you define a shorter length? Which one(s)?
(d) You know that the DFT can be used to define RS and BCH codes. In case of a BCH code, typically, the element at position zero in DFT domain is not put to zero. Why would you not just place zeros starting form zero? In case of an RS code, would you also need to avoid that zero position?

Exercise 20.32

(a) Let an extension field have conjugates z_i, $i = 1, ..., r$. What is the property of the polynomial when you multiply all linear factors $(z - z_i)$?
(b) We use $GF(2^4)$. Compute $(1 + \alpha + \alpha^2)^2$. The primitive polynomial is $x^4 + x + 1$. Describe which modulo operations you applied.

Exercise 20.33

(a) Which two modulo operations need to be done in an extension field.

(b) What kind of modulo operation is needed for exponents?
(c) What are the conjugates of an extension field? List them.
(d) What is an "element of order N"? What is the maximum order?
(e) We use $GF(2^3)$. Compute $(1+\alpha+\alpha^2)^2$. The primitive polynomial is x^3+x+1.
(f) Distinguish irreducible, minimal, primitive polynomials. Describe their definition shortly.

Exercise 20.34 We have a primitive polynomial $p(\alpha)=\alpha^4+\alpha^3+1$.

(a) What is the underlying $GF(2^m)$?
(b) Compute $(1+\alpha^3)^4=...$
(c) Compute $(1+\alpha)^4=...$
Use all the modulo operations that you are aware of to simplify. Then, you should obtain the results very quickly in 2 or 3 steps.

Exercise 20.35 Let the primitive polynomial of GF(2^6) be $\alpha^6+\alpha+1$.

(a) Do a first simplification step for $(1+\alpha)^{70}=$
(b) What is the order of $\beta=\alpha^3$?
(c) You would ideally like to use some kind of FFT for this Galois field GF(2^6). Is this possible in principle? Explain!
(d) What will be the length N of the DFT/FFT using the element β of order N?

Exercise 20.36 Let the primitive polynomial of GF(2^4) be $\alpha^4+\alpha+1$.

(a) Determine the order of α.
(b) Now we assume $\beta=\alpha^5$. Knowing the order of alpha, what is the order of β?
(c) Having determined the order N of β, we write a DFT using β as the element of order N using positive exponents. Assume all components to be 1 in the original domain. Determine all transform domain components using all modulo operations that you are aware of.
(d) Assume this to be an example of a valid codeword of an RS code. How many errors at unknown positions can you correct? This is actually a very simple code, where you could see valid codewords at once and also see the correction capability right away. What simple code is meant and how can you quickly see the correction capability?

20.1.8 Reed-Solomon Codes

Exercise 20.37 Let us consider an RS code with parameters $(N=127, K=117)$ over GF(2^m).

(a) N is the maximum possible length. What is m? Determine the Hamming distance and the correction capability.

(b) You can define an RS code by a degree-limited polynomial. What should be the degree in this case, what should be the samples that one should compute the polynomial for?
(c) Write a polynomial with coefficients A_k and show that this is equivalent to an inverse discrete Fourier transform.
(d) For algorithmic requirements, you are shifting the syndrome in DFT domain to other locations. Which calculations in the decoding process are affected? Explain!
(e) Knowing the relation to the DFT, sketch the generator and check-matrices (assuming encoding in DFT domain). Especially, make clear what the entries look like, what type of matrices you have, what the matrix dimensions are.
(f) Imagine, you would map an element of a Galois field to a permutation matrix, which has single ones in rows and columns. When you then think of the resulting H matrix, does this remind you of another code class?

Exercise 20.38 Let us consider an RS code with parameters $(N = 255, K = 235)$ over GF(2^8).

(a) Why can we not easily increase the length? Why is 255 chosen? What is the minimum Hamming distance? What is the correction capability?
(b) You can define an RS code by a degree-limited polynomial. What should be the degree in this case, what should be the samples that one should compute the polynomial for?
(c) Write a polynomial with coefficients A_k and show that this is equivalent to an inverse discrete Fourier transform.
(d) Please explain, why the shift property of the DFT ensures that you can put the zeroed components in DFT domain at arbitrary, but cyclically consecutive positions.

Exercise 20.39

(a) For an RS code, you may put the information into the DFT domain or the original domain. Explain the decoding steps for both options.
(b) We now circularly shift the code word in time domain. What will be the consequence in the decoding regarding syndrome, error positions, and error values?
(c) We now circularly shift the code word in DFT domain. What will be the consequences then?

Exercise 20.40

(a) Let a code be defined by the generator matrix **G**. How would one define the dual code?
(b) Let a RS code have the parameters (N, K, d). What would be the parameters of its dual code? Assume that the original code has consecutive zeros at the upper end in DFT domain. What would be the positions of zeros for the dual code?

(c) Let us use GF(7). What is the maximum length of an RS code? Use a primitive element and determine the time-domain vector using the information 1, 1, 1, 1. in DFT domain. How many errors could this code correct and what is the minimum distance?
(d) Which vectors in GF(2) would be self-dual? Explain the concept of 'orthogonality' in a finite field.

Exercise 20.41 An RS code is known to fulfill the Singleton bound with equality.

(a) Derive the Singleton bound in general.
(b) How would you prove the minimum distance (min. weight) of an RS code? Note, the proof uses one definition of RS codes.
(c) Another definition uses the DFT. How would you place zeros in DFT domain to realize a minimum Hamming distance d_H (general!)?
(d) Assume a binary symmetric memoryless channel (BSC) with an error probability p. What is the first step for computing the error probability that would also explain why an RS code is not optimum in this situation, although it is optimum in terms of the Singleton bound?
(e) When you consider a BCH code, which component would you not choose to be zero? Choose two zeros for case of GF(2^4) and draw the vector of maximum codeword length and all resulting zeros. What is the corresponding generator polynomial?

Exercise 20.42 We know that an RS code can be defined by means of an IDFT over some number field. The following pictures show the area(s) which are set to zero in DFT domain. Which ones have the same minimum Hamming distance. Mark them by crosses. How big is this minimum distance?

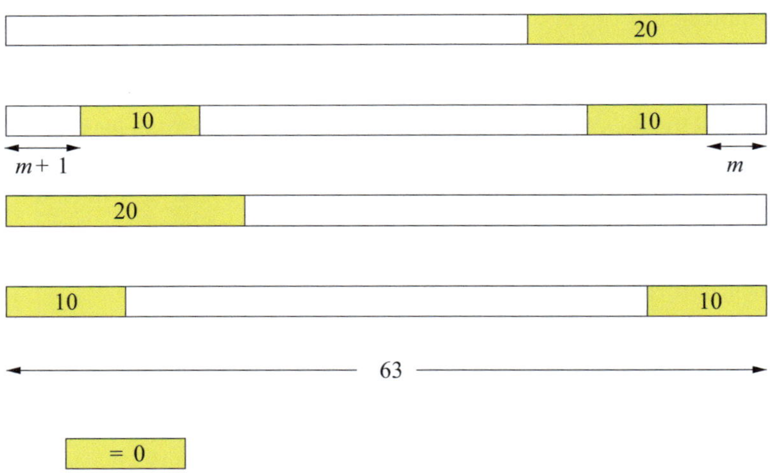

How many symbols can be corrected if the locations are known/unknown?

Exercise 20.43 Show that the degree limitation of a polynomial to $K - 1$, where K is the number of information symbols, results in a DFT with M coefficients set to zero. M is the number of parities. Let the overall codeword length be N.

Which samples of the polynomial do you need to take

(a) assuming complex numbers,
(b) assuming a Galois field $\mathrm{GF}(p^m)$?

For (b) assume the maximum possible length N.

Make clear, how to get from a polynomial description to the DFT using the chosen samples.

Knowing the properties of the DFT, what minimum Hamming distance would result from placing 10 parities at the beginning of the DFT-domain vector and 10 at the end?

Exercise 20.44

(a) What are the samples x of the degree-limited polynomial

$$C(x) = C_0 + C_1 x^1 + C_2 x^2 + \cdots + C_{K-1} x^{K-1}$$

that would make it an RS-code which could be defined by a DFT?

(b) When one would *know the error positions*, how many could be corrected, when N would be the codeword length? How does this relate to the minimum Hamming distance d_{Hmin}?

(c) When the *error positions are not known*, how many errors can be corrected then relative to the minimum Hamming distance d_{Hmin} and the number of parity positions $M = N - K$?

(d) In an extension field $\mathrm{GF}(2^8)$, an RS-Code corrects bytes of errors, regardless of the error structure inside a byte. What would be the byte-error probability p_{Byte} resulting from a binary symmetric channel with bit-error probability p_{BSC}? First compute the probability of a correct byte.
Now, the following computations are based on this p_{Byte}. What would be the probability of not being able to correct, i.e., the word-error probability after decoding of the RS code? What would be the resulting bit-error ratio when assuming that only one bit would be wrong in an erroneous byte?

(e) Why should an interleaver for reshuffling the order in front of an RS code be a byte interleaver, not breaking up bytes into bits?

Exercise 20.45 A codeword c results from the information $\mathbf{i}$ via the generator matrix $\mathbf{G}$, i.e.,

$$\mathbf{c} = \mathbf{i} \cdot \mathbf{G}.$$

Now assume an RS code of length 4 and 2 information symbols and $\mathbf{i}$ should be the information in DFT domain. Construct $\mathbf{G}$ given that we have an element z of order 4. Hint: the 2×4 matrix G is part of the DFT matrix.

The matrix $\mathbf{H}$ is the corresponding parity-check matrix, delivering the syndrome, i.e.,

$$\mathbf{s} = \mathbf{H} \cdot \mathbf{c}^T$$

What would then be a possible formulation of the parity check matrix $\mathbf{H}$?
Which Galois field has an element of order 4? What is the value of N^{-1}, which is part of either the DFT or IDFT?

Exercise 20.46 In a Reed-Solomon-like code of length 255, let the following DFT-domain components be set to zero: 0–9, 20–21, 239–254. What minimum Hamming distance would you expect? Explain your result shortly.

20.1.9 Constructing Long Codes from Short Ones

Interleaving and serial concatenation

Exercise 20.47 An RS code operates on bytes consisting of, e.g., 8 bits. Assume that the RS code has a correction capability of t, Additionally, an interleaver (depth I_D) is provided. The interleaver/deinterleaver change the order of the data.

(a) Should the interleaver be oriented in bytes or bits? Why?
(b) What is the resulting burst-error correcting capability in bytes/bits (choose!)?
(c) Assume that two channels have the same bit-error ratio. One is bursty, one leads to random (i.i.d.) bit-errors. For which channel is the described RS/interleaver configuration more suited.

Exercise 20.48

(a) Imagine a bursty noise channel, e.g., due to impulse noise. Why is an interleaver improving the burst-error correction capability of a code, which originally has an error-correction capability of t? What is the resulting burst-error correction capability?
(b) In a more historical view on serial concatenation, how should the inner code be adjusted to the outer. Assume an outer RS code over GF(2^8). Think of symbol sizes and the code parameters.
(c) Why is typically an RS code chosen as an outer code to a convolutional or Ungerböck-type code? What kind of interleaving should be used in between—bit- or byte-oriented?
(d) Describe the difference between serial and parallel concatenation. You may use a simple example. What kind of concatenation would you see when you think of building blocks like data compression, error-correction coding, equalization, and precoding?

Exercise 20.49

(a) What is the function of an interleaver?
(b) What is/are the advantage/s of a convolutional interleaver compared to a block version?
(c) When the outer code is an RS code over GF(2^8), what should be the symbols treated in the interleaver and why is this important?
(d) Why is an interleaver (e.g., S-random type) needed in Turbo coding and where is the "interleaver" in an LDPC code? e based on bytes or bits.

Product and array codes

Exercise 20.50

(a) A product code, also called array code, is a concatenated coding scheme. You you see it as serial or parallel concatenation? What would you have to change to move to the other kind of concatenation?
(b) Imagine a product code to be a concatenation of single parity-check codes. How can you correct single errors?
(c) Imagine you would determine the parity check code inside a product code over real numbers, i.e., computing the parity check-symbols as the negative sum in rows and columns. What would then be the extrinsic information for a certain component c_{ij} dependent on the corresponding received row and column values?
(d) Look at a single parity-check code. Is there a possibility to also correct an error? How?
(e) Generalized Minimum Distance decoding by Forney makes use of the difference between erasure and error decoding. What is that difference and how can you make use of it?

Exercise 20.51 Let us consider a simple product code (array code), a 3×3 matrix where the rows and columns both are even parity-check codes.

(a) Is this a linear or a non-linear code? What is the necessary condition to be linear and is it fulfilled?
(b) What can you say about the relation of minimum Hamming weight and minimum Hamming distance?
(c) What is the minimum Hamming distance of this product code?
(d) How many errors and erasures could you correct? Note: in the case of erasures, the result depends on the locations of the erasures. How many can you definitely correct, how many at max?
(e) What are the dimensions of the H-matrix of the whole scheme?
(f) Determine the H-matrix, seeing the codeword as a concatenation of the rows of the 3×3 matrix.
(g) Determine the first term of the Union Bound assume a binary symmetric channel with a BER of p.

Shannon limit

Exercise 20.52 We derived a Shannon limit that was the lowest limit for E_b/N_0 where one could hope for diminishing error probabilities, hence, this resembled the lower limit for all codes, especially, Turbo and LDPC codes.

(a) What was the assumption for the channel input distribution that leads to, e.g., –1.6 dB for two-sided noise power spectral density and 2-D signal representation?
(b) What would be the basis for certain given signal formats, e.g., 2-PAM or 8-PSK? Write down the Mutual Information for 2-PAM.
(c) Provide, if possible, a lower limit in E_s/N_0.

Log-likelihood ratios, intrinsic, extrinsic, a-priori information, Turbo, LDPC, and Polar codes

Exercise 20.53

(a) Is MAP or ML the optimum detection rule? Explain! When are both the same?
(b) In Turbo and LDPC decoding, usually so-called log-likelihood ratios are used. Discuss the extremes $L = \pm\infty, 0$!
(c) In the case of puncturing and pruning, what are the assumptions for L-values of punctured or pruned bits.

Exercise 20.54

(a) We are receiving a vector $\mathbf{y}$ which resulted from a transmitted codeword $\mathbf{x}$. To estimate one component x_i, we like to express the log-likelihood ratio (LLR)

$$\ln \frac{P(x_i = +1|\mathbf{y})}{P(x_i = -1|\mathbf{y})}.$$

Reformulate this LLR to recognize the three different information shares.
(b) Assume a binary ± 1 source with the probability of $+1$ to be p. Which parameter has to be addressed among the information shares? Write this information expression.
(c) In Turbo coding, what is the purpose of this information term?
(d) In LDPC codes, the term is typically not even included into the Tanner graph. What is the assumption when not including the term?
(e) What is the assumption at the variable node side when LLRs are simply added?

Exercise 20.55

(a) We are receiving a vector $\mathbf{y}$ which resulted from a transmitted codeword $\mathbf{x}$. To estimate one component x_i, we like express the log-likelihood ratio (LLR)

$$\ln \frac{P(x_i = +1|\mathbf{y})}{P(x_i = -1|\mathbf{y})}$$

Reformulate this LLR to recognize the three different information shares.

(b) In Turbo coding, two of those components are actually changing their function when passing on to the next decoder. Explain shortly!
(c) In LDPC decoding, we ignored the a-priori components. To which nodes should they be added, if we would consider them.
(d) In the Tanner graph of an LDPC code, we can see variable and check nodes as simple individual codes. Which ones are those?

Exercise 20.56

(a) The interleaver has an important function in a Turbo code. Explain, why it is needed.
(b) What information has to be subtracted when forwarding the decoding result to the next decoder in the parallel concatenation?
(c) In case of a serial concatenation, some subtraction seems to be missing. Explain the difference.

Exercise 20.57

(a) Irregular LDPC codes have some irregularities in the, at least, initial quality of the decoding results at the different variable nodes. What should be the variable- and check-node degrees for a "good" variable node, i.e., one where the LLRs will increase first?
(b) When you would shorten an LDPC code by fixing and hence knowing an information bit, say, fixing it to $+1$. What is the effect on the outgoing LLRs from that variable node to check nodes? What is the implication of those LLRs from a check-node perspective, i.e., for the effective degree of the connected check nodes? What will this mean to the other variable nodes connected through these check nodes?
(c) Draw a Tanner graph for the following H matrix

$$\mathbf{H} = \begin{bmatrix} 0 & 1 & 1 \\ 1 & 1 & 0 \end{bmatrix}.$$

(d) How do you obtain a quasi-cyclic code from a protograph?
(e) An LDPC code can also be recognized as a combination of two different code types. What two codes are meant? What does the Tanner graph with its edges then correspond to when you compare this with Turbo codes?

Exercise 20.58 A protograph defines a small H-matrix and with it a small Tanner graph. By copying this Tanner graph many times, which is called "lifting" and permuting the edge endings between those copies, one can obtain a large LDPC code. In the H-matrix, this is equivalent to replacing the one entries by permutation matrices.

We apply this procedure to a tiny example starting from an H-matrix

$$\mathbf{H} = \begin{bmatrix} 1 & 1 & 0 \\ 1 & 0 & 1 \end{bmatrix}.$$

Draw the Tanner graph and then, first duplicate the variable and check-nodes, number them from 1 to 6 and 1 to 4, respectively.

Then replace the ones in the H-matrix by permutation matrices. A permutation matrix has single ones in rows and columns. For 2×2, there are only two possible permutation matrices—which ones? Use them as replacements of the ones in the protograph H-matrix. Do not use the same permutation matrix in a row. Realize that the odd and even rows and columns belong to the left and right half of the duplicated variable and check-node arrangement. This means, number the columns as $1, 4, 2, 5, 3, 6$ and the rows as $1, 3, 2, 4$. Now, draw the new Tanner graph after the lifting. Check that the variable- and check-node degrees are still the same as in the protograph?

Exercise 20.59 Assume the small H-matrix

$$\mathbf{H} = \begin{bmatrix} 0 & 1 & 1 \\ 1 & 1 & 0 \end{bmatrix}.$$

(a) Does this matrix indicate a certain code property? Determine the code and name the type of code.
(b) Bring H into a systematic form and determine the corresponding G-matrix.
(c) Is this a perfect code?
(d) The procedure that you used in (b) is not useful for LDPC codes. Why? Think of starting from a very sparse H-matrix.

Exercise 20.60

(a) How would log-likelihood ratios combine at the variable-node side? Explain, what the underlying assumption is and what the ideal graph would be that would allow for such a combination.
(b) Now assume that the log-likelihood ratios would be Gaussian distributed. What would be the distribution of the messages coming out of a variable node, i.e., how would the incoming ones be combined?
(c) The encoding of an LDPC code could be supported by a special form of the H-matrix. How does it look like?

Exercise 20.61 Source polarization builds on polarizing the entropies, e.g., as $H(U_1) \geq H(X) \geq H(U_2|U_1)$.

(a) Assume a source where the second bit X_2 is dependent on the first bit X_1. What does this mean for $H(X_1) = H(X_2)$ and $H(X_2|X_1)$?
(b) Now, we consider blocks of pairs (X_1, X_2) and would like to apply polarization in a first stage. For simplicity, assume two such pairs. How would one combine the components in a polarization similar to the $(u, u+v)$ or, as described in Section 12.9, $(u+v, v)$? Draw a graph and label the outputs!
(c) Can you already tell for sure, which of the four output entropies are related and how?

20.1.10 *Trellis Structures of Block Codes*

Exercise 20.62 Assume a small check matrix

$$\mathbf{H} = \begin{bmatrix} 1 & 0 & 1 \\ 1 & 1 & 0 \end{bmatrix}.$$

Draw the Wolf trellis.

Exercise 20.63 We construct a trellis of a block code—the so-called Wolf-Trellis. Hereto, we see the rows of the parity-check matrix **H** weighted with 2^i, where i is the row index. Then, the binary codeword components (0 or 1) will be multiplied with a column of that matrix and thus, from every state two possible end states can be reached. We begin with state "0" and the trellis has to end also in state "0", since it has to fulfill the constraint $\mathbf{Hc}^T = \mathbf{0}$. In the figure, we show the beginning and end of this trellis. We use the following parity-check matrix:

$$\mathbf{H} = \begin{matrix} 1 \\ 2 \\ 4 \end{matrix} \begin{pmatrix} 0001111 \\ 0110011 \\ 1010101 \end{pmatrix}$$

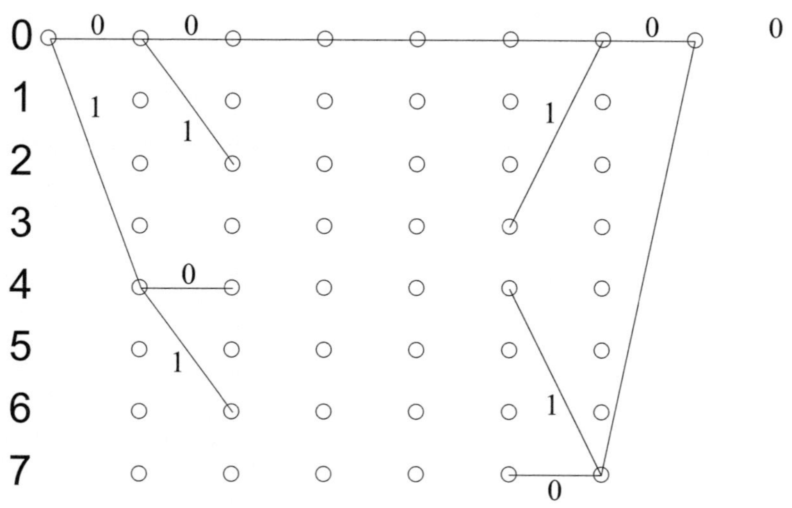

(a) Fill in the missing trellis paths. Make clear which ones are valid and end up in the final zero state.
(b) The code is linear. When you would like to determine the minimum Hamming distance from this trellis, what reference path would you use and why?
(c) Highlight and give the codeword of the minimum-distance path, where the distance is minimum relative to your chosen reference path.
(d) Apply Viterbi's Maximum-Likelihood decoding algorithm for a received word (0, 1, 1, 1, 0, 1, 0).

(e) Practically, you would not use the Viterbi algorithm to do a hard-decision decoding (Hamming-distance decoding) of this code. What property of the parity-check matrix would allow for simplified decoding?
(f) Which form of the H-Matrix would be more suited to determine the corresponding G-Matrix?

Exercise 20.64

(a) Draw a Wolf trellis for the following H-matrix:

$$\mathbf{H} = \begin{bmatrix} 1\,0 & 0\,1 & 0\,0 \\ 0\,1 & 1\,0 & 0\,0 \\ & & \\ 1\,0 & 0\,0 & 0\,1 \\ 0\,1 & 0\,0 & 1\,0 \end{bmatrix}$$

(b) Which decoding algorithm would you favor for such a given trellis? Explain!
(c) Find the minimum Hamming distance. What possibilities would you have to determine it? What is it?

20.1.11 Multilevel Coded Modulation

Exercise 20.65

(a) In convolutional codes, which channels are underlying the use of the Hamming or Euclidean distances?
(b) Which channel is typically used for coded modulation as an assumption? Which metric is used?
(c) Assume a wireless channel, which you could model as a slowly time-varying Gaussian with varying noise variance. What kind of metric would you find suitable to account for this variation?
(d) Let us have a 4-PSK modulation set under set partitioning labeling. Think of multi-stage decoding of a multilevel coded modulation and a Gaussian channel. Draw the point set using ± 1 values for inphase and quadrature. Sketch the set partitioning. Determine the LLR for the first level bit using some received position $y = y_R + jy_I$.

Exercise 20.66

(a) Set partitioning is made use of in two different ways in TCM and multi-level coded modulation. Explain!
(b) Name another possibility of coded modulation and explain the method/structure.
(c) Assume to have a 4-PAM (also named 2B1Q) signal set consisting of $\{\pm 1, \pm 3\}$. Normalize the positions such that the minimum squared Euclidean distance becomes 1. After drawing the set partitions, for TCM, design a trellis with 2

states, only, and label the trellis with the corresponding signal points. It might be convenient to just label them with 0, 1, 2, 3.

(d) Determine the minimum squared Euclidean distance of the TCM scheme.

(e) Determine the minimum squared Euclidean distance of a multi-level code with a repetition code of length N at the first layer and a parity-check code at the second. What would be a suitable choice of N, if only the maximization of Euclidean distance would be the measure and you still like to maximize the overall rate? What other design rule do you know to design the constituent codes of a multi-level scheme?

Exercise 20.67 Consider multilevel coded modulation.

(a) Why are the distances of the codes decreasing and the rate increasing with the level?

(b) Assume the first level to be the code (4, 1, 4), the second (4, 3, 2), the third (4, 4, 1). Draw each trellis of those codes and the overall one for the multilevel code.

20.2 Solutions

Solution 20.1

Sequence Y	Probability
00	p^2
01	$p(1-p)$
10	$p(1-p)$
11	$(1-p)^2$

$$\begin{aligned} H(Y) &= -p^2 \log p^2 - 2p(1-p)\log p(1-p) - (1-p)^2 \log(1-p)^2 \\ &= -p^2 \cdot [\log p + \log p] - 2p(1-p) \cdot [\log p \log(1-p)] \\ &\quad -(1-p)(1-p) \cdot [\log(1-p) + \log(1-p)] \\ &= -\log p \cdot [2p^2 + 2p(1-p)] - \log(1-p)[2(1-p)^2 + 2p(1-p)] \\ &= -\log p \cdot 2p - \log(1-p) \cdot 2(1-p) \\ &= 2 \cdot H(p) \end{aligned}$$

Solution 20.2

1. $P(X_1 = 0) = 1/2$, $P(X_1 = 1) = 1/2$, $H(X_1) = 1$

2.

(X_1, X_2)	$(0,0)$	$(0,1)$	$(1,0)$	$(1,1)$	$H(X_1, X_2)$
$P(X_1, X_2)$	$1/4$	$1/4$	$1/4$	$1/4$	2

3.

$$P(X_1 = 0) = P(X_1 = 1) = 1/2, H(X_2|X_1 = 0) = H(X_2|X_1 = 1) = 1$$
$$H(X_2|X_1) = P(X_1 = 0)H(X_2|X_1 = 0) + P(X_1 = 1)H(X_2|X_1 = 1) = 1$$

4. $H(X_1, X_2, X_3) = 2$

5. $H(X_3|X_1, X_2) = H(X_1, X_2, X_3) - H(X_2|X_1) - H(X_1) = 0$

6. $H(X_3) = 1$

Solution 20.3

$$\begin{aligned} H(X,Y) &= H(Y) + H(X|Y) = H(X) + H(Y|X) \stackrel{!}{=} H(X|Y) + H(Y|X) \\ &\Longrightarrow H(X|Y) = H(X), \quad H(Y|X) = H(Y) \\ &\Longrightarrow H(X,Y) = H(X) + H(Y) \end{aligned}$$

This means X and Y are statistically independent.

Solution 20.4 $H(X|Y) \leq h(P_e^n) + P_e^n \log_2(\nu - 1)$ linearizes for bigger alphabet sizes ν.

Solution 20.5

(a) We observe that the 4ary channel can be split in two independent ones. However, the resulting Capacity will not be twice the Capacity of the individual binary channels!

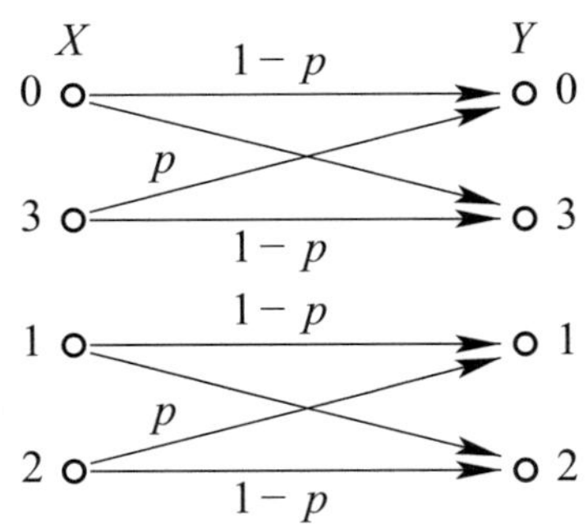

$$H(Y) = 2 \cdot h(p_y)$$

$$-H(Y|X) = (1-p)\log(1-p) + p \cdot \log p$$

$$I(X;Y) = H(Y) - H(Y|X) \leq 2 - h(p)$$

As has been mentioned, we do not obtain twice the individual Capacity. The intuitive reasoning is that you can transmit one bit without errors by choosing the subchannels and once decided you can still transmit $1 - H(p)$, the Capacity of the BSC (binary symmetric channel).

(b)

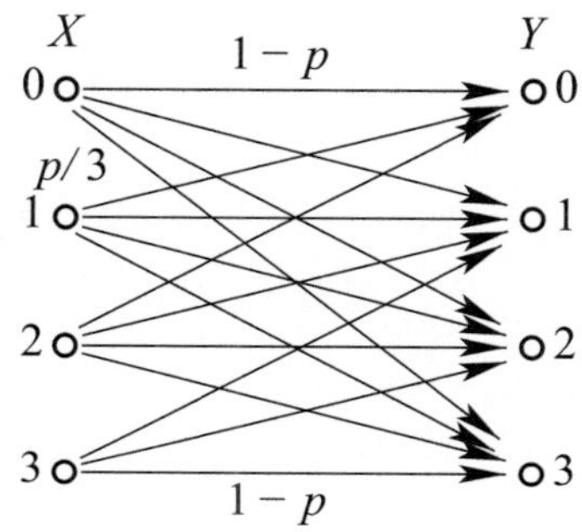

With the results from Solution a, $H(Y) \leq 2$:

$$I(X;Y) = H(Y) - H(Y|X)$$
$$-H(Y|X) = (1-p)\log(1-p) + 3 \cdot \frac{p}{3} \log \frac{p}{3}$$
$$= (1-p)\log(1-p) + p \cdot \log p - p \cdot \log 3$$

And hence,

$$I(X;Y) \leq 2 - h(p) - p \log 3.$$

Solution 20.6

$$I(X;Y) = H(Y) - H(Y|X)$$

Channel matrix:

$$\begin{pmatrix} 1-p_1 & p_1 \\ p_2 & 1-p_2 \end{pmatrix}$$

$$\begin{aligned} H(Y|X) = & -P(x=0) \cdot [(1-p_1)\log(1-p_1) + p_1 \log p_1] - \\ & P(x=1) \cdot [(1-p_2)\log(1-p_2) + p_2 \log p_2] \\ = & -P(x=0) \cdot h(p_1) - P(x=1) \cdot h(p_2) \\ P(y=0) = & P(x=0) \cdot (1-p_1) + P(x=1) \cdot p_2 \\ P(y=1) = & P(x=0) \cdot p_1 + P(x=1) \cdot (1-p_2) \end{aligned}$$

Let $P(x = 0) = q$, correspondingly $P(x = 1) = 1 - q$.

$$\begin{aligned} I(X;Y) &= qh(p_1) + (1-q)h(p_2) + h\left(q(1-p_1) + (1-q)p_2\right) \\ \frac{dI(X;Y)}{dq} &= h(p_1) - h(p_2) + (1 - p_1 - p_2)\left.\frac{dh(x)}{dx})\right|_{x=q(1-p_1)+(1-q)p_2} \stackrel{!}{=} 0 \\ h(x) &= -x\log x - (1-x)\log(1-x) \\ \frac{dh(x)}{dx} &= -\log x + \log(1-x) \end{aligned}$$

Solution 20.7

(a)

$$C = 1 \text{ bit/symbol}$$

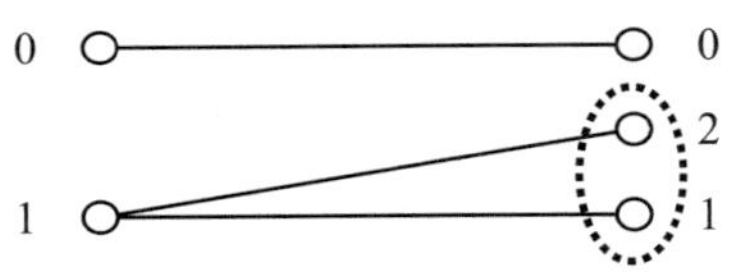

(b)

$$\begin{aligned} &\begin{pmatrix} 1-p_2 & p_2 \\ p_2 & 1-p_2 \end{pmatrix}\begin{pmatrix} 1-p_1 & p_1 \\ p_1 & 1-p_1 \end{pmatrix} \\ &= \begin{pmatrix} (1-p_1)(1-p_2) + p_1p_2 & p_1(1-p_2) + p_2(1-p_1) \\ p_1(1-p_2) + p_2(1-p_1) & (1-p_1)(1-p_2) + p_1p_2 \end{pmatrix} \\ &= \begin{pmatrix} 1 - [p_1 + p_2 - 2p_1p_2] & p_1 + p_2 - 2p_1p_2 \\ p_1 + p_2 - 2p_1p_2 & 1 - [p_1 + p_2 - 2p_1p_2] \end{pmatrix} \\ C &= 1 - H(p_1 + p_2 - 2p_1p_2) \end{aligned}$$

Solution 20.8 The sum of two normal random variables is also normal with mean $\mu_1 + \mu_2$ and variance $\sigma_1^2 + \sigma_2^2$, thus,

$$H(X) = \frac{1}{2}\log_2 2\pi e(\sigma_1^2 + \sigma_2^2).$$

Solution 20.9

$$I(X;Y) = H(Y) - H(N) \leq \frac{1}{2}\log[2\pi e(\sigma_X^2 + \sigma_N^2)] - H(N)$$

Y is Gaussian!

Solution 20.10

$$\begin{aligned}
C &= \sum_i C_i = \sum_i \frac{1}{2} \log_2 \left(1 + \frac{S_i}{N_i}\right) \\
S_i &\geq N_i \\
\Rightarrow C &\approx \sum_i \frac{1}{2} \log_2 [S_i/N_i] = \frac{1}{2} \sum_i \log_2 S_i/N_i \\
&= \tfrac{1}{2} \log_2 \left[\prod_i S_i/N_i\right] = \tfrac{N}{2} \log_2 \left[\sqrt[N]{\prod_i S_i/N_i}\right]
\end{aligned}$$

Solution 20.11

$$\begin{aligned}
\lim_{W\to\infty} C_t &= \lim_{W\to\infty} W \cdot \log_2 \left(1 + \frac{S}{N_0 W}\right) \\
&= \lim_{x\to 0} \frac{\log_2 \left(1 + \frac{S}{N_0} \cdot x\right)}{x} \\
&= \lim_{x\to 0} \frac{\log_2 \left(1 + \frac{S}{N_0} \cdot x\right)}{x} \\
&= \lim_{x\to 0} \frac{1}{\ln(2) \cdot \left(1 + \frac{S}{N_0} \cdot x\right)} \cdot \frac{S}{N_0} \quad \text{(l'Hospital)} \\
&= \frac{1}{\ln(2)} \cdot \frac{S}{N_0}
\end{aligned}$$

Alternative approach:

$$\begin{aligned}
\lim_{W\to\infty} C_t &= \lim_{W\to\infty} W \cdot \log_2 \left(1 + \frac{S}{N_0 W}\right) \\
&= \lim_{W\to\infty} \log_2 \left(1 + \frac{S}{N_0 W}\right)^W \\
&= \lim_{W\to\infty} \frac{S}{N_0} \log_2 \left(1 + \frac{S}{N_0 W}\right)^{W \frac{N_0}{S}} \\
&= \frac{S}{N_0} \log_2 \lim_{W\to\infty} \left(1 + \frac{S}{N_0 W}\right)^{W \frac{N_0}{S}} \\
&= \frac{S}{N_0} \log_2 \lim_{x\to\infty} \left(1 + \frac{1}{x}\right)^x \\
&= \frac{S}{N_0} \log_2(e)
\end{aligned}$$

Solution 20.12 This is the counterpart of the erasure channel and thus, the Mutual Information between $\hat{X}$ and X is given by

$$I(X; \hat{X}) = 1 - D$$

The source symbol $X = 2$ cannot well be represented by $\hat{X}$, i.e., is regenerated randomly from the values 1 or 3.

Solution 20.13 $1 - h(D) = 1 + D\log_2(D) + (1 - D)\log_2(1 - D) = 1 - 0.0114 = 0.98859$ $1/(1 - h(D)) = 1.0115$

Solution 20.14 Dual to each other

Solution 20.15 Zero. Over real or complex numbers, one would conclude orthogonality. There is self-duality in GF(2^m).

Solution 20.16 Due to binary counting procedures in the H-matrix

Solution 20.17 Duals: single parity check and repetition codes

$$\mathbf{G}_{REP} = \mathbf{H}_{PC} = \underbrace{(1, 1, 1, \ldots, 1)}_{N}$$

$$\mathbf{H}_{REP} = \mathbf{G}_{PC} = \begin{pmatrix} 1\,1 & 0 & 0 \cdots 0 \\ 1\,0 & 1 & 0 \quad\; 0 \\ 1\,0 & 0 & 1 \quad\; 0 \\ \vdots & & \ddots \\ 1\,0 \cdots & 0 & 0 \quad 1 \end{pmatrix}$$

Solution 20.18 Even number of ones in the vector.

Solution 20.19 $K = M = 12$
even

Solution 20.20

(a)

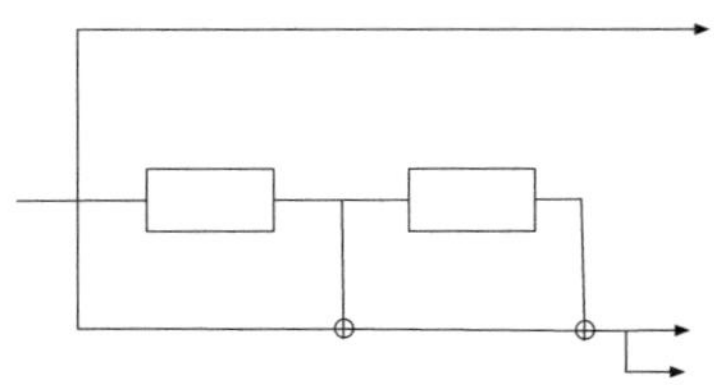

(b)

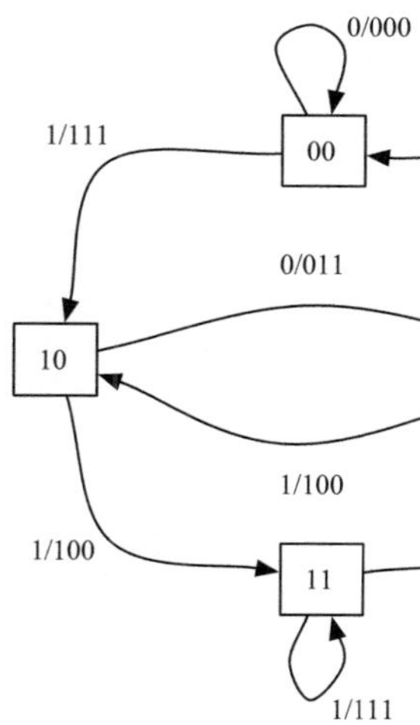
0/000
1/111
00
0/011
0/011
10
01
1/100
1/100
0/000
11
1/111

(c) $d_f = 6$

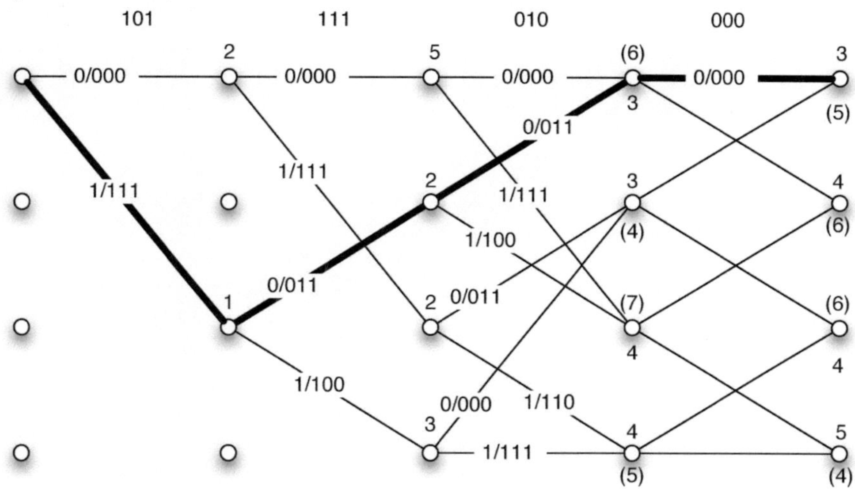
101
111
010
000
0/000
0/000
0/000
0/000
1/111
1/111
1/111
0/011
0/011
0/011
1/100
1/100
1/110
0/000
1/111
2
5
(6)
3
3
(5)
2
3
(4)
4
(6)
1
2
(7)
4
(6)
4
3
4
(5)
5
(4)

Solution 20.21

(a) $\big(15,\ 17\big) = \big(001101,\ 001111\big)$

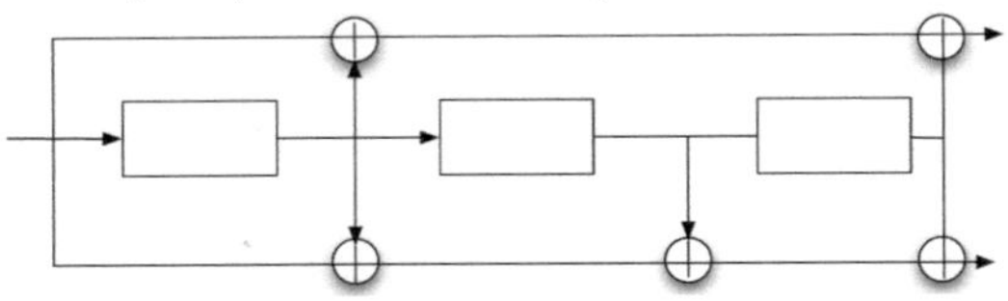

(b) $G = \big(1 + D + D^3,\ 1 + D + D^2 + D^3\big)$

(c)

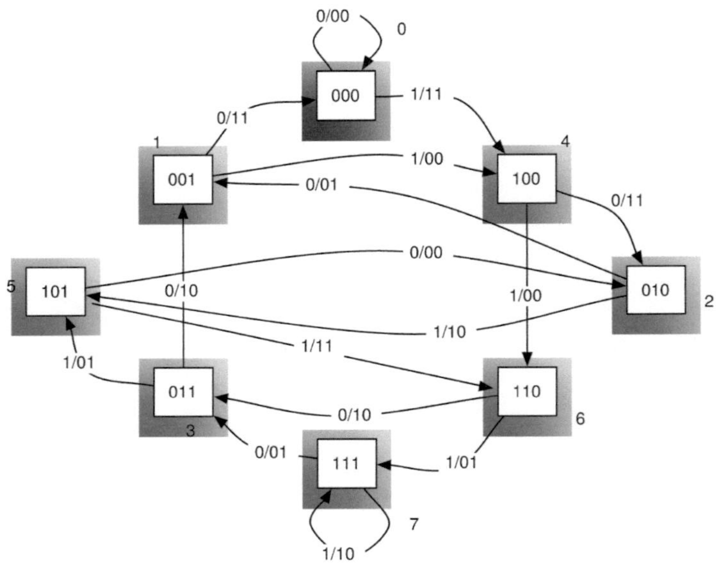

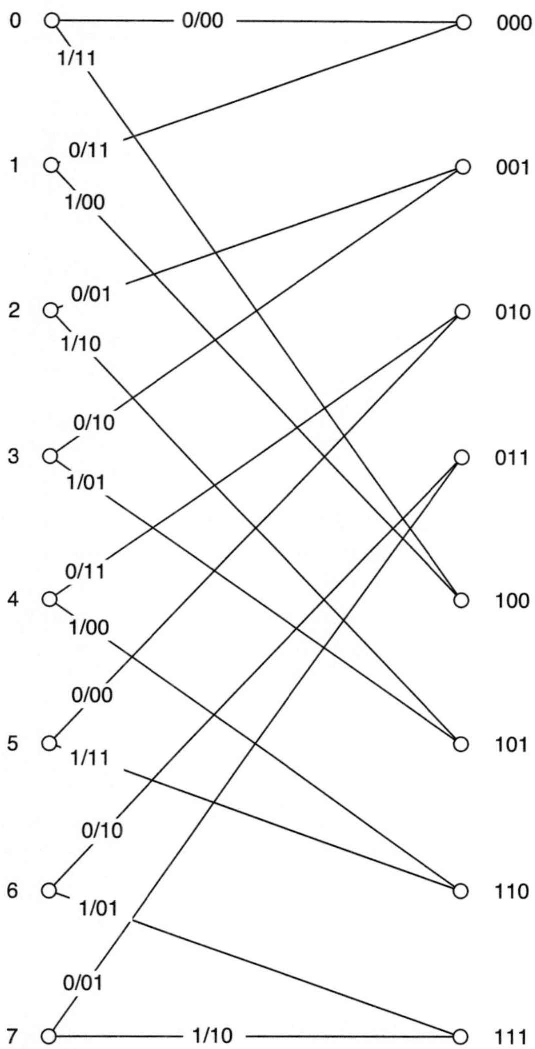

(d) non-systematic, non-recursive

(e) maximum Hamming distance, i.e., opposite output bits

Solution 20.22

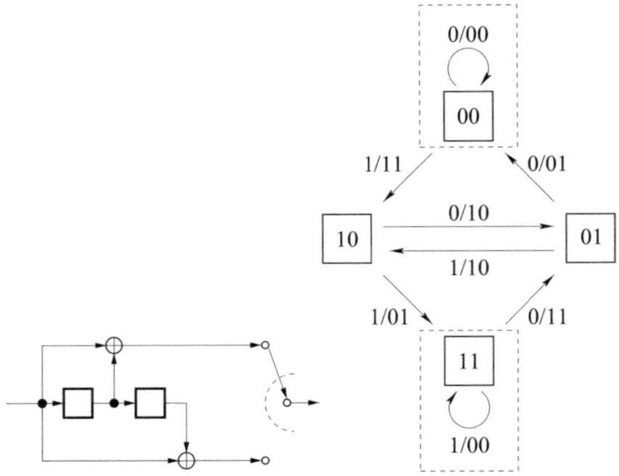

Trellis is the time roll-out of the state diagram (not shown).

The two loops at the states ‘00’ and ‘11’ lead to the same output sequence and thus, do not establish a distance.

A limited number of errors on the channel would lead to an infinite number of errors in the decoded sequence. This is a property of the encoder. A corresponding systematic encoder would not be catastrophic.

Solution 20.23

(a) Linearity
(b) Binary convolutional codes: opposite code bit-pattern or, at least, maximum Hamming distance at common states for incoming and outgoing paths.

Solution 20.24

(a) $\underbrace{P(x|y)}_{MAP} = \underbrace{P(y|x)}_{ML} \cdot \frac{P(x)}{P(y)}$
(b) Both can be ML/MAP. Viterbi: Sequence Estimation. BCJR: Calculation of individual probabilities and LLRs.
(c) $P(x_i|y)$: MAP $P(x_i|y) = P(y|x_i) \cdot \frac{P(x_i)}{P(y)} == [\underbrace{P(y_i|x_i}_{Intrinsic} \cdot \underbrace{P(\mathbf{y}_{\setminus i}|x_i)}_{Extrinsic} \cdot \underbrace{P(x_i)}_{A-priori}]\frac{1}{P(\mathbf{y}_{\setminus i})}$

Solution 20.25

(a) Select the best incoming path according to accumulated metric.
(b) The beginning of all path memories is identical if the decoding delay is chosen long enough (rule of thumb: $5\times$ constraint length).
(c) Linear code.

Solution 20.26 No, It finds the optimum ML sequence, not necessarily leading to the best individual bit estimate.

Solution 20.27

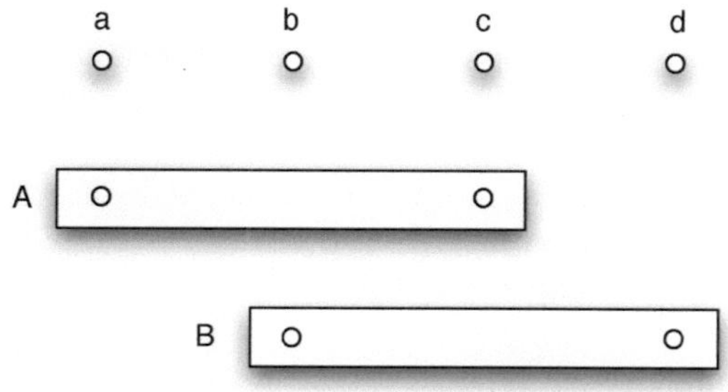

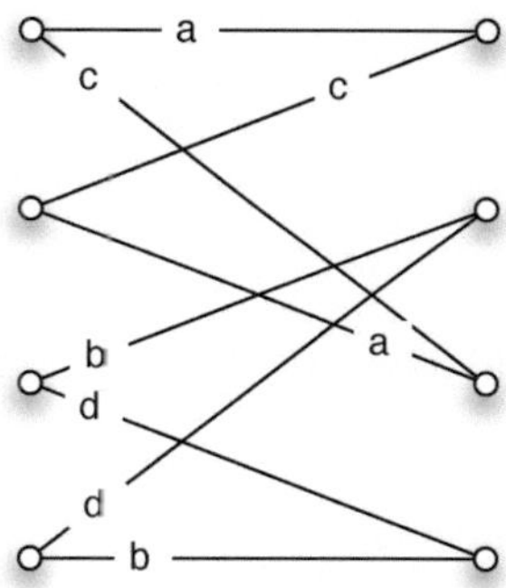

Solution 20.28 $\ln \frac{p(0)}{p(1)} = \ln \frac{\sum_{n=0}^{3} e^{-\frac{|y-e^{j(n\pi/2+\varphi)}|^2}{2\sigma_n^2}}}{\sum_{n=0}^{3} e^{-\frac{|y-e^{j(n\pi/2+\varphi+\pi/4)}|^2}{2\sigma_n^2}}}$

Solution 20.29 $f_X(x) = \int_{-\cos\sin^{-1}(x)}^{+\cos\sin^{-1}(x)} \frac{1}{\pi} dy = \frac{2}{\pi}\int_0^{\sqrt{1-x^2}} dy = \frac{2}{\pi}\sqrt{1-x^2}$

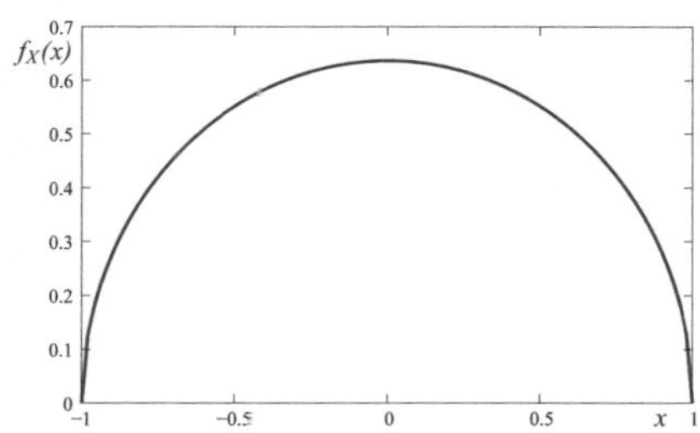

Solution 20.30

(a) $(1+\alpha)^4 = 1+\alpha^4 = 1+(1+\alpha) = \alpha$
(b) $(1+\alpha)^{20} = (1+\alpha)^5 = (1+\alpha)^4(1+\alpha) = (1+\alpha^4)(1+\alpha) = 1+\alpha+\alpha^4+\alpha^5 = \alpha^5 = \alpha+\alpha^2$
(c) $\alpha,\ \alpha^2,\ \alpha^4 = (1+\alpha),\ \alpha^8 = (1+\alpha)^2 = 1+\alpha^2,\ \alpha^{16} = (1+\alpha^2)^2 = 1+\alpha^4 = \alpha$

Solution 20.31

(a) Interpolation possible, not approximation, since there is no size relation of values in a Galois field, i.e., also no bigger or smaller distance to an approximation "curve".
(b) Max order: $N = 2^4 - 1 = 15$. Other orders should divide this N, i.e., 3 or 5 are further possibilities with α^5 and α^3, respectively.
(c) Element of order N (complex case): $e^{\pm j2\pi/N}$
$N = 15$ or 3 or 5
(d) Zero position has no conjugates, hence, no possible improvement in min. Hamming distance. In case of an RS code, any consecutive region of zeros can be chosen.

Solution 20.32

(a) Polynomial has factors from the prime field.
(b) $(1 + \alpha + \alpha^2)^2 = 1 + \alpha^2 + \alpha^4 = 1 + \alpha^2 + 1 + \alpha = \alpha + \alpha^2$

Solution 20.33

(a) $GF(p^m)$ Modulo p, Modulo primitive polynomial
(b) Modulo $p^m - 1$
(c) $\beta, \beta^p, \beta^{p^2}, \beta^{p^3}$
(d) $\beta^N = 1$, Maximum order: $p^m - 1$
(e) $1 + \alpha + \alpha^2 = 1 + \alpha^2 + \alpha^4 = 1 + 2\alpha^2 + \alpha = 1 + \alpha$

Solution 20.34

(a) $GF(2^4)$
(b) $(1 + \alpha^3)^4 = \alpha^{16} = \alpha$
(c) $(1 + \alpha)^4 = (1 + \alpha^4) = (1 + \alpha^3 + 1) = \alpha^3$

Solution 20.35

(a) $(1 + \alpha)^{70} = (1 + \alpha)^7$
(b) 21
(c) Prime factorization: $63 = 7 \cdot 3 \cdot 3$. In principle, FFT with 3 stages would be possible, but not too useful!
(d) 21

Solution 20.36

(a) Order of α: $2^4 - 1 = 15$
(b) Order of β: 3
(c)

$$
\begin{aligned}
F_0 &= 1(\alpha^5)^0 + 1(\alpha^5)^{1 \cdot 0} + 1(\alpha^5)^{2 \cdot 0} = 3 = 1 \\
F_1 &= 1(\alpha^5)^0 + 1(\alpha^5)^{1 \cdot 1} + 1(\alpha^5)^{2 \cdot 1} = 1 + \alpha + \alpha^2 + (1 + \alpha)^2 \alpha^2) = 0 \\
F_2 &= 1(\alpha^5)^0 + 1(\alpha^5)^{1 \cdot 2} + 1(\alpha^5)^{2 \cdot 2} \\
&= 1 + (1 + \alpha^2)\alpha^2 + \alpha^5 = 1 + \alpha^2 + 1 + \alpha + \alpha(1 + \alpha) = 0
\end{aligned}
$$

(d) Error correction capability: $t = 1$
Simple code: repetition code
If one would have a single error, a majority decision would correct it. For two errors this would not be possible any more or lead to the wrong constant codeword.

Solution 20.37

(a) We need an element of order N. The maximum order is $2^7 - 1 = 127$. $d_{Hmin} = 10 + 1 = 11$, $t = 5$.
(b) Degree of polynomial: $K - 1 = 116$. Samples: $z^{\pm i}$ with primitive element z.
(c) $a_i = A_0 + A_1 x + \cdots + A_{K-1}x^{K-1}\big|_{x=z^i} = \sum_{k=0}^{K-1} A_k z^{ki}$
(d) A shift in DFT domain means applying an exponential factor to time domain. This does not affect the calculation of the error-locator polynomial, but it has to be considered when determining the error values.
(e) Vandermonde matrices

$$\mathbf{G}_{K\times N} = \begin{bmatrix} 1 & 1 & 1 & 1 & \cdots & 1 \\ 1 & z^1 & z^2 & z^3 & & 2^{N-1} \\ 1 & z^2 & z^4 & z^6 & & 2^{2(N-1)} \\ 1 & & & & & \\ \vdots & & & & & \\ 1 & z^{K-1} & z^{(K-1)2} & z^{(K-1)3} & & 2^{(K-1)(N-1)} \end{bmatrix}$$

$$\mathbf{H}_{M\times N} = \begin{bmatrix} 1 & 1 & 1 & 1 & \cdots & 1 \\ 1 & z^{-1} & z^{-2} & z^{-3} & & 2^{-(N-1)} \\ 1 & z^{-2} & z^{-4} & z^{-6} & & 2^{-2(N-1)} \\ 1 & & & & & \\ \vdots & & & & & \\ 1 & z^{-(M-1)} & z^{-(M-1)2} & z^{-(M-1)3} & & 2^{-(M-1)(N-1)} \end{bmatrix}$$

(f) LDPC code

Solution 20.38

(a) We need an element of order N. The maximum order is $2^8 - 1 = 255$. $d_{Hmin} = 20 + 1 = 21$, $t = 10$.
(b) Degree of polynomial: $K - 1 = 234$. Samples: $z^{\pm i}$ with primitive element z.
(c) $a_i = A_0 + A_1 x + \cdots + A_{K-1}x^{K-1}\big|_{x=z^i} = \sum_{k=0}^{K-1} A_k z^{ki}$
(d) A shift in DFT domain means applying an exponential factor to time domain, which won't change the Hamming distance.

Solution 20.39

(a) Data in DFT-domain: Syndrome $\longrightarrow$ error-locator polynomial/shift register $\longrightarrow$ Continuing shift register operation outside the syndrome $\longrightarrow$ Subtract error word in DFT domain
Data in original domain: Syndrome $\longrightarrow$ error-locator polynomial $\longrightarrow$ error positions by IDFT $\longrightarrow$ Forney method for error values $\longrightarrow$ subtracting error values

(b) The syndrome will be influenced by exponents of the element of order N. The determined error location will then, of course, be at the shifted location.
(c) The syndrome will be shifted, which has no influence on the error location, but on the error value.

Solution 20.40

(a) The H-matrix is the generator matrix of the dual code.
(b) Dual code parameters: $(N, N-K, K+1)$; zeros at the lower end.
(c) Maximum length: 6

$$C(x) = 1 + x + x^2 + x^3$$

$$\begin{aligned} c_0 &= C(x = z^0 = 1) = 4 \\ c_1 &= C(x = z^1 = 5) = 2 \\ c_2 &= C(x = z^2 = 4) = 1 \\ c_3 &= C(x = z^3 = 6) = 0 \\ c_4 &= C(x = z^4 = 2) = 1 \\ c_5 &= C(x = z^5 = 3) = 5 \end{aligned}$$

(d) Even weight vectors are self-dual. Orthogonality does not exist in a finite field.

Solution 20.41

(a) Single one inside K information symbols $\Longrightarrow w_H = d_H \leq M + 1 = N - K + 1$
(b) Degree-limited polynomial of degree $K-1 \Rightarrow$ max $(K-1)$ zeros $\Rightarrow N - (K-1)$ non-zeros $\Rightarrow d_H \geq M + 1$
(c) M cyclically consecutive zeros.
(d) $p_S = 1 - (1-p)^m$
(e) Not the component at zero.

$$\boxed{0, 1, 2, 3, 4, 5, 6, \boxed{7}, 8, 9, 10, \boxed{11}, 12, \boxed{13}, \boxed{14}}$$

$g(x) = (x - z^1)(x - z^2)(x - z^4)(x - z^8) = x^4 + x + 1$ (primitive polynomial: $p(z) = z^4 + z + 1$)

Solution 20.42 Arrangements 1, 3, and 4 have the same minimum distance $d_{hmin} = 21$.

20 erasures or 10 errors can be corrected.

Solution 20.43

(a) $f_i = F(x)|_{x=e^{\pm j\frac{2\pi}{N}i}} = F_0 + F_1x + F_2x^2 + \ldots + F_{K-1}x^{K-1}|_{x=e^{\pm j\frac{2\pi}{N}i}} = \sum_{k=0}^{K-1} F_k e^{\pm j\frac{2\pi}{N}ik}$

(b) $f_i = F(x)|_{x=\alpha^i} = F_0 + F_1 x + F_2 x^2 + ... + F_{K-1} x^{K-1}|_{x=\alpha^i} = \sum_{k=0}^{K-1} F_k \alpha^{\pm ik}$
$d_{H\,min} = 21$

Solution 20.44

(a) $x = \underbrace{z^l}_{e^{j\frac{2\pi}{N}l}\text{in case of complex numbers}}, l = 0, 1, \ldots, N-1$

(b) number of erasure $\leq N - K = d_{H_{min}} - 1$

(c) number of errors $\leq \lfloor \frac{N-K}{2} \rfloor = \lfloor \frac{d_{H_{min}}-1}{2} \rfloor$

(d)

$$p_{byte} = 1 - (1 - p_{BSC})^8$$

$$p_{nocorr} = \sum_{e=t+1}^{N} \binom{N}{e} p_{byte}^e (1 - p_{byte})^{N-e}$$

$$p_b|_{\text{after dec}} = \frac{1}{8} \sum \frac{e}{N} \binom{N}{e} p_{byte}^e (1 - p_{byte})^{N-e}$$

(e) 1 bit-interleaved erroneous byte would hit many code bytes.

Solution 20.45

$$\mathbf{G} = \begin{bmatrix} 1 & 1 & 1 & 1 \\ 1 & z & z^2 & z^3 \end{bmatrix}, \qquad \mathbf{H} = N^{-1} \begin{bmatrix} 1 & z^{-2} & z^{-4} & z^{-6} \\ 1 & z^{-3} & z^{-6} & z^{-9} \end{bmatrix}$$

GF(5) and $N^{-1} = N = 4$

Solution 20.46

$$d_{H\,min} = M + 1 = (254 - 239 + 1) + (9 - 0 + 1) + 1 = 27$$

Cyclically consecutive parities plus one.

Solution 20.47

(a) In bytes, since an RS code is byte-correcting. Breaking up bursty bytes into smaller units by, e.g., a bit interleaver, would mean to increase the number of erroneous bytes.

(b) The byte-error correcting capability for bursty channels is $t \cdot I_D$.

(c) For bursty noise. Errors should be concentrated, since the RS-code is byte correcting. Interleavers are also only required for bursty errors.

Solution 20.48

(a) Increase the burst-error correction capability by distributing error burst to many codewords, Burst-error correction capability $I_D \cdot t$.

(b) Inner code: $N = 8$.

(c) Decoding of convolutional codes (Viterbi) leads to error burst, asking for a burst-error correcting outer code.
Byte-based interleaving.

(d) Example: product code without parity-of-parities is parallel concatenation, with it is serial concatenation.
Data compr → channel encoder → precoder → channel → equalizer → channel decoder → decompression: serial concatenation.

Solution 20.49

(a) Increase the burst-error correction capability by distributing error burst to many codewords
(b) Half the memory and delay
(c) 8-bit symbols, since otherwise errors would be distributed to more symbols, thereby deteriorating performance
(d) Making noise influence independent for the redundancies resulting from the same information.

Solution 20.50

(a) Serial concatenation due to parity-of-parities. Omit this position to make it a parallel concatenation.
(b) Checking parity violations in rows and columns thereby pointing at the error position.
(c) $c_{ij}^{row} = -\sum_{i'\setminus i} r_{i'j}, \quad c_{ij}^{col} = -\sum_{j'\setminus j} r_{ij'}$
(d) Checking for the analog received value and Wagner decoding.
(e) GMD decoding and similar approaches make use of $t_{erasure} = 2 \cdot t_{error}$, iteratively choosing more or less erasures and trying to correct remaining errors.

Solution 20.51

(a) Linear, contains the all-zero word
(b) $w_{H\,min} = d_{H\,min}$
(c) $w_{H\,min} = d_{H\,min} = 4$
Just check the smallest set of ones, e.g., in the upper left square, i.e., all information components to be one. This is weight 4!
(d) $t_{error} = 1, \quad 3 \leq t_{erasure} \leq 5$
$t_{error} = \left\lfloor \frac{d_{H\,min}-1}{2} \right\rfloor$, $t_{erasure} \geq d_{H\,min} - 1$, e.g., having erasures at positions (1, 1); (1, 2); (2, 1) can be corrected. Having erasures at all parity positions can also be corrected. This represents the upper limit of 5.
(e) 5×9
The number of elements in the 3×3 matrix is, of course, $N = 9$. The number of parities in rows and columns is 5.
(f) $$\begin{bmatrix} 1\,1\,1\,0\,0\,0\,0\,0\,0 \\ 0\,0\,0\,1\,1\,1\,0\,0\,0 \\ 1\,0\,0\,1\,0\,0\,1\,0\,0 \\ 0\,1\,0\,0\,1\,0\,0\,1\,0 \\ 0\,0\,1\,0\,0\,1\,0\,0\,1 \end{bmatrix}$$

Note: there are, of course, other equivalent H-matrices. This one checks

1. 1st row
2. 2nd row
3. 1st col.
4. 2nd col.
5. 3rd col.

of the 3×3 array code.

(g) $p_W \lessapprox \frac{1}{2} A_{d_{min}} p^2 (1-p)^7, \quad A_{d_{min}} = 4 + 4 + 1$
Explanation: Pairwise error probability for minimum distance 4. For even distance, at half distance with 2 errors, one could flip a coin, explaining the factor 1/2.
$A_{d_{min}}$ = [single ones in the four info positions] + [neighboring pairs of ones in rows or columns of the 2×2 info field] + [all ones in the info field]

Solution 20.52

(a) Assumption: Gaussian channel input distribution
(b) For given signal alphabets, numerical Capacity computations/curves need to be used.
$C_{2-PAM} = 1 - 1/2 \cdot \sum_{i=1}^{2} \int_{-\infty}^{+\infty} \cdot \left\{ \begin{array}{c} \frac{1}{\sqrt{2\pi\sigma_n^2}} \\ \frac{1}{2\pi\sigma_n^2} \end{array} \right\} \cdot e^{-\frac{|r-s_i|^2}{2\sigma_n^2}} \log_2 \left(\frac{\sum_{i'=1}^{2} e^{-\frac{|r-s_{i'}|^2}{2\sigma_n^2}}}{e^{-\frac{|r-s_i|^2}{2\sigma_n^2}}} \right)$
$s_i = \pm 1$
(c) No limit!

Solution 20.53

(a) MAP (max $p(x|y)$) optimum, since y is received (given). Both are the same for equally distributed channel input symbols.
(b) $L = \pm\infty$: very reliable ± 1, respectively, 0: erasure or punctured
(c) Punctured: $L = 0$, pruned: $L = \pm\infty$

Solution 20.54

(a)

$$\ln \frac{P(x_i = +1|\mathbf{y})}{P(x_i = -1|\mathbf{y})} = \ln \frac{P(\mathbf{y}|x_i = +1)}{P(\mathbf{y}|x_i = -1)} + \ln \frac{P(x_i = +1)}{P(x_i = -1)} =$$

$$= \ln \frac{P(y_i|x_i = +1)}{P(y_i|x_i = -1)} + \ln \frac{P(\mathbf{y}_{\setminus i}|x_i = +1)}{P(\mathbf{y}_{\setminus i}|x_i = -1)} + \ln \frac{P(x_i = +1)}{P(x_i = -1)}$$

This is the summation of intrinsic, extrinsic, and a-priori contributions.
(b) A-priori information $LLR_{a\ priori} = \ln \frac{p}{1-p}$
(c) In Turbo decoding, the a-priori information is used to feed in extrinsic information from another decoder.
(d) The assumption is equal probability of ± 1.
(e) Independence.

Solution 20.55

(a)

$$\ln \frac{P(x_i = +1|\mathbf{y})}{P(x_i = -1|\mathbf{y})} = \ln \frac{P(\mathbf{y}|x_i = +1)}{P(\mathbf{y}|x_i = -1)} + \ln \frac{P(x_i = +1)}{P(x_i = -1)} =$$

$$= \ln \frac{P(y_i|x_i = +1)}{P(y_i|x_i = -1)} + \ln \frac{P(\mathbf{y}_{\setminus i}|x_i = +1)}{P(\mathbf{y}_{\setminus i}|x_i = -1)} + \ln \frac{P(x_i = +1)}{P(x_i = -1)}$$

This is the summation of intrinsic, extrinsic, and a-priori contributions.

(b) In Turbo decoding, extrinsic become a-priori for the next decoder.
(c) Additional input to variable nodes.
(d) Variable nodes: repetition code, check nodes: single parity-check code

Solution 20.56

(a) Ensuring statistically independent noise or the parities belonging to common information.
(b) A-priori and Intrinsic information.
(c) Intrinsic information is not subtracted after the inner decoder, since it needs to be forwarded to the outer one, which has an access to the channel directly.

Solution 20.57

(a) High variable node degree and low check-node degree at the connected check nodes.
(b) A fixed node leads to LLRs of $\pm\infty$, here, for $+1$ the LLR will be $+\infty$.
From a check-node perspective, the effective degree will be reduced, thereby, improving the performance at connected variable nodes.
(c)

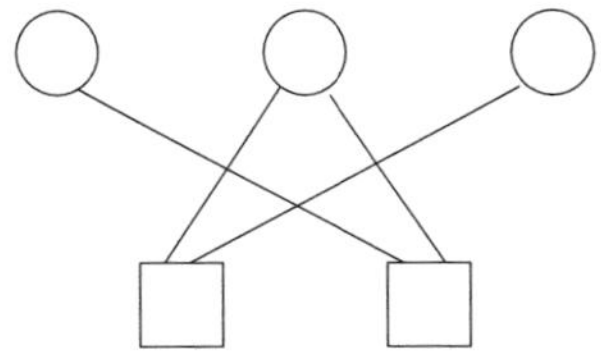

(d) Using cyclic permutation matrices in the lifting.
(e) Repetition and parity-check codes, interleaver

Solution 20.58 Permutation matrices:

$$\begin{bmatrix} 1 & 0 \\ 0 & 1 \end{bmatrix}, \quad \begin{bmatrix} 0 & 1 \\ 1 & 0 \end{bmatrix}$$

$$\mathbf{H}_{lift} = \begin{bmatrix} 1\,0 & 0\,1 & 0\,0 \\ 0\,1 & 1\,0 & 0\,0 \\ 1\,0 & 0\,0 & 0\,1 \\ 0\,1 & 0\,0 & 1\,0 \end{bmatrix}$$

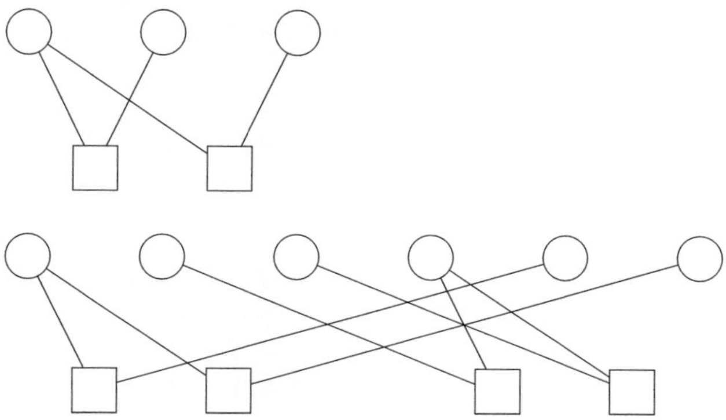

Solution 20.59

(a) Cyclic matrix, hence cyclic code, min. Hamming distance 3, i.e., repetition code.
(b)

$$\mathbf{H} = \begin{bmatrix} 1 & 0 & 1 \\ 0 & 1 & 1 \end{bmatrix}.$$

$$\mathbf{G} = [1\ 1\ 1]$$

(c) Perfect code, since repetition code of odd length
(d) Gauss-Jordan will lead to a non-sparse H-matrix and hence, also a non-sparse G-matrix, leading to high complexity on the transmitter side. The resulting H-matrix shall, of course, not be used for iterative decoding.

Solution 20.60

(a) Under the assumption of statistical independence, log-likelihood ratios add up, ideally true in case of a tree
(b) Convolution leads to adding means and variances
(c) Systematic triangular form

Solution 20.61

(a) $H(X_2|X_1) \leq H(X_1)$
(b) Use the pairs of the two X_1's and the two X_2's as input. One may now omit the first polarization operation as shown below.
(c) Labeling according to Fig. 12.41 and the one presented here.

$$H(U_1) \geq H(S_1) = H(S_2) \geq H(U_2|U_1),$$
$$H(U_3|\mathbf{U}^2) \geq H(R_1|S_1) = H(R_2|S_2) \geq H(U_4|\mathbf{U}^3)$$

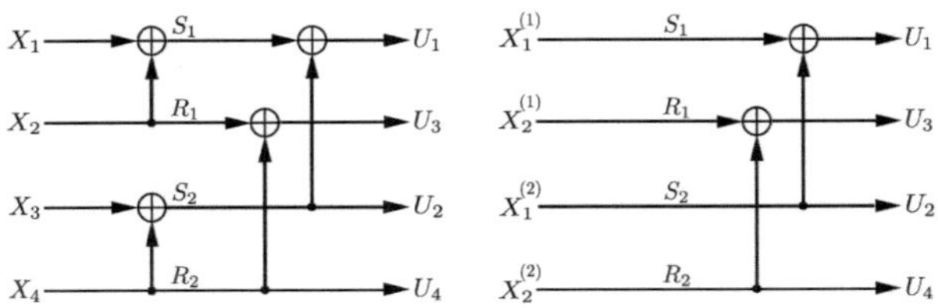

Solution 20.62

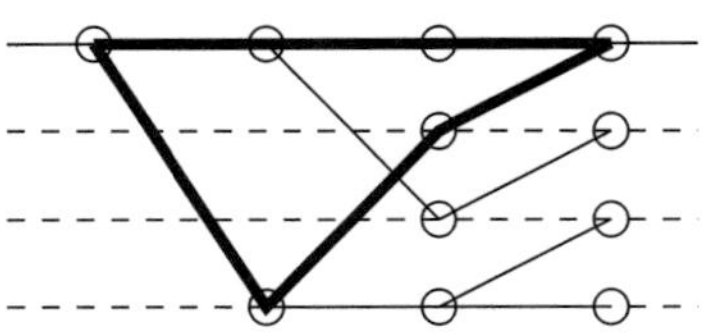

Solution 20.63

a, c, d)

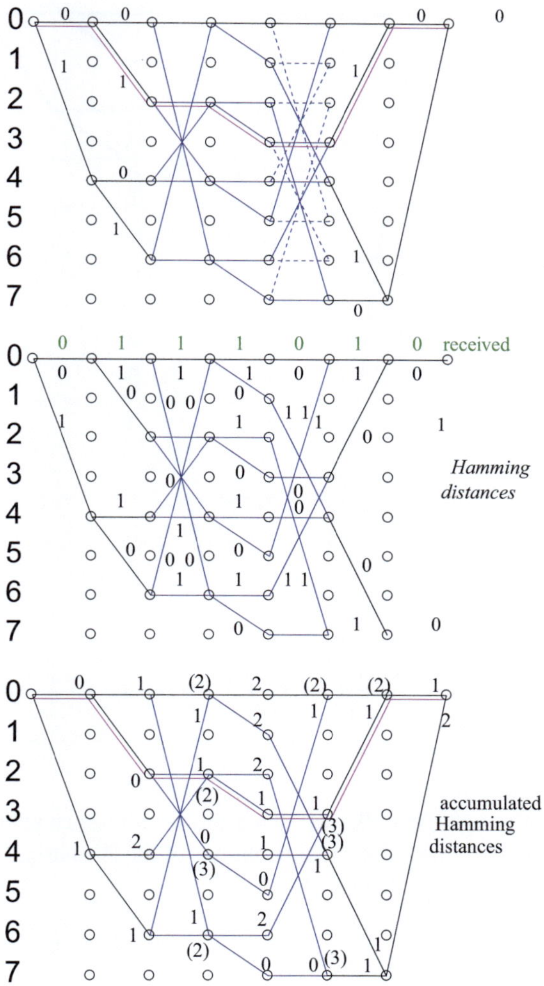

(b)

$$(0 \ldots 0)$$

All-zero path

(c) "magenta" see fig.

(d) see fig.

(e) Hamming code: columns are according to binary counting

(f) "systematic" form with identity matrix being part of the H-matrix.

Solution 20.64

(a)

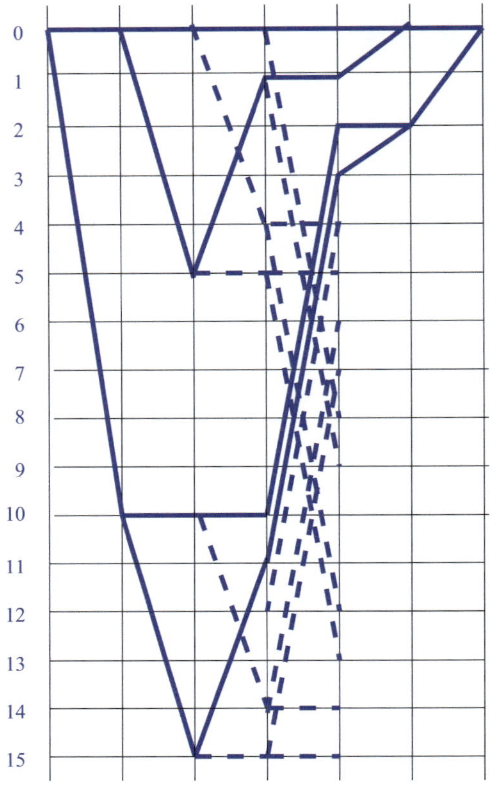

(b) BCJR, blocked trellis
(c) Possibilities through the trellis with an arbitrary reference path or checking for smallest number of linear dependent columns of the H-matrix. Columns 2,3, and 5 are linearly dependent, hence, $d_{H\,min} = 3$.

Solution 20.65

(a) BSC and Gaussian, respectively
(b) Gaussian channel, Euclidean distance.
(c) $|\mathbf{y} - \mathbf{x}_i|^2/\sigma^2$
(d) Point set and Set partitioning
$LLR = \ln \frac{e^{(y_r-1)^2+(y_i-1)^2} + e^{(y_r+1)^2+(y_i+1)^2}}{e^{(y_r-1)^2+(y_i+1)^2} + e^{(y_r+1)^2+(y_i-1)^2}}$
e) Selecting the best incoming path to a state and dismissing all others.

Solution 20.66

(a) TCM: ensuring first level sub-constellations are at a state for outgoing and/or incoming edges. Multi-level coded mod.: choice of rates/ Hamming distances of codes according to Euclidean distances/Capacity differences.

(b) Bit-interleaved coded modulation with binary code, bit-interleaving and mapping to Gray-coded signal points

(c)

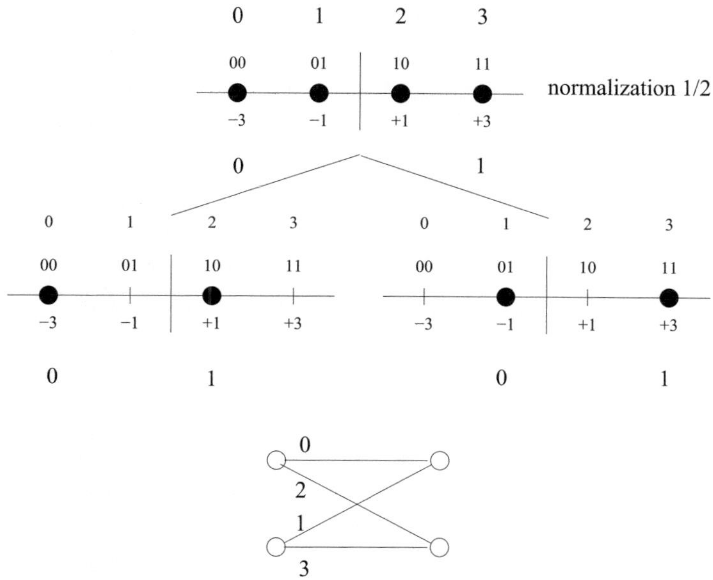

(d) $d_E^2 = 2^2 + 1 = 5$

(e) $\min(N \cdot 1, 2 \cdot 4)$, choice $N = 8$

Other design rule according to Chain Rule of Mutual Information defining the code rates as Mutual Information differences between modulation subsets.

Solution 20.67

(a) The squared Euclidean distances are increasing with the levels, hence code distances can decrease.

(b)

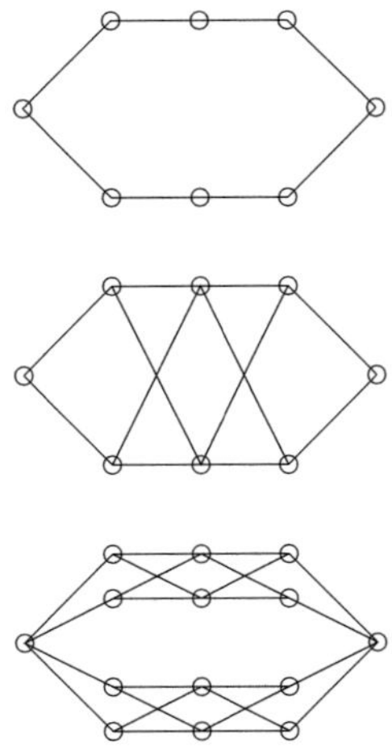

Further Reading

In the following, we give an overview over related literature, certainly not providing a full coverage.

Channel coding

Johnson, S. J., *Iterative Error Correction, Turbo, Low-Density Parity-Check and Repeat-Accumulate Codes*, Cambridge University Press, 2010, ISBN 978-0-521-87148-8.

Declercq, D., Fossorier, M., and Biglieri, E. (ed.), *Channel Coding, Theory, Algorithms, and Applications*, Elsevier Academic Press, 2014, ISBN 978-0-12-396499-1.

Lin, S., Ryan, W., *Channel Codes: Classical and Modern*, Cambridge University Press, 2009, ISBN 978-0521848688.

Lin, S., Costello, D.J., *Error Control Coding*, Pearson, 2004, ISBN 978-013042-6727.

Richardson, T., Urbanke, R., *Modern Coding Theory*, Cambridge University Press, 2008, ISBN 978-0521852296.

Blahut, R.E., *Theory and Practice of Error Control Codes*, Addison Wesley, Reading, Massachusetts, 1983, ISBN 0-201-10102-5.

MacWilliams, F.J., Sloane, N.J.A., *The Theory of Error-Correcting Codes*, North Holland, Amsterdam, 5. Aufl. 1986, ISBN 0-444-85193-3.

Dholakia, A., *Introduction to Convolutional Codes with Applications*, Kluwer, Boston, 1994, ISBN 0-7923-9467-4.

Clark, G.C., Cain, J.B., *Error-Correction Coding for Digital Communications*, Plenum Press, New York and London, 3. Aufl. 1988, ISBN 0-306-40615-2.

Peterson, W.W., Weldon, E.J., *Error-Correcting Codes*, MIT Press, Cambridge, Massachusetts, London, England, 6. Aufl. 1981, ISBN 0-262-16039-0.

Heise, W., Quattrocchi, P., *Informations- und Codierungstheorie*, Springer, Berlin, 2. Aufl. 1989, ISBN 0-387-50537-7 und 3-540-50537-7.

Friedrichs, B., *Kanalcodierung. Grundlagen und Anwendungen in modernen Kommunikationssystemen*, Springer, Berlin, 1995, ISBN 3-540-59353-5.

Bossert, M., *Kanalcodierung*, 3rd edition, Oldenbourg Verlag, Munich, 2013.

W. Henkel, *Channel Coding*, Signals and Communication Technology,
https://doi.org/10.1007/978-3-032-08236-7

Michelson, A.M., Levesque, A.H., *Error-Control Techniques for Digital Communication*, Wiley, New York, 1985, ISBN 0-471-88074-4.

Blahut, R.E., *Algebraic Methods for Signal Processing and Communications Coding*, Springer, New York, Berlin, 1991, ISBN 0-387-97673-6 und 3-540-97673-6.

Mc Eliece, R.J., *Finite Fields for Computer Scientists and Engineers*, Kluwer, Boston, 1987, ISBN 0-89838-191-6.

Viterbi, A.J., Omura, J.K., *Principles of Digital Communication and Coding*, McGraw-Hill, Tokyo, 1979, ISBN 0-07-067516-3.

v. Ammon, U., Tröndle, K., *Mathematische Grundlagen der Codierung*, R. Oldenburg, München, Wien, 1974, ISBN 3-486-34681-4.

van Lint, J.H., *Introduction to Coding Theory*, Springer, New York, Heidelberg, Berlin, 1982, ISBN 0-387-11284-7 or 3-540-11284-7.

Berlekamp, E.R., *Algebraic Coding Theory*, McGraw-Hill, St. Louis, San Francisco, Toronto, London, Sydney, 1968.

Mc Eliece, R.J., *The Theory of Information and Coding*, Addison-Wesley, 1977.

Vanstone, S.A., van Oorschot, P.C., *An Introduction to Error Correcting Codes with Applications*, Kluwer, Boston, Dordrecht, London, 1989, ISBN 0-7923-9017-2.

Anderson, J.B., Mohan, S., *Source and Channel Coding*, Kluwer, Norwell, Massachusetts, 1991, ISBN 0-7923-9210-8.

Duske, J., Jürgensen, H., *Codierungstheorie*, BI, Mannheim, Wien, Zürich, 1977, ISBN 3-411-01527-6.

Pretzel, O., *Error-Correcting Codes and Finite Fields*, Oxford University Press, Oxford, 1992, ISBN 0-19-859678-2.

Berlekamp, E. (Editor), *Key Papers in the Development of Coding Theory*, IEEE Press, Piscataway, N.J., 1974, ISBN 0-87942-032-4.

Kaderali, F., *Digitale Kommunikationstechnik I*, Vieweg, Braunschweig, 1991, ISBN 3-528-04710-0.

Heegard, C., Wicker, S.B., *Turbo Coding*, Springer, New York, 1999, ISBN 978-1-4419-5069-7.

Vucetic, B., Yuan, J., *Turbo Codes: Principles and Applications*, Kluwer, 2000, ISBN 0-7923-7868-7.

Biglieri, E., *Coding for Wireless Channels (Information Thechnology Transmission, Processing and Storage*, Springer, 2005, ISBN 1-4020-8083-2.

Rao, K. D., *Channel Coding Techniques for Wireless Communications*, Springer, 2005, ISBN 978-8132222910.

Information Theory

Cover, T.M., Thomas, J.A., *Elements of Information Theory*, Wiley, New York, 2nd ed., 2006, ISBN 978-0471241959, 978-8126541942.

Csiszár, I., Körner, J., *Information Theory, Coding Theorems for Discrete Memoryless Systems*, Akadémiai Kiadó, Budapest 2011, ISBN 978-0521196819.

MacKay, D.J.C., *Information Theory, Inference, and Learning Algorithms*, Cambridge University Press 2003, http://www.inference.org.uk/mackay/itila/book.html

Gallager, R.G., *Information Theory and Reliable Communication*, John Wiley & Sons, New York, 1968, ISBN W-471-29048-3.

Blahut, R.E., *Principles and Practice of Information Theory*, Addison-Wesley, Reading, Massachusetts, 1987, ISBN 0-201-10709-0.

Slepian, D. (Editor), *Key Papers in the Development of Information Theory*, IEEE Press, Piscataway, N.J., 1973, ISBN 0-87942-027-8.

Gray, R.M., *Entropy and Information Theory*, Springer, New York, Heidelberg, Berlin, 1990, ISBN 0-387-97371-0 or 3-540-97371-0.

Ash, R., *Information Theory*, Dover Books on Mathematics, 1991, ISBN 978-0486665214.

Coded Modulation

Conway, J.H., Sloane, N.J.A., *Sphere Packings, Lattices and Groups*, Springer, New York, Berlin, 1988, ISBN 0-387-96617-X und 3-540-96617-X.

Jamali, S.H., Le-Ngoc, T., *Coded-Modulation Techniques for Fading Channels*, Kluwer, Boston, 1994, ISBN 0-7923-9421-6.

Biglieri, E., Divsalar, D., McLane, P.J., Simon, M.K., *Introduction to Trellis-Coded Modulation with Applications*, MacMillan, New York, 1991, ISBN 0-02-946542-7.

Biglieri, E., Luise, M. (Editors), *Coded Modulation and Bandwidth-Efficient Transmission*, Elsevier, Amsterdam, 1991, ISBN 0-444-89202-8.

Huber, J., *Trelliscodierung*, Springer, Berlin, 1992, ISBN 3-540-55792-X.

Transmission, Signal Processing, and Source Coding

Lee, E.A., Messerschmitt, D.G., *Digital Communication*, Kluwer, Boston, 1988, ISBN 0-89838-274-2.

Proakis, J.G. and Salehi, M., *Digital Communications*, McGraw-Hill, 5th ed., 2007, ISBN 978-0072957167.

Gitlin, R.D., Hayes, J.F., Weinstein, S.B., *Data Communications Principles*, Plenum Press, New York, London, 1992, ISBN 0-306-43777-5.

Sklar, B. and Harris, F.J., *Digital Communications: Fundamentals and Applications*, Prentice Hall, Upper Saddle River, NJ, 2020, ISBN 0134588568.

Ziemer, R.E., Peterson, R.L., *Introduction to Digital Communication*, MacMillan, New York, 1992, ISBN 0-02-946431-5.

Blahut, R.E., *Digital Transmission of Information*, Addison-Wesley, Reading, Massachusetts, 1990, ISBN 0-201-06880-X.

Blahut, R.E., *Fast Algorithms for Digital Signal Processing*, Addison-Wesley, Reading, Massachusetts, 1984, ISBN 0-201-10155-6.

Benedetto, S., Biglieri, E., Castellani, V., *Digital Transmission Theory*, Prentice Hall, Englewood Cliffs, N.J., ISBN 0-13-215062-X.

Carlson, A.B., *Communication Systems*, McGraw-Hill, New York, 2. Aufl., 1987, ISBN 0-07-009960-X.

Schwartz, M., Bennett, W.R., Stein, S., *Communication Systems and Techniques*, John Wiley & Sons, 1995, ISBN 0-78-034715-3

Spilker, J.J., *Digital Communications by Satellite*, Prentice Hall, Englewood Cliffs, N.J., 1977, ISBN 0-13-214155-8.

Salomon, D., *Data Compression, The Complete Reference*, 4th ed., Springer, 2007, ISBN 978-1-84628-603-2.
Gray, R.M., *Source Coding Theory*, Kluwer, Norwell, Massachusetts, 1990, ISBN 0-7923-9048-2.

(The list is not complete. The order is more or less random and should not imply any quality ranking.)

Index

W. Henkel, *Channel Coding*, Signals and Communication Technology,
https://doi.org/10.1007/978-3-032-08236-7

D

E

MIX
Papier aus verantwortungsvollen Quellen
Paper from responsible sources
FSC® C105338

If you have any concerns about our products,
you can contact us on
ProductSafety@springernature.com

In case Publisher is established outside the EU,
the EU authorized representative is:
Springer Nature Customer Service Center GmbH
Europaplatz 3, 69115 Heidelberg, Germany

Printed by Libri Plureos GmbH
in Hamburg, Germany